GERIATRIC EMERGENCIES

Edited by

Richard L. Judd, PhD, EMSI, R-EMTA
Executive Dean and Professor of Emergency
Medical Sciences
Central Connecticut State University
and
Allied Medical Staff
New Britain General Hospital
New Britain, Connecticut

Carmen Germaine Warner, RN, MSN, FAAN
Editor, *Topics in Emergency Medicine*
and
Emergency Health Care Consultant
San Diego, California

Mark A. Shaffer, MD, FACEP
Director/Chairman, Department of Emergency Medicine
Hinsdale Hospital
Hinsdale, Illinois

AN ASPEN PUBLICATION®
Aspen Publishers, Inc.

1986

Rockville, Maryland
Royal Tunbridge Wells

Library of Congress Cataloging in Publication Data

Geriatric emergencies.

"An Aspen publication."
Includes bibliographies and index.
1. Geriatrics. 2. Medical emergencies. I. Judd, Richard L.
II. Warner, Carmen Germaine, 1941-   III. Shaffer, Mark A.
[DNLM: 1. Emergencies—in old age. 2. Emergency Medicine—in old age.
WB 105 G3691]
RC952.5.G436   1986   618.97′025   86-14060
ISBN: 0-87189-378-9

The authors have made every effort to ensure the accuracy of the information herein.
However, appropriate information sources should be consulted, especially for new or
unfamiliar procedures. It is the responsibility of every practitioner to evaluate the
appropriateness of a particular opinion in the context of actual clinical situations and
with due considerations to new developments. Authors, editors, and the publisher cannot
be held responsible for any typographical or other errors found in this book.

Editorial Services: Ruth Bloom

Library of Congress Catalog Card Number: 86-14060
ISBN: 0-87189-378-9

Printed in the United States of America

1 2 3 4 5

To three important women in my life, now in their elder years, who have each made a significant contribution to my life—*Priscilla*, my mother; *Ethel*, my mother-in-law; and *Ida*, my aunt. This does not diminish, of course, the contributions of my family—*Nancy, Sarah, and Jonathan*—who always continue in their steadfast encouragement of my pursuits in emergency medicine.

Richard L. Judd

To *B. Wallace Hood, Jr.* (1942–1985)—my mentor and inspiration for publishing excellence.

Carmen Germaine Warner

To my partner *Anita* who gives meaning to everything I do.
To *Grandmother Esther* who inspired me to become involved in this endeavor.
To *my parents* who are always there when I need them most.
To the memory of *my grandparents, Louis, Isaac, and Elena*. May they be in peace.

Mark A. Shaffer

Table of Contents

v

Foreword

In the practice of medicine it is an accepted fact that the provision of emergency care is fraught with great benefit and great risk for both patient and provider alike. Nowhere is this benefit-risk interface greater than in caring for the elderly. The elderly are subject to all of the life- and limb-threatening problems that confront the younger age group, but are in added jeopardy from a myriad of age-related diseases that confuse their presentation, confound the health care provider caring for them, and complicate our ability to provide prompt and appropriate medical care.

In *Geriatric Emergencies,* Dr. Judd, Ms. Warner, and Dr. Shaffer have combined their emergency management, clinical care, and health systems experience to offer a major new authoritative text directed to the primary health care provider who is called on to diagnose, treat, and/or manage definitively unexpected medical and surgical conditions in the elderly. The editors have gathered a group of recognized specialists and compiled a comprehensive yet succinct summation of problems particularly relevant to the elderly. Providers of emergency care—from field personnel, and emergency nursing to emergency physicians, from nursing home staff to physician specialists in geriatrics—will find this book a major ready resource, a standard reference, and a practical guide for a host of problems that afflict members of our older generation.

In *Geriatric Emergencies,* the editors display a well-ordered approach to a wide variety of emergency problems. A comprehensive review of the broad field of emergency care follows. Diagnostic dilemmas, degenerative diseases, and, appropriately, death and dying are emphasized to remind the reader of the unique challenge posed by an acutely ill or injured elderly patient.

As we enter an era where the elderly constitute an ever-increasing proportion of our population, *Geriatric Emergencies* will increasingly remind us of where we are going and from whence we have come.

Kimball I. Maull, MD, FACS
Professor and Chairman
Department of Surgery
The University of Tennessee
Memorial Hospital
Knoxville, Tennessee

Preface

The elderly, those 65 or older, are the fastest growing age group in the United States. In 1900 this group comprised only 4% of the population; by 1980 their ranks had grown to more than 11%. During these same years, while the population of America tripled, the number of elderly increased eight-fold.

For the first time in the history of the American nation, there are more persons over the age of 65 than under the age of 14. By the year 2030, it is estimated that the elderly will comprise nearly 18% of the population. Older people are not easily categorized into any single entity; they are to be found in every economic stratum, race, religion, occupation, and shading of political belief.

The elderly are likely to be admitted to the emergency medical care facility, at both the basic and definitive care levels, with multiple chronic medical conditions. The management of their critical and traumatic incidents challenges the capabilities of all emergency medical professionals. Understanding the special needs of the elderly, the changes that the aging process brings about in physical structure, body composition, and organ function and these changes' relationship to medical intervention during an emergency is a necessity if mortality and morbidity are to be significantly reduced. Changing patterns of mental and emotional health must also be considered because of their important effect on the elderly person's adjustment to the impact of trauma or critical illness. Physical illness and injury, in fact, must be thought of as a causative factor of mental illness in the elderly. For example, a myocardial infarction or subdural hematoma may trigger mental aberrations, hypercapnia may be the cause of confusion, and toxic states or folate deficiency must be considered in mental status evaluation.

In the management of critial illness or trauma, emergency medical care professionals have come to rely on certain time parameters determined to be valid in preserving and maintaining life. The ''golden hour'' in the trauma patient, for example, has demonstrated the importance of the initiation of definitive care in the last 20 minutes of that hour. In the elderly, that time sequence may not be at all adequate because of factors of declining efficiency of the organism.

Recognizing the special and urgent problems faced by providers in rendering emergency medical care to the elderly, the editors have produced a volume dedicated to the salient and urgent management problems faced by emergency care physicians, nurses, and allied medical personnel. Providing care to this age group is fraught with unusual and challenging decisions that demand often heroic and extraordinary courses of intervention. The authors contributing to this volume bring together in one work an impressive amount of clinical, academic, and research experience. It is hoped that this book will make an important contribution to the growing literature of geriatric medicine.

Richard L. Judd
Carmen Germaine Warner
Mark A. Shaffer
September 1986

Acknowledgments

The concept of this book originated when B. Wallace Hood was publisher of Capistrano Press. Mr. Hood's pursuit of excellence, manifested in numerous emergency care reference books, has affected positively the quality of care nationwide.

In Wally's absence, the development of this book continued through the dedication of two women. Barbara Halliburton, editorial director at Capistrano Press, and Jan Boller, Capistrano's acquisitions editor, have devoted their time, talents, and energies to this book and its intended use in emergency care.

The teamwork of these individuals, complementing the clinical excellence and commitment of our authors, has made this project an exciting and rewarding undertaking.

It has been a joy and a privilege to coordinate this book, as we believe the clinical and technical expertise contained in it will advance the quality of emergency care offered to today's geriatric population.

Contributors

Dominick Addario, MD
Assistant Clinical Professor of
  Psychiatry
University of California, San Diego
School of Medicine
  and
Private Practice
San Diego, California

LCDR Julian E. Allen, MC, USN
Head of the Department of Surgery
U.S. Naval Hospital
Guantanamo Bay, Cuba

Harold F. Bosco, DMD, FACD
Chief of Dental and Oral Surgery
New Britain General Hospital
New Britain, Connecticut

Karen Cervenka, MD
Assistant Clinical Professor
University of Chicago Hospitals and
  Clinics
Chicago, Illinois

Charles E. Copeland, MD, FACS
Chief, General Surgery
Director, Burn Center
Mercy Hospital
Pittsburgh, Pennsylvania

Lewis DeMent, MD, FACEP
Columbia Emergency Medicine
  Associates
  and
Emergency Staff Physician
Good Samaritan Hospital
Portland, Oregon

Martin M. Dinep, MD, FACS
Senior Attending Surgeon
New Britain General Hospital
New Britain, Connecticut

Mary L. Dunne, MD
Attending Physician
St. Francis Hospital
Poughkeepsie, New York

Scott C. Edminster, MD, FACEP
Emergency Staff Physician
Deaconess Medical Center
  and
Clinical Faculty, Family Medicine—
  Spokane and Internal Medicine—
  Spokane (University of Washington
  affiliates)
Spokane, Washington
  and
Private Practice
Colbert, Washington

Peter A. Engel, MD
Assistant Chief of Medicine
New Britain General Hospital
New Britain, Connecticut

Thomas J. Godar, MD
Director of Section of Pulmonary
  Diseases
St. Francis Hospital and Medical
  Center
Hartford, Connecticut
  and
Vice President
American Lung Association

Janet Leigh Haley, BA
Freelance Writer
  and
Member, Institute for Research on
  Aging
University of California, San Diego
School of Medicine
  and
Director of Communications
Sandpiper Communications
Carlsbad, California

James D. Heckman, MD
Professor and Deputy Chairman
Department of Orthopedics
The University of Texas Health
  Science Center at San Antonio
San Antonio, Texas

James J. Jacobson, MD
Chief of Urology
and
Assistant Chief of Staff
New Britain General Hospital
New Britain, Connecticut
  and
Assistant Clinical Professor
University of Connecticut
Farmington, Connecticut

**Richard L. Judd, PhD, EMSI,
  R-EMTA**
Executive Dean and Professor of
  Emergency Medical Sciences
Central Connecticut State University
New Britain, Connecticut
  and
Allied Medical Staff
New Britain General Hospital
New Britain, Connecticut

Peter J. Lynch, MD
Chief of Dermatology
  and
Associate Chairman, Department of
  Internal Medicine
University of Arizona College of
  Medicine
Tucson, Arizona

Peggy L. McCall, MSN, RN, CNA
Nursing Director
Emergency Center/Ambulatory Care
  and Life Flight Nursing
Hermann Hospital
  and

Clinical Assistant Professor
University of Texas School of Allied
  Health Sciences and The School of
  Nursing
Houston, Texas

Edward E. Morse, MD
Professor of Laboratory Medicine
University of Connecticut School of
  Medicine
Farmington, Connecticut

**Mark M. Moy, MD, FACEP,
  FAAFP**
Hinsdale Hospital
Hinsdale, Illinois

C. William Schwab, MD, FACS
Associate Professor of Surgery
UMDNJ Rutgers Medical School at
  Camden
  and
Head, Division of Trauma and
  Emergency Medical Services
Cooper Hospital/University Medical
  Center
Camden, New Jersey

Mark A. Shaffer, MD, FACEP
Director and Chairman
Department of Emergency Medicine
Hinsdale Hospital
Hinsdale, Illinois

Gerald O. Strauch, MD, FACS
Chief of Surgery
New Britain General Hospital
New Britain, Connecticut
  and
Professor of Surgery
University of Connecticut School of
  Medicine
Farmington, Connecticut

and
Clinical Professor of Surgery
Uniformed Services University of the
    Health Sciences School of
    Medicine
Formerly, Vice-Chairman; Chairman,
    Subcommittee on Regional
    Committees; Committee on Trauma
Member, American College of
    Surgeons

Robert W. Strauss, MD
Chairman
Department of Emergency Medicine
St. Francis Hospital
Poughkeepsie, New York

Ronald P. Williams, MD, PhD
St. Francis Regional Medical Center
Department of Orthopedics
Wichita, Kansas

1

Approach to the Elderly Patient

Mary L. Dunne, MD and Robert W. Strauss, MD

The percentage of the American population over 65 years of age will continue to increase in the foreseeable future. In addition, elderly persons have a higher per capita utilization of health care services than the young, and they have a greater propensity to develop acute illness. As such, they will make up an ever more substantial portion of patients seen in emergency departments. It is thus imperative to recognize the particular medical needs of this group and to identify the knowledge and skills within the specialty of geriatric medicine that will become increasingly more valuable to the emergency physician.

Stereotyped views of the elderly warrant re-examination, and health care providers must each address their own attitudes toward this age group. Clinical practice provides limitless examples of wide individual variation in vitality and resilience at any age, and in no group is this range greater than in older persons. A narrow view of an older patient's future is also inappropriate: The average 65-year-old woman can expect to live another 18 years, and a 65-year-old man, another 14; at age 85, there is an average life expectancy of more than 5 years. Physicians' perspectives may be skewed because they habitually deal with the ill or injured, but the elderly tend to report their own health as generally good. Most are self-sufficient or require only minimal assistance; even among those over age 85, fewer than 20% are confined at home. A biased attitude based on age is not only unjust but also inaccurate.

PHYSIOLOGIC CHANGES ASSOCIATED WITH THE AGING PROCESS

Older persons are more susceptible to disease and injury than the population in general, and the course of illness is more complex in the elderly than in younger counterparts. Acute illness or trauma may be superimposed on a background of

1

chronic disease, and a disease process is more likely to alter the function of organ systems beyond the one primarily involved, especially as such stresses may unmask the limited reserves of homeostatic mechanisms.

The elderly as a group are poorly nourished and are more likely than younger adults to have deficient levels of serum albumin, protein, hemoglobin, and vitamins. Nutrition is adversely affected by poverty; physical disability, such as impaired vision or crippling arthritis; inadequate dentition; drugs; and various disease states, including malabsorption and gastrointestinal disorders. A multitude of factors are postulated to be involved in osteoporosis, including inadequate dietary calcium; hypovitaminosis D from drugs, gastrointestinal disease, and decreased exposure to sunlight; decreased physical activity; and menopause.

Humoral and cell-mediated immune responses are impaired in older persons, and the response to autologous antigens is increased. These phenomena may contribute to an increased vulnerability to infection, neoplastic disease, and possibly to vascular injury.

The aging process results in some degree of myocardial hypertrophy and hemodynamic changes leading to diminished cardiac reserve. The older cardiovascular system accommodates filling pressure and volume changes less readily and has less capacity to increase and sustain increased cardiac output. Sudden stress can more easily precipitate cardiac dysrhythmias, heart failure, and sudden death. Although blood pressure rises with age, the prevalence of diastolic hypertension declines slightly after age 60, and the pattern of systolic hypertension predominates. Despite its prevalence, hypertension should not be considered a normal result of aging, although its pathophysiology may differ from that of younger persons.

Some aspects of pulmonary function decline with age, including vital capacity, forced expiratory volume in one second (FEV_1), arterial oxygen tension, and alveolar-capillary gas-diffusing capacity. The elderly have decreased ventilatory response to hypoxia and hypercapnia. The age-related changes of weakened respiratory musculature, decreased thoracic cage compliance, and lessened small airway recoil mimic some components of obstructive lung disease. Many years of exposure to noxious irritants through smoking, environmental pollution, and occupational exposure to toxic agents may be superimposed on purely age-related changes in lung function.

Aging is accompanied by a gradual decline in renal plasma flow, glomerular filtration rate, and renal tubular resorptive capacity, and aged kidneys respond less effectively to hemodynamic stress and fluid and electrolyte imbalance. Moreover, the aging process also limits compensatory pulmonary and endocrine responses to fluid and electrolyte derangements, resulting in further compromise of renal function. Because muscle mass declines concomitantly with glomerular filtration rate, a substantial decrease in filtration rate is not necessarily associated with a rise in serum creatinine. Creatinine clearance, a more accurate estimate of renal function, may be determined relative to age by the following formula:

$$\frac{(140 \ - \ \text{age}) \times \text{body weight (kg)}}{72 \ \times \ \text{serum creatinine}} \qquad (\times \ 0.85 \ \text{in women})$$

With increasing age, a degree of general involution of the gastrointestinal system seems to occur. Changes in cellular number and structure reduce effective surface absorptive area, sphincter activity and gastrointestinal motility decrease, and blood flow through the alimentary system decreases. These changes, however, may result in no discernible dysfunction. Functional disturbances are more likely the result of poor dietary or bowel habits, gastrointestinal or other organ system disease, or the effect of drugs or surgery.

The nervous system is susceptible to the aging process on many levels; a variety of psychologic and neurologic alterations may occur. Although mental status changes very slowly, there is generally some degree of slowing of response and decline in intellectual performance compared with an individual's mature baseline. The brain is especially vulnerable to the vicissitudes of stress, remote disease, and medications. However, decline in vision or hearing should prompt a search for correctable causes, rather than be attributed to aging alone.

There is a gradual decline of glucose tolerance with age; the prevalence of diabetes is estimated to be as great as one in every six persons at age 65, and one in every four persons over age 80. Diabetes may progress insidiously in the elderly, and neuropathy, impotence, or hyperosmolar coma may be the first indication of the disease.

ASSESSMENT OF THE ELDERLY PATIENT

Approach to the Elderly Patient

People come to the emergency department because they feel something is wrong with them. Whether the problem is physical or emotional, it is very real to the patient and is often painful or frightening. Older individuals often come to an emergency department more reluctantly than a younger person; getting there frequently requires a relatively greater expenditure of time and money and may itself be physically exhausting. They generally spend a longer time waiting for their evaluation and disposition and have a greater likelihood of having a serious medical problem. The approach to the elderly patient must take all these factors into consideration.

Emergency medical staff must sometimes react in a most efficient and technical manner. Unfortunately, this behavior pattern may become generalized to situations that do not demand it. Physicians should introduce themselves by name and approach the elderly patient with an attitude of respect, empathy, and thoughtful kindness. The most basic form of respect is to learn and use a person's name, as most older adults are offended by being addressed familiarly by first name. This simple courtesy is not only appreciated by the patient but also puts the person at ease, enhances the gathering of useful data, and fosters patient compliance. Patient behaviors that seem uncooperative, hostile, or distasteful should be recognized as perhaps being beyond that individual's control and should be met with professional equanimity. Rudeness or roughness on the part of the medical care team will be met with conscious or unconscious resistance, whereas a gentleness in manner, voice, and touch is generally welcomed.

Interview Process

The interview of an elderly person often takes longer and may be complicated by barriers to communication, such as hearing loss, visual impairment, distraction, and fatigue, that can be anticipated and minimized. Lighting should be adequate, such background noise as the bedside monitor reduced, and visual distractions removed or, if necessary to the patient's care, explained. The interviewer should speak slowly and clearly in deep tones while facing the patient; this is best accomplished by sitting at the patient's eye level, rather than by looming over the patient or speaking from the foot of the bed.

Patience is a necessary virtue when obtaining a history, as response times and speech are often slower in the elderly. They should be given adequate time to answer the questions. Because older persons frequently underreport important signs and symptoms, these should be sought specifically, as should information about previous hospitalizations, operations, medications, and allergies. Prior medical records should be examined whenever possible. It is prudent to ask particularly about a number of medications, including digoxin, nitroglycerine, diuretics, insulin, corticosteroids, aspirin, and Coumadin.

It is frequently necessary to gather information from other sources. When a patient arrives by ambulance, it is essential to obtain a history from the paramedics concerning both the present illness and the environment from which the patient was received, especially as this may be the only historical information available.

Interviewing family and friends can be critical to the patient's assessment, particularly because their assistance may be necessary in ensuring the patient's compliance with evaluation and treatment. One must not, however, substitute talking with the family for actually interviewing the patient. It is often most productive to conduct conversations with the patient and family separately, lest the more forceful personalities, often of the younger persons who care for the elder patient, dominate the interview. A medical social worker or patient care representative can be invaluable in assessing family dynamics, home environment, and the patient's functional status and can contribute information essential to forming the patient's disposition.

When performing a physical examination, one must bear in mind that older people may be more sensitive to cold and are especially concerned about modesty. They are also more likely to have false teeth, wigs, and breast and limb prostheses. Removal of clothing and cosmetic or functional devices may cause embarrassment, and modesty should be respected as long as health is not compromised. It is equally important to examine the entire patient, as decubitus ulcers, necrotic toes, or evidence of trauma might not be suspected from the historical information supplied.

Laboratory Examination

Although elderly people are more likely to have abnormal laboratory test results, this finding generally reflects their incidence of underlying disease and is not due to old age per se. Those parameters that remain unchanged and those that are commonly altered with age are shown in Table 1–1.

Patients are often left alone while they await laboratory and x-ray results. They should not remain out of sight for long periods of time, and all precautions should be taken to ensure that they do not injure themselves during their stay in the emergency department or literally get lost in transit between locations. Families deserve news of patients, even simply that the evaluation is in progress. When a patient is critically ill, a team approach may best deal with family and friends. There are many personnel that can assist in this area, including patient care representatives, social workers, clergy, hospital volunteers, aides, and orderlies; their only requirement is a sensitive and caring personality. The physician must remember that a personal report to those concerned is a matter of urgency; it should be delivered as soon as circumstances allow.

Therapeutic Recommendations

Recommended care, available alternatives, and anticipated results should be discussed with the patient and family so that a conscientious choice may be made. Discharge from the emergency department must be made with an awareness of the patient's functional status and home environment and the calculated risks and benefits of hospitalization. Hospitals are especially dangerous places for the elderly, as they are at greater risk for nosocomial infection, iatrogenic disorders, and the complications of bedrest or immobility.

Drug therapy should be initiated or changed in the emergency department only when clearly indicated. In general, older persons require smaller doses of drugs than their younger counterparts, and dose regimens should be as simple as possible. Special packaging, clear instructions, and enlisting the aid of a responsible relative to oversee therapy help ensure compliance.

CLINICAL IMPLICATIONS IN THE ELDERLY

Medical evaluation of the elderly requires an awareness of the unique aspects of their health problems, particularly both the incidence of diseases and their complicating factors, and the variety of manifestations of illnesses.

Because older people have higher pain thresholds than younger persons and because they are more likely to minimize habitually the importance of discomfort,

Table 1–1 Laboratory Assessment of the Elderly

Laboratory parameters unchanged
Hemoglobin and hematocrit
White blood cell count
Platelet count
Electrolytes (sodium, potassium, chloride, bicarbonate)
Blood urea nitrogen
Liver function tests (transaminases, bilirubin, prothrombin time)
Free thyroxine index
Thyroid-stimulating hormone
Calcium
Phosphorus

Commonly abnormal laboratory parameters	
Parameter	**Clinical significance**
Sedimentation rate	Mild elevations (10–20 mm) may be an age-related change
Glucose	Glucose tolerance decreases
Creatinine	Because lean body mass and daily endogenous creatinine production decline, high-normal and minimally elevated values may indicate substantially reduced renal function
Albumin	Average values decline (less than 0.5 g/ml) with age, especially in hospitalized elderly
Alkaline phosphatase	Mild elevations common in asymptomatic elderly; liver and Paget's disease should be considered if moderately elevated
Serum iron and iron-binding capacity	Decreased values are not an aging change and usually indicate undernutrition or gastrointestinal blood loss
Urinalysis	Asymptomatic pyuria and bacteriuria are common and generally do not warrant treatment; hematuria is abnormal and needs further evaluation
Chest x-ray	Interstitial changes are a common age-related finding; diminished bone density should prompt consideration of osteoporosis
Electrocardiogram	ST-segment and T-wave changes, atrial and ventricular arrhythmias, and various blocks are common in asymptomatic elderly and may not need specific evaluation or treatment

Source: Reprinted from *Essentials of Clinical Geriatrics* (p 47) by RL Kane et al with permission of McGraw-Hill Book Company, © 1984.

any complaint of pain should be regarded as a significant symptom mandating careful evaluation.

Cardiovascular

Consideration of chest pain in the elderly includes the usual wide differential diagnosis. It must be remembered that intrathoracic pathology may present atypically, eg, painless myocardial infarction or pneumonia without cough or fever. Conversely, acute abdominal emergencies—cholecystitis and perforated ulcer—may present as chest pain. Herpes zoster can cause severe atypical chest pain during its pre-eruptive phase.

Gastrointestinal

Acute abdominal pain in an older person has a high likelihood of representing a surgical emergency. The most common causes include cholecystitis, intestinal obstruction, and appendicitis; less frequent but relatively common causes include perforated peptic ulcer, gallstone ileus or bowel tumor as the cause of obstruction, diverticulitis, pancreatitis, and mesenteric occlusion. Change in mental status, with or without signs of shock, may represent an acute abdominal emergency. In addition, intrathoracic, genitourinary, retroperitoneal, and metabolic disease may cause only abdominal symptoms.

Anorexia is a common complaint of the elderly. In addition to the usual considerations, inadequate or ill-fitting dentures, depression, and drug reactions are important causes in older persons. Weight loss out of proportion to food intake may be due to endocrine disorders, malignant lesions, chronic infections or inflammatory processes, or chronic congestive heart failure.

Endocrine

Thyroid disease is often underdiagnosed because the possibility is not considered. Symptoms and signs may be insidious or atypical and often are either nonspecific or thought to be caused by another organ system. Masked hyperthyroidism may present as weight loss, heart failure, dysrhythmias, angina, or abdominal complaints. Masked hypothyroidism may present with dyspnea, carpal tunnel syndrome, deafness, hypothermia, or unexplained coma.

Neuropsychiatric

Headache, occurring less frequently in the elderly, has greater significance as a symptom of pathology. The possibilities of giant cell arteries, subdural hematoma, metabolic disorders, herpes zoster involving nerves of the face or scalp, trigeminal neuralgia, and tumors should be considered in the differential diagnosis in this age group. Migraine headache is relatively less common, and such a syndrome should prompt consideration of transient ischemic attack or cerebrovascular accident.

Just as medical problems may masquerade as neuropsychiatric disorders so psychiatric syndromes may present with somatic complaints. It is imperative that emergency medical personnel recognize, in particular, that depression is a true life-threatening condition in the older population. The elderly are more successful at killing themselves; they make relatively few suicidal gestures. The suicide rate for white males 80 years of age and older is higher than for any other age group. At particular risk is the older person who lives alone, has a chronic illness, has recently lost a spouse, or who abuses drugs or alcohol.

Alcoholism is thought to be more prevalent in the elderly than is generally recognized, especially as some older people become abusers in late life, often as a result of bereavement. Many do not manifest the typical pattern of intoxication, dependence, and withdrawal, but evidence loss of self-esteem, deterioration in grooming or social behavior, or present with unexplained falls or nonspecific complaints.

Abuse of the elderly is thought to be as widespread as child abuse. It knows no socioeconomic, ethnic, racial, or religious boundaries. It is often, but not exclusively, a family problem and involves physical, psychological, and financial exploitation. Because older persons rarely report or admit to being ill-treated by those on whom they are dependent, medical providers must be alert to that possibility. Risk factors for abuse reflect the stress placed on the caretaker and include older age (with a mean in the eighties), dementia, multiple chronic diseases, incontinence, impaired sleep cycle (especially nocturnal shouting or wandering), and dependence on others for activities of daily living.

Physical signs of abuse are similar to some of those found in abused children. They include cigarette or rope burns and bruises, abrasions, or lacerations on the chest, back, and extremities, particularly if they are in various stages of healing or have unusual patterns that suggest bites or the use of an instrument. A frequently overlooked sign is bleeding beneath the scalp from forceful hair pulling.

Most states have extensive domestic violence or adult protective services legislation governing the handling of cases of suspected abuse. Emergency care providers must maintain a high index of suspicion, provide careful documenta-tion, and initiate ongoing medical and social service involvement. Maintaining a cooperative relationship with the family is essential in seeking a solution, recog-nizing that marital conflict, financial difficulty, exhaustion, and grief contribute significantly to precipitating abusive behavior.

Infection

Several general aspects of bacterial infection in the elderly warrant close attention. The diagnosis may be much more difficult to make than in younger adults, as it is frequently not suggested by the patient's initial complaint, which may be as vague as weakness in the presence of urosepsis or as distracting as abdominal pain in the presence of pneumonia. Some signs may be difficult to appreciate as indicators of infectious processes; confusion may be attributed to senility and neck stiffness attributed to cervical arthritis in a patient with incipient meningitis.

Underlying disease states and environmental circumstances may predispose the elderly to certain infections. The incidence of gram-negative bacillary coloniza-tion of the oropharynx increases with age, and the patient with esophageal motility disorders or decreased gag or incoordination of swallowing secondary to stroke or the lethargic or oversedated patient is vulnerable to aspiration pneumonia. Patients with urinary catheters or prostatism are predisposed to urosepsis. Those who have sensory impairment from stroke or neuropathy or who are immobilized are at greater risk of sepsis from skin breakdown.

Active tuberculosis in individuals over 65 years of age is increasing in Western countries. Although reactivation accounts for most cases, primary tuberculosis may occur with unexpected frequency, and in either case, the classic signs of cough and sputum production may be absent.

The incidence, morbidity, and mortality rates for bacterial infection are higher in the elderly. Older persons are more likely to develop bacteremia and are at greater risk to develop both complications of specific infections, eg, pneumococcal pneumonia progressing to pericarditis or meningitis, and cardiac, respiratory, and renal failure in association with the primary disease process.

Older patients are susceptible to a wider variety of pathogens for most diseases, making empirical therapy more difficult, and they are more vulnerable to toxic reactions to antibiotics.

Drug Reactions

Any abrupt change in an elderly person's physical or mental status should prompt a review of that person's medical regimen. The likelihood of adverse drug reaction rises dramatically among the elderly. It is related to age-associated impairment of organ systems involved in drug distribution and excretion, underlying chronic disease, the often necessary use of multiple drugs and their interactions, and compliance problems. Diagnosis often requires a high index of suspicion, as complaints are often vague and may suggest dementia or depression. Compliance problems are distressingly frequent and may result from physical or mental impairment, drug-induced confusion or sedation, self-adjustment of dosage intervals or amounts, borrowing medication from friends or relatives, or using home remedies or over-the-counter medications without the knowledge of the physician. Duplication of prescriptions, especially if the person is seeing more than one physician, may result in inadvertent drug overdose.

The following medications are most often responsible for adverse drug reactions in older patients: analgesics, antacids, antiarthritics, anticoagulants, antihypertensives, antimicrobials, cardiac glycosides, CNS drugs, diuretics, and corticosteroids.

SUMMARY

Developing an approach to the evaluation of elderly patients is an art that requires a sensitivity to the unique aspects of their presentations. The manifestations of disease are more subtle and the return to health less pronounced. To discern the extent of disease, the emergency physician must be attuned to the clues provided by the patient and family. This evaluation requires gentleness and patience. Treatment should be specific, avoiding the excesses that might otherwise upset a delicate balance.

BIBLIOGRAPHY

Allen CA, Porotman H (compilers): *Chartbook in Aging in America, The 1981 White House Conference on Aging*. Washington, DC, US Government Printing Office.

Harris WR: Leading the health care team for the elderly, in Petersdorf RG, Adams RD, Braunwald E (eds): *Harrison's Principles of Internal Medicine*, New York, McGraw-Hill, 1983.

Kane RL, Ouslander JG, Abrass IB: *Essentials of Clinical Geriatrics*. New York, McGraw-Hill, 1984.

Koin D: Abuse and neglect in the aged, in Schwartz G, Bosker G, Grigsby J (eds): *Geriatric Emergencies*. Bowie, MD, Robert J Brady Co, 1984.

Lamy PR: *Prescribing for the Elderly*. Littleton, MA, PSG Publishing Co, 1980.

McDue JD (ed): *Medical Care of the Elderly*. Lexington, MA, Collamore Press, 1983.

Samiy AH (ed): Symposium on clinical geriatric medicine. *Med Clin North Am* 67:2, 1983.

2

Toxicity of Drugs in the Aged

Peter A. Engel, MD

Older people take more medications, suffer from more illnesses, and experience more adverse drug effects than their younger counterparts. Surprisingly, aging in itself is often not the major factor contributing to this situation. Disease coupled with genetic and acquired impairments in drug metabolism is often a much more important causative factor.

The signs and symptoms of toxic reaction to drugs are nonspecific. A patient might come to the emergency department (ED) with hypotension, arrthymias, nausea, confusion, seizures, urinary retention, fatigue, or other symptoms, any of which could represent a variety of pathologic processes, including an adverse drug reaction.

The goal of this chapter is to make it easier for clinicians to recognize drug-induced illness in the aged and to understand why such illness is so common. It does not review pharmacotherapy or adverse drug effects, for which an extensive literature is available both in general[1-4] and in specific for geriatric pharmacology.[5,6] Instead this consideration of drug-related illnesses (1) reviews the numerous factors that increase the risk of toxic reactions to drugs in the aged, (2) provides sufficient background in pharmacology and age-related physiologic changes to make the toxic effects of drugs more understandable, and (3) illustrates some of these basic principles with clinical examples.

The elderly represent an extraordinarily diverse group. Individual differences in drug sensitivity and metabolism, which are substantial in the young, are even greater in the older population. Furthermore, inherited differences in the ability to eliminate drugs probably do not change much over the life-span, so slow drug metabolizers in youth remain so in old age. The addition of age-associated diseases, such as renal insufficiency and congestive heart failure, compromises drug disposal even further. This subgroup of sick elderly who are also congenitally poor drug metabolizers is most prone to adverse drug reactions. Therefore, that diagnostic possibility deserves greatest attention in these patients.

11

RECOGNIZING DRUG-RELATED ILLNESSES

More than 10% of hospital admissions are drug related, and about 9% of hospitalized patients experience serious adverse drug reactions.[7,8] In an older individual a drug-related illness may stem from a number of factors that deserve attention in an emergency care setting. Consulting the chart and questioning the patient may produce very misleading information, particularly for those who are taking four or more medications. In these individuals perfect compliance is a rarity, and major errors are commonplace. In most elderly patients the relationship between signs, symptoms, and drugs can be characterized as a function of the following:

- too much or too little drug
- drug abuse or drug withdrawal
- any process that increases or inhibits drug action.

The most commonly encountered situations in which drugs contribute to symptoms are as follows:

- The patient who is forgetful, confused, or does not understand the purpose of a drug takes more or less than the prescribed amount. Drug regimens listed in hospital summaries and outpatient notes are often a poor reflection of patient medication use.
- The patient is compliant, but the prescribed dose is excessive.
- The patient receives medications from more than one physician or institution, and each prescription writer is unaware of the other or others. Topical agents must be considered in this instance. Ophthalmic timolol, for example, which is used to control intraocular pressure, can also induce bronchospasm and heart failure.[9]
- The patient resumes the use of old medications, in addition to those prescribed at discharge from the hospital. This error is more likely if different brands of the same agent are prescribed, eg, Lanoxin and generic digoxin.
- The patient fails to mention the use of nonprescription drugs. A patient may develop symptoms of salicylism from excess ingestion of aspirin, for example, or diarrhea from magnesium-containing antacids and not appreciate the connection between the drug and the side effect.
- The patient is a drug abuser, and the signs and symptoms are a manifestation of a drug withdrawal syndrome, eg, acute abstinence from alcohol, meprobamate, barbiturate, diazepam, propoxyphene, or narcotic agents.
- The patient ran out of medications and has a re-emergence of signs and symptoms associated with the treated disease, such as diabetes, heart failure, or angina pectoris.

- The patient has added a new drug to an established regimen, and the addition impairs or exaggerates effects of drugs already in use. For example, tricyclic antidepressants block the antihypertensive effect of methyldopa,[10] cimetidine inhibits the metabolism of propranolol by reducing hepatic blood flow and inhibiting drug-metabolizing enzymes,[11] and phenylbutazone enhances the risk of bleeding associated with warfarin by inhibiting metabolism and displacing this tightly bound drug from albumin.[12]

- The patient changes his or her smoking, alcohol intake, or dietary habits or develops a disease that influences drug metabolism. Smoking increases the activity of drug-metabolizing enzymes in the liver, thereby enhancing the disposal of theophylline, an effect more consistently demonstrated in young as compared to old subjects.[13,14] A theophylline-using smoker who quits cigarettes may develop a toxic reaction to the drug. The xanthines in coffee and tea can also enhance the toxic effects of theophylline.

These examples highlight the uncertainties and complexities of drug therapy and the potential difficulties in obtaining accurate information. The clinician may need to consult not only the patient but also the patient's family, friends, personal physician, pharmacy, and hospital chart. To increase accuracy, one should ask patients for specific information about the times, quantities, and types of medication they have ingested over the past hours or days. Many patients do not consider over-the-counter agents to be drugs and must be directly questioned about them. Patients who are abusing drugs may offer a distorted picture of their actual drug use. A curious, critical, and thorough approach is most likely to define the role of drugs in a given clinical situation.

DRUG METABOLISM AND ACTION IN THE ELDERLY

Drug-related illness in the aged must be viewed from two perspectives: drug metabolism and action, and the physiologic changes of normal aging. Again, the heterogeneity of the aged population means that some of the following principles may not apply to specific individuals. Moreover, geriatric pharmacology is a young science with many areas incompletely investigated and many questions unanswered. Still, enough is known to produce a general understanding of the influences of age, genetic makeup, and disease processes on the actions and toxic effects of drugs.

Absorption

Among the factors that influence drug absorption are gastric pH, motility, and the ingestion of a fatty meal, which slows gastric emptying. Although gastric pH tends to rise with increasing age while splanchnic blood flow falls, no available data convincingly demonstrate a significant age-related change in drug absorption.[15] Most drugs enter the intestinal microcirculation by passive diffusion. Age-related changes in gut membrane properties and blood flow do not seem to be the limiting factors in this process.

Distribution

Drug binding to plasma proteins, pKa, and lipid solubility coupled with body composition of the patient constitute the major determinants of drug distribution to various tissue compartments. Of the many changes associated with aging only the increase in percentage of body fat has a clearly predictable effect on drug distribution.

Drug Binding

Drugs are transported in the blood in free form or bound to plasma proteins, primarily albumin. α_1-Acid glycoprotein and lipoproteins, which are present in much smaller quantities, bind some basic drugs, including propranolol. Because the unbound fraction is pharmacologically active and is distributed to the tissues, the avidity of a drug for albumin binding becomes an important factor in drug action. Acidic drugs, including indomethacin, naproxen, furosemide, tolbutamide, warfarin, and sulfamethoxazole, are highly bound. Simultaneous administration of two such agents may result in the displacement of one or both from binding sites, thus increasing the quantity of free drug in plasma. In most cases this larger fraction of free drug thereby becomes available for metabolism and excretion, so the pharmacologic effects can be complex. Certainly, transient toxic levels of a chronically administered drug may occur when a second agent is introduced that displaces the first from albumin. But if both drugs are continued at regular intervals, the total and free plasma level of the first drug will fall, and free concentration will approach the initial level.[16]

Although displacement of bound drug from albumin seems an attractive mechanism to explain how a drug may reach toxic levels, clinical demonstrations of this metabolism are rare, and its clinical significance is uncertain. In one example, valproate increases the free fraction of phenytoin by displacing it from albumin. Total phenytoin concentration initially falls because more free drug is available for metabolism and excretion. Later, phenytoin levels rise presumably due to inhibition of phenytoin metabolism by valproate.[17] One of the practical consequences of this interaction is a downward shift in the "therapeutic range" of phenytoin plasma levels, which measure total drug, ie, bound and free drug fractions.

In the elderly, plasma albumin concentration drops modestly with age, and the clinical consequences of this change are unlikely to be significant.[15] In disease states in which albumin may be severely depressed, again the major practical impact is that the therapeutic range of total drug concentration is shifted downward because a larger fraction of drug is in free form. This occurs in monitoring total blood levels of the highly bound drugs amitriptyline, imipramine, and phenytoin but not with digoxin, which has little albumin binding.

Change in Body Composition

A considerably more important factor in drug distribution is the well-documented change in body composition associated with aging that is characterized by an increase in body fat, loss of lean tissue mass, and loss of total body water (Figure 2–1).[18] These changes have important effects on the distribution of drugs. Identical weight-adjusted doses of water-soluble agents, such as penicillin, acetaminophen, morphine, and meperidine, reach higher peak plasma levels in old as compared to young subjects because the theoretical space into which the drug can disperse, the volume of distribution (V_d), is smaller.

$$V_d = \frac{\text{Total amount of drug in the body}}{\text{Concentration of drug in plasma}}$$

This change can be clinically significant if the drug has a narrow therapeutic index, as is the case with these narcotic agonists. In addition, these agents have diminished plasma binding in the aged.[19] The increased drug concentration and larger

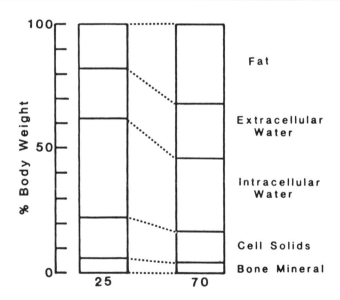

Figure 2–1 Typical change in body composition of men at ages 25 and 70.

Source: Reproduced with permission from RA Kenney: *Physiology of Aging: A Synopsis.* Copyright © 1982 by Year Book Medical Publishers, Inc, Chicago.

free fraction increase the pharmacologic effect of these drugs and necessitate dose reductions.

Drugs that are highly soluble in lipids, such as diazepam, the tricyclic antidepressants, and phenothiazines, which primarily distribute into body fat, have an increased volume of distribution in the elderly. All else being equal, this change alone prolongs the time required for half the drug to be eliminated—the $t_{1/2}$ or elimination half-life—because a given plasma level represents more total drug in the body. A third parameter, clearance—rate of drug elimination/plasma drug concentration—is related to V_d and $t_{1/2}$ by the following formula:

$$t_{1/2} = \frac{0.693V_d}{\text{Clearance}}$$

Either increased V_d, as in the case just mentioned, or diminished clearance increases $t_{1/2}$. The prolonged half-life of diazepam in the elderly reflects increased volume of distribution, whereas clearance is unchanged.[20] Clearance, rather than half-life, is the variable that determines dosage because it is a direct measure of drug elimination.

Clearance

Most drugs are eliminated either by renal excretion or by hepatic metabolism. Both systems undergo age-associated changes that bear on drug disposition, but the decline in renal function is better defined. Reduction in the drug-metabolizing ability of the liver is less clear, but is likely relevant to some cases of adverse drug reactions in the aged.

Renal Function

The aging kidney undergoes a nearly linear decline in glomerular filtration rate of about 50% between ages 20 and 90, a functional loss accompanied by reduced renal blood flow and diminished concentrating ability.[21] Yet serum creatinine is little changed in the aged, who have reduced creatine turnover from a smaller muscle mass. This relative insufficiency calls for a reduction in the dosage of drugs excreted principally by the kidney. Downward dose adjustments are particularly critical for agents that have a low therapeutic index, eg, digoxin, lithium, and the aminoglycoside antibiotics. Fortunately, assays are available to monitor concentrations of these drugs, so their use is safer and more effective. Dose reductions can be based on a formula that estimates creatinine clearance as a function of age:[22]

$$\text{CrCl (expressed as ml/min)} = \frac{(140 - \text{age}) \times (\text{body weight in kg} \div 72)}{\text{Cr (mg/dl)}}$$

Even this approach is still an approximation. Heterogeneity in geriatric renal function is reflected by a gentamycin $t_{1/2}$ that varies more than ten-fold in a large group of elderly patients with normal serum creatinine levels.[23]

Renally excreted drugs are both filtered by the glomerulus and secreted by the pars recta of the proximal tubule and are later reabsorbed along the nephron. Drug secretion can be competitive, and occasionally this is clinically significant. For example, probenecid inhibits the secretion of penicillin as well as methotrexate. The former combination is used to therapeutic advantage in the treatment of gonorrhea; the latter may result in toxic levels of methotrexate.[24]

Tubular reabsorption occurs by passive nonionic diffusion. For a few drugs the degree of reabsorption is significantly affected by urinary pH because the ionized form of the compound is not reabsorbed. The weak acids, phenobarbital, salicylates, and sulfa derivatives are more readily excreted in alkaline urine, whereas urinary acidification enhances the excretion of atenolol, ephedrine, and the tricyclic antidepressants.[22]

The well-documented circadian rhythms of urinary pH are associated with impaired salicylate excretion in the morning when pH reaches its lowest level.[25] Unfortunately, the clinical significance of this observation, particularly the impact on potentially toxic drug levels, has yet to be defined. Moreover, the persistence and significance of biological rhythms in old age remain an uncharted area.

Hepatic Blood Flow and Biotransformation

Clearance of a drug by the liver is a function of two major factors: hepatic blood flow and hepatic drug-metabolizing enzyme activity. For drugs with a high clearance rate, such as lidocaine, propranolol, and morphine, liver blood flow constitutes the rate-limiting step in drug metabolism. For drugs with low hepatic clearance, such as carbamazepine, aminophylline, phenytoin, tolbutamide, and warfarin, the activity of biotransforming enzymes determines the rate of drug clearance.

Because liver blood flow likely declines with age, as well as in the presence of disease, particularly congestive heart failure, the disposal of high-clearance drugs might be expected to decline as well.[26] However, this concept is complicated by several factors. In young healthy subjects hepatic blood flow normally varies up to four-fold, increasing when the subject is supine or eating and decreasing during upright posture and exercise.[27] If such large changes in hepatic blood flow persist into old age, then high-clearance drug metabolism might be substantially influenced by these variables. Unfortunately, no studies have investigated the influence of bedrest or posture on drug metabolism in the elderly. This information could be of great value in the care of aged, bedridden patients. Second, orally administered high-clearance drugs may be extensively metabolized during their "first pass" through the liver after intestinal absorption. If hepatic blood flow is low, a highly cleared drug will be more completely metabolized during its slow first pass through the liver, whereas the remaining fraction that reaches the general circulation will be metabolized more slowly. In old age, clearance of oral propranolol is unchanged, whereas IV clearance declines, suggesting that these opposing effects tend to cancel one another.[26]

In general, hepatic biotransformation increases the polarity of drugs by making them more water soluble. The initial (phase I) reactions include oxidations, hydrolyses, and reductions. These metabolites may be pharmacologically active, eg, some tricyclic antidepressants and benzodiazepine tranquilizers. Phase II reactions further conjugate or attach the drug to glucuronide, sulfate, or acetate. These highly polar, pharmacologically inactive compounds are excreted in the urine.

Many of the phase I reactions involve inducible enzyme systems located on the smooth endoplasmic reticulum of the hepatocyte, and the activity of these enzymes can be modulated by many factors. Smoking, alcohol, phenobarbital, carbamazepine, phenytoin, rifampin, and other drugs can increase activity of the hepatic mixed-function oxidase systems, thereby speeding their own metabolism, as well as that of other compounds.[28] Carbamazepine, for example, induces its own metabolism and the metabolism of warfarin and valproate,[17] whereas cimetidine, a mixed-function oxidase inhibitor, slows the metabolism of carbamazepine. Notably, cimetidine also reduces hepatic blood flow, thereby inhibiting metabolism of high-clearance drugs.[11] High levels of dietary carbohydrates decrease and high protein intake increases the hepatic disposal of theophylline. Charcoal-broiled beef greatly enhances the metabolism of phenacetin and theophylline, whereas cabbage and brussel sprouts also stimulate drug metabolism in humans.[29]

Virtually all this information is derived from studies of young subjects. In the aged, hepatic enzyme induction has been hardly explored, and its contribution to age-related differences in drug metabolism has not been defined. Moreover, drug-metabolizing abilities vary enormously independently of age. Oxidative biotransformations of nortriptyline, tolbutamide, and antipyrine, a low-clearance model substrate, can vary as much as ten-fold in healthy subjects (Figure 2–2).[14,29] Smoking and caffeine appear to enhance antipyrine metabolism more in young than in old subjects, suggesting that in this case induction of some drug-metabolizing enzymes is diminished in the older group.[14]

Despite this observation, and coupled with the diminished liver blood flow and reduced liver mass of old age,[30] very few studies clearly document an age-associated decline in drug clearance. A decline does occur with chlordiazepoxide, diazepam, nortriptyline, and theophylline, but for a number of other drugs, including lorazepam and oxazepam that are directly converted to glucuronides, clearance is unchanged.[28]

In contrast to the mixed picture with phase I reactions, acetylation is unaffected by age. This normicrosomal enzyme system is an important pathway for the metabolism of isoniazid, hydralazine, procainamide, and some sulfonamides. Genetically, populations clearly divide between slow and fast acetylators.[31] Because the slow acetylation defect persists into old age, this group of elderly individuals is more vulnerable to the toxic effects of acetylated drugs. As an example, procainamide-induced systemic lupus erythematosus occurs with considerably

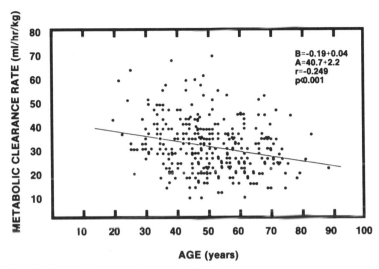

Figure 2–2 Antipyrine clearance rate as a function of age.

Note: Although on average the metabolic clearance rate declines with increasing age, the differences in clearance between individuals can be very great.

Source: Reprinted with permission from *Clinical Pharmacology and Therapeutics* (1975;18:427), Copyright © 1975, CV Mosby Company.

---

greater frequency in slow acetylators.[32] This drug-induced illness is more likely to appear later in life simply because the heart disease and associated ventricular arrthymias that prompt the prescription of procainamide occur far more often in old age than in youth.

Pharmacologic Effect

End organ sensitivity to drugs in the aged remains a largely unexplored area. A handful of studies demonstrate increased sensitivity to benzodiazepine derivatives, whereas the response to β-agonists and antagonists is likely to be reduced.[20,33,34] Although the elderly seem to be more sensitive to drugs, particularly central nervous system depressants, this observation may be related as much to higher drug levels as to increased sensitivity.

CLINICAL ILLUSTRATIONS

The following cases illustrate several important points:

- exaggeration of the usual pharmacologic effect of a drug
- increased drug toxic effects as a result of ingesting two different agents with the same action

- dietary eccentricities
- impaired drug disposal

Case 1

A 68-year-old woman with a 20-year history of diabetes treated with NPH insulin arrived at the ED after 3 days of worsening headache and confusion that culminated in a generalized convulsion. Her long-term medications included 500 mg of methyldopa tid and 800 mg of ibuprofen qd. Four days earlier her physician added hydrochlorothiazide at a dose of 50 mg qd for better blood pressure control. The general physical examination disclosed no significant abnormalities, and the neurologic examination showed no focal signs. Pertinent laboratory data were as follows: serum sodium, 113 mEq/L; serum potassium, 3.3 mEq/L; serum chloride, 81 mEq/L; serum bicarbonate, 25 mEq/L; serum creatinine, 0.7 mg/dL; and blood glucose, 222 mg/dL. After withdrawal of drugs and an infusion of normal saline followed by fluid restriction, she recovered.

Comment

Severe hyponatremia occasionally occurs after 4 to 16 days of thiazide therapy in elderly patients who otherwise have grossly normal renal function.[35,36] Thiazides ordinarily impair urinary-diluting capacity. In this case severe impairment of free water clearance probably developed and resulted in the acute appearance of symptomatic hyponatremia. Ibuprofen, a nonsteroidal anti-inflammatory drug (NSAID), may have exacerbated the hyponatremia by enhancing the effect of antidiuretic hormone.[37]

Case 2

A 66-year-old black man with sickle trait and mild renal insufficiency returned to the ED 6 days after his hospital discharge. He had lower extremity pain and weakness that had worsened over the previous 3 days. He handed the ED nurse three containers of pills prescribed by two physicians: naproxen, 250 mg tid; indomethacin, 25 mg tid; and atenolol, 100 mg qd. The last two medications were dated a day after discharge; the first, 2 weeks before that. He also was taking trimethoprim sulfamethoxazole for a urinary tract infection discovered during the last hospitalization when he was treated for presumed idiopathic pericarditis and hypertension. The physical examination disclosed only diffuse mild muscle weakness and tenderness. The laboratory data were as follows: serum potassium, 8.1 mEq/L; blood urea nitrogen, 32 mg/dL; serum creatinine, 2.6 mg/dL; normal urinalysis; and normal serum creatine phosphokinase. Nine days earlier the first three values were 3.6 mEq/L, 20 mg/dL, and 1.2 mg/dL, respectively. He mentioned that he ate 5 pounds of bananas a day earlier and was using a potassium-containing salt substitute. After withdrawal of drugs and treatment with an oral ion-exchange resin, he recovered.

Comment

This patient was using two NSAIDs prescribed by different physicians. Both drugs have been associated with acute renal failure and interstitial nephritis. In volume-depleted states, heart failure, or cirrhosis, NSAID inhibition of prostaglandin-mediated renal blood flow may produce renal vasoconstriction and reduced renal function. Although the patient did not fall into these categories, his sickle-trait-associated renal failure may have been a predisposing factor. Indomethacin can also induce hyperkalemia, probably by suppressing the renin-angiotensin aldosterone axis with a resultant reduction in cellular potassium uptake.[37]

Because indomethacin, naproxen, and sulfamethoxazole are highly protein bound, one or both NSAIDs may have been competitively displaced from albumin with a transient rise in free drug fraction. In addition, the β-blocker atenolol, which is excreted by the kidneys, may inhibit the sodium-potassium ATPase cell membrane pump, resulting in leakage of potassium into the extracellular space.[38]

This case is an example of complex drug interactions. Additive drug effects led to renal insufficiency that, in turn, exacerbated hyperkalemia by reducing elimination of atenolol and inhibiting excretion of excess dietary potassium. The patient's inclination to consult different physicians for different symptoms and his lack of understanding of the therapy contributed to the problem.

SUMMARY

Drug absorption is not significantly altered in old age, but changes in body composition, reduced renal function, diminished liver blood flow, and selective impairment of hepatic microsomal enzyme systems slow the disposal of some drugs. Interindividual drug-metabolizing ability varies substantially independently of age. Those aged individuals who are genetically poor drug metabolizers or who have liver disease, renal insufficiency, or congestive heart failure, which further impair drug disposal, or who demonstrate increased sensitivity are at greatest risk for toxic reaction to drugs. In an emergency care setting patients with drug-induced illness can have a wide variety of signs and symptoms. The potential contribution of drugs to the clinical picture demands the collection of accurate information on drug use from the patient and the patient's family, friends, personal physician, or pharmacy.

REFERENCES

1. Knoben JE, Anderson PO (eds): *Handbook of Clinical Drug Data*. Hamilton, IL, Drug Intelligence Publications Inc, 1983.

2. Dukes MNG, Ellis J (eds): *Side Effects of Drugs Annual 8*. Amsterdam, Elsevier, 1984.

3. Griffin JP, D'Arcy PF: *A Manual of Adverse Drug Interactions*, ed 3. Bristol, Wright, 1984.

4. Rizak MA, Hillman CDM (eds): *The Medical Letter Handbook of Drug Interactions*. New Rochelle, NY, The Medical Letter Inc, 1986.

5. Conrad KA, Bressler R (eds): *Drug Therapy for the Elderly*. St. Louis, CV Mosby Co, 1982.

6. Vestal RE (ed): *Drug Treatment in the Elderly*. Sydney, Australia, ADIS Health Science Press, 1984.

7. Black AJ, Somers K: Drug-related illness resulting in hospital admission. *J Roy Coll Physicians*. 18:40–41, 1984.

8. Steele K, Gertman PM, Crescenzi C, et al: Iatrogenic illness on a general medical service at a university hospital. *N Engl J Med* 304:638–642, 1981.

9. Zimmerman TJ, Leader BJ, Golob DS: Potential side effects of timolol therapy in the treatment of glaucoma. *Ann Ophthalmol* 13:683–689, 1981.

10. Richelson E: Psychotropics and the elderly: Interactions to watch for. *Geriatrics* 39:30–42, 1984.

11. Freston J: Cimetidine. II. Adverse reactions and patterns of use. *Ann Intern Med* 97:728–734, 1982.

12. Lewis RJ, Trager WF, Chan KK, et al: Warfarin. Stereochemical aspects of its metabolism and the interaction with phenylbutazone. *J Clin Invest* 53:1607–1617, 1974.

13. Cusack B, Kelly JG, Lavan J, et al: Theophylline kinetics in relation to age: The importance of smoking. *Br J Clin Pharmacol* 10:109–114, 1980.

14. Vestal RE, Norris AH, Tobin JD, et al: Antipyrine metabolism in man—influence of age, alcohol, caffeine and smoking. *Clin Pharmacol Ther* 18:425–432, 1975.

15. Mayersohn M: Drug disposition, in Conrad KA, Bressler R (eds): *Drug Therapy for the Elderly*. St. Louis, CV Mosby Co, 1982, pp 31–63.

16. Tozer TN: Implication of altered plasma protein binding in disease states, in Benet LZ, Massoud N, Gamberloglio JG (eds): *Pharmacokinetic Basis for Drug Treatment*. New York, Raven Press, 1984, pp 173–193.

17. Kutt H: Interactions between anticonvulsants and other commonly prescribed drugs. *Epilepsia* 25 (suppl 2):S118–S131, 1984.

18. Kenney RA: *Physiology of Aging, A Synopsis*. Chicago, Year Book Medical Publishers Inc, 1982, pp 22–27.

19. Butler SH: Treatment of pain in the elderly, in Vestal RE (ed): *Drug Treatment in the Elderly*. Sydney, Australia, ADIS Health Science Press, 1984, p 210.

20. Thompson TL II, Morgan MG, Nies AS: Psychotropic drug use in the elderly (first of two parts). *N Engl J Med* 308:134–138, 1983.

21. Rowe JW, Andres R, Tobin JD, et al: The effects of age on creatinine clearance in man: A cross-sectional and longitudinal study. *J Gerontol* 31:155–163, 1976.

22. Crockcroft DW, Gault MH: Prediction of creatinine clearance from serum creatinine. *Nephron* 15:31–41, 1976.

23. Zaske DE, Irvine P, Strand LM, et al: Wide interpatient variations in gentamycin dose requirements for geriatric patients. *JAMA* 248:3122–3126, 1982.

24. Brater DC, Chennavasin P: Effects of renal disease: Pharmacokinetic considerations, in Benet LZ, Massoud N, Gamberloglio JG (eds): *Pharmacokinetic Basis for Drug Treatment*. New York, Raven Press, 1984, pp 119–147.

25. Moore-Ede M, Czeisler CA, Richardson GS: Circadian timekeeping in health and disease. Part 2. Clinical implications of circadian rhythmicity. *N Engl J Med* 309:530–535, 1983.

26. Vestal RE, Wood AJJ, Brance RA, et al: Effects of age and cigarette smoking on propranolol disposition. *Clin Pharmacol Ther* 26:8–15, 1979.

27. Nies AS, Shand DG, Wilkinson GR: Altered hepatic blood flow and drug disposition. *Clin Pharmacokinet* 1:135–155, 1976.

28. Greenblatt DJ, Sellers EM, Shader RI: Drug disposition in old age. *N Engl J Med* 306:1081–1088, 1982.

29. Breimer DD: Variability in human drug metabolism and its implications. *Int J Clin Pharmacol Res* 3:399–413, 1983.

30. Swift CG, Homeida M, Halliwell M, et al: Antipyrine disposition and liver size in the elderly. *Eur J Clin Pharmacol* 14:149–152, 1978.

31. Farah F, Taylor W, Rawlings MD, et al: Hepatic drug acetylation and oxidation; effects of aging in man. *Br Med J* 2:155–156, 1977.

32. Reidenberg MM: Aromatic amines and the pathogenesis of lupus erythematosus. *Am J Med* 75:1037–1042, 1983.

33. Shocker DD, Roth GS: Reduced beta adrenoreceptor sensitivity in the elderly. *Nature* 267:856–858, 1977.

34. Vestal RE, Wood AJJ, Shand DG: Reduced beta adrenoreceptor sensitivity in the elderly. *Clin Pharmacol Ther* 26:181–186, 1979.

35. Ashram N, Locksley R, Arieff AI: Thiazide induced hyponatremia associated with death or neurologic damage in outpatients. *Am J Med* 70:1163–1168, 1981.

36. Booker JA: Severe symptomatic hyponatremia in elderly outpatients. The role of thiazide therapy and stress. *J Am Geriatr Soc* 32:108–113, 1984.

37. Clive DM, Stoff J: Renal syndromes associated with nonsteroidal anti-inflammatory drugs. *N Engl J Med* 310:563–572, 1984.

38. Rosa RM, Silva P, Young JB, et al: Adrenergic modulation of external potassium disposal. *N Engl J Med* 302:431–434, 1980.

SUGGESTED READING

McEvoy GK, McQuarrie GM (eds): *American Hospital Formulary Service*. Bethesda, MD, American Society of Hospital Pharmacists, 1986.

3

Chest Injury and Shock in the Elderly

C. William Schwab, MD and Julian E. Allen, MD

Aging has been described as a process that involves an increase in vulnerability and a decrease in viability that finally lead to death.[1] It is a normal biologic phenomenon intertwined with pathologic causes of deterioration that are difficult to separate, especially when considering whether the elderly tolerate injury any differently from the young. Although some physicians feel age represents a prohibitive risk factor for major procedures, most recognize that attainment of advanced age itself probably represents some form of physiologic superiority.[2] Intermixed with this group of healthy elderly patients is another group: those with chronic illnesses controlled or supported by modern medical means.[3] This second group of patients represents a challenge to the physician caring for traumatized individuals because treatment for their underlying problems must be part of the treatment for any injuries. Some pre-existing diseases represent significant risk factors for ultimate survival and require that thoughtful care be initiated as early as the prehospital phase.[4] Until recently there has been almost no focus on the outcome of elderly trauma victims; even as of 1986, there are but a few published studies.

As the proportion of the elderly in the population has increased, a field of geriatrics has evolved. This, coupled with the contemporary development of trauma care, has provoked a greater interest in geriatric trauma. The geriatric population is projected to increase by 50% over the next 5 years; consequently, more meaningful and thorough information on the effects of trauma on the older patient should become available.[5] At the present, we are forced to draw on our understanding of geriatric physiology and to apply the accepted principles of trauma management—so successful in the usual younger victim—to this older trauma patient.

The change in the lifestyle and greater mobility of the geriatric population account for the fact that trauma is the fifth leading cause of death in patients over

65. Although this age group comprises only 11% of the population, they represent 25% of all injury fatalities (approximately 28,000 deaths per annum).[6] Kohn has demonstrated that the aged have an increased mortality from injury and insults of all types because of their diminished reaction to stress.[7] When a comparison of death rates is made between ages, the death rate from unintentional injury per 100,000 is 57 for all ages combined; it rises to 93 for ages 65 to 74 years, 210 for ages 75 to 84 years, and 625 for all victims aged 84 and older (Table 3–1).[7]

The mechanism of injury in the elderly is slightly different from that of a younger patient, although the usual trauma is blunt.[1] The two most common mechanisms are motor vehicular accidents/auto—pedestrian (as occupants of the car/as victims being struck) and falls (usually while ambulating). Penetrating trauma accounts for only a small percentage of cases, as few elderly are involved in violent crimes or settle their disputes by violent means. The third most frequent injuring mechanism—burning—is not covered in the chapter, except in the discussion of the management of associated shock.

The physiologic differences existing in the elderly, their altered responses to trauma, and differences in the management and treatment of chest injury and shock in the older patient are the main subjects of this chapter. Particular attention is paid to the subtle signs and symptoms of chest injury and hypovolemic shock following the injury of an elderly person.

WHAT MAKES THE ELDERLY "BRITTLE"—UNDERLYING DISEASE AND THE PROCESS OF AGING

Various forms of cardiovascular disease are the most common underlying processes in the elderly; more than 70% of cardiovascular deaths occur in people over the age of 65.[4] Atherosclerotic disease may involve the cerebrovascular circulation, peripheral vessels, or the coronary arteries, and it is these changes that one thinks of most often as making the elderly "brittle." It is the long-standing effects of these diseases that alter the elderly patient's ability to respond to and withstand

Table 3–1 Death Rate from Unintentional Injury (per 100,000)

Age (Yr)	Death Rate (per 100,000)
65–74	93
75–84	210
84–older	625
All ages combined	57

Source: Principles of Mammalian Aging by RR Kohn, Prentice-Hall, Inc., © 1971.

hypoxic and hypovolemic stress. In addition to these disease entities, older people in general have a decreased cardiac output, cardiac index, and oxygen uptake. Peripheral vascular resistance increases progressively with age; this increased resistance to blood flow in the small arterial beds causes a reduction in cellular perfusion and, therefore, oxygenation and glucose delivery. All organs are affected by this decreased flow (Table 3–2).[8] As Table 3–2 indicates, the decreases in flow are progressive with each additional year of aging. However, one cannot assume that the chronological age corresponds to the physiologic age of the individual. Physiologic age is affected by many factors, and no prediction of the adequacy of the patient's physiologic response to stress can be made directly from the chronologic age.

A significant degree of treatable hypertension may frequently be seen, especially among blacks. In considering treatment of the acutely injured elderly patient, the physician must recognize that a "normal" blood pressure may represent a relative hypotensive state that can rapidly lead to cardiac insufficiency in the geriatric victim. Thus, one must not accept a systolic blood pressure of 100 mm Hg as evidence of adequate perfusion. A slightly higher pressure should be restored until more sophisticated measures of adequate perfusion are available.

The effects of age on the lung have been well documented.[4] Major decreases occur in vital capacity, maximal breathing capacity, elastic recoil of the lung, resistance to airway collapse, and the level of blood oxygen. The normal arterial oxygen tension (PaO_2) averages 85–90 torr, but decreases with age; thus a value of 70 torr is an acceptable value in a patient over 60 years of age. The elderly have a reduced vital capacity and forced expiratory volume in 1 second (FEV_1), resulting in a less effective cough. All these changes make the elderly with chest injury a higher risk for respiratory decompensation. The normal respiratory diseases of the elderly also greatly limit pulmonary reserve. The older patient may have a long history of cigarette smoking, resulting in chronic bronchitis, emphy-

Table 3–2 Changes in Regional Circulation

	Average Value at 50 Yrs (liters/min)	Average Rate of Change (%/yr)
Cardiac output	5.01	−1.01
Hepatic portal flow	1.40	−0.3
Renal blood flow	0.91	−1.9
Cerebral blood flow	0.66	−0.5
Remainder	(2.03)	(−1.3)

Source: Adapted from Aging, Some Social and Biological Aspects by NW Shock (Ed) with permission of American Association for the Advancement of Science, Pub No 65, © 1980.

sema, or obstructive lung disease. These diseases themselves pose a threat to life for the geriatric patient. When coupled with any degree of thoracic injury or significant hypotensive episode, they put the elderly victim at a much higher risk from trauma. The use of bronchodilator therapy, mucolytic agents, and oxygen deserves early consideration and is especially important in thoracic injuries occurring in the aged.

Arteriosclerosis is a generalized disease that affects the entire vascular system. As previously discussed, aging itself causes a decrease in flow to all organs (Table 3–2),[7] but this normal physiologic phenomenon is compounded by progressive arterial narrowing from pathologic atheroma. The kidney is especially altered by arteriosclerosis; its function is no better than its blood supply. Besides the deleterious effects of arteriosclerosis, the geriatric kidney can be markedly altered by the long-term effects of hypertensive disease and diabetes. Standard measures of renal function may be misleading as there exists a group of aged patients who have a normal blood urea nitrogen or serum creatinine yet have a markedly impaired renal tubular function. In order to determine accurately the status of the kidney, this group requires a 24-hour urine collection for calculation of creatinine clearance.

The elderly are more likely to have some degree of liver disease, most commonly cirrhosis. The stress of even relatively minor episodes of hypoperfusion and hypoxemia can precipitate liver failure, coma, and subsequent death.

The fluid and electrolyte balance of the older patient may become abnormal in the face of cardiac, renal, or liver diseases. Any degree of chronic cardiac insufficiency leads to an increase in extracellular volume (ECV) and concurrently decreases the serum sodium and potassium. Chronic metabolic alkalosis is common in these situations. In addition, many elderly patients on diuretics lose potassium in the urine and live with some degree of hypokalemia, which is a reflection of low total body potassium as potassium is predominantly an intracellular ion. Decreased stores compound the alkalosis and in extreme cases are associated with cardiac irritability and dysrhythmia. Hypokalemia can also lead to disturbances in muscle contractility, strength, and intestinal function.

The endocrine response to trauma is the same as in the younger population and involves epinephrine, antidiuretic hormone, aldosterone, and glucocorticoids. However, because of the chronic underlying diseases of the cardiovascular system, kidneys, and lungs, the response to these hormones may be altered. Cardiac, renal, and hepatic disease themselves cause a state of chronic hyperaldosteronism and lead to an expanded ECV and total body water. Endocrine disease, such as diabetes, is common in the older age range; Addison's disease (adrenal insufficiency) is more frequently seen in the geriatric trauma patient. These diseases not only adversely affect the body but also complicate management during initial resuscitation and later definitive care. All these conditions lower the margin of safety for successful outcome after injury.

The nutritional status of many elderly patients is poor. Aging is a catabolic phase; it is associated with a decreased body cell mass, decreased rate of wound healing, and marked decrease in muscle strength. The diet of older patients may be inadequate to provide the necessary stores of nutrients (especially protein) needed during periods of stress. For this reason early institution of nutritional support may be lifesaving. Pre-existing nutritional problems as manifested by serum albumin levels of less than 3.0 gm/liter have been used as a predictor of mortality.[3] Patients with serum albumins below this level who underwent emergency abdominal operations had a significantly higher mortality rate than comparable geriatric patients with normal albumin levels.[9] Early enteral nutrition with oral, nasal, or operatively placed feeding tubes has improved the salvage of severely traumatized elderly patients. Parenteral nutrition is also useful and should be utilized if no enteral route is available.

Underlying disease also indicates frequent pre-existing drug therapy. The health care provider should be aware of any additional drugs that must be continued when caring for the traumatized elderly patient. Antihypertensives, cardiotonics, diuretics, and insulin are some medications that require accurate documentation. Each medication should be reviewed for its adverse reactions, side effects, and drug interactions. Alcohol usage and therapy with tranquilizers and antidepressants should also be noted, and the patient should be observed for signs of withdrawal.

In summary, the traumatized elderly patient is much more vulnerable because of the normal aging process and the effects of commonly acquired diseases of later life. All organ systems have less reserve and a greater susceptibility to hypoxia, hypoperfusion, and hypoxemia. However, one cannot assume chronologic age is correlated to physiologic age. In fact, many elderly patients can and do react to trauma in a manner similar to younger patients. However, the majority of patients sustaining a major injury after the age of 65 years are a high risk group and not as competent in their response to trauma nor as successful in their outcome.

CHEST INJURIES

No current reports exist that specifically deal with chest injuries in the elderly. During the 5 years from 1978–1983, the authors' experience with 48 blunt chest trauma patients over the age of 60 provides some insight into their diagnosis and treatment. The average age in this series was 72 years, with 19 patients aged 60–69 years, 20 patients aged 70–79 years, and 9 patients 80 years or older. The normal length of hospitalization was 16 days; 19 (39.6%) patients required intensive care facilities for an average of 10 days.

Table 3–3 depicts the type and location of the chest injuries. The most common injury seen was rib fracture, often multiple, with 162 fractures occurring in 43 patients (average 3.8 rib fractures per patient). Fourteen patients (29%) sustained a flail chest. There were 13 cases (27%) of pneumothorax, and 5 patients (10%) had a hemothorax treated by closed tube thoracostomy. There were four patients (8%) with myocardial contusion. The associated injuries are listed in Table 3–4.

Table 3–3 Site and Type of Chest Injuries in 48 Elderly Patients

	Total Rib Fractures/ Total Patients (range of fractures/patient)	Average Number of Ribs Fractured	Flail Chest	Pneumo-thorax	Hemo-thorax	Pulmonary Contusion
Hemithorax						
Left Side	121 fractures/33 patients (1–7/patient)	3.7	12	10	4	13
Right Side	41 fractures/12 patients (1–8/patient)	3.4	2	3	1	1
Total	162 fractures/45 patients	3.8	14	13	5	14

The mechanism of injury was motor vehicle accident in 20 cases (42%), a fall in 25 cases (52%), and one each of assault, crush, and cardiopulmonary resuscitation (2% each). Table 3–5 relates the mechanism of injury to the age of the patient and frequency of associated injury. Overall there was one death (2%). Of the 47 survivors, 43 (89.6%) were discharged home; only 4 (8.3%) required extended nursing home care.

The following discussion of geriatric chest trauma is derived from this series. An organized approach of initial care is be presented that emphasizes the same ABC approach applicable to all trauma victims.[10] Descriptions of individual injuries and their specific management and recommended therapy are presented next.

Airway—"The Early Killer"

It requires less than 10 minutes of oxygen deprivation for brain death to occur. It is therefore crucial that the first assessment of the patient include a careful

Table 3–4 Associated Injuries in 48 Elderly Patients

Injury	Number	Percentage
Long bone fracture	15	31
Pelvis fracture	5	10
Concussion	7	15
Skull fracture	2	4
Renal contusion	6	13
Splenic rupture	1	2
Diaphragm rupture	1	2

Table 3–5 Mechanism of Injury and Associated Injuries in 48 Elderly Patients

Age Range (Yr)	Injury Type			Associated Major Injury		
	Fall	MVA	Other	Fall	MVA	Other
60–69	7	11	1	2	8	0
70–79	9	9	2	0	8	1
80 and over	9	0	0	1	0	0
Total	25	20	3	3	16	1

evaluation of the airway, with establishment of an adequate airway as the primary goal. Any means necessary should be used, including emergency cricothyroidotomy.

Initial attention should be directed at clearing the oropharynx. In the elderly patient special attention must be directed toward the presence of dental prostheses, and personnel must be certain that no denture, partial plate, or loose teeth are present. Vomitus or other foreign material must be cleared quickly.

The tongue is the most common cause of upper airway obstruction in the unconscious elderly patient. Because of the anatomy of the mandible and tongue, any forward motion of the jaw moves the tongue anteriorly, and either a chin lift or jaw thrust should be used to attain this movement. With either maneuver the cervical spine must be protected with either in-line traction or a rigid cervical collar.

Following this procedure, the placement of some form of airway should be encouraged. Elderly patients have a poorer gag reflex and weaker cough and may not be as capable of maintaining their natural airway as the younger patient. The relative sensitivity of the older patient to hypoxia must always be kept in mind. A soft nasopharyngeal "trumpet" airway may be all that is necessary to prevent the tongue from occluding the airway, but in most elderly patients more aggressive and secure means of airway control are needed. If the patient is obtunded, the clinician's small finger can be used to lubricate and dilate the nasal passage before placement of the nasopharyngeal airway. An advantage of using this airway is that the dilation of nasal passage obtained may prove useful if nasotracheal intubation becomes necessary. The nasotracheal airway also allows for easy, adequate suctioning. In general, nothing more elaborate than a nasal airway should be placed in the conscious, cooperative patient without using some form of local anesthesia; otherwise vomiting with aspiration may be induced. An oropharyngeal airway in the conscious patient should also be avoided for this reason.

The esophageal obturator airway (EOA) may be used in the prehospital phase of patient care; it should rapidly be replaced with a definitive endotracheal tube once the patient arrives in the emergency room. The EOA can only be used in an unconscious patient, is difficult to insert properly without *flexion* of the neck, and is dangerous in the presence of maxillofacial bleeding because the patient may be forced to aspirate blood. It is important that, once placed, the EOA not be removed unless the trachea is intubated or the patient regains full consciousness. Removal of the EOA causes vomiting and can only be done with a protected airway. In general, the use of this airway should be discouraged except in prehospital care systems where endotracheal intubation is not permitted.

If the above mechanical airways fail to establish an adequate upper airway, endotracheal intubation is required. The preferred initial route is nasotracheal. This may be difficult to perform even for experienced personnel, especially with the requirement to protect the cervical spine from movement. Oral tracheal intubation is a less difficult skill and may be the preferred intubation maneuver as long as cervical spine control is maintained. If attempted intubation fails to secure the airway or is contraindicated by maxillofacial trauma or cervical spine fracture, the physician should not hesitate to proceed with needle or surgical cricothyroidotomy.

A needle cricothyroidotomy can be rapidly accomplished by placing a 14-gauge plastic intravenous (IV) catheter through the cricothyroid membrane and attaching a high-flow oxygen tube (15 liters/min) with a Y-connector. The connector is used to cycle the flow of oxygen while the physician is preparing for surgical cricothyroidotomy. This needle method provides adequate oxygen and prevents the early hypoxia so potentially damaging to the elderly patient, but it is inadequate for prolonged ventilation. Unless a larger airway is placed, carbon dioxide will accumulate, leading to hypercarbia and acidosis. Additionally, this needle cricothyroidotomy airway does not protect against aspiration. It may, in fact, force intratracheal blood, teeth, or other foreign material into distal bronchioles, making extraction difficult even with bronchoscopy.

In adults a tracheostomy tube with a low-pressure balloon pressure cuff can be easily inserted through a surgical cricothyroidotomy. A transverse incision is made overlying the cricothyroid membrane and then deepened through the membrane itself. The scalpel handle can then be inserted and rotated 90° to open the membrane, and the tube can be inserted. Tracheostomy is rarely necessary or indicated in the acute management of the trauma patient. A surgical cricothyroidotomy is quicker, safer, and affords a secure airway. The airway is especially crucial in the elderly patient who does not tolerate hypoxia well. A logical, step-wise progression from clearing the oropharynx to cricothyroidostomy will lead to safe attainment of an adequate airway.

Breathing and Ventilation—"Injuries That Kill within Minutes"

Once a sufficient airway is established, adequate ventilation must be provided for the effective exchange of gasses in the lungs. While evaluating the patient's ability to move air, it is important to check for each of the five life-threatening injuries that may lead to death within minutes. These injuries are tension pneumothorax, open pneumothorax, massive hemothorax, flail chest, and cardiac tamponade. As previously noted, the elderly patient is less able to tolerate a period of hypoxia and hypotension, and overlooking one of these injuries may result in serious complications or even death.

Tension Pneumothorax

Tension pneumothorax results when a flap valve effect in the visceral pleura is created by an injury, usually a lung laceration from a rib fracture. This allows inspired air to accumulate within the pleural space of the affected hemithorax, causing total collapse of that lung along with displacement of the mediastinum away from the side of the injury. As a result, not only does hypoventilation occur due to the collapsed lung but there is also a diminution in blood flow returning to the heart. This combination may be rapidly fatal in the geriatric patient. Treatment is release of the tension by placement of a needle into the affected side of the chest. It is immediately accomplished by placing a needle in the second intercostal space in the midclavicular line and then inserting a chest tube in the midaxillary line at the level of the nipple.

Open Pneumothorax

Equally dangerous to the elderly trauma victim is the open pneumothorax caused when a wound in the chest wall provides a continuous communication between the atmosphere and pleural space; this is the sucking or ''blowing'' chest wound. Similar to the tension pneumothorax, the collapsed lung and mediastinal shifting cause hypoventilation and poor venous return. More importantly, an opening in the chest wall that is two-thirds the diameter of the trachea (approximately 3 cm or the size of a 50-cent piece) or larger provides a path of lesser resistance. The continuous diaphragmatic movement causes air to move through the chest wound, rather than through the trachea. This stops ventilation and mandates immediate intubation.

Injuries of this size usually require surgical closure. In the emergent situation, smaller wounds should be treated with an occlusive dressing taped on three sides to create an external flap valve. This allows air within the chest to escape, but not to reaccumulate. Smaller wounds may not require surgical closure, but rather conservative management with debridement, packing, and subsequent dressing changes. *All* wounds, however, require early placement of a chest tube.

Flail Chest

Flail chest is defined as a paradoxical motion of the chest wall with respirations and may be caused by sternal or multiple segmental rib fractures. Usually associated with this injury and more dangerous to the elderly is the underlying pulmonary contusion that results in hypoxia. Stabilization of the flailing segment with sandbags and other bulky padding may increase patient comfort, but it does little to overcome the real problem of hypoxia and hypoventilation. The physician must be aware that deterioration in the elderly patient's status can occur and warrants immediate intubation and ventilatory support.

Arterial blood gas measurement and assessment of the patient's respiratory rate and level of fatigue assist in determining which patients require ventilatory support and which patients can be safely treated with incentive spirometry, adequate pain relief, and close observation but without intubation. Hypoxia (PaO_2 of less than 60 torr on room air), hypercarbia ($PaCO_2$ of greater than 45–50 torr), tachypnea (respiratory rate of 30 or more), or the clinical impression of a tiring patient suggest the need for ventilatory therapy. Although prolonged intubation may lead to pneumonia or other pulmonary complications, ventilation for a period of 24–48 hours is not particularly hazardous and should be used if there is any suggestion of difficulty oxygenating or ventilating the geriatric patient with a flail chest.

Massive Hemothorax

A massive hemothorax occurs when large volumes of blood accumulate in the pleural space. Although more common with penetrating injuries, it can be seen with severe blunt trauma. The diagnosis is suggested by clinical hypovolemia in association with absent breath sounds or a dull percussive note on the affected side. Because the intrathoracic pressure may well be tamponading the bleeding site, placement of a chest tube must temporarily await resuscitation with fluids and blood. Stabilization of shock prior to chest tube insertion is preferred, but massive hemothorax may cause a mediastinal shift with "tension" that is similar to a tension pneumothorax. This condition requires simultaneous repletion of blood volume and placement of tube thoracostomy. An autotransfusion device, such as the Sorenson®, can be used to combine simultaneous removal of blood from the hemothorax with transfusion to treat the shock; it is particularly helpful when immediate blood and blood products are not available.

Pericardial Tamponade

Last among the injuries that can kill within minutes is pericardial tamponade. This condition should be suspected whenever the elderly trauma patient has sustained hypotension associated with jugular venous distension and muffled heart tones. Treatment may be effected by direct aspiration of only a small volume of fluid from the pericardial sac.

As a result of aging, the elderly patient has a more brittle chest wall, which may result in more force being directly applied to the heart, rather than being absorbed by a resilient thoracic wall. This can lead to a more frequent occurrence of tamponade in geriatric patients. The reduced cardiopulmonary reserve of the geriatric patient, together with increased susceptibility to hypotension, makes cardiac tamponade a serious threat. Cardiac tamponade should always be considered in any chest trauma patient who has or develops hypotension and is not responsive to vigorous antishock therapy. In this group of patients, it may be necessary to perform an early pericardiocentesis to gain a higher patient survival.

Circulation

The third component of the primary survey is circulation; this is covered in the following section on shock. The basic goals of this portion of the survey are control of exsanguinating hemorrhage and restoration of adequate tissue perfusion by replenishing the circulating volume.

Blunt Chest Trauma

Of the two prominent mechanisms for chest injury—blunt and penetrating trauma—the elderly patient is much more likely to sustain blunt injury. As noted before, this commonly occurs as the result of a motor vehicle accident or fall.

Chest Wall Injuries

Isolated rib fractures are the most commonly seen form of chest trauma in elderly patients. In the young patient these fractures are often only a troublesome injury and are managed as an outpatient with adequate pain relief. However, in the older patient who has a decreased pulmonary reserve, a pneumonia may easily develop. Consideration should be given to inhospital care in order to provide maximum pain relief and pulmonary therapy. The combination of individual rib blocks with a long-acting local anesthetic and incentive spirometry has been found to give satisfactory results. After several days of inpatient care, the patient may then be discharged for office and visiting nurse care.

First rib fractures represent a controversial area in trauma care. Long considered a fracture the diagnosis of which was indicative of aortic or great vessel injury, it is now appreciated that some patients may have an isolated first rib fracture due simply to the direction of the traumatizing force. Such an example is the rib fracture associated with wearing a shoulder harness. Thus, the mechanism of the injury is probably more important than the site of injury, and a first rib fracture caused by a fall or assault may not be treated the same as one caused by a high-speed motor vehicle accident.

Nonetheless, a high index of suspicion must remain in order to detect potential great vessel injuries, and use of angiography, rather than observation, is prudent, especially in the elderly. The patient who sustains a deceleration injury, such as a head-on motor vehicle accident or fall from a height, is at greatest risk. The presence of mediastinal widening, apical hematoma, or tracheal deviation on upright chest film or the observation of a blood pressure differential between the arms should add further weight to the decision for arteriography.[11]

Flail chest is diagnosed on the basis of the clinical finding of paradoxical chest wall motion, but the extent of the underlying pulmonary contusion and disruption is the real measure of the severity of this injury. Appropriate treatment is controversial, but is generally directed toward early ventilatory support. This may be unnecessary, and the high incidence of pulmonary death from pneumonia in intubated elderly patients may make routine ventilatory care hazardous. Individualization of treatment is essential. One of two treatment regimens is recommended, depending on the severity of the underlying pathophysiology.

If the patient is able to oxygenate and ventilate without difficulty—manifested by a PaO_2 of 60 torr or greater, $PaCO_2$ of less than 50 torr, and respiratory rate of less than 25 breaths per min—then the use of a regimen of rib blockade, supplemental oxygen, fluid restriction, and aggressive pulmonary therapy may avoid intubation and ventilatory support. If, however, the patient is unable to meet the above criteria, intubation and ventilation, usually with some form of positive airway pressure—continuous positive airway pressure (CPAP)—or positive end expiratory pressure (PEEP) is employed. The risk of pneumonia or death from sepsis requires individualization of treatment. Ventilatory support should be reserved for only those patients whose pulmonary dysfunction requires this therapy.

Pulmonary Injuries

Pneumothorax commonly results from blunt chest trauma; it is often the result of a rib fracture lacerating the pleura. The pneumothorax may be simple, tension, or open in nature. Tension and open pneumothorax have been described previously. A simple pneumothorax is detected on physical examination by diminished or distant breath sounds, although it may not be discovered until seen on a chest film. Treatment consists of insertion of a chest tube—in the adult this should be a 32 or 36 French thoracic catheter—in the anterior axillary or midaxillary line at the fifth or sixth intercostal space. An open technique *without* the use of a trocar is safest. The tube is then connected to underwater suction for several days until the pleural injury heals.

Isolated hemothorax is not frequently seen following blunt chest trauma; only five cases (10%) were seen in the authors' series of 48 patients. Massive hemothorax is more likely in penetrating trauma and has already been discussed. In cases not presenting with shock, the most useful diagnostic study is the upright chest film. It is essential that the film be taken with the patient upright, as a liter of blood may accumulate within the pleural space and cause only a diffuse haziness on a supine film. Generally, as little as 300 ml of blood need be present to be seen on upright films. Treatment consists of placement of a chest tube in the fashion described before. It is important to direct the tube posteriorly to provide adequate dependent drainage while the patient remains supine. The chest tube allows re-expansion of the lung, evacuation of blood that may lead to empyema or fibrothorax if not removed, and accurate estimation of continued bleeding that might require operative therapy. Most bleeding is controlled by re-expansion of the lung.

The treatment of pulmonary contusion has been described in the discussion of flail chest injuries. Nearly all contusions of the elderly patient's lung are seen in association with rib fracture. The elderly patient's rib cage is not elastic; forces applied to the bony thorax usually result in multiple rib fractures with contusion. Thus, whenever fractures are seen, the diagnosis of contusion must be considered and therapy instituted according to the aforementioned guidelines.

Cardiac Contusion

A myocardial contusion is classically seen in the patient whose chest strikes the steering wheel during a motor vehicle accident. The diagnosis can be difficult to make, however, because minimal elevations in serum enzymes—creatine phosphakinase (CPK)—may be the only clinical evidence of the injury. Compounding this difficulty is the frequent finding of pre-existing cardiovascular disease in the geriatric patient. Indeed, the cause of the accident may well have been a myocardial infarction, or occasionally the stress of the event may precipitate an infarct. Difficulty arises in making the exact diagnosis; fortunately, treatment is essentially the same in both conditions.

One should consider all elderly severe chest trauma victims to be at risk for myocardial contusion; thus one should evaluate all but the most minimally injured patient for this condition. Symptoms are unreliable because chest pain may be due to associated injuries. Elderly patients should have an ECG done in the emergency department to diagnose any ischemic changes and dysrhythmias, and regardless of the findings on initial ECG, a follow-up study is indicated within 24 hours. Cardiac isoenzymes (MB band) are used to evaluate any elevations in the CPK determination as the MB fraction is diagnostic of muscle injury in the heart. The utility of nuclear cardiology scanning is not yet totally clear.

If the diagnosis of myocardial contusion is suggested, treatment consists of bedrest, fluid restriction with maintenance of hemodynamic stability, and ECG monitoring for dysrhythmias. Observation in an intensive care setting is recommended until enzyme determinations rule out this serious injury. Dysrhythmias are treated according to their individual nature, and close observation is necessary.

The Widened Mediastinum

Evaluation of chest films on older patients often shows a wide mediastinum, suggesting great vessel injury and specifically rupture of the aorta. This widening is often due to atherosclerotic disease of the aorta, rather than to a traumatic injury, although the differentiation may be difficult. Because most patients with aortic rupture who survive long enough to reach the hospital do well with prompt surgical intervention, one should favor prompt angiographic evaluation rather than observation.

Radiologic findings that suggest aortic injury are many, but some more common ones include mediastinal widening, elevation of the left mainstem bronchus, and blurring or loss of the normal aortic knob silhouette. It is imperative that the chest film be of adequate quality to detect these sometimes subtle findings, and an upright AP film should be considered if the patient's status permits.[11] Consultation with the radiologist and thoracic surgeon should be considered if the mechanism of injury is one of rapid deceleration and blunt chest trauma.

Other Injuries

Uncommonly, the tracheobronchial tree or diaphragm may be disrupted by blunt trauma. Most bronchial injuries occur at the level of the mainstem bronchi, and the diagnosis is suggested by a persistent air leak following placement of a chest tube for treatment of a pneumothorax. Mediastinal or cervical subcutaneous emphysema and hemoptysis are also suggestive. This injury is most commonly seen in association with trauma severe enough to fracture several of the upper ribs. The diagnosis is confirmed by bronchoscopy. Repair is indicated for any tear greater than a quarter to a third of the circumference of the bronchus.

Diaphragmatic rupture occurs most commonly on the left side, probably because the liver protects the right hemidiaphragm. Usually the tear is radial and originates in the central tendonous portion. The diagnosis may be difficult, and it depends on proper interpretation of the chest film. The presence of an elevated left hemidiaphragm and radiolucent area above the diaphragm or persistence of a loculated area of pneumothorax following placement of a chest tube should suggest the diagnosis.

Caution in making a diagnosis is important, however. The presence of viscera in the left side of the chest may mimic a hemothorax, and blind placement of a chest tube may injure the herniated abdominal contents. Placement of a nasogastric tube, decubitus chest films, or administration of contrast material either rectally or through the nasogastric tube may be useful in confirming the diagnosis. Once found, a diaphragmatic hernia requires surgical repair, usually through an abdominal approach.

Penetrating Chest Trauma

Frequently seen in the younger urban population, penetrating injuries of the chest are uncommon in the elderly population. In the series presented, blunt injuries were found ten times more often than penetrating ones. However, penetrating injuries may be seen, and the emergency department should be prepared for them.

Stab wounds rarely cause significant injury unless the weapon traverses a vital structure, such as a major vessel or the heart. Often all that is seen after a stab wound is a small hemopneumothorax, which responds well to placement of a chest tube and administration of antibiotics. One should recall the proximity of the abdomen in stab wounds of the lower anterior chest and consider other evaluation, such as peritoneal lavage, if the wound is below the fifth intercostal space or the nipple line.

Gunshot wounds may lead to far more serious injuries as the kinetic energy of the projectile is expended on the soft tissues. Thus, a significant contusion of the lung should be anticipated and treatment begun early. Chest films that show a bullet in proximity to such structures as the esophagus and heart should suggest injury to these organs. Further investigation is generally indicated.

Convalescence

Most elderly victims of trauma are independent before injury. The goal of therapy should be to restore as much of their function as possible.[12] Early use of physical therapy, ambulation, and exercise is necessary to prevent ''freezing'' of joints. This is particularly important in elderly patients who may have underlying joint disease in the form of arthritis. In nonambulatory patients the institution of passive range-of-motion exercises is helpful.[13]

Nutrition undoubtedly plays an important role in the ultimate return of an elderly trauma victim to an independent life. Poor nutrition is correlated with lower survival rates in geriatric patients, and either enteral or parenteral forms of nutritional support should be started early to support potentially nutritionally depleted patients through a period of extreme catabolic stress.[3]

In order to return a large proportion of traumatized elderly patients to an independent life, one must concentrate on every detail of their care. The specific areas of nutrition, physical therapy, early mobility, and respiratory care must be emphasized in each patient.[12,13]

By adopting this approach, a very successful outcome can be achieved. *Ninety percent* of elderly patients returned home following their accident in the authors' series. Most of the remainder were discharged to a nursing care facility. From this experience one concludes that the patient who achieves advanced age can be returned to an independent life following significant trauma, but it is obviously more difficult!

Chest Injury—Management and Treatment Guidelines

The elderly patient who has a chest injury represents both a diagnostic and therapeutic challenge. Although initial evaluation and resuscitation may not differ from the treatment given to a younger person, the clinician must be alert to the specific problems of the older trauma victim. The possibility of underlying disease should be sought by questioning any relatives or friends.[4] As these diseases often include underlying cardiovascular disease, the elderly patient is more vulnerable to hypoxia and hypotension.[2] This makes a rapid and aggressive review for life-threatening injury more important than in the nongeriatric patient. Above all, the geriatric trauma patient requires meticulous attention to detail in order to obtain the best results. The following guidelines, summarized in Table 3–6, may lead to improved survival in the geriatric trauma patient.

Table 3–6 Essential Details for Geriatric Chest Trauma Care

---

1. Correct hypoxia early.
2. Exclude life-threatening chest injury.
3. Maintain hemodynamic stability.
4. Obtain an adequate chest film of the patient sitting.
5. Monitor in the intensive care unit.
6. Investigate for underlying disease.
7. Initiate nutritional support early.
8. Ambulate or exercise early.

The early correction of hypoxia is accomplished by whatever means are necessary, including surgical cricothyroidotomy and ventilation. The five life-threatening injuries—tension pneumothorax, open pneumothorax, flail chest, massive hemothorax, and cardiac tamponade—are initially considered and specifically ruled out in geriatric patients. Because many decisions in chest trauma require examination of a chest film, the clinician must obtain the best possible image.[11] In the elderly patient an upright view is particularly important in order to evaluate the film for subtle findings. A sitting AP view, if clinically possible, should be obtained.

Close monitoring of the elderly patient is paramount. The tiring geriatric trauma victim may deteriorate from adequate ventilation to respiratory arrest in the space of several minutes.[14] It is best to observe any patient over the age of 60 years who sustains major chest trauma in an intensive care unit until all vital functions stabilize. Cardiac monitoring for dysrhythmia associated with myocardial contusion should be continued at least until enzyme determinations are obtained.

The importance of underlying disease and use of medications cannot be overemphasized. If the patient is unable to communicate, relatives and friends may be the best sources of this information. The patient's personal physician should also be consulted.

Nutritional support and early use of physical therapy appear to make a difference for many geriatric patients who sustain chest injury, especially regarding their ability to return to their preinjury level of independence. This support may also help determine the ultimate outcome of death or survival. Attention to these guidelines and a high index of suspicion for rapidly fatal injury are necessary in order to care successfully for the elderly patient with chest trauma.

SHOCK

Definition and History

The modern definition of shock is made in terms of inadequate perfusion, hypoxia, cellular disruption, and accumulation of toxic cellular metabolites.[15] A decrease in blood pressure is in no way a definition of the shock state, but rather is a crude measurement of volume flow that may or may not adequately reflect tissue and cellular perfusion. Shock is not a static event, but rather a dynamic clinical syndrome that can be one of continual decompensation and death at the cellular level, despite the patient's vital signs being restored to normal.

The word "shock" as it is used today was first introduced into the English language about 1743; it was meant to express a reaction to a sudden traumatic occurrence, such as being struck by a bullet.[16] The word then came to mean a collapse from any sudden life-threatening injury. Space does not allow a complete review of the historic aspects of the shock syndrome, but to better understand how shock affects the elderly, it may be wise to review the work of Carl J. Wigger (1883–1963) and the so-called "Wigger's model."[16,17]

Working in the early twentieth century, Wigger developed a method of producing shock in a dog. With a technique of controlled phlebotomy and reinfusion, he was able to vary the amounts of blood lost, the time the animal was in shock, and how adequately or completely reinfusion took place. He found that minor volumes of blood shed for short periods of time were usually well tolerated and reversible, but if the shed volume increased or the time in shock was extended, the animals died. However, in these drastically shocked dogs, reinfusion of the shed blood could transiently restore blood pressure to normal for 30–60 min, but then it again fell to the shocked level and the animal would succumb 4–6 hours later. Wigger's work clarified certain degrees of shock and more importantly demonstrated an existing level of hemorrhage and shock beyond which the animals became refractory to treatment. He concluded this was caused by circulating humoral factors and not what is now recognized as the real problem in shock: cellular hypoxia leading to cell death.

One can speculate from his findings and today's knowledge of the geriatric patient that the distance between the reversible and irreversible shock states is very short. Older people with less cardiac, pulmonary, and renal reserve do not tolerate prolonged hemorrhage; their shock becomes irreversible with less blood loss over shorter periods of time.[5] As an analogy to Wigger's experiments, elderly patients in shock are more likely to have their vital signs restored, yet continue on in the cellular decompensation phase until organs can no longer function, physiologic balance is upset, and death eventually occurs.[5]

Classification of Hemorrhage

Hemorrhage is defined as an acute loss of circulating blood volume and is classified according to the volume of blood lost (Table 3–7).[10]

The normal physiologic responses to these amounts of blood loss are summarized in Table 3–8.[10] For the most part the changes have been documented and recorded in the young patient. Because no specific data are available to develop a classification system for the hemorrhaging elderly patient, it might be wise to analyze the earliest changes seen in the hemorrhagic state and speculate how the

Table 3–7 Classes of Acute Hemorrhage*

Class	Percentage of Blood Loss	mL of Blood Lost
I	Up to 15	Up to 750
II	20–25	1,000–1,250
III	30–35	1,500–1,800
IV	40–50	2,000–2,500

*in a 70-kg male with an approximate blood volume of 5 liters.

Source: Adapted from *Advanced Trauma Life Support Manual* (p 185) with permission of American College of Surgeons, © 1981.

manifestations in the elderly may differ from those in the young patient. There are usually no discernible clinical signs and symptoms of Class I hemorrhage. Class II hemorrhage has more noticeable signs, including tachycardia with a pulse of greater than 100, tachypnea with a respiratory rate of 20–30 breaths per minute, and a positive capillary blanch test. The capillary blanch test is performed by depressing the patient's fingernail or thenar eminence and noting the time it takes for normal color to return. If the color returns to normal within 2 sec—that is the time it takes to say "capillary blanch test" or "capillary return"—it is a normal response and indicates normal tissue perfusion. If the color returns after 2 sec or not at all, the test is termed "delayed" or positive and indicates inadequate tissue perfusion. In addition, patients with Class II levels of blood loss can demonstrate notable mental alterations, usually anxiety, but occasionally combativeness and

Table 3–8 Physiologic Response to Blood Loss

	Class I	Class II	Class III	Class IV
Pulse (bpm)	70–80	100	120	140 or higher
Blood pressure (mm Hg)	120 140/70–90*	110–130/70–90	70–90/50–60	50–60 systolic
Pulse pressure (mm Hg)	36	30	20–30	0–20
Respiratory rate (breaths per minute)	14–20	20–30	30–40	35
Capillary blanch	Normal	Delayed	Abnormal	Abnormal
CNS/mental status	Normal	Mildly anxious	Confused, anxious, lethargic	Confused, lethargic, coma
Skin (color/temperature)	Normal/warm	Normal/cool	Pale/cool	Gray/cool

*After age 65 both systolic and diastolic pressure may be slightly raised.

Source: Adapted from *Advanced Trauma Life Support Manual* (p 185) with permission of American College of Surgeons, © 1981.

agitation. All these changes indicate significant cardiovascular alterations in the shock state.

The cardiovascular changes occurring at these levels of shock are primarily due to the increase in circulating catecholamines (epinephrine and norepinephrine). These hormones have a potent effect; they increase the peripheral vascular resistance and raise the diastolic pressure. At the same time, the shed blood lowers the volume of blood returning to the heart, and thus stroke volume is reduced. As stroke volume falls, the heart rate increases again in response to the high levels of catecholamines. This faster heart rate is a primary attempt of the cardiovascular system to maintain a near-constant cardiac output (CO):

$$CO = HR \times SV, \text{ where } CO = \text{cardiac output, } HR = \text{heartrate, and } SV = \text{stroke volume}$$

Despite the effort to maintain a near constant CO, the fall in stroke volume and effective circulating volume causes a reduction in systolic blood pressure. The synchronous drop in systolic pressure from a lowered blood volume (hemorrhage), combined with an elevated diastolic pressure (increased peripheral vascular resistance from the catecholamine effect), leads to a narrowed pulse pressure. This seems to be a very reliable early sign that an elderly patient has lost significant blood. The normal pulse pressure is about 40 mm HG difference; even when the absolute individual values of systolic and diastolic pressures appear normal, a narrowed pulse pressure of 25–30 mm Hg suggests hypovolemia. The skin color and temperature are altered in early stages of hypovolemia and hypoperfusion. The authors' experience indicates that cool skin is a reliable sign of decreased perfusion, and cool-pale skin indicates serious blood loss. Another excellent early sign of hypovolemia and hypoperfusion in the geriatric is an alteration of mental function. Although the interpretation of the patient's mental capabilities and demeanor is very subjective, alterations in either of these should be interpreted as an early and *cardinal* sign of decreased cerebral blood flow and oxygenation secondary to hypovolemia. One should never interpret these mental aberrations primarily as an alcohol or a drug-induced manifestation. Mental changes coupled with a slight tachycardia, narrowed pulse pressure, and cool skin should be the heralding signs of significant hypovolemia and warrant vigorous fluid resuscitation (Table 3–9).

As one incurs greater blood loss, the signs and symptoms of hypovolemia become more profound; gross abnormalities of pulse, blood pressure, pulse pressure, respirations, and capillary blanch are seen (Table 3–10). However, in Class II hemorrhage—estimated blood loss of 1500–1800 ml—some patients can maintain a *normal* blood pressure in response to their increased circulating catecholamines. This varies according to age, rate of blood loss, and hydrational status, but therefore, blood pressure measurement is discredited as a sound gauge of hypoperfusion. Blood pressure or hypotension is but one determinant of perfusion; in fact, until profound blood loss occurs it can be very inaccurate. Thus,

Table 3–9 Heralding Signs of Early Shock in the Elderly

- Tachycardia
- Narrowed pulse pressure
- Positive or delayed capillary blanch test
- Altered mental status

---

blood pressure, unless obviously very low, should be thought of as a relatively useless tool in the early assessment of hemorrhagic states.

Other criteria for assessing the patient's perfusion status are urinary output, acid-base balance, and central venous pressure. None of these are practical in the prehospital management of traumatized patients and in cases of profound hemorrhage may be too time consuming initially. However, in the hospital setting, these can serve as excellent adjuncts to the assessment of the patient.

Urinary output is an extremely sensitive indicator of adequate perfusion. Both the absolute blood pressure and the rapidity of fall in blood pressure seem to be important in determining urine output. Urine output in the adult usually diminishes rapidly once the systolic pressure falls to 80 mm Hg or below. Urine output is just as sensitive an indicator of normal perfusion as it is of hypoperfusion; once adequate volume replacement has taken place one should expect prompt return of

---

Table 3–10 Fluid Resuscitation of Acute Hemorrhage*

CLASS	Volume Blood Loss (ml)	Fluid	Total Replacement Volume	Estimated Volume of Blood Replacement (whole blood)
I	Up to 750	Crystalloid	Up to 2,250	0
II	1,000–1,250	Crystalloid	3,000–3,750	0
III	1,500–1,800	Crystalloid and Blood	4,500–5,400	1,500–1,800
IV	2,000–2,500	Crystalloid and Blood	6,000–7,500	2,000–2,500

*Calculated by 3:1 formula; actual volumes are best determined according to physiologic response of the individual patient.

urine. An adequate urine output after a hypovolemic episode is approximately 50 ml/hr in the 70-kg adult.

Acid-base balance is best determined by analysis of arterial blood gasses. In the earliest stages of shock, one usually sees mild respiratory alkalosis due to the tachypnea and concomitant blowing off of CO_2. As shock progresses, however, metabolic acidosis becomes the dominant derangement due to obligatory anaerobic metabolism of cellular hypoperfusion and hypoxia. In a milder form this acidosis usually requires no specific therapy other than adequate volume replacement. Severe acidosis—manifested by a pH of 7.20 or less or a HCO_3^- of less than 16 mmol/liter—usually warrants a combination of aggressive volume replacement and *some* $NaHCO_3$. The base deficit should never be totally corrected with $NaHCO_3$, but some buffering of the acidosis at these levels is usually recommended to prevent cardiac irritability and dysrhythmia.[18]

Central venous pressure (CVP) is a measurement that serves as an adjunctive monitoring guide in hypovolemic shock; it records the ability of the right heart to accept and handle a fluid load.[18] The absolute number read from the CVP monitor is not nearly as important as the trend in central pressures. An initially low CVP followed by a sustained rise with volume replacement is a good indicator of appropriate volume expansion. A declining CVP, despite volume replacement, suggests ongoing blood loss and a need for additional fluids, blood, or prompt surgery. An abrupt or continual elevation in CVP suggests possible cardiac problems in the form of cardiac failure with right ventrical dysfunction or possible cardiac tamponade. Other causes of pathologic elevation of CVP include catheter malposition and increased interthoracic pressure from a pneumothorax or hemothorax.[10] Additionally, inflation of medical antishock trousers (MAST) may also cause some elevation, but this varies in individual patients depending on their volume status.[18,19]

Central venous catheters are not to be considered as a primary resuscitation line. The time spent placing and securing this catheter even by experienced personnel is lengthy. In addition, because of the increased catheter length and standard diameters—8–12 in, 14–16 gauge—the flow dynamics are less effective than the standard shorter, peripheral IV catheter (2–3 in, 14–16 gauge). Unless there is no other venous access site available, the central venous line should not replace the peripheral "short and fat" IV catheter as the initial device used for venous access and volume loading.

Shock Management

The standard treatment of shock is based on the volume of blood loss estimated by the clinical and adjunctive signs of hypoperfusion just discussed.[10,18] After a traumatic event all patients should be rapidly evaluated. The management of the resuscitation then depends on the severity of the shock situation.

All patients, regardless of the presence or absence of hypovolemic signs and symptoms, should be initially treated with supplemental oxygen and placed supine on the open MAST device. As the clinical evaluation continues and a better impression of any altered physiology is gained, one can then secure and rapidly inflate the MAST if needed. Obviously, if profound hypovolemia and hypotension—clinical signs, BP ≤ 100 mm Hg systolic in the elderly—are present, the MAST are rapidly inflated to whatever intracompartmental pressure is required to reverse the patient's hypotension. The number of compartments and the degree to which they are inflated are determined by the patient's blood pressure response. Most authorities agree that elevation and maintenance of the patient's systolic blood pressure above 100 mm Hg are the adequate and desirable *initial* responses.[10,18,20] Space limitations do not permit a more complete discussion of MAST, its indications, and complications; however, several references are provided as a review source.[19,20]

If MAST are not immediately available and hypovolemia is suspected, the first therapeutic maneuver should be placement of the patient in the Trendelenburg position (head down, feet up). This simple maneuver is often forgotten or ignored in deference to more technical and modern modalities. It remains, however, a quick and efficacious way of promoting increased venous return to the heart and, consequently, increasing cardiac output.

The Trendelenburg position and MAST application are maneuvers aimed at temporarily restoring and supporting perfusion to critical organ systems. Both sacrifice relative blood flow to the nonessential peripheral vascular beds (skin, muscle, and viscera of lower body). In doing so, they provoke a redistribution of blood flow and increased perfusion to more essential organs (heart, brain, and lungs). Both techniques buy time and require simultaneous IV volume replacement.[15,19,20]

As discussed earlier, the initial IV line should be started in a peripheral site, preferably on the dorsal vein of the hand or forearm. The cephalic vein on the lateral aspect of the upper arm can also be used, but it is not as superficial nor as easy to cannulate as the lower veins of the arm and hand. The antecubital veins are not preferred; any degree of elbow flexion usually causes dislodgement or infiltration. The cannula should be a "short and fat" IV catheter, preferably 2½–3 in and at least 14–16 gauge in size. Ideally, two veins, one on each upper extremity, should be used to allow optimal infusion of large volumes and simultaneous but separate administration of blood, crystalloid, and drugs.

The choice of resuscitation fluid, crystalloid (lactated Ringer's solution) or colloid (albumin, plasma protein solutions, dextran), remains controversial. To date, however, there have been no firm data to support the advantages of colloid solutions, and the cost of any colloid fluid is exorbitant. Therefore, most centers prefer and use lactated Ringer's solution.[10,15,18,21]

Lactated Ringer's solution is the most physiologic solution available for large-volume infusion. About 50% of the lactate is rapidly metabolized to bicarbonate in the liver and serves as a good buffer for the hypoperfusion-induced metabolic acidosis. Normal saline can be used, but remains a solution of second choice as it has no buffering capacity and its high chloride content predisposes the patient to hyperchloremia and further acidosis.

Crystalloid replacement of blood loss is adequate for most Class I and II hemorrhages. The most widely accepted resuscitation formula is the 3:1 rule (Table 3–10). Every milliliter of estimated blood loss is replaced by 3 ml of crystalloid. If, for example, a patient is estimated to have sustained a Class II hemorrhage and based on clinical assessment has lost 1,000 ml of blood, the initial fluid replacement should be 3,000 ml of lactated Ringer's solution. The first 2,000 ml is given as rapidly as possible. Of course, the 3:1 rule is only a "guestimation," and as with any treatment modality it must be guided by clinical response and evaluation.

As greater volumes of blood are lost and one advances to Class III and IV hemorrhages (1,500–2,500 ml blood loss in a 70–kg adult), the replacement rule changes. At these levels of hemorrhage the oxygen-carrying capacity of the blood is dangerously reduced; rapid infusion of blood, along with crystalloid solutions, is necessary. Blood should be replaced on a milliliter-per-milliliter basis so that if one estimates a 2,000 ml blood loss (Class IV) the replacement blood volume should be 2,000 ml. Whole blood can be used if type-specific blood is available. If immediate transfusion is required, low titer "O" negative packed cells should be used.[10] The crystalloid solution is still replaced by the 3:1 rule, and in the 2,000 ml hemorrhage the patient should theoretically receive approximately 6,000 ml of lactated Ringer's solution in addition to the 2,000 ml of blood (Table 3–10).

Regardless of the devices or fluids used, the restoration of the circulating blood volume is key to the successful treatment of shock. This restoration requires reliable and practical means of monitoring. The normalization of pulse and blood pressure, adequate urinary output, and the return of normal mental dysfunction are the key clinical signs of successful shock management. These signs, as well as a progressive elevation and stabilization of the CVP to the 10–12 cm H_2O range, are the more commonly used parameters. Failure to stabilize the patient or an initial stabilization followed by gradual or sudden deterioration should always be thought of as a sign of continual hemorrhage. Other reasons for this failure to respond are possible, but the vast majority of these cases have unrecognized ongoing hemorrhage requiring surgical control.

Shock in the Elderly

Both the normal aging process and the common pathologic causes of deterioration make the elderly less likely to withstand even short periods of hypoperfusion and hypoxia. In one study 100% of traumatized geriatric patients died after sustaining a hypotensive episode (systolic blood pressure less than 80 mm Hg) for 15 min.[5]

The cardiovascular and respiratory systems are the primary responders to the increased catecholamine levels produced as a result of baroreceptor simulation from hypoperfusion.[15] These hormones stimulate the myocardium to contract with increased strength and increased heart rate. They increase peripheral vascular resistance (diastolic pressure), and as blood loss continues, they cause a redistribution of blood within the body. The elderly may be greatly limited in their response to these hormones. Coronary artery disease and its effect on the conducting system and myocardium itself may not allow the increased heart rate or contractility necessary to maintain a normal cardiac output in early hemorrhage and hypovolemia.

Cardiac malfunction in shock may occur directly as a result of reduced blood flow. Autopsy studies on shocked patients have shown that true necrotizing lesions may be found in all parts of the heart, including the conduction system. In one study of patients who expired from hypovolemic shock secondary to blood loss, 36% of all autopsied "shocked" hearts had these necrotic lesions.[16] Pathologically, the evolution of the necrotic lesions of shock is similar to that of a myocardial infarction; they range from single-fiber necrosis to widespread infarction. Because the elderly patient has a diminished cardiac reserve, it makes sense that, as hypoperfusion of the myocardium progresses, more and more ischemic damage is done until an unreversible state occurs and infarction takes place. The clinical situation produced then becomes one of cardiogenic shock: pump failure as a result of myocardial ischemia and infarction. When this occurs in the shocked geriatric is hard to predict, but it is probably an early event and one that could explain the reported high mortality rate.[5] This possibility makes any degree of hypovolemic shock in the geriatric patient potentially lethal. Even Class I or II hemorrhages must be rapidly recognized, aggressively treated, and thoroughly managed. Hypovolemia and shock in the elderly require the same type of resuscitation techniques as discussed, but the inherent brittleness of the geriatric mandates a more aggressive approach that includes stricter monitoring techniques and specific end points.

Since 1980 a specific shock protocol for the elderly trauma patient has been used at the authors' trauma center (Figure 3–1). In general, the protocol follows the lines discussed above; O_2, Trendelenberg position, MAST, large-bore peripheral IV lines, and initial administration of lactated Ringer's solution. However, because of the great risk to the elderly hypovolemic patient from hypoperfusion and hypoxemia, these modalities are modified and supplemented to ensure the most rapid restoration of normal perfusion and maximum oxygenation.

All elderly patients are given at least 5 liters/min of supplemental oxygen through nasal prongs. Although consideration is given to the effect that supplemental oxygen in high concentration has on the "chronic lunger"—that is, decreasing respiratory drive—this effect has rarely been observed in any hypovolemic patient. The airway and breathing status are assessed, and any major chest injuries are rapidly ruled out. Simultaneously a quick clinical assessment is made to determine the degree of hypovolemia and shock. Pale, cool skin and a rapid thready pulse are excellent and easily seen signs of shock in the older patient. The mental status is usually altered, and most frequently patients are agitated or

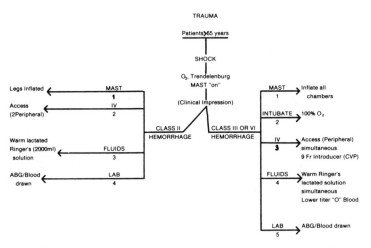

Figure 3–1 Shock protocol for the elderly used at the authors' trauma center.

---

confused. Obtundation can sometimes be observed. In these first few moments, if time permits and a blood pressure can be obtained, special attention is given to the systolic blood pressure and pulse pressure. Any systolic pressure below 120 mm Hg is felt to represent a potential shock state and requires rapid volume replacement. The pulse pressure is usually narrow; if there is less than 35–40 mm Hg difference, it is indicative of hypovolemia.

All patients are initially placed in the MAST garment, and if any of the aforementioned signs or symptoms are present, the two lower extremity compartments are inflated and a response noted. The abdominal compartment is not inflated unless obvious Class III or IV hemorrhage has occurred or specific pelvic or intra-abdominal injury warrants its use. The response to MAST has been not only therapeutic but also diagnostic.[20] If an older person's blood pressure rises in response to MAST inflation, one can consider this as an ancillary sign of hypovolemia and of a need for volume replacement with crystalloid and possibly blood. The advantage of the early use of MAST in the elderly patients is its reversibility. Although the autotransfusion theory of MAST is currently being questioned, the effect of the garment is totally reversible with deflation. This early inflation technique seems more attractive in an older patient with less cardiac reserve than is the rapid administration of 2–3 liters of crystalloid; if given to a patient with an already diseased heart the extra volume can precipitate cardiac decompensation and failure. This is not to say that crystalloid is not administered, but once the patient's blood pressure has been elevated with MAST, the crystalloid can be given more leisurely and its effect monitored more precisely.

At the same time as the MAST inflation, IV lines are secured; in the elderly, two good upper extremity peripheral IVs are started initially. While this is being accomplished, a specially designed CVP device is used to cannulate the internal jugular or subclavian vein. Patients over 60 years of age adjudged to be in shock, to have significant chest injury, or to fit criteria for CVP monitoring should have a 9 French Swan-Ganz introducer sheath inserted as the primary CVP line. This device, when connected to an H_2O manometer, facilitates monitoring of the CVP, and because of its large size it can be used for rapid volume replacement. In addition, a Swan Ganz catheter can be inserted should the situation warrant monitoring of pulmonary artery pressure and attainment of physiologic profiles. This is especially attractive in the geriatric patient for whom more precise volume replacement is needed and careful monitoring of myocardial performance is required.

In the elderly patient with signs of large volume loss, early intubation to maximize oxygenation is used. In severe shock intubation should be a primary part of the antishock therapy, rather than a therapy for airway or breathing problems. As expediently and safely as possible, the patient is intubated and placed on 100% inspired oxygen while the other initial events occur. This aggressive intubation approach is aimed at the most severe hypoperfusion states and is intended to counteract, as best as possible, the significantly reduced oxygen available to the tissues. It is hoped that maximizing the oxygenation of the available intravascular blood will cause some improvement in tissue and cellular oxygenation and avert "irreversible" cell death from hypoxia.

In addition to the early use of intubation, the more severe shock status in the geriatric patient has been treated by initial administration of low-titer "O" blood. Any elderly patient demonstrating signs of Class III or IV hemorrhage is rapidly given two units of low-titer "O" packed cells. This is done *synchronously* with the infusion of the first liter of crystalloid solution. It rapidly restores the red blood cell volume in the intravascular space and affords a great increase in the oxygen-carrying capacity of the blood. Once again, the aim is to perfuse and oxygenate the cells before irreversible changes occur.

When the severity of hemorrhage does not warrant intubation and immediate administration of blood, the geriatric patient is resuscitated in the usual fashion, but kept on "the dry side." Adequate volume expansion can best be monitored by insertion of a Foley catheter with frequent (every 15 min) urine measurements. As the situation stabilizes, more attention can then be given to the CVP (if not previously done), acquisition of arterial blood gasses (ABGs), and ECG. If urine output remains nil despite adequate volume replacement, the patient is still considered to be in shock and needs further volume replacement and surgical treatment for ongoing hemorrhage. Even with the antecedent diseases of the elderly and the possible simultaneous presentation of a myocardial infarction or stroke with trauma, if the geriatric shock patient fails to respond to volume replacement, most often the cause is continuing hemorrhage. The combination of a chest film, peritoneal lavage, and/or intravenous pyelogram (IVP) will determine the bleeding area in greater than 90% of all trauma patients. The hemorrhaging geriatric patient needs rapid surgical intervention even more than the younger person. One cannot assume that the patient is "too old" for surgery; without surgery and hemorrhage control, death is guaranteed.

The resuscitation of the elderly patient should be as drug-free as possible. As with all hypovolemic trauma patients the mainstays of a successful resuscitation are oxygen, crystalloids, and blood. As mentioned before, in some cases with severe metabolic acidosis (pH less than 7.20, HCO_3^- less than 15 mm/L) $NaHCO_3$ can be given to avoid cardiac dysrhythmias, but this is only an adjunct to volume replacement. The authors have not found it necessary to use any of the vasoaction drugs, such as dopamine or dobutamine. If cardiac decompensation and failure become evident, appropriate cardiotonics, vasodilators, or pressors are instituted, based on the need as determined from pulmonary artery catheter data.

Sedatives and narcotics are used sparingly, except to facilitate intubation. It is hard to predict how the geriatric patient will react to these medications, and both categories of drugs can potentiate further hypotension and decrease respiratory drive. Once the patient has become stable, adequate sedatives (usually an anti-histamine derivative) to allay anxiety and narcotics (morphine) are given. When initially prescribing these medicines for the geriatric patient it is better to order small doses until one has a feeling for how the patient reacts and responds to them.

SUMMARY

At the present time there are few studies that focus on trauma in the elderly. Currently, there are approximately 28,000 trauma deaths per year in the over-65 age range. The majority of these are from motor vehicle accidents in which the geriatric patient is usually an occupant. Falls while ambulating are the second most common mechanism of trauma. Because most older people are not usually involved in violent crimes, penetrating trauma comprises only a small percentage of cases. Those older persons that do sustain penetrating injuries are usually victims of crimes, especially assaults.

The initial approach to the elderly trauma patient follows the ABCs. However, the limited reserve of the geriatric patient makes any traumatic event that results in hypoxia and hypoxemia more threatening; even simple injury, if it alters oxygena-tion or leads to shock, must be considered a potentially lethal injury. For this reason, special attention and support are given to any airway or breathing prob-lems. Chest injuries should be rapidly diagnosed and stabilized. Early endo-tracheal intubation is not only a prime treatment for severe chest injury but in the geriatric patient should also be considered and used as a therapeutic modality to counteract shock.

Shock is highly lethal in the elderly patient, and resuscitation must be vigorous. The MAST garment should be used in all severe shock states as a reversible "fluid challenge." This allows time for a more controlled resuscitation and has elimi-nated the need for vast quantities of rapidly administered crystalloids. The early use of a low-titer "O" blood or type-specific blood is recommended as an early volume expander to increase rapidly the oxygen-carrying capacity of the intra-vascular volume and make O_2 available to the tissues and cells. Few, if any, drugs are required initially except to facilitate intubation; if sedation is required, it should be used sparingly in the elderly victim. Although antecedent disease subjects the elderly to simultaneous problems, such as myocardial infarction and multiple injuries, continuous hypotension should always be considered a sign of ongoing hemorrhage. Age alone should not be the deciding factor concerning ability to withstand surgery, as there can be little correlation between chronologic and physiologic age. Thus, surgical intervention to control an unstable situation should be used as aggressively as in the younger population. Once stabilization has occurred, the geriatric trauma patient needs prompt diagnosis and definitive care for injuries.

Lastly, although the recovery and convalescent stages are usually long and complex, most elderly patients can be returned to their families and loved ones. Many can continue to live out their lives as productive and needed people.

REFERENCES

1. Greenfield LF: *Surgery in the Aged*. Philadelphia, WB Saunders Co, 1975.

2. Cole WH: Operability in the young and aged. *Ann Surg* 138:145–157, 1953.

3. Boyd JB, Bradford B Jr, Watne AL: Operative risk factors of colon resection in the elderly. *Ann Surg* 192:743–746, 1980.

4. Rossman I (ed): *Clinical Geriatrics*. Philadelphia, JB Lippincott Co, 1979.

5. Oreskovich MR, Howard JD, Copass MK, et al: Geriatric trauma injury patterns and outcomes. *J Trauma* 24:565–572, 1984.

6. *Accident Facts*. Chicago, National Safety Council, 1971.

7. Kohn RR: *Principles of Mammalian Aging*. Englewood Cliffs, NJ, Prentice-Hall, 1971.

8. Shock NW (ed): *Aging, Some Social and Biological Aspects*. Washington, DC, American Association for the Advancement of Science, Pub No. 65, 1980.

9. Djokovic JL, Hedley-Whyte J: Prediction of outcome of surgery and anesthesia in patients over 80. *JAMA* 242:2301–2306, 1979.

10. *Advanced Trauma Life Support Manual*. Chicago, American College of Surgeons, 1981.

11. Lawson RB, Garland L, Schwab CW: Aortic injury: A comparison of supine versus upright portable chest x-ray films to evaluate the widening mediastinum. *Ann Emerg Med* 13:896–899, 1984.

12. Goldman R: Aging changes in structure and function, in Carnevali DL, Patrick M (eds): *Nursing Management for the Elderly*, ed 3. Philadelphia, JB Lippincott Co, 1979, pp 53–80.

13. Kallenberg GA, Beck JC: Care of the geriatric patient, in Rakel RE (ed): *Textbook of Family Practice*. Philadelphia, WB Saunders Co, 1984.

14. Tinkle JK, Richardson JD, Frant JL, et al: Management of flail chest without mechanical ventilation. *Ann Thorac Surg* 19:355, 1975.

15. Wilson RF, Wilson JA, Gibson D, et al: Shock in the emergency department. *JACEP* 5:678–690, 1976.

16. McGovern VJ, Tiller DJ: *Shock: A Clinicopathologic Correlation*. New York, Masson Publishing USA Inc, 1980.

17. Wigger CJ: *Physiology of Shock*. New York, Commonwealth Fund, 1950.

18. McSwain NE Jr: Objective approach to the management of shock. *Trauma Emerg Med* 7:7–13, 1981.

19. Wasserbert J, Balasubramanum S, Ordog G: Pneumatic antishock trousers: A widening spectrum of uses. *ER Reports* 2:105, 1981.

20. Schwab CW, Gore D: MAST: Medical antishock trousers. *Surg Ann 1983* 15:41–59, 1983.

21. Collins JA, Muawski K, Shafer AW (eds): *Massive Transfusion in Surgery and Trauma,* New York, Alan R Liss Inc, 1982.

SUGGESTED READINGS

Bergqvist D, Hedelin H, Karlsson G, et al: Abdominal trauma in persons older than 60 years. *Acta Chir Scand* 1982;148:569–573.

Besson A, Saegesser F: *Color Atlas of Chest Trauma and Associated Injuries.* New Jersey, Medical Economics Company Inc, 1983.

Daughtry DC (ed): *Thoracic Trauma,* ed. 1. Boston, Little Brown & Company, 1980.

Hanning CD, Ledingham E, Ledingham IM: Late respiratory sequelae of blunt chest injury: A preliminary report. *Thorax* 1981;36:204.

Hogue CC: Injury in late life: Part I, Epidemiology. *J Am Geriatric Soc* 1982;30:183–190.

Landercasper J, Cogbill TH, Lindesmith LA: Long-term disability after flail chest injury. *J Trauma,* in press.

Reiss R, Deutsch AA, Eliashiv A: Decision-making process in abdominal surgery in the geriatric patient. *World J Surg* 1983;7:522–526.

Shackford SR, Smith DE, Zarins CK, et al: The management of flail chest: A comparison of ventilatory and nonventilatory treatment. *Am J Surg* 1976;132:759.

Talley L: Laboratory values, in Carnevali DL, Patrick M (eds): *Nursing Management for the Elderly,* ed 3. Philadelphia, JB Lippincott Co, 1979, pp 81–108.

4

Approach to Multiple System Injury

Gerald O. Strauch, MD

In a society in which the elderly population is increasing at a rather phenomenal rate and in which injury ranks fourth among causes of death, one might expect that data regarding injury in the elderly would be abundant. The actual paucity of such data is a real shock to anyone who examines the problem. However, many researchers have studied the problems encountered by the elderly in surgery, a very controlled form of injury. With some exceptions it is the combination of experience with the management of trauma in a general population and knowledge of geriatric surgery that allows one to describe the approach to multiple system injury in the aged at present. More data specifically on injury in the elderly are clearly needed.

Whereas one might imagine that injuries in older individuals would be caused by blunt forces in all but extraordinary instances, the current epidemic of crimes of violence affects the elderly in two important ways. First, in many urban areas the elderly seem to be prime targets for muggings and robberies. Second, the incidence of injury to innocent bystanders, casualties of the urban warfare waged by criminal elements in many cities today, has increased substantially, and elderly people are among these victims. Consequently, physicians managing the injured must be ready to treat both penetrating and blunt injuries.

PRIORITIES OF EVALUATION AND MANAGEMENT

The priorities of early diagnosis and treatment of multiple system injury in elderly individuals are identical to those of all ages. These have been described in many publications,[1-3] and in-depth consideration of them is beyond the purpose of this chapter. However, special problems encountered in the geriatric age group are discussed below.

At the outset, anyone managing elderly injury victims must recognize that, in general, the aging process places limits on the homeostatic responses ultimately available to assist such victims in their response to injury and, indeed, in their ultimate survival. However, in the absence of pre-existing disease, these limits ordinarily become apparent only if (1) the injury is very severe, (2) appropriate management is delayed, (3) complications of injury ensue, and (4) the nature of the injury dictates a prolonged illness.

Surgeons long ago learned that age in and of itself does not dictate surgical management in most settings. The dictum that the elderly will tolerate a single injury of very impressive magnitude very well, if subsequent complications can be obviated, applies to all forms of injury, not only those planned in the course of surgery.

The priorities in the evaluation and management of the injured aged, then, in decreasing order of immediacy, are as follows:

1. primary survey of injury to detect immediate threats to life and initiation of resuscitation
2. secondary survey of injury to detail all injuries, especially those that could pose early threats to life and/or limb
3. definitive management of injury

This chapter deals largely with the primary survey, initiation of resuscitation, and certain aspects of the secondary survey. Definitive management is beyond its scope.

Primary Survey and Initiation of Resuscitation

The primary survey of injury identifies mechanical and physiologic defects caused by trauma that have the imminent potential for killing the victim within minutes. These defects in the overwhelming majority of instances involve the victim's airway, ventilation, and circulatory volume and are prioritized in that order as the ABCs of primary management: A—Airway establishment and main-tenance, B—Breathing (ventilation), and C—Circulation (external hemorrhage, internal hemorrhage, and shock as a result of hemorrhage).

Airway

Although the usual causes of upper airway obstruction pertain to the elderly patient, some special concerns must be considered in establishing the upper airway in the elderly. Many elderly patients wear dentures, and if they are dislodged during the events surrounding injury, they provide a formidable type of airway obstruction that must be removed or bypassed if the patient is to be ventilated.

Airway compromise in the injured patient is most commonly associated with disturbances in consciousness. In younger injury victims, head injury or alcohol or other drugs are the usual causes of altered consciousness. In elderly individuals, the effects of pre-existing diseases are also of importance. These may or may not have been recognized before the injury and may indeed have been the trigger mechanism for the events producing injury. Primary among these conditions are cardiac disease, with production of arrhythmias or sudden diminution of cardiac output leading to hypotension or syncope, and cerebrovascular disease with brain ischemia, seizure activity, or stroke.

Drugs used for management of pre-existing diseases may also be solely or partially responsible for alterations of consciousness in the elderly and, again, may be the inciting cause of events leading to injury. Chief among these are insulin and drugs used in the management of cardiovascular problems, including hypertension.

Protection of the cervical spinal cord during upper airway management has become a standard corollary of care because of the possibility of producing spinal cord damage by manipulation of the neck during resuscitation of injury victims who may have sustained previously undetected injuries of the cervical spine.

In older persons, degenerative arthritis of the cervical spine may be a source of two problems during the establishment of upper airway control. First, the deformity of the spinal canal may predispose the patient to spinal cord injury from manipulation of the neck, even in the absence of acute injury to the cervical spine. Second, the lack of mobility of the cervical spine may limit efforts to visualize the larynx during attempts at orotracheal intubation, requiring the use of alternate methods of endotracheal intubation if the patient needs intubation for ventilatory assistance.

Carotid occlusion has been reportedly caused by manipulation of the neck on rare occasions,[4] and such occlusion can be anticipated to be a greater risk in the atherosclerotic carotid.

With the exceptions of the foregoing cautions, the management of the upper airway in the injured elderly is essentially identical to that of all injury victims. Recognition of airway obstruction is critical, and the eradication of the obstruction depends on its cause. Maintenance of the airway, once it is patent, is preferably achieved by simple methods, but it frequently requires endotracheal intubation. On rare occasions cricothyroidostomy may be needed, and if injury to the neck is the cause of upper airway obstruction, even tracheostomy may be indicated. In the absence of laryngotracheal injury, the rare adult injury victim who requires an operative procedure for establishing a patent upper airway should have a cricothyroidostomy. Finally, in the author's view, the various "esophageal airways" available provide, at best, inferior airway management modalities and, at worst, a danger to the injury victim.

Breathing

In elderly patients, ventilation after establishing an airway presents few problems that differ from those in other injury victims in the early postinjury phase. The frequency of chronic obstructive pulmonary disease (COPD) in the elderly is so high that surgeons and anesthesiologists deal with ventilatory problems in such individuals almost automatically. For personnel who are not as accustomed to such problems, it is important to know that the mechanism responsible for respiratory drive in patients with COPD may be diminished oxygen levels, rather than the rising levels of carbon dioxide that stimulate ventilatory effort in normal individuals. In such circumstances, provision of oxygen after establishing a patent airway may produce hypoventilation or even apnea in an individual who is otherwise capable of adequate ventilatory effort, and provision for ventilatory assistance is mandatory. An occasional patient with severe, chronic respiratory acidosis may be seen in whom the metabolic compensation for hypercapnea paves the way for a pronounced metabolic alkalosis if aggressive artificial ventilation ablates the respiratory acidosis suddenly. Because the body's homeostatic response to alkalosis is extremely restricted, because injury and operation further compromise the few compensatory mechanisms (primarily renal) for alkalosis that normally exist, and because alkalosis can cause lethal cardiac arrhythmias due to its effects on potassium shifts in body fluid compartments, careful monitoring of blood gases and serum electrolytes is required in such individuals.

Circulation

The management of external hemorrhage in aged individuals is no different from the management in other age groups. Internal hemorrhage in geriatric patients poses all of the same associated problems encountered in younger people, and its cardinal manifestations are those of hypovolemia. The final pathway is shock, unless hemorrhage is so catastrophic that death occurs before signs of shock can supervene.

A surgical axiom states that shock in the injured is caused by hemorrhage until proven otherwise. This axiom applies to the injured elderly, but one must maintain a higher than normal index of suspicion that problems in addition to hemorrhage may contribute to shock that seems to be recalcitrant, despite aggressive blood volume support. Comorbid states involving degenerative diseases of the heart, lungs, and kidneys may introduce cardiac or septic components to shock in these injury victims and may require additional aggressive monitoring and diagnostic studies for proper management.

It is the author's clinical impression that injury in the elderly does not cause shock that is "premature"; that is, shock occurring with losses of amounts of blood that are smaller than those associated with shock in younger victims. In contrast, the elderly frequently display the manifestations of shock in precipitous fashion, providing very little time for intervention between the first manifestations of hypovolemia and blatant shock. For this reason, blood volume support should be very prompt and very precise in these patients.

Many of the drugs prescribed for the diseases afflicting the old are capable of altering the normal responses to hemorrhage. Some may enhance the manifestations of hypovolemia or produce a clinical picture that mimics the symptoms and signs of hypovolemia. High blood alcohol levels seem to accentuate some of the manifestations of shock in some injured persons. Of even more concern are drugs that may delay or mask the appearance of the shock syndrome even when profound hypovolemia exists. β-adrenergic blocking agents, such as propranolol, are noted for such action.

The occurrence of shock in elderly victims of multiple system injury is ominous as an indicator of subsequent survival. In a recent study of geriatric injury victims, all nonsurvivors had been victims of shock, and only 6% of survivors had experienced shock.[5]

Although the logistics of shock management in the elderly are no different from those of other adults, the consequences of overinfusion of fluids in the elderly can be much more serious, albeit subtle, and much more difficult to manage. The difference lies in the frequency of degenerative disease processes that characteristically affect the elderly: diseases of the heart, lungs, kidneys, and liver, which produce a typical systemic metabolic response in addition to their specific organ effects. In the patient with diminished cardiac reserve, overinfusion of fluid during resuscitation from injury may easily precipitate acute pulmonary edema, which is difficult to produce in young patients with sound hearts.

Much more common but less dramatic is the syndrome of the chronically infirm patient that is characterized by waterlogging of the cells and an increase in extracellular fluid volume of the body. It results from the failure of the body's metabolic processes to maintain body fluids and sodium and potassium in the balance identified as characteristic of good health. This tendency exists in virtually all chronic degenerative illnesses, but injury produces an acute energy crisis superimposed on a chronic energy deficit. The pattern is one of intracellular and extracellular edema with increased total body sodium, diminished total body potassium, diminished serum sodium, elevated serum potassium, and sodium and water retention by the kidneys. It is a manifestation of breakdown of the sodium pump of the body's cells that normally maintains the very high differentials in ionic concentrations between an extracellular fluid that is high in sodium concentration and low in potassium concentration, and the interior of cells that are high in concentration of potassium and low in concentration of sodium. This pump requires energy production that cannot be mustered in the presence of chronic disease, and this inadequacy is demonstrated much more vividly when acute stress is applied to the already taxed system. This problem is highlighted here, even though it is very difficult to completely avoid the phenomenon in the emergency setting and even though the consequences of large infusions of fluid may not become apparent for a number of days following injury. The lesson to be learned is the *need to avoid overinfusion of fluids in the infirm elderly during resuscitation from injury*. A corollary of this principle is that, when the need for blood transfusion during resuscitation is clear, transfusion should be undertaken promptly. Certainly these patients need much more careful monitoring of hemodynamics than do their younger counterparts who have no underlying disease, and the installation of central venous or even Swan-Ganz catheters is likely to be appropriate in the elderly earlier and more frequently after major injury than in the young.

Secondary Survey

The secondary survey of injury provides a systematic assessment of the entire body as a prelude to decisions regarding definitive care. The results of that assessment determine whether the victim of serious injury will undergo immediate operation and, if not, where in the hospital (or another hospital) is the most appropriate setting for that victim's care.

Thoracic Injury

A prominent blunt injury to the chest that poses a serious threat to life is thoracic rupture of the aorta. In younger persons with rupture of the thoracic aorta, widening of the mediastinum on a chest roentgenogram, which so frequently triggers performance of aortography to establish whether rupture is present, is almost regularly present if any sign of aortic rupture is seen on the chest film. In contrast, in persons 65 years of age or older who have aortic rupture, widening of the mediastinum may not be seen, and the following indirect evidence of aortic rupture on the chest film may furnish the clue to the diagnosis:[6]

- fractures of first or second ribs
- obliteration of the aortic knob
- deviation of the trachea to the right
- presence of a "pleural cap"
- elevation of the right mainstem bronchus and/or depression of the left mainstem bronchus
- obliteration of the space between the pulmonary artery and the aorta
- deviation of the esophagus to the right, as reflected by the course through the chest of a previously inserted nasogastric tube.

Such pulmonary and chest wall injuries as multiple rib fractures may subject the older patient with chronic pulmonary disease to substantially more ventilatory dysfunction than anticipated. Especially difficult to assess in the immediate postinjury period is pulmonary contusion, which may be an isolated injury, but is much more frequently associated with other thoracic injuries. Because (1) the hallmark of pulmonary contusion is hypoxia, (2) hypoxia is so difficult to diagnose by symptoms and signs, and (3) the elderly are frequently predisposed to post-traumatic pulmonary insufficiency, careful monitoring of arterial blood gases is vital when elderly patients with blunt chest injuries are seen.

Myocardial contusion occurs commonly in victims of blunt chest injury, in some studies as often as one patient in five.[7] Myocardial contusion may be minimal and never become clinically apparent, or it may be rapidly lethal. Establishing the diagnosis may be difficult, especially in the presence of pre-existing myocardial disease. In the geriatric age group, myocardial contusion can present the clinician with real diagnostic dilemmas, which can in turn pose exasperating problems with therapeutic decisions.

Abdominal Injury

Many older individuals in this country have had abdominal operations during their lives. When abdominal injury is suspected in these individuals, they may not be candidates for diagnostic peritoneal lavage because of intra-abdominal adhesions from their earlier operations. In such instances decisions regarding appropriate management of the abdominal component of the patient's injuries may hinge on other data. Computed tomography (CT) of the abdomen may be extremely helpful in these situations.

Cirrhosis is an important disease in the elderly and a major cause of death. The combination of cirrhosis and blunt injury to the liver is a highly lethal combination because of (1) difficulty in managing the injury at operation, (2) coagulopathy that frequently complicates the management of hemorrhage, and (3) deterioration in hepatic function that must be anticipated following major injury of any kind in the cirrhotic patient. If patients with this ominous combination are to be salvaged, admittedly a rare achievement, they require expert management.

Injuries to kidneys occur with increased frequency in diseased kidneys. A distended bladder predisposes the patient to urethral or bladder rupture. Blunt injury in individuals afflicted with renal disease or with prostatism must therefore raise one's index of suspicion for injury to the urinary tract. Conversely, urinary tract injury that seems overly serious in light of the mechanism of injury may require further investigation for underlying urinary tract disease.

As noted previously in connection with carotid occlusion, atherosclerosis may set the stage for sudden vascular accidents in connection with injury. Occlusion of major abdominal arteries may be the result of direct trauma or systemic hypotension, which can precipitate thrombosis in vessels the lumens of which have been compromised by atherosclerotic plaques.

Abdominal injuries in the aged are associated with substantially higher mortality than that seen in younger people; accordingly, they deserve an even higher degree of respect than they ordinarily receive.

Central Nervous System Injury

Interpretation of diffuse and focal neurologic deficits may be difficult in elderly individuals brought to the hospital under circumstances in which injury is obvious. Questions frequently arise whether the injury occurred because the patient suffered a stroke that resulted in neurologic dysfunction, with consequent accident and injury, or whether the neurologic deficit is totally the result of injury. Such questions are even more likely when patients are discovered unconscious in their homes or on the street, and nothing is known of the associated circumstances. Fortunately, the technology of imaging, primarily CT scans, now allows much more expeditious resolution of many of these questions, but they nonetheless must be satisfactorily resolved whenever they arise.

Osteoarthritis of the spine, so common in the elderly that it might be categorized as "normal," may make interpretation of roentgenographic studies of the spine difficult. It is imperative that expert interpretation be available.

Serious head injury gravely compromises the prognosis in old persons. In the recent study of injury in the aged undertaken at the University of Washington,[5] patients who died had over twice the incidence of serious head injury as did survivors.

Extremity Injury

Tetanus prophylaxis is at least as important in the elderly as it is in younger persons. One continues to see older individuals, especially those who have immigrated to the United States from other countries, who have never been adequately immunized against tetanus; in many others, the status of tetanus immunization is very doubtful. Tetanus is even more catastrophic in the old than in the young because of the lethal complications attendant on a disease with a persistently high mortality rate. Because tetanus is so readily preventable, its occurrence is truly tragic.

Fracture of the femoral neck, usually in persons of advanced age, is one of the most common reasons for hospital admission for injury victims in hospitals that are not in urban "battle zones." In a study of more than 6,400 patients who were admitted in 1981 to a consortium of nine Connecticut hospitals because of injuries, fracture of the femoral neck was far and away the most common principal diagnosis, accounting for 12% of admissions.[8] Five percent of these patients died during their hospitalizations, emphasizing the serious problems associated with fractured hips.

Extremity injuries in the older individual are prone to cause vascular complications much more frequently than similar injuries in younger people, primarily when injuries of the legs are involved. Arterial occlusive disease predisposes the patient to problems of acute arterial insufficiency based on arterial thrombosis. Venous thromboembolism following trauma to the lower extremities is a constant threat.

Burns

The significantly higher mortality associated with burn injuries in the aged is well known.[9] If survival is to be achieved in the presence of a serious burn injury in such patients, virtually every aspect of burn care requires detailed attention.

INJURY OUTCOME

Of the 6,400 injury victims admitted to the consortium of Connecticut hospitals, 25 percent were 65 years of age or older.[8] These elderly patients accounted for 53% of all deaths. Some of the characteristics of the elderly discussed in this chapter can be assumed to be responsible, at least in part, for this phenomenon of increased mortality. However, detailed specific knowledge is lacking regarding the relative contributions of various factors that one might suspect would be responsible. Injury severity scoring has provided conflicting data in the injured aged.[10] The contributions of comorbidity and response to specific aspects of management have not been studied in elderly patients with multiple system injury.

Rehabilitation of the elderly individual who has suffered serious injury has received little formal investigation in this country, certainly no more than has rehabilitation of trauma victims in general. In the study by Oreskovich et al., whereas 96% of elderly injury victims were independent in their daily living at the time of their injuries, 92% of surviving patients continued to require some form of assistance at 1 year following injury.[5] Seventy-two percent of patients in the study who required care and surgical intervention at a trauma center required full nursing care at 1 year after the injury.

CONCLUSION

Considered in epidemiologic terms, the data regarding injury in the elderly in the United States are impressive. At least 28,000 persons over the age of 65 die from injuries annually.[5] The death rate is high, accounting for 25% of all deaths due to injury in this country. With more than 26 million people currently over the age of 65 in the United States and with this number increasing annually, it is obvious that the problems of injury in the aged will remain prominent in trauma care. It behooves all who are concerned with care of the injured and care of the elderly to rectify the glaring defects in our knowledge that allow the many problems of prevention, evaluation, and management of the injured aged to remain unsolved. Above all, it is critical that all who care for such fragile lives realize how meticulous and individualized that care must be if success is to be achieved.

REFERENCES

1. Hardy JD (ed): *Critical Surgical Illness*. Philadelphia, WB Saunders Co, 1980.
2. Committee on Trauma, American College of Surgeons: *Early Care of the Injured Patient*. Philadelphia, WB Saunders Co, 1982.
3. Moore EE, Eiseman B, Van Way CW III (eds): *Critical Decisions in Trauma*. St. Louis, CV Mosby Co, 1984.
4. Dragon R, Saranchak H, Lakin P, et al: Blunt injuries to the carotid and vertebral arteries. *Am J Surg* 141:497–500, 1981.

5. Oreskovich MR, Howard JD, Copass MK, et al: Geriatric trauma: Injury patterns and outcome. *J Trauma* 22:565–572, 1984.

6. Gundry SR, Williams S, Burney RE, et al: Indications for aortography in blunt thoracic trauma: A reassessment. *J Trauma* 22:664–671, 1982.

7. Gay WR Jr, McCabe JC: Trauma to the chest, in Shires GT (ed): *Care of the Trauma Patient*. New York, McGraw-Hill, 1979.

8. Strauch GO: Unpublished data.

9. Curreri PW, Luterman A, Braun DW Jr, et al: Burn injury: Analysis of survival and hospitalization time for 937 patients. *Ann Surg* 192:472–478, 1980.

10. Trunkey DD, Siegel J, Baker SP, et al: Panel: Current status of trauma severity indices. *J Trauma* 23:185–201, 1983.

5

Respiratory Emergencies in the Aged

Thomas J. Godar, MD

RESPIRATORY PHYSIOLOGY IN THE AGED

Changes in Lung Volumes

With age there is a decreased compliance or increased stiffness of the chest wall associated with a reduction in intercostal muscle power and calcification of costochondral junctions; as a result the chest cage is less pliable. In addition, the lung loses elastic recoil properties and is more easily distensible, but also empties less completely on expiration so that the patient breathes at a higher lung volume level or functional residual capacity (FRC). The residual air (residual volume) on forced expiration—25% of total lung capacity in young adulthood—slowly increases to 40% or greater by age 70. The residual volume may exceed 50% in adult life in the very elderly patient. The total lung capacity or lung volume at forced inspiration is almost constant or slightly reduced because of reduction in body height caused by gradual flattening of intervertebral discs.

The increased residual volume is associated with a significant and predictable reduction in forced vital capacity (FVC) with age. After age 40 there is a yearly loss in FVC of 25–30 ml per year or approximately 0.5% annually. In patients with established chronic obstructive pulmonary disease (COPD) who have discontinued smoking and have clinically stable disease there is an accelerated loss in FVC closer to 75–80 ml per year, suggesting a deterioration in lung function in excess of that produced by the normal aging process. Lung volumes are routinely measured in the sitting or upright position as patients evaluated in the supine position have smaller volumes because of increased restriction by abdominal contents, with the effect of gravity on the diaphragm eliminated by the supine position. The diaphragm restriction is further increased by progressive levels of obesity, especially when the fat distribution tends to be central as in some older patients. Additional reductions in lung volumes often falsely ascribed to age probably represent the loss of function resulting from recurring respiratory disease.

Changes in Air Flows

With age there is a reduction in lung tissue elastic recoil similar to the change in recoil occurring in a deteriorating elastic band. Accordingly, as the lung is emptied on both forced expiration and a normal expiratory movement, the delicate small airways that lack cartilage in their walls and rely for their support on the integrity of the surrounding tissue and the outward pulling of elastic fibers no longer have these recoil forces to keep them open during the full expiratory movement. Therefore, in the lower portions of the lung where mechanical forces are less capable of keeping the airways open, the airways close before full emptying and collapse at increasingly higher lung volumes until some close during a normal expiratory phase. This premature closing of lung units impairs complete emptying of the lung and is especially exaggerated in the presence of disease, as in the early stages of COPD. It is also common in the postsurgical state and in the supine position. COPD results in the production of lower sections of lung tissue in which premature bronchiolar closure leads to inadequate ventilation of heavily perfused lower lung units. This change results in a reduced ventilation/perfusion ratio that produces a progressive hypoxemia. This phenomenon is common in aged patients, is exaggerated in patients with COPD, and is further increased by the compressing effect of moderate to massive obesity. It partly explains why all obese patients tend to have lower oxygen tensions than patients of the same age who are of normal weight. The reduction in recoil forces that causes small airways to close prematurely also produces excessive turbulent flow with rapid air exchange, as with exercise. Therefore, the maximum voluntary ventilation in such patients is reduced not only by weakening of respiratory muscles due to age with reduction in the excursion of the diaphragm and chest cage but also by the internal forces of airway collapse during rapid air exchange. There is not only an increased resistance to air flow in large airways at high lung volumes and resistance to air flow in small airways at lower lung volumes but also a marked variation in this resistance from one patient to the other. It may be present in elderly patients who appear normal and in whom there is no evidence of a past history of respiratory disease. Any superimposed disease that reduces muscle strength, coordination, or overall conditioning naturally reduces ventilation capacity further.

Changes in Oxygen Tensions

A progressive change in arterial PO_2 from maturity to old age has been well studied and documented, with a gradual decline in PaO_2 occurring when the patient is studied in the sitting position from age 20 to age 80.[1] The mean PaO_2 tends to fall from 90–100 mm Hg to 65–80 mm Hg, resulting not from loss in diffusion surface but from the gradual development of lung zones with a reduced ventilation/perfusion ratio in the normal individual (Table 5–1). Because most blood flow occurs at the lung bases, this decline in PaO_2 probably results from the premature closure of small airways in the dependent lung zones in the aged lung. Moreover, in the patient studied in the supine position and especially one who is mildly or moderately obese, one anticipates a further reduction in PaO_2 of approximately 5–10 mm Hg based on the rearrangement of ventilation/perfusion ratios in the supine position. Obesity further impairs the ventilation of the lung by reducing diaphragm excursion, thereby contributing to increased hypoxemia. Care should be exercised when obtaining arterial blood samples for oxygen tension because those obtained following coughing or changes in position may reveal associated transient hypoxemia. These ventilation/perfusion imbalances in older patients are further compounded by a tendency for reduction in cardiac output and venous oxygen content. Despite these changes, largely brought about by the process of aging, there may be additional undetected lung disease contributing to hypoxemia, which is being ascribed to age alone. Furthermore, the author has observed oxygen tensions of 95–100 mm Hg in elderly subjects with no history of cigarette smoking or known underlying cardiopulmonary disease. This again reflects the increased variability in normal values in the aged patient. Arterial CO_2 tensions are unchanged in the elderly, though there is a reduction in CO_2 sensitivity with advanced age. There is no significant change in arterial pH in the elderly patient, and any change from normal values may be considered evidence of disease.

Respiratory Control

Studies of healthy patients aged 64–75 have demonstrated a significant reduction in heart rate and ventilatory response to hypoxia, as well as to hypercapnia. This finding suggests that in the aging process there is a loss in the protective mechanisms that permit the system to respond to alterations in blood gas levels. In elderly patients who have underlying chronic pulmonary disease, especially COPD, there is a further reduction in response to alterations in both PO_2 and PCO_2. Whether the reduction in ventilatory response to carbon dioxide in the elderly is due to suppression of central nervous system (CNS) receptors or

---

Table 5–1 Normal PaO_2 Values (mm Hg)

Age Group	Mean	Lower Limit of Normal
41–50	88	84
51–60	84	80
61–70	77	73
71–80	75	64

peripheral receptors is not known, but central mechanisms are considered at least partly responsible.

Changes in Exercise Capacity

Because normal exercise capacity limits are based on both genetic and training factors, it is natural that there should be wide variation among normals, including the aged. Lack of physical conditioning significantly reduces maximal oxygen uptake by exercising muscles and therefore limits the level of exercise tolerated. Part of this limitation in exercise capacity may be secondary to a reduction in maximal heart rate or a reduced oxygen extraction by exercising skeletal muscle. It has been established that regular physical training significantly retards the rate of decrease in maximum oxygen uptake that does occur with age, suggesting that some changes ascribed to age are actually the result of deconditioning caused by lack of vigorous exercise.

Changes Associated with Disease Common to the Elderly

In addition to the documented although poorly understood reductions in function of the respiratory system during aging, there are common respiratory diseases seen in the elderly that further reduce respiratory capacity. These diseases may not be recognized, but they may contribute to functional impairment to a significant degree. Because some are very common in the elderly, especially elderly men, they may significantly contribute to further deterioration in function in many patients. These diseases include pulmonary fibrosis resulting from occupational exposures to such minerals as asbestos, silica, and beryllium and processes associated with exposure to organic substances in the workplace. The resultant pulmonary fibrosis produces smaller lung volumes and a reduction in exercise capacity, which sometimes does not affect air flows, but generally leads to increased levels of hypoxemia.

Most associated lung disease in the elderly patient is obstructive airway disease that is largely due to combined chronic bronchitis and emphysema. This condition occurs largely in the cigarette-smoking patient and especially in elderly men, although the incidence is increasing rapidly in women. The presence of airway obstruction markedly reduces exercise capacity by impairing the rapid air exchange required for exercise. Therefore, the loss in function will be greater at any level of disease than is true of patients who have restrictive diseases, such as pulmonary fibrosis. In addition, obstructive diseases are associated with cough and sputum production and, in many cases, with variable elements of bronchospasm. It is important to detect these abnormalities because some are responsive to medication or control of the environment leading to improvement that might not occur if these reductions in functional capacity were ascribed to age alone. In men over 70 years old the incidence of moderate to severe COPD may reach 35% to 40%, and it may be as high as 15% to 20% in women. Although it causes less deaths in elderly patients compared to cardiovascular disease and cancer, COPD plays a major role in producing exercise limitations and functional impairment.

PATIENT ASSESSMENT

History

The Chief Complaint As a Guide

It is vital for the attending nurse or physician to determine the *chief complaint* of the patient. Although the older patient is likely to be restless, agitated, anxious, and confused in the emergency situation, it is also likely that when asked for a chief complaint the patient will clearly state the primary problem. Even if the response is, "I have heart disease," this helps orient the evaluation immediately toward probable cardiac disease and/or complications. In addition, an expression of fear of death helps establish the level of symptoms and also direct one's attention toward myocardial infarction, pulmonary embolism, or other acute conditions commonly associated with a classical sense of impending death. Sometimes the chief complaint is even more directive, such as, "I think I have another blood clot" or "This feels like the pain I had with my last heart attack." Because the older patient is inclined to recurrent episodes of disease, the chief complaint is especially valuable in providing a direction in the first evaluation of an acutely ill patient.

Common Symptoms of Respiratory Disease

It is important to establish early in the evaluation whether symptoms are acute in onset and new or whether they represent a recurrence or exacerbation of chronic symptoms. This finding may immediately orient treating personnel to the nature of the disease in some cases or may establish that the patient's symptoms represent an acute exacerbation of a pre-existing disorder for which the patient is already under treatment and possibly has already undergone extensive diagnostic evaluation. The question "Have you ever had this before?" is superficially naive, but often produces remarkable information from the patient. When symptoms have a truly acute onset, they more likely represent a form of trauma, infection, or a major vascular event. Because older patients frequently receive multiple drugs for treatment of chronic disorders, because their tolerance for drugs is notoriously low and variable, and because the incidence of side effects from multiple drug treatment is very high, a question about new drugs being administered may be very fruitful in explaining the onset of new acute symptoms. The most common new drug-induced symptoms are gastrointestinal, including nausea, vomiting or diarrhea, but may also be palpitations, tremors as from bronchodilator drugs, dizziness, headaches, or somnolence in the case of tranquilizers or sedatives. An increase in dyspnea with reduction in sputum production may result from the desiccation of secretions that is commonly produced by anticholinergic drugs. Drug interaction effects are best analyzed in a more thorough and structured manner when the patient has been safely delivered to the receiving medical care facility.

Dyspnea

Dyspnea may be defined as a sensation of shortness of breath or a distressing sensation associated with breathing; it is a subjective complaint of the patient. A study of dyspnea, its onset, severity, and recurring patterns may be critical in diagnosing the underlying cardiac or pulmonary disease, but it is subject to the patient's own interpretation and must always be separated from such complaints as chest pain and fatigue with which it is frequently confused by the patient. For example, pleuritic pain on full inspiration and the increased work of breathing associated with exercise may both produce dyspnea, as does anxiety-induced hyperventilation that is not associated with any underlying cardiopulmonary disease (Table 5–2). Hypoxemia and hypercapnia do not commonly produce dyspnea, although the conditions that lead to hypoxemia and hypercapnia, such as pulmonary edema, lung trauma, and airway obstruction, may themselves produce dyspnea. In addition, a sense of dyspnea is very common in patients suffering from an anxiety-induced hyperventilation syndrome in which none of the mechanisms listed in Table 5–2 are operative, except for the presence of frequent sighing breaths and an above-normal ventilation level. In the author's experience, the

---

Table 5–2 Causes of Dyspnea

Increased respiratory excursions
　High-altitude response
　Response to exercise
Reduced ventilation
　Breathing muscle fatigue
　Onset of paralysis
　Breath holding
Increased stimulation from lung receptors or chest wall
　Pulmonary edema
　Pulmonary fibrosis
　Hyperinflation—asthma, emphysema
Increased mechanical loading
　Breathing through narrow airways
Increased airway resistance—asthma

Note: A useful approach to analyzing common causes of dyspnea is illustrated. It should be noted that dyspnea may result from increased work of breathing, hyperpnea induced by disease and an increase in mechanical loading on the respiratory system even when increased ventilation does not result.

most commonly confused complaint with dyspnea is that of exercise-induced fatigue. The patient complains of shortness of breath on climbing stairs, but further questioning reveals that the major complaint is actually fatigue of leg muscles, possibly representing deconditioning or cardiac failure with poor muscle circulation, rather than respiratory impairment.

The five most common causes for dyspnea encountered by emergency care personnel are as follows:

1. acute pulmonary edema
2. upper airway obstruction by aspiration or foreign body
3. COPD, such as emphysema or chronic bronchitis
4. asthma or angioneurotic edema
5. hyperventilation syndrome

In the elderly patient, the hyperventilation syndrome is much less likely to be responsible for acute dyspnea; the most frequent mechanism is pulmonary congestion from heart failure or chronic obstructive lung disease.

Cough

Although it is likely that all cough is actually productive of secretions, it is useful to differentiate the very productive from the relatively nonproductive cough because doing so may aid in the initial diagnosis of the etiologic mechanism. The most common causes of chronic cough in the elderly patient are cigarette smoking and the presence of chronic bronchitis. This etiology is confirmed by a history of cough and sputum production that is especially notable in the morning, sometimes clears during the day, but tends to increase with exercise and acute infections. A history of cough producing more than 50 ml sputum per day, especially persistent yellow to green sputum, suggests possible bronchiectasis in which the sputum volume is large and produced daily without interruption, frequently beginning with a history of a severe bacterial pneumonia or chest trauma. A history of cough usually associated with wheeze suggests bronchospasm as the major mechanism. In such patients the cough, often paroxysmal, should be regarded as a wheeze equivalent and is often induced by exposure to cold air, volatile chemicals, or strong odors or by exercise. Both cough and wheeze respond to bronchodilators so the association is important in establishing diagnosis and directing treatment. When cough is a new finding and associated with purulent sputum, fever, chest pain, and dyspnea, especially if preceded by chills, bacterial pneumonia is the likely cause. Patients whose dyspnea and cough with or without wheeze are relieved by expectoration of secretions usually have chronic obstructive lung disease with a predominant element of chronic bronchitis. Dyspnea limited to periods of paroxysmal cough does not require emergency attention.

The cause of the relatively nonproductive cough may be quite different from the cough that is characterized by secretions. Cough is common in cardiac failure, but is generally not productive and tends to be postural, with an increase in the supine position and improvement on standing or sitting as pulmonary congestion subsides. Paroxysmal cough induced by postnasal discharge characteristically begins on assuming the supine position before sleep and tends not to occur as often when the patient is upright. Many patients are unaware of the presence of postnasal discharge because it can be very subtle. Relief by nasal decongestants is diagnostic and therapeutic. The appearance of a nonproductive cough or the increase of a previous cough in an elderly cigarette smoker suggests the need to evaluate for lung cancer. Endobronchial cancer may induce cough and blood streaking of sputum early in its development.

A special problem in the elderly is cough associated with meals and the regular aspiration of oral secretions. In addition, the incidence of symptomatic hiatus hernia with esophageal reflux is higher in the elderly patient. The patient may experience episodes of paroxysmal cough with wheeze associated with midline, substernal burning pain or active symptoms of epigastric distress characteristic of hiatus hernia with reflux. If cough is associated with wheeze and occurs during the sleeping hours, with relief on assuming the erect position, cardiac failure is suggested, but aspiration is also a possible cause. The same complaints may occur when the elderly patient bends forward, thereby increasing intra-abdominal pressure and inducing esophageal reflux with heartburn.

In the elderly patient, underhydration is common, and patients with bronchial secretions tend to inspissate secretions and mobilize bronchial mucus poorly, leading to bronchial obstruction by mucus plugs. This is especially a problem in the winter months when heating causes a drying of the indoor air that dries mucous membranes and airway secretions. It is seen in those patients with poor fluid intake or with fluid restriction combined with the commonly used diuretics. Another hazard in the elderly is the use of anticholinergic drugs for gastrointestinal problems or any drug, such as the commonly employed mood elevators, that may induce dryness of mucous membranes, thereby inducing obstruction by airway secretions with secondary cough, dyspnea, and increased respiratory distress.

Wheeze

The older patient complaining of a wheeze might have cardiac failure, which can induce bronchospasm, but is more likely to have chronic bronchitis, to be a cigarette smoker with daily cough and secretions, and to have a background of asthma or other allergic disease in early life. Nevertheless, wheeze does occur in the older patient for the first time in association with inflammatory airway disease, most commonly with acute postviral bacterial bronchitis or with the chronic bronchitis associated with cigarette smoking. Furthermore, contrary to past teaching, bronchial asthma may occur for the first time in the older patient, even in the absence of a background of allergic disease. This form of bronchial asthma is usually associated with a viral infection that has induced a bacterial bronchitis with cough and wheeze as prominent findings. In general, asthmatic bronchitis is more inclined to remain a chronic disorder requiring continuing treatment in the older patient as compared with the history of intermittent discrete attacks and a tendency for gradual improvement in a younger patient with asthma.

The first step in evaluating the complaint is to determine that the patient is not describing rattling respirations or the presence of secretions in upper airways, but is in fact having episodes of musical expiratory sounds appropriately called a wheeze or a sibilant rhonchus. When wheeze is present only with coughing and is relieved by expectoration, it is usually due to chronic bronchitis in which there is a significant element of bronchospasm or hyperreactive airways. The presence of noisy inspiratory sounds (stridor) should be considered evidence of upper airway obstruction and requires immediate attention, as well as clear differentiation from simple expiratory wheezing. When a wheeze is limited to a small part of the inspiratory phase and has the qualities of a "squeak," especially when it is limited to one lung zone and is persistent, the presence of a foreign body or bronchial tumor must be ruled out. If localized squeaks are heard in conjunction with diffuse wheeze and change with cough and deep breathing, they simply represent local mucus plugs that do not require specific attention. When the older patient is wheezing and short of breath, has a history of cardiac disease, and prefers to sit bolt upright, cardiac failure is likely the cause. The sudden onset of dyspnea and wheeze associated with chest pain, especially in the presence of thrombophlebitis, recent surgery, or immobilization, suggests pulmonary embolism. In pulmonary embolism the wheeze is usually very transient and no longer present on the arrival of the treating personnel. Nevertheless, the author has seen persistent wheeze and hyperinflation in the patient with no previous history of asthma or COPD who has experienced repeated showers of small pulmonary emboli.

Hemoptysis

Coughing up of blood is a common finding, the frequency being underestimated in the presence of chronic lung disease. However, the majority of patients have minimal bleeding with blood streaking of sputum as the most common manifestation. Although not classified as true hemoptysis by many pulmonary physicians, the presence of repeated blood streaking of sputum may have very important diagnostic implications and certainly is a source of anxiety to older patients because they may associate hemoptysis with tuberculosis or lung cancer. Volume estimates of blood are best obtained by using the commonly understood guides of the 5 ml teaspoon, the 15 ml tablespoon, or the 1-oz whiskey jigger, volume guides to which the older patient can relate.

The most common cause of blood streaking of sputum is the simple chronic bronchitis that is associated with cigarette smoking, with blood streaking often occurring after paroxysms of cough; it is generally presumed to be due to a rupture of superficial bronchial mucosal vessels. This should be clearly differentiated from the episode in which there is a "welling up of blood" followed by a cough to clear the secretions and the appearance of a teaspoonful of blood or more. In some episodes the volume reaches several hundred milliliters. The chronic use of anticoagulants, the heavy use of aspirin, or a past history of hemoptysis should be immediately ruled out because these would provide a likely explanation for the coughing up of blood and considerable reassurance about the immediate risk to the patient. It is important to rule out bleeding from the nose (epistaxis) with a clearing of secretions in the throat and expectoration, as this may mimic true hemoptysis. Factitious hemoptysis is very uncommon in the elderly, but may still be present in the highly neurotic patient when chronic bronchitis or bronchiectasis has been ruled out as causes of hemoptysis.

Other prevalent causes should be considered. Pulmonary embolism may cause the appearance of bright red blood in the sputum, but rarely without dyspnea and other findings suggestive of thromboembolism, such as phlebitis, chest pain, or a recent history of surgery or trauma. The rusty sputum characteristic of an acute bacterial pneumonia must never be confused with the bright red blood seen in pulmonary embolism, although hemoptysis may occur in only 30% of patients with pulmonary embolism. Tuberculosis is no longer a common cause for hemoptysis, but when it is the cause, there is a history of weight loss, fever, or sweats. The reactivation of old tuberculosis treated before the chemotherapy era is an increasing problem in elderly patients, especially when associated with immunosuppression or chronic disease. When a heavy cigarette smoker, generally an elderly man, experiences hemoptysis with weight loss and especially with persistent chest discomfort lung cancer should be ruled out, although this is not an emergency.

Massive hemoptysis, or more than 200 ml of blood per day, should be considered life threatening and in the elderly patient is most likely to be due to cavitary lung disease. Massive hemoptysis may occur from a vascular aneurysm and rarely from a carcinoma eroding into a major vessel. These patients require immediate transport to an emergency care facility with monitoring of vital signs and the use of supplemental oxygen. They must be evaluated in order to rule out a coagulation defect and need for transfusion. In addition, chest films may demonstrate the site of the lesion or at least the site of bleeding by showing a localized infiltrate. The patient may then be bronchoscoped while actively bleeding to determine the site and possibly to apply corrective treatment. Because bleeding may be due to a small vascular defect that is generally not visualized, it is not surprising that 10% to 15% of patients with a single episode of spontaneous hemoptysis have neither a recurrence nor the cause established. If there is a history of previous limited hemoptysis, such as blood streaking, and especially when there is evidence of such chronic airway disease as chronic bronchitis or bronchiectasis, the episodes should not be treated as an emergency. These patients should be managed with reassurance and orderly efforts to ensure medical attention so that a significant diagnosis is not missed.

Pain

Pleuritic pain may be dull and gradual in onset as in pulmonary embolism, occurring at the lung bases posteriorly; for some hours it may be confused with simple back pain, but usually it is sharp pain. When it is of abrupt onset, the pain is increased by deep breathing, coughing, yawning, and even postural changes, such as bending forward or turning from side to side. The association with postural changes can create confusion between pleuritic pain and musculoskeletal pain. The latter is well localized and may be intensified by compression of the pain site; this is not true of pleuritic pain. In addition, pleuritic pain is associated with other signs or symptoms of lung disease, such as fever, the appearance of cough, purulent secretions as in pneumonia, or gross hemoptysis as in pulmonary embolism. Pleuritic pain induces involuntary splinting of the chest cage and, when unilateral, leads to asymmetrical expansion of the chest cage or unequal hemi-diaphragm movement that is readily detected on examination. Patients may complain of dyspnea because they are unable to take a normal breath and feel the desire for a deep breath, which is prohibited by pain. They generally splint the chest by holding the area with their arms and may even seek a binding to reduce the movement and control pain. In the older patient who is more likely to have chronic lung disease, a binding of the chest to reduce movement may cause retention of secretions, atelectasis, and further pulmonary complications. Therefore, when pain is truly pleuritic, it warrants evaluation at a medical facility, which may include the private physician's office, but it must never be ignored because some causes of "pleurisy," including pulmonary embolism and bacterial pneumonia, are potentially life threatening in the elderly.

The pain associated with pneumothorax is initially sharp, but then may become generalized and dull and extend over the entire hemithorax; it is associated with dyspnea that may slowly improve over a period of hours after onset. There are splinting and the physical findings of a pneumothorax, although in the elderly patient the pain is likely associated with COPD or trauma. The pain in pneumothorax is characteristically acute in onset, although a gradual onset is not rare. It is not sharply localized and frequently occurs after some form of physical activity, especially that associated with overhead extension of the arm.

A pneumomediastinum is uncommon in the elderly patient, but is associated with vigorous exercise or acute respiratory distress as in status asthmaticus. The onset is acute with midline, substernal pain associated with dyspnea, and there is a gradual improvement over a period of several hours so that most patients do not receive medical attention.

If the older patient has sharply localized pain, a rib fracture or local intercostal muscle injury is suggested. These injuries most commonly occur with paroxysmal coughing and are especially common in older menopausal and osteoporotic women or those receiving chronic steroid treatment. In addition, any chest wall trauma or fall with localized injury would suggest the diagnosis of rib fracture. Compression of the area produces intense localized pain, helping separate the rib fracture from the other forms of pain of pleuritic nature. Chest wall muscle injury is most likely to cause reproducible pain with specific movements and a lack of other signs and symptoms of the respiratory tract, such as dyspnea, cough, or fever. The elderly are less likely to have costochondritis, but it may occur as a unilateral localized pain at the costochondral junction. Pain is increased by breathing and cough, but is frequently not sharp in quality; it is produced by percussion of the area. The best treatment is reassurance and routine medical management, which may include injection for pain relief or the use of anti-inflammatory medications. When pleuritic pain is encountered in any older patient who has undergone trauma, even if there is neither a history nor evidence of chest wall trauma, a thorough evaluation is in order. Many elderly patients experience abdominal pain in the upper quadrant as an early complaint with bacterial pneumonia. Shoulder pain of relatively sudden onset may be due to pulmonary infection involving the pleural surface, especially the basilar lung segments associated with irritation of the diaphragmatic pleural surface.

ASSESSMENT OF UNDERLYING DISEASE

COPD

The presence of nicotine stains on the fingers or evidence of active smoking may lead one to suspect COPD in elderly patients. They may have the COPD posturing; that is, they lean forward, resting on the elbows with the shoulders elevated and use accessory respiratory muscles, including the sternomastoid and trapezius. Patients tend to be elderly men who are thin and have pursed-lipped breathing and visible evidence of anxiety when seen with an acute problem. Their respiratory pattern is one of large tidal volume with a prolonged expiratory phase, often with expiratory grunting. The barrel chest configuration is frequently emphasized, but in thin patients this may not be obvious. Breath sounds are distant, and there may be high-pitched expiratory wheeze.

Cardiovascular Disease

Patients with cardiovascular disease have tachypnea, a nonproductive cough if in left ventricular failure, orthopnea, an unwillingness to lie flat or semirecumbent, and a history of myocardial infarction, angina pectoris, or hypertension. Evidence of cardiac failure is usually present, including an S3 gallop, tachycardia, and inspiratory moist rales at least at the right base posteriorly. It is frequently bilateral, with evidence of right ventricular failure, including venous distention, peripheral edema, and a tender, enlarged liver. A brief history may reveal that these episodes have occurred previously and were treated with diuresis and low-salt diet, as well as by supplemental oxygen, reinforcing the likely cardiac etiology for symptoms.

Musculoskeletal Disorders

It is important to evaluate the use of muscle groups in respiration and to note the presence of any splinting or deformity that might suggest a thoracoplasty, kyphoscoliosis (with the degree of scoliosis the most important criterion from a functional standpoint), or evidence of chest trauma, including open wounds, hematomas, or localized areas of tenderness. A history of injury or fall may be readily available, and there are frequently inspiratory rales and dullness or diminished breath sounds in the zone of injury or tenderness. The patient should be observed for movement of the diaphragm by noting an outward movement of the upper abdomen on inspiration. The power of respiratory muscles can be tested by asking the patient to cough. This cough may reveal the presence of copious secretions, purulent sputum, hemoptysis, or other important information.

PHYSICAL EXAMINATION

One who responds to an emergency must refrain from immediately examining the respiratory system with a stethoscope. It is important to follow an orderly procedure of (1) observation, (2) palpation, (3) percussion, and, finally, (4) auscultation.

Observation

The level of respiratory distress should be immediately assessed to determine the likely level of emergency care needed and the level of decompensation. There should be a comparison between the level of overt anxiety and evidence of cyanosis, tachypnea, or other signs of true respiratory impairment. When the level of anxiety exceeds that of apparent respiratory distress, it is likely that reassurance will be quite effective and that transport can be carried out in a rational and orderly manner. The presence of tachypnea (respiratory rates greater than 20 breaths per min) and evidence of chest wall retractions, the use of accessory respiratory muscles, or classical posturing may be helpful in determining the level of emergency care needed. Cyanosis generally represents an acute emergency, but its absence should never be considered an indication that there is no significant hypoxemia. Patients with a high level of anxiety and frequent sighing breaths, but without tachypnea, probably have acute anxiety and no true respiratory insufficiency.

The respiratory pattern, including inspiration/expiration time ratios, as well as volume and frequency, may be helpful in quickly establishing an initial diagnosis. Figure 5–1 illustrates six commonly encountered respiratory patterns seen in the laboratory when patients are investigated by pulmonary function testing. However, these can also be seen by a trained observer by simply watching the respiratory pattern for a minimum of 30 sec. This may be the most valuable evaluation parameter, as it frequently distinguishes major respiratory disease types almost immediately. The COPD pattern is typical in a patient with severe expiratory airway obstruction and a large dead space, consisting of a large tidal volume and a prolonged expiratory phase, either with grunting or pursed-lipped

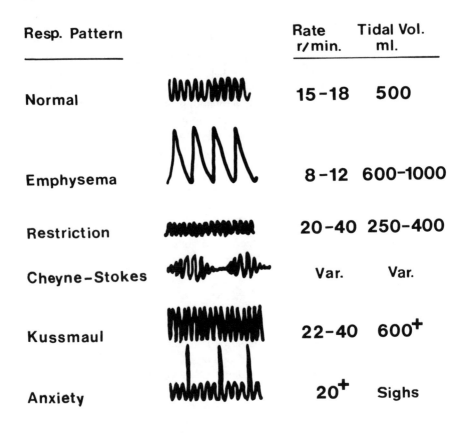

Resp. Pattern		Rate r/min.	Tidal Vol. ml.
Normal		15-18	500
Emphysema		8-12	600-1000
Restriction		20-40	250-400
Cheyne-Stokes		Var.	Var.
Kussmaul		22-40	600^+
Anxiety		20^+	Sighs

Figure 5–1 Six common respiratory patterns. These patterns include the most commonly observed respiratory rates and the most typical tidal volume measurements. Graphic representation is probably most useful in identifying respiratory patterns.

breathing. The addition of accessory respiratory muscle use identifies the patient as having advanced pulmonary emphysema. The pattern in a restrictive disease, such as patients with massive pleural effusions or chronic pulmonary fibrosis, as well as those with impending adult respiratory distress syndrome (ARDS), is manifested by tachypnea and shallow respirations. Shallow respirations produce a high dead space ventilation; the considerable work of breathing results from tachypnea. The pattern typical of cardiac failure or CNS disease is Cheyne-Stokes breathing in which there is a cyclic and reproducible increase in tidal volume, followed by a decrease in tidal volume and variable periods of apnea, with the cycles being repetitive and consistent in their timing and configuration. The period of apnea may be missed if respiratory patterns are observed for only 10 sec. This error could be disastrous if a period of apnea is observed later and it precipitates the inappropriate delivery of CPR because of a mistaken diagnosis of respiratory arrest. The Kussmaul pattern may be seen in patients with recurring pulmonary embolism or other major vascular disorders of the respiratory system, but the vast majority have a serious metabolic acidosis, with the three most common causes being diabetic ketoacidosis, uremia, or a lactic acidosis due to either profound hypoxemia or a prolonged period of shock. The presence of Kussmaul breathing suggests that the respiratory apparatus is rather adequate, and detailed evaluation should probably be carried out in other systems. Because patients with chronic anxiety and the hyperventilation syndrome may have chest pain, sweats, pallor, respiratory distress, tachycardia, dizziness, or near syncope, the detection of sighing breathing with a normal respiratory rate or minimal tachypnea is very important. It permits reassurance of the patient and appropriate management.

Respiratory muscle use should be immediately evaluated to determine if there is use of the diaphragms, splinting of one hemithorax, or the obvious use of accessory respiratory muscles that characterizes severe status asthmaticus and advanced COPD. The elevation of the chest on inspiration with little or no expansion in the lateral or AP dimensions, as well as no obvious movement of the diaphragms, promptly identifies the advanced COPD patient, especially when advanced emphysema predominates (Figure 5–2).

Posturing is an important clue to the underlying disease. It may reveal splinting of the chest, the classical posture of COPD, or a willingness to lie supine, which promptly rules out congestive heart failure. A patient with severe midline chest pain who leans forward with minimal respiratory distress probably has pericar-

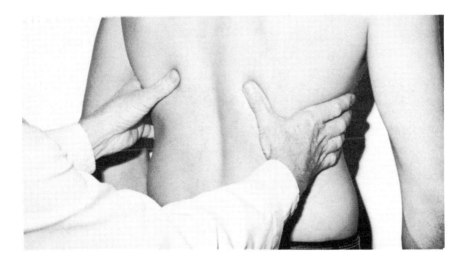

Figure 5–2 The technique for evaluating chest expansion for both adequacy, symmetry, and the absence of a unilateral lag in expansion. The hands must be applied to the chest gently to avoid limiting chest expansion, and the patient should be instructed to inspire and expire maximally to make a proper observation possible.

ditis. One should not forget the high incidence of upper abdominal pain seen early in older patients with bacterial pneumonia.

Movement and symmetry of the chest wall should be evaluated for splinting, such evidence of deformity as flail chest, or fractured ribs. Asymmetrical movement may be a clue to massive pleural effusion or musculoskeletal injury. Intercostal retractions are evidence of severe respiratory distress, including acute upper airway obstruction. Asymmetrical volume or movement may be a clue to the presence of a massive pneumothorax, with the injured side having a larger volume and demonstrating diminished breath sounds and an increased resonance.

Jugular-venous distention should be looked for as evidence of an elevated central venous pressure (CVP) associated with pulmonary hypertension with or without overt right heart failure. Figure 5–3 illustrates that, when the patient is placed with the head and chest at a 45° angle, there should be no distention of the jugular venous system. The CVP can be grossly estimated by measuring the vertical distance from the lower manubrium edge to the upper level of jugular vein distention. If the distention does not clear on early inspiration, this is further evidence of significant CVP elevation. One should be careful to differentiate venous distention from visible jugular veins because patients with emphysema who lose subcutaneous fat may have visible jugular veins without an elevation in pressure. Palpation of the vein for increased pressure may help make the differential diagnosis. Jugular venous distention in the supine patient is significant only

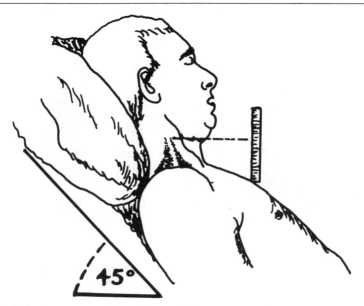

Figure 5–3 Jugular venous pressure. The level of jugular venous distention may be measured from the lower border of the manubrium to the upper level of the jugular vein distention. This provides a gross estimate of CVP if local obstructing lesions can be ruled out.

when the jugular vein does not collapse on full inspiration because in that position the vein is close to the level of the right atrium.

Central cyanosis is an extremely important finding when present, suggesting significant hypoxemia that requires immediate treatment. Peripheral cyanosis of nail beds, extremities, or ear lobes in the absence of cyanosis of oral mucous membranes and lips may reflect only local perfusion defects. Cyanosis is only accurately determined under natural light and is prevented from occurring by moderate to severe anemia. Significant carbon monoxide poisoning may not result in cyanosis, although there may be serious tissue hypoxia. When supplemental oxygen is used and cyanosis does not respond, a serious shunt is implied. This is further discussed in the section on airway management and oxygen therapy.

Clubbing of the digits in the elderly is most likely due to lung cancer or chronic purulent disease, such as bronchiectasis. Other common etiologies are old tuberculosis and moderate to severe pulmonary fibrosis from many causes. In many patients clubbing increases with increased respiratory tract infection and improves with therapy or is associated with progressive hypoxemia. Not all clubbing is readily explained, and in some patients it may be hereditary. When the nails are elevated and the nail bed is spongy, permitting the nail to rock with palpation, the clubbing is called acute and reflects active infection, increased hypoxemia, or the presence of lung cancer. Clubbing does not occur in pulmonary emphysema. Figure 5–4 illustrates the technique for evaluating clubbing by looking at digits from the side, looking for a loss of angle between the skin and the base of the nail bed, and especially using the criterion of the distance across the distal interphalangeal joint from dorsum to ventral surface; that is, when the distance B exceeds the distance A, clubbing is present.

Palpation

Deviation of the trachea can be identified by lining up the trachea with the center of the manubrial notch. This can be done by placing one finger on each side of the trachea or by palpating the tracheal prominence, but the subject's head must be in a neutral forward position or a false impression will be obtained. Deviation of the trachea may reflect old disease with fibrosis pulling it to the disease side as in a thoracoplasty or fibrothorax, or it may be due to a tension pneumothorax pushing the trachea away from the tension pneumothorax side. In addition, a massive effusion may push the trachea to the opposite side if the trachea is movable. In older patients with advanced pulmonary emphysema, the thyroid cartilage is frequently pulled down close to the manubrial notch, leaving very little room for palpation of the trachea.

Chest wall pain may be musculoskeletal when there is evidence of abrasion, contusion, or hematoma and when there is local tenderness on compression. A fractured rib may produce very localized pain on compression, and one may feel the crepitus of the fractured rib ends on inspiration or movement. There tends to be local chest wall splinting, and an associated pneumothorax should be sought. A

Clubbing

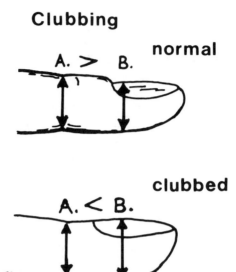

Figure 5–4 Technique for evaluating clubbing. Clubbing is best evaluated by studying the lateral view of the terminal digit. A loss of angulation between the nail bed and the surface of the nail and when dimension B exceeds dimension A may represent two criteria for clubbing.

fractured rib can be ruled out when the chest wall can be gently grasped with both hands and slowly squeezed without eliciting pain. In musculoskeletal pain without rib fracture and in chest pain due to pulmonary disease, this procedure is readily tolerated. The jugular vein can be palpated for tension if jugular venous distention is suspected.

Subcutaneous emphysema should be looked for in chest trauma or a suspected pneumothorax, as well as in patients with midline chest pain and dyspnea who may have a pneumomediastinum. This air will have leaked along vascular planes and into the mediastinum, the neck and upper chest structures serving as a decompression space with air dissecting under the skin and between muscle groups. It can be detected as ''crepitus'' easily felt by compressing tissues at the base of the neck and upper anterior chest wall and, if suggested by palpation, can be confirmed by gently pressing the diaphragm of the stethoscope over the area and noting the ''crackles'' as air is pushed aside. There may also be visible swelling of the lower face and neck where subcutaneous emphysema is moderate or extensive.

Tactile fremitus, or transmitted vibrations, should be evaluated in the posterior lung field by having the patient rotate the shoulders forward when possible and placing the palm of the hand gently over the upper, middle, and lower zones of both lung fields, then repeating the maneuver in the upper anterior chest while the patient repeats a sound designed to produce optimum palpable vibration. Some examiners have the patient repeat ''99'' or ''1-2-3,'' as they look for increased fremitus (vibration) in areas of lung consolidation and loss of fremitus in the pneumothorax or massive pleural effusion.

Percussion

Percussion of the lung field is done by using the third finger of the dominant hand as the striking hammer and placing the terminal portion of the third digit of the other hand on the chest wall as the transmitting sound board. Only the third finger should be placed on the chest wall, although it often appears the entire hand is on the wall, because using the full hand percusses a broad zone and does not distinguish localized changes. This third finger is struck vertically with the hammer finger, a snapping motion that removes the finger immediately after striking and produces the best sound. Figure 5–5 shows the proper percussion technique.

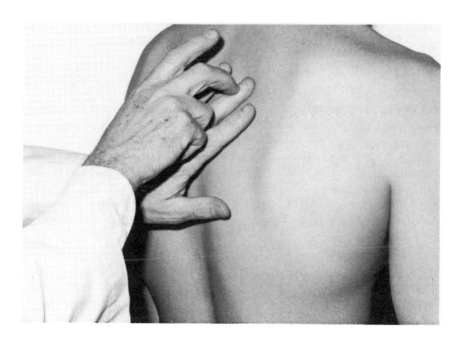

Figure 5–5 Proper percussion technique. Percussion is carried out with the third finger of the dominant hand as the striking hammer and the third finger of the other hand as the sensor. Only the third finger is permitted to touch the chest wall in order to localize the sound to the immediate area. If the entire hand is in contact with the chest wall, a broad zone will be examined and local findings may be missed. The finger should be struck with a snapping motion that requires some practice.

Experienced examiners may attempt to demonstrate resonance by gently slapping the chest wall in the previously noted zones when the patient is heavy or semirecumbent and cannot be moved for standard examination. More information is obtained if percussion is carried out at each level with comparison between the two sides, beginning in the upper lung zone, comparing the right and left upper lung zones, etc. Comparison between the two sides may elicit subtle changes.

Table 5–3 illustrates the four common sounds that can be distinguished by trained observers, including sites where these may be elicited for practice and recognition and common disorders in which they are found.

It is important to practice percussion on many normals because resonance varies with chest wall size, degree of muscular development, and level of obesity. Muscle mass and obesity tend to reduce resonance so an increased resonance in their presence would imply hyperinflated lungs. Percussion of the diaphragm margin posteriorly may be carried out by noting the zone where resonance changes to dullness, then evaluating the movement of this zone on full inspiration and full expiration with a normal zone movement of 1.5–2.5 in in the aged normal patient. The absence of movement with hyperresonance and an increased AP diameter of the chest suggest advanced COPD. Unilateral movement suggests diaphragm paralysis due to phrenic nerve injury or direct trauma to the diaphragm. Patients with COPD generally have hyperresonant lung fields as compared to normals.

Normal and Abnormal Breath Sounds

Most examiners are eventually able to differentiate four basic breath sounds (Figure 5–6), which are normally heard in specific areas but which may represent pathology when heard elsewhere over the chest.

The vesicular breath sounds are sounds normally heard over the lung fields, representing air-filled lung tissue filtering out the large airway sounds and producing a "breezy" sound, which is characterized by a long inspiratory sound and a short expiratory sound with two-thirds of the expiratory phase silent. That is, one hears a soft sound throughout inspiration and only the early portion of expiratory

---

Table 5–3 The Major Percussion Sounds over Lung Fields

Percussion Sound	Practice Sites	Disease States
Resonance	Lung fields	Normal lungs
Dullness	Liver zone (right anterior costal margin)	Pneumonia, atelectasis, pulmonary infarct
Flatness	Patella, anterior thigh	Pleural effusion, fibrothorax
Tympany	Anterior abdomen, epigastrium	Massive bullae, tension pneumothorax

sound is audible, whereas the inspiratory/expiratory time ratio is commonly 1/1.5. The configuration or sound pattern is as important as the quality of the sounds in identifying the vesicular sounds.

Bronchial breath sounds are normally heard over the manubrium of the sternum in the normal chest and are quite different from vesicular breath sounds. They are high pitched and accordingly are frequently graphed as a steep slope on diagrams of breath sounds (Figure 5–6). The sound is harsher in quality, and only the last half of inspiratory sound is audible, with the expiratory phase entirely audible and a distinct pause between inspiratory and expiratory sound. This pattern is the reverse of that seen in the vesicular breath sound, and even if the harsh and high-pitched quality is not identified, the pattern of sound is characteristic. Bronchial breath sounds are commonly heard in chronic bronchitis and pneumonia, as well as in other causes of consolidation of lung tissue, including atelectasis and pulmonary infarction.

Bronchovesicular breath sounds are not readily identified by even experienced examiners because their sound quality is between the vesicular and bronchial

BREATH SOUNDS

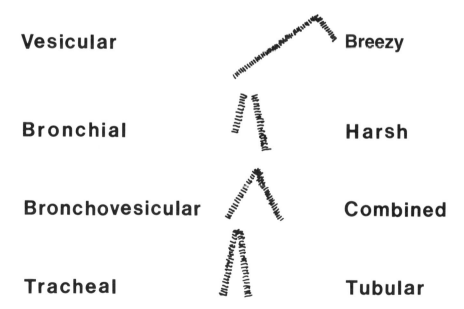

Vesicular	Breezy
Bronchial	Harsh
Bronchovesicular	Combined
Tracheal	Tubular

Figure 5–6 The four generally differentiated breath sounds. These are illustrated with first the inspiratory limb, then the expiratory limb to show the duration of both phases, the pitch of each phase as designated by the slope of the line, and the pause between inspiration and expiration in bronchial breath sounds.

breath sounds, although the configuration of the sound may be more helpful in its identification. As seen in Figure 5–6, the sound time is equally divided between inspiration and expiration, with the entire respiratory cycle usually audible. The harsh quality of the bronchial breath sounds is somewhat diminished, and the pause between inspiration and expiration that characterizes bronchial breath sounds is lacking. Bronchovesicular sounds may be heard in the zone immediately around the manubrium of the sternum in the normal chest as indicated in Figure 5–7. In the abnormal chest they may be heard in pulmonary edema, early cardiac failure, or in an early pneumonia before there is full consolidation and the development of typical bronchial breath sounds.

The tracheal breath sounds or amphoric breath sounds are normally heard over the trachea in the neck (Figure 5–7). The sound is harsh, hollow, and high pitched, with sound heard throughout the inspiration and expiration phases without pause. The sound has often been likened to that made by blowing air across the mouth of a bottle. It may be heard over lung cavities as in an abscess or other ventilated air spaces within the chest.

Table 5–4 lists some common disorders and changes in breath sounds that characterize those conditions.

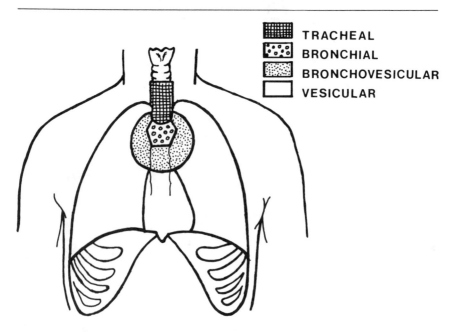

TRACHEAL
BRONCHIAL
BRONCHOVESICULAR
VESICULAR

Figure 5–7 Breath sounds. Tracheal breath sounds are often called tubular or amphoric, a quality illustrated by listening over the anterior trachea in the neck. Bronchial breath sounds are normally heard over the manubrium sternum, and bronchovascular sounds are heard in the zone around the manubrium. Bronchovesicular sounds are the most difficult to identify for the observer, regardless of his or her training.

Table 5–4 Conditions Causing Common Abnormal Breath Sounds

Breath Sounds	Condition
Absent	Complete airway obstruction, pneumonectomy, pneumothorax, massive pleural effusions, paralyzed diaphragm
Tracheal	Cavities
Bronchial	Pneumonia, atelectasis, pulmonary infarction
Bronchovesicular	Pulmonary edema, early edema, early pneumonia

Abnormal (Adventitious) Sounds and Their Significance

Inspiratory stridor is an inspiratory crowing sound heard in patients with almost complete upper airway obstruction, with some observers suggesting that airway obstruction is more than 70% complete before audible stridor can be detected. The sound is most characteristic in epiglottitis, laryngospasm, and croup. However, in the older patient, a persistent stridor represents a serious risk of complete upper airway obstruction with asphyxia. Therefore, it is indicative of upper airway disease, rather than lower airway disease. In the trauma patient it may represent fracture or other injury to the trachea and hematoma or edema of the hypopharynx, requiring rapid identification and treatment of the cause.

Figure 5–8 illustrates the characteristics of the more common adventitious sounds. Fine or crepitant rales are often heard as a shower of discrete, crackling sounds, which are high pitched and tend to be soft or distant to the ear, usually occurring in the late inspiration phase. They are presumed to be due to separation of distal air spaces on expansion of the lung. They may be present in cardiac failure or chronic pulmonary fibrosis and are most commonly heard at the posterior lung bases, more often on the right in the case of heart failure and generally bilateral in the case of pulmonary fibrosis. Unless inspiration is complete, they may not be heard at all because they tend to occur as a burst of sound at the end of a full inspiration. The sound can be imitated by rubbing hair near one's ear.

Coarse or subcrepitant rales are louder crackling sounds, heard earlier on inspiration and variously described by observers as moist or dry based on their perceived quality. The sound is most like that of a crackling fire with crisp, loud popping sounds that extend through much of inspiration. They are most common over areas of consolidation, as with pneumonia and infarction, but they may also be heard in chronic bronchitis. This fact has probably caused pneumonia to be falsely diagnosed very often when other findings for pneumonitis are absent and a chest film is not done for confirmation.

Wheeze or sibilant rhonchi are musical, usually high-pitched, and relatively continuous sounds. They are most often heard in the expiratory phase and are associated with a prolongation of the expiratory sound, as in asthma. The higher

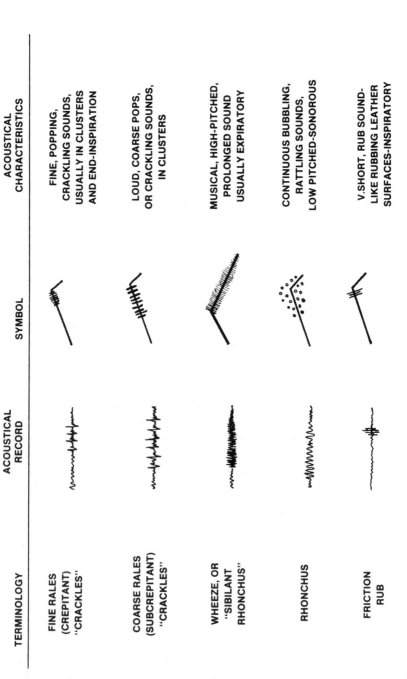

TERMINOLOGY	ACOUSTICAL RECORD	SYMBOL	ACOUSTICAL CHARACTERISTICS
FINE RALES (CREPITANT) "CRACKLES"			FINE, POPPING, CRACKLING SOUNDS, USUALLY IN CLUSTERS AND END-INSPIRATION
COARSE RALES (SUBCREPITANT) "CRACKLES"			LOUD, COARSE POPS, OR CRACKLING SOUNDS, IN CLUSTERS
WHEEZE, OR "SIBILANT RHONCHUS"			MUSICAL, HIGH-PITCHED, PROLONGED SOUND USUALLY EXPIRATORY
RHONCHUS			CONTINUOUS BUBBLING, RATTLING SOUNDS, LOW PITCHED-SONOROUS
FRICTION RUB			V.SHORT, RUB SOUND-LIKE RUBBING LEATHER SURFACES-INSPIRATORY

Figure 5–8 Abnormal lung sounds. The illustrations represent symbols commonly used to describe abnormal lung sounds, as well as the location in the respiratory cycle where they are ordinarily identified. Descriptive words used are selected terms that appear in the literature or on patient records that best represent the examiner's observations.

the pitch and the more distant the sound, the greater the obstruction and the poorer the patient's ventilation. Therefore, loud, low-pitched wheezes are generally associated with less severe obstruction and better air movement because the movement of air in large and small airways is required to generate the sound that is felt to result from vibrating airway structures and secretions. Occasionally the wheeze is relatively short and best described as a squeak, which is most characteristic of a localized obstruction as from a tumor or foreign body in a large airway. The presence of squeaks associated with wheeze simply implies that secretions have accumulated in focal areas. The wheeze or sibilant rhonchus can be induced by hyperventilation or forced expiration if not heard with normal breathing.

The rhonchus is a relatively continuous sound that is not as discrete as the rale nor as musical as the wheeze. Therefore, most sounds described as rattling, bubbling, or gurgling represent rhonchi and are associated with edema or secretions of larger airways. Most observers tend to classify as a rhonchus any continuous sound that does not fit the description of a wheeze. The rhonchus generally changes with deep breathing and coughing, indicating a movement of secretions and the upper airway source of the sound produced by turbulent air flow through irregular airway lumens. Rhonchi are characteristic of patients with chronic bronchitis or those with secretions in the larger segments of the tracheobronchial tree. They may be heard in patients with pulmonary edema and pneumonia as well.

The pleural friction rub is an inspiratory sound usually limited to late inspiration, which is due to friction between pleural surfaces. It is well localized, associated with pleuritic pain, and is very short, very loud, and harsh, with a squeaky or rubbing quality. It is frequently described as similar to the sound heard when two pieces of leather are rubbed together. It is not changed by cough or deep breathing.

ACUTE ANXIETY AND THE HYPERVENTILATION SYNDROME

The term "hyperventilation syndrome" describes a group of symptoms producing a pattern of acute complaints, including an atypical dyspnea, in the absence of a causative organic disease. Although the syndrome is far more common in young people and slightly more common in women than in men, it may also be seen as the result of chronic anxiety in the elderly patient with known cardiac or pulmonary disease, making diagnosis even more difficult.

Mechanisms

The respiratory centers control breathing primarily in response to the $PaCO_2$ and secondarily in response to pH changes in the blood. Oxygen tension is not an important controlling mechanism except in those patients with severe hypoxemia, especially when it is due to chronic lung disease in which the hypoxemia becomes a progressively more significant respiratory driving mechanism. Almost anyone, including patients with known COPD, may override respiratory control mechanisms and hyperventilate at will or in response to stimulants, including stimulation from commonly employed bronchodilator drugs, other drugs with a similar pharmacologic result, and from external stress. Chronic anxiety is a very common cause of intermittent, symptomatic hyperventilation. It is most prevalent in the very young but even more subtle in the elderly who have underlying cardiopulmonary disease that might otherwise explain similar complaints.

Although ordinary exercise induces hyperventilation to compensate for oxygen need and an increased carbon dioxide production, the increased ventilation that normally results precisely matches carbon dioxide elimination with the steady-state exercise CO_2 production. When increased ventilation occurs at rest, as when the patient's breathing is driven by chronic anxiety, it may become symptomatic because there is an increased elimination resulting in hypocapnia without an increased carbon dioxide production. These episodes generally occur at rest and are evanescent, producing frightening symptoms secondary to hypocapnia and alkalosis. Alkalosis induces not only a reduction in ionized serum calcium but also vigorous cerebrovascular arterial constriction resulting in widespread neurologic symptoms that are so similar to many produced by acute cardiac and pulmonary disease that their acute onset and severity may lead to misdiagnosis.

Diagnosis

The diagnosis is readily made when one has a high index of suspicion arising from the pattern of respiratory symptoms. The episodes are intermittent, last from several minutes to many hours, and characteristically occur with the subject at rest, rather than during exercise, thereby immediately distinguishing this form of dyspnea from that due to cardiopulmonary diseases. The episodes are most frequent in the evening hours, and there is no pattern of progression that would suggest organic disease. When one suspects the diagnosis, it is not difficult to elicit the presence of increased anxiety and stress and sometimes even the cause for that stress. The following six symptoms are common, and most present in the average patient.

1. *Shortness of breath.* The dyspnea is described as a "desire for a deep breath" or an inability to inhale deeply enough to satisfy the patient, rather than air hunger or tachypnea. When asked to describe the breathing pattern, the patient commonly states that it is not associated with increased breathing rate, but rather with frequent sighing breaths.
2. *Lightheadedness, dizziness, blurred vision, or a sensation of near syncope that are virtually always present.* Some patients can only describe an altered mental state, but usually this is with a change in visual acuity. Many say they feel faint but true syncope is rare.

3. *Palpitations.* Patients often describe a rapid or pounding cardiac action or arc aware of an irregular rhythm that generally follows the onset of the other complaints, rather than being the initial symptom. This description is important in differentiating the symptoms of hyperventilation syndrome from those induced by a sudden arrhythmia or tachycardia.

4. *Pain.* Almost all patients complain of substernal pain or pain over the left precordium that is dull in nature, not pleuritic, and almost never has the radiation that is typical of angina pectoris. The substernal pain generally does not begin suddenly and has a tendency to wax and wane over long periods of time. The patients deny any relationship to digestive tract symptoms and do not experience nausea, although they may describe sweats similar to those seen with angina pectoris.

5. *Paresthesias.* The paresthesias may be described as "pins and needles" or as "numbness," whereas others can only describe an altered sensation that may be more prominent in one extremity than in the other, but almost without variation is bilateral and usually quite symmetrical. It is common for the hands and feet, occasionally the perioral area or the tongue, and on rare occasion the remainder of the face to be involved. The bilateral nature of paresthesias occurring at rest are quite characteristic, even though symptoms may be more intense on one side of the body.

6. *Sweats, nausea and vomiting, and classical pain radiation.* These are notable by their absence if observed while symptoms are severe and acute. When the symptoms begin at rest and the patient has a somewhat rapid but full pulse, one can readily rule out hypotension. As these episodes may awaken patients from a sound sleep, that pattern should not rule out the diagnosis of hyperventilation syndrome.

Physical Examination

Although the most typical patient is young and more often a woman, hyperventilation syndrome is probably more common in the elderly patient than is realized because its symptoms are often falsely ascribed to significant cardiac or pulmonary disease. The patient appears quite tense and anxious, generally demonstrating frequent sighing breaths during evaluation and an absence of acute findings to explain dyspnea (see Figure 5–1). On examination of the chest the patient hyperventilates further, and symptoms may intensify. Observing the response to hyperventilation while examining the lung fields is one way of verifying the mechanism causing the patient's symptoms. At this time breath holding frequently produces mild relief within 15–20 sec, further demonstrating that the examiner has elicited the mechanism for the symptoms.

Laboratory Data

Arterial blood gas analysis reveals alkalosis and significant hypocapnia with a $PaCO_2$ generally well below 35 mm Hg. Chronic hyperventilation can be detected by the presence of significant hypocapnia associated with a normal or near-normal arterial blood pH. If patients are studied in a pulmonary function laboratory, the baseline breathing pattern recorded documents frequent deep sighing breaths that often reach a frequency of 2 or 3 per min and are sufficient to induce significant hypocapnia and symptomatic alkalosis.

Treatment

The first step in treatment is making the proper diagnosis and ruling out significant cardiac or pulmonary disease as a cause for such symptoms as shortness of breath, chest pain, and dizziness. The fact that these symptoms occur at rest should be pointed out to the patient to demonstrate that these are very unlikely to be associated with organic disease. One must emphasize that the symptoms are real, but are not due to underlying cardiac or pulmonary disease. It may be helpful to explain the mechanism to the patient while demonstrating breath holding as a technique for controlling hypocapnia. The author finds it helpful to induce an episode and promptly control it by instructing the patient to carry out a prolonged breath hold, further documenting the innocent nature of the symptoms. Some episodes are sufficiently severe to induce carpopedal spasm, and although syncope is quite uncommon, it probably periodically occurs. Rebreathing carbon dioxide by breathing into a paper bag is a time-honored mechanism for controlling symptoms.

The individual responds best to management of the anxiety, either by identify-ing and removing its cause or by the use of drugs on a short-term basis while the underlying problem is approached. The prognosis is excellent, especially when the cause for chronic anxiety is subject to correction. Certainly prompt diagnosis can not only provide relief to the patient but also prevent an extensive and unnecessary cardiac or pulmonary evaluation. This is especially important in the elderly patient where some underlying cardiac or pulmonary disease may actually exist to obscure the true diagnosis. When the constellation of symptoms is not absolutely typical, when there is a history of dyspnea both on exertion and at rest, or when there is any doubt whether the symptoms are due to hyperventilation syndrome or may be due to existing cardiac or pulmonary disease, the safest course is reassurance and general support measures while transporting the patient to a medical facility to rule out serious organic disease. The presence of a normal pulse and blood pressure, the intermittent nature of the symptoms, and the history of episodes extending back for many months or even years generally permit a more conservative approach, such as simply contacting the patient's physician for advice, support, and such evaluation as the physician deems necessary.

UPPER AIRWAY OBSTRUCTION ABOVE CARINA

Definition

Upper airway obstruction is characterized by *inspiratory* obstruction or, in some cases, total obstruction to flow of air on either inspiration or expiration. It is defined as airway obstruction in the upper respiratory tract, which extends from the carina upward to the nose and mouth, including the nasopharynx, oropharynx, glottis, and trachea (Figure 5–9). The clinical syndromes and mechanism of obstruction are quite different from lower airway disease, and the two are easily differentiated in most instances. Because acute upper airway obstruction often presents a life-threatening problem requiring prompt diagnosis and treatment in the field and special attention to maintenance of a patent airway to avoid lethal asphyxia, it calls for the highest level of diagnostic and therapeutic skills by emergency medical personnel. There are almost 3,000 deaths a year in the United States from acute upper airway obstruction.[2] Some patients have subtle signs of incomplete obstruction for some time before total occlusion of their airways.

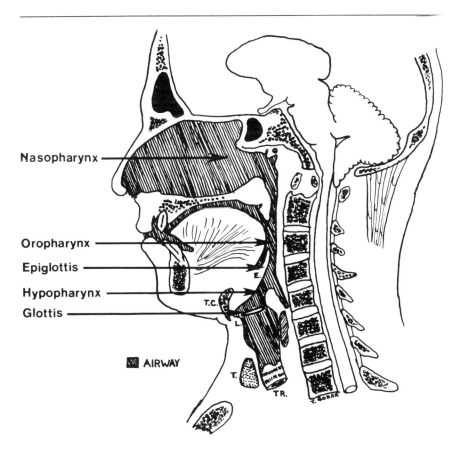

Figure 5–9 Upper airways. A lateral view of the upper airways illustrates critical zones in which airway dimensions are small, predisposing to upper airway obstruction. Note that the epiglottis is ordinarily not visible on routine examination and that the air space between the posterior tongue and the posterior wall of the oropharynx is normally limited.

Etiology

Table 5–5 describes some of the most common causes of upper airway obstruction. These causes are artificially subdivided into simple anatomic or physiologic abnormalities of the upper airways, local diseases that may cause airway obstruction, and obstruction due to aspiration of foreign bodies.

Clearly the most common cause of upper airway obstruction is the tongue falling back against the posterior wall of the hypopharynx, occluding the airways and producing either partial obstruction with intermittent snoring respirations or complete obstruction with respiratory efforts but no air movement. Ordinarily obstruction is readily corrected by using the head tilt (Figure 5–10), with one hand behind the neck and one pressing down on the forehead to hyperextend the head, thereby raising the floor of the mouth and elevating the posterior tongue away from the oropharynx. Another common procedure is the triple airway maneuver. The attendant places fingers behind the angles of the jaw, displacing the lower jaw forward while tilting the head backward and retracting the lower lip with the thumbs. These maneuvers are used with caution or modified for patients who are

---

Table 5–5 Causes of Upper Airway Obstruction

Anatomic
   Unconsciousness with hypopharyngeal obstruction due to a flaccid tongue against the
      posterior pharyngeal wall
   Paralysis of neck muscles
   Tracheomalacia—uncommon in the aged
   Substernal thyroid (usually nonobstructive)

Local Disease
   Severe tonsillitis or peritonsillar abscess
   Angioneurotic edema due to drugs, bites, or insect stings
   Neck trauma—tracheal fractures, lacerations or hematoma
   Neoplasms—extrinsic (lymphoma, carcinoma), intrinsic (adenoma, bronchogenic carcinoma)
   Epiglottitis—acute form is rare in the aged
   Acute laryngospasm—usually transient
   Flash burns or chemical burns

Obstruction due to Foreign Bodies
   Teeth or dentures
   Candy, peanuts, fruit pits, etc.
   Food aspiration—"café coronary"

Note: Anatomic causes of upper airway obstruction are almost invariably chronic; obstruction induced by local disease may be very acute as in allergic reactions or laryngospasm, and tonsillitis and neoplasms may produce obstruction on a subacute basis with the subtle development of symptoms. Obstruction due to foreign bodies is almost invariably very acute and may represent the largest group of true emergencies among patients with upper airway obstruction.

Tongue Obstructing at the Oropharynx

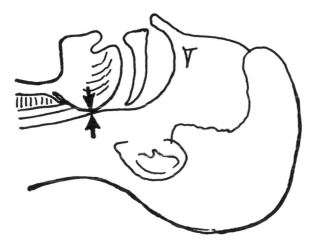

Cleared by Hyperextension

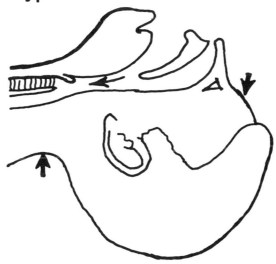

Figure 5–10 Correction of airway obstruction. Note that a re-establishment of the upper airway may only require hyperextension of the neck and head with the force applied at the location of the two arrows.

suspected of cervical spine injuries. One technique for reducing movement of the neck is moving the jaw forward and up without hyperextending the neck.

Patients with residual neurologic disease or those obtunded and under the influence of sedatives or tranquilizers may have frequent and prolonged bouts of airway obstruction due entirely to a flaccid tongue and muscles of the floor of the mouth. Periods of obstructive apnea with evidence of respiratory efforts but no air movement are common in the very elderly during sleep. These periods of apnea are usually not an emergency requiring immediate treatment. However, in the acutely ill aged patient and in cases of trauma, establishing an adequate airway is the first priority in acute medical management.

Most causes of subacute or acute upper airway obstruction are visible by examination of the neck and oropharynx, as one looks for evidence of inflammatory masses, foreign bodies, contusions, or other injuries suggesting a hematoma or edema of the upper airways or for evidence of acute inflammatory disease secondary to burns. Most causes of upper airway obstruction, with the exceptions of food aspiration or angioneurotic edema, which is almost always associated with an allergic reaction to drugs or insect bites, cause subacute obstruction and some early warning signs before complete obstruction occurs.

The usual symptom of incomplete obstruction is ''difficulty getting air in'' and frequently dyspnea on exertion, although not at rest. When a higher level of obstruction occurs, the following eight signs may be noted:

1. hoarseness
2. a barking cough
3. inspiratory stridor or crowing
4. paradoxical breathing
5. intercostal and superclavicular retractions
6. evidence of respiratory distress
7. cyanosis and signs of sympathetic discharge
8. aphonia—no voice and no air movement

When inspiratory stridor appears, airway obstruction is 70% complete or more, and it should never be ignored without ensuring rapid medical evaluation to determine its cause and prevent total obstruction with asphyxia.

When obstruction is due to muscle paralysis or a flaccid tongue, an oral airway and hyperextension are effective. A foreign body is readily ruled out in the presence of swelling of upper airways or obvious trauma to upper airways, and an endotracheal tube should be inserted as soon as possible to stabilize the airway. Unnecessary manipulation should be avoided to prevent increasing edema further.

Acute laryngeal obstruction due to angioneurotic edema, usually the result of allergic reaction, is treated by establishing an airway and administering oxygen and epinephrine (1:1,000) 0.3 ml subcutaneously. The patient should also receive epinephrine in aerosol form from a nebulizer, employing five or six deep inhalations to provide more rapid local effect. Diphenhydramine (Benadryl) 25 mg intermuscularly is a commonly employed treatment. It does not have an immediate effect, but may help maintain airways during patient transport to a medical facility. In all aged patients a search should be made for aspirated dentures or other foreign bodies.

Total Upper Airway Obstruction by an Aspirated Foreign Body

A common cause of sudden death in the elderly is aspiration of a foreign body during meals, usually produced by a bolus of food lodged in the hypopharynx or glottis. The typical patient is an older person with an abnormal swallowing function, who generally wears dentures and often has ingested alcohol. The usual obstructing bolus of food is meat that is aspirated into the upper airways, which does not produce the usual transient laryngospasm followed by paroxysmal cough, but rather causes complete airway obstruction with aphonia and apnea. In a short period the patient becomes agitated, frequently leaving the room unobserved and rapidly developing an ashen cyanosis with intercostal retractions and unconsciousness. The duration of total airway obstruction that can be tolerated with survival is based on the oxygen stores available in circulating blood, tissues, and in the lung air compartment at the time of obstruction. Survival time is shortened by vigorous physical activity on the part of the patient that causes an accelerated oxygen consumption.

The usual oxygen stores at the time of total airway obstruction approximate 11 ml/kg, which would mean a survival time of 4–5 min assuming an oxygen consumption of 200–250 ml/min at rest with no anemia and an average lung functional residual capacity (FRC) at the moment of total airway obstruction. Not all the oxygen can be utilized because as it is consumed the PaO_2 falls to levels below 25 mm Hg and oxygen delivery to tissues ceases for lack of a driving pressure gradient.

Treatment

The first step is identification of complete airway obstruction characterized by apnea and respiratory distress, but especially by aphonia. If upper airways can be visualized, the food may be removed by forceps or by a finger sweep. The recommended procedures are those adopted by the American Heart Association, which involve a sequence of maneuvers.[2] ╯

Patients having total obstruction, with no air movement and no cough available to help dislodge the obstructing bolus, are managed with the Heimlich maneuver. The subdiaphragmatic abdominal technique for foreign body obstruction removal from the airway is the only recommended emergency treatment of choice. This method is considered more effective and considered safer than other methods, such as the back-blow technique. Back blows are *no longer* included in emergency management of airway obstruction in adults.

The Heimlich maneuver is employed by delivering upward thrusts to the subdiaphragmatic area (see Figure 5–11). In the conscious patient there is no recommended number of thrusts to be delivered. Thrusts are to be continued until the obstruction is cleared or the patient becomes unconscious. With the patient sitting or standing, but still conscious, the rescuer stands behind the patient and wraps the arms around patient's waist, placing a fist, thumb side in, against the epigastrium and grasping the fist with the other hand. The first is then vigorously pushed inward and upward to elevate intra-abdominal and intrathoracic pressures and force the foreign body loose.

The Heimlich maneuver can be done from many positions, but the position of choice is astride the supine patient. The astride position provides the optimum

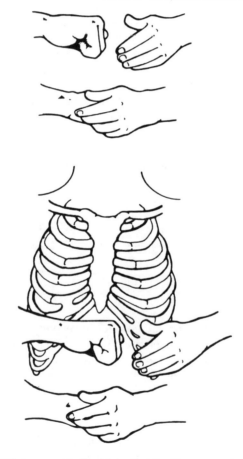

Figure 5–11 The hand placement for the abdominal thrust maneuver is illustrated.

Source: Reprinted with permission from *The Journal of the American Medical Association* (1980;244:464), Copyright © 1980, American Heart Association, Inc.

capability to deliver the thrusts mid-line and avoids complications caused from delivering thrusts from aside.

In the unconscious patient (or one who becomes unconscious during obstructed airway management maneuvers) do the following:

- position the patient in a supine position,
- check the airway,
- perform a finger sweep for any dislodged objects,
- attempt 2 ventilations,
- perform 6–10 abdominal thrusts,
- repeat the procedure from the beginning step (checking airway).

Once the Heimlich maneuver has been used successfully, because of the risk of laceration of the liver or other injury to internal organs, the patient should be seen at a medical facility and quickly examined to determine that there are no injuries or consequences of prolonged hypoxia requiring treatment, such as a change in mental status or arrhythmia.

When the patient is unconscious and the cause of airway obstruction is not detectable, or the patient does not respond to the above maneuvers although total obstruction by a food bolus is suspected, other procedures are available to provide an emergency airway.[3] However, emergency tracheostomy in unskilled hands may be more disastrous than beneficial. A less hazardous technique for establishing an airway in complete upper airway obstruction is the cricothyrotomy. In this procedure a cannula is placed below the thyroid cartilage and above the cricoid cartilage through the cricothyroid membrane. Very few emergency medical staff are qualified to carry out this procedure. In general, the aged patient found unconscious with complete airway obstruction who fails to respond to standard resuscitation techniques is likely to have serious and permanent brain damage by the time emergency surgical procedures to establish an airway have been carried out. Therefore, the heroic efforts universally employed in resuscitation of the young patient with airway obstruction are generally not justified in the case of the very aged and chronically ill patient, whose tolerance for even brief periods of hypoxemia is quite limited. The emergency attendant must use his or her judgment, because a surviving patient with brain death may result when standard resuscitation efforts are unsuccessful and additional time is taken to carry out surgical procedures to establish an airway. Even when the skill of the operator permits, a more aggressive approach may rarely be life saving.

ACUTE OBSTRUCTION OF AIRWAYS BELOW CARINA

Aspiration of Stomach Contents

Gastric aspiration, or Mendelsohn's syndrome, is a toxic aspiration pneumonitis characterized originally in experimental animals and younger subjects whose aspirated stomach contents had a pH below 2.5. Mendelsohn first pointed out that gastric acid was the main mechanism for lung injury, although associated aspirated food might be responsible for major airway obstruction.[4] The morbidity and mortality appeared to depend on the volume of aspirate, the pH and character of the aspirate, and the extent and distribution of aspiration, with many patients aspirating while in the lateral decubitus position and distributing aspirate largely to the dependent lung. A number of predisposing conditions exist, including drug overdose, such as with sedatives, tranquilizers or narcotics. The risk is increased by associated alcohol abuse. Aspiration is common in trauma victims in whom the aspirate may contain stomach contents, blood, dentures, or other foreign objects as well. Especially predisposed patients are the very aged, the debilitated, patients with a defective gag reflex or significant reduction in state of alertness, and all those with esophageal disease or hiatus hernia who have known esophageal reflux or a history of esophagitis. In addition, bowel obstruction and acute gastritis may induce repeated vomiting with a high risk of aspiration of stomach contents in the presence of the use of drugs or alcohol, or of neurologic disease or in the old, debilitated patient.[5-10]

Pathophysiology

There is an immediate risk of serious airway obstruction from aspirated food material. Because the older patient's stomach acid generally does not have a pH below 2.5, the chemical reaction from aspirated hydrochloric acid tends to be more subtle and less intense than in the young patient who aspirates during intubation or inhalation anesthesia. Although the aspiration of less acidic material may produce a less intense reaction and be less likely to lead to adult respiratory distress syndrome, older patients do have reduced defense mechanisms, a weak cough, and a reduced tolerance for the resulting hypoxemia.

Elderly patients with hyperreactive airways or COPD may have airway constriction that further intensifies the poor ventilation, resulting in profound hypoxemia. Bacterial infection is a later problem, generally occurring several days after aspiration.

Initial findings are dyspnea; tachycardia; significant hypoxemia, frequently with cyanosis; variable levels of bronchospasm; and copius secretions, varying in character based on the content of food material, blood, or other aspirates. Physical findings may reveal coarse rales and rhonchi consistent with aspiration at both smaller and larger airway levels. Inspiratory or expiratory squeaks are common, which represent obstructing fluid or food in the bronchial tree. With aspiration of gastric aspirate having a pH above 2.5, there is generally only mild capillary permeability with increased lung water and findings of pulmonary congestion. With more extensive aspiration, associated generally with profound hypoxemia, there is hypotension, which is considered by some to be reflex in nature. Fever is low grade or absent at the time of first encounter. The presence of shock or apnea shortly after aspiration is associated with a grave prognosis. Early improvement in clinical status may be followed by slow deterioration in subsequent hours or days.

Evaluation and Treatment

The first priority is securing an airway, and it is generally recommended that the patient be placed in a head down, left lateral decubitus position during early treatment and evaluation.[3] This position may prevent further aspiration during initial examination and treatment. Examination of upper airways for aspirated food particles and a general suctioning of the mouth and oropharynx are in order, but early attention should be given to oxygen supplementation, preferably by nasal cannula or mask. This supplementation generally requires an FIO_2 of 40% or more, based on the patient's clinical status. When aspiration is massive, there is a substantial risk of ARDS, which requires a higher level of treatment, including intubation and total ventilation support during transportation to a treatment facility. It is reasonable to employ 100% oxygen in this situation in the older patient who must be considered to have a compromised coronary and cerebral circulation and to be more susceptible to prolonged hypoxemia. Pulmonary edema resulting from capillary leak following the acute insult responds to aerosol bronchodilators. Because the use of corticosteroids is controversial and because their effect is delayed for hours after administration, they should not be administered until the evaluation in the receiving facility has been completed. The receiving facility should be warned of the potential for the need to treat a resultant ARDS.

On arriving at a treatment facility, immediate arterial blood gas analysis, chest film, and evaluation to determine the need for bronchoscopy should be carried out. Bronchoscopy should be avoided if there appears no evidence of large particulate matter in the airways. X-ray films invariably demonstrate patchy infiltrate or a pulmonary edema pattern, suggesting the development of ARDS.

Between 25% and 50% of patients will develop a bacterial pneumonia, but prophylactic antibiotics have never been shown to reduce the morbidity or mortality in aspiration pneumonia.[8] The incidence of gram-negative pneumonias is higher in patients who have received prophylactic antibiotics. Approximately 15% of patients have profound hypoxemia and shock and will die within the first 24 hours. Approximately 50% to 60% stabilize and show progressive clinical improvement. One-third may show early improvement, but their conditions deteriorate later, with a bacterial pneumonia manifesting on the third to fifth day as the most common late complication. Mortality is high among those with severe aspiration, shock, and bacterial superinfection, approximating 60% to 90%. [11–13]

Aspiration of Foreign Bodies

Elderly patients sustaining severe abdominal or thoracic trauma and those obtunded by alcohol, drugs, or neuromuscular disease are especially likely to aspirate foreign bodies, including food, dentures, gum, candy, or other small objects. The risk is increased by confusion, agitation, and a reduction in the gag reflex, which is common in the elderly under the influence of stimulants, alcohol, or antidepressant drugs. It may result from eating, drinking alcohol, and talking simultaneously or carrying out physical activities. If aspiration of a foreign body does not obstruct upper airways, such common foods as candies, peanuts, seeds, or small food particles may be aspirated into a lobar or segmental bronchus, inducing a cough paroxysm often after an initial reflex inspiration. If the cough is not effective in producing expectoration of the foreign body, it may become trapped in the bronchial tree, inducing edema and sometimes producing a check-valve mechanism leading to local hyperinflation. In other cases, atelectasis results, with continued cough, local pain, and, in some patients, a profuse bronchorrhea from local response to the foreign body. In the older patient the acute episode may not be recognized or remembered, and the patient may later have symptoms of a recurring pulmonary infection and persistent cough.

Diagnosis

In an older patient with a history of possible aspiration followed by paroxysmal cough, the diagnosis is easily suspected. When there is an impaired gag reflex or the known use of alcohol or drugs and especially when there have been periods of unconsciousness or known difficulty in swallowing, the diagnosis may be made by the use of key findings on physical examination and chest film. It is common for foreign bodies to permit air entry at the end of inspiration and to present with an end-inspiratory squeak or transient wheeze at the site of the obstruction. This finding may be localized and may persist, despite deep breathing and repeated cough. Although a foreign body may induce generalized wheeze in a patient with hyperreactive airways, more commonly there are local findings. The same area may reveal a decrease in breath sounds or bronchial breath sounds with inspiratory crackling rales. A chest film often reveals atelectasis or a pneumonia associated with a reduced lung volume, suggesting a postobstructive infection. Temperature tends to be low grade, and the white count may be normal. Sputum tends to have a benign character, but there may be intermittent blood streaking following parox-ysmal cough and local irritation by the foreign body. This picture of low-grade fever with an unimpressive white blood count and sputum character, especially combined with a history of sudden paroxysmal cough, should readily lead one to the correct diagnosis.

Treatment

A foreign body lodged in the bronchial tree below the carina may be observed and removed through bronchoscopy. Edema and granulation tissue formation, as well as local bleeding, may obscure the foreign body, but proper technique usually makes the diagnosis and reveals the mechanism. Bronchodilators may be helpful in relaxing the bronchial tree to permit clearing of the foreign body, and postural drainage after humidification of the secretions with specific attention to the anatomic location of the foreign body may be effective in completing the clearance process. Local physical findings should rapidly clear, and the chest film should show the clearing of infiltrate and any lung collapse.

ACUTE RESPIRATORY FAILURE

Definition

The terms "respiratory failure" and "respiratory insufficiency" are frequently confused and used inappropriately. When there is sufficient abnormality of the respiratory apparatus to produce an awareness of breathing difficulty (dyspnea), the patient has respiratory insufficiency, although not necessarily respiratory failure. Because dyspnea is highly subjective, it may be associated with minimal respiratory apparatus abnormality or due entirely to anxiety with associated hyperventilation in the absence of significant respiratory disease.

True acute respiratory failure is defined as a condition in which the gas exchange function of the respiratory system is impaired, but the diagnosis can only be established by arterial blood gas analysis to detect either significant hypoxemia, significant hypercapnia, or both. The definitions of significant hypoxemia or hypercapnia are arbitrary, but, by consensus, respiratory failure is considered to be present when the PaO_2 on ambient air falls below 55 mm Hg or the $PaCO_2$ reaches 45 mm Hg or greater.

To describe respiratory failure in an orderly fashion, it is common to subdivide patients into three groups. In the first group are those patients who have respiratory failure associated with a failure of the respiratory bellows in the absence of any primary lung disease, eg, a patient with drug overdose or a CNS lesion that depresses respirations. The second group is composed of patients who have a history of hypoxemia and hyperventilation with hypocapnia, in whom serious hypoxemia is the primary marker of respiratory failure, eg, those with pneumonia, pulmonary embolism, or chronic pulmonary fibrosis. In the third group are the more readily recognized patients who have underventilation associated with significant ventilation/perfusion abnormalities, usually exemplified by the patient with obstructive airway disease in whom respiratory failure is associated with both progressive hypoxemia and hypercapnia. Clearly, it is important that all treating personnel recognize that respiratory failure can occur with a simple neuromuscular disorder and relatively normal lungs. One must remember that patients who are tachypnic and are actually hyperventilating may be dying of hypoxemia and that profound hypoxemia is sufficient to diagnose respiratory failure. The classical respiratory failure more readily recognized by the emergency medical personnel is the patient with COPD or status asthmaticus who commonly has both serious hypoxemia and hypercapnia. Such patients are of greatest concern to the management team because the presence of acute hypercapnia induces respiratory acidosis and further impairs oxygen transport by reducing hemoglobin saturation, as well as reducing the airway response to such β-receptor drugs as the commonly employed bronchodilators. Table 5–6 illustrates one classification of causes for respiratory failure: (1) those related to physiologic abnormalities with normal lungs, (2) those associated with neuromuscular disease associated with normal lungs, (3) those found in patients who have respiratory failure with restrictive disease characterized by hypoxemia, and (4) those found in patients with obstructive airway disease generally characterized by both hypoxemia and hypercapnia. No single classification is ideal, but this schema does provide a framework for determining the likely primary defect in the first encounter with the patient, thereby providing a better guide for rational therapy.

The patients classified as having restrictive disease are most likely to have profound hypoxemia as their main or perhaps only evidence of respiratory failure when first observed. They often have increased respiratory drive and actually are hyperventilating, demonstrating hypocapnia but profound hypoxemia. Patients with neuromuscular disorders, CNS depression of respirations, or those with COPD generally have not only hypoxemia but also hypercapnia as markers of respiratory failure.

Figure 5–12 represents the PaO_2 and $PaCO_2$ values anticipated in a normal adult with a normal alveolar ventilation of 3.5 to 5 liters per minute (L/min), based on body metabolism and size. If one assumes a normal alveolar ventilation of 4 L/min, the arterial PCO_2 is 50 mm Hg and the PaO_2 95 mm Hg for a normal young adult.[14]

As ventilation is increased, the $PaCO_2$ falls and the PaO_2 rises in a predictable fashion. With the patient breathing ambient air, when the PaO_2 is 95 mm Hg (torr) and the PCO_2 is 40 mm Hg (torr) the sum of the two tensions is 135 mm Hg. If the patient increases alveolar ventilation to lower the $PaCO_2$ to 30 mm Hg, the PO_2 should rise to 105 mm Hg. Again, the sum is 135 mm Hg. This sum of oxygen and CO_2 tensions applies to young adults in the sitting position who have entirely normal lungs. When there is a reduction in ventilation, the rise in $PaCO_2$ and the fall in PaO_2 are predictable and accelerate with each unit reduction in ventilation below the normal range. In fact, there are both hypoxemia and hypercapnia at a ventilation level of 2 L/min and even a slight reduction of that level causes an exaggerated increase in hypercapnia and hypoxemia. It has often been stated that hypercapnia could not reach levels sufficient to produce coma (90 mm Hg or greater) without the patient first encountering lethal hypoxemia resulting in a fatal arrhythmia or cardiac arrest. Therefore, it is necessary that patients receive supplemental oxygen, thus having a higher oxygen tension line, if they are to reach sufficient levels of underventilation to result in hypercapnia that can produce coma. This underscores the importance of identifying and treating hypoxemia in respiratory failure, rather than emphasizing the risks of hypercapnia excessively. It should also be noted that patients with significant hypercapnia may have a striking reduction in $PaCO_2$ by modest increases in ventilation because the slope of the PCO_2/ventilation relationship is steep at hypoventilation levels. Simple cor-

Table 5–6 Classification of Acute Respiratory Failure

General Alveolar Hypoventilation

Physiologic (normal respiratory apparatus)
   Sleep—significant in the aged with COPD
   Metabolic alkalosis
      Hypokalemic alkalosis
      Hypochloremic alkalosis
      Primary hydrogen ion depletion (vomiting)
   CO_2 retention (severe hypercapnia depresses respirations)

Neuromuscular Disorders
   Poliomyelitis
   Guillain-Barré syndrome
   Myasthenia gravis
   Multiple sclerosis
   Amyotrophic lateral sclerosis
   Toxic myopathy of carcinomatosis
   Neuromuscular blockade
      Curare, succinylcholine
      Drug synergism—aminoglycosides

   Pseudocholinesterase
   Electrolyte abnormalities
   Diseases of the respiratory centers
      Sedative, narcotic, tranquilizer overdose
      CNS trauma, tumors, vascular disease
      Primary hypoventilation (Ondine's curse)
      Obesity hypoventilation—nonobstructive
      sleep apneas

Trauma—Spinal cord, phrenic nerves, etc.

Myxedema (Hypothyroidism)

Hypoventilation Associated with Ventilation/Perfusion Abnormalities

Restrictive diseases
   Extensive pneumonias
   Pneumothorax
   Flail chest, lung contusion
   Adult respiratory distress
      syndrome (ARDS)
   Pulmonary edema (cardiogenic,
      noncardiogenic)
   Chest cage deformity
      Thoracic scoliosis (kyphoscoliosis)
      Thoracoplasty
      Fibrothorax
   Restrictive lung disease
      Diffuse pulmonary fibrosis
      Granulomatous disease

Obstructive Pulmonary Disease
   Acute bronchial asthma
   Chronic bronchitis exacerbations
   Emphysema—complicated
   Bronchiectasis
Mechanisms
   Airway collapse
   Bronchial secretions (mucoid, purulent)
   Bronchial edema
   Airway inflammation
   Bronchospasm
Vascular disease
   Acute pulmonary embolism
   Chronic, recurrent pulmonary embolism
   Pulmonary hemorrhage

Note: Because acute respiratory failure may be associated primarily with alveolar hypoventilation characterized by hypercapnia or may be characterized by severe hypoxemia in the presence of hyperpnea, it is convenient to analyze respiratory failure using this classification based on the presence or absence of predominant ventilation/perfusion abnormalities.

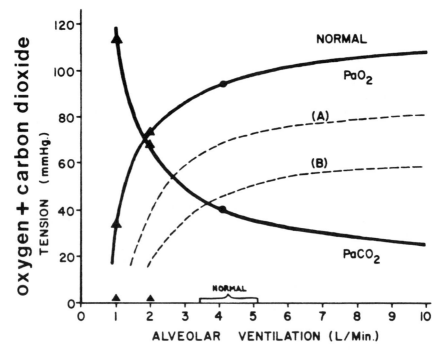

Figure 5–12 Arterial oxygen and carbon dioxide tensions are plotted for a normal individual at variable alveolar ventilation levels. Note that changes in gas tensions are more rapid at low ventilation levels, such that each unit change in alveolar ventilation makes a greater change in blood gas tensions. *Line A* illustrates the oxygen tension line for an aged patient compared to the normal line for young adults. *Line B* illustrates the oxygen tension line for a patient with underlying pulmonary disease.

rection of underventilation may elevate a dangerous PaO_2 level to one that is relatively safe without the need for supplemental oxygen. If one continues to use the sum of ambient air $PaCO_2$ and PaO_2 to identify the lungs that do not have ventilation/perfusion abnormality, in the patient with drug overdose with a PCO_2 of 65 mm Hg, a PaO_2 of 70 mm Hg is anticipated and would represent the response of normal lungs to hypoventilation. In contrast, a patient with underlying pulmonary disease would be more likely to have a PaO_2 in the range of 40–60 mm

Hg when the PCO_2 reaches 65 mm Hg. If the sum of the two tensions with ambient air breathing does not reach 135, it can be assumed the young adult has an abnormal lung. This implies a need to evaluate the possibility of aspiration, atelectasis, pneumonia, or other mechanisms that would induce a ventilation/ perfusion abnormality.

In many cases the aged patient has an oxygen tension line closer to line *A* in Figure 5–12 because ventilation/perfusion abnormalities and hypoxemia characterize the aged lung. Accordingly, in a patient with a 4 L/min alveolar ventilation, when the PCO_2 is 40 mm Hg the PaO_2 may be 70 mm Hg rather than 95, and the sum of the two tensions does not equal that of the young adult. However, the same principle applies: As ventilation is increased there is a gradual reduction in $PaCO_2$ and a gradual corresponding increase in PaO_2, with both lines being relatively flat at high ventilation levels. This means lowering a PCO_2 from 30 mm Hg to 20 mm Hg requires a considerable increase in ventilation and a 50% increase in alveolar ventilation. However, the same rules apply as one looks at hypoventilation zones in which there is a gradually accelerating increase in hypercapnia and hypoxemia as ventilation moves below normal levels by equal increments. At low levels, even a modest further reduction in alveolar ventilation causes significant hypercapnia and hypoxemia. Accordingly, patients with chronic CO_2 retention may appear stable for extended periods, but then deteriorate suddenly because of a minimal shift in ventilation to the left. However, this is a double-edged sword, and minimal improvement in ventilation also causes striking improvement in both hypercapnia and hypoxemia. But, if one follows the oxygen tension line *A* one finds that before significant hypercapnia occurs, lethal hypoxemia has supervened, probably explaining why many patients have lethal arrhythmias or cardiac arrest during acute respiratory failure without ever achieving serious hypercapnia or even approaching hypercapnic coma. Furthermore, PaO_2 line *B* might better describe the oxygen-carbon dioxide tension relationship of a patient who is both aged and has an acute respiratory disorder or an exacerbation of a chronic disorder, such as pulmonary fibrosis or COPD. These patients have a more significant hypoxemia even when hyperventilating and maintaining hypocapnia. Again this finding underscores the need to use supplemental oxygen in virtually all patients, with special caution directed toward those patients known to have chronic COPD who may have been chronic CO_2 retainers and have a ''reset'' of their respiratory center, as well as an abnormal hypoxic respiratory drive mechanism. It is clear that hypoxemia may be contributed to by both alveolar hypoventilation and the reduction in ventilation/perfusion ratios that characterize so many pulmonary disorders. Those patients with respiratory failure characterized by severe hypoxemia in the presence of hyperventilation have predominantly ventilation/perfusion mismatch, some so profound that it is referred to as a shunt. In patients with simple respiratory center depression, hypoxemia is milder and related to the level of ventilation. As such patients encounter the complications of aspiration, atelectasis, or pulmonary infection, hypoxemia is increased by the development of ventilation/perfusion mismatch.

The arterial $PaCO_2$ is the best indicator of ventilation level because there is a linear relationship between ventilation and the CO_2 tension. Hypoxemia is too common with age and underlying lung disease and is too variable to be used as a marker of ventilation. For example, it is common for the PaO_2 to fall 5 mm Hg when the patient is supine, rather than sitting, and abdominal distention, cough, and splinting due to pain have significant effects on oxygen tension that are not related to the ventilation level. Furthermore, oxygen tensions are commonly affected by supplemental oxygen in the acute emergency, thereby reflecting oxygen application, rather than ventilation level.

Hypoxia

An element of arterial hypoxemia is common to the aged and all patients with underlying respiratory disease, but tissue hypoxia may be more severe than the level of arterial blood hypoxemia suggests. Anemic patients may suffer hypoxia of such sensitive tissues as in the brain and heart due to underlying local arterial disease common to the aged and the fact that oxygen transport is largely dependent on hemoglobin so that a significant anemia represents an important deficiency in oxygen transport to vital tissues. The same concerns apply where there is a risk of carbon monoxide poisoning affecting oxygen association on the hemoglobin molecule or with tissue poisons, such as cyanide that impairs oxygen use even when oxygen tensions appear adequate. Furthermore, such abnormal hemoglobin as methemoglobin may impair oxygen transport even in the presence of high oxygen tensions. The oxygen tension may then be used as a marker of the adequacy of the oxygen exchange surface of the lung and does not guarantee adequate oxygen content or delivery to the tissues. A further defect occurs when perfusion is inadequate due to local vascular disease or shock.

Table 5–7 lists common symptoms and signs of tissue hypoxia that is usually produced by hypoxemia in conjunction with respiratory failure, but is at times aggravated by defects in the transport mechanism, including abnormalities or perfusion defects. Because acidosis is common in respiratory failure associated with hypercapnia or when hypoxemia is sufficiently profound to produce lactic acidosis, hemoglobin oxygenation may be defective due to a shift to the right of the hemoglobin-oxygen dissociation curve, impairing oxygen loading in the lung (Figure 5–14).

Cyanosis is not a reliable sign and may never appear in the presence of severe anemia because it requires 5 gm% of reduced hemoglobin and is affected by

Table 5–7 Hypoxia

Symptoms	Signs
Confusion	Tachycardia
Impaired judgment	Mild hypertension
Altered personality	Skin pallor
Restlessness	Sweats
Dizziness	Tachypnea
	Cyanosis
	Bradycardia

available light, observation error, and underlying skin color. In addition, peripheral tissues may be cyanotic due to impaired circulation and venous stasis in the presence of adequate oxygen tensions. When central cyanosis does appear, significant hypoxemia requiring treatment can be assumed to be present. Oxygen should never be withheld because of a lack of cyanosis if other signs of hypoxemia are present.

Hypercapnia

Hypercapnia in the aged patient is generally produced by alveolar hypoventilation, most commonly in the presence of obstructive airway disease and less often due to an abnormal chest bellows or CNS depression. The CO_2 tension remains the primary marker of the ventilation level because it is relatively unaffected by ventilation/perfusion mismatch and is so diffusable that diffusion disorders do not exist for all practical purposes. It is important to recognize that chronic hypercapnia with a ''reset'' of the respiratory center may exist at the time of acute respiratory failure, but this condition is almost entirely limited to patients with advanced COPD, especially in which chronic bronchitis is a predominant feature. In intermittent bronchial asthma chronic hypercapnia is rare, and most patients with restrictive disease have hypoxemia with hyperventilation and hypocapnia for the better part of their disease lifetime. Such patients may develop hypercapnia acutely when a superimposed insult precipitates respiratory failure or in the terminal stages of disease.

Hypercapnia has several effects, including stimulation of the respiratory center with mild elevations, although tensions over 80 mm Hg tend to be sedating and cause further underventilation. Therefore, carbon dioxide at high levels acts as a narcotic on the respiratory centers. Hypercapnia dilates cerebral arteries, thereby increasing cerebrospinal fluid pressure and producing papilledema. It also causes loss of concentration, irritability, insomnia, and anorexia and frequently leads to throbbing morning headaches when hypercapnia occurs during sleep and reverses on awakening. At higher levels hypercapnia induces asterixis (a flapping tremor of the hands). CO_2 tensions above 100 mm Hg generally produce coma. See Table 5–8 for common symptoms and signs of hypercapnia.

Acidosis

Acidosis occurs when carbon dioxide retention is acute, depending on the rate of change and the level of hypercapnia, as well as the adequacy of bicarbonate stores to buffer hypercapnia.[15] There may be an additional metabolic component produced by lactic acidosis resulting from tissue hypoxia, whether due to prolonged periods of intense hypoxemia or shock. Patients unable to hyperventilate to compensate for metabolic acidosis develop profound acidosis, which further impairs oxygen transport by producing hemoglobin desaturation. Table 5–9 illustrates a crude rule of thumb for predicting arterial pH with acute changes in $PaCO_2$. When a given $PaCO_2$ fails to produce the anticipated level of acidosis, some chronic compensation may be presumed to be present, or the disease may be associated with another cause of metabolic alkalosis, such as vomiting.[16]

Acidosis seriously affects the patient with status asthmaticus or COPD in which bronchospasm is a significant component, because an arterial pH below 7.25 commonly reduces responsiveness to β-adrenergic stimulating drugs used as aerosol or systemic bronchodilators. In addition, acidosis contributes to pulmonary arterial vasoconstriction that is commonly produced by hypoxemia in which the PaO_2 falls below 50 mm Hg, thereby inducing acute cor pulmonale with right cardiac failure. The presence of cardiac failure is suggested by venous distention, a tender enlarged liver, and especially bilateral edema of the lower extremities. Because correcting hypoxemia produces a rapid reversal of this process, it is extremely important to recognize the presence of both significant acidosis and hypoxemia. Treatment can begin immediately, before patient transport.

Pathophysiology of Respiratory Failure and Cor Pulmonale

As is illustrated in Figure 5–13, restrictive disorders may induce hypoxemia and produce cor pulmonale by virtue of the physiologic effects of severe hypoxemia on the pulmonary vascular bed, whereas most disorders are associated with

---

Table 5–8 Hypercapnia

Symptoms	Signs
Mild sedation	Vasodilatation of skin—flushing
Impaired concentration	Sweats
Irritability	Mild hypertension
Insomnia	Tachycardia
Anorexia	Papilledema (optic disc)
Headaches, throbbing	Bounding pulses

Table 5–9 Predicting Arterial pH with Acute PCO_2 Changes

PCO_2 mm Hg	pH	
20	7.65	HYPERVENTILATION
30	7.50	
40	7.40	
50	7.33	
60	7.26	HYPOVENTILATION
70	7.19	
80	7.12	

Note: For each 10 mm Hg rise in PCO_2, the pH falls 0.07 unit. A corresponding PCO_2 fall causes greater changes in pH than a rise in carbon dioxide.

alveolar hypoventilation that induces both hypoxemia and hypercapnia simultaneously. Hypoxemia may then be further aggravated by acidosis that produces a more intense reflex constriction of the pulmonary vascular bed and induces pulmonary hypertension leading to right cardiac failure. Precipitating or aggravating factors that may induce or accelerate the process of respiratory failure depend partly on the clinical circumstances and the nature of the underlying disease. However, the most common factor is a superimposed acute process, such as a respiratory infection; another common precipitating mechanism is bronchospasm induced by an infection, aspiration, or exposure to environmental irritants. In patients with COPD, even small doses of tranquilizers, sedatives, or antihistamines that produce mucous plugging and sedation, may precipitate respiratory failure in marginal patients. Other common aggravating factors are left cardiac failure, pneumothorax, trauma, or nonrespiratory disease, such as an acute abdomen. Thus patients may have marginal potassium levels or have significant hypochloremia that may produce weakness and respiratory muscle fatigue in the presence of an acute infection so that a relatively minor event appears to precipitate respiratory failure in the marginal patient. Because the aged patient invariably has a contracted blood volume and a chronic state of dehydration compared to young adults, any febrile illness or dehydrating process, such as vomiting or diarrhea, may be sufficient to precipitate mucous plugging, thereby intensifying hypoxemia and precipitating respiratory failure.

Treatment of Acute Respiratory Failure

The treatment of respiratory failure is based on identifying the probable underlying disease and precipitating factors, recognizing the physiologic abnormalities, and tailoring therapy accordingly. [17,18] The principle is to ''let the punishment fit the crime.'' That is, patients with severe hypoxemia should receive oxygen supplementation sufficient to correct visible cyanosis when it exists or to improve

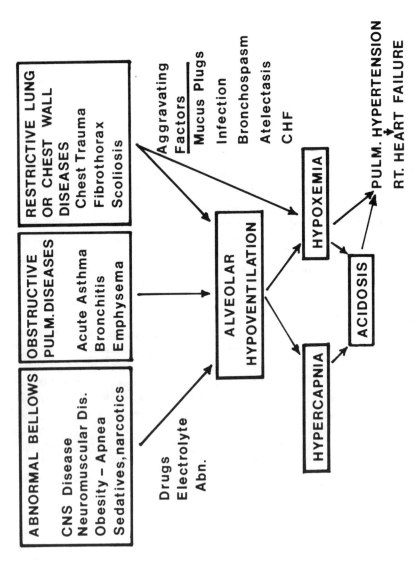

Figure 5–13 Pathophysiology of Cor Pulmonale. The development of cor pulmonale occurs largely as a consequence of hypoxemia, with acidosis as an aggravating factor. In restrictive lung disease the hypoxemia is primary and may be severe even when alveolar ventilation is normal or increased. Patients with abnormal respiratory bellows tend to have matched CO_2 abnormalities.

oxygen tension sufficiently to stabilize the patient during transport. For most patients this can be accomplished with nasal cannula at 2 L/min. Even an elevation of PaO_2 to 50–60 mm Hg is sufficient to improve the saturation of hemoglobin but not seriously affect any existing hypoxic respiratory drive. When possible, hypercapnia should be identified by looking for its signs and symptoms, although there may be few with a $PaCO_2$ of 45–60 mm Hg. Patients known to have COPD may be treated by the Venturi-type mask, preferably at 24% oxygen, unless oxygen tolerance is known and cyanosis persists, in which case 28% may be used for short transport periods. The significant improvement in hemoglobin oxygen saturation produced by even slight improvement in PaO_2 can be seen in Figure 5–14.

Note that in the presence of acidosis the hemoglobin dissociation curve shifts to the right and saturation is less at any given PaO_2 level. Those patients who do not have COPD, including patients with status asthmaticus and all those with pulmonary fibrosis or pneumonia, pulmonary embolism, or pulmonary edema, may be given oxygen at higher levels with relative safety. It would be preferable to treat such patients with 28% to 35% oxygen by Venturi mask or achieve comparable levels using oxygen via nasal prongs.

When there is gross evidence of respiratory failure with hypercapnia and an altered mental status and when respirations appear to be failing, with irregular shallow respirations and cyanosis, patients should be ventilated by at least an oral airway and bag-and-mask ventilation using 30% to 50% oxygen to correct signs of hypoxemia. There should be no limitations or concerns about oxygen application as long as ventilation is being maintained. Once there is ventilation support, hypercapnia ceases to be an issue, and the greatest risk might be overventilation of the patient that produces a significant alkalosis and impairs blood supply to the brain. Intubation should be considered when secretions are excessive and cannot be managed by suction or the patient's cough.

In the presence of bronchoconstriction, aerosol bronchodilators may be administered initially and as often as every 1–2 hr. The safest regimen is to administer 0.3 ml of isoetharine with 2 ml of diluent via a nebulizer or an intermittent positive pressure breathing (IPPB) where required. The patient must be monitored for a tachycardia because isoetharine is a β_2-stimulating drug, but does have β_1 activity as well. Another choice would be the use of isoproterenol (Isuprel) in a dose of 1.5 mg (0.3 ml of a 1/200 solution) diluted with 3 ml of saline or water by nebulizer or IPPB where necessary. When an IV line is available and when there are adequately trained EMTs with appropriate medical supervision, aminophylline may be administered to patients known to have received the drug for clinical bronchospasm. A safe dose for the aged patient is 4 mg/kg infused slowly over 15 min to avoid the risks of nausea, vomiting, hypotension, or arrhythmias. It is unlikely that a repeat dose will be required during transport. Patients require careful monitoring of vital signs, commonly requiring transport in the semirecumbent or sitting position if desired.

Reassurance is an important treatment modality and should not be overlooked. Such patients may have evidence of congestive heart failure or a history of

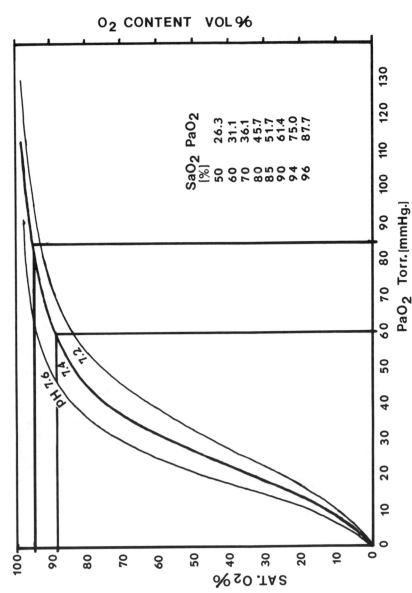

Figure 5–14 Hemoglobin oxygen dissociation in the aged. Both the normal oxygen tension range for the aged patient and the limited range of oxygen saturation when the arterial pH is 7.40 are illustrated. A significant reduction in saturation occurs at lower oxygen tensions with the pH reduced to 7.20 so that the combination of acidosis and low-normal oxygen tensions in the aged patient can lead to significant desaturation.

arteriosclerotic heart disease (ASHD) with chronic use of digitalis and diuretics so that pulmonary edema may supervene in the course of the acute illness and management. It is important to carry as much information about the patient's medical management, including the drug regimen, with the patient wherever possible so that intelligent management can begin immediately at the receiving facility. The emergency treatment facility should be warned that ventilator support or other more sophisticated modalities will be required. The treatment of acidosis should usually be limited to controlling hypercapnia and hypoxemia using clinical judgment because correcting acidosis by the use of sodium bicarbonate may aggravate or precipitate congestive heart failure from a sodium overload.

ACUTE AND CHRONIC BRONCHIAL ASTHMA IN THE ELDERLY PATIENT

Definition

Bronchial asthma is characterized by hyperreactive airways, including both bronchioles and bronchi; is intermittent and reversible; and results in increased production of a tenacious mucous, edema, and inflammatory changes in the airways. There is intense bronchospasm with eventual smooth muscle hypertrophy, which results in a dynamic obstructive airway disease with mucous plugging characterized by hypoxemia in all episodes and by hypercapnia in asthmatic crisis. Asthma is categorized as acute and intermittent or chronic, depending on its clinical course. A more meaningful differentiation is between extrinsic or allergic asthma and intrinsic or nonallergic asthma. Extrinsic asthma is associated with a positive family history of asthma, elevated levels of serum IgE, and common association with other allergic disorders, such as hay fever, food or drug allergies, allergic rhinorrhea, nasal polyps, or anaphylaxis. The form of asthma most common to the elderly patient is nonallergic or intrinsic asthma, which is characterized by bronchospasm, edema, and mucus production produced generally by stimuli other than pure allergens. In the older patient attacks result from exercise, exposure to cold air, and exposure to various fumes and ambient pollutants, and they are aggravated by anxiety. Most often a chronic, indolent asthmatic bronchitis exists with a variable course, but one that is less characterized by brief, intermittent episodes than is the allergic variety. The most common precipitating event is a viral infection because the virus invades the tracheobronchial tree where the hyperreactivity of the airways is centered.

It is estimated that between 7% to 8% of the population have bronchial asthma at some time, and the incidence is highest in older patients with associated COPD.[19] In addition, the prognosis is less favorable in the aged, and the disease tends to be chronic, requiring therapy over many years. As with allergic asthma, patients' conditions deteriorate following viral infections and exposure to various air pollutants, including ozone and sufur dioxide; an increase in wheeze and dyspnea is associated with cough or laughter, and there may be a tendency for increased symptoms in the nocturnal hours. In general, desensitization is not effective in intrinsic asthma, and some patients even respond to desensitization injections with increased symptoms occurring hours after injection. Older patients with intrinsic asthma may have increased symptoms within one hour after meals, probably due to increased vagal tone; they generally have increased symptoms after ingestion of cold food or fluids and frequently have an intolerance for red wine and similar fluids containing substances that promote bronchoconstriction. Patients with a known allergy to aspirin may have an increase in bronchospasm after ingestion of foods containing tartrazine dyes or a number of food preservatives, such as meta-bisulfite used commonly in restaurants to preserve salads. Older asthmatics also have paroxysmal cough as a wheeze-equivalent, with coughing induced by exercise or exposure to cold air or to a large variety of volatile chemicals and fumes, with diesel exhaust, perfumes, and second-hand cigarette smoke among common aggravating exposures.

Physiology of Intrinsic Asthma in the Aged

Airway obstruction is especially severe during the expiratory phase, but may also be present on inspiration with narrowing of all airways from trachea to bronchioles. Obstruction is caused by edema of the airway wall with hypertrophy and excess mucous production by deep mucous glands, followed by progressive hypertrophy of smooth muscle that becomes increasingly more powerful and hyperreactive. In the uncomplicated case lung tissue may escape pathology, but the accumulation of mucus with mucus plugs characteristically produces hypoxemia because of widespread reduction of ventilation/perfusion ratios. Many segments of lung are being perfused, but receive little or no ventilation because of mucus plugs, bronchospasm, and edema. Occasionally air enters these zones and is trapped in the expiratory phase providing a one-way ball-valve phenomenon leading to local distention. As the patient's symptoms increase, distention increases, with the gradual increase in residual air encroaching on the forced vital capacity and forcing the patient to breathe in a higher and higher lung position as symptoms progress. The result is always hypoxemia at all stages of asthma from the mild to the most severe stage, which is commonly termed ''asthma in crisis'' or ''status asthmaticus.'' As mucous plugging and ventilation/blood flow discrepancies increase, hypoxemia progresses, and eventually total ventilation is impaired, with hypercapnia characterizing the severe stages of acute asthma. Early stages are characterized by hyperventilation with hypoxemia but still hypercapnic. [20–22]

Some clinicians classify asthma as mild when the FEV_1 is greater than 2.0 liters, as moderate when the FEV_1 ranges from 1.0–2.0 liters, and as severe when the FEV_1 is below 1.0 liter. In general, these categories correlate relatively well with levels of hypoxemia, but the exact PaO_2 is partly based on the presence or absence of coexisting primary pulmonary disease at the onset of the acute episode. In most elderly patients, COPD is common, and patients begin with at least mild hypoxemia prior to even early stages of acute asthma. Accordingly, the major risk from status asthmaticus is always profound hypoxemia resulting in serious cardiac arrhythmias, cardiac arrest, or acute cerebrovascular insufficiency. For many decades the term "status asthmaticus" has been reserved for those patients who receive medication and fail to show a response, but instead have further deterioration, because it underscores those patients at risk of death.

The dehydration and underlying vascular disease of the older patient may intensify mucous plugging and levels of hypoxemia. In asthma, mucous secretion is not only markedly exaggerated but bronchial secretions also tend to be viscous and unusually tenacious.

Differential Diagnosis in the Aged

In older patients with persistent or intrinsic asthma, other possible causes for cough, dyspnea, and wheeze must be carefully considered and ruled out. They may have more symptoms in the winter months with viral infections and tend to have acute episodes resulting in respiratory insufficiency that require treatment in a medical care facility.

The differential diagnosis should not be difficult in patients with a known history of cardiac disease, a history of employing cardiac drugs, or a history of orthopnea and paroxysmal nocturnal dyspnea. The cardiac patient responds quickly to supplemental oxygen in the upright position. The majority are on diuretics and have other evidence of left heart failure, including rales at lung bases and an S_3 left ventricular gallop. However, left heart failure may mimic status asthmaticus because of copious secretions, although generally they are pink or blood streaked, and because the asthma may be aggravated in the evening hours after the patient has been supine for some time. Paroxysmal nocturnal dyspnea is associated with bronchospasm in patients with hyperreactive airways.

Pulmonary embolism may occasionally be responsible for cough and bronchospasm associated with severe hypoxemia and dyspnea and thus may be confused with status asthmaticus. In general, the response to bronchodilators is poor and atypical for asthma. One-third of patients with pulmonary embolism present with evidence of thrombophlebitis, and the remainder have blood streaking of sputum, pleuritic chest pain, or a very abrupt onset without the history of chronic intermittent symptoms that characterizes status asthmaticus in the older patient.

Chronic aspiration due to esophageal reflux associated with a hiatus hernia may induce acute cough and bronchospasm in discrete episodes that are most common in the nocturnal hours. Patients generally have a history of epigastric distress or substernal burning characteristic of esophageal reflux, or they may be aware of an acid taste in the mouth and of the presence of a symptomatic hiatus hernia, often having received previous treatment. The episode is often associated with a prominent paroxysmal cough, and bronchospasm is secondary.

Physical Findings

The older patient may have underlying COPD with the characteristic physical findings for chronic bronchitis or emphysema; a musical wheeze is heard in all lung fields with the wheeze higher in pitch and more distant with increasing severity of airway obstruction. Inspiratory wheeze may be present in more severe cases. Patients demonstrating restlessness and anxiety with distant high-pitched wheezes are the sickest and most at risk of fatal hypoxemia or respiratory failure from exhaustion, whereas those with low-pitched, loud wheezing probably have better air movement and are not quite as sick. Most patients have some cough and sputum. They tend to sit bolt upright, using accessory respiratory muscles, and to show progressive distention with flattened diaphragms, hyperresonance of lung fields, and distant breath sounds. The expiratory phase is prolonged and generally occupied entirely by an audible wheeze. The retraction of sternocleidomastoid muscles is usually associated with an FEV_1 under 1 liter. A paradoxical pulse may be identified, with a loss of systolic sounds on inspiration for greater than 10 mm below the systolic pressure, indicating a severe stage of asthma. The paradoxical pulse deficit on inspiration may exist for up to 50 mm below systolic pressure and is a good marker of severe disease. Respiratory fatigue and exhaustion may be clinically evident, but the adequacy of ventilation is best determined by arterial blood gas analysis and a search for severe hypoxemia, the development of hypercapnia, and the development of acidosis, usually from combined hypercapnia and hypoxemia. As the disease progresses, hypoxemia becomes more severe and may become hazardous even before significant hypercapnia results. Cyanosis may be present where the arterial pH and hemoglobin levels permit. Some patients have evidence of right heart failure with the development of ankle edema, a tender enlarged liver, jugular venous distention, tachycardia, and an S_3 gallop heard over the right ventricular zone (body of the sternum).[19,23]

Laboratory Findings

Most patients have increased eosinophils in secretions and in their blood count, but this is of little consequence in determining the etiology or severity of the asthmatic attack. The sputum should be examined for evidence of infection manifested by a purulent appearance and an increase in neutrophils with a gram stain for identification of bacterial flora. Some clinicians use the FEV_1 as an indicator of disease stage, with an FEV_1 of 2.0 liters representing mild disease, an FEV_1 under 1.0 liter representing severe disease, and an FEV_1 below 0.75 liter representing an advanced status asthmatic. Others employ peak expiratory flow rates (PEFR), with a level of 200 L/min indicating mild disease, with severe disease characterized by a PEFR of under 80 L/min, and with the most advanced stages resulting in a PEFR of below 60 L/min, this stage being associated with hypercapnia.

Arterial blood gas analysis is a critical element in laboratory evaluation of the patient with status asthmaticus, with all patients showing hypoxemia, which may be profound in the advanced stage, and hypocapnia in early stages. In the advanced stage the arterial $PaCO_2$ rises to approximately 40 torr and then above 40 in the late stages when respiratory failure supervenes and ventilatory support becomes necessary. Patients have an alkalosis with hypocapnia until late stages at which time the pH may fall rapidly as a result of both increased CO_2 tension and a metabolic acidosis produced by profound hypoxemia. It is important to detect acidosis, especially with a pH below 7.25, because it may render patients unresponsive to sympathomimetic bronchodilator drugs.

The chest x-ray generally reveals hyperinflation, but may reveal streak densities radiating from the hilar areas consistent with local atelectasis associated with mucus plugs. A significant infiltrate suggests that infection has precipitated the attack, and cardiomegaly with engorgement of pulmonary vascular tree suggests left heart failure as a precipitating or aggravating factor. As airway obstruction with progressive distention continues, diaphragms become flattened, and the AP diameter may increase to resemble emphysema to the casual observer. A careful search should be made for pneumothorax or pneumomediastinum—the latter identified by air lines extending from the mediastinum into the neck and best seen in the lateral chest film—because these complications may accelerate respiratory failure. A pneumothorax requires immediate treatment with a thoracotomy tube, whereas the pneumomediastinum is likely a single event that does not seriously impair lung function and does not recur. A pneumomediastinum may also be identified by the presence of subcutaneous air in the anterior chest and neck.

The ECG generally reveals only tachycardia and nonspecific ST-T wave changes associated with the aged heart in conjunction with tachycardia and hypoxemia. In some cases it may reveal evidence of right heart strain or a right axis shift.

Clinical Staging of Status Asthmaticus

Table 5–10 provides a useful structured approach to evaluating the severity of status asthmaticus. [24–26] Because the underlying disease may be more significant

Table 5–10 Staging of Status Asthmaticus

Stage	FEV_1 (liter)	pH	PaO_2 (mm Hg)	$PaCO_2$ (mm Hg)	Pulsus Paradoxus
I	2.0+	Alkalosis	70–85	28–35	None
II	1.0–2.0	Alkalosis	65–80	30–38	None
III	<1.0	7.35–7.45	55–70	35–45	+
IV		<7.35	40–60	50–80	+ + +

in the older patient, the numbers displayed in Table 5–10 should be used only as a guide. Some patients have significant COPD and begin with significant hypoxemia even during the early stages when they hyperventilate and may have lethal hypoxemia before significant hypercapnia can occur. Therefore, oxygen tensions must be observed very carefully. Generally, when wheezing becomes less prominent and restlessness and cyanosis increase, serious deterioration is present, and there is a need to consider intubation and ventilation support. During stage IV intubation and support on a ventilator are required because patients' conditions may continue deteriorating during the period between full administration of bronchodilator drugs and an adequate response. It is hazardous to delay intubation waiting for acute deterioration because it may be associated with serious or fatal cerebral or cardiac hypoxia. This is especially important in older patients with underlying cerebrovascular disease.

In Table 5–11 are noted the most common indicators of disease severity.

Acute Treatment

After initial evaluation demonstrating the presence of bronchospasm with distention and respiratory distress and with the knowledge that all patients, particularly the older patient, have an element of hypoxemia, all patients should receive oxygen at a level of 3–4 L/min by nasal cannula or 30% oxygen by mask where tolerated. In the presence of severe bronchospasm and acute respiratory distress, depression of respirations by the use of oxygen during transportation to a medical facility is unlikely, and the risk from failing to give supplemental oxygen

---

Table 5–11 Indicators of Severe Status Asthmaticus

- Severe reduction of FEV_1
- Poor bronchodilator response
- Central cyanosis
- Retraction
- Heart rate >130 bpm
- Pulsus paradoxus
- PaO_2 under 50 mm Hg
- $PaCO_2$ greater than 50 mm Hg
- Mental obtundation
- Pneumothorax or pneumomediastinum
- Malignant ECG rhythm
- Silent chest
- Exhaustion with absent cough

Note: Indicators of severe status asthmaticus generally occur in clusters, with more than half of the listed indicators present in the vast majority of patients who are developing a life-threatening respiratory failure.

is much greater. Because most patients are dehydrated, IV fluids may be initiated when expertise and facilities permit, although aggressive hydration of the older patient is hazardous and proper hydration should await arrival at a medical care facility. The IV line will be useful for the administration of drugs.

Based on the patient's age and recent use of bronchodilators, patients should receive IV theophylline in the form of aminophylline, with proper attention to the recent history of its use. In a patient who has not previously received aminophylline, a loading dose of 6 mg/kg should be administered intravenously over a period of 30–60 min, although in older patients and those previously receiving aminophylline, this should be reduced to 2–5 mg/kg. A maintenance infusion in a younger asthmatic patient usually requires 0.9 mg/kg/hr in a cigarette smoker and 0.5 mg/kg/hr in a nonsmoker. In the presence of COPD or when aminophylline metabolism is characteristically impaired a maintenance dose of 0.25 mg/kg/hr is employed. Patients who metabolize the drug slowly and are more at risk of toxicity include those with severe hypoxemia, febrile states, known liver disease, cardiac decompensation, pneumonia, severe airway obstruction, and advanced age. Despite a potential for toxicity, the drug is employed for its action as a respiratory stimulant and its excellent action as a bronchodilator with relatively rapid onset and only nominal cardiac effects. Aminophylline is rapidly cleared by heavy cigarette smokers, thereby resulting in a need for higher doses.[27]

Sympathomimetic bronchodilators should be administered immediately in aerosol form because of their rapid effect, which alleviates acute anxiety, and relatively selective β_2 effects. The value of calm procedures and patient reassurance cannot be overestimated because anxiety greatly exaggerates the respiratory distress and accelerates failure. The author prefers isoetharine 0.3 cc nebulized with 2 cc of sterile saline by powered aerosol and where necessary by IPPB. If IPPB is used, it should be used intermittently with a 1-min interruption after each 15–20 breaths to avoid overdistention or increasing toxic side effects. Isoetharine is preferable in patients over age 70 because of its selective β_2 effect and short duration, which reduce the risk of increasing tachycardia and cardiac arrhythmias. However, many patients obtain a longer and more beneficial effect from the use of metaproterenol in a dose of 0.2–0.3 ml, with 2 ml of normal saline diluent also by powered aerosol.

Subcutaneous epinephrine and sedatives must never be employed in the elderly patient during transportation because they require careful monitoring due to hazards of tachyphylaxis and respiratory failure, respectively.

Emergency department triage consists of immediately examining the patient for critical signs of impending respiratory failure, including determining the levels of air exchange and distention, the presence of a cough, the mental status of the patient, and any suggestion of fatigue, impending exhaustion, or failure to cooperate, all of which lead to the need for intubation and mechanical ventilation. Arterial blood gas analysis should be performed immediately to provide a proper scientific basis for staging, keeping in mind the patient's age and the possible presence of underlying cardiopulmonary disease that would otherwise modify the staging of hypoxemia and hypercapnia. Profound hypoxemia and significant acidosis require immediate correction because they may prevent an appropriate response to therapeutic drugs. In that respect, IV steroids may help reduce the blockade of β-receptors and improve the response to other drugs, although after an IV bolus of corticosteroids, there is a lag of 4–6 hr before a significant effect can be detected. In the meantime, the patient may receive supplemental oxygen, continued reassurance, and hourly treatment with β-adrenergic aerosol bronchodilators, such as isoetharine and continuous IV aminophylline. A chest film should be done at the earliest convenience and cardiac monitoring established on arrival in the emergency treatment area. After the initial evaluation of the patient's status there should be a review of previous medication and medical conditions with information provided by the transporting EMT team.

CHRONIC OBSTRUCTIVE PULMONARY DISEASE

Vital statistics for the United States reveal that chronic obstructive pulmonary disease (COPD) is the sixth ranking cause of mortality, being responsible for 50,488 deaths or 21.2 deaths/100,000/year in 1978, or 2.6% of all deaths. [28,29] It is more common in men, and in the age group 55–74 it is the fifth cause of death in men, but eighth in rank as cause of death among women, with no change in rank for individuals over age 75. However, national statistics include emphysema as a ninth ranking cause of death in patients over 55 because it is often recognized as an isolated entity; if it was not calculated separately, COPD would rank even higher as a cause of death.

The term "COPD" was developed to describe patients who have combined and variable degrees of both chronic bronchitis and pulmonary emphysema, with the clinical picture varying from one dominated almost entirely by chronic bronchitis to one characterized almost entirely by pulmonary emphysema. In Great Britain the clinical picture in obstructive airway disease has been predominantly one of chronic bronchitis, whereas in the United States the picture of the average aged patient with obstructive airway disease is closer to that of the emphysema pattern as indicated by both pulmonary function testing and clinical appearance. Some authors have included bronchial asthma in the category of COPD, but the vast majority differentiate bronchial asthma because of its intermittent and reversible nature, as well as its entirely different etiology. However, in the author's experience, approximately one-third of patients with COPD do have significant bronchospasm, even if low grade, and therefore respond to bronchodilators in clinical management. The incidence of COPD increases with age and is highest in the elderly man with a history of cigarette smoking, with the rate increasing rapidly in women as a result of their becoming heavy cigarette smokers in recent decades. Patients with predominant and severe chronic bronchitis may have respiratory failure and require emergency management at an earlier age (age 45–65), whereas patients with predominantly emphysema are more often men over age 60. The

EMT and other treating medical personnel responding to emergencies in such patients are not likely to see them as stable chronically ill patients, which is their usual status. Rather, they are seen with acute deterioration, usually precipitated by an infection that is often viral or when their disease is complicated by congestive heart failure, dehydration, exposure to irritant fumes, or extremes of heat and humidity.

Definition

Chronic Bronchitis

Chronic bronchitis has been defined by the American Thoracic Society as a disease characterized by daily cough and sputum production for a minimum of 3 months a year and for a minimum of 2 consecutive years, if other common causes such as bronchiectasis, tuberculosis, or lung cancer can be ruled out.[30] It is associated with chronic cigarette smoking, and its incidence correlates with the level of cigarette consumption. It remains reversible for many years and can be significantly improved when individuals discontinue smoking. The productive cough is most evident in the early morning, and many patients consider themselves relatively normal after clearing secretions on arising. Some patients develop a low-grade chronic bronchitis as a result of repeated industrial exposures.

The incidence of bronchitis increases with each decade of age, is highest in urban communities, is two to three times more common in males, and appears to have an increased frequency with ambient air pollution and the respiratory infections of the winter months. The role of infection in chronic bronchitis is controversial, although most patients with chronic bronchitis have contamination of bronchial secretions by either *Haemophilus influenzae* or *Streptococcus pneumoniae,* whereas normal airways are sterile below the vocal cords. Chronic bronchitis tends to exacerbate with recurring respiratory infections, and there is evidence that antibiotic treatment may improve the overall course of the disease.

The pathophysiology is characterized by an increase in mucous glands throughout the tracheobronchial tree, with the appearance of mucus-secreting cells in small airways and the presence of inflammatory changes and edema in all airways. In chronic bronchitis an increase in bronchial smooth muscle has been demonstrated, especially in those who have associated bronchospasm. Chronic bronchitis does not itself affect the alveolus or the distal lung unit where gas exchange takes place, but is characterized by airway obstruction, bronchial edema, inflammation, and increased secretions. These factors not only produce significant expiratory airway obstruction that is especially notable in large airways but also cause some damage to bronchioles as well. Lung elastic recoil is normal, and the obstructive airway disease shows a modest response to bronchodilators, frequently improving 5% to 15% shortly after an aerosol bronchodilator is administered. Dyspnea is not striking because distention of the lung is minor compared with emphysema. Airway obstruction leads to very significant hypoxemia that is often more striking than that seen in emphysema; in addition, hypercapnia occurs earlier than in advanced emphysema. To describe the patient with severe chronic bronchitis who has cyanosis but does not have the weight loss seen in emphysema, the term "blue bloater" has been used.

Because the patients have more significant hypoxemia (PaO_2 of 40–60 mm Hg) for extended periods and because the respiratory drive is lower than in the patient with advanced emphysema due to less chest distention found in chronic bronchitis, it is common for patients to have an insidious and gradual progression of hypercapnia and the development of a hypoxic respiratory drive that is not seen in normals. Therefore, correction of hypoxemia traditionally requires monitoring of arterial blood gases and careful oxygen supplementation to avoid further depressing respirations. [31,32]

Pulmonary Emphysema

Pulmonary emphysema, which is not reversible, is defined as a destruction of the air spaces distal to the terminal bronchioles, including the alveolar units where gas exchange takes place. It is characterized by loss of capillary bed, loss of alveolar units, the development of expiratory airway obstruction beginning in bronchioles and progressing to large airways, and a reduction in lung elastic recoil that impairs normal emptying during expiration. The progressive loss of both lung tissue and impaired function are so subtle and slowly progressive that patients often are unable to date the onset of their shortness of breath and are only aware of a very slow progression often extending over decades.

It is several times more common in males with an incidence that increases with age, although the rate in women is rapidly increasing. A long history of cigarette smoking is a constant finding, and most patients have an associated chronic bronchitis. The increased incidence in males appears to parallel that of heavy cigarette consumption, with a lag period of two or more decades for the moderate or severe disease. The incidence is also increased in heavily industrialized communities and by certain industrial exposures. It is also partly related to genetic factors, which are not clearly defined, although only the rare case can be ascribed entirely to a genetic defect of enzyme inactivation systems in which cigarette smoking has not played a role in the development of the disease.

Emphysema should not be confused with "senile emphysema," which represents the hyperinflated lung that is normal with age and is not emphysema at all. Local areas of emphysema may be seen in chronic inflammatory scars as with tuberculosis or bronchiectasis, but generally do not affect overall lung function.

Patients have a markedly hyperinflated lung with a barrel chest and very slow expiration due to airway collapse. The diaphragm is often flattened by the hyperinflated lung, and the patient is forced to use intercostal and accessory respiratory muscles, which markedly increases the work of breathing. Accordingly, patients have a high level of dyspnea and have more respiratory distress than the patient with chronic bronchitis alone, although the levels of hypoxemia are generally less striking. They frequently purse their lips during the prolonged expiratory phase to maintain pressure in the airways and avoid collapsing small branches of the bronchial tree and further air trapping. Patients are accordingly described as "pink puffers." In advanced stages they have weight loss due to the high energy costs of breathing and are generally very dyspneic with even minimal exertion. In advanced cases large meals, bathing, shaving, or dressing may induce shortness of breath relieved only by rest. Hypercapnia tends to occur in late stages when the disease is complicated by acute infections, congestive heart failure, pneumothorax, or medications that depress respiration. Pure emphysema does not respond to bronchodilator therapy unless low-grade bronchospasm is also present. Right heart failure tends to occur much later in emphysema compared with patients with severe bronchitis.

The average patient seen during a respiratory emergency has combined chronic bronchitis and emphysema, and the majority have deterioration induced by an acute respiratory infection. A simple viral infection is the most frequent type of infection, but during influenza epidemics there is increased incidence of acute respiratory distress. Patients are also known to have increased respiratory insufficiency in association with other infections or diarrhea that induce dehydration and with exposure to noxious fumes or ambient air pollution. Acute stress and anxiety are common factors in accelerating deterioration and exaggerating the level of dyspnea. [33,34]

History—Common Elements in COPD

Although the patient with COPD may have an increase in dyspnea and evidence of respiratory insufficiency when seen in the emergency situation, there is invariably a history of cigarette smoking on a chronic basis, a long history of cough and sputum production that is daily and generally more significant in the morning, and invariably a gradual progression of dyspnea on exertion that is more obvious in the patient with predominant emphysema. Brief questioning about the patient's tolerance for routine activities, such as climbing stairs, walking distances, and the routines of daily living, quickly documents their level of impairment. In contrast to patients with chronic left heart failure, they tend not to have orthopnea or paroxysmal nocturnal dyspnea, and the cough is generally productive. Furthermore, there is a pattern of improvement in dyspnea following expectoration of secretions or treatment of bronchospasm if it coexists. In contrast to acute bronchial asthma, patients do not have intermittent periods of normal function associated with brief attacks of cough, wheezing, and dyspnea, but rather describe a long history of gradual progression of dyspnea (see Table 5–12).

Physical Findings

Patients with COPD commonly have cough with a "loose" quality that suggests significant secretions. Patients with severe bronchitis may have cyanosis of

Table 5–12 History and Symptoms in COPD

History or Symptom	Chronic Bronchitis	Emphysema	Asthma
Smoking history	Present	Present	Variable
Allergic syndromes	Uncommon	Uncommon	Usual
Normal periods	None	None	Usual
Chronic progressive	Variable	Usual	Uncommon
Wide symptom fluctuations	Variable	Uncommon	Typical
Productive cough	Daily, productive especially in morning	Mild, minimally productive, or absent	Common with exercise, URI, or nocturnal
Dyspnea	Only present in advanced disease	Prominent, with insidious onset, persistent, and progressive	Episodic, associated with increased cough and wheeze

mucous membranes and nail beds, but patients with predominant emphysema show no cyanosis. In emphysema, respiratory rates are not much increased in acute illness because of the expiratory airway obstruction that causes pursed-lipped breathing and an almost mandatory prolonged expiratory phase. Patients generally are found in the sitting or standing position, leaning forward, either supporting themselves on their elbows or with the shoulders elevated, and using accessory respiratory muscles, including the sternomastoid, scalenus, and trapezius muscles. They frequently show evidence of weight loss that makes the jugular vein and neck muscles more prominent. They use pursed-lipped breathing with a grunting or expiratory wheeze and a high level of anxiety. Table 5–13 summarizes these common signs of COPD.

Distention of neck veins with a tender right costal margin or palpable tender liver with bilateral ankle edema suggests acute right heart failure. Lethargy or stupor suggests the presence of more than mild hypercapnia. The patient is frequently dehydrated with very dry mucous membranes and poor skin turgor.

Examination of the chest reveals distant breath sounds that may be absent at lung bases due to the hyperinflated lung and lack of diaphragm activity. Inspiratory rales are common in bronchitis, and a high-pitched, prolonged, distant-sounding wheeze is not uncommon in severe airway obstruction when bronchospasm plays some role in the acute illness. Elevation of the chest on inspiration with a lack of lateral or AP expansion may be associated with a lack of outward abdominal wall movement on inspiration and suggests the patient is breathing only

Table 5–13 Signs in COPD

Signs	Chronic Bronchitis	Emphysema	Asthma
Wheeze (sibilant rhonchi)	Transient and uncommon	Usually absent, or soft and high pitched, with exacerbations	Predominant, with infections and allergen exposures
Expiratory airway obstruction	Present and variable	Constant, often severe, and progressive	Associated with acute episodes, often minimal
Distended chest	Mild	Marked	Present only with acute episodes
Absent breath sounds at lung bases	Uncommon	Common	Only with acute, severe episodes
Rales	Present occasionally at bases posteriorly	Absent	Usually absent
Rhonchi	Usual, change with cough	Absent or minimal	Striking, musical, high pitched, expiratory
Weight loss	Uncommon	Typical	Absent
Clubbing	Present occasionally	Absent	Absent
Plethora	Common	Uncommon	Absent
Cor pulmonale	Frequent, will occur early in disease	Only in far advanced disease with complications	Absent

with accessory respiratory muscles. A marker of disability is also the strength and quality of the patient's cough.

Laboratory Findings

Pulmonary function testing reveals moderate to advanced expiratory airway obstruction, with no response to aerosol bronchodilators in pure pulmonary emphysema but a modest response (5% to 15%) in patients with chronic bronchitis.

There is a mild to moderate increase in residual volume in chronic bronchitis, but in advanced pulmonary emphysema the residual volume and total lung capacity may be massively increased. In both cases there is a reduced FVC. In emphysema the respiratory rate is normally 8–14 breaths per min, with tidal volumes of 500–1,000 cc and a prolonged expiratory time of 4–8 sec. This rate changes with acute distress, but the same pattern remains, with more shallow breathing and a mild increase in rate. The work of breathing is very great in pulmonary emphysema, which is characterized by an increased oxygen requirement for respiratory muscles. Intrapulmonary gas mixing is abnormal in emphysema but generally normal in chronic bronchitis, and the diffusion capacity is impaired in emphysema but not in bronchitis. In advanced disease, the average PaO_2 is 60–85 mm Hg in pulmonary emphysema at rest and 45–65 mm Hg in predominant bronchitis. Patients with advanced emphysema have a normal CO_2 tension until there is acute respiratory infection or other complication, whereas those with far advanced bronchitis have chronic hypercapnia, with a $PaCO_2$ of 45–60 mm Hg being commonly observed.

The chest x-ray in chronic bronchitis may show mild hyperinflation and increased peribronchial markings, often termed ''a dirty lung.'' In emphysema, hyperinflation is likely to be present with the diaphragm flattened, especially notable on the lateral view, with or without a mild diffuse fibrosis, but with a reduction in vascular shadows in the peripheral third of the lung fields.

Staging COPD

In 1965, guides to the evaluation of respiratory impairment were developed based on four grades of dyspnea to standardize terms used to describe functional status.[35]

1. *Class 1*—(0% impairment): when dyspnea occurs, it is consistent with the circumstances of activity.
2. *Class 2*—(20%–30% impairment): does not occur at rest and seldom occurs during the performance of the usual activities of daily living. The patient can keep pace with persons of same age and body build on level surfaces without breathlessness, but not on hills or stairs.
3. *Class 3*—(40%–50% impairment): does not occur at rest, but does occur during the usual activities of daily living. However, the patient can walk a mile at his or her own pace without dyspnea although he or she cannot keep pace on level surfaces with others of the same age and body build.
4. *Class 4*—(60%–90% impairment): occurs during such activities as climbing one flight of stairs or walking 100 yards on a flat level, using less exertion, or even at rest.

Respiratory failure can only be diagnosed by demonstrating significant hypoxemia and/or hypercapnia, but respiratory insufficiency is relatively common even when respiratory failure is not present. Respiratory insufficiency implies an increase in dyspnea, an increased sense of the work of breathing, or respiratory distress associated with an increased level of disease even when respiratory failure is absent. Acute deterioration is most commonly due to infection and next most often due to environmental factors, including ambient air pollution, cigarette smoke or irritants, and exposure to sharp changes in temperature, such as cold air or extremely hot, humid air. Less often, dehydration with inspissation of secretions and mucous plugging causes a deterioration in function. Additional factors that may precipitate sudden deterioration are pneumothorax, left heart failure, or any febrile illness that increases body temperature and metabolism and thereby increases the discrepancy between gas exchange requirements and the capacity of the respiratory system. The condition of patients with advanced COPD may also deteriorate as a result of chronic use of sedatives or antihistamines used for minor upper respiratory tract symptoms. They may produce progressive effects due to the impaired metabolism of drugs by the elderly patient.

Acute Treatment and Transportation

Immediate treatment begins with a careful observation of the patient's appearance, looking for the stigmata of COPD and estimating the level of respiratory distress. A few questions may clarify the reason for deterioration in respiratory status, which may be an acute respiratory infection, a failure to take bronchodilator drugs, the presence of overt left heart failure, or evidence of dehydration. There is an increased incidence of respiratory distress in summer months characterized by heat and humidity and especially when air pollution is a significant problem. Unless the patient is obtunded and appears to be a "blue bloater" with ankle edema and a history of lethargy, oxygen is required and should be used either in the form of 2 L/min by nasal cannula or 25% to 30% by mask.

The patient should be asked to cough to determine the presence of copious secretions and estimate the power of the cough. If the cough is very weak or the patient responds poorly, it is likely that ventilation support will be required, with minimum treatment consisting of an oropharyngeal airway and a bag-and-mask ventilation support to stabilize the patient during transport to a treatment facility. When bronchospasm is prominent, a bronchodilator may be administered in the form of metaproterenol administered by aerosol in a standard dose of 0.3 cc with 2 cc of normal saline or other sterile diluent. If there has not been a recent administration of theophylline, the patient may receive IV aminophylline at a rate of 80–100 ml/hr through an IV line kept open with 5% DW. Epinephrine 1:1,000 in a dose of 0.2–0.5 ml subcutaneously has been recommended for severe bronchospasm, but is not desirable in the aged patient because of the risk of tachyphylaxis, especially where there is significant acidosis. In addition, most patients have an element of cardiac disease that increases the risk of using epinephrine without the monitoring and support available at the emergency treatment facility. Despite restlessness and agitation, sedation should never be administered. Patients with known advanced COPD, especially those having used IPPB equipment under physician supervision, may benefit from intermittent use of IPPB for 15–20 breaths every 2–5 min for its psychological support and to relieve the work of breathing. During such therapy it is permissible to use high oxygen mixtures as long as the patient is being ventilated and as long as therapy is intermittent. In general, however, this modality is not encouraged because the hazards may outweigh the benefits, and some patients increase distention by persistent use of positive pressure devices. An important key to supportive care of the COPD patient during transportation is the presence and reassurance of treatment personnel because anxiety is a common cause of accelerated deterioration in many patients.

ADULT RESPIRATORY DISTRESS SYNDROME

Definition

The adult respiratory distress syndrome (ARDS) is a form of acute respiratory failure associated with profound hypoxemia. It begins either within minutes to hours or as late as 1 day after a variety of insults to the lung from various but generally recognized sources and leads to stiff, noncompliant, atelectatic lungs altered by diffuse edema and hemorrhage within lung tissue and air spaces. The disease generally spares the airways. There is a marked reduction in lung distendibility with a decrease in the functional residual capacity (FRC), which leaves the lungs with a small mixing chamber for exchange of oxygen and carbon dioxide and makes the work of breathing extremely difficult because of low lung compliance.

Physiology—Mechanisms of Disease

Shortly after an insult to the lung by one of the disorders noted in Table 5–14, there is both interstitial and alveolar edema, as well as hemorrhage into the air spaces produced by a massive ''leak'' of the pulmonary capillaries associated with microscopic accumulation of platelets and white cells. In addition, there is damage to the cells producing surfactant, which permits increased surface tension and promotes alveolar collapse with widespread atelectasis. The lungs become heavy with protein-containing fluid and blood, resulting in the loss of gas exchange compartments, which are no longer ventilated but may continue to receive blood flow. This leads to the common characteristics of profound hypoxemia that is resistant to supplemental treatment with oxygen and hyperventilation with tachypnea and a shallow tidal volume. The syndrome has previously been called ''shock lung'' or ''congestive atelectasis.''

History and Clinical Course

Minutes to hours and occasionally even days after an acute insult, including remote trauma distant from the chest, hypoxemia steadily develops, with progressive reductions in lung volumes and a gradual increase in respiratory rates that often reach levels of 30–40 breaths per min. There is generally a correlation between falling oxygen tensions and increasing respiratory rates. The process always involves both lungs, although it may not be symmetrical. Identifying a

Table 5–14 Disorders Associated with Adult Respiratory Distress Syndrome

Shock from any cause	*Inhalation toxins*
Trauma	*Oxygen toxicity, smoke inhalation*
Fat embolism	Corrosive gases (NO_2, SO_2, NH_3, Cl_2,
Lung contusion	phosgene)
Head injury	*Drug overdose*
Nonthoracic trauma	Heroin
Extensive burns	Methadone
Gram-negative sepsis	Barbiturates
Pneumonia	Propoxyphene
Viral	Aspirin
Bacterial	Paraquat
Aspiration	*Miscellaneous*
Gastric contents	Pancreatitis
Near-drowning (fresh or salt water)	Uremia
Hydrocarbon fluids	Massive blood transfusion
	Cardiopulmonary bypass
	Radiation
	Hanging
	Lung re-expansion

Note: This table includes only the more commonly recognized causes of adult respiratory distress syndrome (ARDS). Up to half of the patients with ARDS have more than one known cause present.

medical or surgical condition known to lead to ARDS and observing the patient developing increasing respiratory distress with tachypnea and profound hypoxemia should immediately lead to a suspicion of ARDS. It should dictate immediate emergency medical attention in a treatment facility capable of management of patients in intensive care units who require complex monitoring of physiologic parameters and advanced ventilatory support. Because patients are usually hyperventilating before the final stages of cardiopulmonary collapse, it is likely they have a respiratory alkalosis improving oxygen saturation and partly masking hypoxemia, thus delaying the onset of clinical cyanosis.[36]

Physical Findings

The older patient is more likely to develop ARDS from gram-negative sepsis, bacterial pneumonia, shock from any cause, or aspiration. Other causes might be more likely in the younger patient. Physical findings include those of the precipitating event, such as shock, evidence of aspiration, or signs of bacterial pneumonia associated with marked tachypnea, cyanosis in most cases, shallow respirations, and dullness over lung fields associated with the presence of rales and rhonchi. Dyspnea is intense, and the patient is anxious and often confused because of severe hypoxemia. Invariably tachycardia, tachypnea, and frequently cyanosis are present. Failure to improve cyanosis with high oxygen mixture administration is additional evidence of the shunt hypoxemia characteristic of the disorder.

Laboratory Findings

Some clinicians have defined ARDS as a diffuse lung disorder in which the PaO_2 is 50 mm Hg or less with the patient on 60% oxygen or more. All patients have severe hypoxemia. Despite the atelectatic, heavy, wet and hemorrhagic lung that characterizes ARDS, patients generally hyperventilate until terminal stages and have hypercapnia, with the $PaCO_2$ ranging from 30–35 mm Hg. Alkalosis may be present initially, but as hypoxemia persists and tissue perfusion is impaired, a metabolic acidosis is likely. In addition, those cases beginning with an episode of shock or significant hypotension may have a metabolic acidosis early in their course. Chest films generally reveal fluffy or diffuse bilateral infiltrates, in some cases producing a "white out" of the lung fields. The pattern may resemble pulmonary edema, and in all cases simple pulmonary edema from primary cardiac disease must be ruled out. When the process has been initiated by hemorrhagic shock, evaluation of hemoglobin and hematocrit may be helpful in determining its cause.

Early Recognition and Acute Therapy

Because ARDS can be rapidly lethal, it is important to suspect its early development by monitoring oxygen tensions to detect progressive hypoxemia with increased tachycardia and respiratory rates. The earlier the patient receives full ventilatory support and correction of atelectasis and hypoxemia, the more likely that he or she will survive. Mortality may reach 70% when ARDS is secondary to gram-negative sepsis, but may be much lower when due to aspiration or bacterial pneumonias. During transport patients should receive the highest oxygen supplementation possible and in most cases should have airways in place with careful monitoring for arrhythmias, including profound bradycardia. Artificial ventilation is not practical during transport because of the marked tachypnea and the high inflation pressures required to improve oxygen transfer in the wet, hemorrhagic, and stiff lungs of ARDS. Alerting the emergency medical facility that the patient may have ARDS could prove life saving by enabling full support services, including monitoring and continuous ventilation, to be available immediately on arrival, thus reducing the risk of cardiac arrest during the critical period between transport and stabilization in the receiving facility. With recognition of the syndrome, the patient should receive supplemental oxygen at 10–12 L/min by nonrebreathing mask to permit the administration of concentrations as high as 90%. When transport facilities and trained personnel are available, endotracheal intubation and delivery of 100% oxygen are ideal because the older patient with ARDS is more likely to be at risk of fatal CNS or cardiac events as a result of profound hypoxemia.

PNEUMONIA IN THE AGED

Incidence

Data from the U.S. Bureau of Statistics indicate that pneumonia and influenza combined continue to be the fifth leading cause of death in the United States, resulting in 58,319 deaths, or 23.6 deaths per 100,000 per year.[28] In the age group 55–74, it is the sixth leading cause of death among women and the seventh cause among men, but in the age group of 75 or over it is the fourth leading cause of death for both men and women. At one time the leading cause of death, acute bacterial pneumonias continue to account for 10% of hospitalizations in the United States. Among the bacterial pneumonias there is an increased recognition of *Legionella* pneumonia, but *Streptococcus pneumoniae* is still responsible for 70% to 80% of bacterial pneumonias in the adult population.

Untreated pneumococcal pneumonia continues to have a 40% mortality rate due to error in diagnosis, delay in treatment, and increased age of the patient. Factors responsible for increased infection, morbidity, and mortality in the aged patient include:

- reduced salivation and increased aspiration of oral pharyngeal organisms
- chronic disease, including diabetes mellitus, alcoholism, and COPD
- impairment of normal defenses in the mucous membranes of the upper and lower respiratory tract, including reduced immune globulins and the reduced integrity of the mucociliary clearance mechanism
- abnormal cough reflex
- metabolic acidosis or hypoxemia
- altered mental status, especially with neurologic disease that increases the frequency of aspiration
- instrumentation of the respiratory tract
- residence in chronic care facilities where altered bacterial colonization exists.

The older alcoholic man poses a special problem, especially if pneumonia is associated with COPD, because gram-negative bacterial pneumonias (including *Klebsiella*) are common and carry a high morbidity, a high complication rate, and a very high mortality. Added to these risks is the more subtle and frequently undetected onset of bacterial pneumonia that delays diagnosis and treatment and also predisposes the patient to increased morbidity and mortality.

Viral Pneumonias

Viral or mycoplasma pneumonias are far more common in young patients and are less likely to be diagnosed in the elderly. The exception is the pneumonia caused by influenza virus that occurs during epidemics and may be complicated by secondary staphylococcal infection or may result in combined infection with influenza virus and *Staphylococcus aureus* leading to a fulminant course and very high mortality. The high mortality in older patients during past influenza virus epidemics has partly been secondary to the associated bacterial superinfection.

Because the typical viral pneumonia has a gradual onset, frequently with signs and symptoms of a classical upper respiratory infection, including rhinorrhea, sore throat, low-grade temperature, malaise, and scant sputum, such infections tend to be underdiagnosed. In the absence of the lobar consolidation typical of a bacterial pneumonia and with tachypnea and tachycardia less common, patients generally receive only symptomatic care and do not present for emergency management or hospitalization. It is more likely that the patient will come to the attention of the EMT and medical care team when a bacterial superinfection occurs with more serious systemic signs and symptoms.

Pneumonias caused by influenza viruses may have a fulminant course, with rapid progression of dyspnea, hyperventilation, serious hypoxemia, and temperatures of 38–40°C. Often, older patients with COPD or bronchospasm have tachycardia and respiratory failure. They appear to be flushed and dehydrated with tachypnea, tachycardia, and mental changes caused by toxic reactions. There may be few physical findings and no rales or evidence of consolidation, partly because of the diffuse nature of the infection and partly because of the dehydration common to older patients with acute infection. The occurrence during epidemics of influenza virus in the late winter months suggests the diagnosis, and in the presence of respiratory distress at an advanced stage, hospitalization for diagnosis and treatment is indicated. Many of these patients require respiratory support and a careful search for superinfection by either *Staphylococcus aureus* or gram-negative organisms. Because the primary cause of death is respiratory failure or fatal arrhythmia associated with profound hypoxemia, all patients should be transported in the most comfortable position and be given supplemental oxygen at 3–4 L/min by nasal cannula or, preferably, a relatively safe 30% oxygen mixture given by face mask. To assist in evaluating the risk of superinfection, any antibiotics or other medications the patient is receiving should be noted or taken to hospital with the patient.[37-39]

Bacterial Pneumonia

Community-acquired bacterial pneumonia is usually due to *Streptococcus pneumoniae,* but in older patients, especially those with a background of COPD and/or alcoholism, infection by gram-negative organisms, including *Klebsiella,* must be considered. In differentiating the bacterial pneumonia from a viral pneumonia, the characteristics shown in Table 5–15 have been traditionally used.

Overall mortality in bacteremic pneumococcal pneumonia is 20%, but over age 50 it is 50%, largely due to untreated hypoxemia. The most common cause is *Streptococcus pneumoniae,* which is a normal inhabitant of the nose and throat.

Table 5–15 Characteristics of Community-Acquired Pneumonias in the Elderly

Symptoms or Signs	Bacterial	Viral
Onset of illness	Abrupt	Gradual
Chills	Common at onset	Uncommon
Pleurisy	Common	Uncommon
Temperature	High (>39.5°C)	Low grade (<39.5°C)
Tachypnea (>25 bpm)	Common	Rare
Sputum	Purulent, rusty	Scant, mucoid
Tachycardia (>120 bpm)	Common	Rare
Distribution	Lobar, segmental	Patchy, diffuse
Leukocytosis, left shift	Common	Uncommon
Pleural effusion	Common	Rare

The frequency of carriers is 4.5% in all seasons, but the majority of infections occur in the winter months. Increased risk factors are advanced stage alcoholism, COPD, congestive heart failure, and diabetes mellitus. Increased morbidity is associated with sickle cell disease, lung cancer, other malignancies, and hypogammaglobulinemia. Increased mortality is associated with age over 60, multilobe involvement, leukopenia with immature neutrophils, delay in diagnosis and treatment, the presence of bacteremia, and alcoholism. In addition, patients who have had splenectomies or who are functionally asplenic have a high incidence of pneumococcal sepsis with bacteremia and lethal vascular complications. Bacteremia increases the mortality by a factor of 6, and the mortality in patients without bacteremia over age 50 increases to more than 10% with a 5% to 10% further increase for each subsequent decade. In all age groups the incidence is higher in men, with an overall male/female ratio of 3:1.[40–42]

Klebsiella pneumoniae infection represents up to 5% of bacterial pneumonias and is more common in the older patient (average age 52); the male/female ratio is 7–9:1. It is endemic throughout the year with an increased frequency in summer months. Up to 25% of normal adults are oropharyngeal carriers, and this incidence increases sharply with pre-existing chronic obstructive lung disease. The incidence is increased in the chronically debilitated patient, especially those with alcoholism, diabetes mellitus, chronic renal disease, chronic cardiac disease, COPD, and neoplasms. The likely mechanism of infection is aspiration of oropharyngeal secretions, so the frequency is increased in the presence of alcoholism and with neuropathy or altered mental status. As with the pneumococcal pneumonia, the onset is abrupt, and there are substantial toxic reactions with prostration.

The typical patient is an aged man with a history of alcoholism and COPD. The complication rate is high because *Klebsiella* produces a necrotizing pneumonia with a tendency for abscess, empyema, and more serious morbidity. The mortality rate is still 20% to 54% despite antibiotic treatment.

Hospital or Institution-Acquired Pneumonias

The most common institution-acquired pneumonias are due to gram-negative organisms. Enteric gram-negative bacilli and *Pseudomonas aeruginosa* represent the most common infecting organism. The mechanism of infection is usually endogenous aspiration of oropharyngeal flora; particles of 10 micra diameter readily reach the terminal bronchi, causing plugging and setting up local infection in the predisposed host. The most common organisms are *Escherichia coli, Pseudomonas aeruginosa, Klebsiella pneumoniae, Enterobacter* organisms, and *Haemophilus influenzae,* also a cause of community-acquired pneumonia.

Predisposing factors are altered consciousness as in alcoholism (advanced stage), following a CVA, seizures, drug overdose or sedation, smoke inhalation, esophageal disease, liver disease, and COPD. There is an increased carrier state in the patients who have chronic illness or who are institutionalized. The rate in persons over age 60 reaches 9% in populations residing in chronic care facilities; rates are 60% in patients receiving chronic treatment in acute hospital wards. The leading organism in patients with COPD is *Pseudomonas aeruginosa,* but this varies with the medical institution and the characteristic resident bacterial flora. Infections have been ascribed to poor handling of urinary incontinence and drainage equipment or to contamination of respiratory therapy equipment with a frequency inversely related to the quality of medical care.[43–46]

With an increased recognition of *Legionella* infections occurring as a community-acquired pneumonia in older men, especially heavy smokers with COPD and an alcohol abuse history, this organism may be found in both community and hospital settings.

Pathophysiology

The predominant disorder in the older patient with bacterial pneumonia is a profound hypoxemia due to consolidated lung with a reflex tachypnea generally associated with hypocapnia. Hypoxemia is the major cause of fatal arrhythmias or sudden death and is a mechanism for associated congestive heart failure. Bronchospasm is generally not a significant factor in bacterial pneumonia although there may be some wheezing in patients with very hyperactive airways. Older patients usually are quite dehydrated and may be disoriented and restless from both toxic reactions and hypoxemia. The presence of airway secretions and consolidation produces respiratory muscle fatigue so that respiratory failure is a risk.

Physical Findings

The typical patient is febrile, appears severely ill, and is dyspneic with tachypnea and evidence of hypoxemia, including cyanosis, restlessness, and tachycardia. There may be expectoration of purulent sputum, but debilitated and severely ill older patients may be sufficiently dehydrated so that sputum is not being mobilized. When present it tends to be purulent and rusty. The presence of bright red blood is more suggestive of pulmonary embolism. Patients with a leukopenia may not have purulent sputum initially. There is evidence of pleuritic pain in 40% to 70% of patients, with splinting. Upper quadrant abdominal pain is common with the onset of bacterial pneumonia and often confuses early diagnosis. With lobar pneumonia there is local consolidation, usually with findings in the posterior lung field consisting of local dullness to percussion, bronchial breath sounds, and coarse, crackling inspiratory rales that are associated occasionally with rhonchi and a local friction rub. Delirium may be due to cerebral vascular disease and hypoxemia, but meningitis must be ruled out. Shock due to vascular collapse is rare. Improvement in the patient's color should be anticipated with the immediate use of supplemental oxygen, but there should be no reduction in tachypnea or respiratory distress because they are based on local reflexes originating from the consolidated lung.

Laboratory Findings

A sputum smear should reveal gram-positive or gram-negative organisms with a predominant organism associated with many leukocytes. The WBC count generally peaks at 15,000–40,000/ml on the third day of illness, and there is usually an acute shift with an increased number of band forms. The presence of leukopenia, especially with immature neutrophils, suggests a fulminant course, bacteremia, and a poor prognosis. Blood cultures are positive in only 30% of cases, and there is a significant discrepancy between smear and culture results in identification of the organism. For example, almost one-half of patients with a gram stain positive for *Streptococcus pneumoniae* have a negative sputum culture. In contrast, up to 25% of patients with pneumonia due to *Haemophilus influenzae* who have a negative smear ultimately have a positive sputum culture. Approximately 60% of culture-positive sputum specimens can be properly identified by prior gram stain. Some authorities prefer using tracheal aspiration to obtain samples for culture, but this is usually not necessary. The chest film should reveal a consolidation that is lobar and segmental or multilobed. In older patients with COPD, especially with advanced pulmonary emphysema and dehydration, there may be neither pulmonary infiltrate by initial chest film nor rales or signs of consolidation, despite the overwhelmingly suggestive picture of rusty sputum, high fever, and onset with chills. With hydration of the patient it is common for the film to be more revealing, with the appearance of consolidation and the subsequent development of local findings, including rales.

Differential Diagnosis

Acute bacterial pneumonia must be differentiated from pulmonary embolism, acute bronchitis, or congestive heart failure in the usual clinical setting involving the older patient. Pulmonary embolism does not begin with a shaking chill, the sputum is not purulent, and bright red blood is noted in contrast to the rusty sputum of a bacterial pneumonia. In addition, there is often evidence of thrombophlebitis—in 30% of cases—or other predisposing disorders, including recent surgery, prolonged immobilization, or underlying malignancy.

The hypoxemia of pulmonary embolism is more profound and responds poorly to supplemental oxygen compared with that of the bacterial pneumonia. In pulmonary embolism, fever is low grade, if present. Acute bacterial bronchitis may be associated with sudden onset and fever with purulent sputum, but a shaking chill, pleuritic pain, and rusty sputum are rare. Furthermore, there are no signs of consolidation although rales may be heard over lung fields in acute bacterial bronchitis. Congestive heart failure associated with left ventricular failure produces dyspnea, cough, hypoxemia, and respiratory distress with both tachycardia and tachypnea, but chill, fever, rusty sputum, and pleuritic pain do not occur. The presence of blood streaking in the sputum and copious thin, non-purulent secretions suggest cardiac failure, especially in the presence of tachycardia, an S_3 gallop over the left ventricle, and either a known history of arteriosclerotic heart disease or previous myocardial infarction.

Complications of Pneumonia

The complications of bacterial pneumonia are based on the extent of infection, the nature of the infecting organism, and the status of the underlying host. The ultimate complication is early death, which still occurs despite appropriate antibiotic treatment, although it is usually due to known predisposing factors. Fever predisposes the older patient to severe dehydration, hypotension, and oliguria. Hyperpyrexia may produce disorientation and lack of cooperation. Pleuritic pain and inadequate cough predispose the patient to retained secretions with increasing infection and progressive abnormality of ventilation/perfusion matching, resulting in profound hypoxemia and death, at times due to malignant arrhythmias. Pre-existing COPD, a poor WBC response to infection, a prior history of alcoholism, underlying malignancy, and multilobed involvement are all factors that increase mortality and complication rates. The author is convinced that late diagnosis and treatment are major causes of complications and poor resolution of bacterial pneumonia in the older patient. In delayed resolution of pneumonia, the associated empyema, bronchopleural fistula, multiple lung abscesses, meningitis, pericarditis, or metastatic brain abscess are largely based on the quality of the host defenses, late diagnosis and treatment, and the nature of the underlying organism.

The greatest complication rates occur in pneumonia due to such organisms as *Staphylococcus aureus* or the gram-negative bacteria that tend to produce necrotizing pneumonias that destroy lung tissue.

Treatment

After initial evaluation, patients should receive supplemental oxygen in every case because hypoxemia is the major cause of early death. Oxygen should be administered either by face mask with 30% to 40% oxygen or, when this is not tolerated, by nasal cannula at 3 L/min. Transportation should take place in the most comfortable position for the patient, which is in the sitting position for the majority. Pleuritic pain should not be treated until the patient has arrived in the treatment facility, and the diagnosis is established. Efforts should be made to observe expectorated secretions. Supplemental oxygen may improve the patient's mental status and restlessness, but should not be expected to alter the tachypnea because it is not produced by hypoxemia. Monitoring of vital signs is indicated in older patients with obviously severe illness. Patients who deteriorate during transport with progressive cyanosis or hypotension should receive ventilatory support with an oropharyngeal airway and bag-and-mask ventilation using the highest achievable oxygen concentration. Up to 80% oxygen can be administered when there is high oxygen flow and a reservoir bag system is used. Periodic suctioning may be required, but it reduces oxygen tension sufficiently so that it should not be used when lung expansion appears adequate and there is not undue resistance to ventilation with bag and mask.

Evaluation and treatment in the receiving emergency hospital are facilitated by the history provided on arrival. Abdominal pain may initially confuse the diagnosis, but with a history of shaking chills, high fever, and purulent sputum, the diagnosis should not present a problem. Evaluation of the WBC and sputum smear by gram stain usually provides an indication of the likely organism. Hydration can be carried out with IV fluids, according to the patient's cardiovascular status, age, and level of dehydration. There tends to be increasing consolidation on chest films and increased presence of rales and physical findings as the patient undergoes hydration over the first few hours of medical treatment. The fact that physical findings change with time should not cause alarm because the diagnosis is always more obscure on initial evaluation than after multiple forms of treatment and the performance of tests. Treating personnel must remember that the older anemic patient may not manifest cyanosis readily, and therefore oxygen should not be withheld until the appearance of cyanosis.

PNEUMOTHORAX IN THE ELDERLY

Incidence and Classification

Pneumothorax is defined as an escape of air into the pleural space secondary to trauma or rupture of a subpleural bleb, with the leak of air causing lung collapse. Pneumothorax is ordinarily classified as spontaneous (not associated with trauma or disease) or as a simple pneumothorax, which may be associated with a disease. Pneumothorax associated with trauma can be viewed as a separate problem, although common principles apply to its treatment. Two forms of special interest to all emergency treatment personnel are an open pneumothorax, known also as sucking chest wound, and the extremely dangerous tension pneumothorax that is associated with increasing lung collapse and results in cardiovascular collapse and death if not identified and treated.

The majority of patients with pneumothorax are men, with a ratio of men to women of 2:5–3:1; men outnumber women increasingly with advancing age.[47] In the age group 60–89, the ratio is 6:1. Weeden and Smith, who studied 233 patients, found that the mean age was 41, with a range extending to age 87. The majority occurred on the right side (60%), with 12% of patients having bilateral episodes. Additionally, 39% had more than one pneumothorax. The highest incidence was in the third decade, but there was a secondary peak in the sixth decade. Only 25% of patients were over age 60, and the vast majority of these were men. In this group, 70% had associated COPD. There were 78 patients with COPD, including 6 with pulmonary fibrosis and 8 with bronchial asthma, suggesting that the vast majority of older patients with spontaneous pneumothorax had underlying obstructive airway disease and were males.

Spontaneous Pneumothorax

Spontaneous pneumothorax is defined as a pneumothorax occurring without trauma or penetrating chest wound, although subpleural blebs or bullae may be present. The characteristic onset is sudden, occurring at rest without special preceding physical activity. However, the author has seen many examples of spontaneous pneumothorax after activity with elevation of the arms or stretching, producing an increased incidence during showering, dressing, or on awakening from sleep. Characteristic findings are sudden and sharp chest pain confined to one hemithorax and associated with shortness of breath. The pain is frequently diffuse and overlying the entire hemithorax, rather than localized. Pain is often anterior, but may radiate to the neck, back, or even the upper abdomen. The radiation of pain toward the sternum suggests an associated pneumomediastinum. Severity of pain has no relationship to the extent of collapse. Dyspnea occurs generally in relation to the proportion of lung collapse and the state of the underlying lungs, especially the contralateral lung. If the air leak is small and the pleural defect seals rapidly, dyspnea may be brief and may slowly clear in the absence of treatment. In older men with advanced COPD, larger pleural tears are likely, and the pneumothorax is ordinarily more extensive and persistent, requiring aggressive medical management for relief of symptoms.

Physical findings are those of a dyspneic patient with evidence of splinting due to pain. The diseased hemithorax may have a slight increase in volume that is subtle and is associated with marked reduction of breath sounds and an increase in resonance compared with the opposite side. Often present are tachycardia and invariably, hypoxemia, which often produces an ashen appearance and cyanosis initially, with gradual improvement within minutes of the acute event. When the episode represents a recurrence, patients frequently recognize the onset of symptoms and relate it to a previous episode of pneumothorax. Diagnosis is not difficult when there is sudden onset of unilateral chest pain and dyspnea associated with ipsilateral hyperresonance, diminished breath sounds, and especially when there is a history of a previous similar event.

Treatment consists of transportation to a treatment facility to confirm the diagnosis, where full inspiratory and expiratory chest films reveal the pneumothorax; the expiratory film often delineates the outer edge of the lung more clearly. The chest film also reveals the ipsilateral increased hemithorax volume and often a small fluid level at the costophrenic angle. It may also suggest underlying COPD. Evaluation at a medical facility is advised because the patient may have a more extensive pneumothorax than realized, and it can be complicated hours to days later by a tension pneumothorax. In addition, a thoracotomy tube is often required for re-expansion of the lung in the presence of extensive COPD, especially when there is a history of cough and sputum production and the risk of atelectasis. Furthermore, re-expansion is often effective in correcting significant hypoxemia.[47]

Transportation can be carried out in an orderly fashion, generally with the patient in a sitting or semirecumbent position and always with the use of supplemental oxygen, the most useful and safe concentration being 25% to 30% by nasal cannula or mask.

Simple Pneumothorax

A simple pneumothorax is defined as one in which there is not a progressive air leak, a sucking chest wound, or a tension pneumothorax. However, it may represent a pneumothorax that is spontaneous or one associated with some form of pulmonary disease that predisposes the person to the pneumothorax. The simple pneumothorax is spontaneous in onset in most instances.

Treatment is based on the level of dyspnea and associated cardiopulmonary disease, as well as the extent of collapse. With minimal dyspnea, no underlying COPD, and a collapse rate estimated at 25% or less, bedrest and conservative management are usually adequate. With moderate to severe dyspnea, a high percentage of collapse, and especially in the presence of COPD or cardiac disease, immediate re-expansion with a thoracotomy tube is advisable to prevent complications and accelerate resolution.

Traumatic Pneumothorax

The traumatic pneumothorax may be limited, may result in an open sucking chest wound as a result of chest wall trauma, or may lead to a tension pneumothorax. Unlike a simple pneumothorax, it is more likely to be associated with other abnormalities in the chest wall or lung, such as rib fractures, flail chest, lung contusion, or lacerations of lung or major airways. In this form, there is more likely to be an associated subcutaneous emphysema and evidence of chest wall injury. In addition, the levels of hypoxemia and respiratory distress are likely to be higher, and there is a greater need for careful monitoring and the use of supplemental oxygen.

A traumatic pneumothorax is more likely to represent a hemopneumothorax. Bleeding may be secondary to trauma to chest wall vessels or bleeding from within thoracic structures, including sites of lung laceration. The accumulation of blood in the pleural space impairs lung expansion and leads to atelectasis, also impairing ventilation/perfusion matching with resultant hypoxemia. Bleeding is generally not massive, but when it is, it may impair both venous return and respirations and so compromise both the respiratory and the circulatory system. The signs of a hemopneumothorax are respiratory distress with tachypnea, dullness to percussion over the lower thorax on the injured side due to the accumulated fluid, marked reduction or absence of breath sounds, and occasionally deviation of the trachea away from the affected side.

Management of the patient involves an awareness of the possibility of extensive blood loss in the thorax and monitoring for signs of hemorrhagic shock. Patients require control of any visible bleeding, the placement of an IV line or infusion, administration of oxygen by mask or cannula at levels of 30% to 40%, and immediate transportation to a treatment facility. The patient must be observed for signs of exsanguination and impending shock, such as restlessness, cool clammy extremities, a rapid thready pulse, hypotension, and complaints of severe thirst similar to that frequently observed during active gastrointestinal bleeding. The active treatment of shock from internal bleeding can be initiated during transport based on the level of available facilities and especially on the expertise of the EMT and support teams.[48]

Open Pneumothorax

The open pneumothorax or sucking chest wound represents a traumatic defect in the chest wall that permits air leak into the pleural space. Air is drawn into the pleural space during inspiration and frequently escapes during expiration (Figure 5–15). Lung collapse is generally extensive, and gas exchange is poor on the affected side with an atelectatic lung and significant hypoxemia. Because the movement of air into and out of the pleural space impairs effective ventilation on the affected side, one approach to treatment is to seal the chest wall defect with a large gauze, then commonly overlaying plastic or aluminum foil and applying the bandage sealed on three sides (thereby allowing a modified flap-valve) at the end of expiration to reduce the volume in the pleural space to its absolute minimum. The patient can then be placed on the injured side to permit maximum ventilation of the unaffected lung. Patients generally require supplemental oxygen at substantial levels, such as 30% to 40% by face mask. Positive pressure ventilation should be avoided if at all possible to prevent increasing the collapse should there be a defect in the pleural surface of the lung (visceral pleura). Patients with an open pneumothorax are at risk of developing a tension pneumothorax and must be observed extremely carefully during transportation. Any progressive deterioration in respiratory status or evidence of vascular collapse that may result from a

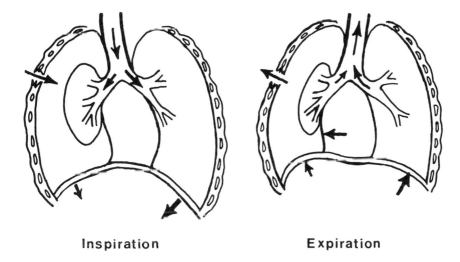

Inspiration   Expiration

Figure 5–15 Open pneumothorax. Note that in the open pneumothorax, air enters the abnormal side on inspiration through both internal airways and the external chest wall defect, limiting ventilation on the injured side. On expiration, air escapes through the chest wall on the diseased side, and the deflation of the normal lung causes a shift of the mediastinum and, at times, the trachea toward the diseased side.

developing tension pneumothorax and obstruction of venous return should be treated by removing the occlusive chest bandage.

Tension Pneumothorax

A tension pneumothorax is a pneumothorax in which the air in the pleural space is under increased pressure or tension. This causes a shift of the mediastinum away from the affected side that induces venous collapse, thus occluding venous return and resulting in cardiovascular collapse with shock. A tension pneumothorax may develop within minutes to hours and occasionally days after a pneumothorax that is either open or closed as in a simple pneumothorax, but where there is a pleural defect that has not sealed. This area may then operate as a ball-valve, allowing one-way movement of air into the pleural space, but prohibiting egress during exhalation. The gradual increased entry of air on the affected side increases the pressure and causes complete collapse of the affected lung with a shift of the mediastinum to the opposite side. The increase in pressure on the affected side may reach a level that occludes vena caval flow, causing a drop in cardiac output and shock (Figure 5–16).

Patients may manifest symptoms of a simple pneumothorax followed by the gradual or rapid development of increasing respiratory distress, with respirations becoming increasingly shallow and rapid. There is increasing hypoxemia, rest-

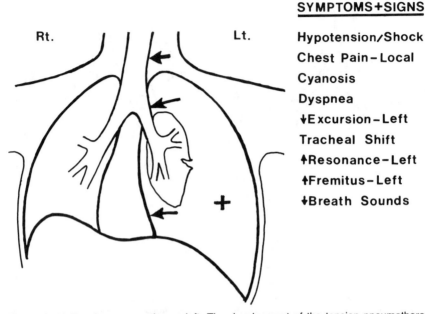

SYMPTOMS+SIGNS

Rt.   Lt.

Hypotension/Shock
Chest Pain-Local
Cyanosis
Dyspnea
✦Excursion-Left
Tracheal Shift
✦Resonance-Left
✦Fremitus-Left
✦Breath Sounds

Figure 5–16 Tension pneumothorax–left. The development of the tension pneumothorax tends to cause an increased distention of the diseased side with a shift of cardiac and mediastinal structures to the opposite side, often causing a tracheal shift that can be identified by inspection. The characteristic symptoms and signs are illustrated.

lessness, and the development of cyanosis. There may be distention of jugular veins, and the trachea may be deviated away from the affected side by the increased intrathoracic pressure. Gradually there is a fall in blood pressure and the development of a rapid, thready pulse, followed by shock. The affected hemithorax reveals absent breath sounds and a marked increase in resonance. Occasionally there is evidence of subcutaneous emphysema. Some observers have described a high-pitched voice in the patient with increasing tension pneumothorax.

Treatment consists of standard treatment for a pneumothorax, including the use of supplemental oxygen to alleviate dyspnea and cyanosis and monitoring for early detection of the development of a tension pneumothorax. If signs and symptoms suggest a developing tension pneumothorax with impaired venous return, it is necessary to decompress the affected side immediately. When a syringe and needle are used, it is not rare for the rush of air under pressure to force the syringe plunger out of the barrel under extreme force, often propelling it many feet. There is a dramatic change in color and relief of vascular collapse. Ordinarily the needle is instantly removed to await placement of a thoracotomy tube or catheter at the receiving facility. The author has employed an IV line and needle with the IV tubing under water at the time of needle insertion, permitting rapid egress of air through the IV line and water and providing an automatic underwater seal. This procedure is not recommended for general use, but can be lifesaving. When a tension pneumothorax is relieved there is some risk of redevelopment, but this is rare and delayed in onset. By that time it is likely that the patient will have reached a treating facility, be more completely evaluated, and have received standard management with thoracotomy tubes, supplemental oxygen, and appropriate monitoring.

Emergency Room Evaluation and Treatment

When the pneumothorax is small and the diagnosis is not certain, the patient should have blood drawn for analysis and immediate chest films done (both full inspiration and full expiration) to demarcate better the outer rim of lung tissue. If there is chest trauma, films may reveal rib fractures, lung contusions, or extensive effusion, which may represent a hemothorax. Evacuation of the hemothorax permits better lung expansion and a better estimate of blood loss, thereby accelerating the healing process and reducing the risk of chronic pleural scar. In the older patient with a history of smoking, the film may also reveal underlying bullae or generalized COPD that requires a more aggressive approach to management, including earlier use of a thoracotomy tube and a more rapid re-expansion of the lung to ensure adequate cough and control of secretions. Doing so prevents the morbidity of atelectasis, respiratory failure, progressive bronchospasm, and pneumonia. In addition, hypoxemia is more rapidly corrected, which may be important in the elderly patient with coronary artery disease or cerebrovascular disease. Patients with significant pulmonary emphysema tend to have large pleural tears that do not seal spontaneously. They generally do better with aggressive re-expansion of the lung via the use of a thoracotomy tube and either underwater seal or negative pressure.[49] IPPB should not be used for the delivery of bronchodilator drugs unless a thoracotomy tube is in place and even then is generally restricted to patients with the most advanced disease in whom distribution of bronchodilators by aerosol is extremely poor. The safest course is to use nebulized aerosol bronchodilators and parenteral bronchodilators without resorting to IPPB. Patients with underlying COPD should be carefully observed for subsequent collapse of the opposite lung, which occasionally occurs when a pneumothorax is associated with chest trauma.

PULMONARY THROMBOEMBOLISM/INFARCTION

Pulmonary thromboembolism is considered a leading cause of death in hospitalized patients, which is especially true when one looks at the chronically ill elderly patient. Embolization to the pulmonary circulation from a venous thrombus site is the usual mechanism, and current data suggest that 80% to 90%

originate from deep leg veins. Because only 25% to 30% of patients have evidence of thrombophlebitis at the time of pulmonary embolism, this suggestive finding is not always present when a patient has a pulmonary emergency secondary to embolism.[50,51] Some series have documented multiple pulmonary embolism in up to 64% of lungs at postmortem.[52]

The incidence is several times higher in patients with pre-existing heart disease, particularly in the presence of atrial fibrillation or congestive heart failure, which are both recognized to be predisposing factors and both common in the older patient. Pulmonary embolism superimposed on pre-existing cardiopulmonary disease clearly increases both morbidity and mortality. Furthermore, in one series only 11.5% of patients with pulmonary embolism were correctly diagnosed before death.[53] In addition, the frequency of thrombophlebitis predisposing to pulmonary embolism is variable, being as high as 50% to 60% for orthopedic procedures and the postthoracotomy state and varying from 25% to 30% in patients undergoing urologic procedures, such as prostatectomy, or in general surgical patients over the age of 40.

Many studies have determined that 50,000 deaths or more per year in the United States can be ascribed to pulmonary embolism and that in three times this number pulmonary embolism is a contributing cause for death. It is estimated that 500,000–600,000 individuals experience pulmonary embolism annually in the United States, with less than 10% of these being fatal. Fatality increases with age, increasing the necessity of early diagnosis and treatment.

Identifying the Predisposed Patient

Table 5–16 lists some medical and surgical conditions that predispose the patient to thrombophlebitis and pulmonary embolism. Studies have demonstrated that pulmonary embolism is three to four times more frequent in patients with heart disease and that this is the most common predisposing factor. Additional predisposing factors are atrial fibrillation and congestive heart failure,[50] which presumably impair circulation and predispose to clot formation. The risk of pulmonary embolism is increased several hundred times by trauma to the leg, particularly when deep vein thrombosis occurs. Hip and pelvic fractures are especially important predisposing events in the elderly. Underlying cancer of the lung, gastrointestinal tract, or genitourinary tract significantly increase thromboembolism. Embolism associated with malignancies has a tendency to recur and to be resistant to treatment.

Medical or surgical conditions predisposing the patient to increased clotting activity, such as surgical procedures or acute stress followed by prolonged bedrest with poor venous blood flow, represent significant predisposing states for pulmonary embolism. In addition, patients with polycythemia vera have an increased tendency to coagulation and an increased incidence of pulmonary embolism. The famous pathologist, Virchow, correctly outlined the three predisposing causes for pulmonary embolism by describing the three factors of (1) stasis of venous blood,

Table 5–16 Conditions Predisposing to Pulmonary Embolism

- Age over 60
- Congestive heart failure, atrial fibrillation
- Acute trauma
- Hip and pelvic fractures
- Major surgery—abdominal, thoracic
- Chronic obstructive pulmonary disease
- Polycythemia, primary or secondary
- Prolonged bedrest
- Carcinoma—lung, bowel, gastrointestinal tract, etc.
- Obesity, moderate to marked

Note: The conditions that predispose to pulmonary embolism are not listed in the order of either frequency or significance as predisposing factors. However, advanced age, circulatory abnormalities, and major trauma or surgery remain among the most prominent factors.

(2) damage to the vascular lining, and (3) increased blood clotting tendency.[54] The conditions in which pulmonary embolism is common are those where one or more of these factors are present.

Pathophysiology

The physiologic changes in acute pulmonary embolism are very dynamic, with symptoms often beginning very quickly and changing at first minute by minute, then hour by hour, and eventually showing a gradual improvement over days and weeks. Therefore, the physical findings and complaints are partly based on how soon after onset of pulmonary embolism the patient is seen. When the embolized clot lodges in the lung, it may occlude more than 50% of the pulmonary circulation. In the presence of underlying cardiopulmonary disease it may result in sudden death by so obstructing pulmonary blood flow that there is inadequate venous return and cardiac output from the left ventricle. The patient collapses with rapid onset of shock and death. Patients with occlusion of 25% to 50% of the pulmonary vascular bed have an acute onset of symptoms and evidence of vascular compromise, including shock and hypotension that respond poorly to vasopressor therapy. With the fragmentation of clots and movement of the clot to smaller branches of the pulmonary artery, there may be sufficient improvement in circulation to allow the patient to survive with optimum therapy, although with some risk to residual lung damage after recovery.

It is likely the majority of episodes of pulmonary embolism produce transient and minor symptoms and are in fact never diagnosed or treated. Medical personnel must assume that they see only a small percentage of episodes, those producing sufficiently acute symptoms to be identified and treated.

When the clot affects the pulmonary circulation there is a massive release of mediators that produces widespread constriction of airways, including such small airways as bronchioles and alveolar ducts. There may be virtually no air movement for the first minute or two and then a gradual increase in ventilation as the constriction slowly releases; this leads to the finding of wheeze shortly after the acute event, although it commonly has cleared prior to evaluation by trained personnel. When the patient is first evaluated, the characteristic findings are those of hyperpnea and tachypnea with hypocapnia. Also present are hyperventilation and profound hypoxemia, which are characteristically resistant to oxygen supplementation, unlike pulmonary edema, pneumonia, or other conditions with a similar appearance. Hypoxemia is undoubtedly the result of widespread narrowing of the airway in response to mediators that are released within the lungs so that supplemental oxygen does not necessarily reach areas being perfused with blood. Therefore, these patients characteristically manifest the shunt phenomenon.[50]

Because older patients are more predisposed to embolism and because they are more likely to have underlying cardiopulmonary disease, they are especially susceptible to profound hypoxemia. Therefore the correction of hypoxemia is critical if the patient is to reach a medical facility for definitive diagnosis and treatment. Table 5–17 shows the usual laboratory findings relevant to lung function after acute pulmonary embolism.

History and Differential Diagnosis

Patients usually have a history of chronic disease, trauma, major surgery, or prolonged immobilization including simple bedrest. The majority of older patients have underlying cardiopulmonary disease. The onset of symptoms is often acute, but may be gradual with an increase in symptoms over a period of minutes to

Table 5–17 Lung Function Alterations with Pulmonary Embolism

Elements	Changes
Respiratory rate	Increased
Forced vital capacity	Decreased
Expiratory flow rate	Decreased
Compliance	Decreased
Arterial PO_2	Decreased
Arterial PCO_2	Decreased
Alveolar-arterial CO_2 difference	Increased
Arterial pH	Increased
Dead space	Increased

hours. Table 5–18 shows the frequency of signs and symptoms common to pulmonary embolism.

The first question that should be asked of the patient with a suggestive history and onset is whether the symptoms are familiar. Recurrent pulmonary embolism is common, and patients often identify the stages and symptoms as being identical to a previous episode.

Physical Findings

The physical findings are dynamic, often sudden in onset, and change continuously from minute to minute or hour to hour during early observation. With massive embolism there are shock or serious hypotension and both peripheral and central cyanosis from poor perfusion of tissues and intrapulmonary shunting. Commonly tachycardia and evidence of acute respiratory distress associated with signs of pulmonary hypertension and right ventricular overload are present. Some of the more common findings on examination are transient and may be seen only in

Table 5–18 Symptoms and Signs in Acute Pulmonary Embolism

Symptom	Frequency (%)
Dyspnea	75–95
Chest pain—nonpleuritic	50–60
Pleuritic pain	70–75
Cough	50–60
Fever	40–50
Apprehension—anxiety	55–65
Thrombophlebitis symptoms	25–35
Sweats	25–30
Palpitations	25–35
Hemoptysis	30–40
Syncope	10–15
Back pain	5–10
Sign	
Tachycardia (pulse >100 bpm)	40–50
Tachypnea	80–95
Hypotension, shock	5–10
Fever	35–50
Sweats	25–45
Prominent or split P_2	45–60
Phlebitis	20–45
S_3 or S_4 gallop	20–45
Cyanosis	10–30
Local Physical Findings	
Rales	50–60
Pleural friction rub	15–50

early stages (Table 5–18). In a major embolism, the signs of pulmonary hypotension and right ventricular overload may be quite persistent. In addition, when embolism leads to infarction, which occurs in less than 5% of patients, there are local findings associated with infarction, eg, evidence of pleural fluid, consolidation, and local rales generally confined to the lower lung field and usually heard best in the posterior lung fields.

Up to 50% of patients complain of cough that is generally nonproductive, but is in a small number associated with hemoptysis. The absence of purulent sputum with acute onset rules out a bacterial pneumonia, which would be the other most common clinical entity presenting with these findings in the older patient. In general, the more significant the embolism and the underlying cardiopulmonary disease, the more abnormal the physical findings and the larger number that the observer will find on the initial examination. The absence of certain "classical" findings should therefore not rule out the diagnosis. The absence of phlebitis, pleuritic chest pain, and hemoptysis has often led to pulmonary embolism being erroneously excluded from the diagnosis. Because further embolization may lead to sudden death, this is a serious error.

Laboratory Findings—Relationship to Treatment

The most important finding is that of profound hypoxemia with a poor response to treatment with supplemental oxygen. In the urokinase pulmonary embolism trial, 89.5% of patients had a PaO_2 below 80 mm Hg despite hyperventilation in a majority of patients studied, 42% had a PO_2 below 60 mm Hg, and 16% had a PO_2 below 50 mm Hg.[55] These levels of hypoxemia, combined with the often poor response to treatment with supplemental oxygen in an older patient with underlying cardiopulmonary disease, may represent a mechanism for a lethal arrhythmia and sudden death.

The majority of patients have hyperventilation with hypocapnia and alkalosis, though hypoxemia and hypotension may rapidly produce a progressive metabolic acidosis requiring detection and treatment. Frequently correction of profound hypoxemia is sufficient to reverse this trend.

The chest film is often not helpful, except in demonstrating the absence of a bacterial pneumonia. The chest film is most useful in ruling out other diagnoses. The most common findings are those of an elevated diaphragm and a plate-like atelectasis at the base seen in 20% to 25% of patients. Only 20% to 25% have a pleural effusion. There may be evidence of enlarged main pulmonary arteries with lung fields that show a reduction in perfusion. Only 5% to 10% of patients show definite evidence of right ventricular dilation or a prominence of the outflow tract.

The ECG is most often abnormal in a nonspecific way; the most characteristic finding is ST-T abnormalities, which are present in 40% to 50% of patients. About 65% of patients have QRS abnormalities, but the majority are nonspecific and show a right axis deviation compared with previous ECGs or, in 10% to 15% of patients, a very suggestive right bundle branch block. Arrhythmias are common with both atrial and ventricular premature beats, but a small number of patients develop atrial fibrillation with the acute event. A change in electrical axis for either the P wave or the QRS complex that suggests right heart strain may be helpful. In some series, the ECG was of diagnostic help in only 15% to 25% of patients.[51]

Transportation and Emergency Department Management

The first step in management is to suspect the diagnosis, suspect intense hypoxemia, and immediately begin correction with high oxygen mixtures. Oxygen concentrations of 60% to 90% should be provided via a nonrebreathing system, particularly when cyanosis is present. The absence of a visible response in the patient's color should not cause treatment to be terminated. When the patient is hypotensive and nonresponsive, when signs are deteriorating, or when cyanosis does not respond to high oxygen supplementation by mask, intubation and ventilation support with 100% oxygen are indicated. Until arterial blood gas analysis is available this should be the recommended procedure to avoid unnecessary patient death or deterioration during transportation to the medical facility. Although bronchodilator drugs do produce transient improvement in ventilation, such treatment would have a low priority before reaching a treatment facility. Vasopressor agents when facilities and qualifications permit may improve hypotension, although they are quite ineffective when hypotension is produced by inadequate left ventricular output. Receiving facilities should be informed of the possible diagnosis of pulmonary embolism so that immediate monitoring and diagnostic procedures are available on arrival. An IV line should be immediately established, and analysis of arterial blood gases has a high priority until it has been established that profound hypoxemia and acidosis have not developed.

When the clinical picture is typical, heparin can be administered intravenously for its immediate effects, which include a reduction of airway resistance. However, before either heparin or thrombolytic therapy is instituted the diagnosis must be substantiated by adequate studies, which include a positive perfusion scan in the presence of a typical clinical picture and after a chest film fails to reveal pneumonia, pneumothorax, or other causes of similar symptoms. In the absence of thrombophlebitis, which is true of most patients, and when there are relative contraindications to treatment, angiography is essential to prevent potentially inappropriate treatment.[56]

Thrombolytic therapy with streptokinase can be used to improve hemodynamics and oxygenation rapidly. Additional benefits to lytic therapy are a reduction in the risk of permanent pulmonary impairment after recovery and improved blood flow at the venous site of thrombosis. Contraindications to thrombolytic therapy are recent surgery (within 10 days), recent extensive trauma with multiple bleeding sites, severe hypertension, active gastrointestinal bleeding, and a recent CVA (within 2–3 months).

When cardiac arrest occurs shortly after massive pulmonary embolism and when CPR is not effective in establishing a pulse, blood pressure, or evidence of adequate circulation, the mortality in the best of hands is 100%.

FAT EMBOLISM

Incidence and Predisposition

Fat embolism is common in both elderly and young subjects after major trauma or after extensive dissection of fat tissue as occurs in surgery on the morbidly obese patient.[57] With a variable onset from 8 hr to 4 days after a fracture of long bones, the pelvis, or multiple ribs and also after major contusion of adipose tissue as in the multiple trauma patient associated with automobile accidents, there is the onset of symptoms of respiratory distress and the subtle onset of CNS changes, including disorientation, restlessness, confusion, and/or bizarre behavior. The incidence after trauma is so high that fat embolism was found to be present in 65% of patients dying from battle wounds during World War II.[58] Studies of civilians after long bone fractures confirmed the high incidence, although the diagnosis is often not made because symptoms may not be sufficiently intense to be identified and also because other traumatic injuries receive the full attention of treatment personnel. Fat embolism may also be seen in nontraumatic conditions, such as extensive burns, pancreatitis, and coma associated with diabetic ketoacidosis. It can be the result of a very prolonged and traumatic CPR in an obese patient.

Pathophysiology

Although it is commonly held that the liberation of free fat from fat depots is the major mechanism, especially because it occurs with massive contusions and fractures of long bones with a fatty marrow, other mechanisms may play a role in producing the fat embolism syndrome. One explanation for fat embolism associated with a nontraumatic condition is that blood lipids are rendered less stable and tend to aggregate with platelets, causing local aggregation of red blood cells, a stasis of blood flow, and occlusion of capillary vessels, especially in the lung, which leads to tissue hypoxia that releases more fat from local depots. Experimental models with oleic acid injected into the circulation produce all of the clinical and laboratory findings seen in the fat embolism syndrome. Some clinicians, therefore, believe that free fatty acids are released following injuries, leading to a chemical pneumonitis resulting in the changes seen physiologically and on chest films. This is further supported by beneficial results of treatment with steroids that tend to block the chemical reaction in the pulmonary capillaries.

Clinical Manifestations

Symptoms begin variably from 8 hr to 4 days after the acute event, which is usually of a traumatic nature, with the gradual onset of respiratory distress with dyspnea characterized by tachypnea, tachycardia, and hypoxemia that responds relatively well to supplemental oxygen. Most patients have at least mild CNS symptoms, including confusion, change in personality, restlessness, or the more severe findings of convulsions and coma. There may be low-grade fever and cough, but no significant sputum. Hemoptysis is uncommon. The sicker patients manifest cyanosis. Petechial hemorrhages occur in the skin, usually over anterior axillary folds or the flanks. It is common to find petechiae in the conjunctivae or the oral mucous membranes. The presence of petechiae with dyspnea, tachypnea, and recent trauma should immediately suggest the diagnosis. In many cases the onset is so subtle and delayed following acute trauma that the diagnosis is only made later following an abnormal chest film or the appearance of petechiae with an unexplained anemia. Pulmonary hypertension may occur.

Laboratory Findings

Virtually all patients have hypoxemia and hypocapnia as evidence of hyperventilation, with the hypoxemia responding readily to supplemental oxygen treatment. More than half have a reduced platelet count and evidence of anemia, presumably due to hemolysis. Jaundice is rare, but a gradual progression of anemia is not uncommon, frequently being noted on days 2–4 of the illness. Lung compliance is markedly reduced, and pulmonary hypertension is not rare. The chest film reveals diffuse bilateral pulmonary infiltrates consistent with bronchopneumonia or atypical pulmonary edema. Free fat is found in the urine in more than half of the patients, and examination of retinal vessels may reveal small defects, probably representing fat in retinal vessels. Quick frozen blood specimens reveal fat globules in large numbers, suggesting the diagnosis.

Transportation and Early Treatment

Because death does occur as a result of massive fat embolism, prompt transportation to a diagnostic facility is indicated, although the vast majority of patients have a gradual onset of symptoms that begin after arrival at the treatment facility. The presence of injury with dyspnea and petechiae in the mucous membranes or skin warrants a preliminary consideration of the diagnosis. Patients may respond to IV corticosteroids, which presumably reduce further chemical reactions in the pulmonary capillaries secondary to either free fatty acids or liberated neutral fats passing through the pulmonary capillary bed. Intravenous heparin has been used as a lipolytic agent and to reduce coagulation presumed to be secondary to the aggregation of platelets by fat. Corticosteroids in doses ranging from 200–500 mg of cortisone IV are more effective. Ethyl alcohol has been used for its lipolytic effect. Supplemental oxygen by nasal cannula or mask (30% to 40% FIO_2) is indicated. During transport, the broad differential diagnosis of mild pulmonary edema, aspiration pneumonitis, and lung contusion must be considered until a diagnosis of fat embolism is substantiated by supportive laboratory evidence.

SMOKE INHALATION—AIRWAY BURNS

Smoke is a suspension of solid and liquid particles in a gas medium, including toxic gases. Inhalation injury resulting from smoke exposure is defined as an injury of the respiratory system caused by inhalation of thermal, particulate, gaseous, and chemical products of combustion. As a result, there may be thermal injuries, injury due to particulate matter that is deeply inhaled, chemical pneumonitis resulting from both particulates and gaseous elements, and the ever-present problem of carbon monoxide poisoning, a risk common to all fires. Burns of the respiratory zone including the face and upper airways not only contribute to morbidity and mortality but also often dictate the course of immediate treatment and subsequent hospital management.

Smoke inhalation injuries usually result from structural fires, including industrial fires, and may be a component in vehicle accident injuries. Although fire is a leading cause of accidental death in the United States, there has been little understanding of its physiologic effects until recent years.

Respiratory Effects of Common Gases and Fumes

Carbon dioxide, which is a product of combustion of any materials containing carbon, is present in all fires. Because it is a potent respiratory stimulus, levels as low as 2% to 3% may increase ventilation of the exposed individual by 50% to 100%, thereby increasing exposure to other toxic gases and particulates. Its major role is increasing ventilation and exposure to other more toxic gases. Exposure to greater than 10% carbon dioxide for more than 5–10 min is likely to be lethal.

Hydrogen chloride is a product of combustion of chloride-containing plastic materials, including polyvinyl chloride, which is found in electrical wire coating, insulation, and pipes used in industry and home construction. It is irritating, has a pungent odor, and is associated with exposures to chlorine and phosgene. It is capable of inducing irritation of the upper airway mucous membranes, chest tightness, bronchospasm, and pulmonary edema.[59,60] It is very hazardous to the elderly and makes electrical fires especially dangerous, a finding confirmed in major fires in high-rise hotels and apartments.

Nitrogen dioxide is a very toxic reddish-brown gas. Exposure to concentrations as low as 0.02% to 0.05% is fatal. Common to most fires, it forms when organic and inorganic nitrates are heated or burned and where nitric acid and metals are found. Injury caused by nitrogen dioxide is characterized by a delayed chemical pneumonitis that often occurs many hours after exposure; it is the result of deep inhalation permitted by its tendency to go into solution in airway secretions very slowly. This permits a selective effect in the small airways of the lung, rather than in upper airways.

Sulfur dioxide is the product of combustion of organic materials containing sulfur. Because of its high solubility, it enters solution in the upper airways and causes intense irritation or burning of the eyes, nose, throat, and trachea, inducing cough and local discomfort.[61]

Ammonia is a very irritating and highly soluble gas produced by combustion of nitrogen-containing materials, such as nylon, silk, wool, and acrylic plastics. In addition, ammonia is released by damage to refrigeration systems, as it is a commonly employed refrigerant. It produces intense irritation of the eyes, nose, and throat. Because of the intense irritation of upper airways produced by its pungent qualities and high solubility, prolonged exposure is unlikely except in the case of a trapped or unconscious patient.

Acrolein, formaldehyde, and acetic acid are common products of combustion of wood, particularly such soft wood as pine, fats, some fabrics, and paper. Inhalation of these substances causes severe mucosal irritation.

Hydrogen sulfide gas is formed by partial combustion of organic materials containing sulfur and is easily identified by its characteristic rotten-egg odor. It is a product of combustion of rubber, hair, wool, and certain animal hides. However, rapid tolerance develops, and prolonged exposure may then result in the development of dizziness, dryness of mucous membranes, and airway pain. It may increase respirations and lead to respiratory paralysis at higher levels.

Hydrogen cyanide is a very toxic and dangerous gas resulting from incomplete combusion of polyurethane, nylon, silk, and a variety of acrylics. It is less common in the average fire in which an older individual might be exposed, but has produced large numbers of deaths in fires involving x-ray film and similar products.

Phosgene is a toxic gas resulting from combustion of polyvinyl chloride and from burning of chlorinated materials, such as carbon tetrachloride. It may produce a fulminant pulmonary edema and rapid death.

Carbon Monoxide Poisoning

Acute carbon monoxide poisoning is considered responsible for approximately 4,000 accidental or suicidal deaths in the United States annually.[62] It poses a special risk to the elderly who may live in apartments adjoining a garage where an automobile may be left running, because this relatively nonviolent mode of suicide is appealing to depressed older patients; in addition, the elderly have a reduced ability to escape from fires in which prolonged exposure in a confined space may lead to collapse and death from carbon monoxide poisoning. The mechanism of death has been known since the 19th century, when Claude Bernard reported death by hypoxia resulting from a reversible combination of carbon monoxide with hemoglobin.[63] The effects of carbon monoxide are based on its concentration and the degree to which it has combined with hemoglobin.

Because the affinity of CO for hemoglobin is approximately 250 times as great as that of oxygen, carbon monoxide can rapidly displace oxygen on hemoglobin and impair oxygen delivery to the tissues. In addition to displacing oxygen on the hemoglobin molecule, carbon monoxide alters the hemoglobin-oxygen dissociation curve, which improves the combination of oxygen and hemoglobin at lower oxygen tensions but results in poor unloading of oxygen at the tissue sites, again leading to reduced oxygen transport to tissues.[64] Those tissues with the highest oxygen requirements, including the brain and myocardium, are most subject to carbon monoxide-induced hypoxemia. Because the older patient may already have abnormal arterial supply to both structures and may be mildly anemic, this reduction in oxygen transport to key tissues results in severe morbidity or rapid death. There is evidence that COHb concentrations of below 20% do not produce permanent CNS damage, but both cardiac and CNS symptoms may occur below this level with physical exertion, particularly in the presence of underlying arteriosclerotic heart disease or cerebrovascular insufficiency.[62,65,66] Many patients are thought to die from fatal arrhythmias before the levels of carbon monoxide become lethal. Among survivors, there is a significant incidence of deterioration of personality or impairment of intellectual function. Table 5–19 outlines the common symptoms and signs noted at various carboxyhemoglobin levels.

Table 5–19 Clinical Manifestations of Carbon Monoxide Poisoning

COHb%	Signs and Symptoms
3–10	Increased blood flow to vital organs. Usually no change in respiration Flushing of skin Visual discrimination of light intensity impaired May interfere with short interval time judgments Treadmill exercise time to exhaustion may be decreased and time to angina may be decreased in patients with heart disease
10–15	Above clinical manifestations, as well as polycythemia from chronic exposure. Headaches rare.
15–20	Mild headache, subtle diminution in manual dexterity
20–30	Throbbing headache, nausea, weakness
30–40	Severe headache, vomiting Syncope with exertion in elderly Skin and mucous membranes may be cherry red even to untrained eye Increased depth of respiration
50–60	Confusion, collapse on exertion, fainting Seizures may occur
60–70	Unconsciousness, seizures Acidosis, hypotension, death likely if untreated
80–90	Rapidly to immediately fatal

Note: CO uptake and COHb levels are dependent on CO concentration, duration of exposure, alveolar ventilation, inspired oxygen concentration, circulation time, and Hgb concentration. Onset of symptoms depends not only on COHb level but also on O_2 requirements.

Evaluating the Victim at the Site

Immediate death may result from asphyxia secondary to rapid oxygen consumption by a violent fire, as well as from displacement of oxygen by carbon dioxide and other gases.

It is important to evaluate the mental status of the patient and identify coma or vascular collapse, as well as physical injuries associated with the fire. There should be a quick evaluation of vital signs to ensure that respirations and circulation are intact. Patients with burns of the respiratory zone should receive preferential treatment, with rapid transport to a hospital and special attention to maintaining an airway. All patients should be suspected of having carbon monoxide poisoning and risk of inhalation injury, but the following six risk factors are most important:

1. persons who are or have been unconscious
2. persons found in a confined or closed space
3. persons with associated chest or other traumatic injuries
4. persons suspected of prolonged exposure to smoke
5. persons having obvious facial burns, especially in the respiratory zone
6. anyone with the following: dyspnea, chest pain, older patients with COPD, brassy cough, wheeze, singeing of nasal hairs or mustache, soot in sputum, and conjunctivitis

In addition, it is useful to observe the burning material to help treatment personnel predict the agents to which the patient might have been exposed.

Criteria for Early Treatment and Transportation to a Medical Facility

Patients who manifest signs and symptoms of significant respiratory distress or who run the highest risk of carbon monoxide intoxication, as well as all patients with facial burns and unconsciousness, should receive priority treatment. They should be immediately removed from further exposure to toxic chemicals or smoke and should receive supplemental oxygen by nasal cannula or mask to deliver 40% oxygen or more. Transportation to a treatment facility should be immediate for patients who have significant facial burns, obvious respiratory distress, inspiratory stridor, or a history of underlying COPD or cardiac disease. Because carbon monoxide poisoning may induce hypoxia and death without cyanosis, cyanosis should not be looked for as evidence of need for priority treatment. Aerosol bronchodilator drugs should not be administered in the presence of a mild wheeze because the patient may be far more susceptible to such toxic effects as arrhythmias. The use of IPPB with mask or mouthpiece may be more helpful in delivering high oxygen concentrations and reducing pulmonary edema induced by reaction to inhaled toxic chemicals. Oxygen is not withheld from patients with known COPD, but rather their respiratory status is observed carefully and they are given ventilation support when respirations appear to be failing during transport.

Evaluation and Triage in the Emergency Department

At the emergency department patients should have a survey history of smoke exposure, possible unconsciousness, and a survey of facial burns done immediately. Once an airway has been ensured and the integrity of respirations and circulation are confirmed, arterial blood gas analysis is done to evaluate the oxygen tension with regard to possible pulmonary damage and provide early analysis for carboxyhemoglobin. Oxygen tension reflects the adequacy of oxygen transfer in the lung, but does not reflect the level of carboxyhemoglobin.

The elderly patient with burns over 20% of the body should be admitted for treatment of smoke inhalation and postburn pulmonary complications. Patients with extensive orofacial burns should undergo nasotracheal intubation or tracheostomy and support on a ventilator when severe hypoxemia and hypercapnia are documented. In those patients still hyperventilating with hypocapnia but with profound hypoxemia (PO_2 below 50 mm Hg), consideration should be given to nasotracheal intubation, with a possible need for later mechanical ventilation. However, these patients can be temporarily observed closely with frequent monitoring of arterial blood gases and continued oxygen supplementation by the use of mask and high concentrations. Patients are generally kept in the sitting position and are encouraged to cough with suctioning as needed. Most patients are treated with IV aminophylline and a large bolus of IV corticosteroids, such as methylprednisolone at 30 mg/kg while chest films, ECG, and other studies are being conducted.

Those patients who have been unconscious or have significant respiratory symptoms and have known underlying COPD should automatically receive nasotracheal intubation and ventilator support when their PaO_2 approaches 50 mm Hg and there is any evidence of hypercapnia (a PCO_2 >45 mm Hg). Close observation is required because the latent period for effects from steroids may permit further deterioration before the beneficial response is manifest.

Those patients who do not have orofacial or body burns are admitted to the hospital for observation and treatment in the presence of any of the following ten symptoms:

1. respiratory distress and cough
2. serious hypoxemia
3. rales, rhonchi, or wheezes on auscultation
4. a history of unconsciousness
5. hoarseness
6. singeing of nasal hairs
7. restlessness

8. confusion or irrational behavior
9. soot in sputum
10. exposure to explosion or steam

Chemical pneumonitis caused by inhalation of particulates and gases may have a delayed onset, and some patients deteriorate late but rapidly (in a period anywhere from hours to days), producing a classical picture of ARDS and requiring full support with intubation, high oxygen mixtures, and ventilation support. The earlier one detects deterioration, the more likely is the patient's survival. All patients with underlying COPD and those with significant hypoxemia, dyspnea, rales, wheeze, or tachycardia should be hospitalized for initial treatment. Patients with chest films that reveal diffuse or patchy infiltrates should also be hospitalized for further diagnosis and management.

All patients require early treatment for probable carbon monoxide intoxication, and treatment should be more intensive for those with known COPD or coronary artery disease. Approximately 40% develop significant airway obstruction requiring treatment with expectorants, bronchodilating agents and, in some cases, broad spectrum antibiotic treatment. Hypoxemia is an excellent indicator of the patient's progress.

Carbon monoxide poisoning is currently treated by administering 100% oxygen to wash carbon monoxide off hemoglobin as rapidly as possible. One atmosphere of oxygen reduces carboxyhemoglobin levels by 50% within 1–2 hr; breathing ambient air would require 4–6 hours for the same change. Breathing 100% oxygen also rapidly increases the dissolved plasma oxygen, adding a further source for tissue delivery. When a hyperbaric chamber is available, 100% oxygen can be administered at 2 atmospheres for 1 hr. This procedure produces very rapid clearing of carbon monoxide in virtually all patients. CNS symptoms are expected to clear during treatment; otherwise, they are evidence of hypoxic cerebral damage or cerebral edema. The use of high oxygen concentrations combined with 5% carbon dioxide to stimulate breathing during carbon monoxide washout is no longer recommended. If an elevated carbon monoxide level is the only manifestation under treatment, treatment need not continue once a COHb of 5% is reached. This rule might be modified in the older patient, especially with coexisting anemia or significant ASHD with a history of angina pectoris or cardiac failure.

Significance of Burns of the Respiratory Zone

Thermal injury to the tracheobronchial tree is rare, except where there has been exposure to steam. Even intense dry heat is less effective in breaking down the protective barrier of the respiratory tract mucous membranes, but superheated steam can produce severe damage of the respiratory tract extending to the small bronchi. In determining whether respiratory tract burns have occurred, it is useful and safest to consider significant airway damage to have occurred in the presence of (1) burns about the face, (2) singeing of the nasal hairs or mustache, or

(3) extensive burns associated with unconsciousness. Because pneumonia is a major cause of late complications and high mortality and because facial burns are frequently associated with pneumonia, these burns represent a significant reason for hospitalization and careful attention not only to establishing an airway but also to resultant late complications. Patients with significant airway burn damage have edema, usually an element of stridor or hoarseness, and respiratory distress associated with severe hypoxemia.

Major attention in the early phase of evaluation and treatment should be paid to maintaining an adequate airway. Early use of antibiotics has not been shown to be effective, and the use of corticosteroids is controversial. Treatment consists of supplemental oxygen, adequate fluid, hydration of mucous membranes, and bronchodilators as indicated.[67–69]

Airway Complications

Patients with significant smoke inhalation may not only have burns and trauma with resultant scar and stricture of upper airways, including the trachea, but also may develop the complications of tracheal stenosis from traumatic intubation or suctioning. In addition, some patients suffer the late development of a small airway syndrome, generally because of the effect of toxic gases and chemicals inhaled during smoke exposure, in addition to residual complications of infection, aspiration, or the development of ARDS. In the vast majority of patients with upper airway disease following smoke inhalation, documented resolution is almost complete, although a few may have a residual chronic bronchitis.[70–72] Most studies of firefighters who have repeated exposures to smoke with periodic minor symptoms requiring evaluation show little evidence of any chronic loss of lung function as a result.

ACUTE LUNG INJURY FROM IRRITANT GASES/CHEMICAL PNEUMONIA

Exposure in the Elderly Patient

The majority of lung injuries from toxic or irritant gases are the result of either a fire or intense exposure secondary to occupational activity or accidents. Early detection and treatment is especially important in the elderly patient with a high frequency of underlying cardiopulmonary disease.

For those acid solutions toxic to the lung, particle size and level of ventilation are important in producing exposure of the respiratory tract.

The solubility in water of toxic gases determines the site of primary reaction in the respiratory tract. It is also important to recognize the principal toxicity of the gas or liquid aerosol, as well as any characteristic latent period between exposure and acute respiratory symptoms. In general, larger particles tend to lodge in the upper respiratory tract, and particles of smaller size (0.5–3 microns) tend to reach distal air spaces and produce bronchiolitis or pneumonitis. In addition, highly soluble gases, such as ammonia and sulfur dioxide, tend to have a major effect in the upper respiratory tract because they enter solution rapidly; they tend to induce bronchitis. There is a high level of correlation between sulfur dioxide exposure, including concentration and duration of exposure, and the level of the bronchitis syndrome. This is seen daily in industrial exposures, accidental exposures, and air pollution disasters. During major air pollution inversions acute symptoms occur in a large percentage of the susceptible population, and there is increased death associated with severe episodes of pollution characterized primarily by high levels of sulfur dioxide from high sulfur-containing fuel combustion.[73]

Less soluble agents, such as chlorine and nitrogen dioxide, a byproduct of the internal combustion engine and certain industrial processes, including welding, mining, and the silo storage of grains, characteristically produce fewer upper respiratory symptoms and more lower respiratory symptoms because of the decreased solubility as the gas is inhaled. This produces a delay in the reaction, with symptoms appearing hours to days after exposure. These agents are likely to produce either small airway disease or a clinical picture resembling pneumonitis or pulmonary edema.

Ozone, which is generated by arc welding and is a common air pollutant during the summer months, characteristically produces small airway disease, as well as upper respiratory tract symptoms due to irritation of mucous membranes. Ozone levels reach a peak in summer months in many communities because they result from ultraviolet light activity on the common precursors, which are hydrocarbons and NO_2 that are usually produced in large measure by such mobile sources as the automobile. Levels tend to be highest several hours after peak traffic and in areas of heavy traffic congestion, such as in major metropolitan areas of the Northeast. This form of pollution exposure also is found in the Los Angeles area, which presents special problems of acute bronchitis and upper respiratory tract irritation in older patients with underlying COPD, especially where bronchospasm is a significant component of disease. Elderly patients with underlying COPD are particularly susceptible to acute symptoms in the summer months based on exposure to intense heat and humidity in association with increased levels of ozone. However, although ozone may alter lung function temporarily, it does not tend to produce severe parenchymal disease or a chemical pneumonitis.

Acute lung injury may result from intense exposures to toxic gases, such as ammonia, chlorine, nitrogen dioxide, and especially phosgene. With exposure to phosgene and nitrogen dioxide, a clinical picture similar to pulmonary edema is produced, whereas the more soluble ammonia and chlorine gases are more likely to produce acute laryngitis, tracheitis, or bronchitis. Table 5–20 lists common irritant gases that cause lung injury and indicates their usual source and the clinical syndromes they commonly produce.

Table 5–20 Irritant Gases Producing Lung Injury

Gas	Usual Exposure Source	Solubility	Clinical Syndrome
Ammonia (NH_3)	Manufacture of fertilizers, explosives, and chemicals and product of some fires	Very soluble	Tracheitis, bronchitis
Sulfur dioxide (SO_2)	Chemical manufacture, bleach, air pollution inversions	Very soluble	Acute laryngitis— tracheitis or bronchitis
Chlorine (Cl_2)	Manufacture of plastics, chemicals, and paper and the product of fires	Moderately soluble	Tracheitis, bronchitis, pulmonary edema
Nitrogen dioxide (NO_2)	Arc welding, explosives, silage, burning of cellulose, automobile exhaust	Relatively insoluble	Bronchiolitis— pneumonitis
Ozone (O_3)	Bleach, electric power stations, welding, photochemical smog	Low solubility	Aggravation of asthma, emphysema, increase in airway obstruction
Phosgene ($COCl_3$)	Pesticides, chemicals, plastics, and some fires	Insoluble	Pneumonitis/pulmonary edema
Polyvinyl chloride	Plastics, floor and wall coverings, textiles; is degraded to chlorine, phosgene, and hydrochloric acid when burned	Insoluble	Severe pulmonary irritation with shock, unconsciousness, and toxic death

Patient Transportation and Treatment

The history of exposure and identification of the noxious agent are very important in determining treatment and which level of the respiratory tract will be the site of primary reaction. For example, upper airway disease is most likely to occur with exposure to ammonia and sulfur dioxide and to some extent with chlorine, whereas nitrogen dioxide, ozone, and especially phosgene with lower solubility tend to produce a higher incidence of chemical pneumonitis or a pulmonary edema-like picture that may occur many hours after exposure. Because there may be a substantial time lag between exposure to acute symptoms and eventual chemical pneumonitis or pulmonary edema, it is reasonable to ensure transportation of the patient to a proper medical facility for evaluation. That evaluation should include examination for the presence of bronchospasm or rales and any evidence of undetected hypoxemia. Abnormal x-ray films may show patchy infiltrates or evidence of incipient pulmonary edema.

During transport, oxygen therapy is a reasonable recourse and should be administered at levels of 40% to 100%, based on symptoms and clinical findings. Mucous membranes exposed to high levels of gases should first be washed. Signs of airway constriction, hoarseness, or stridor should be noted and the possible need for emergency airway management considered. The presence of bronchospasm requires vigorous treatment with bronchodilators and may require early IV use of corticosteroids. In the presence of rales, bronchospasm, tachypnea, respiratory distress, or hypoxemia, oxygen therapy and respiratory support with plans to admit the patient to a receiving facility for prolonged observation should be instituted. Because lower respiratory symptoms with the development of a bronchiolitis obliterans or respiratory failure associated with pulmonary edema may occur hours to days after the acute event, prolonged observation is indicated when examination reveals rales, bronchospasm, tachypnea, or significant hypoxemia or when the history indicates a pre-existing cardiopulmonary disease, particularly some form of obstructive airway disease. The use of corticosteroids and antibiotics is based on the underlying disease and the nature of the physical findings; bronchodilators are used as indicated.

In every case, every effort should be made to identify the agent to which the patient has been exposed. This is best accomplished by the initial treating personnel in the field because patients may not be able to give useful information once acutely ill, and later treating physicians may have little access to this information.

ASPIRATION PNEUMONIA—A SPECIAL PROBLEM OF THE ELDERLY

Incidence

Chronic aspiration pneumonia in the elderly is a very frequent cause of chronic or recurring cough, low-grade fever, and variable levels of dyspnea. It must be differentiated from the acute aspiration pneumonia that involves aspiration of gastric contents, which may follow abdominal or thoracic trauma. Conditions leading to chronic aspiration pneumonia are a diverticulum of the hypopharynx (Zenker's diverticulum), esophageal strictures, or stenosis (either due to malignant tumors or benign disease), achalasia (representing a massively dilated esophagus with poor emptying), or neuromuscular disturbances in the swallowing mechanism associated with progressive neurologic disease commonly found with advanced age. Surveys of chronic care facilities and the experience of all community hospitals suggest that older patients develop abnormalities in swallowing function that slowly progress and present increasing risk of recurring bouts of aspiration of either oral secretions or small amounts of food retained in the upper digestive tract, including the esophagus. It has been estimated that more than half the patients over age 70 have abnormal swallowing function.

Some observers estimate that the majority of patients over 70 aspirate regularly. These patients present with low-grade fever, cough, a benign-appearing sputum and variable transient infiltrates on x-ray films, which suggest pneumonitis but without the usual purulent sputum, chills, or pleuritic chest pain on onset. Many of these episodes are subacute; the vast majority are not identified or treated.[74,75]

Studies of patients with neuromuscular disturbances that increase with age reveal slow clearance of material from the hypopharynx and frequent aspiration into airways, commonly with patients unaware of aspiration.[75] The less alert and the older the patient, the more likely that aspiration will be a source of recurring respiratory infections.

Underlying Mechanisms

The most common causative factor is a deterioration in neuromuscular function associated with advanced age, but abnormalities of the upper digestive tract or hypopharynx as noted are additional etiologic factors. The oropharynx contains a large bacterial population, yet in the normal individual the lower respiratory tract is sterile, suggesting excellent defense mechanisms. It is likely that the aspiration of small quantities of oropharyngeal secretions is very common in all patients with a reduction in consciousness and advanced age, as well as in all individuals during deep sleep. In older patients, the respiratory tract defense mechanisms are impaired, and patients may acquire a change in bacterial flora, including not only the usual anaerobic organisms but also chronic care facility and hospital-acquired gram-negative bacteria. These bacteria may then be aspirated to cause gram-negative bacterial pneumonia or mixed infections associated with anaerobes. Generally, there is a history of a period of unconsciousness, seizures, or some form of neurologic disease. The process is very common in heavy smokers and those consuming large amounts of alcohol.

The defense mechanisms that may be deficient in the elderly and permit the establishment of infection associated with oropharyngeal aspiration include chronic pharyngeal and esophageal disease, stenosis or malignant tumors, deficiencies in the mucociliary system of the tracheobronchial tree due to cigarette smoking, and reduced ciliary function associated with age. A poor gag reflex is associated with chronic alcohol use, neurologic disease, or advanced age. Deficiencies exist in immune factors and lung defense cells, such as alveolar macrophages and neutrophils, the migration and capacity of which to ingest organisms are reduced with age.

Clinical Picture

The patient has a history of cough and difficulty in swallowing and frequently a period of unconsciousness or reduction in state of alertness, with or without recent trauma. There is a history of periodic lung infections or episodes of pneumonia associated with low-grade fever but rarely with chills or purulent sputum. A history of weight loss, deterioration in neurologic function, or known esophageal carcinoma is very suggestive.

Laboratory Findings

Patients with a lung abscess secondary to oropharyngeal aspiration may have a foul odor to the breath and expectorate purulent and foul-smelling sputum, occasionally with hemoptysis. They may also complain of a chest ache and have a significant fever and evidence of toxic reactions. Other patients with aspiration pneumonia due to oropharyngeal secretions do not appear acutely ill and do not require special treatment during transport to a treating facility.

Treatment

Treatment is based on accurate diagnosis of an aspiration pneumonia or lung abscess, which requires evaluation of sputum, blood cultures, chest film, and an analysis of blood count for leukocytosis. Special attention is given to recovering an anaerobic organism, and in older patients with previous hospitalizations and chronic lung disease, the risk of gram-negative organisms causing infection receives special attention.[76–78] Detecting and treating obstructive esophageal lesions are critical when that mechanism is primary, but in many patients advanced age and neurologic deterioration lead to continued episodes of aspiration with infection despite the best medical management. Feeding via a nasogastric tube may be helpful, but aspiration may continue even with this modality. In selected cases, a feeding jejunostomy may be used. Adequate oral hygiene and treatment for dental caries and gingival disease may reduce the incidence of significant pulmonary infection by anaerobes.

NEAR DROWNING

Approximately 8,000–9,000 people die annually from drowning in the United States, and an equal number suffer from near drowning. The highest incidence is in the second decade of life.[78] Near drowning is uncommon in the elderly patient, except for accidental immersion and near drowning associated with reductions in cardiopulmonary function.

It is estimated that approximately 10% of drowning victims do not aspirate water, but die of asphyxia and respiratory obstruction that are produced by laryngospasm after minor water aspiration. However, a postimmersion syndrome may occur many hours after apparently successful resuscitation and recovery, with a recurrence of respiratory distress, pulmonary edema, and severe hypoxemia that may result in death. Many days after the acute event some patients may then suffer a delayed death from pulmonary injury, irreversible cerebral anoxia, or gram-negative bacterial infections. Drowning has been associated with hyperventilation before entering water, a technique employed to lower the PCO_2 so that the individual may remain under water longer but one that predisposes to the development of serious levels of hypoxemia, producing unconsciousness and secondary drowning. In the elderly patient, immersion in cold water may also bring into play the effects of hypothermia with reduction in sensation and consciousness, as well as arrhythmias.

Ultimately death is associated with hypoxia, although for several decades changes in electrolyte and fluid balance were considered critical factors in causing death associated with drowning. The work of Modell and associates showed that the underlying mechanisms for death were asphyxia, rather than electrolyte abnormality. They demonstrated that 35% of patients had a PaO_2 below 60 torr after near drowning at the time of hospital admission. The majority had values below 100 torr, despite the application of FIO_2 ranging from 21% to 100%.[79–83]

Pathophysiology

Experimental and clinical data in the years 1940–1960 demonstrated that in fresh water drowning there was almost immediate absorption of hypotonic water via the pulmonary capillary bed, which led to dilution of serum electrolytes, significant hemolysis, and elevation of serum potassium with a resultant high incidence of ventricular fibrillation.[79] In salt water drowning, there appeared to be a transfer of plasma water to the pulmonary alveolar space, causing aspirated water to increase in volume and thereby producing ventilation/perfusion mismatch with hypoxemia. Ventricular fibrillation and hyperkalemia were uncommon in salt water drowning so the thesis that different treatment was required in the two forms of near drowning evolved from experimental data. The work of Modell subsequently revealed that these water transfers and electrolyte abnormalities are acute changes that are rapidly reversed and almost never demonstrable by the time of hospitalization 30–60 min after near drowning. In addition, it became clear that 10% to 15% of near drowned victims do not actually aspirate fluid, but suffer hypoxemia from either breath holding or laryngospasm.

When fluid is aspirated, as is true in 80% to 85% of cases, the aspiration of even small amounts of water may produce significant hypoxemia. A mere 11 ml/kg of aspirated fresh or salt water may produce profound hypoxemia within 1–2 min, with the condition persisting for 24–72 hr in survivors. The hypoxemia is associated with hypercarbia and a mixed respiratory and metabolic acidosis. The hypercarbia and respiratory acidosis are readily reversed by resuscitation or mechanical ventilation. The level of metabolic acidosis is dependent on the duration of the hypoxemia. It is postulated that aspiration of fresh water causes an increase in surface tension by damaging the pulmonary surfactant layer and leading to unstable alveoli and diffuse atelectasis. This produces a reduction in ventilation/perfusion matching and leads to hypoxemia that has some of the characteristics of shunting with a variable response to supplemental oxygen. In addition, the clinical picture of pulmonary edema may supervene after aspiration of small amounts of fluid. It has been demonstrated that the application of continuous positive airway pressure can reduce this hypoxemia, probably by correcting atelectasis and increasing the gas exchange surface, thereby improving ventilation/perfusion matching.

In the absence of pre-existing cardiovascular disease, the correction of hypoxemia and acidosis results in a stable patient. Although ventricular fibrillation is common in fresh water drowning with experimental animals, the volume of fresh water aspiration required to produce this mechanism of death in humans does not occur frequently.[84] Similarly, although hemolysis may occur with the aspiration of large volumes of fresh water, it is more common in the experimental animal than in the human experience because the volume of fresh water aspirated (44 ml/kg) required in animals is rarely achieved in the human subject. There is a transient reduction in cardiac output and a risk of additional effects from hypothermia, including ventricular fibrillation that generally occurs when body temperature falls below 28°C.

In the older patient the critical factor is not only cardiac function but also CNS integrity because the CNS is most susceptible to an extended period of hypoxemia. Up to 30% of survivors revealed neurologic dysfunction after near drowning, and efforts at evaluation of the near-drowning patient have concentrated on detecting neurologic deficits.[84] In studies of patients arriving at a hospital awake and alert, although having suffered cardiopulmonary arrest, survival without neurologic deficit was the rule. A second group arriving with some alteration in their state of consciousness and found to be lethargic, disoriented, confused, or semicomatose usually survived with minimal or no neurologic sequelae. Patients arriving at an emergency facility in a comatose state revealed up to a 25% neurologic deficit;[84,85] this would be a special problem for the elderly patient with cardiopulmonary disease and a compromised cerebral circulation.

Transportation and Treatment of the Elderly Patient

Because the outcome of treatment is largely dependent on resuscitation at the scene, the control of hypoxemia and acidosis represents the keys to survival. Cardiopulmonary resuscitation as recommended by the American Heart Association should be applied at the scene, including mouth-to-mouth ventilation during the rescue procedure. In general, mouth-to-mouth ventilation should begin while the subject is still in the water because precious moments may be saved in the elderly patient with a compromised cerebral circulation, possibly pre-existing hypoxemia from underlying cardiopulmonary disease, and exercise losses prior to the near-drowning event. When the lung is noncompliant and atelectatic it may be necessary to apply continuous airway positive pressure and to use mechanical ventilators to ensure adequate oxygen transfer. The Heimlich maneuver proposed for the purpose of removing aspirated fluids from the lungs is not recommended because of the risk of trauma and the possibility of increasing the hazard of aspiration.[86] In addition, the fluids aspirated are so rapidly absorbed that the maneuver is not likely to affect intrapulmonary water content. CPR is applied as indicated after evaluation of the cardiovascular status.

When rescue personnel are sufficiently skilled to carry out endotracheal intubation, this should be used in the patient who is comatose or apneic to establish suitable oxygen tensions as rapidly as possible. Personnel skilled in mouth-to-mouth or bag-and-mask ventilation are likely to do better by that modality, using oxygen supplementation at the highest concentrations feasible under the circumstances.

If the patient appears to revive, it is important to remember that transfer to a medical care facility is required to continue evaluation and to avoid the subsequent postimmersion syndrome, which may result in late respiratory failure and death after an apparent dramatic recovery. Oxygen is continued, as are monitoring and respiratory support until the patient reaches a medical care facility and is appropriately stabilized and placed on continuing monitoring.

Comatose or apneic patients require intubation and should be treated with a minimum FIO_2 of 0.4% to 1.0% with continuous positive airway pressure (CPAP) as indicated. Because overtreatment is not a problem and undertreatment may cause ultimate failure.

On arrival in the emergency department, the patient who has not had a cardiopulmonary arrest requires IV fluids and evaluation of intake and output, as well as monitoring of blood pressure and pulse. Ventilation can be evaluated by performing arterial blood gas analysis on a regular basis, and treatment for significant acidosis should be carried out immediately. At the same time the patient's neurologic status should be evaluated. Those patients who remain obtunded or have an abnormal CNS evaluation or persistent hypoxemia require intubation and continuous mechanical ventilation with supplemental oxygen, as well as admission to an intensive care unit and prolonged monitoring.[85]

Bronchospasm may be treated as indicated with IV theophylline or aerosol bronchodilators. There is no consistent benefit obtained with the use of IV steroids, but the decision to use steroids may be made on an individual basis.[87,88] Prophylactic antibiotics have not been demonstrated to be effective, but it may be assumed that many patients aspirating water known to be contaminated with coliform organisms may respond to immediate antibiotic treatment because such treatment is probably not prophylactic. Superinfection with gram-negative bacteria is a common cause of late death after fluid aspiration.

Special techniques are required for patients who are comatose or show evidence of more serious levels of neurologic impairment on reaching the treatment facility. Such patients have often been treated with sedation, hypothermia, and full support with corticosteroids and oxygen supplementation. Treatment must be directed to the reduction of cerebral edema with such techniques as hyperventilation and the judicious use of diuretics.

Complications

One late complication is a prominent neurologic deficit, which is best prevented by rapid resuscitation at the scene, the application of appropriate oxygen therapy during transport, and ventilatory support as indicated. Because acidosis further desaturates hemoglobin and impairs oxygen transport in the presence of an already abnormal PaO_2, it is important to prevent it from developing into both hypercapnia and lactic acidosis associated with prolonged bouts of hypotension or tissue anoxia. Careful monitoring, the use of antibiotics, and routine airway management may permit survival in spite of aspiration of fluid contaminated with gram-negative bacteria. Late deaths are generally due to CNS damage or, more commonly, gram-negative sepsis associated with pulmonary infection. Survival is largely dependent on the quality of resuscitation at the scene and not the full array of sophisticated support modes available in the treating hospital.

HEMOPTYSIS IN THE ELDERLY

Definition and Identification

Hemoptysis, or the coughing up of blood, is not only an important sign but also one least likely to be ignored by the patient or treating personnel. Although hemoptysis is a term reserved by some clinicians for the spitting up of gross pure blood in minimal amounts of at least 5–10 ml, the most common presentation is that of blood-streaking of sputum, rather than expectoration of pure blood. The most common cause of simple blood streaking of sputum is the paroxysmal coughing of chronic bronchitis in elderly cigarette smokers, although blood streaking may also be the first manifestation of lung cancer. Accordingly, streak hemoptysis should never be ignored, but warrants at least evaluation of the patient, although not requiring emergency attention.

Massive hemoptysis is variously defined as in excess of 200 ml of blood per 24 hr to in excess of 600 ml in 24–48 hr. It requires immediate attention, not so much because of the risk of hemorrhagic shock but because of the risk of severe hypoxemia from extensive bleeding into the lung parenchyma. Copious intrapulmonary bleeding is life threatening because it may produce lethal hypoxemia with death from cardiac arrest or arrhythmia, rather than from exsanguination. The vast majority of patients with massive bleeding have a past history of previous hemoptysis.

To the elderly patient, hemoptysis is almost synonymous with tuberculosis or lung cancer; in fact, lung cancer is one of the leading causes for hemoptysis in the older patient, especially the older male cigarette smoker who is most at risk. Hemoptysis occurs in over 60% of patients with lung cancer at some point in their course. However, the majority have less than massive hemoptysis, and many have persistent blood streaking of sputum for long periods of time before reaching medical attention. Table 5–21 lists the most common causes for hemoptysis as grouped in categories of disease, rather than order of frequency.

Table 5–21 Common Causes of Hemoptysis

Infection
    Chronic bronchitis
    Bronchiectasis
    Tuberculosis
    Lung abscess
    Gram-negative pneumonia
    Fungus ball (aspergilloma)
Tumors
    Pulmonary carcinoma
    Bronchial adenoma
Trauma
    Lung contusion
    Flail chest
    Multiple rib fractures
Vascular Disease
    Pulmonary thromboembolism
    Cardiac failure
    Mitral stenosis, chronic
    Pulmonary vasculitis
Bleeding Disorders
    Hereditary bleeding disorders
    Acquired disorders (drugs)
    Anticoagulant treatment
Idiopathic (10% to 15%)

Note: Although there are many potential causes for hemoptysis, pulmonary infection and tumors remain the most frequently encountered causes in the elderly patient.

Differential Diagnosis

The first step is to verify that hemoptysis has occurred and that blood is present in the expectorated secretions and to differentiate blood streaking from the expectoration of pure blood. It must then be determined that blood was not vomited and is not the product of nasal bleeding or lesions of the pharynx, either inflammatory, traumatic, or self-induced. Factitious bleeding due to self-induced trauma to the oral mucous membranes is uncommon in the elderly, but must be considered in the manipulative patient at any age. When an obvious nasal or oral bleeding source has been ruled out by quick examination, and because bleeding is frequently not present or evident on first examination, the patient warrants an orderly examination for its source, including chest films, evaluation for coagulation abnormalities, and bronchoscopy to determine the site of bleeding.

Infection of the bronchial tree or lung parenchyma is a common cause of bleeding, but generally there is also a history of chronic cough and sputum production. The most common cause for blood streaking in an active cigarette smoker is chronic bronchitis. The rusty sputum of a bacterial pneumonia should not be confused with frank hemoptysis, although in gram-negative bacterial pneumonia, such as that due to *Klebsiella,* frankly bloody sputum is not rare. A common cause of hemoptysis due to infection in elderly patients is tuberculosis, which should be associated with chronic cough and weight loss and is also frequently accompanied by night sweats or low-grade fever. Bronchiectasis characteristically leads to repeated bouts of pulmonary infection and is at times preceded by episodes of hemoptysis before the appearance of fever and the typical purulent sputum. Patients with a past history of a necrotizing pneumonia or lung trauma followed by bronchiectasis should have a long, subsequent history of daily cough and sputum, with a sputum volume generally exceeding 30–50 ml/day, and recurring bouts of bronchial infection. The presence of finger clubbing supports a diagnosis either of bronchiectasis or bronchogenic carcinoma in the older patient, although clubbing is chronic in bronchiectasis and of recent origin in lung cancer. Because adenomas are more common in younger patients, a bronchial tumor is likely to be malignant when associated with hemoptysis in the elderly.

In the presence of chest trauma, bleeding may be found with lung contusion or from secondary lung injury associated with flail chest or fractured ribs. If bleeding is brisk, the possibility of a lacerated vessel dictates that the patient receive emergency handling and attention at a treatment facility capable of bronchoscopy and emergency thoracic surgery as indicated, although surgical treatment is not commonly required.

In the older patient the relatively sudden onset of hemoptysis consisting of frank blood in the absence of purulent sputum, when it is associated with dyspnea, cough, or pleuritic pain, should immediately suggest pulmonary thromboembolism with pulmonary infarction. This diagnosis is especially likely in the debilitated patient who has been bedridden or immobilized after major surgical procedures and in patients with COPD or arteriosclerotic heart disease with atrial fibrillation. Further predisposing factors are obesity, left ventricular failure, and underlying malignancies, because these all increase the frequency of thrombophlebitis and pulmonary embolization. This is an important diagnosis to make because the patients require transport to a diagnostic and treating medical facility and commonly require supplemental oxygen for hypoxemia.

Patients with left heart failure, especially patients with mitral stenosis, traditionally experience hemoptysis due to pulmonary venous hypertension that causes capillary bleeding. In addition, several forms of pulmonary vasculitis may lead to substantial and vigorous bleeding, which at times reaches proportions requiring transfusion. However, these diagnoses are not commonly established without medical evaluation, and certainly they would be difficult to make in the field. A history of recurring left ventricular failure or known rheumatic heart disease and the presence of physical findings for congestive heart failure or mitral valve disease are helpful in establishing the etiology when these are causative. In general, when there is an extensive history of recurring hemoptysis, it is rare for a true emergency to exist, and orderly transport to an evaluation and treatment facility is the most rational course.

Emergency Management and Transportation

Patients with hemoptysis, however minor, have considerable anxiety and usually have a mild tachycardia. If vital signs are stable and there is a history of repetitive blood spitting with small volumes of blood, no real emergency exists and the patient can be transported to a treatment facility in a routine manner; however, monitoring of vital signs is still necessary. The patient can benefit from continued reassurance during transport. It is also reasonable to attempt to estimate blood loss while the patient is being evaluated and transported to a treatment facility. When bleeding is massive and when training and facilities permit, it is prudent to establish an IV infusion with a large-bore needle, which may be helpful in expediting volume replacement at the receiving facility. Supplemental oxygen may be given by nasal cannula or, when the patient's anxiety permits, by face mask at levels of 25% to 30% or 2 L/min by nasal cannula. Major indications for administering oxygen are the presence of underlying lung disease or arteriosclerotic heart disease with known left ventricular failure, or where any underlying condition suggests that significant hypoxemia exists. A history of a bleeding disorder or the use of anticoagulants could direct immediate treatment on arrival at the emergency facility. Significant anemia may mask hypoxemia by retarding the appearance of cyanosis due to the increased difficulty in generating 5 gm/% of reduced hemoglobin that is generally required for visible cyanosis.

Because most patients with active hemoptysis that is more extensive than blood streaking of sputum are considered to require diagnostic bronchoscopy to determine the cause, as well as the site, of bleeding, communication with the receiving facility may permit appropriate personnel to be available for early study of the patient. The more extensive the hemoptysis, the more imperative it is that the patient have early bronchoscopy performed by a qualified thoracic surgeon. A localization of the bleeding site and surgical intervention may be required on an emergency basis. Despite these cautions, however, the majority of patients with hemoptysis may be handled in a routine manner with speed and dispatch but with calm and reassurance because they are not at risk of exsanguination.

AIRWAY MANAGEMENT—OXYGEN THERAPY AND ARTIFICIAL VENTILATION

Evaluating and Establishing the Airway

Checking and clearing the upper airway is the first priority in the trauma patient and in those in whom vomiting with aspiration or injury to upper airways is suspected.[89,90] The presence of respiratory distress and stridor calls for immediate inspection of the oropharynx for a foreign body, hemorrhage, or edema. Patients with high levels of airway obstruction are agitated and reveal an exaggerated respiratory effort with retractions, probably with cyanosis and an altered mental status.

The first step in ensuring the establishment of an adequate airway is to tilt the head backward, producing hyperextension and an elevation of the floor of the mouth to free the tongue from the posterior pharyngeal wall. This is done if a cervical cord injury is considered unlikely. When the patient is apneic despite hyperextension, positive pressure inflation efforts should be attempted with manual inflation using an oral airway and a bag-and-mask apparatus. This may establish ventilation and also documents the ease with which lungs can be inflated. Evaluating resistance to lung inflation is best done by the manual bag-and-mask technique, although it can also be done with mouth-to-mouth resuscitation techniques. The oropharynx should be surveyed for foreign material, which should be removed if present, with suctioning used for retained secretions. Solid particles may be removed by wiping. The presence of continued obstruction after these maneuvers may call for further hyperextension while displacing the mandible, using the operator's fingers to push the descending ramus of the mandible forward. In the elderly, it is very important to seek out and remove any partial dentures loose in the oropharynx.

Oropharyngeal and nasopharyngeal airways may be helpful, but the oropharyngeal airway is generally limited to use in the comatose patient and is strictly a temporary device. Patients who are conscious and have respiratory distress generally fight the oropharyngeal airway, which produces gagging and vomiting, but this airway is helpful in preventing the teeth from sealing off the oral cavity for suction and evaluation. The oropharyngeal airway is strictly a temporary device in the unconscious patient.

The nasopharyngeal airway is a better technique for maintaining an upper airway; it consists of a hollow latex rubber tube shaped to correspond to the contours of the nasopharynx. By using lubrication and a topical anesthetic it is easily placed through the nasal passage that is the largest on inspection. The primary hazard is trauma to the nasal mucous membranes with bleeding. The nasopharyngeal tube provides an excellent route for posterior pharyngeal suctioning.

Endotracheal Intubation

Specific indications for the use of endotracheal intubation, either by the nasal or oral route, are

- the need to maintain a patent airway in a deeply unconscious patient with underlying cardiopulmonary disease
- the need to protect against aspiration when it has either occurred or there is a high likelihood of it occurring
- when deep tracheobronchial suctioning is required because of the patient's mental status or the failure of the cough mechanism to clear secretions

- where positive pressure mechanical ventilation is required as in ARDS
- when there is chest trauma and severe respiratory insufficiency.

Endotracheal intubation is commonly used in the patient in whom high concentrations of oxygen must be administered in a closed system, who has severe pulmonary embolism with shunting resistant to routine oxygen supplementation, or in the patient with ARDS where hypoxemia is profound and likely to induce a metabolic acidosis.

The orotracheal intubation technique has the advantage of speed, with rapid establishment of an airway possible and a potential for using a larger endotracheal tube. In acute resuscitation, the oral route is generally utilized to provide a stable airway in as rapid a fashion as possible. However, for the conscious patient an oral tube is less comfortable, and stabilization of the tube is more difficult. Common accidents are extubation or accidental advancement of the endotracheal tube into the right mainstem bronchus. Nasotracheal intubation provides more comfort and a more stable tube, but requires more technique than is commonly available at a trauma site, except for the emergency management of airways within hospitals or other emergency care facilities. Figure 5–17 illustrates the configuration of standard disposable endotracheal tubes with a large-volume cuff that are currently used to provide a good airway seal and minimum trauma to the tracheal mucosa. The high-volume, low-pressure cuff greatly reduces the frequency and severity of

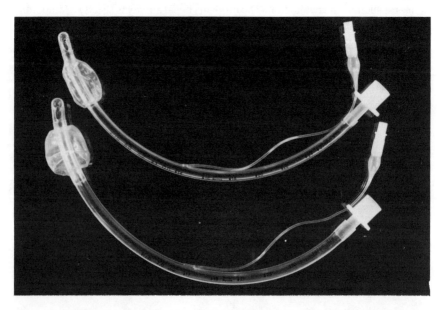

Figure 5–17 Two sizes of standard disposable endotracheal tubes are illustrated utilizing the large volume/low pressure cuff to reduce trauma to the tracheal mucosa.

tracheal damage and later tracheostenosis. However, care should be taken not to overinflate the cuff; inflation should be sufficient to provide a seal.[91,92]

Figure 5–18 illustrates the use of the laryngoscope to expose the glottis and permit safe and rapid insertion of the endotracheal tube with minimal trauma to the vocal cords.

The lubricated endotracheal tube is inserted atraumatically between the vocal cords under direct visualization. The endotracheal tube must not be passed blindly because it will most often enter the esophagus or traumatize the cords. Once the cuff has passed approximately 1 in beyond the vocal cords, the cuff can be inflated and ventilation attempted, as one looks for simultaneous and symmetrical expansion of both hemithoraces. Once it is properly placed, it may be secured, and ventilation with a manual bag may be initiated, utilizing an enriched oxygen mixture routinely in early stages of respiratory support. It is desirable to use 100% oxygen for 2–3 min before suctioning through the endotracheal tube be-

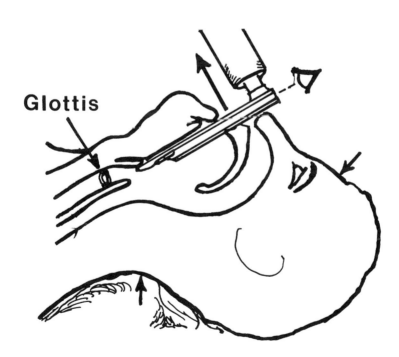

Glottis

Figure 5–18 Laryngoscopy to visualize the glottis for the purpose of inserting an endotracheal tube requires extension at the neck and depression of the epiglottis to bring the vocal cords into view.

cause suctioning, although it may clear away secretions, also induces profound hypoxemia.

If intubation is not successful, the patient should be returned to ventilation using an oropharyngeal airway and a bag-and-mask technique, using 100% oxygen to stabilize the patient and provide adequate ventilation before making a second attempt at intubation.

Esophageal Obturator Airway

The esophageal obturator airway (EOA) is somewhat controversial and limited to use by the status of the patient and the nature of the EMT's expertise and experience. The insertion of a tube into the esophagus with side vents to permit ventilation via the hypopharynx is easier than endotracheal intubation or may represent an alternative when intubation cannot be achieved.[93,94] The device consists of a mask fixed to a tube with a blind end and an inflatable cuff, with side holes designed to permit ventilation via the hypopharynx without intubation of the trachea (Figure 5–19). Sealing the esophagus with an inflated cuff permits air to enter the trachea and is also helpful in reducing the risk of aspiration of stomach contents. Because the aged patient may have osteoarthritis of the cervical vertebrae and limited extension of the head and neck, the EOA is seen as a superior device in the aged patient, although it should be noted that extension of the head

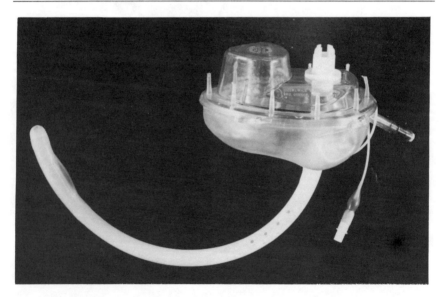

Figure 5–19 The esophageal obturator airway is made up of a tight-fitting face mask and an inflatable cuff to seal the trachea and permit diversion of inspired air into the tracheobronchial tree. Because ventilation is then indirect, it is recommended for use in the comatose patient requiring intubation.

and neck is also required for its insertion and function. Its use should probably be limited to patients who are unconscious because there is substantial risk of gagging and vomiting in the semicomatose patient.

Hazards include trauma to the esophagus, gastric distention despite the inflated cuff, inadvertent tracheal intubation, and trauma to the upper airways. Experience with small esophageal perforations has led to the recommendation that only 20 ml of air be used to inflate the esophageal cuff. The greatest limitation to this technique is the lack of experience on the part of the operator and the fact that its use is restricted to comatose patients. Standard texts should be consulted for further details about the insertion of the EOA and its applications.

Tracheostomy and Cricothyrotomy

Tracheostomy is a dangerous surgical procedure to perform in the field because of the risk of severe bleeding and most emergency medical personnel's lack of experience with it. In the presence of complete airway obstruction that is not corrected by clearing of the upper airways or manual thrusts, however, it is rarely possible for the safer cricothyrotomy to be lifesaving. Tracheostomy is only performed when all attempts at ventilation have failed and endotracheal intubation is unsuccessful. It is likely to be employed when there is severe trauma to the upper airways, including upper airway burns, edema, or hematoma above the larynx.

Using a standard cricothyrotomy kit an incision is made in the cricothyroid membrane between the thyroid cartilage above and the cricoid cartilage below, and a small airway is established with the use of a metal cannula or large-bore plastic catheter.[95] The membrane is punctured with a transverse incision using a blade with the cannula introduced through the incision and directed downward so as not to traumatize the cords. It is necessary to control local bleeding and to evaluate the location and adequacy of the tube immediately by identifying the presence of ventilation through auscultation and chest movement and by feeling air movement through the cannula. The cannula is stabilized and both tied and taped in place. In the presence of spontaneous respirations, a high oxygen mixture may be delivered by placing a mask set at 40% oxygen mixture over the cannula opening. Oxygen catheters should never be inserted in the cannula because it greatly increases air flow resistance. This is an emergency airway and is only intended to permit survival during transportation to a medical care facility (Figure 5–20).

Oxygen Therapy and Artificial Ventilation

Body oxygen stores partly determine the patient's tolerance for apnea or complete airway obstruction and vary widely, generally providing up to 5 min of vital organ life after complete cessation of respirations. The normal individual is estimated to have 11 ml/kg of body weight, which is sufficient to sustain life for 3–5 min if the patient has a normal oxygen consumption and is at rest. The

CRICOTHYROTOMY SITE •

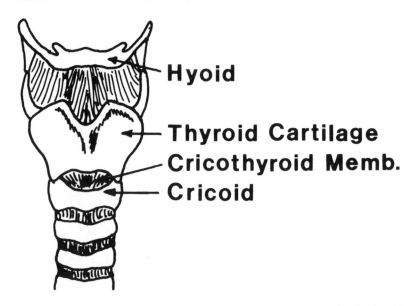

Hyoid

Thyroid Cartilage
Cricothyroid Memb.
Cricoid

Figure 5–20 The cricothyroid membrane is readily identified as the soft zone below the thyroid cartilage and above the cricoid cartilage. The vocal cords lie immediately above this site.

presence of high temperature, agitation, or physical activity, coupled with anemia, low oxygen levels in the lung and tissue stores, or other causes of reduced oxygen stores, greatly limits the patient's tolerance for apnea.

The signs and symptoms of hypoxemia were described in the section on acute respiratory failure. Table 5–22 illustrates oxygen tensions that would be anticipated in the normal individual based on age, revealing a progressive fall in PaO_2

Table 5–22 Effect of Age on PaO_2

Age Group	PaO_2 mm Hg Mean	PaO_2 mm Hg Lower Limit of Normal	A–aDO_2 mm Hg Mean	A–aDO_2 mm Hg Upper Limit of Normal
31–40	93	82	11	22
41–50	93	77	11	24
51–60	88	67	14	24
61–75	87	64	16	28
76–90	82	60	18	30

with age, assuming the absence of cardiopulmonary disease. It is clear that serious hypoxemia could easily occur with alteration of the lung ventilation/perfusion balance in the presence of trauma or other pulmonary disorder. In addition, significant acidosis may alter oxygen loading on hemoglobin and reduce oxygen transport to the tissues.

One indication for the use of supplemental oxygen is the presence of anemia as an underlying disorder or as secondary to active bleeding. The effect of anemia on oxygen content is illustrated in Table 5–23 as a reminder that significant anemia may lower oxygen content at any oxygen tension and that transport of oxygen may be critical in the presence of anemia combined with a reduced oxygen tension.

Oxygen is indicated in those patients who are apneic and in those with respiratory distress associated with signs of hypoxemia, such as cyanosis, tachycardia, and restlessness. It is also indicated when there is any clinical evidence of respiratory insufficiency, including pulmonary edema, acute myocardial infarction, drug overdose, CVA, chest trauma, COPD, shock from any cause, smoke inhalation, fume exposure, or pneumonia.

In general, oxygen can be administered at concentrations of 25% to 30% with minimal hazard and only those patients established to have chronic hypercapnia are at risk of the oxygen treatment suppressing respirations. Such patients are readily identified. Many patients require even higher concentrations of oxygen if there is an inadequate response to initial treatment.

Oxygen Sources and Equipment

Oxygen is generally used in emergency medical care from steel cylinders, with D, E, or M cylinders most commonly used. The pin-indexing safety attachment system permits the safe use of gas with only appropriate pressure regulators fitting oxygen tanks. Oxygen is always obtained through a pressure regulator that reduces the pressure to levels suitable for use with medical equipment, in the range of 40–70 psi. Humidification is generally employed to avoid drying the patient's

Table 5–23 Arterial O_2 Content in Anemia

PO_2	Sat O_2%	VOL % O_2 CONTENT (Hb)		
20	32	6.5	4.3	3.2
30	58	11.7	7.9	5.9
40	75	15.1	10.2	7.5
50	85	17.3	11.6	8.7
60	91	18.5	12.4	9.3
70	94	19.1	12.8	9.7
80	96	19.5	13.1	9.9
90	97	19.8	13.3	10.1

secretions, although there is some evidence that humidification may not be critical in the case of oxygen administered for short periods by nasal cannula or mask. Despite this evidence, it continues to be standard practice to employ humidification when delivering dry oxygen to any oxygen supplementation device.[96]

Selection of Oxygen Concentration and Mode of Administration

Patients with respiratory distress generally require supplementation to deliver an FIO_2 of 25% to 30% oxygen, with some conditions requiring a closed system and higher concentrations. Modes of oxygen delivery in common use are listed in Table 5–24.

The response to increased oxygen concentration is relatively good in such disorders as pneumonia, pulmonary edema, and respiratory failure associated with respiratory infections. However, in such conditions as massive pulmonary embolism and ARDS, the response to oxygen supplementation may be remarkably poor due to high levels of venous admixture or shunting. Table 5–25 illustrates the approximate PaO_2 to be anticipated with oxygen concentrations varying from ambient air to 100%, based on the percentage of approximate shunt, although these levels are not modified to take into account the reduced resting oxygen tension seen in the older patient. The normal adult lung has a 3% to 5% shunt that is anatomic and this is probably doubled in the very aged patient. Figure 5–21

Table 5–24 Oxygen Supplementation Modes

Device Used	O_2 Flow Rates (L/min)	O_2 Concentration Delivered (%)
Nasal cannula or catheter	1	24
	2	28
	3	32
	4	35
	5–6	38–44
Nasal catheter	6–8	35–50
Face mask	5–6	40
	6–8	50–60
Venturi mask		
24%	4	24
28%	4	28
35%	8	35
40%	8	40
Rebreathing mask	6–10	35–60
Nonrebreathing mask with bag	6	60
	7	70
	8–10	80–95+

Table 5–25 Effect of FIO_2 and Shunt on Arterial PO_2

	Approximate Shunt (%)							
FIO_2	0%	5%	10%	15%	20%	25%	30%	50%
0.21	100	90	80	65	60	55	50	42
0.35	210	150	110	85	65	57	52	45
0.40	250	185	180	90	70	65	60	47
0.60	390	315	235	160	105	75	65	52
0.80	—	460	360	265	180	110	70	55
1.00	—	—	475	400	290	170	100	60
				PaO_2 mm Hg				

illustrates oxygen tensions and shunt percentage, reflecting several literature sources and the author's experience. It is clear that, with high degrees of shunt, such as 50%, the response to an FIO_2 of 1.0 is negligible. It is in such patients that proper management requires the use of either a mask with reservoir bag at 9–10 L/min or, when the respiratory bellows are insufficient, the addition of an endotracheal tube and 100% oxygen by bag utilizing a reservoir to approach 100% oxygen administration.

Nasal Cannula or Catheter

The nasal catheter is useful in the uncooperative patient who is unable to keep a cannula in place, but has no other advantage over the nasal cannula, even in a patient with predominant mouth breathing. The catheter is inserted after measuring the distance from the tip of the patient's nose to the ear lobe and marking this distance on the catheter. After lubrication of the catheter and carefully avoiding obstruction of the lumen, it is inserted into the nasal passage that is largest until it is visible behind the uvula. Insertion should be gentle to avoid trauma to mucous membranes with resultant bleeding. The catheter is withdrawn until the tip is just out of sight above the uvula and is then taped to the patient's nose and cheek, permitting considerable freedom of movement so that it is not dislodged or used as a vehicle to traumatize the nasal mucous membranes. Humidified oxygen is then delivered through the catheter.

The nasal cannula is more comfortable and quite suitable even with patients who are mouth breathers. It is the preferred mode of oxygen delivery when only mild supplementation is required and the patient is not restless, agitated, or uncooperative. It may be used when a mask is desired but ineffective because of the patient's intolerance.

A simple face mask, usually of translucent plastic, may be used to deliver oxygen concentrations as high as 60%. The levels achieved are based on oxygen flow and the patient's exchange level. The most accurate oxygen concentrations are achieved with higher flow rates and low tidal volumes. The simple mask contains no valves or reservoir bag and prevents rebreathing of CO_2 by the use of

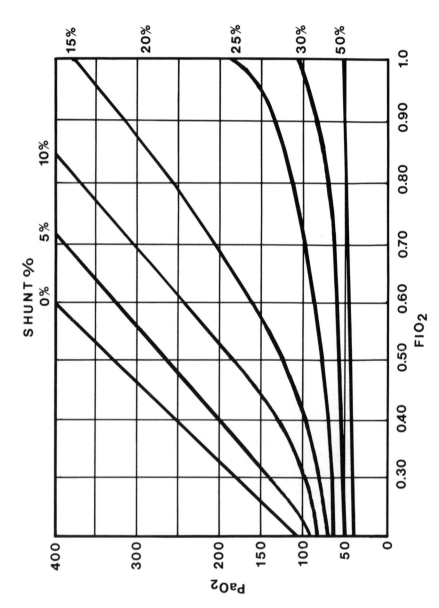

Figure 5–21 Common oxygen tensions are illustrated with the use of supplemental oxygen at an FIO_2 of 0.21 to 1.0, illustrating the progressive drop in oxygen tension as percentage shunt increases. Note that the lines only represent mean values and that some variation should be expected.

high oxygen flows. Ambient air enters the mask through the side holes to provide the predicted mixtures.

The Venturi mask employs the Venturi principle and is especially useful when precise oxygen concentrations are required, as in patients with established COPD in whom chronic hypercapnia may dictate cautious use of supplemental oxygen to avoid reducing a possible hypoxic respiratory drive. Figure 5–22 illustrates a typical disposable Venturi mask device that is partly trimmed to reveal oxygen concentration settings. The Venturi mask can generally be operated at oxygen flows 50% below those prescribed without significantly affecting the oxygen concentration delivered, although the prescribed flows provide comfort and control heat within the mask. As with other devices, humidification is recommended for the aged patient because those patients with shock or significant respiratory disease generally have dessicated secretions and dry mucous membranes prior to therapy and have further dessication with the prolonged use of dry oxygen during transport. Manipulation of the Venturi mask by sealing ambient air entrainment openings to provide higher O_2 concentrations should be discouraged because higher oxygen concentration requirements would dictate a change in delivery system, such as the use of a mask with a reservoir bag.

A partial rebreathing mask is a simple mask with an attached reservoir bag into which O_2 is delivered. On inspiration, the reservoir mask gas is inspired along with that in the reservoir bag. During the expiratory phase, the reservoir is filled with pure oxygen from an oxygen source, thus maintaining relatively high oxygen mixtures even for patients who are tachypneic and have high tidal volumes. It is necessary to adjust the oxygen flow so that the reservoir bag remains relatively inflated to provide adequate oxygen levels. Oxygen flows of 6–10 L/min are adequate to provide oxygen concentrations of 35% to 60% in the average patient with mild tachypnea.

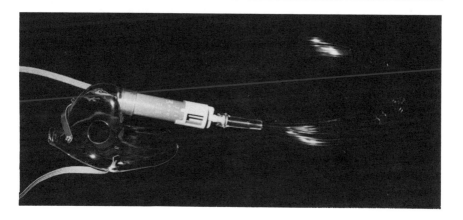

Figure 5–22 One type of disposable Venturi mask is illustrated with its multiple settings to permit standard oxygen enrichment mixtures, as shown in Table 5–24.

The nonrebreathing mask, seen in Figure 5–23, provides a reservoir of oxygen in both the bag and the mask; it also includes a valve that permits inspiration to occur only from the reservoir bag and expiration to occur only to the outside, which then provides the potential for almost 100% oxygen delivery at oxygen flows of 9–10 L/min. This system is preferred for patients who have large shunts, but do not require ventilation support during transportation to a medical facility.

The bag-valve-mask resuscitator is utilized to ventilate the patient who requires both mechanical ventilation support and high oxygen concentrations in a relatively closed system. When an endotracheal tube is inserted, it is useful to increase the oxygen tension before intubation. Ventilation support can then continue by removing the mask and using the bag and reservoir to ventilate via the endo-tracheal tube. This system is preferable to the use of mechanical ventilators because it allows the operator to sense or feel pulmonary resistance and changes in lung compliance in the course of treatment. In addition, the gentle and controlled application of pressure is safer than that delivered by a fixed mechanical device. A typical disposable model utilizing a bag with oxygen supply line and an attached oxygen reservoir is illustrated in Figure 5–24.

The bag-valve-mask system requires:

- a resilient and self-filling bag with a valve system that permits 15 L/min oxygen input,
- a transparent plastic face mask permitting a tight fit and visualization of vomitus or secretions

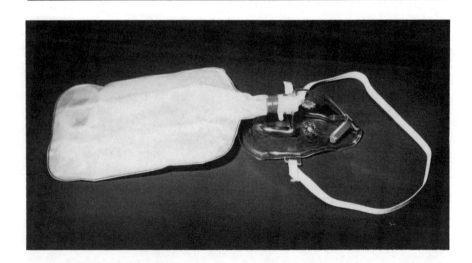

Figure 5–23 The nonrebreathing mask with reservoir bag provides the highest oxygen concentrations available without a closed system. The reservoir bag permits delivery of over 95% oxygen at oxygen flows of 9–10 L/min.

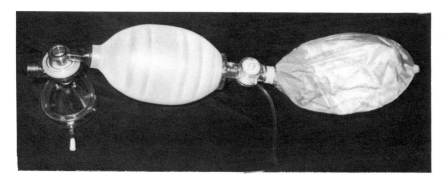

Figure 5-24 The bag-valve-mask system is designed to deliver high oxygen mixtures, delivering close to 100% oxygen with even the highest ventilation rates. The face mask should be tight fitting and made of transparent plastic to permit visualizing the respiratory zone.

- an oxygen reservoir bag that is large enough to permit close to 100% oxygen to be delivered at very high ventilation rates.

With good technique, an experienced operator can use this system to support the patient's spontaneous respirations, thereby providing not only oxygen enrichment but also a very reassuring and responsive system that reduces the patient's work of breathing and also reduces any tendency for the patient to fight or resist ventilation support. Coaching of the patient and constant conversation reassure the patient and may also improve the coordination of the patient's breathing with the use of the resuscitation bag. It is very important to avoid overventilating patients with COPD who may have had previous hypercapnia, especially as the lung slowly becomes more compliant in a patient with pulmonary edema that is improving, in whom the risk of excessive ventilation increases as the lung clears. One clue that alkalosis from hyperventilation has occurred is improvement in the patient's color and mental status, followed by slow onset of a semicomatose state with muscle twitching. Once this system is employed in the ventilation of a patient, it is very important to continue support because withdrawing it may result in apnea with progressive hypoxemia due to the patient having been rendered hyperoxic, alkalotic, and hypocapnic, thus obliterating all respiratory drive. Profound hypoxemia may occur before hypocapnia and alkalosis reverse to permit the resumption of spontaneous respirations.

Mechanical ventilators are not commonly required during patient transport, although a pressure-regulated portable ventilator operating from an oxygen source may be useful in delivering interrupted mechanical support or aerosol bronchodilator drugs to patients with severe COPD. In general, their use should be very brief and intermittent to avoid increasing distention in patients with COPD.

Hazards of treatment are hyperventilation and pneumothorax due to barotrauma, although these are infrequent when inflation pressures are maintained at 15 CMH_2O or less. The hazard of distention due to gas trapping following prolonged use of IPPB is more common and important.

Suctioning

Suctioning should always be done with a catheter fitted to a Y-connector that permits intermittent application of suction. In that way the catheter may be inserted after oxygen enrichment with 100% oxygen for 2 min in the case of an endotracheal tube, with gradual intermittent suctioning as the catheter is slowly withdrawn, thereby avoiding trauma to the mucosa from continuous suction. Suctioning of the oropharynx may be somewhat more continuous, but it is still useful to apply suction for 3–5 sec, then withdraw it for 2 sec, to avoid drawing mucous membranes into the suction tip and producing trauma by movement of the catheter. Blind nasotracheal suctioning can be hazardous because it may induce arrhythmias or bradycardia by stimulation of the vagus nerve through both direct suctioning of mucous membranes and the physical trauma of introducing a suction catheter. Suctioning should never continue beyond 15 sec, even when done in an interrupted manner, and repeated suctioning requires the use of supplemental oxygen to avoid generating profound hypoxemia. When suctioning via an endotracheal tube, it may be possible to suction both mainstem bronchi by turning the head to one side and then the other prior to completing catheter insertion and the application of suctioning. However, in the author's experience, the catheter tends to repeatedly enter the right mainstem bronchus, despite these maneuvers. It is helpful to turn the patient on the right side in the right lateral position with the left chest uppermost and to suction after that position has been maintained for approximately 1 min to remove secretions that are presented to the catheter by gravity drainage from the left mainstem bronchus.

REFERENCES

1. Sorbini CA, Brassi V, Solinas E, et al: Arterial oxygen tension in relation to age in healthy subjects. *Respiration* 25:3–13, 1968.

2. Standards and guidelines for cardiopulmonary resuscitation (CPR) and emergency cardiac care (ECC). *JAMA,* June 6, 1986.

3. Caroline NL: *Emergency Care in the Streets,* ed 2. Boston, Little Brown & Co, 1983.

4. Mendelsohn CL: The aspiration of stomach contents into the lungs during obstetric anesthesia. *Am J Obstet Gynecol* 52:191–205, 1946.

5. Awe WC, Fletcher WS, Jacob SW: The pathophysiology of aspiration pneumonitis. *Surgery* 60:232–239, 1966.

6. Pamintuan R, Brashear RE, Ross JC, et al: Cardiovascular effects of experimental aspiration pneumonia in dogs. *Am Rev Respir Dis* 103:516–523, 1971.

7. Hamelberg WV, Bosomworth PP: *Aspiration Pneumonitis.* Springfield, IL, Charles C Thomas, 1968.

8. Bynum LJ, Pierce AK: Pulmonary aspiration of gastric contents. *Am Rev Resp Dis* 114:1129–1136, 1976.

9. Lefrock JL, Clark TS, Davies B, et al: Aspiration pneumonia: A ten-year review. *Am Surg* 45:305–313, 1979.

10. Arms RA, Dines DE, Tinstman TC: Aspiration pneumonia. *Chest* 65:136–139, 1974.

11. Wynne JW, Modell JH: Respiratory aspiration of stomach contents. *Ann Intern Med* 87:466–474, 1977.

12. Landay MJ, Christensen EW, Bynum LJ: Pulmonary manifestations of acute aspiration of gastric contents. *Am J Roentgenol* 131:587–592, 1978.

13. Murray HW: Antimicrobial therapy in pulmonary aspiration. *Am J Med* 66:138–190, 1979.

14. Sykes MK, McNichol MW, Campbell EJM: *Respiratory Failure,* ed 2. Oxford, Scientific Publications, 1976.

15. Brackett NC, Cohen JJ, Schwartz WB: Carbon dioxide titration curve of normal man, effect of increasing degrees of acute hypercapnia on acid-base equilibrium. *N Engl J Med* 272:6–12, 1965.

16. Filley GF: *Acid-Base and Blood Gas Regulation.* Philadelphia, Lea and Febiger, 1971.

17. Campbell EJM: The J. Burns Amberson lecture—The management of acute respiratory failure in chronic bronchitis and emphysema. *Am Rev Resp Dis* 96:626–639, 1967.

18. Pontoppidan H, Geffin B, Lowenstein E: *Acute Respiratory Failure in the Adult.* Boston, Little Brown & Co, 1973.

19. Mathews KP: Respiratory atopic disease. *JAMA* 248:2587–2610, 1982.

20. Thurlbeck WM: Pathology of status asthmaticus, in Weiss EB (ed): *Status Asthmaticus.* Baltimore, University Park Press, 1978, Chapter 3.

21. McFadden ER Jr, Lyons HA: Arterial blood gas tensions in asthma. *N Engl J Med* 278:1027–1037, 1968.

22. McFadden ER Jr, Kiser R, DeGroot WJ: Acute bronchial asthma: Relation between clinical and physiological manifestations. *N Engl J Med* 288:221–225, 1973.

23. Rebuck AS, Read J: Assessment and management of severe asthma. *Am J Med* 51:788–798, 1971.

24. Bocles JS: Status asthmaticus. *Med Clin North Am* 54:493–509, 1970.

25. Weiss EB: Status asthmaticus, in Weiss EB, Segal MS, (eds): *Bronchial Asthma, Mechanisms and Therapeutics.* Boston, Little Brown & Co, 1976, pp 875–914.

26. Snider GL: Staging therapeutic schedules to clinical severity in status asthmaticus, in Weiss EB (ed): *Status Asthmaticus,* Baltimore, University Park Press, 1978.

27. Jusko WJ, Koup JR, Vance JW, et al: Intravenous theophylline therapy: Nomogram guidelines. *Ann Inter Med* 86:400–404, 1977.

28. Silverberg E: Cancer statistics. *Ca—A Cancer Journal for Clinicians* 33:9–25, 1983.

29. *The Health Consequences of Smoking: Chronic Obstructive Lung Disease: A Report of the Surgeon General.* US Department of Health and Human Services, prepublic ed. Public Health Service, Office of Smoking and Health, Rockville, MD, 1983, pp 215–246.

30. *Chronic Obstructive Pulmonary Disease,* ed 5. American Lung Association and American Thoracic Society, 1977, pp 11–70.

31. Thurlbeck WM: *Chronic Airflow Obstruction in Lung Disease.* Philadelphia, WB Saunders Co, 1976, pp 96–234, 253–287.

32. Guenter CA, Welch MH: *Pulmonary Medicine.* Philadelphia, JB Lippincott Co, 1982, pp 566–688.

33. Matthay RA (ed): Obstructive lung diseases, *Med Clin North Am,* 65:453–645, 1981.

34. Hodgkin JE: *Chronic Obstructive Pulmonary Disease,* Park Ridge IL, American College of Chest Physicians, 1979.

35. Guides to the evaluation of permanent impairment—The respiratory system. *JAMA* 194:919–926, 1965.

36. Bone RC (ed): Adult respiratory distress syndrome. *Clinics Chest Med* 3:1–212, 1982.

37. Fraser RG, Pare JAP: Infectious Diseases of the Lungs, in *Diagnosis of Diseases of the Chest,* vol 2, ed 2. Philadelphia, WB Saunders, 1978.

38. Liu C: Nonbacterial Pneumonia. In Hoeprich PD (ed): *Infectious Diseases,* ed 2. Hagerstown, MD, Harper & Row, 1977, pp 283–294.

39. Hand WL: When to suspect a viral cause of pneumonia. *J Resp Dis* 2:36–43, 1981.

40. Austrian R, Gold J: Pneumococcal bacteremia with especial reference to bacteremic pneumococcal pneumonia. *Ann Int Med* 60:759–776, 1964.

41. Lerner AM, Jankauskas K: The classical bacterial pneumonias. *Dis Month* February 1975, pp 1–46.

42. Austrian R: Pneumococcal infection and pneumococcal vaccine. *N Engl J Med* 297:938–939, 1977.

43. Johanson WG Jr, Pierce AK, Sanford JP, Thomas GD: Nosocomial respiratory infections with gram-negative bacilli: The significance of colonization of the respiratory tract. *Ann Int Med* 77:701–706, 1972.

44. Mostow SR: Pneumonias acquired outside the hospital. *Med Clin North Am* 58:555–564, 1974.

45. Johanson WG Jr, Higuchi JH: Common gram-negative bacillary pneumonias, in Braude AL (ed): *Medical Microbiology and Infectious Diseases.* Philadelphia, WB Saunders, 1981, pp 918–921.

46. LaForce FM: Hospital acquired gram-negative rod pneumonias: An overview. *Am J Med* 70:664–669, 1981.

47. Weeden D, Smith GH: Surgical experiences in the management of spontaneous pneumothorax, 1972-1982. *Thorax* 38:737–743, 1983.

48. Moser KM, Spragg RC: Spontaneous pneumothorax, in *Resp Emergencies,* ed 2. St. Louis, CV Mosby Co, 1982, pp 176–193.

49. George BB, Herbert SJ, Shames JM, et al: Pneumothorax complicating pulmonary emphysema. *JAMA* 234:389–393, 1975.

50. Sasahara AA: Current problems in pulmonary embolism: Introduction, in Sasahara AA, Sonnenblick EH, Lesch M (eds): *Pulmonary Emboli.* New York, Grune & Stratton, 1975, pp 1–4.

51. Sharma GVRK, Sarahara AA, McIntyre KM: Pulmonary embolism: The great imitator. *Dis Month* 22:438, 1976.

52. Freiman DG, Suyemoto J, Wessler S: Frequency of pulmonary thromboembolism in man. *N Engl J Med* 272:1278–1280, 1965.

53. Horowitz RE, Tatter D: Lethal pulmonary embolism. *Thrombosis,* National Academy of Sciences 19, 1969.

54. Virchow R: Weitere untersuchungen uber die verstopfung der lungenarterie und ihre folgen. *B eitr exp pathol physiol* 2:21, 1846.

55. Sasahara AA, Hyers TM, Cole CM, et al: The urokinase pulmonary embolism trial: A national cooperative study. *Circulation* 47(suppl 2):1–108, 1973.

56. Belenkie I: Pulmonary vascular disease, in Guenter CA, Welch MH (eds): *Pulmonary Medicine,* ed 2. Philadelphia, JB Lippincott Co, 1982, pp 475–509.

57. Benator SR, Ferguson AD, Goldschmidt RB: Fat embolism: Some clinical observations and a review of controversial aspects. *Quart J Med* 41:85–96, 1972.

58. Evarts CM: The fat embolism syndrome: A review. *Surg Clin North Am* 50:493–500, 1970.

59. Terrill JB, Montgomery RR, Reinhardt CF: Toxic gases from fires. *Science* 200:1343–1347, 1978.

60. Dyer RF, Esch VH: Polyvinyl chloride toxicity in fires. *JAMA* 235:393–397, 1976.

61. Charan NB, Myers CG, Lakshminarayan S, et al. Pulmonary injuries associated with acute sulfur dioxide inhalation. *Am Rev Resp Dis* 119:555–560, 1979.

62. Winter PM, Miller JH: Carbon monoxide poisoning. *JAMA* 236:1502–1504, 1976.

63. Bernard C: *Lecons sur les effects des substances toxiques et medicamenteuses*. Paris, Baillere, 1857.

64. Haldane J: The relation of the action of carbonic oxide to oxygen tension. *J Physiol* 18:201–217, 1895.

65. Done AK: Carbon monoxide: The silent summons. *Emergency Medicine* 5:268–269, 1973.

66. Myers RA, Linberg SE, Cowley RA, et al: Carbon monoxide poisoning: The injury and its treatment. *JACEP* 8:479–484, 1979,

67. Pruitt BA, Erickson DR, Morris A: Progressive pulmonary insufficiency and other pulmonary complications of thermal injury. *J Trauma* 15:369–379, 1975.

68. Fein A, Leff A, Hopewell PC: Pathophysiology and management of the complications resulting from fire and the inhaled products of combustion. *Crit Care Med* 8:94–98, 1980.

69. Wroblewski DA, Bower GC: The significance of facial burns in acute smoke inhalation. *Crit Care Med* 7:335–338, 1979.

70. Tashkin DP, Genovesi MG, Chopra S, et al: Respiratory status of Los Angeles firemen: One-month follow up after inhalation of dense smoke. *Chest* 71:445–449, 1977.

71. Loke J, Farmer W, Matthay RA, et al: Acute and chronic effects of fire fighting on pulmonary function. *Chest* 77:369–373, 1980.

72. Peters JM, Theriault GP, Fine LJ, et al: Chronic effect of fire fighting on pulmonary function. *N Engl J Med* 291:1320–1322, 1974.

73. Amdus MO: Toxicologic appraisal of particulate matter, oxides of sulfur and sulfuric acid. *J Air Pollut Control Assoc* 19:639–643, 1969.

74. Rebaudo CA, Grace WJ: Pulmonary Aspiration. *Am J Med* 50:510 519, 1971.

75. Huxley E: Pharyngeal aspiration in normal adults and patients with depressed consciousness. *Am J Med* 64:564–568, 1978.

76. Johanson WG, Pierce AK, Sanford JP: Changing pharyngeal bacterial flora of hospitalized patients. Emergency of gram negative bacilli. *N Engl J Med* 281:1137–1140, 1969.

77. Johanson WG, et al: Nosocomial respiratory infections with gram negative bacilli. *Ann Intern Med* 77:701–706, 1972.

78. Lorber B, Swenson RM: Bacteriology of aspiration pneumonia. *Ann Intern Med* 81:329–331, 1974.

79. Modell JH: Biology of drowning. *Ann Rev Med* 29:1–8, 1978.

80. Modell JH (ed): *The Pathophysiology and Treatment of Drowning and Near Drowning*. Springfield, IL, Charles C Thomas, 1971.

81. Hasan S, Avery WF, Fabian C, et al: Near-drowning in humans: A report of 32 patients. *Chest* 59:191–197, 1971.

82. Clarke EB, Niggemann EH: Near-drowning. *Heart and Lung* 4:946–955, 1975.

83. Modell JH, Graves SA, Ketover A: Clinical course of 91 consecutive near-drowning victims. *Chest* 70:231–238, 1976.

84. Modell JH, Graves SA, Kuck EJ: Near-drowning: Correlation of level of consciousness and survival. *Can Anaesth Soc* 27:211–215, 1980.

85. Heimlich HJ: The Heimlich maneuver: First treatment for drowning victims. *Emerg Med Serv* 10:58–61, 1981.

86. Siesjo BK, Carlsson C, Hagerdal M, et al: Brain metabolism in the critically ill. *Crit Care Med* 4:283–294, 1976.

87. Downs JB, Capman RL Jr, Modell JH, et al: An evaluation of steroid therapy in aspiration pneumonitis. *Anesthesiology* 40:129–135, 1974.

88. Calderwood HW, Modell JH, Ruiz BC: The ineffectiveness of steroid therapy in treating fresh water near-drowning. *Anesthesiology* 43:642–650, 1975.

89. Safar P, Elam JO (eds): *Advances in Cardiopulmonary Resuscitation.* New York, Springer-Verlag, 1977.

90. Gann DS: Emergency management of the obstructed airway. *JAMA* 243:1141–1142, 1980.

91. Danzl DF, Thomas DM: Nasotracheal intubations in the emergency department. *Crit Care Med* 8:677–682, 1980.

92. DeLeo BC: Endotracheal intubation by rescue squad personnel. *EMT J* 2:60–62, 1978.

93. Berdeen TH: One-year experience with the tracheo-esophageal airway. *Ann Emerg Med* 10:25–27, 1981.

94. Meislin HW: The esophageal obturator airway: A study of respiratory effectiveness. *Ann Emerg Med* 9:54–59, 1980.

95. Brantigan CO, Grant JB: Cricothyroidotomy: Elective use in respiratory problems requiring tracheotomy. *J Thorac Cardiovasc Surg* 71:72–81, 1976.

96. *Emergency Care and Transportation of the Sick and Injured,* ed 3. American Academy of Orthopedic Surgeons, 1981.

6

Gastrointestinal Hemorrhage in the Geriatric Population

Karen Cervenka, MD and Mark A. Shaffer, MD, FACEP

Gastrointestinal (GI) hemorrhage is a common clinical problem in emergency medicine, and the elderly patient with this condition poses a unique challenge in diagnosis and management. Clinical features may be subtle, with merely a change in mental status, development of anorexia and weight loss, or symptoms secondary to anemia present. Conversely, asymptomatic anemia or occult blood loss in the stool may be detected only on routine screening.

Blood loss in the stool may be manifested in several ways. The history may be significant for hematemesis, which is emesis of either bright red blood or coffee-ground-like material. Melena is black, tarry malodorous stools, and the physician should realize that what the patient actually calls black stools may just be dark-colored stools secondary to ingestion of iron or bismuth-containing compounds. Melena usually is caused by approximately 500 ml of blood loss, whereas a loss of 25 ml causes heme-positive stools. The passage of bright red blood through the rectum—hematochezia—can indicate a rapid upper GI hemorrhage suggesting a blood loss of 1 liter (L) or more, but it more commonly indicates lower GI hemorrhage. Standard estimates of blood loss, however, can be misleading and even dangerous in the older patient who can decompensate with much less loss of blood than the younger person. Caution must be observed in replacing fluids and blood, as there is an increased need for monitoring cardiovascular status. Chronic illnesses, such as chronic heart failure (CHF), chronic obstructive pulmonary disease (COPD), and renal insufficiency, make management more difficult and increase morbidity and mortality.

INITIAL ASSESSMENT AND STABILIZATION

Any information that can be obtained about the patient's condition is helpful; particularly valuable is information about previous similar episodes; use of alcohol, aspirin, and prescription and nonprescription drugs; or any past abdominal surgeries. History of any anticoagulant therapy should be sought. Hematemesis and melena place the source of bleeding proximal to the ligament of Treitz. Hematochezia, usually caused by a lower GI hemorrhage, can also represent a massive upper GI hemorrhage of approximately 1 L. Any patient with a history of hematemesis, melena, or rectal bleeding should have a nasogastric tube inserted. Aspiration of blood or coffee-ground-like material establishes the diagnosis, but a negative aspirate, although ruling out an esophageal or gastric cause, does not necessarily rule out a postpyloric source nor indicate that hemorrhage may have stopped.

Gastric lavage with iced saline or water should be performed until bleeding clears; room temperature fluids may be effective also. Lavage can require various amounts of fluid, which are then drained by gravity. Only a small amount of fluid is actually absorbed from the stomach, so the procedure can be done safely in the geriatric patient without worrying about electrolyte abnormalities or further hemodilution. Eighty-five to 90% of all patients clear with lavage. Lavage provides a measure of the severity of bleeding and allows for the removal of blood clots, thus letting the stomach contract and causing hemostasis.

If hemorrhage ceases, one can begin therapy empirically for peptic ulcer disease or hemorrhagic gastritis. Hourly titration of gastric pH and doses of antacids should be instituted to keep the pH near 7. Cimetidine can also be started, although in actively bleeding patients it has not been shown to be any more effective than placebo.[1] Diagnostic workup can then proceed; this includes endoscopy and upper GI x-ray films but rarely arteriography.

If bleeding does not stop, early endoscopy should be attempted to establish a diagnosis. If the source of bleeding cannot be visualized, arteriography may be necessary, with subsequent treatment consisting of intra-arterial or intravenous (IV) vasopressin for varices and gastritis. Intravenous vasopressin should be used cautiously in the elderly because of its vasoconstrictive effects. Nasogastric infusion of levarterenol (8 mg in 100 ml of saline)[2] can serve as a temporizing measure, but its efficacy has not yet been established. Barium studies are never appropriate in the actively bleeding patient.

Laboratory Tests

The examining physician should be aware that the hemoglobin and hematocrit values that are obtained are usually unreliable in the setting of acute hemorrhage for any cause. At least 12 hr may be required before the hematocrit accurately reflects the extent of hemorrhage. An initial low hematocrit in an otherwise healthy patient suggests either chronic blood loss or massive acute loss. The patient with upper GI hemorrhage typically has leukocytosis and an elevated BUN secondary to increased urea synthesis from hemoglobin. Reticulocytosis occurs with any source of hemorrhage. Prothrombin and partial thromboplastin times mark the effect of anticoagulation and indicate coagulopathy from liver disease. Liver function tests and possibly a serum ammonia level can be especially helpful in determining etiology if there is a history of alcohol abuse. An ECG is necessary in this population to document ischemic changes secondary to blood loss.

The patient's condition may not allow for an extensive physical examination so attention should be directed to vital signs, especially orthostatics, and a complete abdominal examination. Does the patient exhibit a resting tachycardia, or is the heart rate low secondary to the use of β-blockers? Examination of the skin for telangiectasias or jaundice and the presence of hepatosplenomegaly may point to the cause of bleeding.

Stabilization

Initial resuscitation of the older patient proceeds in the same course as in any emergent situation; airway, breathing, and circulation are the first priorities. Fluid resuscitation with large-bore IV catheters is preferable, but in the geriatric population, it becomes even more important to establish a central venous line for cardiovascular monitoring, via a central venous pressure (CVP) or Swan-Ganz catheter. CVP readings in this population often do not accurately reflect left heart function, especially in those with baseline cardiovascular disease. Extremes of measurements and response to fluid challenges can provide a rough guideline in conjunction with serial examinations until left heart monitoring is available. Fluid challenges should be smaller than with other patients—200 ml to 500 ml boluses of saline or lactated Ringer's solution—and there should be continuous monitoring of vital signs, urine output, CVP or wedge pressure, and serial physical examinations. MAST trousers can be used early in resuscitation without extensive fluid replacement until more proper monitoring is established.

The elderly patient may not tolerate volume deficits as well as a younger person; these deficits may cause mental confusion, myocardial decompensation, or shock. Therefore transfusions may be required earlier than in younger patients. Conversely, this sensitive response to changes in volume makes it advisable to treat elderly patients with packed RBCs, rather than whole blood, because of the increased risk of volume overload.

UPPER GASTROINTESTINAL HEMORRHAGE

Inflammation of the stomach mucosa known as gastritis can be localized to a certain portion of the stomach, or it may be diffuse. Further division into acute and chronic forms is based on endoscopy, histology, and response to therapy. Acute gastritis eventually resolves with therapy, whereas chronic gastritis is a long-standing disease.

Acute Gastritis

The elderly patient may be especially prone to acute gastritis because numerous substances are known to damage gastric mucosa. Aspirin, alcohol, bile salts, and nonsteroidal anti-inflammatory drugs (NSAIDs), especially indomethacin and corticosteroids, are thought to interfere with the mucosal barrier. In addition, gastritis is known to develop in the course of such medical or surgical illnesses as trauma, hypotension of any cause, sepsis, and renal or respiratory failure. Gastritis caused by any of these conditions or by drugs is also known as erosive or hemorrhagic gastritis.

Clinical Features

Clinical manifestations may occur in otherwise healthy persons. These patients also show classic findings on endoscopy. Patients may complain of epigastric pain, nausea, vomiting, hematemesis, or melena. The physical examination is unremarkable unless other disease entities are present.

Diagnosis

If significant bleeding has occurred, the patient's hematocrit may be decreased, the BUN may be increased, and nasogastric aspirate from stomach or stool may test positive for blood. Definitive findings with endoscopy and biopsy are superficial ulcerations, erosions, and inflammation.

Treatment

By definition, acute gastritis is reversible, with healing within 48 hours after cessation of bleeding. The patient who has acute gastritis and no other medical problems does not necessarily require therapy. The effective antacid dose is still in question.

Patients with more significant gastritis—with evidence of GI bleeding—or underlying diseases should be given antacids hourly to keep the gastric pH near 7 for several days. The frequency of antacids is then reduced to 1 and 3 hr after meals, and cimetidine is added at bedtime. This regimen is continued for 4 to 6 weeks. Effective prevention of hemorrhagic gastritis is also accomplished with titration of gastric pH over 3.5.[1] Cimetidine is not as effective as antacids.

Chronic Gastritis

The exact cause of chronic gastritis is unknown, but the frequency seems to increase with age. Repeated long-term damage to gastric mucosa may play a role, eg, through the chronic use of aspirin or alcohol. Immunologic factors are important in patients with pernicious anemia who have antibodies to parietal cells and intrinsic factor.

Clinical Features

Most patients do not display the symptoms of gastritis; therefore a patient with known chronic gastritis who has hematemesis or melena should have other causes ruled out.

Diagnosis

Mucosal biopsy is the best means of diagnosis. In addition, laboratory findings may be consistent with pernicious anemia or abnormal secretion of gastric acid, pepsin, and gastrin.

Treatment

Most patients do not require therapy, especially because no studies have established that therapy prevents atrophy, pernicious anemia, or the higher-than-normal incidence of gastric cancer.[2]

PEPTIC ULCER DISEASE

Peptic ulcer disease is thought to occur secondary to an imbalance between acid-pepsin and mucosal resistance. It is the commonest cause of upper GI hemorrhage in the nonalcoholic patient.[2] Those areas of the GI tract prone to develop peptic ulceration include the lower esophagus, stomach, the first portion of duodenum, and any small bowel that has been surgically anastomosed to the stomach.

Acute peptic ulcer disease usually consists of multiple superficial lesions that do not penetrate the muscularis mucosa. Chronic peptic ulcer disease, in contrast, consists of single ulcers that have penetrated the muscularis; it therefore leads to scar formation on healing. Morbidity from duodenal ulcer is greater than that from gastric ulcer, but the number of deaths is similar in uncomplicated cases.

As the person ages, the incidence of gastric ulcer tends to increase, because there is a decrease in the ability of the stomach to secrete acid. In addition, gastric ulcers tend to bleed more frequently, and therefore mortality increases. The reduced ability of the stomach to secrete acid may explain the declining incidence of duodenal ulcer in older age groups.[3] Still, in several studies of hospitalized patients with duodenal ulcer, the elderly accounted for approximately one-third of the total patients.[3] Peptic ulcer disease affects more elderly women than elderly men. The association of smoking and increased frequency of peptic ulcers, increased morbidity and mortality, and slower healing is well known. Occupation is not an important risk factor, and the role of psychological factors is still questionable.

Again, a thorough medication history must be sought; salicylates, indomethacin and other NSAIDs, and glucocorticoids all block prostaglandins, which are thought to protect mucosa. The elderly are also prone to peptic ulceration from many of the same medical or surgical illnesses that predispose to gastritis: sepsis, shock, trauma, major surgical procedures especially involving the brain, extensive burns, acute respiratory insufficiency, and any cerebrovascular accident.

Clinical Features

Typically, peptic ulcer pain is described as a burning or gnawing pain located in the epigastrium without radiation. It is not dependent on movement, and it may or may not fluctuate in intensity. Pain is classically absent in the morning when acidity is low and increases hours after a meal, with increased acid secretion. Complaints in the elderly may be vague or nonspecific with poor localization of pain, or they may involve left-sided or lower chest discomfort, heaviness, or nausea. In addition, the patient's family may note a loss of appetite or weight in the elderly person. Bleeding may be occult or go unnoticed until the patient's anemia is significant, at which time the patient has pallor, palpitations, mental confusion, or lightheadedness. Hemorrhage is the commonest sign of peptic ulcer disease, with an incidence of 15% to 20%; it causes hematemesis, melena, or occult blood in the stool. Patients with underlying cirrhosis with a coagulopathy or on anticoagulant therapy may have spontaneous bleeding. The physical examination can be unremarkable with only minimal to no epigastric tenderness or can reveal evidence of other diseases, eg, ascites, telangiectasias, arthritis.

The incidence of perforation is highest in the fifth and sixth decades of life, and approximately 10% of these patients hemorrhage at the same time. Classically, the patient experiences a sudden onset of intense constant abdominal pain with signs of peritonitis, but the older patient may show no such change. In general, the entire course of illness may be more severe, especially when complicated by bleeding, perforation, or underlying illnesses. Once hemorrhage occurs, the incidence of re-bleeding is increased, and to an even greater degree in the elderly.

Treatment

The basic principles of fluid replacement and the need to monitor the older person have already been discussed. The decision to transfuse blood products, however, must be based on each individual patient's condition. Time and the status of the patient dictate the type of blood products to be administered.

Continuous nasogastric suction is thought to empty at least 90% of gastric acid secretions, which is one of the therapeutic goals. Cimetidine has shown to be no better than placebo in the acute hemorrhagic stage;[1] however, it does promote healing of duodenal and benign gastric ulcers.[4] Antacids are effective with active duodenal ulcer, but the therapeutic effect of antacids on bleeding gastric ulcers has not been established.[4] Fifteen to 30 ml, depending on the specific antacid, should be used hourly in the bleeding patient to keep the gastric pH near 7; cimetidine should be administered concomitantly every 4 to 6 hrs. After the patient is stabilized and bleeding is under control, antacids can be used 1 to 3 hr after meals for treatment of duodenal and gastric ulcers. In patients with impaired renal function, magnesium-containing antacids should be used with caution, if at all, as elevated magnesium levels can lead to hypotension or respiratory arrest. Aluminum-containing antacids can decrease phosphorus, which can benefit the patient with renal insufficiency. Oral calcium-containing antacids can cause a secondary increase in acid secretion after the buffering effect has ceased.

Well-known side effects of cimetidine include mental confusion in the elderly, especially those with liver or renal impairment; decreased liver metabolism of warfarin-type anticoagulants; elevation of SGOT and SGPT; and rare granulocytopenia. Gynecomastia and impotence also occur. Reduction of doses are necessary for patients with impaired renal function.

Ranitidine, a more potent H_2 receptor-blocking antihistamine, has been approved for use in treatment of duodenal ulcer and Zollinger-Ellison syndromes only.[5] The higher cost of this drug may assume lesser importance if patient compliance increases on a twice a day dosage, but reports of side effects, such as confusion and interaction with drugs metabolized by the cytochrome P 45-system, are beginning to accumulate. Carafate, in contrast, has minimal effects on acid-neutralizing capacity and is thought to work by forming an ulcer-adherent complex. There are no contraindications to the drug, and it is approved only for treatment with duodenal ulcers four times daily.[6]

Finally, indications for surgery may be different in the geriatric population. On the one hand, one may choose to operate sooner because of the increased incidence of rebleeding in the elderly or the need for large amounts of blood products within the first 24 to 48 hours of bleeding. On the other hand, surgery may be delayed because of the high risks posed by underlying diseases in the older patient. Morbidity and mortality in peptic ulcer disease, regardless of complications, are significantly increased in persons over the age of 50.

Zollinger-Ellison Syndrome

The Zollinger–Ellison syndrome is caused by a gastrin-secreting tumor, two-thirds of which are malignant on biopsy, that is usually located in the pancreas. Seventy-five percent of patients have a postbulbar or bulbar duodenal ulcer. Clinical features are the same as those of any ulcer and include abdominal pain, hematemesis, and/or melena. However, what should make the physician especially suspicious is a history of recurrent or previous ulcer disease, any ulcer symptoms that are refractory to medical treatment, and recurrent ulceration after surgery for peptic ulcer disease. Treatment consists of ranitidine or cimetidine to decrease gastric acid secretion and total gastrectomy.[5] There is no evidence that either modality decreases the incidence of metastatic disease.

Mallory-Weiss Tears

Mallory-Weiss tears occur in the gastric mucosa below the gastroesophageal junction secondary to vomiting. The patient gives a history of emesis initially of gastric contents and later of bright red blood. Diagnosis is made by endoscopy, and treatment is conservative as the tears usually heal spontaneously.

Variceal Bleeding

Bleeding from esophageal or gastric varices is a complication of portal hypertension. The most common clinical presentation is that of massive or recurrent hematemesis. Melena or hematochezia is infrequent. Evidence of liver disease is often found on physical examination, and definitive diagnosis is based on the results of endoscopy. Therapy consists of adequate blood and fluid replacement. However, volume overload can lead to ascites in a patient with liver disease or to recurrent variceal bleeding. Refractory bleeding is treated by IV or intra-arterial vasopressin and endoscopic sclerotherapy. Again, one must be cautious about administering vasopressin IV to a patient with cardiovascular disease who could possibly develop myocardial ischemia.

Malignancy

Erosion of esophageal tumor may cause hematemesis, as well as the more common signs of progressive dysphagia and odynophagia. Patients with gastric carcinoma typically do not have gross hematemesis, but one-half of patients do exhibit occult blood loss with iron deficiency or megaloblastic anemia.

Admission Criteria

As emphasized previously, the course of illness in the older patient is often more severe, with increased incidence of complications and increased morbidity and mortality.[7] Therefore, criteria for admission should be more liberal. Outpatient evaluation is reasonable in the patient who has occult blood in the stool in whom there is no evidence of circulatory compromise. Vital signs and orthostatics should be normal. If anemia is significant, it is wise to admit the patient. Any patient with hematemesis or melena should be admitted.

VASCULAR DISEASE OF THE INTESTINE

The GI tract is usually spared from ischemic injury because of its extensive overlapping blood supply. However, with significant atherosclerosis acute or chronic ischemic changes can occur in either the small or large bowel.[8]

Normal Anatomy

There are three major arterial branches of the aorta: (1) the celiac trunk at the T-12 level, which gives rise to hepatic, splenic, gastric, and gastroduodenal branches; (2) the superior mesenteric artery, which arises just below the celiac and has branches extending from the distal duodenum to the distal transverse colon; and (3) the inferior mesenteric artery which arises from the aorta at L-3 and supplies the distal transverse colon to the proximal rectum. All three major arteries are interconnected by an extensive collateral system; thus a slowly progressive occlusion or blockage of a small vessel may not produce any classical manifestations. Ischemic syndromes depend therefore on the size and location of the vessel and the rapidity of the occlusion.

Chronic Ischemia of the Bowel

Chronic ischemia of the bowel is a rather uncommon syndrome that occurs only when two of the three major vessels have significant (greater than 50%) atherosclerosis. Patients complain of dull or cramping epigastric or midabdominal pain, otherwise known as abdominal angina. Pain usually begins 15 to 30 min after a meal and lasts for a few hours. Or, the patient may be anorexic and report losing weight only to reveal the long history of abdominal angina. When questioned in detail, heme-positive stools and complaints of diarrhea are less common. The physical examination gives nonspecific results, and even the presence of an abdominal bruise is nondiagnostic. Angiography reveals significant occlusions, and surgical revascularization is the treatment of choice.

Acute Bowel Infarction

Acute occlusive disease may occur with advanced atherosclerosis that does not allow time for collaterals to develop, dissecting aortic aneurysm, vasculitis, or emboli. Most patients (75% to 98%) have a sudden onset of severe diffuse abdominal pain.[3] Pain often is out of proportion to physical findings. The onset may be associated with forceful emesis, low-grade fever, and leukocytosis. The patient may be confused from volume depletion or ensuing shock. Hematemesis and rectal bleeding are common and can occur early or late in the condition's course. With more advanced ischemia, signs of peritonitis and obstruction can occur.

Diagnosis

Without a previous history of abdominal angina, one must have a high index of suspicion in order to make the diagnosis. Plain films of the abdomen should be obtained to rule out other obvious causes, such as obstruction or perforation, that can also be a result of infarction. Angiography establishes a definitive diagnosis.

Treatment

Massive amounts of protein-rich fluid are lost early; therefore, IV fluids, blood, and possibly other colloid replacements, such as dextran and albumin, are given to correct losses. Broad spectrum antibiotics should be started early because there is a high incidence of bacteremia and positive blood cultures. A nasogastric tube can be used to bring about decompression. Digoxin should be used cautiously because of its possible vasoconstrictive effects on mesenteric blood flow. Anticoagulants should also be avoided as they may provoke spontaneous bleeding. Such supportive therapy is continued until surgical revascularization and resection of the infarcted bowel are carried out. Mortality under the best of conditions is 60% and without surgical intervention reaches 100%.

Mesenteric Artery Embolism

The severity of an embolism of the mesenteric artery and whether chronic or acute symptoms develop depend on the size of the embolus and the extent of occlusion. Emboli may originate from a fibrillating left atrium, a mural thrombus after a myocardial infarction, valvular vegetations, and prosthetic valves. Fifty-five percent of emboli lodge at the middle colic artery, 20% at the origin of the superior mesenteric artery, and 17% at the right colic artery.[9]

Clinical Features

The onset of signs and symptoms is more acute and noticeable than in bowel infarction. There is a sudden onset of severe constant abdominal pain that is more frequently localized periumbically and is followed by nausea, vomiting, and bloody diarrhea. If ignored, the signs and symptoms progress to those of bowel infarction with hematemesis, continued rectal bleeding, and indications of intestinal obstruction.

Treatment

Urgent surgical exploration is indicated with embolectomy and resection of any infarcted bowel. Prognosis with surgery carries a mortality rate less than 60%.

Nonocclusive Infarction

Nonocclusive infarction is necrosis of the bowel secondary to ischemia when mesenteric blood flow is preferentially shunted to vital organs for various reasons, ie, hypotension. Clinical manifestations are similar to those of occlusive infarction and include onset of severe abdominal pain, rectal bleeding, or blood-tinged diarrhea progressing to findings of obstruction and shock. Treatment consists of blood pressure support as necessary, adequate oxygenation, and surgery for bowel resection.

Ischemic Colitis

Any patient over 50 years of age who complains for the first time of symptoms resembling ulcerative colitis should be suspected of having ischemic colitis until proven otherwise.[6] The disease may result from extensive atherosclerosis of the inferior mesenteric artery or from damage sustained during aortic surgery. In addition, any vasculitis, hypercoagulable state, or amyloidosis may also be the cause. Typically the patient has a sudden cramping abdominal pain, usually located on the left side, followed by the onset of bright red or dark rectal bleeding or bloody diarrhea. In addition, the patient may have a low-grade fever and leukocytosis. The commonest sites of involvement are the splenic flexure and the descending and rectosigmoid colon.

Clinically the patient may not appear very ill, and physical findings can be minimal other than mild left-sided abdominal tenderness and heme-positive stools. The amount of blood loss varies, but it is usually not massive, so indications of volume depletion may not be present. Clinical symptoms abate within 24 hours and resolve completely in 7–10 days.[10]

The diagnosis is made on the basis of physical examinations, sigmoidoscopy, and barium enema. Even on sigmoidoscopy, findings can frequently resemble those of ulcerative colitis. In classic ischemic colitis sigmoidoscopy reveals discrete ulcers or bluish-black mucosa. A barium enema should be performed approximately 48 hours after the acute phase of bloody diarrhea and pain. It typically shows "thumbprinting" as a result of mucosal edema and hemorrhage. Radiologic findings resolve in 1–2 weeks. Involved mucosa typically regenerates in approximately 4 weeks, but stricture formation can develop if impairment of flow is severe enough.

If signs and symptoms do not abate and the patient begins to develop signs of obstruction or peritonitis, one must consider infarction and urgent surgery becomes essential. Otherwise treatment is conservative and includes follow-up studies to document healing.

Abdominal Aortic Aneurysm

Aneurysms of 4 to 5 cm are rarely symptomatic, nor are they associated with increased morbidity and mortality. Those of 6 to 7 cm or those that show any increase in size place the patient at risk as they can lead to rupture into the peritoneal cavity or retroperitoneum. A pulsating abdominal mass and rapid onset of shock indicate exsanguinating hemorrhage. There may be an interval of hours between the first episode of bleeding and exsanguination; the patient may have a sudden onset of severe abdominal pain radiating to the back. This may lessen after the initial episode only to reappear with further bleeding. Retroperitoneal bleeding can be diagnosed on physical examination by the finding of a pulsatile abdominal mass that is very tender. This progresses to generalized fullness of the midabdomen and the development of shock. Aggressive fluid replacement and immediate surgery are indicated.

Prosthetic-Enteric Fistula

Acute massive GI hemorrhage or intermittent episodes of bleeding can occur any time between 21 days to years after surgical placement of an abdominal aortic graft. Fistula formation can result from erosion and occurs up to 15 years after surgery. The patient may have intermittent episodes of hematochezia, hematemesis, or melena with or without abdominal pain. Vital signs vary according to blood loss. Findings on physical examination may be unremarkable if the bleeding is enteric; if it is retroperitoneal, a tender abdomen may be found. Any patient who has this symptomatology and a history of aortic graft should be presumed to have a fistula between the graft and the bowel, and immediate surgery is necessary. Treatment in the emergency department should consist of resuscitation and support until surgery. Nasogastric aspirate can be clear if bleeding is into the duodenum or below. The results of endoscopy, as well as arteriography, may show no signs of a fistula; therefore a high index of suspicion is necessary to detect it.

Vascular Ectasias

Vascular ectasias are an important cause of lower GI bleeding in patients over 60 years old.[11] These are small arteriovenous communications thought to be the result of years of low-grade obstruction of capillaries and venules in the submucosa.[12] They may also represent one end of a continuum of angiodysplasia of the bowel. At one end are the hereditary arteriovenous malformations that may also involve skin and other organs, eg, hereditary telangiectasias; at the other end of the continuum is angiodysplasia in which lesions have developed over several years particularly in the cecum and right colon and often existing in association with aortic valve disease.[13]

The typical patient is over 60 years of age with a history of repeated episodes or admissions for GI bleeding. These bleeding episodes may be frequent episodes of low-grade rectal bleeding or of infrequent but massive hemorrhage. Thus, one sees various clinical manifestations of angiodysplasia from signs and symptoms secondary to anemia with heme-positive stool to hypotension, confusion, and melena. Lesions occurring in the stomach or proximal to the ligament of Treitz may cause hematemesis or melena. Although one may suspect vascular ectasias as a cause of hemorrhage, definitive diagnosis is usually made by upper or lower endoscopy or angiography. Diagnosis may require repeated endoscopic examinations before the ectatic lesions are recognized.

Lesions of the ascending colon may be removed via right hemicolectomy or endoscopic coagulation; they may also respond to intra-arterial vasopressin. Indications for surgery depend on the frequency and severity of hemorrhage.

LOWER GASTROINTESTINAL BLEEDING

The patient's history is important in diagnosing and treating this condition. Has there been any anorexia, weight loss, or change in bowel habits? Has the patient had previous rectal bleeding, history of diverticulosis, familial polyps, or surgery for aortic bypass graft? Or, is this a new onset of painful bloody diarrhea? The physical examination should include a search for abdominal and rectal masses, including hemorrhoids or any extraintestinal manifestations of diseases. Signs of increased fatigue, weakness, or confusion may be noted, as well as near-syncope, angina, or rapid onset of shock. Anoscopy can be performed in the emergency department to look for local pathologic changes. Resuscitation measures are basically the same as for upper GI hemorrhage. Placement of a nasogastric tube should always be done to rule out a proximal source of hemorrhage.

If bleeding stops spontaneously during these measures, the patient should still be admitted for a diagnostic workup, which begins with a proctoscopy and 24–48 hours of observation for any rebleeding. If the patient does hemorrhage again, angiography should be considered at this time, as well as possible embolization or infusion of vasopressin to control hemorrhage. A further workup includes barium enema and colonoscopy. Barium enemas should be deferred until bleeding stops so as not to obstruct angiography or colonoscopy. Because a history of hemorrhage or diverticulosis does not exclude other causes, a colonoscopy should be performed in any anemic patient with heme-positive stools whose proctoscopic and barium enema examinations give normal findings even if diverticuli are seen, because these latter two tests can miss 20% of the significant lesions.[14]

Diverticulosis

It is estimated that one-half of this population over 60 years of age exhibits diverticula.[15] Seventy to 90% of diverticula occur in the sigmoid and descending colon, but bleeding more commonly occurs with those located on the right side. The bleeding source is from arterioles located in the mesenteric walls that show areas of focal weakening; therefore the bleeding is bright red. Patients have various degrees of blood loss and complaints. They may exhibit massive red rectal bleeding with no complaint of pain, or they may have occult-positive stools with or without symptoms of anemia and localized tenderness on examination, perhaps with palpation of a mass and some amount of obstruction. There is no fever or leukocytosis. A barium enema shows an irregular contour of the lumen and possibly extravasation outside the lumen perforation or evidence of fistula formation. If bleeding ceases in response to initial resuscitation therapy, the workup can then proceed as discussed earlier. If bleeding continues or recurs, angiography and colonoscopy should be considered to observe the actual bleeding site.

Treatment is therefore varied and can consist of intra-arterial vasopressin at angiography. Surgical resection of that portion of colon with bleeding diverticulae depends on the severity of hemorrhage, whether or not it stops spontaneously, and the frequency of recurrences.

Diverticulitis

Diverticulitis is a complication of diverticulosis and is thought to result from microscopic or larger perforations of diverticulae. The patient complains of steady pain, usually in the left lower quadrant as the descending and sigmoid colon are the commonest sites.[2] These sites rarely bleed. Low-grade fever and leukocytosis are very common. Palpation may reveal a tender mass/abscess on abdominal or rectal examination.[2] A flat plate of the abdomen can show generalized free air. Generalized or localized ileus can be seen over the left lower quadrant. Air-fluid levels in the left lower quadrant can be a sign of abscess formation. Typically, the workup—namely, a barium enema—does not begin until the acute phase is over. However, if one is considering ischemic colitis or perforation secondary to carcinoma of the colon, then sigmoidoscopy and colonoscopy should be performed. Otherwise, therapy consists of antibiotics (gentamicin and clindamycin) and surgical consultation for evidence of mass, abscess, or perforation.

Polyps

Polyps are growths of epithelial tissue protruding into the bowel lumen. They may be sessile or pedunculated, benign or malignant. As many as 5 to 10% of patients over age 40 are found to have asymptomatic polyps on routine proctosigmoidoscopy.[2] Most are asymptomatic, and rarely do they become so large as to cause obstruction or pain. The most frequent signs, if they do occur, consist of rectal bleeding, usually hematochezia or occult blood loss leading to iron-deficiency anemia. Therefore, patients may have signs and symptoms of anemia also. What is most important about polyps is their potential for malignant change. Adenomatous polyps, especially those with villous components, do have this potential, as do those inherited syndromes of family polyposis or Gardner's syndrome.

Polyps can usually be removed endoscopically. There is some controversy whether polyps greater than 2 cm should be removed by endoscopy or by surgery. If carcinoma is found to penetrate the muscularis mucosa, segmental resection is indicated.

Neoplasms of the Small Intestine

Neoplasms of the small intestine are relatively rare. The asymptomatic benign carcinoid tumor found at autopsy is seen most often. The commonest tumors diagnosed are those from metastases, eg, carcinoma of the breast, ovary, kidney, or lymphoma.[3] Both these and larger carcinoid tumors can produce symptoms by obstruction or hemorrhage. Apparent risk factors for development of small bowel neoplasms include Crohn's and celiac disease. Treatment is surgical, with or without postoperative radiation or chemotherapy.

Neoplasms of the Large Intestine

The incidence of adenocarcinoma of the colon begins to increase at age 40 and then approximately doubles with each decade after age 50; the peak incidence occurs at age 75.[7] Its development is thought to be associated with high-beef, high-fat, and low-fiber diets that increase bowel transit time and allow bacteria to convert certain food metabolites into carcinogens. Other risk factors include long-standing ulcerative colitis; inherited cancer syndromes, such as Gardner's syndrome, polyposis, and Peutz-Jahger's syndrome; and history of a previous colorectal cancer or adenoma. One-half of all adenocarcinoma occur within the distal 25 cm of the colon.

Presentation

Cancer on the left side tends to obstruct, whereas masses on the right side may be silent for a period of time. They all, however, have a tendency to ulcerate and bleed. Lesions in the cecum and ascending colon rarely obstruct early in the course of the disease. Therefore there may only be generalized signs and symptoms associated with malignancy, such as anorexia, weight loss, weakness, or indications of anemia. The physical findings of the examination are nonspecific, except for the presence of occult blood in the stool. Patients with masses on the left side may complain of a change in bowel habits, hematochezia, or signs and symptoms consistent with obstruction. A mass may or may not be palpated on abdominal or rectal examination. Perforated adenocarcinoma leads to signs of peritonitis, fever, and leukocytosis. Evidence of metastasis to the liver, lung, brain, and bone should also be sought. Important in the differential diagnosis are angiodysplasia, diverticulosis, ulcerative colitis, and the various ischemic syndromes. Diagnostic workup includes protosigmoidoscopy before barium enema to rule out a distal lesion that could perforate and colonoscopy with biopsy of any lesions.[16] Treatment consists of resection with or without radiation or chemotherapy.

Ulcerative Colitis

Patients with ulcerative colitis may have rectal bleeding, diarrhea that may or may not be bloody, anorexia, weight loss, malaise, and low-grade fever. Severity of signs, including bleeding and diarrhea, are often in proportion to the exacerbation. The disease has a peak incidence in persons between 15 and 20 years old and a lesser increase in those between 55 and 60. The physical examination should be notable for signs of fluid depletion and generalized abdominal tenderness with heme-positive stool. Absent bowel sounds, abdominal distention, and signs of peritoneal irritation warn of toxic megacolon. Diagnosis is made with proctosigmoidoscopy and biopsy; barium enema is avoided in the acute stage. Treatment includes IV fluids, low-fiber or nothing-by-mouth diets, IV corticosteroids, and sulfasalazine. Indications for surgery include perforation, severe colitis or megacolon refractory to medical therapy, and carcinoma. Crohn's colitis rarely causes rectal bleeding or bloody diarrhea. Whenever a patient over 50 has these or similar complaints for the first time, the physician is obligated to rule out ischemic colitis before establishing a diagnosis of ulcerative colitis.

Diseases of the Rectum

Typically the type of rectal bleeding does not indicate the type of disorder or its origin. Blood supply to the rectum is abundant, so ischemic disease is rare. The superior hemorrhoidal artery arises from the inferior mesenteric artery; the middle hemorrhoidal artery arises from the internal iliac artery, and the inferior hemorrhoidal artery arises from the internal pudendal artery.

Hemorrhoids

The cause of hemorrhoids is still controversial. They are dilated veins from hemorrhoidal plexuses thought to occur either secondary to increased intra-abdominal pressure or perhaps arteriovenous shunts. Approximately 50% of the population by age 50 have hemorrhoids.[7]

Red blood found on toilet paper is most commonly a result of hemorrhoids or fissures. Chronic bleeding can lead to iron-deficiency anemia. Unless hemorrhoids are actively bleeding and inflamed, one cannot assume that they are the cause of blood loss and proctosigmoidoscopy is indicated.

External hemorrhoids develop from inferior hemorrhoidal plexuses and are covered by anoderma and skin. The patient with external hemorrhoids usually seeks treatment when they have thrombosed and cause pain on defecation. Physical examination reveals a tender, round, bluish mass that arises from the anal orifice, thus distinguishing internal from external hemorrhoids. Treatment consists of topical anesthetics or corticosteroid preparation, sitz baths, and stool softeners. External hemorrhoids can be excised.

Internal hemorrhoids develop from superior hemorrhoidal venous plexuses and are covered by rectal mucosa. They can be treated with band ligation or hemorrhoidectomy.

Anorectal Fistula

An anorectal fistula is a fibrous tract connecting the rectum with perianal skin. It may result from recurrent perianal abscesses, Crohn's disease, rectal cancer, tuberculosis, radiation therapy, or lymphogranuloma venereum. The patient complains of purulent and bloody drainage or mucus-like discharge; bleeding is often minimal. One must consider the possible causes mentioned here and proceed with further workup if indicated. Definitive treatment is surgery.

Anorectal Fissure

An anorectal fissure is a painful ulcer located at the anal orifice. It is thought to arise from trauma, hard feces, inflammatory bowel disease, carcinoma, tuberculosis, or venereal disease. The patient complains of burning or a tearing sensation on defecation and has minimal rectal bleeding. These fissures heal spontaneously, and treatment is the same as for hemorrhoids.

Nonspecific Ulcerative Proctitis

Nonspecific ulcerative proctitis can occur secondary to radiation, trauma, or ischemia. Signs and symptoms usually are minimal rectal bleeding, tenesmus, local pain, and a mucus-like discharge. No change in bowel habits occurs. Diagnosis is made on protosigmoidoscopy, which is used to document inflammation of rectal mucosa only. Examination of biopsy specimens shows changes that look similar to those associated with ulcerative colitis. Treatment includes topical, not oral, corticosteroids, and sulfasalazine to decrease inflammation. Long-term follow-up is required in these patients to observe for the progression to ulcerative colitis, the risk of which is less than 15%. The risk of rectal cancer is also small.

Infectious Proctitis

Patients with infectious proctitis have much the same signs and symptoms as in nonspecific ulcerative proctitis, but the causes include gonorrhea, syphilis, amebiasis, and lymphogranuloma venereum. Therefore, any patient with proctitis should always have cultures and serologic tests done to exclude an infectious cause.

Rectal Cancer

Rectal cancer makes up about 2% of all large bowel cancers. The clinical features are not distinctive. Rectal bleeding, pain with defecation, and change in bowel habits are common, as is pruritus secondary to a mucus-like discharge. Diagnosis is made on the basis of a sigmoidoscopy examination and a biopsy. Therapy is resection.

Admission Criteria

The decision to admit the patient is made as with upper GI hemorrhage, provided that vital signs and orthostatics are within normal limits and anemia is not significant. With lower tract hemorrhage in the older patient however, one must consider both vascular ischemic disease and colon carcinoma as part of the differential diagnosis. This complicates the admissions decision, but if these indeed are diagnostic possibilities, it is wise to admit the patient even with stable vital signs, hemoglobin, and hematocrit.

REFERENCES

1. Priebe HJ, et al: Antacid versus cimetidine in preventing acute gastrointestinal bleeding. *N Engl J Med* 302:426–430, 1980.

2. Wyngaarden JB, Smith LH: Chapter on gastrointestinal disease, in Cecil (ed): *Textbook of Medicine.* Philadelphia, WB Saunders Co, 1982, pp 589–737.

3. Permutt RP, Cello JP: Duodenal ulcer disease in the elderly patient, *Dig Dis Sci* 27:1, 1982.

4. Healing of benign gastric ulcer with low dose antacids or cimetidine. *New Engl J Med* 308: 1983.

5. Collen MJ, et al: Comparison of ranitidine and cimetidine in the treatment of gastric hypersecretion. *Ann Intern Med* 100:52–58, 1984.

6. McCarthy BM: Ranitidine or cimetidine. *Ann Intern Med* 99:445, 1983.

7. Altman BF: Gastrointestinal diseases in the elderly: Symposium on clinical geriatric medicine. *Med Clin North Am*, 67:2, 1983.

8. Ockner RK: Vascular diseases of the bowel, in Sleisenger MH, Forbtran JS (eds): *Gastrointestinal Disease*, ed 2. Philadelphia, WB Saunders Co, 1978.

9. Boley SJ, Brandt LJ: Ischemic disorders of the intestines. *Current Probl Surg* 15:1, 1978.

10. Dawson M, Schaefer J: The clinical course of reversible ischemic colitis. *Gastroenterology* 60:577, 1981.

11. Boley SJ, Sammarthano R, Dibase A, et al: On the nature and etiology of vascular ectasias of the colon. *Gastroenterology* 72:650, 1977.

12. Meyer CT, Troncale FJ, Calloway S, et al: Arteriovenous malformations of the literature. *Medicine* 60:36, 1981.

13. Weaver GA, Alpern HB, Baris JS, et al: Gastrointestinal angiodysplasia associated with aortic valve disease: Part of a spectrum of angiodysplasia of the gut. *Gastroenterology* 77:1, 1979.

14. Tedsco FJ, Waye JA, Raskin JB, et al: Colonoscopic evaluation of rectal bleeding. *Ann Intern Med* 89:907, 1978.

15. Meyers MA, Aloso BR, Gray GF, et al: Pathogenesis of bleeding colonic diverticulosis. *Gastroenterology* 71:577, 1976.

16. Winawer SJ, Sherlock P, Schottenfeld D, et al: Screening for colon cancer. *Gastroenterology* 70:783, 1976.

7

Hematologic Emergencies in the Elderly

Edward E. Morse, MD

There are little firm data on the frequency of hematologic emergencies in individuals over 64 years of age. The best estimates can be made only by inference from several sources. A review of emergency medical service utilization by the elderly in Akron, Ohio,[1] showed that 22% of the calls were from patients over 64 years of age; this represented a utilization rate 1.7 times that of younger individuals. Cardiovascular disease predominated, accounting for 37% of the calls. Central nervous system (CNS) complaints (19.6%) and trauma (18%) were the only other substantial categories isolated in this study, but there was a significant grouping (25,4%) of "other." Hematologic emergencies would fall in this category, but they were not noted specifically.

Yet, there is substantial information from several reviews[2,3] and studies[4-7] that indicates anemia may be present in 14% to 20% of people over 60 years of age in certain selected populations. Hedstrand and Killander[8] estimated that 1% of middle-aged men had iron-deficiency anemia. Although it is difficult to obtain accurate information about the exact frequency of hematologic emergencies, there are abundant data concerning specific hematologic problems that develop (Table 7–1).

ANEMIA

Anemia appears to be the most common hematologic problem in the elderly. Although the level of hemoglobin that separates normal from abnormal in those over 65 years of age is debated, the lowest level agreed to for both men and women is 12 gm/dl. In the United States or England, well-fed businessmen over 65 years of age have the same hemoglobin levels as their younger colleagues. In contrast, in less well-fed men over 65 years of age in rural areas of England, 14% to 20% have hemoglobin levels less than 12 gm/dl.[2] Studies of rural populations in Israel[9] and

Table 7–1 Hematologic Abnormalities in the Geriatric Population

Anemia
  Senescence
  Nutritional or chronic disease
  Iron deficiency (bleeding)
  Megaloblastic
  Preleukemia syndrome
Polycythemia
  Primary
  Secondary (pulmonary disease or renal tumor)
Multiple Myeloma
  Hyperviscosity syndrome
  Hypercalcemia
  Renal impairment
Chronic lymphocytic leukemia
  Hypoglobulinemia (infection)
  Pancytopenia
Hemorrhage
  Platelet abnormalities
  Anticoagulants

Sweden[7] indicate that nutritional deficiencies and other chronic disease states are frequent contributing factors to anemia (Table 7–2).

Pathophysiology

Lipschitz et al.[10] described a group of 222 people older than 65 years of age in a community center in Arkansas; 51 of these were found to be anemic without other obvious signs of disease. They coined the term ''anemia of senescence'' to describe this phenomenon. Of these 51, only three had iron deficiency, two had

Table 7–2 Anemia in the Elderly

Type	Incidence (%)		Comments
Anemia of senescence	Women 21	(42/196)	Age 65 years; community center
	Men 35	(9/26)	in Little Rock, Arkansas[10]
Nutritional or "simple"		14–20	Rural areas of England,[2] Israel,[9] Sweden[7]; other than U.S.[4]
Iron deficiency		3	Geriatric hospital[12]
(blood loss anemia)		17	Chronic disease facility[13]
Megaloblastic anemia	1 or less		Borderline vitamin B_{12} levels[2]
Preleukemia	Rare[19]		

anemia of chronic disease, none had B_{12} or folate deficiency, and none had hemolytic anemia. The authors noted that leukopenia was also prevalent in the persons with anemia and suggested there was a general depletion of marrow activity with age. Only 3 of 15 treated individuals responded to iron with a rise in hematocrit. Several others had decreased total iron-binding capacity (TIBC) (< 250 mg/dl) or elevated ferritin measurements, which were interpreted to indicate chronic disease. The vast majority of these subjects showed no evidence of altered iron metabolism or chronic disease. The authors suggested that a reduced lean body mass may decrease oxygen requirements with aging and that reduced androgen levels may contribute to a reduction in hemoglobin; therefore, the apparent anemia is in fact physiologic.

Bone marrow scans of erythroid elements labeled with radioactive iron show diminution of active marrow in the elderly. It has been estimated that the cellularity of the marrow in a person over 80 years of age is 30% of the maximum cellularity in a young individual.[11] It is general practice to obtain marrow from the iliac crest in the elderly because it is more cellular than sternal marrow. Sternal aspiration of marrow in the elderly sometimes causes fractured ribs, producing flail chest, or the needle punctures large vessels, such as the aorta.

Vogel[2] points out that it is difficult to determine the role of erythropoietin lack in the simple chronic anemia of the elderly because even normal levels of this substance are difficult to measure. However, the advent of radioimmunoassay of erythropoietin may eliminate this difficulty. Clearly, elderly patients with renal disease sufficient to raise the urea nitrogen level may have anemia caused by a lack of erythropoietin.

The finding of mild (Hb 12 g/dl) normocytic, normochromic anemia as part of an emergency workup is most likely due to physiologic changes of aging and rarely to chronic disease.

Causes of Severe Anemia

The prevalence and cause of severe anemia found in the elderly vary depending on the study. Croker and Beynon[12] found a hemoglobin of less than 10 g/dl in 18 (4 men, 14 women) of 511 patients (3.5%) admitted in 1 year to the Middlesex Hospital Geriatric unit in England. These patients were 75 to 100 years of age. Three patients were too frail for full workup, but the anemia in the other 15 patients could be explained by gastrointestinal lesion and bleeding. Four patients had colon cancer, and three had gastric cancer. There were also individual cases of gastritis, esophagitis, ulcers, and polyps. Ten recovered uneventfully after definitive treatment.

Kalchthaler and Tan[13] examined 161 residents of a long-term facility in New York and found 64 (40%) were anemic (Hb less than 12 g/dl). Twenty-seven patients (42%) responded to iron therapy. These patients had gastrointestinal hemorrhage, hemorrhage secondary to anticoagulant therapy, and hemorrhage associated with surgery. Many of the nonresponding patients had widespread malignancy, which eventually led to their deaths.

Matzner et al.[5,6] looked at two populations of elderly patients. One group of 142 individuals over 60 years of age found to be anemic in a small rural village in Israel did not respond to folic acid, but one-half did show an increase in hemoglobin when treated with iron tablets. The remaining patients were presumed to be suffering from anemia of chronic disease. In Jerusalem, in contrast, these investigators examined 106 hospitalized elderly patients with anemia and found that their anemias were due to renal failure, metastatic carcinoma, infection, gastrointestinal (GI) hemorrhage, and pernicious anemia or hemolysis.

Reizenstein et al.[7] showed that 70% of people receiving iron supplements in Sweden had no documentable reason for this therapy. However, 30% had various causes of iron deficiency, including malignancy. One hundred fifty-seven records were reviewed. Of 60 patients with evidence of iron deficiency, 10 had inoperable tumors at the time of presentation. He urged that tumors in the GI tract be sought in all patients.

Another review of the causes of anemia[14] in patients of different ages revealed iron deficiency in 12.3% of those over 60 years of age. Anemias associated with inflammatory disease of infection (23.4%) or malignancy (35.1%) were more common, but iron deficiency is easily treatable and if properly followed up may lead to early diagnosis of malignancy in the bowel, particularly in the cecum.[15,16]

Hiatus hernia is a common source of bleeding in those over 65. The lower bowel is another common bleeding site. The observation of hemorrhoids should not deter careful examination of the lower bowel for other bleeding sites. Although a positive stool guaiac test encourages further diagnostic workup, a negative test should not deter further stool examinations because many lesions bleed intermittently. Iron-deficiency anemia should be considered to be evidence of bleeding from the gastrointestinal tract until proven otherwise.

The fact that aging, chronic disease, and nutritional deficiency are common causes of anemia in the elderly should not discourage the emergency physician from doing a few inexpensive and rapid tests to diagnose specific treatable causes of anemia, such as GI bleeding, pernicious anemia, and folate deficiency. Similarly, when anemia is severe, it becomes an emergency in itself. Most commonly, weakness, dizziness, fainting, and hypotension with tachycardia are its symptoms and signs, but the astute emergency physician will recognize that pulmonary edema, angina pectoris, buzzing in the ears, mental confusion, or unexplained apathy may be the first signs of severe anemia in the elderly. Pallor should be sought in the nail beds and buccal mucosa, rather than in the skin, which is often sallow in the aged.

Diagnosis and Treatment of Iron-Deficiency Anemia

Much of the time a low hematocrit, coupled with a hypochromic microcytic smear, is sufficient for diagnosis of iron-deficiency anemia, particularly if there is previous evidence of normal blood counts. A centrifuged hematocrit obtained on capillary blood from a fingerstick and a blood smear can be examined by the physician, often in the emergency area. Supplies for this purpose should be readily available.

A more specific test for iron deficiency is measurement of ferritin, but a report is not available for several days because it is done by radioimmunoassay. Aspiration of bone marrow, however, can be done the day the patient is seen. If negative, a properly done iron stain of the marrow is sensitive and specific for iron deficiency. A low serum iron measurement is less useful unless accompanied by a sufficiently high TIBC so that iron saturation is less than 16%. Negative bone marrow iron stain or ferritin levels less than 12 ng/ml are specific for diagnosis. Bone marrow is examined also if there is another indication to suggest intrinsic marrow disease, eg, abnormal white cells, megaloblasts, or decreased platelets in the peripheral blood smear.

Treatment for the severely anemic, iron-deficient individual can begin in the emergency room while the definitive diagnostic workup is underway. Although transfusion is the quick and easy answer for some patients, it is not without grave hazards. If the patient is comfortable lying down and the hematocrit is more than 25%, the patient can be treated with injectable iron, preferably intravenously, to ensure that the entire dose is given. This avoids poor compliance, a common problem with the elderly.[17]

Megaloblastic Anemia

Another type of anemia that can cause severe symptoms is megaloblastic anemia. The diagnosis can be suspected from the very low hematocrit and a smear that shows macrocytes, Howell-Jolly bodies, thrombopenia, and leukopenia with hypersegmented polys. A British survey[2] showed that 10% of elderly subjects had serum B_{12} levels of 110–199 pg/ml, whereas fewer than 1% had levels less than 110 pg/ml, clearly in the deficient range. Changes in the GI tract with aging and loss of intrinsic factor are the major reasons for pernicious anemia, although other malabsorption mechanisms, such as blind loop, fish tapeworm, and pancreatic insufficiency, can occur. Folic acid deficiency is a result of alcoholism and poor diet and is usually seen in a young population, but 8% to 14% of elderly people have serum levels below 3 ng/ml.[2]

The diagnosis of vitamin B_{12} deficiency is particularly important, because it is associated with neurologic changes—loss of vibration and position sense—and dementia, which become irreversible if not treated early. If the diagnosis is suspected from symptoms, signs, and blood smear, blood samples can be obtained from serum for levels of B_{12} and red cell folate levels, and the patient can be started on injections of cyanocobalamin.

The Schilling test is still the most specific test of malabsorption of vitamin B_{12}, but it must be scheduled for an 8-hr blood sample or a 24-hr urine collection after administration of 0.5 μCi ^{57}Co B_{12}. Because the malabsorption defect does not change with administration of the vitamin, beginning therapy early does not interfere with the definitive diagnosis and may alleviate the need for blood transfusions and prevent the progression of neurologic changes. Specific therapy with injections of cyanocobalamin is preferable, but occasionally the patient's anemia is so severe that transfusion is necessary to alleviate symptoms.

In the elderly patient with pernicious anemia the anemia has developed slowly, and the patient is not likely to be hypovolemic. In fact, the patient may be on the verge of congestive heart failure from the hypoxia of severe anemia and fluid overload. Transfusions of packed cells should be administered very slowly (100 ml/hr).

Learning as much as possible about the patient on the first visit is important because follow-up is often difficult in the emergency service setting and the elderly patient may be lost to follow-up for weeks or months. The ideal emergency service should not let the seriously ill patient out of its doors until there is a definitive diagnosis and a treatment plan is begun. If days are required for scheduled tests or for results of tests to be returned, then the patient may need to be admitted to a hospital for interval observation and care. Eventually surgery, radiation, or chemotherapy may be required for definitive care of underlying disease, thus removing the patient from the province of the emergency service.

MYELOPROLIFERATIVE BLOOD DISEASES

Preleukemia syndrome may be a cause of anemia or indeed of reduction in any of the cellular elements of the blood. As age advances, morphologic abnormalities of the myeloid and/or erythroid series may be observed, but after age 55 an evolving picture of acute myelocytic or monomyelocytic leukemia is much more common than acute lymphocytic leukemia.[18] Hypoplastic acute leukemia affects patients over 55 (median age of 68). The pancytopenia of the peripheral blood is accompanied by a hypoplastic marrow with more than 30% myeloblasts. These patients do not tolerate chemotherapy well. Low-dose cytosine arabinoside (10 mg/m^2 bid) was reported to produce a remission in an 80-year-old man.[19] Myelodysplastic syndrome itself has also been reported to respond to cytosine arabinoside in the elderly.[20] Six patients aged 62 to 86 received 10–20 mg twice a day for 14–21 days. All demonstrated a reduction in abnormal cells, and one showed a remission of hypoplastic acute myeloid leukemia.

A recent study of marrow dysplasia in elderly patients showed 54% were myelodysplastic, and almost one-third went on to develop acute myelocytic leukemia. The other 46% showed erythroid dysplasia, and only 12% went on to develop acute leukemia.[21] In some instances overt leukemia did not develop for more than 5 years. Poor results from chemotherapy have led leading blood specialists to discourage aggressive treatment.[2]

Aplastic anemia is uncommon. Less than 0.2% of patients over 65 years of age have anemia as a result of markedly reduced marrow cellularity.[15]

Myelofibrosis and myeloid metaplasia are seen in the population over 50 years of age. Some patients give a history of radiation or exposure to benzene solvents, but in most there is no definable initiating event. The patient may complain of weakness and fullness in the abdomen and have anemia and hepatosplenomegaly. The peripheral blood smear is striking: myelocytes, nucleated red cells, and, particularly, teardrop forms may be abundant. Marrow aspiration is difficult, and a biopsy specimen obtained by needle usually shows fibrosis. Sometimes the specimen shows hypocellularity or hypercellularity. Patients should be followed for a time to determine the progress and tempo of the disease for the course can persist for 5 years before complications begin. The patient may come to the emergency department with pain in an enlarged spleen. The pain is usually caused by localized infarction or rupture after trauma. These symptoms or marked pancytopenia from hypersplenism requiring transfusion are indications for splenectomy. However, splenectomy is not undertaken lightly in this disease because almost one-half the patients have postoperative infections, bleeding, or further liver enlargement, which eventually are associated with debility and death.

POLYCYTHEMIA

Several reports[22-26] indicate polycythemia can be found in patients from 50 to over 80 years of age and at a rate of about 185 cases per year in the United States. Although compatible with a long survival, the disease progresses slowly like a growing malignant clone. Some patients make the transition to frank leukemia, whereas others do not. Acute emergencies develop as a result of hyperviscosity and thrombosis due to increased hematocrit and red blood cell mass.[26]

Although patients with primary polycythemia (vera) may show thrombocytosis and/or leukocytosis, as well as erythrocytosis and splenomegaly, patients with secondary erythrocytosis because of chronic lung disease or malignancy seldom do and this can be a helpful differential point. The following two recent case histories illustrate some of the interesting features of primary and secondary polycythemia that might bring the elderly patient to the emergency service.

A 72-year-old woman living in a nursing home was seen by a physician because she had suddenly developed dizziness and weakness. She gave a past history of some blood disease, but did not know its exact nature. Blood drawn by the physician revealed a hematocrit of 32%, with marked microcytosis and hypochromia. The physician diagnosed iron-deficiency anemia and began iron therapy. Within a month the woman's hematocrit increased to 45%, and she felt better. However, in another month her hematocrit reached 56%, and she complained of headache and dizziness. She was again seen in emergency circumstances and referred for hospitalization.

It was clear at this time that she had polycythemia vera and that her increased red cell mass and blood volume needed to be reduced. For phlebotomies a large syringe (60 ml), a large-bore needle (16 gauge), and a three-way stopcock were necessary to transfer blood rapidly to a blood bag. The viscosity of the blood did not allow sufficiently rapid bleeding into a blood bag by gravity to avoid clotting in the tubing. The daily bleedings (450 ml each) were well tolerated. Iron deficiency can be therapeutic in patients with polycythemia vera.

The other patient was a 69-year-old man who collapsed in a shopping mall and was admitted to his local hospital. He was found to have a hematocrit of 61%, and a "spleen-mass" on the left side. After four phlebotomies to reduce his red cell mass, he developed a renal vein thrombosis and was transferred for further care to a university hospital.

Review of the intravenous pyelogram (IVP) showed a mass arising from the left kidney, not the spleen. After fluid therapy, the tumor—a renal cell carcinoma—was removed, but postoperatively the patient suffered thrombosis of the right kidney and renal shutdown and died.

Critical observations in this case were that his red cell mass was minimally elevated and plasma volume was normal. Polycythemia vera patients usually have increased plasma volume, as well as increased red cell mass. The apparent spleen mass turned out to be a renal mass. The mild leukocytosis ($13,000/\mu l$) without thrombocytosis together with the previous observation made a difficult differential diagnosis.

A high hematocrit in an elderly patient must be evaluated with caution. Polycythemia vera[18] can be diagnosed only by determining that the red cell mass is increased, the oxygen saturation is normal, and there is either splenomegaly or two of the following conditions present: leukocytosis, thrombocytosis, elevated B_{12}-binding capacity, elevated B_{12}, or increased leukocyte alkaline phosphatase.

MULTIPLE MYELOMA

Patients with multiple myeloma or Waldenströms macroglobulinemia can also have difficulties with blood viscosity, which may at times be severe enough to cause blindness, congestive heart failure, stroke, and renal shutdown.[27] Myeloma patients have anemia, bone pain, and/or renal failure. Viscosity of serum plasma may be increased if there is an M component, a large polymer of IgG_3, or a macroglobulin of IgM-type.

These abnormal proteins decrease the flow of cells in the vascular bed and create circulatory disturbances, resulting in symptoms of headaches, dizziness, stupor, and coma. Polyneuropathy of unknown cause in the elderly patient may be a sign of myeloma.[28] Observations of the fundi may reveal a sausage-link deformity of the retinal veins, or observation of rouleaux (coin stacking) of the red blood cells on the blood smear may be a clue to the hyperviscosity state.

Measurement of viscosity is relatively simple. Using an Oswald viscometer (U tube), EDTA-treated plasma from the patient is timed while it runs through a capillary in the U tube; this time is compared to the time it takes water to run through the tube. Normal plasma has a relative viscosity compared to water of 1.6. Few patients are symptomatic up to a relative viscosity of 4, but the likelihood of symptoms increases as relative viscosity increases to 8, and almost all patients are symptomatic at a relative viscosity greater than 8. Plasma exchange is immediately effective—2–4 liters every few weeks depending on the patient's rate of production of abnormal protein. Chemotherapy of the underlying disease aids in reducing the synthesis of the abnormal protein.[18]

Multiple myeloma occurs mostly in individuals over the age of 50 years. The abnormal growth of plasma cells leads to several complications that may cause the emergency visit. Bone pain or pathologic fractures are common in those patients with widespread osteoclastic activity. Plasma cell tumors may be found in multiple sites in the skull, ribs and pelvis, or long bones. The increased activity of osteoclasts causing lytic lesions in bones is thought to be caused by the release of osteoclast activating factor (OAF).[18] Severe neurologic problems can develop that require emergency treatment. One of the most crippling is compression of the spinal cord. Paraparesis or paraplegia may require surgical decompression immediately with follow-up radiation therapy to control paraspinal tumors. Hypercalcemia also associated with widespread bony lesions may cause coma, delirium, and confusion (both in the patient and in the physicians).

Back pain and poor urine output are clues that myeloma may be present. Widespread routine use of serum protein electrophoresis has led to more frequent recognition of the disease.

Excessive excretion of light chains in the renal glomeruli damage the tubules when they are unable to reabsorb the massive protein load. Hypercalcemia and hyperuricemia may add to the renal problems, causing acute failure.

Hydration and reduction in tumor mass and protein production are the goals of therapy. Phenylalanine mustard and prednisone are commonly used forms of chemotherapy in the elderly, although other drugs are often added in younger, more vigorous patients. Plasma exchange by plasmapheresis can reduce viscosity and alleviate symptoms almost immediately.

CHRONIC LYMPHOCYTIC LEUKEMIA

Chronic lymphatic leukemia occurs in the over-50 population almost exclusively.[18] The disease may be manifest for several years by simple lymphocytosis that hardly requires a visit to the emergency room. Later, however, hypogammaglobulinemia and neutropenia may result in susceptibility to infections with *Streptococcus pneumoniae*, herpes zoster, and, eventually, gram-negative organisms.

In the elderly, chlorambucil can be used to reduce tumor burden along with supportive care to keep the patient comfortable. In the face of pancytopenia and a large spleen, examination of the bone marrow (quick, easy, and inexpensive) may differentiate a hyperplasia (response to hypersplenism), hypoplasia (response to chemotherapy), and leukemic infiltration (active disease), each of which requires a different therapeutic approach.

Prognosis seems to depend on the extent of disease on presentation. Severe anemia and thrombocytopenia with splenomegaly are poor prognostic signs. Hypogammaglobulinemia increases the likelihood of infection, but does not itself shorten survival. There is great individual variation in the course of the disease.

Therapy should be delayed until complications develop because the asymptomatic lymphocytosis may last 5–10 years. When the tumor burden becomes large or the spleen becomes tender, then a trial of corticosteroids (1 mg prednisone/kg/day) can be initiated. Usually the lymph nodes and spleen shrink, and anemia and thrombocytopenia improve. Infections may be a recurrent problem and a major source of mortality. Corticosteroids may be useful for treatment of autoimmune hemolytic anemia or thrombocytopenia caused by generation of abnormal antibodies. Chlorambucil or cyclophosphamide has been used to control lymphocyte proliferation. Hematopoietic values must be monitored appropriately. Patients so treated may come to the emergency room with infections that require treatment with antibiotics. Administration of γ-globulin adds little to this regimen because antibodies to the infecting organism are seldom present. When herpes zoster develops in the immune-deficient patient, herpes zoster immune globulin (HZIG) may be helpful. Chemotherapy should be interrupted until the complication is controlled. Irradiation of the spleen to treat hypersplenism and to reduce tumor size has been used for decades. Treating with chemotherapy intermittently reduces toxic reactions and produces relief of symptoms, but does not appear to prolong life.[18]

HEMORRHAGE

Bleeding in the elderly is usually caused by specific injury, malignancy, or ulcerative inflammatory lesion, but hemorrhagic manifestations in several different sites are likely to be due to a more general disturbance of the hemostatic system. Thrombocytopenia is the most likely cause of skin and mucus membrane hemorrhage. Petechiae over the extremities are also a clue to thrombocytopenia. Petechiae distal to the blood pressure cuff after a blood pressure reading may alert the observant physician to this defect.

Hemorrhages in the retina indicating leakage from arterioles and venules are sometimes a sign of severe thrombocytopenia. A platelet count and/or review of the blood smear confirms the presence of thrombocytopenia. In contrast to younger age groups, most of the thrombocytopenia in the elderly is secondary to some underlying disease or to drug ingestion.

A study by Bottiger and Westerhohm[29] found that 54% of patients with thrombocytopenia from a regional health service in Upsala, Sweden, were over 50 years old and 25 were over 70. In the older group, 15 patients died of cerebral or GI hemorrhage, and women predominated: 8.1/100,000 to 4.2/100,000 men. In 152 patients younger than 55, no etiologic factor could be found.

Many of the cases were related to medication: 126 of 359 patients, most of whom were over 55, had a history of taking medications associated with thrombocytopenia.[30] Medications can cause thrombocytopenia by several mechanisms, including immunologic damage, intravascular coagulation, toxic destruction, and reduced marrow production because of alterations in megakaryocyte or stem cell precursors. Oral diuretics were most commonly the cause of thrombocytopenia, with the risk of the condition being 1/15,000 in patients taking oral diuretics. The incidence of thrombocytopenia seemed to parallel the increased ingestion of diuretics with advancing age. Chlorothiazide and other sulfa ring compounds also seem particularly likely to cause thrombocytopenia, possibly by selective megakaryocytic suppression. As many as 25% of patients taking chlorothiazide may have mild thrombocytopenia.[31] Recovery can be slow after discontinuing the drug. Alcohol also can be a cause of marrow depression and toxic vacuolization of megakaryocytes.

Other drugs taken by elderly patients, such as quinidine, gold, and sulfa-containing antibiotics, may stimulate antibody formation and complexes of antibody, drug, and complement that damage platelets, shortening platelet survival. Quinidine and quinine caused one-half as many cases of thrombocytopenia as did oral diuretics. Withdrawal of these drugs is usually followed by a prompt remission within 1–2 weeks.

Chemotherapy with marrow-suppressive drugs causes thrombocytopenia to some degree in all patients. The patient's disease history usually makes the pathogenesis obvious.

Marked thrombocytopenia may occasionally be a symptom of megaloblastic anemia with ineffective hematopoiesis. Macrocytes and neutropenia are clues to a more general disease of the marrow causing the thrombocytopenia. The examination of bone marrow to determine whether there are sufficient megakaryocytes present sometimes reveals the presence of megaloblasts and makes the alternative diagnosis.

Autoimmune thrombocytopenia (ITP), thought to be rare in the elderly from studies done in the 1950s, has been recognized with greater frequency in the elderly since the 1960s.[29,32] With the availability of tests for platelet antibodies, the diagnosis of immune thrombocytopenic purpura need no longer be one of exclusion. In patients without evidence of marrow disease or splenomegaly, 65% have evidence of platelet antibodies.[33] If there are no drugs involved to explain the antibody phenomenon, then the diagnosis of ITP is appropriately applied. Only one series of patients selected for platelet survival studies had a high proportion over 55 years of age (11/15).[32]

Thrombocytopenia in the elderly may be due to a malignancy (carcinoma or leukemia) in the marrow or to ineffective hematopoiesis (vitamin B_{12} or folic acid deficiency). Rarely is it due to a hypoplastic marrow. In any event, a bone marrow examination is required to establish whether precursor megakaryocytes are present in sufficient quantity to warrant further diagnostic search for a platelet-destructive process. Usually a disease involving the marrow that causes secondary thrombocytopenia is obvious. Hypocellular aspirates necessitate bone marrow biopsy (usually by needle) to detect tumor, fibrosis, granulomata, or true aplasia.

Petechial bleeding in a patient with a normal platelet count may be a sign of a defect in platelet function. A template bleeding time prolonged beyond 9–10 min further suggests the presence of a platelet function abnormality. The patient should be warned against taking any aspirin-containing compounds for a week prior to platelet function studies. Platelet aggregation studies using adenosine diphosphate, collagen, epinephrine, and ristocetin detect any of the acquired function defects of platelet membrane structure or release activity.

It is extremely unlikely that a congenital malfunction would go undetected until age 60, but the astute physician should not ignore that possibility. A good example of acquired platelet abnormality in the elderly is the patient with abnormal proteins produced by myeloma cells. These proteins sometimes form complexes with the surface glycoproteins of platelets and prevent adhesion and aggregation from occurring.[34]

TRANSFUSION

Transfusion therapy in the elderly, which is designed to replace malfunctioning or missing cells or proteins, can usually be accomplished with today's modern blood banking facilities. Much of the blood collected from normal donors (60% to 80%) is processed into red cells, platelets, fresh frozen plasma, or derivatives thereof (albumin, γ-globulin, Factor VIII, factors of the vitamin-K-dependent complex—II, VII, IX and X), thus enabling individual treatments for individual diseases. Red blood cells are used by those over 65 three times more frequently than their younger counterparts, mostly to support surgical procedures required more frequently in the age group.

The major consideration in the emergency department should be volume replacement in the traumatized patient, which can be accomplished with saline or plasma expanders stored in the department. Elderly patients tend to tolerate fluid replacement poorly, so a CVP line should be put in place. If major blood loss or marked anemia requires replacement with red blood cells, a blood sample should be sent to the blood bank for type-specific red blood cells. Clearly, if the patient is clinically stable, the cause of the anemia should be determined as quickly as possible and specific treatment given.

Transfusion should be used as emergency treatment in the symptomatic, unstable patient. Symptoms usually occur at hematocrits of 25% or less, especially if the anemia has developed rapidly. In this situation, replacement of blood volume may alleviate symptoms and stabilize the patient until definitive diagnosis and treatment can be made.

Transfusion should be given cautiously in the elderly, for although it can be lifesaving in the proper circumstances, it can be lethal. In the emergency situation where many procedures are being carried out at the same time in diagnostic or therapeutic care, volume overload is a distinct complication that is probably responsible for more deaths than is commonly recognized. Sudden congestive heart failure, pulmonary edema, or arrhythmia and death have occurred during transfusion, but are rarely reported. According to reports to the Federal Drug Administration, 3 of 70 fatal transfusion reactions occurred in emergency departments, and 4 occurred in intensive care units.[35]

In addition, hemolytic transfusion reactions from mixups and clerical errors are still being reported. Hepatitis, malaria, and other infections are transmitted by blood products. Immunization to leukocytes because of multiple transfusions has been associated with chills, fever, and severe respiratory reactions. Blood products should be administered slowly to elderly patients to reduce the severity of some of these reactions.

REFERENCES

1. Gerson LW, Skvarch L: Emergency medical service utilization by the elderly. *Ann Emerg Med* 11:610–612, 1982.

2. Vogel JM: Hematologic problems of the aged. *Mt Sinai J Med* 47:150–165, 1980.

3. Walsh JR: Hematologic disorders in the elderly. *Geriatr Med West J Med* 134:446–454, 1981.

4. Freedman ML, Marcus DL: Anemia and the elderly: Is it physiology or pathology? *Am J Med Sci* 280:81–85, 1980.

5. Matzner Y, Levy S, Grossowicz N, et al: Prevalence and causes of anemia in the elderly. *Isr J Med Sci* 14:1165–1169, 1978.

6. Matzner Y, Levy S, Grossowicz N, et al: Prevalence and causes of anemia in elderly hospitalized patients. *Gerontology* 25:113–119, 1979.

7. Reizenstein P, Ljunggren G, Smedby B, et al: Overprescribing iron tablets to elderly people in Sweden. *Br Med J* 2:962–963, 1979.

8. Hedstrand H, Killander A: Anemia in middle aged men. *Scand J Haematol* 19:417–423, 1977.

9. Hershko C, Levy S, Matzner Y, et al: Prevalence and cause of anemia in the elderly in Kiryat Shmoneh Israel. *Gerontology* 25:42–48, 1979.

10. Lipschitz DA, Mitchell CO, Thompson C: The anemia of senescence. *Am J Hematol* 11:47–54, 1981.

11. Hartsock RJ, Smith EB, Petty CS: Normal variation with aging of the amount of hematopoietic tissue in the bone marrow from the anterior iliac crest. *Am J Clin Pathol* 43:326–331, 1965.

12. Croker JR, Beynon G: GI bleeding—a major cause of iron deficiency in the elderly. *Age & Aging* 10:40–43, 1981.

13. Kalchthaler T, Tan MER: Anemia in institutionalized elderly patients. *J Am Geriatr Soc* 28:108–113, 1980.

14. Mackawa T: Hematologic disease, in Steinberg FU (ed): *The Care of the Geriatric Patient*. New York, CV Mosby Co, 1976, pp 152–166.

15. Robinson RC, Nansom EM: Anemia in the elderly: Caveat caecum. *NZ Med J* 81:379–382, 1975.
16. Evans DMD, Pathy MS, Sanerkin NG, et al: Anemia in geriatric patients. *Gerontol Clin* 10:228–241, 1968.
17. Wright WB: Iron deficiency anemia of the elderly treated by total dose infusion. *Gerontol Clin* 9:107–115, 1967.
18. Wintrobe MM (ed): *Clinical Hematology*, ed 8. Philadelphia, Lea & Febiger, 1983, pp 42–43, 1498, 1686, 1732, 1740.
19. Manoharan A: Low dose cytarabine therapy in hypoplastic acute leukemia. *N Engl J Med* 309:1652–1653, 1983.
20. Mufti GJ, Oscier DG, Hamblin TJ, et al: Low dose cytarabine in the treatment of myelodysplastic syndrome and acute myeloid leukemia. *N Engl J Med* 309:1653–1654, 1983.
21. Rosenthal DS, Maloney WC: Refractory dysmyelopoietic anemia and acute leukemia. *Blood* 63:314–318, 1983.
22. Modan B: Polycythemia: A review of epidemiological and clinical aspects. *J Chronic Dis* 18:605–645, 1965.
23. Gunale SR, Zelkowitz L: Polycythemia vera in a nonagenerian. *JAMA* 228:1148, 1974.
24. Cutler SI, Devesa SS, Scotto J: The 3rd National Cancer Survey. *JNCI* 58:1568–1575, 1974.
25. Devesa SS, Young JL, Williams RR: Polycythemia among the elderly. *JAMA* 232:706–707, 1975.
26. Freedman ML: Common hematologic problems: Diagnosis and treatment. *Geriatrics* 38:119–134, 1983.
27. Bloch KJ, Maki DG: Hyperviscosity syndromes associated with immunoglobulin abnormalities. *Semin Hematol* 10:113–124, 1973.
28. Rogers JS: IgE myeloma with osteoblastic lesions. *Blood* 49:295, 1977.
29. Bottiger LE, Westerhohm B: Thrombocytopenia. I: Incidence and etiology. *Acta Med Scand* 191:535–540, 1972.
30. Bottiger LE, Westerhohm B: Thrombocytopenia. II: Drug induced thrombocytopenia. *Acta Med Scand* 191:541–548, 1972.
31. Hussain S: Disorders of hemostasis and thrombosis in the aged. *Med Clin North Am* 60:1273–1287, 1976.
32. Aster RH, Keene WR: Sites of platelet destruction in idiopathic thrombocytopenic purpura. *Br J Haematol* 16:61–73, 1969.
33. Karpatkin M, Siskind GW, Karpatkin S: The platelet factor 3 immunoinjury technique reevaluated: Development of a rapid test for antiplatelet antibody. *J Lab Clin Med* 89:400–414, 1977.
34. Cohen AM: Coagulation abnormalities in myeloma. *Am J Med* 48:766–774, 1970.
35. Honig CL, Bove JR: Transfusion-associated fatalities: Review of Bureau of Biologics reports 1976–78. *Transfusion* 20:653–661, 1980.

8

Nutritional Emergencies

Peggy L. McCall, MSN, RN, CNA

Traditionally, life after the age of 65 was known as the "golden years" or as a period of blissful disengagement. It is recorded in literature as the age when the "best is yet to be." However, it is actually viewed by our society as a time of life with more social, physical, emotional, and financial problems than ever before. The health care system has been instrumental in advancing the quantity of years lived. Currently a 65-year-old woman can be expected to live an additional 18.4 years, and a 65-year-old man can live another 14 years.[1] However, modern medicine has not provided a meaningful and valued quality for those added years. Consequently, aging brings increasing risks of illness, isolation, and loss of physical and emotional support.

The elderly tend to use emergency services for regular as well as preventive health care.[2] For some, the emergency department is the only available access point to the health care system. A lack of transportation, financial insecurity, inadequate information about available community resources, and discriminatory practices have contributed to the elderly's inability to obtain health care. Some studies have shown that the proportion of emergency department (ED) patients with nonemergent problems is as high as 58%.[2,3] Persons over 65 require one-third of all medical care given and one-fourth of all medications prescribed and are responsible for one-fourth of all EMS responses. Are emergency health care providers prepared to meet the needs of this rapidly increasing population? Or, are the elderly a population at "risk" in the ED.[2,4]

The function of the ED has been expanded from its traditional role as an "emergency" and "trauma" center to include evaluation and care of patients with nonemergent health care problems. The older patient population provides a challenge because of the number of complex problems with which they are likely to present. Because of the episodic nature of the ED's services, only chief complaints are generally evaluated. Therefore, elderly patients who use the ED for a primary care source are at special jeopardy because their other more serious problems may be overlooked. In addition, they often find themselves in an environment that is fast paced, noisy, confusing and frequently insensitive to their needs. Historically, EDs have been staffed by young health care providers who enjoy delivering short-term, acute care with limited long-term patient involvement. This type of provider is ill-prepared to meet the needs of the elderly population.

Nutritional imbalances are recognized as a major contributor to illness in the elderly.[5] Patients with these problems are seen frequently in the ED as geriatric emergencies.[6] Age affects the older person's nutritional requirements in many ways, and special nutritional concerns and problems may result in life-threatening emergent conditions.

The purpose of this chapter is to identify these nutritional emergencies, to outline their early signs and symptoms, to recommend treatment protocols, to discuss special assessment techniques, and to convey a holistic approach to patient care and discharge planning.

ASSESSMENT

Clinical Assessment

Clinical assessment and diagnosis are as essential to the proper management of elderly patients as they are for their younger counterparts, but the assessment and diagnostic process of the older patient differs in four important ways:[7]

1. Multiple pathology is more the rule than an exception, so multiple rather than single diagnoses should be sought.
2. Special assessment techniques are required for the clinical history.
3. Individual symptoms and their interpretation differ in the elderly.
4. Clinical examination requires that a number of important differences be considered.

Multiple Pathology

With old age, health problems frequently come in clusters. Although one problem predominates, it may open the door to others. An assessment and diagnostic process that assumes that only one condition accounts for most of the patient's problems is totally unrealistic. For example, an elderly patient with malnutrition and anemia may have tachycardia. The tachycardia in turn may lead to decreased coronary blood flow and angina. The patient presents to the ED with chest pain and is assessed and diagnosed as a myocardial infarction, and the precipitating nutritional problem is often not addressed.

Special Assessment Techniques

A number of special concerns must be considered in the initial assessment phase. A person's biological age does not necessarily reflect that person's ability to function. Thus, an individual assessment is essential. In addition, a belief that being old is synonymous with being dependent and dying hinders the assessment. Although many aged individuals have multiple health problems and are unable to make adaptations past mid-life, a number of biologically superior individuals will enjoy a middle age that extends well into their nineties.

Communicating with the elderly is often reported to be difficult.[7,8] This difficulty can be the result of deafness or impairment of memory and concentration. However, changes in an elderly person's brain, e.g., such as fewer neurons, reduced blood flow, and metabolism, appear to have little functional significance. Intellectual ability remains stable, some cognitive processes actually improve, and others are maintained, although at a slower pace.[8] The best-documented major CNS change in the elderly is a gradual slowing of the conscious and reflex reaction time because of a decrease in nerve conduction velocity. This slowing affects the multisynaptic neural pathways more than the simple pathways.[7,8] Therefore, the elderly react more slowly; they need stronger stimuli and more time to respond. The elderly usually compensate for their slower pace by emphasizing accuracy and clarity, rather than speed.

In emergency medicine, where time is of the essence, one must immediately "change gears" to adapt to their pace. To assess these patients appropriately, one must speak slowly and clearly and face them so that they may actually see the words formed. Speaking this way facilitates hearing and allows the elderly patient to focus on the questions that are being asked. Other techniques that might assist in communicating are the use of written questions and the assistance of a relative or friend.

Differences In Interpretation of Symptoms

Elderly patients do not always show the expected signs and symptoms. The most striking single alteration in specific symptoms is the reduction in the intensity of visceral pain. This is especially apparent in cardiac infarction, which may be painless even in patients in whom pain is not overshadowed by breathlessness or confusion. The aged may have pneumonia without pain or fever, or appendicitis without pain, nausea, or vomiting. Both perforated peptic ulcers and acute cholecystitis may be painless. Headache is a relatively rare symptom in the elderly patient and must be taken seriously when it is present. In contrast, the experience of pain from bones and joints seems much less altered, so rib fractures and fractures of the long bones are usually extremely painful.

Four common nonspecific symptoms occur in a variety of illnesses in the elderly: confusion, falls, immobility, and incontinence. Any of these may be due to conditions as diverse as myocardial infarction, nutritional deficiencies, pneumonia, cerebral infarction, and toxic reactions to drugs. These four common symptoms are examined specifically as they relate to nutritional conditions later in the chapter.

Differences in Clinical Examination

Many essential procedures and observations of the clinical examination of an elderly person are the same as those for a patient of any age. However, there are also many differences. It is important to establish the patient's mental state. As previously stated, there are very few age-related changes in a person's brain that appear to have functional significance; therefore, any changes in mental status are usually the result of illness, not aging. Structured psychometric tests that assist in the evaluation of mental status are recommended. Yet, several neurologic abnormalities are extremely common in the elderly, and therefore, their presence cannot be taken as evidence of neurologic disease. These include small, slightly irregular pupils; impaired upward gaze; absent abdominal reflexes; absent ankle jerks; and reduced vibration and position sense in the lower limbs.[7] Another sign that is frequently present but open to different interpretation is local muscle wasting. Its common cause is joint disease, which is immediately apparent in the quadriceps and usually accompanies osteoarthritis of the knee. Also, wasting in the small muscles of the hand accompanies rheumatoid arthritis and, occasionally, osteoarthritis.[7,8] Knowing what to look for in assessing the elderly patient's clinical condition and knowing the differences in interpretation that must be considered make one better prepared to administer the care that is specific to the person's needs. As a final precaution, on completing the assessment, keep in mind that even though the elderly can have many complex problems, they are more than a set of symptoms. Just like any other patient of any other age group, the geriatric patient deserves careful attention to the person, not just the disease.[8]

Prehospital Assessment

Because of the increasing number of EMS calls by the elderly—greater than 25%[9]—emergency medical technicians (EMTs) and paramedics (EMTP) are frequently the first providers to initiate treatment to the geriatric emergency patient. The aged have many fears that are difficult for the young and healthy to appreciate fully, and these can make the elderly patient hostile. These fears include the fear of being hospitalized or institutionalized and the loss of self-sufficiency or control. The elderly may frequently deny or minimize their symptoms. Therefore, the prehospital provider must be aware of these tendencies and avoid being misled.[10]

It is often difficult to distinguish the symptoms of acute, emergent conditions from the physical findings of multiple chronic diseases. For example, the elderly often have nonpathologic rales, they mouth breathe, exhibit loss of skin elasticity, and give the appearance of being dehydrated when actually they are not. The prehospital provider may, in turn, start an IV of normal saline at a rapid rate and immediately greatly increase the patient's risk of congestive heart failure.

Prehospital providers must understand the delicate balance that is vital in the emergency treatment of the elderly. Treatment protocols should be prepared and closely followed. The following ten recommendations can he applied appropriately to a variety of emergent conditions. These recommendations are extremely important and should be considered as priorities in the prehospital care of the geriatric patient.[9]

1. Be aggressive.
2. Oxygenate rapidly.
3. Clear secretions and maintain an open airway.
4. Maintain blood pressure.
5. Avoid excessive fluid overload.
6. Avoid drugs (if possible).
7. Keep body temperature normal.
8. Observe sterile technique.
9. Monitor the ECG.
10. Provide psychological support.

History

Diet

Acute illness greatly increases patients' nutritional requirements while at the same time depressing their appetite. Many geriatric patients have protein-calorie malnutrition, as well as vitamin and trace mineral deficiencies.[5] These conditions are caused by a combination of physical, psychological, social, and environmental factors. Nutritional assessment is an essential early step in the management of an acutely ill elderly patient, and a complete diet history is an extremely important evaluation tool. A common mistake frequently made is assuming that the elderly need fewer nutrients than younger people. Many older people live alone on a fixed low income. They have a decreased appetite and a reduced motivation and ability to shop for fresh foods. They tend to rely solely on ''ready to serve,'' nonperishable, or processed foods. Elderly people frequently believe that the amount and quality of their diet are adequate when, in actuality, gross deficiencies exist.

When obtaining the diet history, be aware of the factors that affect the patients' responses and develop methods that facilitate obtaining an accurate assessment. The diet history should be directed toward obtaining information about preparation and purchase of food, patterns of eating, the frequency of the meals, and the kinds and amounts of food consumed. A combination of methods to obtain this information can be used. A 24-hr recall or food diary yields the most information. However, these methods are not feasible for the ED. Answers to such questions as the following—How many times did you eat today? What is your favorite food? Do you cook for yourself? Do you go to the grocery store? Do you take vitamins? Do you eat fruit daily? Do you eat between meals?—together with input from the patient's family or friends, will help establish a valid diet history.[11]

Dental

The condition of the patient's gums and teeth is another important evaluation tool. Does the patient wear dentures? Do the dentures fit? Are the dentures comfortable? An analysis of the dental needs of the elderly revealed the following:[12] (1) approximately 50% of the elderly over the age of 65 have lost all their teeth, (2) periodontal disease affects 90% or more of the elderly population, (3) the average age of dentures is greater than 10 years, (4) the average time between dental visits is more than 6 years. Nutritional and digestive problems certainly begin in the mouth, so the patient's ability to chew is very important in the selection and intake of food.

Any type of swallowing problems should also be included in the history. The elderly's saliva production is usually about one-third the amount of a younger person. Therefore, there is increased difficulty in swallowing, and elderly patients choke easily because their mouths are dry.[8] Often, older people, even with evidence of gross water depletion, are also not thirsty. Although elderly patients rarely complain of thirst or ask for water, they drink avidly if encouraged.

Drugs

It is essential to have accurate information on what medication an elderly patient is taking. Studies have shown that elderly patients use one-quarter of all prescribed and over-the-counter drugs.[2,4] They are prescribed an average of six drugs on discharge from hospitals, many of which are to be taken over extended periods of time. In the ED, it is not unusual to see elderly patients with a large sack full of drugs that they are not sure why or how long they have been taking. Therefore, the elderly are likely to be exposed to a large mixture of medications, some of which are very potent and many of which are very capable of producing toxic actions and interactions. Moreover, the aging process affects the absorption of drugs and their distribution throughout the body. Therefore, if the drug is taken over a long period of time, it may accumulate and cause adverse reactions, such as tremors, confusion, and coma.

It is often difficult and not always possible to obtain a detailed accurate history of what medications the patient is taking, despite the fact that it may be the medications that have predisposed the patient to acute injury or illness. Questions about medications should be directed toward the patient, if possible. Otherwise, family, friends, or the medical record from prior admissions may be helpful. If the patient is transferred from another facility, a medication record should be requested if not included.

Special attention should be paid to drugs such as diazepam (Valium) that depress the CNS. Diazepam is one of the most widely prescribed drugs in the United States.[10] A multipurpose drug prescribed as a minor tranquilizer, it is also used to relax cardiac patients, to relieve muscle pain, and to combat insomnia—all frequent conditions in the elderly.

Analgesics that contain aspirin and laxatives should also be objects of concern. Aspirin is a significant cause of gastrointestinal blood loss, and laxatives cause diarrhea and potassium depletion. One should determine whether the patient takes any drugs that may depress the bone marrow, such as chlorpromazine HCl (Thorazine) or phenylbutazone (Butazolidin). Digitalis and aminoglycoside antibiotics are likely to have toxic effects caused by decreased renal function.[7]

One must also establish which prescribed drugs are *not* being taken. For example, recurring cardiac failure may be due not only to a recent myocardial infarction or pulmonary infarction but also to the discontinuance of drugs prescribed to control the cardiac failure. The importance of a complete and accurate drug history can not be overemphasized in geriatric emergencies.

Drug interactions as they relate to nutrition are just beginning to be understood. For example, isoniazid-type drugs can result in symptoms of vitamin B_6 deficiency, phenytoin (Dilantin) can precipitate folic acid deficiency anemia, and colchicine may reduce vitamin B_{12} absorption. Nutrition and drugs in association with underlying medical problems are often involved in the development of geriatric emergencies.

Elimination—Bowel Habits

Constipation is probably the most common problem occurring in the elderly. The term "constipation" means different things to different people. For some, it may mean a decrease in the frequency of their normal elimination pattern; for others, it may mean an increased difficulty in passing stool. The most frequent causes of constipation in the elderly are slower peristalsis, inactivity, and less bulk and fluid in the diet. To assess the elderly patients' bowel habits, ask if any particular food causes a problem, how easy is defecation, what is the consistency of the stools, and whether laxatives or enemas are taken regularly. The type of laxative taken is important as well. Mineral oil taken to promote regularity blocks the absorption of fat-soluble vitamins A, D, and K.

If the patient's definition of constipation includes an *acute* onset of decrease in the frequency of stools, then this change in bowel habit represents true constipation. An acute onset of true constipation is considered more ominous than chronic constipation and warrants a more complete workup. Constipation should be considered a symptom, rather than a disease, and it should be completely evaluated.

Physical Examination

Evaluation of the nutritional state of the elderly in the absence of severe malnutrition is extremely difficult. However, it should be included in the physical examination of all elderly patients who come to the ED.

Body weight is the most useful single observation for assessment of nutritional status. However, in the elderly, care should be taken in interpreting an individual's weight in relation to his or her nutritional state. For example, most height and weight tables are based on the average weight and height of the 25–29 age population. Weight gain after this age usually results in an increase in fat and not muscle mass. Difficulty in interpretation occurs when a patient is within or near the desired chart weight, and due to a change in body composition associated with aging, has an increase in fatness, a decrease in musculature, and a demineralization of bone. Therefore, it is possible for the elderly patient at a desirable weight to be in a poor nutritional state. An additional consideration in the evaluation of weight is fluid retention. Prolonged malnutrition may result in an increase in extracellular fluid that may not be apparent as edema, may add sufficient weight, and may mask soft tissue wasting so that by weight and appearance the patient does not look undernourished. It is also important to obtain some estimation of body fatness to determine the significance of relative body weight. The thickness of skin folds, for example, over the triceps, subscapular area, and lateral abdominal wall normally provides a good correlation. The measurement and inspection of skin folds can assist in the interpretation of relative weight in terms of lean body mass and fatness.

Physical Signs of Malnutrition

Physical changes related to malnutrition (Table 8–1) often are overlooked in the elderly because they are viewed as part of the normal aging process. Another frequent error is overlooking the elderly obese individuals who are just as likely to be deficient in protein or other nutrients as are the slim elderly.

Certain changes in the skin and mucous membrane are associated with nutritional deficiencies. When these are present, they should be considered in the differential diagnosis. Glossitis is a common finding in the elderly. It can result from vitamin B group deficiency, but such other causes as irritants, systemic antibiotics, and uremia should be considered. A tongue that is pale and atrophied may be related to an anemia, which can be either nutritional or nonnutritional. Another frequent finding is the breaking and fissuring of skin at the corners of the mouth. This sign has been associated with deficiencies of niacin, riboflavin, or pyridoxine, but it can also be a result of poor dental care or gum disease. Dryness and pigmentation of the skin, increased thickness over pressure points, follicular hyperkeratosis, and nasolabial seborrhea may be associated with nutritional deficiencies and should be investigated. Vitamin A deficiency can be exhibited as a thickening and opaqueness of the bulbar conjunctivals. Other physical findings that could possibly have a nutritional etiology are liver enlargement, parotid gland enlargement, calf tenderness, loss of vibratory sense, absent tendon reflexes, petechiae, and ecchymoses. Dry cracking lesions on the hands or other areas exposed to the sun and symmetrical hyperemia could indicate pellagra.

Routine laboratory tests that can be helpful in the assessment of the elderly nutritional state are measurements of hemoglobin, hematocrit, and serum albumin. Some studies have stated that the elderly normally have a reduction of the

Table 8–1 Physical Signs of Malnutrition

Signs and Symptoms of Malnutrition
General: weight loss or excessive weight, muscle wasting, weakness, lethargy, confusion, irritability
Hair: dull, dry, sparse, depigmented, plucks easily
Skin: dry, scaly, follicular hyperkeratosis (sandpaper feel of skin), petechiae, loss of fat under skin, dyspigmentation, dermatitis, ulcerations
Face: depigmentation, supraorbital pigmentation, flaky skin around nose and mouth
Nails: brittle, ridged, spoon-shaped
Eyes: conjunctival pallor, infection, or redness; fissuring of eyelids, dull cornea
Lip: denuded, red, swollen, angular fissure; scars
Tongue: loss of filiform papillae; hypertrophy of fungiform papillae; tongue smooth, fissured, red, swollen
Teeth, jaws: dental caries, missing teeth, gums spongy, bleed easily, recessed
Glands: enlarged thyroid or parotids
Musculoskeletal: muscle atrophy, wasting, dependent edema, bow legs, bending of ribs, edema in dependent parts
Neurologic: irritability, confusion, lethargy, apathy, anorexia, motor weakness, walking difficulty, sensory loss, burning, tingling
Cardiovascular: tachycardia, cardiac enlargement, arrhythmia
Gastrointestinal: constipation, diarrhea, liver enlargement

Source: Adapted with permission from *American Journal of Public Health* (Supplement, Nutritional Assessment in Health Programs), (1973;63:19), Copyright © 1973, American Public Health Association.

hemoglobin and hematocrit concentration as a process of aging.[13] However, well-nourished older persons may show hemoglobin values within the normal range for younger adults. Hematocrits below 40 in men and below 38 in women should not be accepted as normal without further evaluation of possible iron or protein deficiency, as well as of blood loss or specific diseases associated with anemia.[5]

Serum albumin concentration is not considered a sensitive indicator of protein nutrition because severe protein deprivation must occur before the level of serum albumin is sufficiently low to result in edema. Serum albumin levels below 3.5 gm/dl should be considered below normal and indicate a reduced intake or utilization of protein.[5] Overnutrition may be indicated by the lipid concentration in the serum. Elevation of the cholesterol level and hypertriglyceridemia may indicate the need for further tests, such as serum lipid electrophoresis. The laboratory findings should always be consistent with the history and physical findings before such a diagnosis as a deficiency is acceptable.

Nutritional Requirements

Age affects the elderly's nutritional requirements in many ways. Their caloric requirements are less than those of younger people, their requirement for certain vitamins and trace elements are probably greater, and they are more likely to suffer from digestive disturbances.

The quality of life of the elderly individual depends greatly on what he or she chooses to eat. Eating habits are a complex set of behaviors that evolve over a lifetime. During the lifetime of today's elderly, there have been vast changes in the food supply, and their memories of "good home cooking" are probably very different from what they eat now.

A number of factors affect the nutritional status of the elderly: a limited knowledge of the nutritional value of food, loss of appetite, changes in economic circumstances and lifestyle, poor dentition, and the increasing incidence of disease and disabilities that lead to alterations in absorption and metabolism of nutrients.

The Recommended Dietary Allowances (RDAs)[14] are the acceptable standards of nutrition established by the U.S. Food and Nutrition Board. These standards are designed for the healthy adult. Even though individual variability of nutrient requirement is taken into consideration in establishing them, the elderly are much less uniform as a group than are most younger age groups. Variability in the physiologic aging process and susceptibility to disease further influence the elderly's nutritional needs (Tables 8–2 and 8–3). One standard could hardly be devised that takes all these factors into consideration.

Table 8–2 Recommended Requirements

	MEN	WOMEN
Protein (g)	56	44
Vitamin A (μg RE)*	1,000	800
D (μg)	5§	5
E (mgα-TE)†	10	8
Ascorbic acid (mg)	60	60
Thiamine (mg)	1.2	1.0
Riboflavin (mg)	1.4	1.2
Niacin (mg NE) ‡	16	13
Vitamin B_6(mg)	2.2	2.0
Folacin (μg)	400	400
Vitamin B_{12}(μg)	3	3
Calcium (mg)	800	800
Phosphorus (mg)	800	800
Magnesium (mg)	350	300
Iron (mg)	10	10
Zinc (mg)	15	15
Iodine (μg)	150	150

Note: *RE = retinol equivalents. 1 μg (3.33 IU) retinol or 6 μg (10 IU)
β-carotene = 1 RE.
†α-TE = α-tocopherol equivalents, 1 mg (1.49 IU) d-α-tocopherol = 1α-TE.
‡NE - niacin equivalent. 1 mg niacin or 60 mg tryptophan = 1 NE.
§5 g vitamin D = 200 IU of vitamin D.

Source: Recommended Dietary Allowances, 9th ed, National Academy of Sciences—National Research Council, © 1980.

Table 8–3 Estimated Adequate Daily Intake of Vitamins and Minerals

Vitamin K (μg)	70–140
Biotin (μg)	110–200
Pantothenic Acid (mg)	4–7
Copper † (mg)	2.0–3.0
Manganese* (mg)	2.5–5.0
Fluoride† (mg)	1.5–4.0
Chromium† (mg)	0.05–0.20
Selenium† (mg)	0.05–0.20
Molybdenum† (mg)	0.15–0.50
Sodium (mg)	1,100–3,300
Potassium (mg)	1,875–5,625
Chloride (mg)	1,700–5,100

Note: * – Retinol equivalents.
† = For many trace elements, consumption of several times the usual daily intake may be toxic. Upper levels given in this table should not be habitually exceeded.

Source: Recommended Dietary Allowances, 9th ed, National Academy of Sciences—National Research Council, © 1980.

There are several areas of controversy concerning acceptable standards of nutrition for the elderly:

- What is the appropriate calcium intake for the elderly, especially post-menopausal women at risk of developing osteoporosis? The question of whether calcium intake above the RDA of 800 mg/day is beneficial remains in dispute.[15] Most international standards recommend 500 mg/day or less.
- The RDA for Vitamin D is 5 μg/day, whereas international standards recommend 2-5 μg/day, depending on exposure to sunlight.
- Fiber is a food component that is not considered essential by the RDA. In the elderly a moderate intake of fiber, achieved through fruits, vegetables, and cereal products, has been found to contribute to the reduction of constipation and to improve intestinal musculature.[15]

Associated Signs and Symptoms of Nutritional Emergencies

Falls are cited as the single greatest cause of accidental death in the elderly,[16] and injuries associated with falls frequently bring the patient to the ED. A number of nutrition-based illnesses can contribute to confusion, dizziness, and dehydration, and thereby result in falls and serious injuries in the elderly. Vitamin deficiencies may result in weakness and a tendency toward more accidents. For example, symptoms of early niacin deficiency include mental confusion, dizziness, syncope, paresthesias, and palpitations; early signs and symptoms appear long before the classic signs of diarrhea, dermatitis, etc. Early scurvy or vitamin C deficiency presents with joint stiffness and pain, pain with motion, unsteadiness of gait, and signs of confusion. Again, these symptoms appear before the classic signs of skin and hair changes or bleeding gums. Chronic thiamine deficiency as seen frequently in elderly ethanol abusers appears as dizziness or syncope. These early symptoms can occur even when the elderly patient has not used alcohol for weeks and so can be very confusing for the ED diagnostician.

Malnutrition is always considered a potential threat to the aged. It may first be demonstrated as mental confusion and dizziness, again resulting in accidents and injuries. A more complete review of vitamin deficiencies and malnutrition is presented later in the chapter.

Almost any metabolic and endocrine emergency can occur in the elderly. They are prone to dehydration and problems associated with fluid, electrolyte, and acid-base balance. Hypokalemia due to inadequate food and fluid intake or overuse of drugs is seen frequently. These conditions again cause weakness, confusion, and unsteady gait, resulting in accidents and falls that require immediate emergency care.

SPECIFIC NUTRITIONAL EMERGENCIES

Malnutrition

Malnutrition is a serious potential threat to the aged and should be closely looked for in the ED. It is an inclusive term that involves the lack, imbalance, or excess of one or more of approximately 40 nutrients required by the body.[17] The causes of malnutrition are complex and include conditions that preexist with the individual (the host), the quality of the environment, and the specific agents that provoke the problem.

Primary nutritional deficiencies are caused by inadequate or imbalanced intake of food. Usually these conditions are the results of many environmental factors. Secondary deficiencies result from some pathogenesis in digestion, absorption, or metabolism, so that the tissue needs are not met even though the diet would be adequate in normal circumstances. The elderly population as a whole are very susceptible to both primary and secondary deficiencies because of changes in economic circumstances or lifestyle.[17,18]

The literature states that malnutrition occurs in as many as three out of every 10 elderly individuals.[17] As age increases, so does the incidence and risk of malnutrition.[17,18] Presenting signs and symptoms are fatigue, anemia, variations in body weight and body fat, changes in the mucous membrane and skin, glossitis, petechiae, loss of muscle tone and coordination, and loss of hair. Other physical findings include liver enlargement, parotid gland enlargement, calf tenderness, loss of vibratory sense, and absent tendon reflex.[5] Many of these signs and symptoms are associated with a variety of other conditions seen in the elderly.

However, when they are present, they should alert the emergency medicine provider to consider nutritional deficiencies in the differential diagnosis.

Emergency Treatment

The first step in emergency treatment of malnutrition is immediate replacement of deficient nutrients, eg, IVs with multivitamin preparations. Hospital admission is then required to:

- establish acceptance by the patient and/or family
- rule out organic disease
- establish causative factors
- provide appropriate dietary counseling
- refer to community service agencies.

If hospital admission is not possible, dietary counseling with the patient and/or family should occur in the ED with appropriate referral to community resources, such as the Visiting Nurse Association or Meals on Wheels Program.

Acute Vitamin Deficiencies

Vitamin deficiencies are rare in this country in younger age groups. However, in the elderly they are more common and assume greater clinical importance.[5,18] Precipitating factors include low dietary intake and chronic disease, which may interfere with the intake, absorption, metabolism, and utilization of vitamins. Most frequently, the low dietary intake and endogenous factors act in combination, and the deficiency is caused by a complex set of problems not easily defined. The most important clinical deficiencies seen in the elderly are related to B group vitamins, folic acid, and vitamins B_{12}, C, D, and K. Disorders of the liver and biliary system frequently produce vitamin K deficiencies.

Vitamin B Complex—Niacin

Niacin is similar to other B complex water-soluble vitamins in that it is a constituent of coenzymes involved in the metabolism of carbohydrates, fats, and proteins. The B complex vitamins are needed in proportion to the individual's calorie requirements, which are somewhat lower in the elderly.

Signs and symptoms of early niacin deficiency include irritability, fatigue, headaches, loss of appetite, sleeplessness, dizziness, syncope, paresthesias, palpitations, and depression. These appear well before the classic signs of pellagra, dermatitis, diarrhea, and dementia. Acute nicotinic acid deficiency, which is found mainly in alcoholics with severe cases of malnutrition, produces Holliffe's syndrome, an acute encephalopathy characterized by clouding of consciousness and extrapyramidal rigidity.[17]

Thiamine Deficiency

Only a minimal amount of thiamine is stored in the body. The liver, kidneys, heart, brain, and muscles have somewhat higher concentrations than the blood; therefore, the tissues are rapidly depleted during thiamine deficiency. The functioning form of thiamine is cocarboxylase, also known as thiamine pyrophosphate (TPP). TPP has a critical function in carbohydrate metabolism in the oxidative process of pyruvic acid and the formation of acetyl coenzyme A, which in turn enters the Kreb's cycle. This is one of the most complex reactions in carbohydrate metabolism. Thiamine is required for the metabolism of alcohol as well.

Elderly persons appear to utilize thiamine less efficiently; therefore, supplements are recommended even though their calorie requirement is lower. Studies have indicated thiamine deficiencies as great as 37% in 233 elderly subjects aged 44-90 years.[19]

Thiamine deficiency is not rare in the U.S.; however, it is confined principally to the alcoholic population and a significant increase is reported in hemodialysis patients.[5,19] Alcoholics ingest little thiamine in their limited food intake. The problem is compounded in the elderly alcoholic who is less efficient in utilizing thiamine. Early signs and symptoms of chronic thiamine deficiency may be dizziness, memory lapses, or syncope.[6] These can occur with only intermittent excessive use of alcohol.

Ethanol Abuse

Wernicke's encephalopathy and Korsakoff's psychosis occur frequently in the elderly nutritionally deficient alcoholic. The most marked signs in Wernicke's disease are the ocular findings of nystagmus (horizontal and vertical), oculomotor paralysis, and palsies. Ataxia and mental changes are also present. Often the ocular changes and ataxia precede the mental changes by several days to several weeks. Korsakoff's psychosis occurs very often in patients with Wernicke's disease. The patient exhibits a distinct impairment in short-term and long-term memory, disorientation, confabulation, and hallucinations. In the elderly, accidental hypothermia has been described in association with Wernicke's disease, which is likely due to hemorrhagic lesions in the region of the hypothalamus that are responsible for problems in temperature regulation.[19] Cardiac manifestations, such as heart enlargements and CHF, are reported in severe cases of thiamine deficiency.[19] They should always be ruled out in malnourished elderly patients.

The treatment of Wernicke's disease and Korsakoff's psychosis consists of the following six steps:

1. Administration of large doses of thiamine in association with other B vitamins dramatically improves the symptoms. The eye signs especially respond rapidly. Ataxia may respond more slowly, and mental confusion may or may not improve, depending on such other underlying conditions as liver disease.

2. Special attention should be paid in the ED to airway management, respiratory depression, and possible aspiration. In comatose patients who are suspected alcoholics, IV thiamine should be given prior to 50% dextrose so that Wernicke's disease is not further precipitated.
3. Seizure precautions should be taken.
4. Blood levels of alcohol and reduced red cell transketolase activity are recommended to confirm the diagnosis.
5. Hospital admission is recommended.
6. Referrals should be made to appropriate community services.

Vitamin C Deficiency

Scurvy, an ancient disease that plagued the seagoing adventurers of the 16th and 17th centuries, is still occasionally seen in this country in the elderly, especially in men.[18,19] The body stores of ascorbic acid in many older people are diminished due to poorly balanced meals; in addition, the institutionalized aged may be subject to a delay in consumption or delivery of meals and inadequate supply of fruit and juices. Low leukocyte ascorbic acid levels are not always associated with a low intake of vitamin C. They may be found in association with gastrointestinal disease, hepatic cirrhosis, cancer, and acute myocardial infarctions. Heavy smokers also are reported to have lower levels of Vitamin C because of the destruction of vitamin C by tobacco products.[19]

Common signs and symptoms of early scurvy include joint pain, stiffness, and pain with motion; unsteady gait; and signs of confusion. Scurvy does not appear suddenly; there is a slow insidious progression of these subtle manifestations before the classic signs and symptoms occur. These signs cannot easily be detected by the ED practitioner because they are so similar to frequent complaints of aging or chronic illness. However, the ED provider should be aware that, when there is an infection or other signs of stress, there may be a rapid development of such symptoms as bleeding gums, skin changes, hair changes, depression, and eventually death.[6]

Acute scurvy responds to the administration of 100-200 mg of ascorbic acid. However, in the elderly administration of vitamin C does not always increase the leukocyte ascorbic acid (LAA) level. The LAA appears to correlate with the severity of the illness, which in turn influences the tissue stores of vitamin C. Therefore, it is believed that many illnesses occurring in the elderly patient depress LAA concentration. In addition, a number of drugs used frequently in clinical practice, such as tetracycline, are reported to also depress LAA levels.[19]

Anemia and Diet

It is difficult to obtain accurate figures about the incidence of anemia that is solely due to nutritional factors in the elderly. Frank anemia due to nutritional deficiency alone appears to be uncommon in old age. However, nutritional factors often play a major role in the pathogenesis of anemia in the elderly. For example, iron-deficiency anemia in elders is more often associated with chronic gastrointestinal blood loss than with inadequate iron intake alone; however, both factors are frequently implicated.[20]

Predisposing factors to anemia include the following:

- reduced dietary intake due to social and environmental factors
- increased incidence of gastric mucosal abnormalities
- reduced efficiency of iron absorption; reduced efficiency of nutrient absorption
- increased use of drugs
- ethanol abuse
- multiple pathology

Iron-Deficiency Anemia

Iron requirements are increased in old age at a time when iron intake is low. A number of studies have indicated that the RDA of 10 mg is rarely achieved, and actual intake may often be less than 5–8 mg/day. Many foods that are important items in the diet of the elderly, including bran, eggs, milk, and tea, inhibit iron absorption. Iron absorption may be greater than 25% from meat and less than 10% from vegetables. However, meat is eaten much less frequently by the elderly.[20,21]

Plasma iron and total iron binding capacity (TIBC) decrease as the individual ages. Iron is transported in plasma in combination with protein, which is also decreased in old age. Iron stores increase in the bone marrow with increasing age, and at all ages men have greater iron stores than women. There is increased iron loss in the elderly. Pathologic blood losses commonly occur from the gastrointestinal tract because of such chronic diseases as hemorrhoids, hiatal hernias, bowel carcinoma, and frequent use of such drugs as salicylates.[21] In summary, elderly patients are extremely susceptible to iron-deficiency anemias because of impairments in iron requirements, iron transport, iron utilization, iron stores, and loss.

Patients may be asymptomatic or may attribute early symptoms to old age. This is especially true if the onset of the anemia is insidious. By the time patients arrive in the ED they may be acutely ill with signs and symptoms of cardiovascular failure such as SOB, edema, confusion, dizziness, left ventricular failure, agitation, delusions, or hallucinations. Pallor of the mucosa or nail beds is a more useful sign than pallor of the skin.

Treatment includes the following components:

- full diagnostic workup, including complete blood studies
- radiologic workup
- detailed drug and diet history to search for the other coexisting cause of the anemia
- hospital admission

Oral iron therapy is recommended in all cases unless contraindicated. One 200 mg dose of ferrous sulfate provides 60 mg of iron, about one-third of which can be absorbed. Vitamin C increases the absorption of iron but also increases its side effects. Parenteral iron therapy may be required when there are problems with malabsorption or other conditions. Imferon should be avoided in uremic patients. Intravenous iron, such as Ferrivenin or Astrafer, provide total dose iron infusion and are recommended for the elderly, if given with care. However, they can produce local irritations, venous spasm, or phlebitis. General reactions include nausea, vomiting, fever, tachycardia, headaches, and abdominal pain. Intravenous iron is reported to cause fewer reactions in cases of severe iron deficiency, presumably due to increased plasma iron-binding capability.[20]

Blood transfusions are not recommended in iron-deficiency anemia unless there is acute blood loss. In chronic anemias, blood transfusions are contraindicated due to the blood volume, which is maintained or possibly increased.

Megaloblastic Anemias

Megaloblastic anemias are macrocytic anemias characterized by oversized abnormal red-cell precursors or megaloblasts in the bone marrow. These anemias occur more frequently in the elderly and may produce a severe illness because of the late diagnosis. Common features include leukopenia and hypersegmentation of the neutrophil nuclei.[20] This type of anemia is usually due to a deficiency of vitamin B_{12} or folic acid. A deficiency of either of these nutrients leads to a defective nucleic acid synthesis, which progresses to megaloblastosis in the bone marrow.

Vitamin B_{12} Deficiency

There is no convincing evidence of an age-related decline in the absorption of vitamin B_{12}. However, there are documented decreases in serum B_{12} levels and liver stores of B_{12} in the elderly.[19,20]

Vitamin B_{12} is found in all foods of animal origin, such as milk, eggs, and meat. Vegetable foods contain virtually no B_{12}. Dietary deficiencies of vitamin B_{12} are rare except in pure vegetarians. Therefore vitamin B_{12} deficiency is usually due to impaired absorption of the vitamin and not to a dietary deficiency. Malabsorption of vitamin B_{12} is most frequently related to gastric lesions, intestinal lesions, drug-induced malabsorption, or severe pancreatic disease.[19,20]

Pernicious anemia is the most common type of megaloblastic anemia seen in the elderly.[20] The onset is insidious and contributes to a late diagnosis. The elderly patient may be severely anemic before the condition is recognized. Manifestations include severe mental changes, such neurologic changes as peripheral neuropathy, and subacute combined degeneration of the cord. The ED provider should be aware of predisposing causes, such as gastric surgery, strict vegetarianism, or a family history of pernicious anemia or autoimmune disease.

Treatment includes (1) administration of parenteral vitamin B_{12} injections given long-term (regularly for life) and (2) referral to appropriate community resources.

There is significant evidence of latent pernicious anemia or vitamin B_{12} deficiency in the elderly without anemia. However, there appears to be no symptomatic benefit from vitamin B_{12} therapy in the absence of anemia.[19]

Folic Acid (Folate) Deficiency

Several forms of folic acid are utilized in the body, most of which are stored in the liver. The conversion of folic acid to folinic acid, the biologically active form, occurs in the liver and requires ascorbic acid. Folinic acid is the coenzyme for a number of other enzyme systems. For example, it facilitates the synthesis of nucleoproteins and the maturation of red blood cells, and its action is interrelated with Vitamin B_{12}.

Folate deficiency should be suspected in any elderly patient with an unexplained neuropathy, megaloblastic anemia, confused state, or changes in the mucous membrane of the tongue. Neurologic features may include symptoms of cord degeneration.

The main causes of folate deficiency in the elderly are inadequate intake, malabsorption, increased utilization, and impaired effectiveness. Major contributing factors are anticonvulsant therapy, skin diseases, alcoholism, and chronic diseases, such as rheumatoid arthritis. In the elderly inadequate dietary intake is usually an important cause of the deficiency in contrast to vitamin B_{12} deficiency, which is usually the result of malabsorption. Studies report a significant relationship between organic brain disease and low folate levels.[19,20] It has been thought that dementia leads to inadequate dietary intake and folate deficiency; however, the possibility that folate deficiency leads to impaired mental function cannot be excluded. Treatment includes identification of the deficiency, appropriate nutritional replacement, and community referral for long-term dietary counseling.

Vitamin K Deficiency

The major causes of vitamin K deficiency are obstructive jaundice, which causes impaired absorption of vitamins K_1 and K_2, and hepatocellular damage, in which there is impaired synthesis of the coagulation factors. However, deficiencies of vitamin K may develop in malnourished elderly patients who are given broad spectrum antibiotics. The antibiotics interfere with the bacterial synthesis of vitamin K in the gut. Anticoagulant therapy also antagonizes the effects of vitamin K by reducing the hepatic synthesis of the coagulation factors.[19]

Vitamin K operates at several points in the blood coagulation mechanism. Deficiencies lead to a reduction in prothrombin (Factor II) and in Factors VII, IX, and X. Signs are subcutaneous hemorrhages and bleeding from other sites. The treatment of vitamin K deficiency in biliary obstruction is administration of vitamin K parenterally. However, if the cause of the deficiency is liver damage the response to vitamin K is generally poor.[19]

FRACTURES

Fractures are a common occurrence among the elderly. In those over the age of 65, fractures from falls and the resulting complications are cited as a major cause of death.[22] Older women have a higher incidence than older men. Research indicates that the problem of fractures in the elderly has both dietary and hormonal implications.[21,22] All persons begin losing bone minerals around the age of 40; however, women's rate of bone loss is greater than men's and increases significantly after menopause.[21] The most common age-related fractures are lower forearm fractures (especially in women of 50 and over), vertebral compression fractures, and femoral neck fractures.[22,23]

Nutritional Factors in Adult Bone Loss

Approximately 90% of the body's calcium is found in the bones. Absorption of calcium is enhanced by the presence of lactose, certain amino acids, and vitamin D. Women in the United States over the age of 50 are reported to consume less than the RDA of calcium in their daily diet which for women 51 and older is 800 mg.[14,21]

Phosphorus is a major bone mineral. Dietary deficiency of phosphorus is unlikely. However, in the elderly, the frequent use of phosphate-binding antacids may contribute to a phosphate deficiency. The ratio of calcium to phosphorus is important and contributes to loss of bone and inadequate calcium absorption. The normal ratio is greater than 2:1 Ca:P; however, the calcium:phosphorus ratio of the typical American diet is 1:1.6. An important nonnutritional factor that prevents or slows bone loss is the estrogen hormone. When estogens are given within 3 years following menopause, they can prevent bone loss and actually increase mineral content. Also immobilization due to cast or prolonged bedrest can contribute to serious bone loss.[14,21,24]

Osteomalacia

Osteomalacia is a well-documented condition in the elderly.[21,24] Frequently referred to as adult rickets, it is a condition characterized by abnormal mineralization of the bone. Calcium absorption decreases with age, which is thought to be due to abnormal metabolism of vitamin D that is needed for absorption of calcium in the intestines. In osteomalacia there is frequently a calcium bone loss. Osteomalacia may be secondary to any of the following factors or a combination of factors:

- inadequate dietary intake of Vitamin D
- inadequate exposure to the sun
- intestinal malabsorption
- renal tubular disease
- use of anticonvulsants, particularly phenytoin (Dilantin)

Signs and symptoms include generalized skeletal pain, muscle weakness/gait disturbances, and pathologic fractures.

In the laboratory evaluation the levels of calcium and phosphorus depend on the underlying etiology of the osteomalacia and may be confusing to the emergency diagnostician. For example, patients with osteomalacia secondary to vitamin D deficiency may have a normal or low blood calcium level and a low phosphorus level. In patients with renal tubular problems, the calcium level is normal, phosphorus level is decreased, and alkaline phosphatase is normal or elevated.

Osteoporosis

Osteoporosis is a condition commonly associated with the elderly in general and aged women in particular. It is seen much more frequently in the United States than osteomalacia, affecting as many as 14 million elderly American women.[21] Osteoporosis is characterized by a decrease in bone mass. Bone formation and reabsorption take place continually through one's lifetime. The delicate physiologic balance necessary for bone formation depends on a number of factors, including (1) sufficient dietary intake of calcium and phosphorus, (2) adequate dietary intake of vitamin D or adequate exposure to the sun, and (3) the presence of hormones to stimulate bone tissue activity.

In order to maintain calcium homeostasis the skeleton acts as a reservoir. Conditions that cause more bone reabsorption than formation result in loss of bone density. The reduction in bone mass that occurs after age 40–50 is known to affect women at a faster rate than men because of a lack of estrogen.[22] This condition is commonly called postmenopausal osteoporosis. Five other types of osteoporosis can be classified by etiology:

1. disuse, eg, immobilization, paralysis
2. drug induced, eg, steroids, anticonvulsants, anticoagulants, antacids, alcohol, aspirin
3. endocrine, eg, parathyroid hormone, insulin
4. nutritional, eg, calcium or vitamin D deficiency
5. miscellaneous causes, including trauma and renal disease.

The patient may be completely asymptomatic or may have pain secondary to pathologic fractures. The fractures may occur from minor or no apparent trauma. The most common sites are the vertebrae and femur. There may be spinal tenderness and postural changes as well. Radiologic studies show a decrease in bone density or evidence of pathologic fracture. Serum calcium, phosphorus, and alkaline phosphatase levels are within normal limits.[23,24]

Paget's Disease

Paget's disease is a skeletal disease associated with chronic inflammation of the bones that results in thickening and softening of bones and bowing of the long bones. The patient may initially have a pathologic fracture. The early course of the disease may be asymptomatic or may be associated with vague bone pains and headaches. The disease is characterized by an increased reabsorption of bone.[25]

Laboratory findings include normal serum calcium and phosphorus levels and an increased alkaline phosphatase. A raised alkaline phosphatase in the elderly is more commonly due to Paget's disease or liver damage than to osteomalacia. However, as always, the clinical picture is further complicated by the presence of multiple pathology in the elderly. For example, osteoporosis, osteomalacia, and Paget's disease may coexist in the same patient.[25]

NUTRITION-RELATED METABOLIC EMERGENCIES

Diabetes

Geriatric Differences

Diabetes is a major illness in the elderly. The highest incidence of diabetes is reported in the sixth decade of life, and more than one-half of cases of diabetes are detected between the ages of 40 and 60. The diabetic population is now reported to be doubling every 15 years, primarily because of the increased longevity of the elderly.[26]

Diet is considered the cornerstone of all diabetic therapy. However, for a number of physical, environmental, and social reasons, achieving an adequate diet for the elderly diabetic is difficult. Therefore, the elderly diabetic has frequent metabolic emergencies that demand prompt medical attention in the ED.

Glucose Tolerance

A number of factors affect glucose tolerance in the elderly:

- decreased and delayed insulin release
- peripheral insulin resistance
- obesity
- hyperlipemia
- increased percentage of body fat and decreased muscle mass

- increased proinsulin blood levels
- increased glucagon blood levels
- decreased physical activity
- drug therapy
- trauma

Many of these factors are directly related to nutritional status. Obesity and hyperlipemia tend to increase with age and raise glucose intolerance, because both lead to peripheral insulin resistance. With aging there is an increase in the percentage of body fat and a decrease in muscle mass available to metabolize a glucose load. The degree of physical inactivity also affects the efficiency of glucose utilization.[26] In addition, widespread use of thiazide diuretics in the treatment of chronic cardiovascular diseases contributes to glucose intolerance.

Diagnostic Criteria

Guidelines for interpretation of glucose tolerance tests in the elderly can be confusing, although there are published criteria that make allowances for age in setting diagnostic limit levels.[24,26,27] These age adjustments should be carefully considered in the ED. Studies have indicated that as many as 50% of patients over the age of 60 will have abnormal glucose tests[26,28] (Figure 8–1).

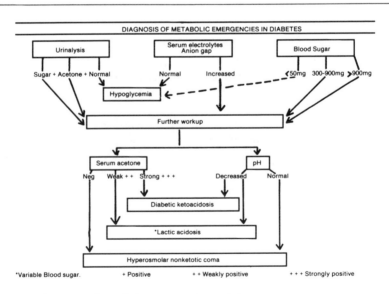

Figure 8–1 Diagnosis of metabolic emergencies in diabetes.

Source: Adapted with permission from *Geriatrics* (1981;36), Copyright © 1981, Harcourt Brace Jovanovich.

Diabetic Ketone Acidosis

It is a serious misconception that ketoacidosis is a disease of younger people. The elderly are at great risk for this condition, and some studies have reported a mortality rate as high as 50%.[23,27] Frequently, diabetic control is nutritionally based. In addition, multiple pathology occurring concurrently in the elderly greatly increases the risk of diabetic emergencies and makes treatment and dietary control more difficult.

The classical presentation of diabetic ketone acidosis (DKA) may occur in the elderly patient, but the presentation is often atypical. Most frequently, there is a relatively slow onset with several days or even longer of polydipsia, polyuria, weight loss, vomiting, dehydration, and overbreathing.[24] The patient may become confused and drowsy. Hypothermia may occur, and bronchopneumonia frequently precipitates or is caused by this emergency. DKA usually occurs in the insulin-dependent diabetic. Other major precipitating factors include trauma, infections, and systemic illness.[27]

ED treatment includes IV fluid replacement with insulin infusion. CVP monitoring should be started immediately, and detailed laboratory workup should be initiated. However, a rapid infusion of fluids, especially in elderly patients with heart disease, may create serious problems. Dextrose 5% should be administered instead of saline when the blood glucose level falls below 10 mg/L. (Insulin replacement can be slowed or stopped when blood glucose falls below 10 mg/L.) Intravenous potassium is usually needed in large amounts. Careful cardiac monitoring and immediate transfer to an intensive care setting are recommended.[24,27]

Hyperosmolar Hyperglycemic Nonketotic Coma (HHNC)

This syndrome occurs usually in the elderly, noninsulin-dependent diabetic. The patient may be a known diabetic, but often the patient presents for the first time with HHNC. Symptoms may be spontaneous or precipitated by drugs or a major stressful event, such as surgery or peritoneal dialysis. Signs and symptoms include abdominal pain, marked hyperglycemia, dehydration, stupor, and coma. Focal grand mal seizures occur frequently. Localizing signs of a cerebrovascular accident, such as a positive Babinski sign, may be confusing to the ED diagnostician.[29]

The primary difference between HHNC and DKA is that in HHNC there is enough insulin in the circulation to inhibit lipolysis. Certain laboratory values differ markedly between DKA and HHNC as well. For example, in HHNC the serum glucose is usually much higher than in DKA, with values often reaching 2800 mg/ml. Also, serum ketones are absent in HHNC.[29,30]

The management is similar to DKA and includes insulin, careful monitoring of fluid and electrolyte replacements, and antibiotics. Less insulin and half-strength saline, rather than isotonic saline, is usually indicated.[24] The mortality rate is 40% to 70% unless early management is aggressive and appropriate. Complications include cerebral edema, thrombophlebitis, and acute electrolyte disturbances, such as hypokalemia and hyperkalemia.

Adult Hypoglycemia

Adult hypoglycemia is a serious and frequent complication of diabetes in the aged. It may be caused by several factors, including excessive administration of insulin or oral antidiabetic medications, inadequate carbohydrate intake due to delayed or missed meals, excessive exercise (rarely a cause in the elderly), or drug interactions (a frequent cause in the elderly).

Hypoglycemia may occur without any warning symptoms; however, common clinical features include intense hunger, sweating, palpitations, confusion, unsteadiness, and tremors. In several reported cases hemiplegia and seizures have occurred.[24]

Management includes administration of 50 ml of 50% glucose by IV bolus and continuous IV administration of glucose. In the elderly, the urine test may be confusing because it does not accurately reflect the blood-glucose levels due to an elevated renal threshold. Serum electrolytes should be closely monitored.

Glucose-Induced Hyperkalemia

Hyperkalemia can occur in response to the administration of hypertonic glucose. This phenomenon occurs in elderly patients who are insulinopenic and who have hypoaldosteronism or who take potassium-sparing diuretics. Close monitoring of serum potassium levels is recommended to avoid serious cardiotoxicity.[30]

Hypothyroidism (Myxedema)

There is an age-related rise in thyroid disease in the elderly. It is reported to be significantly more common in elderly women (especially myxedema) than men.[24]

Hypothyroidism is classically insidious at any age; however, in the elderly it is easily confused with a variety of other chronic conditions. Signs and symptoms include myopathy, confusion, lethargy, constipation, obesity, deafness, dislike of cold, joint pain, coarse skin, hair loss, and depression. Anemia is present in one-third of patients with hypothyroidism. Nutritional deficiencies or a poor appetite that is influenced by the myxedema may further complicate the anemia. Hypothyroidism should always be considered in patients who come to the ED in a coma with hypothermia.[24,29] The coma of myxedema is usually precipitated by poor ventilation, hyponatremia, and hypothermia. Emergency management includes maintenance of the airway, thyroid and steroid replacement, cardiac monitoring, sodium replacement, and complete laboratory evaluation. External rewarming of the patient in the ED is not recommended.[29]

Hyperthyroidism (Thyrotoxicosis)

Hyperthyroidism (thyrotoxicosis) is predominantly a disease of middle and old age. The most common presentation in the elderly is of mental changes, arrhythmia, and heart failure. Most old people with thyrotoxicosis are lethargic and even apathetic, rather than anxious and overactive.[23] Weakness, exhaustion, immobility, and falls are frequently present. The disease is usually caused by an autoimmune pathology (Grave's disease) or Plummer's disease (modular goiter). Thyrotoxicosis might also be induced after the administration of iodine in dietary supplements. Diabetes frequently coexists with thyrotoxicosis.

Management with carbimazole is recommended. Propranolol may improve symptoms, and many consider radioiodine-131 the treatment of choice in the elderly.[24]

Adrenal Insufficiency

Adrenal hypofunction or Addison's disease in the elderly causes a high serum potassium, decreased sodium, decreased fasting blood sugar, and increased BUN. Patients with long-standing Addison's disease usually exhibit darkened pigmentation of the skin on the elbows, knees, hands, and lips. The adrenal cortex produces glucocorticoids, mineralocorticoids, and androgens. The deficiency of either glucocorticoids or mineralocorticoids can be life threatening. The patient in crisis comes to the ED with a history of fatigue, nausea, vomiting (dehydration), anorexia, weight loss, weakness, and postural hypotension. Fever, tachycardia, and shock are profound.[29] Adrenal crisis should always be suspected in patients whose hypotension cannot be explained. Precipitating factors include stress, infection, trauma, recent surgery, or sudden discontinuation of oral steroids, all of which occur frequently in the elderly patient. Management includes laboratory evaluation, careful fluid replacement, steroid therapy, and immediate admission to an intensive care setting.[29]

Fluid Electrolyte Imbalance Related to Nutritional Deficiency

Hypokalemia

Depletion of potassium is common in the elderly and is attributed to several factors including the process of cell aging, abnormal urinary excretion due to a misuse of diuretics, increased fecal elimination due to misuse of laxatives, and inadequate dietary intake.

The source of body potassium is the diet, which is more than adequate in middle life. However, in the elderly the intake of potassium is often much lower. Studies have shown that as many as 60% of women and 40% of men failed to satisfy the daily dietary intake of potassium.[24,31] Therefore, as a direct result of poor intake many elders are at risk of developing hypokalemia.

Signs and symptoms are muscle weakness, muscle tenderness, apathy, confusion, abdominal distention, and arrhythmias. All of these could easily be confused with signs of a number of other conditions frequently seen in the elderly. Muscle weakness is cited as the most striking symptom of hypokalemia.[32]

Successful management of hypokalemia depends not only on replacement of the potassium but also on recognition and correction of the underlying cause of the potassium deficiency. Complete diet history, laboratory evaluation, and potassium replacement are recommended in the ED.

Hyperkalemia

Retention of potassium occurs in the elderly following the use of potassium-sparing diuretics and potassium supplements. Significant hyperkalemia is seen primarily in patients with renal insufficiency. However, such factors as acidosis, gastrointestinal bleeding, and drug therapy may precipitate hyperkalemia in otherwise stable patients.

The signs and symptoms of lethargy, anxiety, restlessness, confusion, and cardiac arrhythmias can easily be confused with those of hypokalemia or other chronic conditions. The clinical symptoms are subtle and appear late, often only shortly before death from cardiac arrhythmias or complete heart block occurs.[31]

Initial management is aimed at lowering serum potassium by antagonizing its physiologic effects with sodium or calcium salts. Emergency management includes infusion of hypertonic glucose, complete laboratory evaluation, and the administration of calcium and Kayexalate. Hemodialysis or peritoneal dialysis is the treatment of choice for patients with moderate or severe renal failure.[23]

Hyponatremia

Hyponatremia in the elderly is best divided into three categories: (1) with decreased extracellular volume (ECFV), (2) with extracellular volume expansion, and (3) with normal extracellular volume.[24] Hyponatremia with decreased ECFV almost always results from loss of body fluids with inadequate replacement. Diuretic-induced hyponatremia (type 1) is probably the single most common cause in the elderly of this condition. It may be present even when there is peripheral edema.[32] Young persons on restricted salt intake are capable of lowering urinary sodium levels. However, elderly persons, especially those with renal disease or hypertension, are unable to conserve sodium; therefore, they can become salt depleted on severe salt-restrictive diets.

Signs and symptoms are muscle weakness, apathy, headaches, postural dizziness, and muscle cramps. In more severe cases, delirium, stupor, and coma may develop. Skin turgor and skin elasticity decrease. Orthostatic hypotension and tachycardia occur as early symptoms, and clinical shock occurs later.[24] Hyponatremia with increased extracellular volume occurs commonly in patients.

Cardiac, liver, or renal failure can also occur. Hyponatremia with normal extra cellular volume is commonly seen in patients with chronic pulmonary disease, arteriosclerosis, or malnutrition. It is distinguished from water intoxication and salt depletion by its chronic nature and lack of acute symptoms.[24]

Emergency management includes identification of the type of hyponatremia and the underlying chronic disease. Complete laboratory evaluation is required, and appropriate saline replacement is administered as indicated by the laboratory values.

Hypernatremia

Hypernatremia and dehydration occur frequently in the elderly because of their inability to obtain sufficient water to replace their losses, which may be due to their inability to communicate. Patients in nursing homes are highly susceptible to dehydration. Precipitating factors are vomiting, diarrhea, tachypnea, and hyperthermia during hot weather or fever. Almost all cases of hypernatremia are due to a deficit of body water (TBW) and not to a sodium excess.

Diagnosis is aided by complete laboratory evaluations and clinical signs, such as loss of skin turgor, hypotension due to hypovolemia, dry mucous membranes, confusion, and oliguria.

Emergency management depends on the severity or degree of dehydration. Careful replacement of fluids and saline over a prolonged period of time (48 hours) is recommended.[32]

Hypocalcemia

Hypocalcemia in the elderly is frequently related to an inadequate intake or absorption of calcium or vitamin D. Other causative factors include excessive gastrointestinal calcium loss (as seen in osteomalacia), excessive urinary calcium loss (as seen in renal tubular disease), and uremia associated with elevated serum phosphorus.

The most prominent sign of hypocalcemia is tetany. Other signs and symptoms include numbness, tingling, various muscle cramps, diarrhea, fatigue, depression, and convulsions. In most patients with hypocalcemia this disorder is established before they reach old age; the exception is the elderly patient with terminal renal disease.[31]

Emergency management includes complete laboratory evaluation, radiologic evaluation, and calcium replacement. Nutritional evaluation and community referral are indicated. Hospital admission depends on the signs and symptoms; however, it is usually recommended in the newly symptomatic elderly.[31]

Hypercalcemia

Hypercalcemia develops in the elderly from either excessive absorptions of calcium from the GI tract or increased reabsorption of bone, as seen in Paget's disease or hyperparathyroidism. The most common cause in the elderly is the latter, due to malignancies associated with bone metastasis and multiple myeloma.[31] The early symptoms of hypercalcemia are often subtle and difficult to differentiate. They include malaise, weakness, and anorexia. Patients with severe cases may have nausea, vomiting, constipation, polyuria, polydipsia, and confusion.

Emergency management includes laboratory evaluation, and in symptomatic hypercalcemia, normal saline should be administered. Many of these patients are dehydrated, and CVP monitoring may be indicated. Admission to the ICU is usually indicated in the symptomatic elderly.[24,31]

Hypomagnesium

Hypomagnesium in the elderly may result from gastrointestinal fluid losses, misuse of diuretics, inadequate diet, acute pancreatitis, treatment for diabetic acidosis, hypoparathyroidism, and hypercalcemia. Also, low serum magnesium levels are commonly seen in chronic alcoholics. Hypomagnesium is related to the clincal syndrome of delirium tremens; however that relationship is not clearly understood. It is also reported to be related to digitalis toxicity in certain types of patients.[32] The clinical picture is primarily one of neuromuscular and CNS hyperirritability. Tremors, disorientation, confusion, hallucinations, convulsions, hypertension, and tachycardia may be seen.[31]

Emergency management includes laboratory evaluation, hospital admission, and careful magnesium replacement. These patients are usually extremely ill with a number of associated chronic conditions that require intensive long-term management.

Hypermagnesemia

Hypermagnesemia is primarily associated with chronic renal disease. It is also seen in elderly patients with long-term use of antacids that have impaired their renal function or diminished their ability to excrete potassium. The symptoms are usually CNS depression or cardiovascular related. Patients may have bradycardia, hypotension, and occasionally, heart block. However, vomiting, nausea, and confusion may also occur.[31]

Emergency management includes laboratory evaluation and calcium chloride administered intravenously. Hospital admission is frequently indicated for long-term evaluation and/or dialysis.

CONSTIPATION

Constipation is a common problem among the elderly. It should be considered a symptom, rather than a disease, and it can result from poor bowel habits and the formation of dry hard stool that is difficult to pass. The formation of dry hard stool may be caused by a lack of proper fluid in the diet, organic disease, anorexia due to depression, and such drugs as iron preparations, anticholinergics, antihyperten-sives, and analgesics.[33]

Flatulence is also a common problem in the elderly. Contributing factors include constipation, irregular bowel movements, intake of certain foods, and poor neuromuscular control of the anal sphincter.

Fecal impaction occurs frequently in the elderly as a result of constipation. Signs and symptoms include distended rectum, abdominal and rectal discomfort, oozing fecal material around the impaction that is easily mistaken for diarrhea, and palpation of a hard fecal mass.[33]

Treatment for constipation and flatus should focus on preventive measures. Emergency personnel must be aware of the concern the elderly have regarding their bowel habits and should attempt to understand their feelings. Nutritional counseling should encourage adequate intake of fruits, vegetables, and fluids. Physical activity and providing regular and adequate times for bowel movement should also be encouraged. Laxatives should only be considered after other measures have proven ineffective. Mineral oil should not be recommended in the elderly, because it can dissolve and be excreted with the fat-soluble vitamins A, D, and E.[22]

A complete diet history including bowel habits and character of movements should be obtained. Medications or a rectal tube may be prescribed for gas. Enemas should be prescribed carefully and infrequently, because the elderly are at risk for dehydration and electrolyte disturbances. A fecal impaction should be gently removed digitally and followed by a bisacodyl (Dulcolax) or Senokot suppository. Other laxatives are not recommended.[22]

BOWEL OBSTRUCTION

It is difficult to diagnose bowel obstruction in the elderly. Normally patients have intermittent abdominal pain accompanied by tenderness, vomiting, and abdominal distention. These signs and symptoms may or may not be present in the elderly. Frequently tachycardia, mild to moderate abdominal pain, and heme-positive stools may be the only findings.[34]

Any patient who has had a significant change in bowel habits or a combination of the above symptoms should have a complete laboratory evaluation including CBC, hemoccult x3, SMA12, and U/A electrolytes. Radiologic evaluation, including abdominal x-ray, proctoscope, and barium enema, should be obtained as indicated. A complete physical examination including an abdominal and rectal examination should be performed. Hospital admission is recommended.[22]

OBESITY

Obesity is the most common nutritional disorder in the United States.[22,35] It is defined as an excessive accumulation of fat in the body that results in the body weight exceeding the desirable weight for the person's height, age, and bone structure. An individual who weighs 15% more than the ideal body weight is considered obese.[22] Adiposity is defined as an excess of fat accumulation in the body. It is difficult in the elderly to determine what degree of adiposity is normal with aging because fat to muscle proportion increases in both men and women. Therefore, the elderly may be relatively adipose and not obese. Because of the changing fat accumulation and deposition, the diagnosis of obesity in the elderly should be made carefully, using both ideal weight tables and skinfold measurements.

Several distinguishing characteristics occur in obesity in the elderly: (1) obesity, particularly severe obesity, is almost entirely found in women, (2) obesity to men is life threatening because of major complications of hypertension and vascular disease, (3) obesity in the elderly is usually a long-term chronic condition, and (4) high incidences of such complications as osteoarthritis and diabetes mellitus (non-insulin dependent) occur in this group.[22,35] Other complications include coronary artery disease, hypertension, dyspnea, joint strain and pain (osteoarthritis), and increased surgical risk.

Causes

Many factors lead to a greater incidence of obesity in the elderly, including the following: (1) food is readily available for many and is enjoyed; 2) physical activity is minimal; 3) elders frequently buy and eat improper foods. Many aged people like convenience foods that have excess empty calories and are easy to fix. Also, such emotional factors as depression and loneliness can contribute to obesity. Underlying organic causes of obesity, such as hypothyroidism or Cushing's syndrome, are rare and usually cause less than 1% of all cases of obesity.[22]

Treatment

The treatment of obesity in the elderly is difficult; the components include the reduction of adipose tissue and the long-term maintenance of this reduced state. Caloric restriction and reduction of food intake are considered the established therapy. Drug therapy, psychotherapy, and surgical procedures have proven to be less beneficial in the elderly obese patient.

Emergency management includes:

1. complete history
   - social
   - weight
   - diet
   - postmedical
   - family

2. complete physical examination
3. laboratory evaluation
   - CBC
   - SMA
   - U/A
   - thyroid function studies
   - blood glucose studies
   - stool hemocult x3
4. chest film
5. possible hospital admission for complete evaluations
6. community referral for dietary counseling

Dieting

The diet of the elderly should contain a lower quantity and higher quality of food. Less carbohydrates and fats and more of certain types of protein and minerals are recommended. Fad diets or any type of "quick" weight loss diets should always be avoided.[11,5] Many of these diets contain high amounts of carbohydrates, which stimulate an abnormally high release of insulin. This type of dieting can easily precipitate hypoglycemia and associated metabolic emergencies in the elderly.[6]

Signs and symptoms of quick weight loss diets include syncope, confusion, and falls. Emergency management should include complete diet history; laboratory evaluation (CBC, U/A, and SMA), hospital admission if indicated, and community referral for further dietary counseling.

PATIENT EDUCATION

Patient education in the ED is considered by emergency practitioners to be one of the most important aspects of patient care. The opportunity for patient and family teaching is as available in the ED as in almost any other hospital department or health care agency. However, there are several obstacles that can interfere with this opportunity. The rushed environment, the increased anxiety levels of the patient and family, and the multiple varieties of health problems frequently become obstacles to patient education.[36,37] The psychosocial and physical constraints demonstrated frequently by elderly patients are further barriers to patient education.

Emergency health care providers must be aware of the steps in the teaching-learning process. Special attention should be paid to identifying the learning needs and assessing the learner. Considerations should be made for the patient's physical constraints, such as impairment of sight and hearing.

The ability to learn does not decrease with advancing age. However, such factors as disease, anxiety, motivation, and provision of irrelevant information significantly affect learning. To improve patient compliance in the ED one should consider the following:

- Keep the instruction as simple and untaxing as possible.
- Remove as much extraneous noise and movement as possible.
- Give the elderly patient time to recall or rehearse material to be learned.
- Provide written instruction sheets in simple meaningful terms.
- Involve the family and other sources of support.
- Provide community referrals.

SUMMARY

The elderly are particularly vulnerable to nutritional deficiencies and imbalances due to chronic diseases that put added stress on the body systems. The social environment of the elderly further adversely affects their nutritional status.

Emergency health care providers have the opportunity and the challenge to increase their knowledge base to provide better emergency care for this growing population. They have the privilege of being close to the patient and the opportunity to direct them to the most appropriate source of care. Fortunately there are a number of resources available in most communities to assist the elderly to achieve better nutrition. Most frequently they are under the direction of local or county agencies, such as church groups or community action programs. The congregate eating program has proven very beneficial to a large number of elderly citizens. The meals are well balanced and are served in community centers free of charge. Many churches also deliver hot meals to elderly shut-ins.

Emergency health care providers have the opportunity to improve the quality of care provided to the elderly patient by developing a holistic approach to their special needs. One must apply the precepts of human regard and demonstrate respect for their individuality to achieve this goal. Emergency care should be directed toward the goal of returning the elderly individual to an independent life and the opportunity to achieve the highest level of function possible for each individual.

REFERENCES

1. *Statistical Abstract of the United States,* US Dept of Commerce, Bureau of the Census, ed 102, National Data Book and Guide to Sources, 1981.
2. Wilson L, Simson S: *Establishing a Data Base on Emergency Services and the Elderly: Planning for Linkages Between Emergency Services, Long Term Care, and Health Related Services.* Dallas, Gerontology Services Administration, The University of Texas Health Science Center, 1981.

3. Jacoby L, Jones S: Factors associated with ED use by repeater and non-repeater patients. *J Emerg Nurs* 8:243–247, 1982.

4. Podgorny G: Emergency medicine must plan now to control the future of graduate education. *JACEP* 8:337–338, 1979.

5. Weir DR, Houser HB, Davery L: Recognition and management of the nutrition problems of the elderly, in *Working With Older People, Clinical Aspects of Aging*, vol 4. Washington, US Department of Health Education and Welfare, 1973, pp 267–278.

6. Schwartz GR: Geriatric Emergencies. *Geriatrics*, June 1980, pp 32–33.

7. Caird FI: Physical examination of the elderly, problems and possibilities, in Folmer AR, Schouten J (eds): *Geriatrics for the Practitioner*. Amsterdam, Excerpta Medica, 1981.

8. Hudson MF: Safeguard your elderly patient's health through accurate physical assessment. *Nursing 83*, November 1983, pp 58–64.

9. Wilder RS: Trauma in the elderly. *Emerg Med Services*, March/April 1980, pp 61–62.

10. Garvin J: Caring for the geriatric patient. *Emerg Med Services*, March/April 1980, pp 75–76.

11. Schaffer JB: Getting elderly patients to eat properly. *Geriatrics* 36:76–82, 1981.

12. Simpson R: Analysis of dental needs of the elderly. *J Amer Dent Soc* 106:178–181, 1982.

13. Wintrope M: *Clinical Hematology*, ed 6. Philadelphia, Lea and Febriger, 1967, p 92.

14. *Recommended Dietary Allowances*, ed 9. Washington, DC, National Academy of Sciences—National Research Council, 1980.

15. Harper AE: Dietary guidelines for the elderly. *Geriatrics* 36:34–42, 1981.

16. Chipman C: What does it mean when a patient falls, pinpointing the cause. *Geriatrics* 36:83–85, 1981.

17. Robinson CH: *Normal and Therapeutic Nutrition*. New York, Macmillan Company, 1972.

18. Exxon-Smith AN: Nutritional status: Diagnosis and prevention of malnutrition, in Exxon-Smith AN, Caird FI (eds): *Metabolic and Nutritional Disorders in the Elderly*. Chicago, Year Book Medical Publishers, 1980, pp 66–73.

19. Exxon-Smith AN: Vitamins, in Exxon-Smith AN, Caird FI (eds): *Metabolic and Nutritional Disorders in the Elderly*. Chicago, Year Book Medical Publishers, 1980, pp 26–73.

20. Hyams DE: Nutrition and anemia, in Exxon-Smith AN, Caird FI (eds): *Metabolic and Nutritional Disorders in the Elderly*. Chicago, Year Book Medical Publishers, 1980, pp 100–119.

21. Yen PK: Fractures and diet—What's the relationship. *Ger Nurs*, September/October 1981, pp 327–328.

22. Pearson LF, Kotthoff ME: *Geriatric Clinical Protocols*. New York, JB Lippincott Company, 1979.

23. Nordin BEC: Calcium metabolism and bone, in Exxon-Smith AN, Caird FI (eds): *Metabolic and Nutritional Disorders in the Elderly*. Chicago, Year Book Medical Publishers, 1980, pp 123–145.

24. Green MF: Metabolic emergencies, in Coakley D (ed): *Acute Geriatric Medicine*. Littleton, MA, PSG Publishing Company, 1981.

25. Windsor ACM, Nutrition in the elderly. *The Practitioner* 222:625–628, 1979.

26. Levin ME, Diabetes: The geriatric difference. *Geriatrics* 37:41–45, 1982.

27. Gitman L: Diabetes mellitus in the aged, in *Working With Older People, Clinical Aspects of Aging*, vol 4, Washington, DC, US Department of Health, Education and Welfare, 1973, pp 219–224.

28. Keen H, Fuller JH, The epidemiology of diabetes, in Exxon-Smith AN, Caird FI (eds): *Metabolic and Nutritional Disorders in the Elderly*. Chicago, Year Book Medical Publishers, 1980. pp 146–159.

29. Budassi SA, Barber JM: *Emergency Nursing: Principles and Practice*. St. Louis, CV Mosby Co, 1981.

30. Sivaprasad R, Rodolsky S, Katta TJ: Diabetic emergencies and how to handle them. *Geriatrics* 36:34–39, 1981.

31. Lindeman RD: Application of fluid and electrolyte balance principles to the older patient, in *Working with Older People, Clinical Aspects of Aging,* vol 4. Washington, DC, US Department of Health, Education and Welfare, 1973, pp 229–240.

32. Brenner BE: Electrolyte Abnormalities, in Kravis TC, Warner CG (eds): *Emergency Medicine: A Comprehensive Review.* Rockville, MD, Aspen Publishers, 1983, pp. 191–215.

33. Eliopoulos C: *Gerontological Nursing.* New York, Harper and Row, 1979, pp 110–117.

34. Krome RL: Gastrointestinal emergencies, in Kravis TC, Warner CG (eds): *Emergency Medicine: A Comprehensive Review.* Rockville, MD, Aspen Publishers, 1983, pp 325–326.

35. Schroeder HA: Nutrition, in Steinberg FU (ed): *Cowdry's The Care of The Geriatric Patient,* ed 5. St. Louis, CV Mosby Co. 1976, pp 191–195.

36. Yen PK: Helping seniors shop for food. *Ger Nurs,* July/August 1982, pp 222–226.

37. Miller M: Patient teaching in the emergency department, in Budassi SA, Barber JM, (eds): *Emergency Nursing: Principles and Practice,* St. Louis, CV Mosby Co, 1981, pp 214–227.

9

Environmental Emergencies

Richard L. Judd, PhD, EMSI, R-EMTA and Martin M. Dinep, MD, FACS

The ability of the human body to adjust to variations in the ambient temperature is dependent on many factors, including the state of one's health, existence of such pathologic conditions as hypothyroidism and diabetes mellitus, diet, and the capability to alter environmental conditions through such means as air conditioning or artificial heat sources.

The elderly, as do the very young, have a difficult time adjusting to radical changes in ambient temperatures. In addition to altered thermoregulatory mechanisms, altered cardiovascular, respiratory, and CNS function affect the body's ability to adjust to climatic changes Use of multiple medications may also drastically alter neurologic control, circulation, electrolyte balance, or excretory function and so affect temperature regulation.

Physical changes in lean body mass, abnormalities in fluid level, and the proportion of fatty tissue can further affect temperature regulation. Add to these factors the exacerbating complications and sequelae of multiple system trauma, and one can understand the importance of evaluating environmental temperature factors that may affect patient mortality and morbidity.

HEAT ILLNESS

Heat illness encompasses several entities, ranging from heat edema, the least severe, to hyperpyrexia (heatstroke), the most severe. These illnesses, once thought to be isolated phenomena, may be related and progressive. It is therefore important for emergency medical personnel to assess, monitor, and manage the initial problem as one stage of a continuum, with a keen eye toward escalation of the situation.

The body's adaptation to heat is dependent on many factors. The elderly generally are less adaptable to changing ambient temperatures. Abnormalities in

255

internal control mechanisms, such as hypothalamic lesions, circulatory disorders, and tumor invasion, may add to problems of thermal regulation.

Infection, chronic illness, cardiovascular disease, substance abuse (both alcohol and other), and certain prescribed drugs, such as the phenothiazines (chlorpromazine, butyrophenones), haloperidol, antihistamines, propranolol, or anticholinergics, may predispose the elderly to a higher risk of heat illness because of the likely inhibition of the perspiration mechanism of the body. Obesity, fatigue, and the general state of health must also be considered. Lack of proper fluid and electrolyte replacement, lack of protective clothing, such as a sunhat or other lightweight clothing, strenuous exertion, and/or poor ventilation contribute to the probability of heat illness.

In the elderly heat illness is predictable because of the longer time the body takes to acclimatize to changing weather conditions. Health care providers should be alert that when the average outside temperature exceeds 32°C (90°F) for 2 or more days and the relative humidity has been in the 50% to 75% range, heat illness problems may be expected to occur. This is especially true if the community is located near a large body of water.

Heat Edema

Heat edema occurs frequently in the elderly, particularly in those who may not be acclimatized to the changes in the ambient weather conditions. It may occur when an individual visits a semitropical or tropical climate and has not become acclimatized to the new environment. It is not usually a problem of great seriousness.

Signs of this condition are swollen feet and ankles; swelling can be relieved by elevation of the lower extremities and wearing support hose. The elderly person with cardiovascular conditions in which fluid retention is a problem should have diet, drug therapy, and electrolyte evaluation as well.[1]

Heat Syncope

Fainting sometimes occurs when persons are exposed to rising temperatures, especially when acclimatization has not occurred or when an individual has been standing in a hot environment for a long period of time, such as watching a parade. The resultant pooling of blood in the lower extremities is the likely cause of the syncope. If perspiration has been excessive, the condition is more likely to occur.

Care in this situation involves removing the patient from the hot environment to one that is cooler, placing the person in a supine position, monitoring the ABCs, and administering fluid replacement, if indicated.

Heat Exhaustion

Heat exhaustion occurs as a result of a failure to hydrate adequately in the face of excessive fluid loss and prolonged exposure to heat, usually with high humidity and overexercise or hard work. All or some of these factors may cause low blood volume peripheral vasomotor circulatory collapse. The condition is usually transient, and mortality is low unless it is complicated by cardiac or other existing pathology.

The usual clinical picture may include the following:

- severe frontal headache
- nausea, sometimes accompanied by vomiting, which will likely exacerbate the already serious problem of fluid depletion
- profuse perspiration, often drenching sweats; pale, cool and clammy skin
- thready, rapid pulse
- low and imperceptible blood pressure
- temperature below normal, but other variations are possible
- level of consciousness: confused, "V" level or lower AVPU; anxious
- visual problems, eg, inability to focus
- fatigue and weakness, which are usually gradual but often profound
- diarrhea, which will likely aggravate the already serious problem of fluid depletion
- muscle spasms

Emergency management consists of the following five steps:

1. Move the patient to a cooler environment.
2. Treat for hypovolemic shock to optimize brain perfusion: lay the patient flat and moderately elevate the feet and legs 10–20 degrees. Administer small amounts of slightly salty fluids (hypotonic salt solution—1 teaspoon table salt to 8 oz (250 ml) water) orally every few minutes, if the patient is conscious. If not, and in the more serious cases, administer normal saline IV.
3. Administer fluids judiciously to avoid overloading an already embarrassed circulatory system.
4. Order laboratory studies, including serum electrolytes, hematocrit, and urinalysis.
5. Monitor the patient carefully and watch for progression to hyperpyrexia. If recovery is slow, other causative factors must be investigated.

Hyperpyrexia

Heatstroke is a catastrophic environmentally induced hyperpyrexia with core temperature above 94°C (104°F), hot dry skin, and a disturbance of the sensorium. It results from an extensive disturbance of the body's temperature regulatory apparatus that causes a failure to eliminate metabolic heat. This condition requires rapid intervention of massive dimensions. If untreated, hyperpyrexia has a high mortality (50%) for a person of any age, but especially for the elderly.

When the weather has been hot and sticky for several days, the environmental temperature reaches 37°C (100°F), and the humidity is high (over 50%), heatstroke may develop.

This condition usually develops after strenuous activity or prolonged exposure to severe hot weather conditions. Problems are likely in the elderly population who may not be able to afford air conditioning or who use more modest means of cooling the inside environment. The heat wave that affected much of the United States in the closing days of July 1980 produced grim evidence of the elderly's incapacity to deal with this problem. Cited as the worst heat wave since 1954, temperatures soared to 47°C (117°F) in Texas. The death toll was in excess of 1,200 persons, a high proportion of whom were elderly.[2,3]

Predisposing Factors

Risk of hyperpyrexia may increase if underlying pathology, pre-existing febrile illness, infection, recent immunization, or severe agitation, such as in the psychoses or delirium tremens, are present. Patients with skin disease, such as ectoderm dysplasia, in which the sweat glands are absent, or those who have lost sweat glands from burns are at high risk. Potassium depletion from use of diuretics is another causative factor because it impairs urine concentration and decreases myocardial output. Drug use is yet another factor, particularly the use of drugs that inhibit the sweat response (phenothiazines, antihistamines) or the thirst mechanism (haloperidol, propranolol). Amphetamines, excess thyroid medication, LSD, and PCP increase susceptibility. There is also consideration, although poorly documented, that alcohol consumption predisposes to heat illness through a complex set of mechanisms.[4,5]

Other underlying major problems to be considered together with hot weather conditions include chronic dehydration, hypokalemia, heat cramps, and heat exhaustion.

Clinical Picture

The classic triad of hyperpyrexia is (1) hot, dry skin and no perspiration, (2) high body temperature—40°C (94°F) or higher, and (3) mental aberrations, including combativeness, euphoria, irritability, and disorientation.[6]

Symptoms of hyperpyrexia include prodromal headache, dizziness, muscle cramps (sometimes with twitching), and mental status changes, including confusion, combativeness, delirium, and declining levels of consciousness.

Signs of hyperpyrexia are hot skin lacking in perspiration; a high core temperature above 40°C (104°F) and increasing; respiratory rate of 20 and higher, with Cheyne-Stokes breathing in the late stages; pulse rate of 160 bpm and higher; contracted pupils in the early stages, and dilated pupils in late stages; and blood pressure that is probably within normal limits, but may be slightly elevated with a widened pulse pressure and later falling.

In the elderly, the usual course is marked by gradual dehydration, confusion, delirium, lethargy, and combativeness that may persist for 2 or 3 days; then the patient may slip into coma. The prognosis at this stage is dim.

The pathologic effects are many. The likely cause of organ damage is ischemia, probably because the metabolic demand for oxygen has exceeded the supply. The cerebellum is usually affected, and dysarthria, ataxia, wide-based gait, and loss of fine motor control may be expected. The coronary arteries may show signs of infarction. Renal failure occurs in about 10% of heatstroke victims.[3] Disseminated intravascular coagulation (DIC) in which local areas of intravascular coagulation develop may lead to in situ thrombosis and further contribute to multiple organ dysfunction and pulmonary and cardiac insufficiency.[2] Electrolyte disturbances, such as in serum sodium and potassium levels, may also be seen.

Emergency Management

Heatstroke is an acute medical emergency and requires rapid intervention. The first goal, after airway management, is the rapid and immediate cooling of the body.

In the prehospital environment care is as follows:

- Monitor and ensure ABCs.
- Wrap the patient in cold, water-soaked sheets, or douse with ice water; fan the patient; and elevate legs for management of shock. Temperature (rectal) reduction goal is 38°C (102°F): dropping it lower may cause the patient to slip into mild hypothermia.
- Administer oxygen to assist in meeting metabolic demands.
- Provide fluid therapy judiciously to avoid pulmonary edema.

For definitive care, the following seven steps should be undertaken:

1. Continual reduction of body temperature is imperative. Use ice tub baths, ice compresses, and sponging with ice and alcohol, with assistance by fanning and vigorous massage or application of the hypothermia blanket.
2. Cold, isotonic saline peritoneal lavage may be helpful. Inserting a nasogastric tube and administering iced fluids may also prove to be beneficial.
3. Assessment of rectal temperature every 5 minutes is necessary (chilled saline enemas will eliminate this measurement and are not recommended).
4. Control of convulsions with diazepam may be necessary.
5. In the comatose patient, treatment of cerebral edema, if found, should be managed initially with mannitol 1 gm/kg IV as a 20% solution initially and

then 0.3 gm/kg/h IV infusion for approximately 3 hr. A neurosurgical consultation is advised to determine if surgical decompression is indicated.

6. Baseline studies should be obtained and acidosis and hypokalemia corrected as indicated. Electrolyte studies should guide the IV therapy.
7. Renal function should be assessed as failure is a significant problem; ensure adequate urine output.[7,8]

A complete diagnostic workup should include the following studies:

- complete blood count
- electrolytes
- urinalysis
- BUN, creatinine
- ABGs
- CPK
- SGOT, LDH, SGPT, bilirubin and alkaline phosphatase
- prothrombin time (PT) and partial thromboplastin time (PTT), platelet count, and fibrinogen levels
- serum or urinary amylase or both
- chest x-ray film
- ECG
- stool for occult blood
- lumbar puncture and EEG (generally unhelpful and not routinely indicated unless neurologic syndromes develop)
- CVP and Swan-Ganz catheterization, when necessary.[2]

HYPOTHERMIA

Accidental hypothermia (core temperature below 34°C (94°F) occurs when the body is unable to maintain normal core temperature in the face of environmental cooling as a result of a single catastrophic event and or some combination of mental, physical, or pharmacologic insults.

Hypothermia is a serious and often fatal environmental emergency, especially in the elderly. As with heat illness, exposure to the cold or living in inadequately heated homes, coupled with the elderly's decreased ability to cope with the effects of changes of ambient temperature, decreased metabolism and fat, less efficient peripheral vasoconstriction, poor nutrition, lower income, and marginally heated homes, presents a problem of significant dimension.[9,10]

In Great Britain, where more study has been made of the hypothermia problem in the elderly, it has been estimated that 20,000 to 100,000 hypothermia deaths occur yearly. Taylor[10] found that the temperature in a substantial number of his patient's rooms were only, on the average, 1–2 degrees above the outside air temperature and that the patient's average oral temperature was 94°F, with a range of 89°F to 96.2°F. He estimated that between one and five elderly persons per 2,500 died from diseases related to hypothermia during the cold months of the year.

The evidence in the United States has not been as definitive because the substantial increase in the cost of heating fuels has occurred more recently. Williamson et al.[11] note that, although the elderly consume less energy than other age groups, a larger share of their income is expended on energy-related functions, such as heating the home. It is estimated that 50,000 to 60,000 older persons are admitted to U.S. hospitals each year for hypothermia. The emergency medical provider may not recognize the problem as hypothermia immediately because of associated problems, such as trauma, pulmonary and cardiovascular failure.

Clinicians should be aware that factors other than exposure to a cold environment may have contributed to the problem. Alcohol use or abuse may significantly alter CNS regulation of temperature. It may cause hypoglycemia and thereby reduce metabolic energy sources. Because of the vasodilatory effect of ethanol, blood may be shifted from central core areas to the peripheral vasculature. All of these factors exacerbate the cooling down of the body. Such drugs as the barbiturates and phenothiazines induce hypothermia, and their use must be considered.

Hypofunction of the thyroid gland that causes myxedema must be part of the differential diagnosis because its signs and symptoms are similar to those of hypothermia. Other endocrinopathies, such as hypopituitarism, hypoadrenalism, and hypoglycemia associated with hypothermia, require consideration as well. Trauma, such as hip fractures, cerebrovascular accidents, acute febrile illness, senility, lesions, and some hypothalamic disorders have the potential to affect thermal regulation of the body and therefore must be considered in patient assessment.[12]

Clinical Picture

The critical body systems that are immediately affected are the cardiac, respiratory, and CNS. In assessing clinical status these systems should be carefully monitored. Physical findings and other diagnostic studies will reflect functions controlled or regulated by them. Tables 9–1, 9–2, and 9–3 show the characteristics of mild, moderate, and severe hypothermia.

When the core (rectal) temperature is below 34°C (95°F), physical findings include the following:

- lack of coordination, lethargy, stiffness of muscles, and rigidity as core temperature drops
- shivering (ceases as hypothermia progresses)
- level of consciousness impaired, progressing to coma (use AVPU or Glasgow Coma Scale to determine accurate level)

Table 9–1 Characteristics of Mild Hypothermia

Core Temperature		
Degrees C	*Degrees F*	*Characteristics*
37.6	99.6	Normal rectal temperature
37	98.6	Normal oral temperature
36	96.8	Increase in BMR
35	95	Maximum shivering thermogenesis, which may be absent in the elderly because of illness or drugs
34	93.2	Amnesia and dysarthria, blood pressure within normal range
33	91.4	Ataxia

Note: A rectal hypothermia thermometer capable of measuring to 68 F (20 C) is required.

Table 9–2 Characteristics of Moderate Hypothermia

Core Temperature		
Degrees C	*Degrees F*	*Characteristics*
32	89.6	Disorientation, decreased sensorium
31	87.8	Absent shivering thermogenesis
30	86	Atrial fibrillation and other arrhythmias develop; poikilothermia; cardiac output and pulse decreased 33%; insulin ineffective
29	85.2	Progressive decrease in status of cardiac, respiratory and CNS systems, pupils dilated
28	82.4	Susceptibility to ventricular fibrillation; oxygen consumption and pulse rate decrease
27	80.6	Reflexes and voluntary motion decline

Table 9–3 Characteristics of Severe Hypothermia

Core Temperature		
Degrees C	*Degrees F*	*Characteristics*
26	78.8	Reflexes absent; unresponsive to pain
25	77	Cerebral blood flow decreased 66%; cardiac output less than half of normal
24	75.2	Hypotension
23	73.4	Corneal reflexes absent
22	71.6	Ventricular fibrillation at maximum risk; oxygen consumption at 25%
20	68	Lowest resumption of electromechanical activity
19	66.2	Flat EEG
18	66.4	Asystole

- decreased mentation (becomes progressive as hypothermia increases)
- cardiac manifestations usually include arrhythmias, such as atrial fibrillation; in severe cases, bradycardia is common. A 12-lead ECG should be in place; ECGs frequently show T-wave inversion and prolonged PR, QRS, and QT intervals, as well as the pathognomonic J wave (Figure 9–1) at the end of the QRS complex. As the hypothermia becomes more severe, with core temperatures below 30°C (86°F), the myocardium becomes irritable, and ventricular fibrillation ensues.[1,11,13,14]

No patient should be pronounced dead until the core temperature has been elevated to 33–36°C (93–96°F). Until the patient is warmed, one cannot presume the occurrence of death.

Emergency Management

Treatment depends on the degree of hypothermia. The first consideration after airway management has been ensured is raising the patient's temperature by approximately 1°C (1.8°F) an hour. There is considerable controversy about the proper techniques for rewarming, which can be either passive or active.

In the less severe cases of hypothermia, reducing the loss of body temperature by controlling radiation, conduction, convection, and evaporation is all that is required. This is accomplished by using passive techniques, such as removing the person from the cold environment, removing wet clothes, wrapping the person in a blanket, and so on. Passive rewarming has no complications, except that it does take time and if the core temperature is below 32°C (90°F) more aggressive means must be considered.

Active rewarming is an aggressive process that is undertaken when there is a suspicion of cardiac irritability or suppression. It consists of active external rewarming and or active core rewarming. A number of authors discuss in some detail the effectiveness of these processes.[10,12–17]

Prehospital Care

One must perform a primary survey of the ABCs. Accurate assessment in the presence of hypothermia may take up to 1 min.

For mild cases treatment is as follows:

- Reduce heat loss by insulating the patient with blankets. If the patient is on the ground, place insulation beneath the body as well.
- Assess the vital signs: pulse, respiratory rate, and blood pressure.
- Obtain a core temperature.

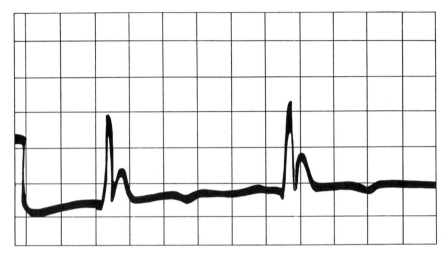

Figure 9–1 Pathognomonic J wave at end of QRS complex.

- Evaluate CNS status, and pupil size and response (PERLA). Determine the presence of slurred speech, staggering gait, and level of consciousness (AVPU).

For moderate and severe cases, repeat the steps for mild cases and add the following seven steps:

1. If both pulse and respirations are absent, begin basic life support.
2. Administer heated, humidified oxygen by nasal cannula.
3. In *severe* cases give nothing by mouth, especially warm or hot fluids, in view of possible airway maintenance problems, as well as the danger of innervating the shunt reflex in the throat, which may cause further shifting of blood from central body areas to the periphery.
4. If the victim is alert, small quantities of warm food and drink may be given. Do not give fluids by mouth. In any case do not give alcohol.
5. If IV fluids are administered in the field, D5W or D5NS is recommended. Do not administer cold IV fluids.[18]
6. Protect the extremities. Do not let the patient walk or move about!
7. Handle the patient gently, because of the instability of the cold myocardium.

Definitive Care

In mild cases, in addition to the treatment measures for prehospital care, the following steps are indicated.

- Place the patient on the hypothermia blanket; the hypothermia blanket should be set 1.8°C (2–3°F) above the patient's core temperature.

- A heating pad, hot water bottles (packs), or placing the patient in a warm bath with appropriate safeguards may be efficacious. However, these techniques may cause rewarming shock in which the peripheral vasculature dilates, pooling of blood occurs, and intravascular volume is depleted. Also, as cold blood returns to the central body organs, a further core reduction in temperature may occur, as well as an increased risk of acidosis and hyperkalemia. Exercise *caution* in turning on the hypothermia blanket until the treatment modality is defined.

- Active external rewarming should be truncal; heating the extremities eliminates peripheral vasoconstriction and allows sudden return of hyperkalemic acidotic blood, which is cold, to the depressed cardiovascular system.[14]

For moderate and severe cases there are various modalities for rewarming, each with its own advocates. The choice of modality depends on the depth of the hypothermia, its course, duration, the age of the patient, what is available at a particular hospital, and the experience of the staff in using the various methods.

In addition to external rewarming techniques, active core rewarming must be considered. The most invasive of the procedures—mediastinal irrigation, hemodialysis, and extracorporeal blood rewarming—should be reserved for patients with no intrinsic mechanical cardiac activity. The temperature must be rapidly elevated in the patient in ventricular fibrillation. Peritoneal dialysis with the dialysing fluid at 40.6–42.2°C (105–108°F) is considered useful in any patient whose stability is questionable.[14] The solution should be kept in for 15 min and then drained; use a total of 4 L/hr.

Other steps include:

- administer 100% oxygen; intubate as necessary and ventilate by bag mask valve unit as required or adjunctively by heated humidified oxygen (maximum temperature 113°F (45°C) administered by nasotracheal tube.
- insert large-bore line and administer 1,000 ml normal saline.
- give fluid as rapidly as possible for the first 200 to 300 ml, then reduce the rate to provide 1 liter in the first hour. Warm the IV solutions; caution is advised in administering bicarbonate in view of a too-rapid correction of acidosis; acidosis tends to be self-correcting in the hypothermic patient as warming occurs. The correction of alkalosis by the body is much more difficult, and the risk of ventricular fibrillation is great.
- insert a nasogastric tube
- monitor cardiac activity continuously by 12-lead ECG
- insert a Foley catheter in most patients
- protect extremities from injury; provide soft splinting and pad between digits. Evaluate for frostbite.

The use of a pressor agent prior to rewarming is controversial, but if indicated dopamine is preferred. The antiarrhythmic of choice for premature contractions is lidocaine and is not to be used prophylactically. Procainamide is ineffective.[19]

Laboratory assessment of the hypothermia patient is essential in carrying out required emergency and definitive management. Laboratory tests should be carried out at appropriate intervals during resuscitation and follow-up care. Initially the following values should be obtained: ABGs (corrected to the patient's temperature), serum potassium, and blood glucose. These tests should be followed by CBC, BUN, serum enzymes, and chest x-ray studies.[10]

REFERENCES

1. Judd RL, Ponsell DD: *The First Responder: The Critical First Minutes*. St. Louis, CV Mosby Co, 1982.

2. The misery spreads. *U.S. News & World Report* 89:14–16, August 4, 1980.

3. Wagner AJ: Worst heat wave in 26 years. *Weatherwise* 33:168–169, August 1980.

4. McElroy CR: Update on heat illness. *Top Emer Med* 3:1–17, 1980.

5. Cummings P: Felled by the heat. *Emer Med* 15:94–110, 1983.

6. Mangi R: Runners in the sun. *Emer Med* 13:135–144, 1981.

7. Cain HD: *Flint's Emergency Treatment and Management*. Philadelphia, WB Saunders Co, 1980.

8. Berkow R: *The Merck Manual, ed 14*. Rahway, NJ, Merck, Sharp & Dohme Research Laboratories, 1982, pp 2124–2126.

9. Editorial: Hypothermia. *Ann Emer Med* 89:565–567, 1978.

10. Bangs C, Hamlet M: Out in the cold: Management of hypothermia, immersion, and frostbite. *Top Emer Med* 2:19–37, 1980.

11. Williamson JB, Munley A, Evans L: *Aging and Society: An Introduction to Social Gerontology*. New York, Holt, Rinehart and Winston, 1980, p 268.

12. Hoffman JR: Clinical settings of accidental hypothermia. *Dig Emer Med Care* 2:1, 1982.

13. Welton DE, Mattox KL, Miller RR, et al: Treatment of profound hypothermia. *JAMA* 240:2291–2292, 1978.

14. Martinez JE, McSwain NE, Adinolfi MF, et al: Trauma rounds: Problem: hypothermia. *Emerg Med* 16:55–59, 1984.

15. Reuler JB, Parker RA: Peritoneal dialysis in the management of hypothermia. *JAMA* 240:2289–2290, 1978.

16. Johnson LA: Accidental hypothermia: Peritoneal dialysis, *JACEP* 6:556–561, 1977.

17. O'Keeffe KM: Accidental hypothermia: A review of 62 cases. *JACEP* 6:491–496, 1977.

18. Steinman AM: The hypothermic code. *J Emer Med* Ser 8:32–35, 1983.

19. Guidelines for treatment of hypothermia. Fairview Hospital, Great Barrington, MA.

SUGGESTED READINGS

Bristow G, Smith R, Lee J: Resuscitation from cardiopulmonary arrest during accident hypothermia due to exhaustion and exposure. *Can Med Assoc J* 117:247–249, 1977.

Chilled to the core. *Emer Med* Jan 15, 1979, pp 173–175.

Mittman N, Nussbaum SJ, Sowinski SL, et al: Core rewarming with peritoneal dialysis for profound accidental hypothermia. *NY Med Q* 4:35–37, 1983.

Winter hazard for the old: accidental hypothermia. US Dept of Health and Human Services Publication No. 81-1464. National Institute on Aging, 1980.

10

Orthopedic Emergencies

James D. Heckman, MD and Ronald P. Williams, MD

The life-span of the general population has continued to increase throughout this century to the point that the average woman's life expectancy in the United States is now 78 years.[1] Associated with this prolonged life expectancy has been an exponential increase in the incidence of fractures of the vertebrae, distal forearm, proximal femur, proximal humerus, and pelvis.[2,3] Fractures in the elderly are a significant cause of both morbidity and mortality. Falls are the leading cause of accidental death among men and women older than 75.[4] Hip fractures per se cause a 12% reduction in life expectancy, primarily in the first 4 months following the fracture.[5,6] The attendant morbidity of fractures in the elderly is also high. For example, at least half of the patients who were ambulatory before hip fractures are unable to walk after the fracture. Similarly, the mean hospital time required for fracture management more than doubles after age 65 (13.6 days age 24 to 44 versus 32.6 days age 65 and older). Fractures of the proximal femur account for more than half of all hospitalization days for limb fractures.[6] The cost of management of fractures in the elderly has also risen dramatically. Acute care for proximal femur fractures alone is estimated to cost more than $1 billion annually in the United States.[6,7] The cost of acute care of Colles' fractures in adults may reach $140 million per year.[6]

Many factors predispose elderly patients to fractures. Osteoporosis is a prevalent disorder that weakens the bone and predisposes it to fracture. Other bone diseases common in the elderly that weaken the bone include osteomalacia, Paget's disease, osteolytic bone metastases, and primary bone tumors, such as multiple myeloma. All of these disorders make the elderly patient more prone to fractures after minor injuries. Simultaneously, the elderly are more prone to minor trauma, especially simple falls, because of the numerous other chronic diseases associated with aging.[8-10]

A second group of musculoskeletal problems seen frequently in the elderly are the arthropathies: primarily degenerative joint disease, acute gouty arthritis, and

267

acute exacerbations of rheumatoid arthritis. The less frequent problems of psoriatic arthritis and the special case of the arthropathy of unknown etiology are also seen in the elderly. In the evaluation of arthritis one must always rule out septic arthritis, especially as a complication of the other joint diseases in the elderly.[11,12]

Complications of peripheral vascular insufficiency also frequently result in extremity problems. Nonhealing ulcers, infections, and progressive gangrene of the lower extremity occur often as sequelae of diabetes mellitus or severe atherosclerotic disease.

The loss of independence by the elderly patient is the most serious consequence of most of these musculoskeletal problems. This physical impairment can place a severe burden on both the patients and their families. The loss of the ability to perform the basic survival skills—eating, moving about, dressing, and personal hygiene—often represents the end of the patient's ability to lead an independent life. For the patient this usually means a decrease in activity level that further perpetuates and aggravates the existing problems. For the family, the dependent person becomes a problem in providing direct care, a financial liability, or both.[9,13,14]

The goal of this chapter is to emphasize the unique aspects in the emergency care of the elderly that are necessary to help the patient remain independent or to resume an independent life as soon as possible after sustaining an orthopedic injury.

GENERAL PRINCIPLES

The overriding consideration in the management of geriatric orthopedic patients is to enable them to return to their previous level of independent activity as rapidly as possible. The corollaries to this cardinal rule include the following:

- Prolonged immobilization is contraindicated in elderly patients,[9] because it exacts such a toll on the elderly that it may result in permanent loss of independence for these patients. Prolonged bedrest causes multiple functional losses in patients of any age, but the effect on the elderly is profound:
  —rapid loss of cardiorespiratory tone, which may lead to insurmountable orthostatic changes in the elderly
  —increased risk of pneumonia from both atelectasis and aspiration
  —increased risk of urinary tract infection
  —increased risk of deep venous thrombosis leading to pulmonary emboli or cerebral vascular thrombosis
  —loss of muscle tone
  —joint contractures
  —acceleration of osteoporosis
  —skin breakdown leading to decubiti

—sensory deprivation, which can exacerbate confusion and dementia[9,15] (Figure 10–1).

- To avoid prolonged periods of bedrest following injury, surgical treatment should be used when possible to mobilize the patient and provide rapid return of function. For most elderly patients the risks of anesthesia and surgery are usually outweighed by the risk of morbidity from immobility and loss of independence. However, surgical management is not indicated when it does not allow immediate activity, because then the patient must recover from both the injury and the operation without achieving the desired goal. Sometimes operative techniques can be modified to decrease the immediate risk of prolonged anesthesia, blood loss, and infection by using less invasive surgical approaches that result in acceptable functional, but not perfect anatomic results.

- An adequate functional result should be the intended therapeutic goal. Anatomic reduction and full range of motion, if they cannot be easily obtained, are not always necessary. Cosmesis, athletic strength, and full joint mobility are not often of significant concern to the elderly. In fact, repeated manipulations of fractures or overmanipulation of joints is contraindicated in the elderly because it only subjects the patient to unnecessary stress when the patient may have a limb that is fully functional, despite some minimal residual deformity or loss of motion.[9]

CAUSES OF FRACTURES

Certain features distinguish fractures in the elderly from those seen in younger persons. The incidence rates are greater among women than men, the rate of fracture increases dramatically (often exponentially) with age, and the fractures occur at sites containing large proportions of trabecular bone. The cause of these distinguishing features can be roughly divided into two categories: (1) disease that leads to osteopenia, which therefore predisposes a patient to fracture after minor trauma, and (2) a propensity for trauma because of other complications of aging.

Factors that Predispose to Fractures

The metabolic bone diseases that most frequently cause osteopenia in the elderly are osteoporosis, osteomalacia, osteolytic bone metastases, primary bone tumors (most common multiple myeloma), and Paget's disease of bone. Osteoporosis is the generalized loss of bone mass caused by imbalance in bone formation and resorption. Postmenopausal osteoporosis is by far the most common form and is, in fact, the most commonly observed form of metabolic bone disease (Figure 10–2). Clinically significant postmenopausal osteoporosis occurs in 30% of elderly women[1,16] and is the basic cause of vertebral body collapse, hip fractures, and forearm fractures in elderly women.

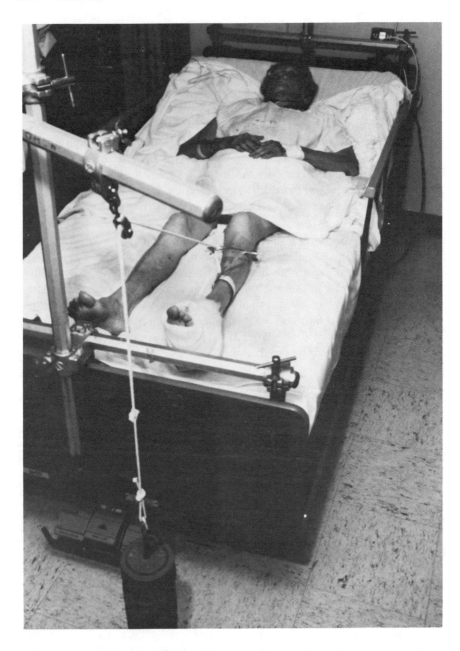

Figure 10–1 This previously healthy 75-year-old woman who suffered a femoral neck fracture was treated with bedrest and skeletal traction. She became demented after only 3 days of immobilization, which necessitated removal of the traction. Dementia is but one of many complications that result from prolonged bedrest in the elderly.

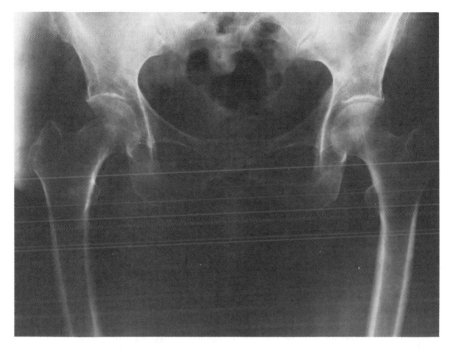

Figure 10–2 Diffuse osteoporosis of the pelvis in a postmenopausal woman—a fracture just
waiting to happen.

No specific etiology of postmenopausal osteoporosis is known, although many
hormonal, genetic, and dietary factors have been implicated. At present it appears
that all three types of factors play a significant role in the progression of the
disease. Thus, serum estrogen, parathyroid hormone, vitamin D_3, and calcium
levels do not follow a consistent pattern that is related to the diagnosis.

However, a number of specific risk factors have been correlated with the disease
and help define the diagnosis. The major risk factors are as follows:

(1) white women (blacks have a distinctly lower incidence),
(2) small skeleton,
(3) small fat mass,
(4) poor general physical condition associated with a sedentary lifestyle, poor
    diet, and malabsorption, and
(5) early menopause, biological or surgical.[17–19]

At present this form of osteoporosis is considered irreversible, but its inexorable
course may be slowed by estrogen and calcium supplements.[16,20–22]

Other common causes of osteoporosis in the elderly, which may appear alone or
superimposed on any other form of osteoporosis, are (1) functional inactivity

("senile osteoporosis") seen prominently in the paralyzed limbs of hemiplegic stroke victims and frequently predisposing elderly patients to femoral neck fractures; (2) hypercortisonism, frequently due to excessive exogenous steroid intake; and (3) male hypogonadism or pelvic irradiation secondary to treatment for prostatic or cervical carcinoma.[23,24]

Osteomalacia is another form of osteopenia. It is caused by the inadequate mineralization of newly formed bone matrix (Figure 10–3). This disorder may be caused by a number of factors, of which the following are the most commonly seen in the elderly:

(1) dietary vitamin D deficiency or chronic malabsorption syndromes, especially following gastric surgery;
(2) prolonged anticonvulsant therapy;
(3) chronic renal insufficiency;
(4) renal tubular acidosis; and
(5) hypophosphatemia associated with excess antacid consumption.[23]

The characteristic laboratory findings of hypophosphatemia with normal or low serum calcium levels, elevated serum alkaline phosphatase, and metabolic acidosis help confirm the diagnosis in many cases.[24] The radiologic findings of Looser's zones (pseudofractures) may also aid in diagnosis (Figure 10–4). The reversibility of osteomalacia is solely dependent on the reversibility of the underlying disease. As does osteoporosis, osteomalacia predisposes the elderly to vertebral body collapse and long bone fractures, either stress fractures or fractures following minor trauma. The clinical picture of osteomalacia may be very similar to that of osteoporosis because the classical findings of diffuse bone pain and muscle weakness may not appear until late in the course of the disease. Thus, serologic, careful roentgenographic and, if necessary, bone biopsy evaluation should be carried out in elderly patients who are thought to have osteomalacia to identify this reversible systemic disease so that corrective therapy can be instituted to minimize the risk of future fractures.

Skeletal metastases of tumors are a frequent cause of pathologic fractures in the elderly.[9,16] In particular, breast, kidney, prostatic, thyroid, and lung tumors have a predilection for bone. Because the spread of these tumors is primarily hematogenous, the bones most frequently involved are those with the greatest proportion of marrow: the vertebrae, pelvis, proximal femur, proximal humerus, skull, and ribs. The metastases seed in the medullary canal and secondarily invade the cortex, usually without significant periosteal reaction. In most cases the diagnosis can be made from the history of prior treatment for cancer. In the unusual case of an unknown primary site, a diligent search must be made for the suspected primary site, and biopsy of the bone lesion may be necessary to help establish the diagnosis. In either case, once a bone metastasis has been identified, a bone scan and bone survey should be carried out to find other metastatic sites.

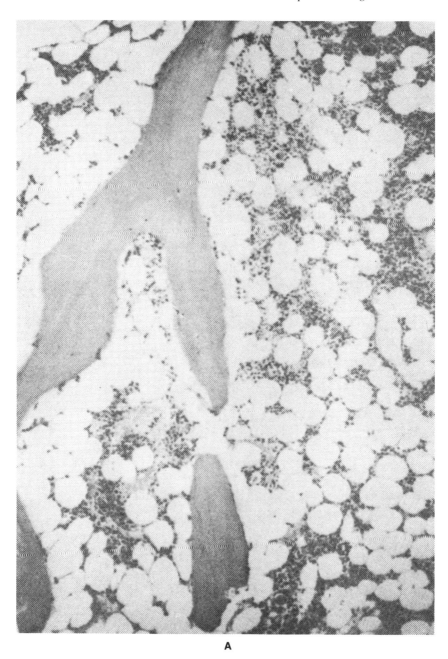

A

Figure 10–3 A: Normal trabecular bone. Compare this with **B**: diminished trabecular bone in osteoporosis, and **C**: widened osteoid seams in osteomalacia.

Source: **A** and **B**, reprinted from *Postgraduate Textbook of Clinical Orthopaedics* (p 308) by N Harris (Ed) with permission of John Wright & Sons Ltd, © 1983;

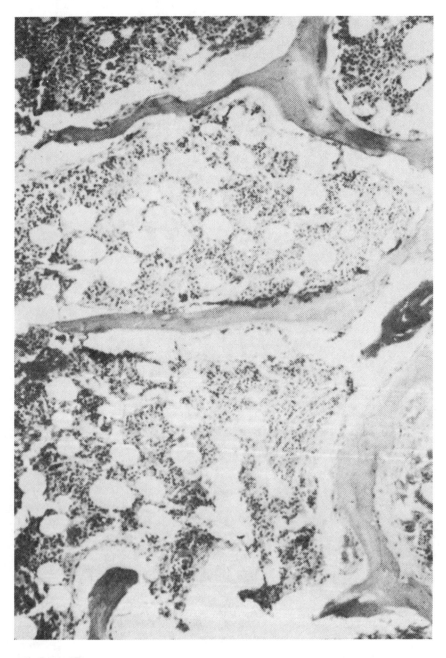

Figure 10–3B

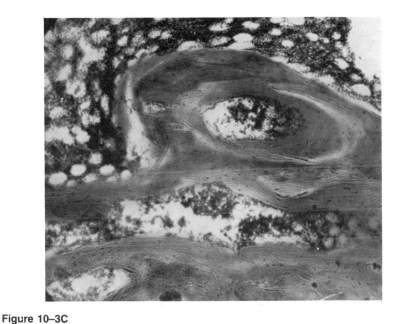

Figure 10–3C

Source: **C**, reprinted from *Orthopaedics Principles and Their Application*, 4th ed (p 228) by S Turek (Ed) with permission of JB Lippincott Company, © 1984.

Although primary bone tumors are an infrequent cause of fractures, multiple myeloma should always be considered in the differential diagnosis of a pathologic fracture in an elderly patient.[9,25,26] Multiple myeloma is one of a group of malignant plasma cell neoplasms. The disease is believed to originate from a single plasma cell clone, which produces a large quantity of abnormal immunoglobulin molecules. The rapid growth of the tumor cells in the marrow results in bone destruction, marrow failure, and hypercalcemia. The production of large quantities of abnormal proteins leads to renal failure and recurrent infections. This disease has the highest incidence of pathologic fractures of all malignant tumors of bone and commonly causes bone pain from pathologic fractures, especially in the vertebral bodies and ribs.[25,26] The radiologic findings of multiple cystic tumors in the spine, skull, ribs and long bones should suggest the diagnosis (Figure 10–5A, B). A laboratory finding of a monoclonal globulin peak on serum or urine protein electrophoresis helps confirm the diagnosis. The associated findings of ''Bence-Jones'' proteins in the urine, a markedly increased erythrocyte sedimentation rate, and hypercalcemia suggest a more advanced disease stage and a poorer prognosis.

Paget's disease of bone (osteitis deformans) is another common cause of pathologic fractures in the elderly. This disease of unknown etiology is characterized by a localized and very gradual replacement of normal lamellar bone with disorganized, poorly mineralized matrix and vascular connective tissue. The disease

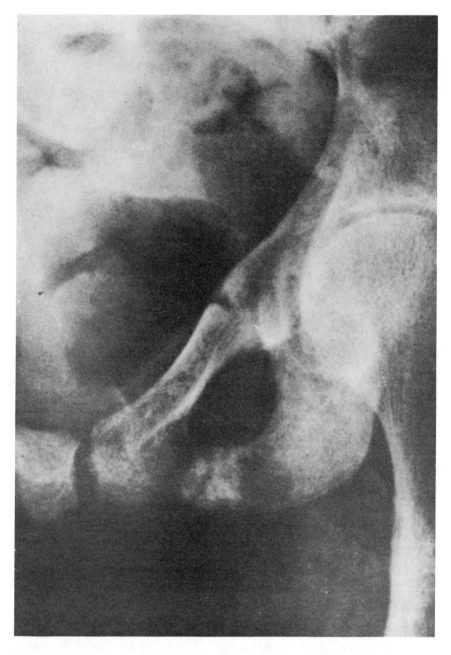

Figure 10–4 Looser's zones (pseudofractures) in the pubic rami of a patient with osteomalacia.

Source: Reprinted from *Postgraduate Textbook of Clinical Orthopaedics* (p 321) by N Harris (Ed) with
permission of John Wright & Sons Ltd, © 1983.

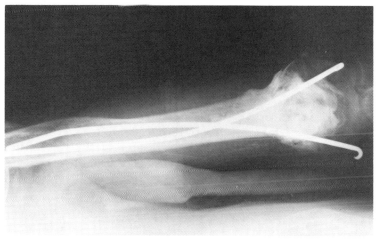

Figure 10–5B The same lesion as in Figure 10–5A treated by internal fixation with Rush rods and methylmethacrylate cement to restore stability and function promptly.

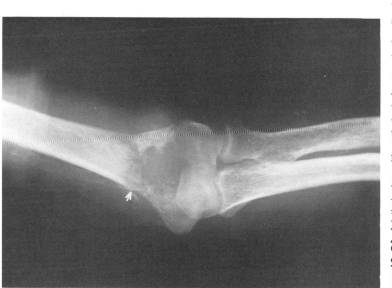

Figure 10–5A A lytic lesion with pathologic fracture in the distal humerus of a 65-year-old man with multiple myeloma.

usually appears as either a monostotic form, which usually involves the tibia or femur, or as a polyostotic form, which usually involves the pelvis, skull, and spine. The disease is usually described as progressing in stages. First, the original lamellar bone is resorbed and is replaced by vascular connective tissue intermixed with woven bone. This woven bone in turn is reorganized into new lamellar bone, which is poorly mineralized and produces osteoid seams on the margins of the new bone. Thus, although the new bone is thick, it is structurally unsound. It develops multiple cracks in response to stress and is predisposed to fracture from minor trauma. The increased thickness of the bone and the multiple cracks lead to progressive deformity. The characteristic roentgenographic features are irregular deposits of numerous trabeculae, appearing first subperiosteally then in the medullary cavity (Figure 10–6). The outstanding laboratory finding to suggest the

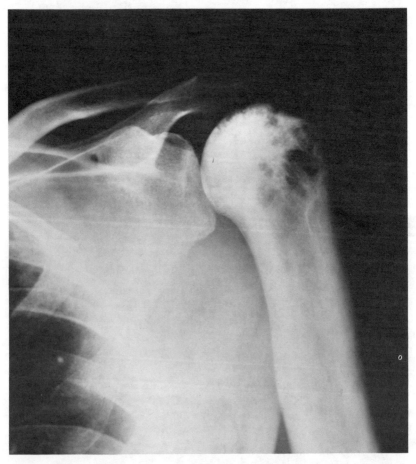

Figure 10–6 Paget's disease. Note the thickened cortex of the bone and the irregular trabecular pattern around the lesion in the proximal humerus.

active disease is a dramatically increased serum level of alkaline phosphatase. The serum calcium, parathyroid hormone, and phosphorus levels are usually normal. In addition to the multiple fractures, especially of the spine, pelvis, tibia, and femur, the patient may have bone pain in a region that is enlarged and hypervascular. A serious complication of this disease, which occurs in 1% to 10% of patients, is the evolution of an osteogenic sarcoma within a Pagetic lesion.[16,24,26]

Factors That Predispose to Minor Trauma

The elderly patient is distinctly at risk for fractures occurring with minor trauma, the vast majority of which are caused by a simple fall from a standing height or less. At least one-third of elderly individuals are subject to such a fall each year.[10] The causes of these falls are numerous. One-half or more are induced by a specific dysfunction, such as diminished postural control, gait change, muscular weakness, decreased reflexes, poor vision, postural hypotension, vestibular disorders, confusion, and/or dementia.[4,8] Such environmental hazards as scatter rugs, slippery surfaces, stairways, and electric cords may also be primarily responsible for the falls in one-third of the cases. A few falls can be directly related to specific conditions, such as parkinsonism, stroke, cardiac dysrhythmias, pneumonia, syncope, alcoholism, oversedation, and overtreatment of hypertension.[9]

Many of these risk factors are synergistic. For example, the loss of visual acuity and equilibrium causes a decrease in mobility with a resultant loss of muscle strength and bone mass. The physician should also keep in mind that the discovery of a specific cause greatly improves the prognosis because the problem can then be avoided or treated. In most of these patients, the injury has occurred during the course of their normal, independent lifestyle, and the physician should be able to return the patient to the previous level of activity. Conversely, patients who cannot give a specific cause for their injuries have a much more guarded prognosis. Their present injury may be the precipitating event that leads to loss of independence.

Causes of Arthritis

Degenerative joint disease (osteoarthritis) is a universal problem in the elderly. Continued wear and tear on the joint leads to the loss of joint cartilage and hypertrophy of subchondral bone. The continuous mechanical compression of the articular cartilage causes a breakdown in the specialized type II articular cartilage. Simultaneously, the articular chondrocytes proliferate and produce proteases and other enzymes that further degrade the articular cartilage. The new chondrocytes then replace the type II cartilage with the less malleable type I cartilage. In addition to the cartilage changes, the subchondral bone develops multiple microscopic fatigue fractures. The healing of these fractures results in subchondral bone sclerosis and marginal bone overgrowth (spurs)[11,27] (Figure 10–7). This process occurs to some extent in all joints, but is more severe in the weightbearing joints. Thus, the spine, hips, knees, and ankles are the most commonly and severely af-

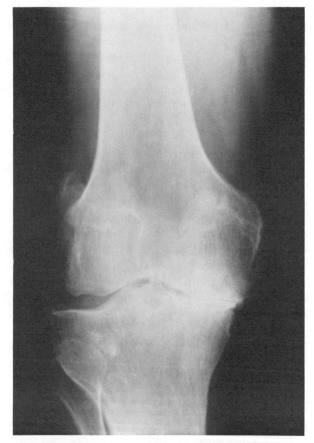

Figure 10–7 Degenerative joint disease in the knee demonstrating subchondral bone sclerosis, narrowing of the medial joint space, and osteophytes.

fected joints. A secondary form of degenerative joint disease also occurs in joints that have sustained a mechanical injury. Any joint that has been infected, fractured through the cartilage, or has had ligamentous injury resulting in joint laxity, malalignment, or abnormal motion can be expected to show early and more severe degenerative changes.

Rheumatoid arthritis is a chronic systemic autoimmune disorder of uncertain etiology. Specific autoantibodies (rheumatoid factors) form immune complexes in the synovium of the joint. These complexes apparently activate complement, which leads to the generation of chemotactic substances that attract neutrophils into the synovium. The activated neutrophils release lysosomal enzymes that are responsible for joint destruction. During the inflammatory response the synovium expands to form a pannus, a large fold of hypertrophied synovium, which extends over the articular cartilage. The lysosomal enzymes in the pannus are responsible for destruction of the articular cartilage, subchondral bone, and joint capsule. In addition, there is a variably present microvascular vasculitis characterized by lymphocytic infiltration into the vascular wall. This vasculitis contributes to muscle atrophy, formation of rheumatoid nodules, myositis, and the numerous other complications of rheumatoid arthritis[11,28] (Figure 10–8).

Gouty arthritis seen in the elderly population is usually a complication of a 20- to 30-year history of persistent hyperuricemia. Although multiple factors— genetic, environmental, and hormonal—are involved in the generation of hyperuricemia, the condition most consistently associated with it is obesity. Associated with the obesity are hypertriglyceridemia, hypertension, atherosclerosis, and diabetes. In addition, a common cause of secondary hyperuricemia is diuretic therapy, which enhances renal urate retention. The excess urate is deposited in microtophi about the joint. Minor trauma, alcohol ingestion, or temperature change then induces the release of the urate crystals into the synovial fluid. The released urate crystals trigger an acute inflammatory response that results in the release of lysosomal enzymes from activated leukocytes into the synovial fluid. The lysosomal enzymes digest the articular cartilage; hence recurrent attacks lead to joint destruction.[29]

Septic arthritis, usually of bacterial etiology, is a rare but serious and potentially lethal form of arthritis. It occurs in the elderly usually by hematogenous spread from other infection sites in the urinary, biliary, and intestinal tracts and seeds in joints that are predisposed to infection. Joints damaged by rheumatoid arthritis,

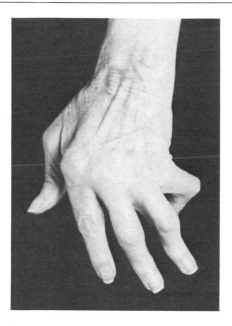

Figure 10–8 The typical hand deformity of rheumatoid arthritis.

gout, or degenerative joint disease are distinctly at risk for developing secondary bacterial infections. Thus, infection must be ruled out in the management of any acutely or persistently inflamed joint.[30]

Finally, in unusual cases the cause of an arthropathy may not be clinically apparent. In these patients, especially if they have a significant history of smoking, one should consider the possibility of the arthropathy being associated with a neoplasm. In most of these cases the neoplasm is bronchogenic in origin. The cause of this association is unknown, and no systemic factors have as yet been implicated.

COMPLICATIONS OF PERIPHERAL VASCULAR DISEASE AND DIABETES

A third group of problems seen frequently in elderly patients consists of the complications of peripheral vascular insufficiency and diabetes. The majority of these involve the lower extremity, especially the foot. Nonhealing ulcers, progressive infections, and gangrene frequently threaten the function and viability of the affected limb, and sometimes are an acute threat to life (Figure 10–9).

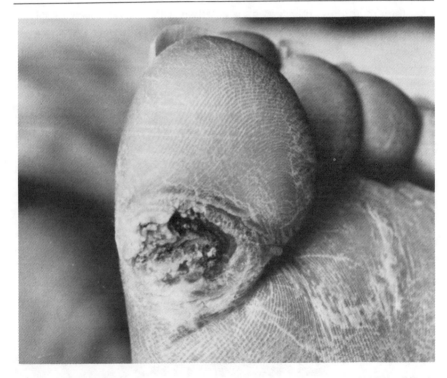

Figure 10–9 A nonhealing ulcer ("mal perforans") in the great toe of an elderly diabetic patient.

There are three distinct factors involved in producing these problems in a patient with diabetes mellitus: ischemia, peripheral neuropathy, and infection. Ischemia in the diabetic foot has two contributing causes. Atherosclerotic or thrombotic disease of the large and middle-size arteries decreases the perfusion of the limb. Atherosclerosis appears to be primarily related to age but may be accentuated by diabetes. Thrombosis is often a result of inactivity. A second problem is the specific microangiopathy of diabetes, which causes narrowing of the small arterioles and capillaries that further impairs perfusion. This microangiopathy can produce ischemia even in the presence of adequate large vessel perfusion.[31–33]

Peripheral neuropathy is another common complication of diabetes. This loss of protective sensory function, usually in a stocking-type distribution, predisposes the patient to skin breakdown from trivial trauma. Corns, calluses, deformed toenails, and skin abrasions or blisters caused by minor injury or by poorly fitting shoes occur frequently. Because of the lack of protective pain sensation, the patient ignores the lesions and delays treatment until the lesions have become infected or deeply ulcerated.[34–37] Once a lesion on the foot becomes infected, the immunocompromised diabetic patient is unable to mobilize an effective response. Thus, the infection persists and progressively extends deep into the foot and up the limb.[36] These factors work synergistically to place the elderly diabetic patient at high risk of developing nonhealing ulcerative lesions, cellulitis, and gangrene in the lower extremities.

MANAGEMENT OF FRACTURES

The primary goal of fracture management in the elderly patient is to restore adequate function of the injured part as rapidly as possible (Figure 10–10). Rapid restoration of a functional limb is necessary to maintain or restore quickly the patient's independence and thus prevent the development of insurmountable complications that can cause a permanent loss of independence. The specialized care of the elderly patient with a fracture should begin as soon as the patient is seen. It is of utmost importance to protect the skin of the elderly immediately by eliminating point pressure with adequate padding and proper positioning. Skin breakdown can occur after as few as 2 hr of moderate direct pressure over a bony prominence. This is well within the time frame of transport, emergency evaluation, and initial treatment. Primary care providers must be acutely aware of this potential problem because it is not uncommon for an elderly patient to lie, sit, or even be restrained in one position for several hours.

Initial Care

Once the patient has arrived at the hospital, a brief evaluation of the general physical condition, as well as the type and severity of the fracture, should be carried out. An elaborate medical evaluation should not be performed at this time.

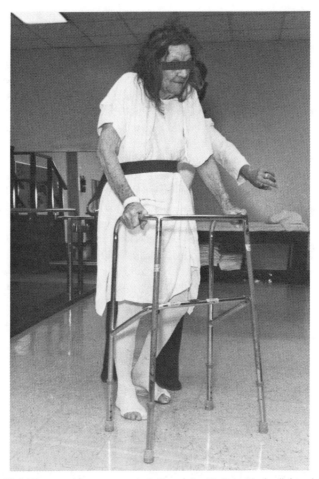

Figure 10–10 A 78-year-old woman ambulating well with the aid of a lightweight walker 3 days after stable internal fixation of a femoral neck fracture.

The examination should focus on identifying problems that may prevent immediate treatment of the fracture. Foremost among these are congestive heart failure or unstable arrhythmias, infections (especially urinary tract infections and pneumonia), uncontrolled diabetic ketoacidosis, anemia, and hypothermia. These problems should then be aggressively managed so that treatment of the fracture is minimally delayed. Ideally, reduction and fixation of extremity fractures should be accomplished within hours after arrival in the emergency department (ED).

Once the immediate care of the fracture is complete, a thorough evaluation of the cause of the fracture and the cause of the injury that produced the fracture should be completed. Reversible causes of osteopenia should be searched for. Pathologic fractures should lead to a careful evaluation for the underlying disease, such as malignancy, myelomatosis, or Paget's disease. The history should direct the physician toward continued evaluation of the cause of the injury: changes in vision or equilibrium, cardiac dysrhythmias producing syncopal episodes, orthostatic hypotension, transient ischemic attacks, or any other of the other numerous problems that predispose the elderly to minor trauma.

Special Considerations

The elderly fracture patient should be managed as an outpatient if at all possible in order to promote independence. The decision to admit a patient should be based on the need to facilitate the restoration of function so that return to independence is not delayed. The high morbidity associated with extensive immobilization of the elderly should be one of the primary considerations in fracture management. Old age per se should not be considered an indication for internal fixation. However, when internal fixation can provide a more rapid return to any of the basic functions—ambulation, feeding, and hygiene—it should be chosen over cast immobilization even when it is known that casting will result in fracture healing. Furthermore, once the decision to operate has been made, surgery should not be delayed.

Occasionally the surgical technique used in the elderly should also be modified. A procedure that provides adequate stabilization of the fracture with minimal anesthesia time and blood loss should be employed to ''get the job done'' with less concern about such late sequelae as secondary degenerative joint disease or minor cosmetic deformities that would be of greater concern with a younger patient. The surgeon must also be aware of the need to compensate for osteoporotic bone. The fixation may need to be extended well above and below the fracture site to provide adequate structural support for early mobilization. Load-sharing devices, such as intramedullary rods, as opposed to plates, should be used whenever feasible, and often, particularly with pathologic fractures, reinforcement of the fixation with methylmethacrylate is required.[38–40]

The nonoperative management of fractures may also need to be modified. Plaster casting is usually acceptable in the upper extremity. However, immobilization of the lower extremity may immobilize the entire patient. Immobilization of the ankle in a long leg cast for example, in a person with poor muscle tone and decreased equilibrium, may make ambulation impossible. Thus, a short leg cast may be more appropriate even though the ankle is not totally immobilized. This compromise is possible in the elderly because they are not as mobile as young people, and the decreased strength of the muscles minimizes the risk of movement at the fracture site. The eventual slight displacement of the fracture fragments, when healed, will be tolerated better by an elderly individual because there will be less stress applied to the joints.

In following the progress of the patient one must remember that osteoporotic bone heals at the same rate as ordinary bone. Therefore, rehabilitation should not be delayed because of the patient's age. Rehabilitation should not be overly aggressive, however, because excessive stress on an osteoporotic bone may cause a second fracture adjacent to the site of fixation. Thus, rehabilitation should be aimed at an early but gradual return to the patient's previous level of function.

Fractures of the Proximal Humerus

Fractures of the proximal humerus in the elderly population have all of the epidemiologic characteristics of osteoporosis-related fractures. The vast majority occur after a fall from a standing height or less, and the incidence increases with age. There is a 2:1 female predominance, and the severity of the fracture increases with age.[41] These fractures are common in the elderly, occurring with 70% of the frequency of proximal femur fractures. There are two common mechanisms of injury: a fall onto the outstretched hand and a fall onto the lateral side of the shoulder.

The diagnostic features of a proximal humeral fracture are (1) a history of a recent fall, (2) loss of contour of the affected shoulder, (3) pain and refusal to move the shoulder, and (4) edema and ecchymosis about the shoulder. In the elderly it must be remembered that the patient may not recall a recent fall or may deny pain. Thus, unconscious splinting or refusal to cooperate with the examination of the shoulder may be the first diagnostic clue. Once the diagnosis is suspected, a rapid neurovascular examination of the entire upper extremity should be performed. Then, before transport, the shoulder should be immobilized in a sling and swathe, and peripheral pulses should be reexamined after splinting.

In the ED a repeat neurovascular examination should be performed with special attention to the function of the axillary, median, radial, and ulnar nerves. Initial radiologic evaluation of the shoulder with an anterior-posterior and true lateral view of the shoulder should then be performed, with the arm still supported in a sling. The radiologic analysis helps determine the appropriate treatment. Most (85%) of these fractures are minimally displaced, impacted fractures, which are satisfactorily treated with a collar and cuff sling to support the arm[42] (Figure 10–11A, B). Active motion of the elbow, wrist, and hand should be carried out immediately. Gentle active motion of the shoulder with pendulum exercises should be started in about 4 days with gradual increase in motion. This treatment usually results in full functional recovery in 6–8 weeks.[9,43]

Management of the more severely displaced three-part and four-part fractures and fracture-dislocations usually requires open reduction and internal fixation to restore the anatomy and allow early return of function.[44,45]

Complications of the conservative management of minimally displaced fractures of the proximal humerus are unusual and are usually the result of overtreatment. Moderate residual deformity is usually of little consequence, but shoulder and elbow stiffness from prolonged immobilization will result in a weak, stiff, painful, and often useless extremity. Thus, these patients should be encouraged to maintain motion in the hand, wrist, and elbow while in the sling and to begin pendulum exercises at an early date and not await full bony union. Nonunion is a

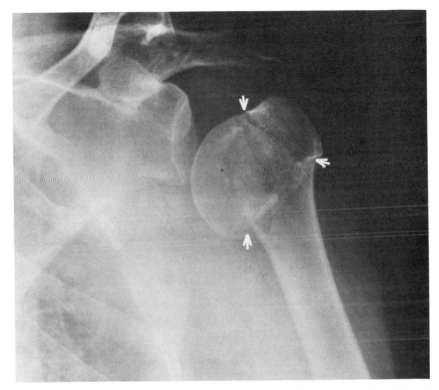

Figure 10–11A A displaced three-part humeral neck fracture that was caused by a fall onto the outstretched hand.

rare complication of this fracture, even with minimal immobilization and early motion. In severely displaced fractures, the complications of nonunion and avascular necrosis can be minimized or obviated by early surgical treatment followed by an early, progressive rehabilitation program. The primary goal of treatment in fractures of the proximal humerus in the elderly is the restoration of painless shoulder motion.[43,46]

Fractures of the Distal Radius

Fractures of the distal radius are quite common in all age groups, but are especially prevalent in the elderly; they are second only to proximal femur fractures in incidence.[2,47] The fracture occurs six times more frequently in women than men and is typically the result of a fall from a standing height or less.

Three basic anatomic fracture patterns occur in the distal radius. The Colles' fracture is certainly the most frequent pattern of injury. This injury occurs as the result of a fall on the outstretched hand with a force applied to the palm and supina-

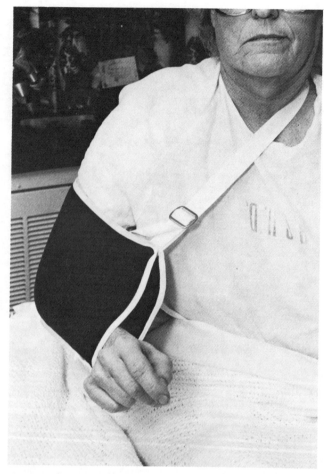

Figure 10–11B A sling applied to afford pain relief for fracture of the proximal humerus. The sling is applied loosely to allow early pendulum exercises and thus avoid persistent shoulder stiffness.

tion of the forearm. The distal radius fractures, and the distal fragment displaces dorsally, producing the characteristic "silver fork deformity" of the wrist (Figure 10–12A, B). The forearm is shortened, and frequently the wrist is deviated radially. The displaced distal radius fragment can often be seen or palpated dorsally.

A second fracture pattern is the reversed Colles' (or Smith's) fracture in which the distal radial fragment is displaced toward the palmar aspect of the wrist. This pattern of injury is much less common than dorsal displacement and is thought to be the result of a fall onto the dorsal aspect of the flexed wrist.[48]

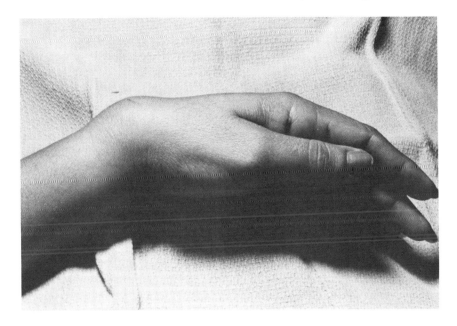

Figure 10–12A The silver fork deformity of the wrist in a patient with a Colles' fracture.

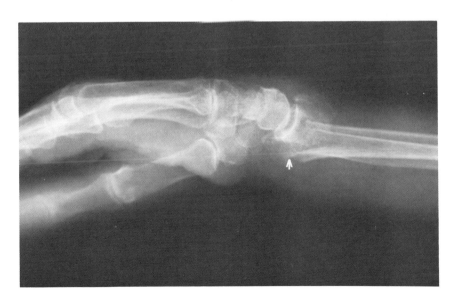

Figure 10–12B A radiograph of the Colles' fracture seen in 12A demonstrating the dorsal displacement of the distal radial fragment.

A third variant, named the Barton's fracture, is an injury in which only part of the distal radius is fractured. The fracture line passes through the articular surface of the radius. Either the dorsal or the palmar lip of the radius is broken off, resulting in either dorsal or palmar displacement of the fracture fragment along with the wrist. Roentgenographs are required to distinguish this variant from Colles' or Smith's fractures.[48]

Fractures of the distal radius are often nondisplaced. In these cases there is minimal or no deformity, except for swelling. Ecchymosis of the wrist and thumb and tenderness over the styloid processes of the distal radius and ulna are the characteristic signs of a nondisplaced fracture. With minimally displaced fractures, shortening of the radius occurs. Normally the tip of the styloid process of the radius is 1cm distal to that of the ulna. With radial shortening following a fracture, the tips of the styloid processes may be palpated at the same level, or with greater displacement, the ulnar styloid is more distal. The immediate care of a distal radius fracture should consist of a rapid neurovascular assessment of the involved hand and immobilization with a padded board or air or pillow splint. In the ED a repeat neurovascular examination should be performed with particular attention to the sensory and motor distribution of the median nerve. Radiologic evaluation should consist of anterior-posterior and lateral views of the forearm and wrist.

In treating Colles' fractures, one must remember that an untreated fracture usually results in a fully functional hand and forearm.[48] Thus, the negative results of overly aggressive treatment, such as prolonged traction, repeated manipulations, or immobilization in a nonfunctional position should be avoided.[49] The fracture should be reduced immediately following diagnosis. Bier's block or hematoma block usually provides adequate anesthesia for reduction, although occasionally general anesthesia is needed to achieve adequate muscle relaxation.[9,48]

Most fractures can be reduced by traction applied to the thumb with countertraction above the elbow, followed by manual manipulation of the distal radial fragment. The reduction can then be maintained by a circular plaster short arm cast or sugar tong splint. The fingers should always be left free to allow a full range of motion and to prevent stiffness. Immobilization in 10 degrees of palmar flexion with moderate ulnar deviation usually provides the best results with minimal inconvenience to the patient.[50,51] More severe palmar flexion (the Cotton Loder position) or above-the-elbow immobilization may sometimes be necessary to maintain reduction of unstable fractures. However, the extensive complications—particularly elbow and finger stiffness—accompanying these extreme forms of immobilization have led to the use of external fixation techniques, such as pins and plaster or metal external fixation frames. These devices provide rigid immobilization of the reduced fracture, yet allow free elbow and finger motion.[48] The neurovascular status of the involved hand must be followed carefully for the first 24 hr following reduction of a distal radius fracture. Rehabilitation in the form of self-care, normal household activities, and vigorous active range of motion exercises for the shoulder, elbow, and fingers should begin immediately. The fracture should be immobilized for 6 to 8 weeks.

Complications from the management of a Colles' fracture are unusual. The late development of median nerve compression in the carpal tunnel is most frequently seen. This condition should be managed the same as a primary carpal tunnel syndrome.[48] Distal radial fractures almost always unite, although there may be some residual radial shortening and a dorsal bony prominence at the wrist. These mild deformities are usually compatible with good wrist function. If symptoms, particularly pain with pronation and supination, result from malunion of a Colles' fracture, they can usually be relieved by excision of the distal ulna.[48] Sudeck's atrophy and shoulder-hand syndrome may also occur after a Colles' fracture. These disorders are characterized by pain and stiffness in the hand, wrist, and fingers and redness and swelling of the hand. If allowed to progress, a ''frozen shoulder'' results. This problem is a result of immobilization of the limb. Thus, active exercises should be instituted immediately after fracture reduction to prevent its occurrence. Once the syndrome has occurred, extensive rehabilitation is required to reverse the process, and usually only fair results are possible.[48] Finally, rupture of the extensor pollicis longus tendon occurs as a late complication in about 0.2% of Colles' fractures. This usually results in little deformity and is of little consequence in the elderly. Surgical repair by transfer of the extensor indices proprius tendon can be performed if the patient has a significant functional impairment.[52]

Fractures of the Proximal Femur

Fractures of the proximal femur (''hip fractures'') are the most common fractures in the elderly.[2,53,54] The mortality associated with fractures about the hip is high. Approximately 25% of patients die within 6 months of the fracture, which is 20 times the expected death rate of an age-matched population.[54-56] Morbidity is also high and is primarily a result of the loss of the ability to walk.[53] For these reasons the treatment of hip fractures should be aggressive, with the goal of restoring ambulation as rapidly as possible.

Most hip fractures resulting from simple falls are either femoral neck fractures or intertrochanteric fractures. In addition, stress fractures of the femoral neck occur spontaneously in osteopenic bone. Stress fractures, when left untreated with continued weightbearing, will almost always displace. Therefore, the early diagnosis of a stress fracture can be lifesaving by allowing early surgical stabilization to prevent its inevitable progression.[57]

One must have a high index of suspicion to diagnose a nondisplaced stress fracture of the femoral neck. The patient may complain of only minimal pain in the groin, nonspecific pain about the hip, or pain along the medial side of the knee. The patient is usually walking, but with an antalgic gait. The physical signs are often nothing more than minor discomfort with active or passive motion, some muscle spasm, and a minimal decrease in range of motion of the hip. Because patients with rheumatoid arthritis and degenerative joint disease are at increased risk of developing a stress fracture, these historical and physical findings do not provide specific diagnostic clues. Thus, the physician must suspect a stress fracture in the characteristically osteopenic patient who complains of a new onset of pain or increasing pain about the hip or knee with no history of injury or after a trivial injury.

According to Devas[58] almost all of these fractures can be diagnosed at the time of first presentation by meticulous roentgenographic evaluation. A properly positioned anterior-posterior x-ray of the hip usually reveals a lucency along the superior surface of the femoral neck (Figure 10–13). If this is not apparent, computed tomography (CT) or bone scan may be necessary to identify the fracture. Often stress fractures are bilateral. Thus, when evaluating a patient for a stress fracture, both hips should be thoroughly examined.

Stress fractures should be treated as surgical emergencies. Full weightbearing should be prohibited until the fracture is stabilized surgically because of the high

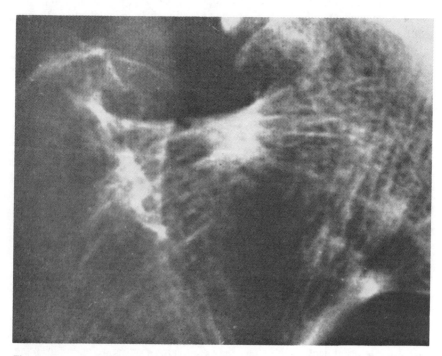

Figure 10–13 A stress fracture in the superior cortex of the femoral neck of an 88-year-old woman who developed pain in the right hip.

Source: Reprinted with permission from *The Journal of Bone and Joint Surgery* (1965;47B:732), Copyright © 1965, Journal of Bone and Joint Surgery, Inc.

risk of displacement of the fracture. Internal fixation with pins is usually required to stabilize the fracture. Complications of this treatment are unusual, and following fixation, the patient will be able to resume partial weightbearing and most activities of daily living quite rapidly.

After a fall, patients with displaced femoral neck fractures have pain in the hip and/or knee region. The leg is in external rotation and abduction and is slightly shortened (Figure 10–14A, B, and C). Intertrochanteric fractures cause a similar deformity, but the degree of shortening and external rotation is more exaggerated. There is often edema and ecchymosis about the hip. The greater trochanter is tender on palpation and percussion. Any motion of the limb is quite painful.

Attenborough[14] has emphasized that treatment of these patients should begin as soon as they are seen. There is substantial pain in the affected hip, and therefore movement of the extremity should be avoided. It is essential that all skin pressure points be padded, especially over the sacrum and heels. Although some clinicians have recommended that traction splints be used to transport these patients,[59] the author feels that effective immobilization can be achieved by placing the patient on a spine board, a scoop stretcher, or simply on the ambulance litter with pillows and rolled blankets used to support the injured limb (Figure 10–15).

The patient may sustain significant blood loss with the fracture. Pre-existing anemia and dehydration frequently compound this problem, and hypovolemic shock may occur. This complication is especially dangerous in the elderly person with poor coronary and cerebral perfusion and may precipitate myocardial infarction or cerebral vascular ischemia, leading to the patient's demise.[5,55]

ED management must consist of a rapid evaluation of the patient's cardiovascular, neurologic, respiratory, and renal status. Before fluid therapy is initiated, the patient must be assessed for congestive heart failure and diabetes. Immediate laboratory evaluation should include blood hemoglobin and hematocrit, urea, and glucose levels. The patient should be typed and cross-matched for two units of packed red cells. The leg may be splinted with 5 pounds of nonadhesive (Buck's) skin traction to control pain prior to surgery. Radiologic evaluation should consist of anterior-posterior and cross table (or "OR") lateral views of the hip.[60]

Most femoral neck and intertrochanteric fractures require some form of operative treatment. As Clawson and Melcher have stated, "The more debilitated the patient, the more emergent the indications. The goal of treatment must be to restore the patient to preoperative status at the earliest possible time, and this can be achieved best through reduction and internal fixation in a stable fashion that allows early ambulation."[61] Operative treatment may consist of nailing and pinning, compression plate and screws, or primary hemiarthroplasty, depending on the surgeon's expertise, the assessment of the condition of the patient, and the type of fracture[43] (Figure 10–16A, B). Operative treatment should rarely be withheld because of the poor general medical condition or short expected life-span of the patient. Even if the patient is nonambulatory, stable internal fixation can permit increased mobility without pain and thus enable the best quality of life possible.

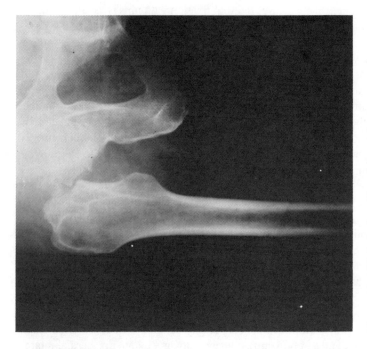

Figure 10–14B A displaced femoral neck fracture.

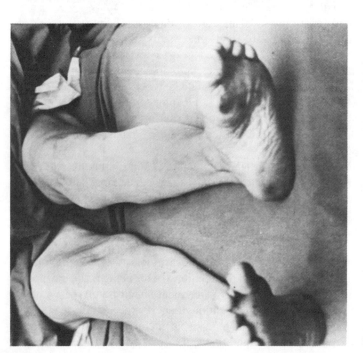

Figure 10–14A A shortened and externally rotated left lower extremity of an 80-year-old woman who sustained an intertrochanteric fracture of the femur after a simple fall.

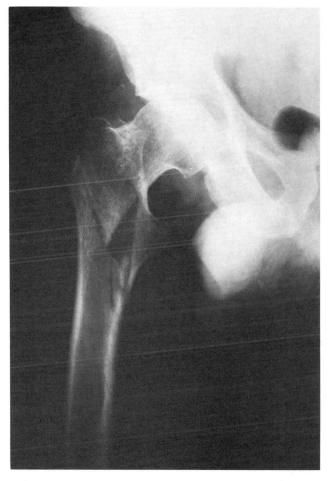

Figure 10–14C An intertrochanteric fracture of the femur.

For patients returning to an active lifestyle after the fracture is treated, their neurologic and cardiac status should be carefully assessed before discharge. This evaluation should include complete electrocardiographic testing and, if indicated, Holter monitoring to detect cardiac ischemia and arrhythmias. Electroencephalographic evaluation for reversible neurologic deficits also helps identify problems that may precipitate a second fall.[54] In addition, patients and their families should be educated about environmental hazards that may cause another fall and be encouraged to rearrange the patients' home environment to minimize these risks.[4,62]

The complications of proximal femur fractures are numerous, including thromboembolic problems, failure or migration of the fixation device, avascular ne-

Figure 10–15 The use of a spine board and pillows to splint a hip fracture.

Source: Reprinted from *Emergency Care and Transportation of the Sick and Injured*, 3rd ed (p 159) by J Heckman et al with permission of American Academy of Orthopaedic Surgeons, © 1981.

crosis of the femoral head, and infection. These can best be minimized by prompt treatment, meticulous surgical technique, and aggressive postoperative rehabilitation.

Fractures of the Spine

The pathologic compression fracture of a vertebral body usually causes a sudden onset of severe back pain. This may occur spontaneously but, more frequently, follows minor stress on the spine, such as coughing, sneezing, opening a window, or falling. The acute pain at the time of the fracture has been described as an incapacitating, severe "catching" pain in the back that is aggravated by rotational movements and flexion of the spine.[63] The patient holds the trunk rigid and lies quite still on one side because changing positions increases the pain. On physical examination there is point tenderness or pain on gentle percussion over the spinous process of the involved vertebra. The fracture is usually at the thoracolumbar junction (T_{11}-L_2).[64] There is usually no neurologic deficit, although transient radicular pain may be present. It is not uncommon for these patients to have a transient paralytic ileus. The diagnosis of the fracture can be confirmed by anterior-posterior and lateral roentgenograms of the spine (Figure 10–17).

Although the majority of these fractures are caused by osteoporosis, a significant number are also produced by osteomalacia, rheumatoid arthritis, multiple myeloma, Paget's disease, and breast or prostatic carcinoma. Thus, laboratory evaluation of the patient must include a complete blood count; erythrocyte sedi-

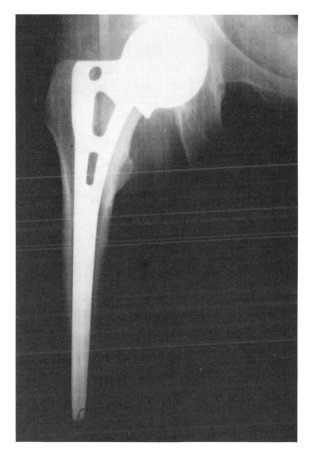

Figure 10–16A An Austin-Moore prosthesis used for primary replacement of a displaced femoral neck fracture.

mentation rate; urinalysis, including electrophoresis for Bence-Jones proteins; serum protein electrophoresis; and serum levels of calcium, phosphate, and alkaline phosphatase.[62]

Treatment of the fracture begins in the ED by creating an environment conducive to rehabilitation.[9] The patient should first be made comfortable by positioning and the use of mild analgesics. Occasionally, orally administered muscle relaxants help relieve the acute pain. Patients should then be told that they have bruised a bone in the back and that, although the pain is severe now, it will quickly subside over the next few days. Their need to move as much as possible should also be emphasized. The patients should not be told that they have a "broken back." They must then be continuously encouraged to begin sitting, standing, and walking as soon as possible, within the limits of pain.[65] Because the fracture is stable, nothing is achieved by delaying rehabilitation. Moist heat, deep heat dia-

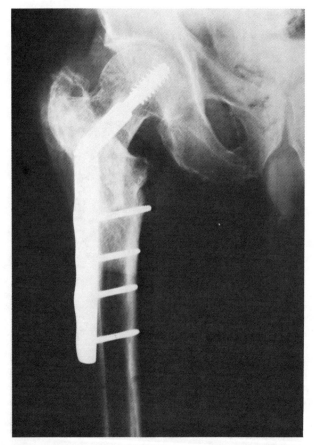

Figure 10–16B A compression plate and screw used for stable fixation of an intertrochanteric fracture of the femur.

thermy, massage, and transcutaneous electrical nerve stimulation may all be used to control pain and muscle spasm while minimizing the use of analgesics. The temporary use of a lumbosacral corset can assist ambulation and perhaps minimize the development of deformity.[43] Many patients can be managed on an outpatient basis, with hospitalization being reserved for those patients with severe pain or a poor home environment.

Other Fractures

There are an infinite number of fractures that may be seen from time to time in the elderly population. The general principles outlined earlier should be kept in mind when dealing with these problems. For example, fractures of the pelvis occur as the result of osteoporosis. These fractures, as are spinal fractures, are usually

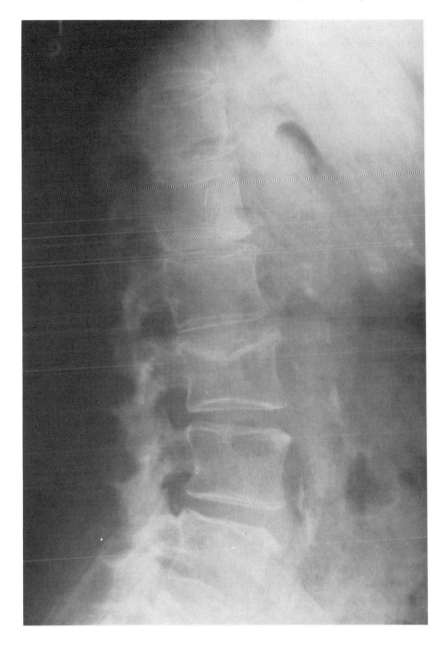

Figure 10–17 A compression fracture of the third lumbar vertebra that occurred spontaneously in the osteoporotic spine of an elderly woman.

stable and can be treated by early ambulation.[9,66] The use of cast bracing for the treatment of tibial plateau fractures[43,67] allows early ambulation of most of these patients (Figure 10–18A, B). Similarly, fractures about the foot can usually be treated adequately with compression bandages in lieu of plaster casts to provide unimpeded ambulation. Lightweight synthetic casting materials can also be used to provide immobilization of many limb fractures with minimal functional impairment.[68] Finally, impending pathologic fractures from metastases to bone should be treated by internal fixation before fracture to facilitate radiotherapy, relieve pain, and avoid the complex surgery often necessary for complete pathologic fractures.[9,68]

MANAGEMENT OF JOINT DISEASES

In evaluating patients with arthritic complaints it is necessary to perform a complete history and physical to assess for systemic diseases and to obtain a careful description of the evolution of the signs and symptoms. The initial laboratory assessment should include a complete blood count, sedimentation rate, rheumatoid factor, and serum uric acid level. Arthrocentesis is often necessary to confirm the diagnosis and to detect complicated problems, such as septic arthritis superimposed on a rheumatic or degenerated joint. Synovial fluid analysis should include cell count and gram stain, polarized light examination for urate crystals, and always a routine culture and sensitivity.[12] Radiologic assessment should also be performed with a minimum of two views at right angles to one another to aid in diagnosis.

The most common cause of joint problems are periarticular conditions, such as tendonitis and bursitis, most commonly around the shoulder, the greater trochanter of the hip, and the knee.[69] These periarticular inflammatory disorders should be distinguished from arthritis by physical examination. Periarticular problems result in fairly well localized pain and swelling in contrast to the more diffuse presentation of arthritis. In addition, a patient with tendonitis or bursitis usually has more pain on active range of motion of the involved limb than on passive range of motion. In contrast, when the joint itself is inflamed, active and passive motion are usually equally painful.[70] Patients with periarticular disorders should be treated with nonsteroidal anti-inflammatory drugs (NSAIDs) followed by gentle range-of-motion exercises to maintain limb mobility and function. Occasionally, local injections of anesthetic and corticosteroids are indicated to relieve acute tendonitis or bursitis.[12]

Degenerative Joint Disease

Degenerative arthritis is a universal problem in the elderly. Although it is found most commonly in weightbearing joints, it may occur in any joint following injury or simply as a slowly progressive degeneration from many years of use. The

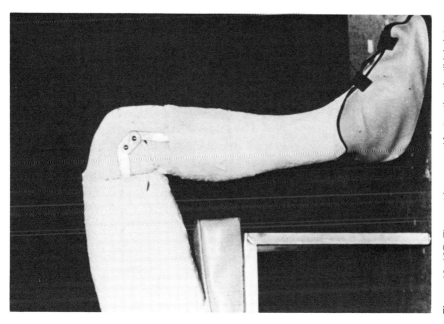

Figure 10–18B The cast-brace used for treating the tibial plateau fracture in Figure 10–18A.

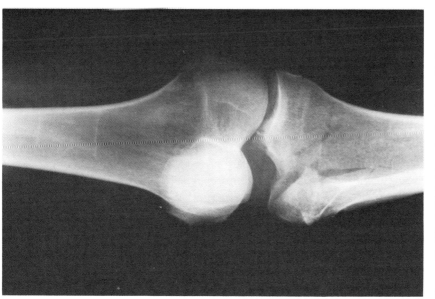

Figure 10–18A A tibial plateau fracture in an elderly woman that was satisfactorily treated by cast-bracing and early ambulation.

patient with degenerative arthritis has a gradual onset of low-grade aching pain in the joint associated with decreased range of motion and swelling. The pain is more severe with weather changes or with excessive use of the joint. On physical examination there is generalized joint tenderness, limited range of motion, and joint swelling. Occasionally, on motion of the joint, crepitus is felt as the roughened articular surfaces move against one another. Osteophytes, subchondral bone sclerosis, and narrowing of the joint space are the characteristic roentgenographic features of this disorder. The white blood cell count and sedimentation rate should be normal, and rheumatoid factor in the blood should be negative. Aspirated joint fluid should be sterile and have noninflammatory characteristics.[12,27,71]

Occasionally, particularly following excessive use of the joint, the patient has an acute exacerbation of symptoms with severe pain and swelling of the joint. At times it is difficult to distinguish this acute inflammatory reaction from gout and septic arthritis. In these cases it is necessary to aspirate the involved joint to establish the correct diagnosis so that proper treatment can be instituted.

The treatment of degenerative arthritis includes physical modalities, such as physical therapy, heat, and ultrasound; restriction of physical activities; and the use of ambulatory aids (cane or crutches) along with one of a variety of NSAIDs. These arthritis medications can cause gastrointestinal (GI) irritation. Prolonged use of these drugs occasionally causes chronic bleeding into the GI tract, which frequently produces secondary anemia, especially in the elderly. Thus, the use of these drugs should be confined to the treatment of acute joint pain.[27]

Rheumatoid Arthritis

The onset of rheumatoid arthritis is insidious, with fatigue, weakness, and joint and muscle pains preceding the appearance of specific joint swelling. Usually, several joints are involved, especially in the hands and feet, with further joint involvement spreading symmetrically. Morning stiffness becomes more prominent as the disease progresses. Physical examination reveals warmth, tenderness, and swelling about the joints, which usually develop significant deformities and contractures as the disease progresses. The presence of rheumatoid factor in the serum and an elevated sedimentation rate help confirm the diagnosis. Roentgenograms will show erosions about the joints and periarticular osteoporosis.[11,28] Synovial fluid is turbid with increased neutrophils (10,000–50,000/μl) and a decreased viscosity.

The initial treatment usually consists of salicylates or other NSAIDs. However, as the disease progresses, steroids, gold, antimetabolites, and other more potent drugs may be required to control the patient's symptoms. The progression of the disease and the side effects of the drugs can combine to produce severe osteoporosis, fragility of the skin, and a propensity toward infection, all of which are magnified in the elderly.[71]

Gout

Gout occurs commonly in the elderly. It usually develops over just a few hours with redness, heat, swelling, and intense pain in a single joint. Most frequently, gout affects the metatarsophalangeal joint of the great toe, but may also develop in the knee or ankle. Frequently, the attack begins at night. The laboratory findings of hyperuricemia and urate crystals in the synovial fluid help confirm the diagnosis. X-rays reveal asymmetrical swelling of the joint or subcortical cysts without erosion.

Initial treatment consists of indomethacin or phenylbutazone and temporary protection of the joint to control pain.[29,71]

Septic Arthritis

Any patient with chronic arthritis whose condition suddenly worsens or who has an acute exacerbation of the disease in any single joint may have septic arthritis because these diseased joints are more prone to develop infection.[72] Transient bacteremia, which occurs frequently in everyone, is considered to be the cause of septic arthritis in patients with arthritic joints. Although a normal joint can remove bacteria seeded there following an episode of bacteremia, a diseased joint cannot clear them as effectively, allowing a full-blown joint infection to develop. The mortality rate from this complication is high and is primarily the result of delayed diagnosis or inadequate treatment. The infected joint is painful, edematous, and erythematous and has a limited range of motion. A fever with a temperature greater than 101°F with a white blood cell count of greater than 10,000 cell/μl and a sedimentation rate greater than 20 should suggest the diagnosis of a septic joint. These findings, along with cell count and gram stain of the joint fluid, should provide adequate indication for hospitalization and beginning IV antibiotic therapy. Joint fluid should also be sent for culture and sensitivity tests. Surgical drainage or repeated needle aspiration is usually required to complete the treatment.

MANAGEMENT OF THE COMPLICATIONS OF PERIPHERAL VASCULAR DISEASE AND DIABETES

Diseases in the lower extremity caused by advanced atherosclerotic disease and diabetes are some of the most frequently occurring musculoskeletal problems seen in the elderly.[9,31,73,74] It is important that these diseases be diagnosed and treated promptly to prevent further complications, such as life-threatening infections or amputation. The problems most often seen are ischemia, gangrene, nonhealing ulcers, and infections.

Ischemic Pain

The patient with ischemic pain due to chronic arteriosclerotic vascular disease has a history of a gradual onset of burning pain and cramps in the foot and leg, which worsen at night and are aggravated by heat. The patient usually has intermittent claudication; cramping and pain in the legs are produced by such simple muscular activities as walking and resolve with rest. As the disease progresses the patient develops pain at rest and dependent rubor. The patient often has developed the habit of hanging the leg off of the bed at night to relieve the pain. Seventy-five percent of these patients are smokers.[31,33,73]

The ischemic foot is cool with diminished or absent peripheral pulses. The skin is pale and waxy without hair and with thickening and tubular curling of the nails. There is loss of subcutaneous tissue, with the skin drawn tightly over the bony prominences.

The sudden onset of severe, unilateral, unremitting leg and foot pain, which is usually associated with diminished pulses and foot pallor, should make one very suspicious of acute femoral or popliteal artery occlusion.[31]

In contrast, diabetic neuropathic pain usually consists of leg cramps, numbness, or tingling or stabbing pain of sudden onset. The foot may feel "dead" to the patient, giving the sensation of walking on air. There are various degrees of anesthesia (usually in a stocking-type distribution), diminished proprioception and vibratory sense, and decreased ankle reflexes. Both sensory and motor deficits are likely to be present bilaterally.[31,33,37]

Initial treatment of the arteriosclerotic ischemic limb consists of careful protection from further injury and further evaluation of the patient's potential for vascular reconstruction. The patient should be placed at bedrest, the heels should be protected with woolen booties, and lamb's wool should be placed between the toes. The foot can then be protected by a bed cradle.[74] If the ankle systolic pressure is less than 60 mm Hg, there is persistent ischemic pain at rest, and there is prominent dependent rubor or prolonged venous filling time (greater than 20 sec), the ischemia is probably irreversible, and an amputation is required. In many cases however, angiography should be performed to assess the potential for vascular reconstruction.[33,75,76]

Acute femoral or popliteal artery occlusion is a surgical emergency, which can often be corrected by removal of an obstructing blood clot or by bypassing the diseased vessel. Treatment must be started within a few hours to prevent gangrene of the extremity distal to the site of vessel obstruction.

Diabetic neuropathic pain is best treated with tranquilizers and certain mood-elevating drugs. Preservation of the ischemic or neuropathic foot over the long term requires meticulous attention to foot hygiene and protection from injury.[33,37,77]

Gangrene

Ischemic gangrene starts as a purple-black, painless discoloration of the distal portion of one or more toes. The lesion may remain localized or spread proximally. If pain, erythema, moisture, lymphangitic streaking, or a poorly demarcated border are seen, an infection is probably present, and emergency amputation is usually necessary.[31,33] The best management of a gangrenous extremity is amputation at the most distal point at which healing is likely to occur. For example, gangrene confined to a digit can often be successfully treated by amputation of the toe or ray resection of the metatarsal. If the gangrene extends onto the dorsum of the foot and pulses about the ankle are strong, a transmetatarsal amputation usually heals successfully. If ankle pulses are weak or absent, a below-the-knee amputation is necessary. Oakley et al.[31] have shown that delaying amputation for gangrene is detrimental to the patient and should be avoided.

Nonhealing Ulcers

The neuropathic ulcer ("mal perforans") is a unique problem of the elderly diabetic patient.[31] It is characteristically an ulcer within a thickened callus under a bony prominence in the foot. The ankle pulses are usually adequate, and the ulcer has abundant blood supply with rich granulation tissue but refuses to heal. Treatment consists of meticulous care of the callus and removal of the pressure from the underlying bony prominence. Pressure can be relieved by the use of extra depth orthopedic shoes or a lightweight short leg walking cast.[33] More severe ulcers may require excision and grafting.[36]

Infections

Infection is a common foot problem in patients with peripheral vascular insufficiency and diabetes. The diabetic patient's propensity to develop foot ulcers, the impaired ability to heal soft tissue lesions, and the impaired peripheral circulation combine to make lower extremity infections a particularly common and often difficult problem to treat. An infection may cause a dorsal phlegmon, plantar abscess, interdigital infection, osteomyelitis, or septic arthritis. Dorsal phlegmon is a nonsuppurative infection of the dorsum of the foot that produces local edema, erythema, and systemic signs of infection. Often it progresses rapidly to necrotizing fasciitis of the entire limb, a life-threatening problem. Plantar abscesses develop in the lateral, medial, or central plantar spaces, usually as a direct spread from a cutaneous lesion (usually a chronic, nonhealing ulcer). These abscesses can dissect along tendon sheaths and ascend into the leg or progress to septic arthritis or osteomyelitis.

The same general principles apply to the management of all types of infection. Prompt incision and drainage with collection of samples for culture are of primary importance. Proper broad-spectrum antibiotic coverage for the most likely causative organisms is also imperative.[36] Roentgenographic assessment during the course of treatment is necessary to detect osteomyelitis. Repeat attempts at incision and debridement of a deep infection are rarely successful in saving the limb. Thus, if prompt healing does not follow the initial drainage, amputation of the infected part is usually necessary.[31]

MANAGEMENT OF THE GERIATRIC AMPUTEE

The mortality rate of elderly patients after amputation is quite high. Approximately 35% die within 6 months and 50% in 2 years.[74,78] This is primarily due to the poor general physical condition of the patients who have diseases requiring amputation. However, Hyland and co-workers[74] point out that the fate of many geriatric amputees can be improved by early diagnosis and treatment of ischemic limb disease and early intensive physical rehabilitation. This concept has led to the development of lightweight prosthetic devices and early walking aids,[13,74,78] which allow even debilitated and weakened amputees to ambulate (Figure 10–19). The patient can begin exercising in bed within a few days after amputation and begin ambulating within 2 weeks. This early mobilization prevents most of the complications of immobilization, as well as maintaining and improving muscle tone and decreasing stump problems. Thus, although the life expectancy may be short, the quality of life can be greatly improved for those

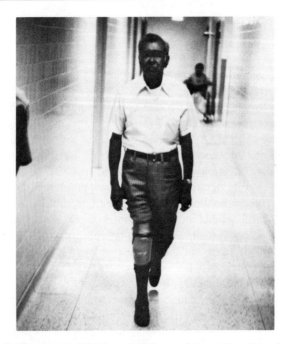

Figure 10–19 A 62-year-old diabetic ambulating well 3 months after a below-the-knee amputation.

patients in whom independent ambulation can be retained following amputation.[13,78]

REFERENCES

1. Frame B: Aspects of osteoporosis. *Transition* 1:17–36, 1983.

2. Knowelden J, Buhr A, Dunbar O: Incidence of fractures in persons over 35 years of age: A report to the MRC working party on fractures in the elderly. *Br J Prev Soc Med* 18:130–141, 1964.

3. Jensen G, Christian C, Boesen J, et al: Epidemiology of postmenopausal spine and long bone fractures. *Clin Orthop* 166:75–81, 1982.

4. Rodstein M: Accidents among the aged: Incidence, causes and prevention. *Br J Chron Dis* 17:515–526, 1964.

5. Beals R: Survival following hip fracture: Long follow-up of 607 patients. *J Chron Dis* 25:235–244, 1972.

6. Melton L III, Riggs B: Epidemiology of age-related fractures, in Avioli L (ed): *The Osteoporotic Syndrome: Detection, Prevention, and Treatment.* New York, Grune and Stratton, 1983, pp 45–72.

7. Owens R, Melton J III, Gallagher J, et al: National cost of acute care of hip fractures associated with osteoporosis. *Clin Orthop* 150:172–176, 1980.

8. Clark A: Factors in fracture of the female femur: A clinical study of the environmental, physical, medical and preventative aspects of the injury. *Gerontol Clin* 10:257–270, 1968.

9. Devas M: Fractures in the elderly: Introduction, in Devas, M (ed): *Geriatric Orthopaedics.* New York, Academic Press, 1977, pp 99–114.

10. Wild D, Nayak U, Isaacs B: How dangerous are falls in old people at home? *Br Med J* 282:266–268, 1986.

11. Duthie R, Bentley G (eds): Arthritis and rheumatic diseases, in *Mercer's Orthopaedic Surgery*, ed 8. Baltimore, University Park Press, 1983, pp 610–716.

12. Preslar A, Heckman J: Emergency department evaluation of the swollen joint. *Emerg Clin North Am.* 2:425–440, 1984.

13. Devas M: The geriatric amputee, in Devas M (ed): *Geriatric Orthopaedics.* New York, Academic Press, 1977, pp 175–183.

14. Attenborough C: Fractures near the hip, in Devas M (ed): *Geriatric Orthopaedics.* New York, Academic Press, 1977, pp 115–123.

15. Corcoran P: Disability consequences of bed rest, in Stolov W, Clowers M (eds): *Handbook of Severe Disability*, US Dept of Education, Rehabilitation Services Administration, publication no. 017-090-00054-2, 1981, pp 55–63.

16. Spencer H, Lender M: The skeletal system, in Rossman I (ed): *Clinical Geriatrics*, ed 2. Philadelphia, JB Lippincott Co, 1979, pp 460–476.

17. Aloia J: Estrogen and exercise in prevention and treatment of osteoporosis. *Geriatrics* 37:81–85, 1982.

18. Palma L: Postmenopausal osteoporosis and estrogen therapy: Who should be treated? *J Fam Prac* 14:355–359, 1982.

19. Raisz L: Osteoporosis. *J Am Geriatr Soc* 30:127–138, 1982.

20. Hutchinson T, Polansky S, Feinstein A: Post-menopausal estrogens protect against fractures of hip and distal radius: A case-control study. *Lancet* 2:705–709, 1979.

21. Weiss N, Ure C, Ballard J, et al: Decreased risk of fractures of the hip and lower forearm with post-menopausal use of estrogen. *N Engl J Med* 303:1195–1208, 1980.

22. Jensen F, Christiansen C, Travsbol I: Treatment of postmenopausal osteoporosis: A controlled therapeutic trial comparing oestrogen/gestogen, 1,25 dihydroxy-vitamin D_3 and calcium. *Clin Endocrinol* 16:515–524, 1982.

23. Krane S, Holick M: Metabolic bone disease, in Isselbacher K, Adams R, Braunwald E, et al (eds): *Harrison's Principles of Internal Medicine*, ed 9. New York, McGraw-Hill Book Co, 1981, pp 1849–1860.

24. Baryel U: Common metabolic disorders of the skeleton in aging, in Reichel W (ed): *Clinical Aspects of Aging*, ed 2. Baltimore, Williams & Wilkins, 1983, pp 360–370.

25. Alexanian R: Plasma cell neoplasms and related disorders, in Isselbacher K, Adams R, Braunwald E, et al (eds): *Harrison's Principles of Internal Medicine*, ed 9. New York, McGraw-Hill Book Co, 1981, pp 333–338.

26. Wilson J: Pathological fractures, in Wilson J (ed): *Watson-Jones Fractures and Joint Injuries*, ed 6. New York, Churchill Livingstone, 1982, pp 1207–1280.

27. Mannik M, Gilliland B: Degenerative joint disease, in Isselbacher K, Adams R, Braunwald E, et al (eds): *Harrison's Principles of Internal Medicine*, ed 9. New York, McGraw-Hill Book Co, 1981, pp 1894–1896.

28. Gilliland B, Mannik M: Rheumatoid arthritis, in Isselbacher K, Adams R, Braunwald E, et al (eds): *Harrison's Principles of Internal Medicine*, ed 9. New York, McGraw-Hill Book Co, 1981, pp 1872–1880.

29. Kelley W: Gout and other disorders of purine metabolism, in Isselbacher K, Adams R, Braunwald E, et al (eds): *Harrison's Principles of Internal Medicine*, ed 9. New York, McGraw-Hill Book Co, 1981, pp 479–487.

30. Hirschmann J, Gilliland B: Osteomyelitis and infectious arthritis, in Isselbacher K, Adams R, Braunwald E, et al (eds): *Harrison's Principles of Internal Medicine*, ed 9. New York, McGraw-Hill Book Co, 1981.

31. Oakley W, Catterall R, Martin M: Aetology and management of lesions of the feet in diabetes. *Br Med J* 2:953–957, 1956.

32. Ellenberg M: Interplay of autonomic neuropathy and arteriosclerosis. *NY State J Med* 82:917–921, 1982.

33. Owen J Jr: How to treat the diabetic foot. *Diabetes* 37:57–69, 1982.

34. Newman J: Non-infective disease of the diabetic foot. *J Bone Joint Surg* 63-B:593–596, 1981.

35. Arenson D, Sherwood C, Wilson R: Neuropathy, angiopathy and sepsis in the diabetic foot: I. Neuropathy. *J Am Podiatry Assoc* 71:618–624, 1981.

36. Arenson D, Sherwood C, Wilson R: Neuropathy, angiopathy and sepsis in the diabetic foot: III. Sepsis. *J Am Podiatry Assoc* 72:35–40, 1982.

37. DiPalma J: Therapy of diabetic peripheral neuropathy. *Diabetes* 37:43–46, 1982.

38. Harrington K: The use of methylmethacrylate as an adjunct in the internal fixation of unstable comminuted intertrochanteric fractures in osteoporotic patients. *J Bone Joint Surg* 57-A:744–750, 1975.

39. Habermann E: Orthopaedic aspects of the lower extremities, in Rossman I (ed): *Clinical Geriatrics*, ed 2. Philadelphia, JB Lippincott Co, 1979, pp 477–501.

40. Lewallen R, Pritchard D, Sim F: Treatment of pathologic fractures or impending fractures of the humerus with Rush rods and methylmethacrylate. *Clin Orthop* 166:193–198, 1982.

41. Rose S, Melton L III, Morrey B, et al: Epidemiologic features of humeral fractures. *Clin Orthop* 168:24–30, 1982.

42. Neer C: Displaced proximal humeral fractures: I. Classification and evaluation. *J Bone Joint Surg* 52-A:1077–1089, 1970.

43. Freehofer A: Injuries to the skeletal system of older persons, in Reichel W (ed): *Clinical Aspects of Aging*, ed 2. Baltimore, Williams & Wilkins, 1983, pp 371–383.

44. Neer C: Displaced proximal humeral fractures: II. Treatment of three-part and four-part displacement. *J Bone Joint Surg* 52-A:1090–1103, 1970.

45. Lee C, Hansen H: Post-traumatic avascular necrosis of the humeral head in displaced proximal humeral fractures. *J Trauma* 21:788–791, 1981.

46. Kessel L: Injuries of the shoulder, in Wilson J (ed): *Watson-Jones Fractures and Joint Injuries*, ed 6. New York, Churchill Livingstone, 1982, pp 513–571.

47. Owen R, Melton L III, Johnson K, et al: Incidence of Colles' fracture in a North American community. *Am J Pub Health* 72:605–607, 1982.

48. Benjamin A: Injuries of the forearm, in Wilson J (ed): *Watson-Jones Fractures and Joint Injuries*, ed 6. New York, Churchill Livingstone, 1982, pp 650–709.

49. Pool C: Colles fracture: A prospective study of treatment. *J Bone Joint Surg* 55-B:540–544, 1973.

50. Sarmiento A, Pratt G, Berry N, et al: Colles' fractures: Functional bracing in supination. *J Bone Joint Surg* 57-A:311–317, 1975.

51. Van der Linden W, Ericson R: Colles' fracture. *J Bone Joint Surg* 63-A:1285–1288, 1981.

52. Helal B, Chen S, Iwegbu G: Rupture of the extensor pollicis longus tendon in undisplaced Colles' type of fracture. *Hand* 14:41–47, 1982.

53. Devas M: Geriatric orthopaedics. *Br Med J* 1:190–192, 1974.

54. Lewis D: Fracture of neck of the femur: Changing incidence. *Br Med J* 283:1217–1220, 1981.

55. Ceder L, Elmquist D, Svensson S: Cardiovascular and neurological function in elderly patients sustaining a fracture of the neck of the femur. *J Bone Joint Surg* 63-B:560–566, 1981.

56. Mikhail S, Sonn M, Lawton A: Optimism in the management of hip fracture in elderly patients. *J Am Geriatr Soc* 26:39–42, 1978.

57. Sloan J, Holloway G: Fractured neck of the femur: The cause of the fall? *Injury* 13:230–232, 1982.

58. Devas M: Stress fractures of the femoral neck. *J Bone Joint Surg* 47-B:728–738, 1965.

59. Wilson J: Injuries of the hip, in Wilson J (ed): *Watson-Jones Fractures and Joint Injuries*, ed 6. New York, Churchill Livingstone, 1982, pp 878–973.

60. Devas M: Fractures in the elderly. *Geront Clin* 6:347–359, 1964.

61. Clawson D, Melcher P: Fractures and dislocations of the hip, in Rockwood C, Green D (eds): *Fractures*. Philadelphia, JB Lippincott Co, 1975, pp 1012–1074.

62. Sheldon J: On the natural history of falls in old age. *Br Med J* 2:1685–1695, 1960.

63. Brower T: Pathologic fractures, in Rockwood C, Green D (eds): *Fractures*. Philadelphia, JB Lippincott Co, 1975, pp 243–263.

64. Rowe C, Sorbie C: Fractures of the spine in the aged. *Clin Orthop* 26:34–49, 1963.

65. Devas M: Fractures in the elderly—General considerations, in Devas M (ed): *Geriatric Orthopaedics*. New York, Academic Press, 1977, pp 125–151.

66. Melton L III, Sampson J, Morrey B, et al: Epidemiologic features of pelvic fractures. *Clin Orthop* 155:43–47, 1981.

67. Scotland T, Wardlaw A: The use of cast-bracing as treatment for fractures of the tibial plateau. *J Bone Joint Surg* 63-B:575–578, 1981.

68. Huckstep R: Early mobilization and rehabilitation in fractures and orthopaedic conditions. *Aust NZ J Surg* 47:344–353, 1977.

69. Calin A, Fries J: Polyarthralgia and polyarthritis. *Compr Ther* 2:11–16, 1976.

70. Marino C, Greenwald R: Acute arthritis. *Med Clin North Am* 65:177–188, 1981.

71. Grob D: Prevalent joint diseases in older persons, in Reichel W (ed): *Clinical Aspects of Aging*, ed 2. Baltimore, Williams & Wilkins, 1983, pp 344–359.

72. Gristina G, Rovere G, Shoji H: Spontaneous arthritis complicating rheumatoid arthritis. *J Bone Joint Surg* 56-A:1180–1184, 1974.

73. Brodibb H: Diabetes and the geriatric orthopaedic patient, in Devas M (ed): *Geriatric Orthopaedics*. New York, Academic Press, 1977, pp 49–56.

74. Hyland J, Nolan D, Browne H, et al: Factors influencing the outcome of major lower limb amputations. *Irish Med J* 75:58–60, 1982.

75. Shanik D, Atkinson P: Limb salvage following digital amputation. *Irish Med J* 75:52–53, 1982.

76. Wheelock F: Transmetatarsal amputations and arterial surgery in diabetic patients. *N Engl J Med* 264:316–320, 1961.

77. Helfond A: Foot health for the elderly patient, in Reichel W (ed): *Clinical Aspects of Aging*, ed 2. Baltimore, Williams & Wilkins, 1983, pp 384–395.

78. Devas M: Early walking of geriatric amputees. *Br Med J* 1:394–396, 1971.

11

Dental-Oral-Maxillofacial Injuries

Harold F. Bosco, DMD, FACD

Injuries to the oral and maxillofacial structures represent 12% of all injuries seen in individuals 65 years old and over. What is often a minor injury in a young patient turns out to be serious and often fatal in the older age group.

Many predisposing factors contribute to dental, oral, and maxillofacial injuries in the aged. Both local and general physical problems and socioeconomic factors contribute to these injuries. General physical problems include decreased reflexes, postural hypotension, lack of adequate mobility and agility, decreased visual and auditory acuity, early senile dementia of the Alzheimer-type syndrome, and osteoporosis.

Local factors are the lack of natural teeth and atrophy of the alveolar bony structures of the jaws (Figure 11–1). Many of the elderly wear prosthetic appliances, which act as secondary missiles during trauma and cause much soft tissue damage (Figure 11–2). Tooth structures in the aged are very brittle and fracture easily. In addition, an increase in air spaces diminishes the strength of the bony structures of the face. Residual bone pathology in the jaws also predispose the aged to easy fractures, such as retained root fragments, teeth, and osteolytic bone lesions (Figure 11–3).

Many socioeconomic factors contribute to dental, oral, and maxillofacial injuries. Elderly people often live alone and therefore attempt to do activities that are beyond their capabilities. Driving, shopping, housekeeping, and cleaning can lead to injury. The interval between time of injury and the time that treatment is received is often quite lengthy. Consequently, mortality and morbidity are increased. Side effects of drugs, which the aged take for a variety of medical conditions, must also be considered as causative factors.

EVALUATION AT THE ACCIDENT SCENE

Preliminary evaluation at the scene of the accident must be done systematically and carefully. Proper early action greatly reduces the morbidity and mortality in this age group of patients.

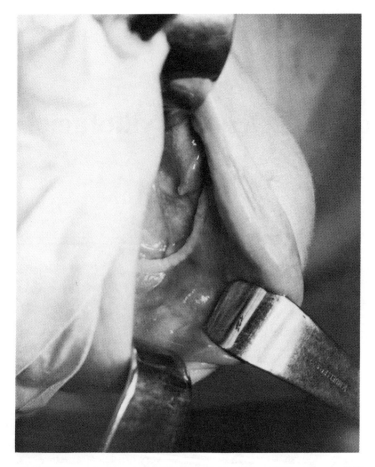

Figure 11–1 Note extensive atrophy of this patient's mandible, which predisposed this woman to easy fracture of the mandible.

The primary consideration is evaluation of the general condition of the patient. When checking the patient for adequate respiration, one must look carefully for obstructions secondary to fragmented prosthetic appliances or dental structures. In many cases of fractured jaws, a posterior displacement of the proximal segments can cause obstruction of the airway (Figure 11–4). In these cases, the tongue and entire lower jaw may be clamped and pulled forward to improve breathing. Often times a safety pin inserted through the tongue and then drawn forward and attached to some of the clothing greatly aids respiration.

After adequate consideration and evaluation of the patient's respiration, attention should be given to other surgical emergencies, such as abdominal and intracranial damage. The EMS personnel at the scene of the accident should obtain some information either from the patient, neighbors, friends, or witnesses of the acci-

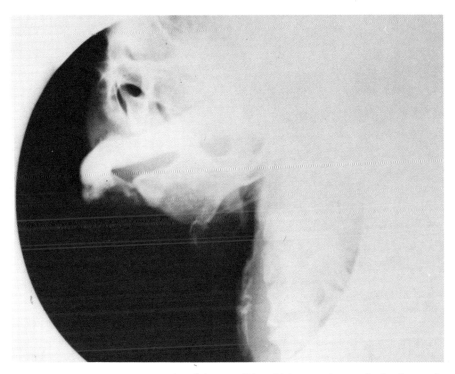

Figure 11–2 Note extensive atrophy of the mandible, which caused an earlier fracture and subsequent complication of osteomyelitis.

___

dent. It is very helpful to know the nature of the blow or the force of the blow to the head or to the face. The past medical history, if obtainable, can be very beneficial. It would certainly be advantageous to know whether the patient is a diabetic, has a history of cardiac disease, or is on medication. Close observation, inspection, and examination of the head, ears, eyes, nose, face, mouth, and neck should be done next.

The head should be observed closely for injury to the scalp and skull. Loss of consciousness, dizziness, nausea, and headaches must be noted because they can indicate intracranial damage. While inspecting the patient's head, one should look for the Raccoon sign—a bilateral periorbital ecchymosis usually resulting from fracture of the maxilla involving the ethmoids and cribriform plate area—and the Battle sign, ecchymosis in the mastoid area that often indicates a fracture of the base of the skull.

Trauma to the ears involving the mandible and mandibular condyle and to the tympanic portion of the temporal bone leads to autological manifestations, including hemorrhage from the ear, loss of hearing, and injury to the 7th cranial nerve. The 7th cranial nerve is a motor nerve controlling muscle action on the affected side.

314 GERIATRIC EMERGENCIES

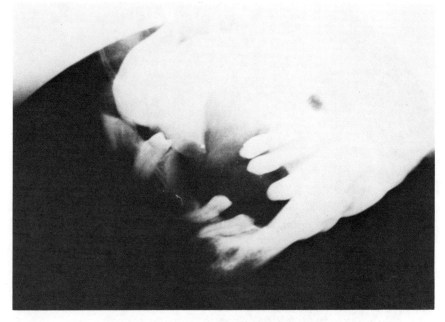

Figure 11–3 Note the loss of teeth in this 65-year-old individual. There is a retained tooth in the line of the fracture.

The eyes must be observed for diplopia, subconjunctival hemorrhage, and tenderness in the orbital rim. These signs are pathognomonic of zygomatic-maxillary complex fractures. Other signs are nasal bleeding and crepitus of the tissue in the area because of the presence of air resulting from fracture of the antral wall. The pupils may be dilated and fixed, indicating a serious prognosis with extremely high mortality. The 3rd, 4th, and 6th cranial nerves are often involved in fractures of the orbit, and injuries to these nerves are often manifested by abnormal eye mobility. Nystagmus—involuntary eye movements—may be indicative of brainstem injury. Blindness resulting from fractures through the optic nerve area have often been reported. Diplopia (double vision) with endophthalmus indicates blow-out fractures of the floor of the orbit, in which much of the orbital contents are found in the maxillary sinus.

Lid lacerations, corneal lacerations, and penetrating foreign bodies of the eye also are seen and are extremely painful wounds. The care of these wounds is discussed elsewhere in this text.

The nose should be checked for fluid discharge. If clear fluid is noted, one should suspect a leakage of cerebrospinal fluid resulting from a fracture of the skull in a cribriform plate. If this fluid is noted the nose should not be packed. Nasal fractures are the most common of all facial fractures. Deformity, crepitus, and ecchymosis are the most common signs.

Figure 11–4 A partial denture, which can cause secondary damage to the mouth in an elderly trauma victim. Prosthetic appliances can also cause respiratory obstruction.

The face should be examined for asymmetry, crepitus, and hematomas (Figure 11–5). Areas of anesthesia result from compression or tears to one of the three divisions of the 5th cranial nerve. Anesthesia is most commonly noted in the infraorbital area, lip, and chin. One should look for emphysematous tissues that crackle on palpation and for occlusion of teeth. Malocclusion is the most common finding in jaw fractures.

The mouth must be observed for hematomas, lacerations, swelling, and perforation. Specific attention should be given to the lips, cheeks, tongue, floor of the mouth, palate, gingival tissues, and the oropharynx. Tongue lacerations bleed profusely, and the tongue may fall back to cause obstruction of the airway.

The neck must also be observed for penetrating wounds that may enter the oral cavity and cause injuries to the jaw and dental structures.

SPECIFIC INJURIES TO TEETH, SUPPORTING STRUCTURES OF TEETH, AND JAWS

Teeth

Teeth may be completely avulsed, partially avulsed or luxated, impacted, displaced, or fractured. Bridges and dentures may be fractured, displaced, or lost.

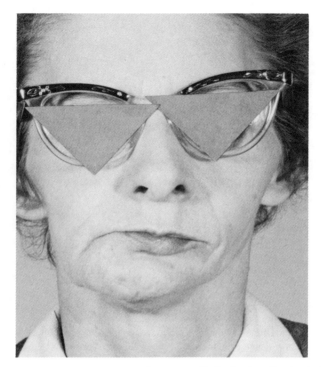

Figure 11–5 Note facial asymmetry secondary to mandibular fracture. The jaw is shifted to the right.

Avulsed teeth or teeth that have been completely removed may often be found at the scene of the accident. If possible, they should be placed in a wet sponge and brought to the ED with the patient as they can be reimplanted in many cases. Partially avulsed teeth or displaced teeth can be repositioned and splinted or wired into position. Teeth that are impacted into the bone can be brought down into correct position and wired or splinted.

Artificial full or partial dentures must be recovered from the scene of the accident. These dentures are often used to reduce and maintain fractured maxillas or mandibles. Even when they are broken, they can be utilized in the repair of the injury. It is very important to save all parts of teeth and dentures!

Dental injuries in the elderly are classified as Type I, II, III, and IV (Figure 11–6):

- Type I: involvement of tooth enamel only
- Type II: involvement of enamel and underlying dentin
- Type III: involvement of enamel, dentin, and pulp
- Type IV: fractures of the tooth in the root area

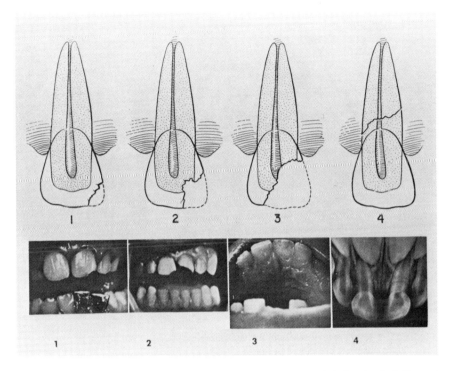

Figure 11–6 Four types of fractures involving teeth: *1*: Enamel only is involved; *2*: Enamel and dentine are involved; *3*: Enamel, dentine, and pulp are involved; *4*: Fracture below the gum line and in the bone.

Source: Reprinted from "Traumatic Injuries of the Teeth and Alveolar Process" by ML Hale in *Textbook of Oral and Maxillofacial Surgery*, 6th ed, by GO Kruger (ed), with permission of The CV Mosby Company, © 1984.

These dental injuries are not life threatening. They are usually treated by the family dentist at a later date.

Mandibular Fractures

The deformity of the mandible is often dependent on the direction of the force, the location of the fracture, the direction of the line fracture site, and the muscles involved (Figure 11–7). Mandibular fractures are classified as simple, greenstick, compound, comminuted, and compound comminuted.

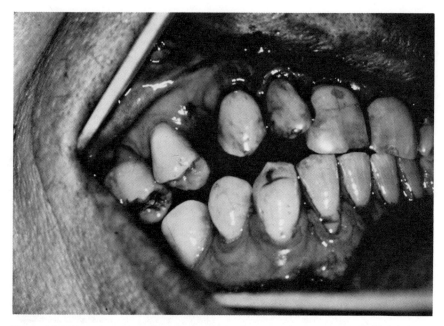

Figure 11–7 Note the malocclusion, the most common finding in jaw fractures. Also note the gingival bleeding that results.

Malocclusion is the single most important finding in mandibular fractures. It results from displaced segments of the mandible, which contain teeth and muscle pull. Abnormal mobility, which is determined by bimanual examination of the mandible; pain on movement of segments with oral palpation or function; disability in function; trismus; and lacerations and bleeding at the floor of the mouth are other characteristics of fractured mandibles. Crepitus can be felt or heard on palpation in a fractured mandible, resulting from the ends of the fractured bone rubbing against each other. Anesthesia occurs when a mandibular fracture is located in the area of a nerve. In addition, ecchymosis is usually indicative of a fracture. On examination oral odor (bad breath) is a sign of stagnant blood or early infection.

All mandible fractures must be confirmed by the following x-ray films: PA views, right lateral view, and left lateral view.

Maxillary Fractures

There are four types of maxillary fractures: the Horizontal LeFort I, Transverse LeFort II, Pyramidal LeFort III, and the Alveolar (fracture) process (Figure 11–8).

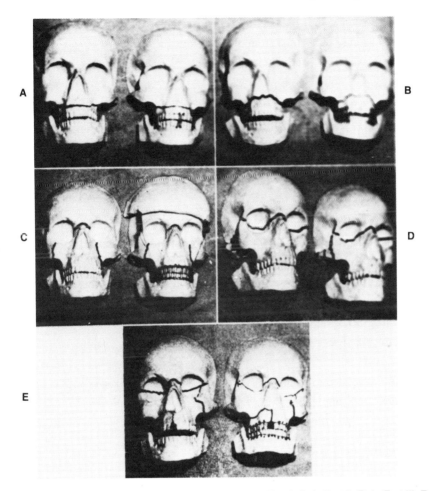

Figure 11–8 Three types of maxillary fractures **A, B**: LeFort I; **C**: LeFort II; **D**: LeFort III; **E**: LeFort III and complex zygomatic-maxillary fracture.

LeFort I Horizontal Fracture

The LeFort I Horizontal Fracture presents bilaterally above the alveolar process of teeth through the floor of the maxillary sinuses. Both perpendicular palates of pterygoid are fractured. Signs of this fracture are as follows:

- malocclusion open bite resulting from muscle pull on posterior aspects of maxilla
- mobility of entire maxilla on palpation
- crepitus (air in tissue) resulting from cracks in the sinus walls

- obstructed airway if the maxilla is displaced posteriorly
- nose bleeding (epistaxis) from blood in maxilla sinuses
- ecchymosis, intra- and extraorally.

LeFort II Fracture

The LeFort II fractures of the maxilla are pyramidal in shape and involve nasal, lacrimal, ethmoid, and sphenoid bones. Signs and symptoms of these fractures include the following:

- subconjunctival hemorrhage
- subscleral hemorrhage
- ecchymosis of eyelids with swelling of facial tissues
- bleeding from the nostril
- crepitus in facial tissues resulting from air in maxilla and sinuses
- mobility of midface
- dishpan face profile
- neurologic signs resulting from intracranial bleeding or swelling

X-ray studies needed to confirm this type of fracture are the PA view of the skull and the right and left lateral view of the skull, as well as a Waters view and CT scan.

LeFort III Transverse Fracture

In the LeFort III transverse fracture the entire face is displaced from the cranium. Nasolacrimal and ethmoidal, zygoma, and the maxillary bones are separated from the cranium. Signs and symptoms of this type of fracture are as follows:

- ecchymosis of eyelids (Raccoon signs)
- diplopia (double vision)
- mobility of maxilla
- crepitus
- malocclusion
- nasal bleeding
- rhinorrhea/cerebrospinal fluid leaks/nasal discharge
- loss of vision due to fractures involving the optic nerve.

Alveolar Fracture

In alveolar fractures there are segments of alveolar bone, with the teeth being mobile. Malocclusion results with laceration of gingival tissues (Figure 11–9).

Trimalar Fractures

Signs of a zygomatic-maxillary complex fracture (trimalar fracture) include facial swelling with distortion, flatness of face, and ecchymosis with swelling of the face. In addition, mandibular limitation of motion due to coronoid process impingement onto the zygomatic arch and subconjunctival hemorrhage with flaming red flare are seen in the outer corners of the eyes. Additional signs of a zygomatic-maxillary complex fracture are nasal bleeding, emphysematous tissue, diplopia, crepitus, and anesthesia of the intraorbital nerve.

The two most important signs of a zygomatic arch fracture are (1) depression and deformation of the face with dimple effects and (2) trismus due to coronoid process impingement of the zygoma (Figure 11–10).

FACIAL INJURIES

Soft tissue wounds resulting from foreign bodies, burns, lacerations, abrasions, and contusions often occur in oral injuries. Penetrating wounds and burns of the

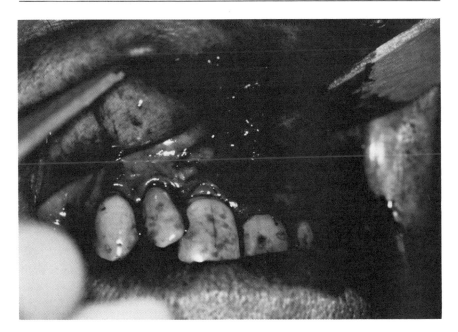

Figure 11–9 Laceration of gingival mucosa in an alveolar fracture of the maxilla.

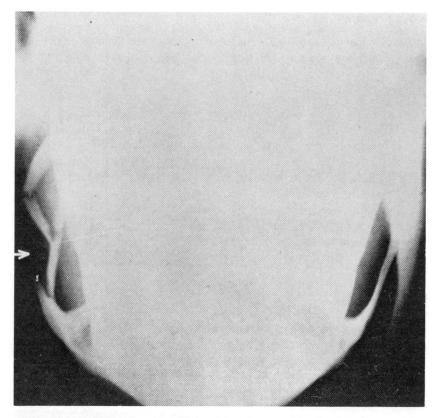

Figure 11–10 Roentgenogram showing a fracture of the zygomatic arch.

face are described in other chapters in this text. There are, however, a number of other anatomic structures specific to the oral and facial area that must be considered when trauma victims are seen. The protection and preservation of these structures are important in minimizing morbidity.

Facial Nerves

The motor nerve that controls facial movements may be affected by facial lacerations or tears in the parotid gland region or ears.

The trigeminal nerve, the branches of which supply sensitivity to the lips and other facial structures, is often affected in facial lacerations. Areas to observe are in the supraorbital, infraorbital, and the mental area of the chin.

The parotid (Stenson duct) may secrete saliva when lacerated. Also fistula formations are often seen in knife injuries to the face.

In cases of severe hemorrhage the following four areas should be compressed:

1. carotid artery pressure against carotid notch of cervical vertebra, which may help control hemorrhage from mouth, nostrils, and face
2. external facial artery and vein pressure placed ¾ inch from the angle of the jaw
3. pressure on both supra- and infraorbital areas, which contain vessels that may bleed profusely
4. large superficial vessels, which may be clamped with care to avoid damaging motor or sensory nerves (Figure 11–11).

GUIDELINES FOR EMERGENCY CARE

For the emergency personnel who are the first people to arrive at the scene of an accident, the following list of nine "Do's and Don'ts" must be adhered to after

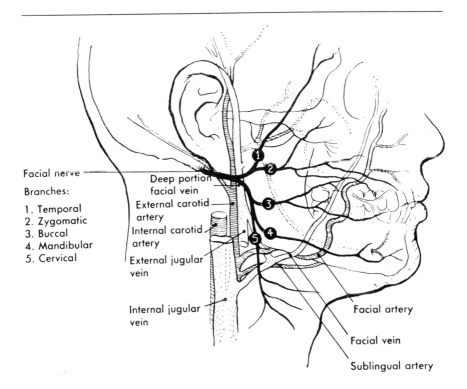

Figure 11–11 General distribution of facial nerve, arterial blood supply to face, and venous return from face.

Source: Reprinted from "Traumatic Injuries of the Teeth and Alveolar Process" by ML Hale in *Textbook of Oral and Maxillofacial Surgery,* 6th ed, by GO Kruger (ed), with permission of The CV Mosby Company, © 1984.

basic emergency measures have been performed. Proper early emergency care can often make the difference between life and death and can produce better cosmetic results.

1. Remove foreign bodies, teeth, and broken dentures from the oral cavity.
2. Save all parts of tissue, bone, teeth, dentures, and parts of dentures. Put teeth in wet gauze.
3. Replace flaps of tissue to normal positions.
4. Support bony structures with temporary splints (Barton ace bandages).
5. Apply pressure to areas to control bleeding. Clamp off vessels with hemostats; be careful not to tear much soft tissue present or damage vital structures, eg, nerves.
6. Do not pack the nasal cavity to stop bleeding in LeFort II and LeFort III type fractures as doing so may lead to cranial infections.
7. Suture the tongue to clothing to maintain an airway.
8. Perform an emergency tracheostomy-cricoid type with tube if necessary.
9. In all cases of maxillofacial injuries, suspect cranial and cervical vertebrae injuries. Support and move the head gently and with great care.

SUGGESTED READINGS

Bosco HF: Reconstruction of mandible. *J Oral Surg, Oral Med & Oral Path* 12:663–667, 1960.

Creighton JL, Dychtwald K: *Alternative, Therapies and Management of Stress and Catastrophic Diseases*, 1981, pp 307–317.

Glick SM: Preventive medicine in geriatrics. *Med Clin N Am* 60: 1976.

Hale Merle L: Traumatic injuries of the teeth and alveolar process, in Kruger GO (ed): *Textbook of Oral and Maxillofacial Surgery*, ed 6. St. Louis, CV Mosby Co, 1984.

Hogue CC: *Injury in Late Life*. Washington, DC: National Institute on Aging, 1982.

Shafer N: Trauma to the elderly. *Med Trial Tech Quart* 25:187–203, 1978.

12

Genitourinary Emergencies in the Elderly

James J. Jacobson, MD

Distressing symptoms and anxiety characterize the presentation of most genitourinary problems in the elderly, in whom these problems are most common. Urinary retention, infections, and neoplasms with bleeding are all seen with increasing frequency as the population ages. Bleeding may not be associated with pain or discomfort, but it causes extreme anxiety and demands a diagnostic evaluation and explanation. In the intellectually diminished elderly, it may be difficult to pinpoint symptoms, and a simple problem, such as a ureteral calculus, may become a diagnostic dilemma. Other diseases increasingly mimic genitourinary symptoms, the most serious of which is the leaking aortic aneurysm.

Congenital defects are usually discovered long before the sixth decade, but obstruction at the ureteropelvic junction is not unknown, and even testicular torsion has been reported in this age group. Renal and ureteral anomalies can lead to the silent formation of calculi over a period of many years; these calculi may suddenly become symptomatic late in life.

Recent surgery may lead to specific acute problems that cause a return visit to the ED. Past surgery causes anatomic changes that may lead to specific problems, obscure an otherwise simple diagnosis, or create difficulties in treatment. Removal of the bladder with diversion of the urine to an ileal conduit is a major urological operation for cancer and is typical of other major surgical procedures (Figure 12–1). When evaluating a patient who has had this procedure, consideration must be given to the previous operation as the cause of symptoms or as a modifier of them. A bowel obstruction, for instance, should be seriously considered if this patient develops an acute abdomen.

The elderly take many medications and their effects must be evaluated in all areas of medical care. Well known to urologists are the effects of Coumadin, an anticoagulant that causes hematuria, and α-adrenergic drugs (ephedrine or phenylpropanolamine), which increase urethral tone and cause urinary retention in men with prostatic obstruction. Medications must be prescribed with great care in genitourinary disease because renal function at age 75 is 20% less than at age 30.[1]

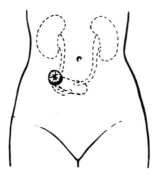

Ileal-conduit
urinary diversion

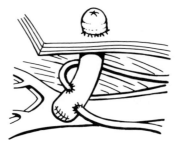

Figure 12–1 Ileal conduit urinary diversion.

It is not uncommon to find a patient who has suffered kidney failure and is being treated by dialysis in an emergency situation. Estimates in 1980 placed the number of patients on dialysis in the United States at about 48,000 and increasing.[2] The average age of this group is over 46 and is also increasing.[2] These patients usually have an arteriovenous shunt in one arm, which produces very large superficial vessels in the arm, with a palpable thrill over them. These patients are extremely fragile and respond very poorly to blood loss because they are anemic from their renal disease. All medications and fluid therapy must be decreased as in those patients with acute renal failure.

Because of these many variables, the history becomes extremely important and should include the prior medical record. It may be necessary to confirm events and medications with one or more relatives. A careful physical examination, including pelvic and rectal examinations, pertinent x-ray films and laboratory tests should follow.

SIGNS AND SYMPTOMS

Bleeding

Bleeding from the genitalia and urinary tract is always alarming, and it may be impossible for an elderly person to differentiate bloody urine from actual blood (Figure 12–2). This event generally leads to a visit to an emergency facility for explanation and reassurance. A careful history must be taken that investigates past and recent surgery, trauma, previous bleeding episodes from the area, other illnesses, and usage of medications. It is important to establish the use of anticoagulants or aspirin.

Bloody urine should be described by the patient or relatives, if possible, to assist in locating its source. A bloody urinary stream that clears as the act of voiding continues indicates bleeding distal to the bladder neck. Terminal bleeding, or blood in the last few drops of urine, is usually from the bladder and is typically seen in cases of hemorrhagic cystitis. The painless passage of totally bloody urine often means cancer somewhere in the urinary tract.

Blood may be seen grossly on the genitalia, particularly in women. It can come from the uterus, vagina, urethra, anus, or some other superficial site. Determining the exact site usually requires a clinical setting, a cooperative patient, good light, examining gloves, a speculum, and a urethral catheter. The female perineum and proximity of orifices and anus are first inspected for lesions, such as hemorrhoids,

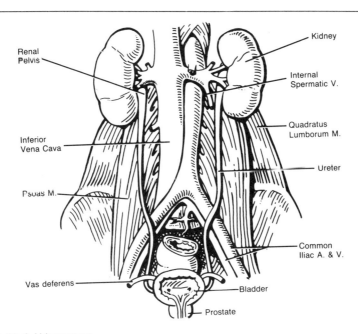

Figure 12–2 Urinary tract.

a urethral caruncle (a large area of erosion on the urethral meatus), or superficial lacerations (Figure 12–3). The vagina and cervix are then carefully inspected. Rectal examination and examination of stool for blood may be indicated. A urine sample is obtained by voiding or catheterization.

The site of origin of blood from the male genitalia or anus can usually be pinpointed by the patient or by careful inspection. Microscopic examination of the urine should be carried out because beets, excreted phenolphthalein (a laxative), and bilirubin can color the urine red or brown.

The abdomen is examined for masses in the renal and suprapubic areas or for signs of trauma. In gross total painless hematuria, immediate cystoscopy, if available, may localize the bleeding site quickly. However, it is satisfactory to do excretory urography first, followed by cystoscopy. The choice of other specific radiologic studies is determined by the findings of urography and cystoscopy. The hematocrit should be established and blood coagulation investigated when indicated clinically.

Urinary bleeding in the elderly is presumed due to cancer or other catastrophe until proven otherwise with appropriate x-ray films and cystoscopy. Presumptions of benign bleeding from infection or overanticoagulation may be a tragic mistake.

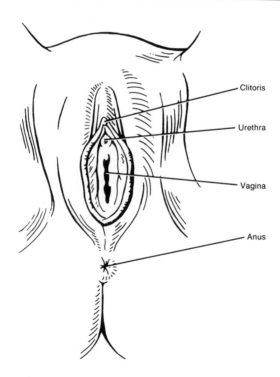

Figure 12–3 Female perineum and proximity of urethra, vagina, and anus.

Pain

Pain from the urinary tract is felt below the ribs and extends down the trunk to the genitalia. Occasionally pain is felt on the inner thigh, but generally urinary tract pain does not radiate down the legs. The anatomic site of the pain points to the urinary tract as its source, although in the very elderly, as in the very young, pain may be felt more diffusely.

Renal pain is felt in the flanks and radiates around to the front, down across the inguinal region to the genitalia. This pain can be dull and is usually felt directly in the flank. The colicky pain of acute ureteral obstruction is typically felt in the flank and referred down over the course of the ureter into the pelvis and genitalia. This type of pain is described as the most excruciating ever experienced by the patient. It is usually accompanied by random movement as the patient tries to find a comfortable position.

Bladder pain is felt directly over the bladder and is severe and constant, as in overdistention, or acute and associated with urination. Pain as the bladder empties is seen with cystitis, bladder calculi, and abscesses adjacent to the bladder. Burning on urination is typical of cystitis.

The prostate gland when infected causes local pain and perineal pain with burning on urination. Prostatic cancer is painless until the cancer invades other organs locally. Unexplained back pain or bone pain elsewhere may be caused by metastatic prostatic cancer.

Penile pain can be due to infection or trauma, but is most often referred from the bladder or prostate gland.

Testicular pain is dull and visceral, and its source can usually be found by careful physical examination of the testes and inguinal region.

Although the distribution of pain may point to the urinary tract as its source, other serious problems must be ruled out as the patient is evaluated (Figure 12–4). The most important of these problems is a leaking aneurysm of the abdominal aorta, which may cause pain in the left side of the abdomen or in the left lower quadrant. Diverticulitis of the colon also causes pain in the left lower quadrant. Pain in the left upper quadrant may be caused by the pancreas or the stomach. Gall bladder disease causes pain in the right upper quadrant, and biliary colic is very similar to renal colic.

Fever

Pathogens in the urine and in the urinary conduit system usually do not lead to fever because these ducts are impermeable to urine and other substances. Fever associated with urinary infection indicates involvement of the solid organs of the urinary tract. Shaking chills associated with a urinary infection are a sign of bacterial infection in the bloodstream, a potentially serious problem that can lead to bacteremic shock. A temperature elevation to 100–101°F can also occur

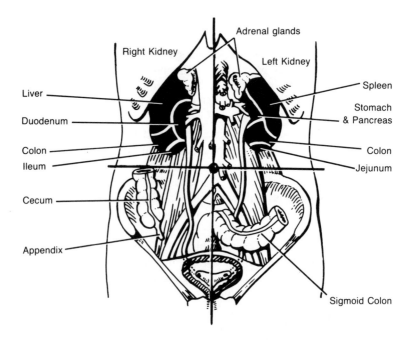

Figure 12–4 Anatomic relationship of urinary tract to other organs.

---

because of simple extravasation of urine outside the urinary tract. Tumors, particularly kidney tumors, and infarction of the kidney can also cause fever.

Change in Evacuation of Urine

The outflow of urine may be altered. The most serious sign specific to the outflow of urine is its complete retention. When this occurs acutely, it is usually accompanied by a severe and urgent need to void and by severe pain in the suprapubic area. If it occurs slowly, it may be painless and almost symptom-free and detected only by physical examination and discovery of the distended bladder. Urinary retention is most commonly associated with prostatic disease in men and rarely occurs in women.

Incontinence or spontaneous loss of urine, although distressing, is not usually a serious problem per se. In the elderly age group, it is often due to neurologic disease or pelvic relaxation, but it can be due to overflow from an extremely distended bladder. Perceived retention or incontinence is often seen, which is usually due to infection or irritation of the bladder and which gives the patient the sensation of fullness and the extreme need to empty the bladder frequently. Measuring the amount of urine remaining in the bladder after voiding will confirm if the problem is one of retention.

Other Symptoms

Systemic symptoms of weight loss, weakness, and nausea are nonspecific, but can be caused by renal failure, chronic infection, or metastatic genitourinary neoplasm.

GENITOURINARY DISEASES

Benign Prostatism

Diseases and afflictions of the prostate gland begin in adult life with prostatitis and increase in severity and frequency until age 100 when autopsies show virtually 100% of men have changes in the prostate consistent with adenocarcinoma (Figure 12–5).

Chronic prostatitis or prostatosis begins in the second decade and causes local pain and tenderness in the perineum and pelvic area. The cause of this disease remains a mystery, and it responds poorly to myriad treatments; however, it usually remits by the time the patient reaches age 50.

Acute and chronic bacterial prostatitis begins during the second decade, but can be seen at any age and should always be included in the differential diagnosis of urinary retention. Infection of the prostate causes edema, which, when combined

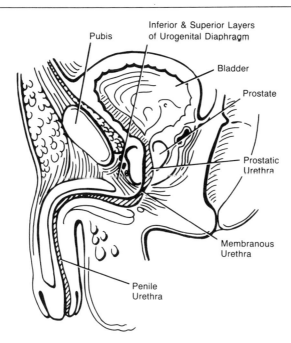

Figure 12–5 Sagittal view of prostate gland.

with early benign hyperplasia, leads to urethral closure and obstruction. Pyuria, fever, and leukocytosis are common and do not easily differentiate benign prostatism with urinary infection, retention, and pyelonephritis from acute prostatocystitis with urinary retention.

The patient with acute prostatocystitis should give a history of normal voiding prior to the acute onset of symptoms. If benign prostatic hyperplasia is the problem, there has usually been a slowing of the stream for several months or years. Physical examination of the patient with acute prostatocystitis reveals the distended bladder in the suprapubic region. The genitalia show no specific changes. On rectal examination, the infected prostate is enlarged, tender and distended, and firm to hard. It may be so hard as to suggest the presence of prostatic cancer. The enlarged benign prostate, on the other hand, is rubbery, symmetrical, and nontender.

Emergency treatment in either case is the relief of obstruction; one should obtain urine for a culture and begin parenteral antibiotic therapy. An aminoglycoside with ampicillin is a good choice until the culture report returns. Later definitive treatment depends on the exact diagnosis because only true prostatic obstruction requires surgical resection.

Benign prostatic hyperplasia (BPH) develops after age 40 and increases in severity into the seventh and eighth decade (Figure 12–6). By age 80, 75% of men can be demonstrated to have BPH.[3] The hyperplastic changes occur in the glands around the urethra, compressing it inward and the normal prostate outward. Through the rectal wall, the prostate feels larger and rubbery; the size is graded subjectively from 1 plus (slight enlargement) to 4 plus (huge). The size gives an

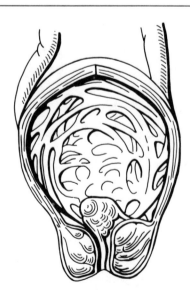

Figure 12–6 Benign prostatic hypertrophy with obstructive changes in the bladder.

indication of the degree of obstruction within. However, there may be significant obstruction without an increase in prostatic size.

The history is of a slow increase in difficulty voiding with hesitancy, terminal dribbling, and nocturia. Acute retention from BPH is usually precipitated by overdistention of the bladder, leading to decompensation of the detrusor muscle. The use of α-adrenergic (decongestants) or anticholinergic (antispasmodics) drugs can also precipitate retention if significant prostatic obstruction is present.

Examination of the abdomen reveals a distended bladder that may be visible or palpable. If distention occurs rapidly over several hours, it is very painful; however, it may occur very slowly and painlessly over several days. A distended bladder is the most common cause of a lower abdominal mass in an elderly man, and it is this problem that usually precipitates a search for medical care and relief of symptoms. Diagnosis does not require sophisticated x-ray studies or ultrasound examination of the pelvis. The patient is best served by urethral catheterization and drainage of the bladder, thus relieving distress and confirming the initial diagnosis. Drainage should be immediate and not delayed, and the amount of urine in the bladder must be measured and recorded as objective evidence of the obstruction. Hematuria may develop as the bladder is decompressed, but this rarely obstructs the catheter and stops in 24 to 48 hr.

Urinalysis indicates the sterility of the urine, and a culture may be done if infection is suspected. Blood urea nitrogen, serum creatinine, and electrolyte levels are checked to see if the bladder neck obstruction has impeded renal function. If the levels are elevated, urinary output should be measured hourly for several hours to detect any diuresis. Prolonged obstruction at the bladder neck causes renal failure and may affect the ability of the kidneys to concentrate urine. In such a case, the urinary output may rise above 200 ml/hr.[4] If this is observed, 0.5 normal saline should be started intravenously at a rate that replaces one-half of the hourly output.[5]

Rectal examination should not be performed until after the bladder is drained because the distended bladder makes the prostate feel much larger than its actual size.

Prostate Cancer

Prostatic cancer is the second most common form of cancer in white males and the most common malignancy in black males.[6] It begins in the posterior lobes of the prostate adjacent to the rectum and is palpable as a small hard nodule very early. Unfortunately, only 5% of prostatic cancers are discovered at this early asymptomatic and curable stage. This lesion, as does BPH, becomes an emergency when it causes urinary retention. At this stage it causes extensive anatomic changes in the prostate. The history may be one of increasing difficulty voiding over a period of weeks, rather than months or years as in BPH. There may be pain from bony metastases, and renal failure can be present because of obstruction of the bladder neck and ureters.

Physical examination is directed to the lower abdomen to look for a distended bladder, which, as in BPH, is relieved by catheterization. Rectal examination reveals a hard irregular prostate. The seminal vesicles are not ordinarily palpable, but when infiltrated with prostatic carcinoma they become very hard and distinct.

Blood tests of immediate importance are the BUN, creatinine, electrolytes, and a *baseline* acid phosphatase. If renal function is abnormal, ureteral obstruction should also be suspected. This is investigated with excretory urography or ultrasound studies in the case of acute renal failure in a critically ill individual. A urologist must then make the critical decisions regarding treatment of this problem.

Urethral Stricture

Stricture or closure of the urethra because of injury and healing is certainly not an emergent problem, but it often leads to more serious illness and is more likely to be found in the elderly population. One reason for this increased incidence is that penicillin, the first antibiotic that could cure gonorrhea, was not discovered until 1940, so in the 50-to-80 age group strictures from this disease can still be found. Both blunt external and internal urethral trauma also cause strictures. And as a person ages, the urethra becomes subject to an increasing number of insults from instruments and catheters.

Strictures cause problems when the urethra is narrowed to a pin-sized hole. Urethral pressures on voiding are higher proximal to the stricture, and there is residual urine in the system, thus making it more susceptible to infection. Cystitis and prostatitis become more common, and if these infections are untreated, a urethral abscess may develop at the site of the stricture. The abscess usually erodes through the fascial layers, and pus spreads over the perineum and up under the abdominal integument. These abscesses may open and drain spontaneously.

It is this type of infection that causes emergency visits. Careful management of these patients is essential because instrumentation (eg, urethral dilatation) in the face of a urinary infection can cause bacteremia, septicemia, and death. A urine culture is appropriate because strictures rarely cause complete retention of urine, and parenteral antibiotic therapy is begun as with most infections in this group. An aminoglycoside plus ampicillin should be used. If the patient is voiding, is not in urinary retention, and has normal renal function studies (BUN, creatinine), instrumentation is then delayed for 24 hours. If there is a severe problem voiding, instrumentation or dilation of the stricture may be carried out after IV antibiotics have been started (Figure 12–7). A catheter should be passed until it meets obstruction to pinpoint the site of the stricture. An injecting and voiding urethrogram may also be carried out.

A special filiform or catheter is then used to bypass the strictured area, and larger followers attached to the filiform are used to open the strictured area. Consideration should be given to taping these followers in place overnight if great

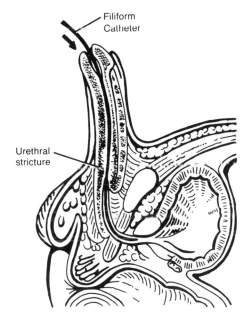

Figure 12–7 Dilation of urethral stricture.

difficulty is encountered in dilating the stricture, but it is usually possible to enlarge the area enough to insert a small no. 14 F catheter for drainage. If there is an associated perineal abscess, it must be opened surgically and drained.

Urinary Calculi

Urinary calculi occur in the adult age group primarily, but are less common in the very elderly. Bladder calculi are seen more often in the elderly man in association with benign prostatism, but it is renal and ureteral calculi that cause severe and emergent symptoms. As previously described, this pain is so severe that its immediate relief should be the first step in management. The signs and symptoms of ureteral colic should be so well known to emergency personnel that it should never be necessary to make the patient suffer without analgesic medication until the diagnosis is made. Meperidine or morphine must be used in carefully calculated amounts in the elderly because they are very sensitive to narcotics, which may cause respiratory depression.

There is often a history of previous urinary calculi in these patients. Gouty arthritis may be present. The body temperature is very important in detecting associated infection. Urinalysis should reveal many red blood cells in the urine, but perfectly clear urine may be seen when calculi completely occlude the upper urinary tract. Many pus cells in association with a calculus indicate associated infection and the possibility of bacteremia and shock.[7] A blood count usually shows a slight increase in the white blood cells, but with infection there is a marked upward shift. A plain x-ray film of the abdomen is a basic test to look for opacities over the area of the upper urinary tract, although only calcium stones are radio-opaque. Uric acid stones are radiolucent. A formal excretory urogram should be done as soon as possible. Establishing the size of the stone and its position in the ureter is necessary before treatment. A calculus less than 5 mm in the lower one-third of the ureter should pass, and a knowledgeable patient can return home to await its elimination (Figure 12–8).

However, hospital admission usually follows because of the severity of the pain. Analgesic medication and extra fluids help most small stones to pass in 1–2 days. Other stubborn lower ureteral calculi can be manipulated by the urologist. Stones greater than 6 mm may require surgical removal. Urinary infection, if present, is cultured and treated with appropriate antibiotics; then everything possible is done to relieve the patient's obstruction. The stone may be removed at the same time or after the infection is under control.

Neoplasms

The cancers that affect the urinary tract become medical emergencies when they bleed and produce blood in the urine. Although the bleeding itself may not be life threatening, it causes great anxiety and sometimes pain. The carcinomas that commonly occur in the elderly are the transitional cell group, which arise from the lining of the urinary tract. These can affect the kidney, ureter, and more commonly the bladder (Figure 12–9). Renal cell carcinoma arises within the kidney. Cancer of the prostate is usually found on an emergency basis because of urinary obstruction, rather than hematuria.

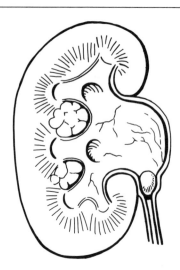

Figure 12–8 Obstructing renal calculus.

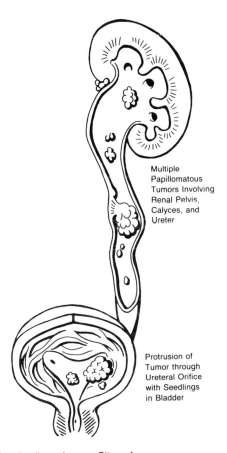

Multiple
Papillomatous
Tumors Involving
Renal Pelvis,
Calyces, and
Ureter

Protrusion of
Tumor through
Ureteral Orifice
with Seedlings
in Bladder

Figure 12–9 Transitional cell carcinoma: Sites of occurrence.

Transitional cell carcinomas of the kidney and ureter and renal cell carcinoma cause bleeding and often pain on the side of the lesion, which may be associated with passage of clots down the ureter. Frank bleeding in the ureter can lead to fish-worm type clots in the urine. Patients with renal cell cancer may have a palpable flank mass, as well as other systemic symptoms, such as fever and jaundice caused by dysfunction of the liver. The triad of flank pain, hematuria, and a flank mass is a classic presentation of renal cell carcinoma.

There are usually no physical findings associated with bladder and ureteral tumors, although a very large bladder tumor may be palpable.

Cancer of the testicle, a serious illness in the male, rarely occurs in the elderly age group.

Cystoscopy pinpoints the exact site of the bleeding. Bladder tumors are easily seen, or blood may be noted spurting from a ureteral orifice. Excretory urography, ultrasound, CT scanning, and angiography are also used to evaluate urinary neoplasms. These lesions are treated by excision whenever possible. Bladder tumors are the only tumor treated by endoscopic excision.

Infections

Urinary tract infection occurs with equal frequency among elderly men and women. This is rarely a problem for adult men until after the age of 60, when the incidence rises because of prostatism and instrumentation associated with medical care. Women show an increase because of a lack of estrogen and poor emptying of the bladder. Such associated medical conditions as diabetes mellitus cause an increased susceptibility for both men and women.[8] In addition to being a single disease process in the elderly, urinary infection may be a symptom of some other more serious obstructive problem, such as a renal calculus.

The symptoms of a simple bladder infection are urgency, frequency, and burning on urination, usually of a short duration. The urine often has a foul smell, and there may also be blood in it. Associated fever indicates infection of a solid organ: either one or both kidneys, the prostate gland, or the epididymis and testicle. Physical examination is extremely important in infection because fever must be documented, and there is often tenderness that localizes the infection to a specific organ. The epididymis and testicles develop marked swelling and tenderness. The flank should be carefully palpated and inspected for tenderness or a bulging mass. Diabetic patients are prone to develop perinephric abscess or papillary necrosis, and these must be considered if fever and flank pain are present.

Additional studies include routine urinalysis, urine culture, and blood cultures when there is high fever. An excretory urogram is usually done to visualize the urinary tract, but it should be avoided in diabetics with renal insufficiency because the contrast media may cause renal failure. Ultrasound is the best and safest way to examine the kidneys in a diabetic patient. Catheterization may be necessary to relieve lower urinary tract obstruction.

Treatment consists of administration of antibiotics and fluids and prompt drainage of any urinary obstruction. The sooner that treatment is started, the less chance that septic shock will occur, which may be seen with urinary tract infection and in which there is a mortality rate of approximately 40%. An aminoglycoside and ampicillin together remain an excellent choice for the severe infection and should be given intravenously. For cystitis and other less severe infections, oral antibiotics, such as ampicillin, sulfisoxazole-trimethoprim, or the cephalosporins, are a good choice. Antibiotics and IV fluids should be reduced in dosage to accommodate the elderly patient's decreased glomerular infiltration and cardiac output.

Renal Failure

There are five different presentations of renal failure in an emergency setting: (1) anuria, (2) oliguria, (3) the uremic syndrome, (4) edema and heart failure, and (5) asymptomatic failure. Chronic renal failure may cause symptoms in any organ system in the body.[9] In every case of renal failure the single most important factor is the serum potassium level. Failure to excrete adequate amounts of urine leads to retention of potassium, as well as of urea, sodium, creatinine, and uric acid; and a serum potassium of greater than 7 mg/L may cause cardiac asystole or fibrillation. A serum potassium of 6 mg/L is cause for alarm, particularly if the case is complex with no immediate improvement in urinary output anticipated. It is critical at this point to do an ECG. Hyperkalemia results in progressive peaking of the T wave, prolongation of the QRS complex, and, immediately before asystole, absence of the P wave. These changes require immediate treatment.

The most rapid treatment is the IV push of one ampule (44 mg) of sodium bicarbonate while monitoring the ECG. This may be repeated as needed. The slow IV infusion of 10 to 20 ml of 10% calcium gluconate decreases myocardial irritability very rapidly. It should not be given in the same solution with sodium bicarbonate or even in the same arm. Intravenous glucose and insulin drives potassium back into the cells, but this is not as rapid, taking 1–2 hr. One should use a 10% or 50% glucose solution containing 1 unit of regular insulin for 5 gm of glucose and monitor the ECG changes. Kayexalate is a potassium exchange resin that can be given by mouth or enema, usually 150 mg diluted to a drinkable solution with 70% sorbitol. It takes 1–2 hr to lower potassium by this method.[10] Hemodialysis or peritoneal dialysis are the last measures in treatment because it may take hours to get either procedure underway.

If the serum potassium level is not elevated above 6 mg/L and the patient is stable, the first step is to look for either prerenal or postrenal causation for the renal failure because these problems are for the most part treatable and correctable. Prerenal causes include dehydration, heart failure, increased muscle catabolism, and blood breakdown in the GI tract. Postrenal causes are those that cause obstruction to the outflow of urine from the end of the urethra to the ureteropelvic junction on each side.

While evaluating the serum potassium, a careful history and physical examination should be carried out, focusing on past illnesses and medications, in particular analgesics. Blood chemistries and electrolytes are checked, as well as serum osmolality. A urethral catheter is inserted to check for distal outflow obstruction, to obtain a urine sample, and to monitor the urinary output. The urine sodium and osmolality are measured. The kidneys are examined with a plain x-ray film of the abdomen and an ultrasound examination. These two studies give renal size and shape, identify dilation of the collecting system as would be seen with ureteral obstruction, and also identify opaque calculi.

In prerenal failure, the urine sodium is low, less than 15 mg/L, and the urine osmolality is greater than the serum osmolality. The urine is usually free of cells and casts.

Renal failure due to renal cause (eg, acute tubular necrosis) is characterized by a urine sodium greater than 40 mg/L and urine osmolality less than 350 msm/L. The urine contains casts and RBCs. The findings in postrenal failure are similar, but there may be pus, blood, or crystals in the urine.

Emergency treatment includes giving IV fluids, usually one-half normal saline at a slow rate to rehydrate the patient. If edema and heart failure are present, fluids are withheld. Dialysis may be necessary later to decrease excessive salt and water loads. Cystoscopy and retrograde pyelography may also be carried out later to establish patency of the ureters.

Vascular Emergencies

Renal vascular emergencies occur only in the elderly and are extremely rare. The most common type is infarction from embolization that is seen in the patient with valvular heart disease, atrial fibrillation, or myocardial infarction with formation of mural thrombus that becomes an embolus. Flank pain, similar to renal colic, with microscopic hematuria is the usual presentation. Aneurysms of the renal artery may occur, and 15% of these rupture.[11] Trauma may also occlude or divide the renal artery. To make the diagnosis, one must consider the possibility of trauma.

Excretory urography demonstrates a normal-sized but nonfunctioning kidney, and retrograde pyelography rules out obstruction. Angiography will then precisely demonstrate the lesion.

Early management consists of stabilization of vital functions with IV fluids, a transfusion as needed, prompt diagnosis, and preparation for surgery. The status of both kidneys must be determined. Surgical treatment is indicated, either an embolectomy, resection of an aneurysm, repair of the artery, or nephrectomy.

TRAUMA

Traumatic injury, although certainly not as common in the elderly population as in the young, is nonetheless a significant health problem. The loss of a vital 70-year-old because of trauma is certainly as tragic as the loss of a younger person, yet saving these older individuals in such situations may be considerably more difficult. Decreased renal reserve, poor blood flow to tissues, poor nutrition, and various medical problems all contribute to the challenge of enabling an elderly individual to survive a serious traumatic accident.

Renal and Ureteral Trauma

Trauma to the kidney and ureter may occur from either a blunt or penetrating injury. A penetrating injury caused by some type of instrument or a gun shot usually can be visualized. Blunt injury is more difficult to evaluate, but there are often signs of injury to the flank, such as abrasion and ecchymosis of the skin; swelling due to underlying bleeding, broken, and/or tender ribs; or a history of a blow to the area of either kidney. Urinalysis is performed to look for blood, which is usually present. An excretory urogram is necessary to determine if the kidney is functioning and to give an indication of the severity of the injury.

Laceration of the renal pedicle or avulsion of the pedicle causes total nonfunction of the kidney. A simple contusion of the kidney, although it may cause blood in the urine and flank pain, causes no roentgenographic changes and requires only simple supportive measures. Between these extremes are various degrees of renal laceration with urine extravasation and bleeding. In general, these injuries are managed conservatively without surgery.

Injury to or laceration of the ureter is a different problem because it always leads to urine extravasation, which does not heal by itself. This injury is seen with gunshot or stab wounds and usually not with blunt injury. It can also be iatrogenic and be seen in the hospital setting. It always requires repair of the ureter by open surgery. Early management consists of IV fluids and preparation for transfusion and surgery.

Bladder Trauma

Bladder injuries are open or closed or blunt or penetrating and lead to bleeding into the urine and extravasation of urine outside the bladder. The opening into the bladder is either intraperitoneal through the dome of the bladder or extraperitoneal. Intraperitoneal rupture of the bladder is caused by blunt injury to a full bladder, leading to fracture at its weakest point where it is covered only by peritoneum. This injury may be associated with very little bleeding or trauma to other organs.

Extraperitoneal rupture is usually associated with pelvic fracture and perforation of the bladder wall by bone fragments. The pelvic fractures cause massive retroperitoneal bleeding that is not visible. Therefore, treatment begins with access to the bloodstream, fluid replacement with saline or lactated Ringer's solution, and blood transfusion. The signs and symptoms include contusions around the pelvis, pain on motion of the pelvic bones, and pain and tenderness at fracture sites. X-ray studies confirm the clinical impressions. Bleeding from the urethral meatus is usually seen with urethral injuries, but even if this symptom is absent, urethral injury should also be suspected.

Because injury to the urethra and bladder occurs with pelvic injury, films of these areas are obtained at the same time. Under sterile conditions, the urethra is injected with sterile IV venous contrast media; this establishes its integrity. A catheter is then inserted, and the bladder is filled with contrast media. If there has been an opening into the bladder, contrast media will be identified in the pelvis or peritoneal cavity. The catheter should be connected to a sterile, closed drainage system until the bladder can be repaired.

Trauma to the Urethra

The posterior urethra extends from the bladder neck to the urogenital diaphragm, and it is surrounded in the male by the prostate gland. The female urethra corresponds to this part of the male urethra. Injury to this area is extremely rare in either sex and is caused by a penetrating wound or very severe blunt trauma. The more common injury involves rupture of the prostatomembranous urethra, and this occurs in 5% of all cases of pelvic fracture[12] (Figure 12–10). This rupture may be complete or partial, and every effort is directed toward not worsening the injury. Great care should be taken because the external sphincter in the urogenital diaphragm may be all that remains of the patient's mechanism of continence. A prior prostatectomy may have rendered the internal sphincter or bladder neck nonfunctional.

To manage this problem properly, the urethral meatus is inspected for bleeding. Next, rectal examination is carried out in search of the prostate gland. If the prostatomembranous urethra has been ruptured, the prostate floats up in the pelvis, and all that can be felt is the boggy hematoma. If either sign is present, a urethrogram must be done by injecting parenteral contrast media through the urethra. If there is extravasation, the patient is asked to refrain from voiding, and no attempt should be made to introduce a urethral catheter. Preceding and during the diagnostic workup, every attempt is made to obtain homeostasis by administering IV fluids and blood as necessary. Urinary drainage is ultimately obtained by suprapubic cystostomy.

The anterior urethra from the urogenital diaphragm to the tip of the penis is injured usually by a blow to the perineum or direct trauma to the penis, leading to bleeding from the penis and into the tissues around the injury site (Figure 12–11). The patient is asked to refrain from voiding, and an injecting urethrogram is carried out with parenteral contrast media under sterile conditions to determine the extent of the injury.[11] Pressure should be applied to the penis and bulb of the

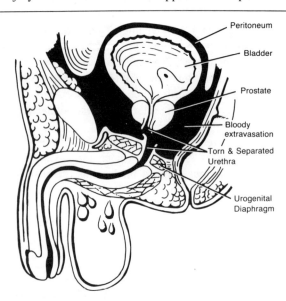

Figure 12–10 Ruptured prostatomembranous urethra.

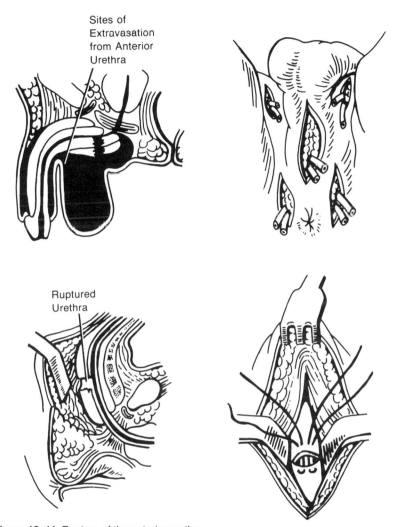

Figure 12–11 Rupture of the anterior urethra.

urethra to stop persistent and troublesome bleeding. Catheterization should be avoided. Urinary retention can be relieved by inserting a small trocar catheter into the bladder just above the pubis. The surgical treatment depends on the severity of the lesion. Minor contusions may be managed by urethral catheter, whereas a major disruption requires suprapubic drainage and repair of the urethra.

Penis

Trauma to the penis without urethral injury should be treated by controlling the bleeding and doing appropriate suturing if lacerations are superficial. Blunt trauma is best treated initially with ice packs followed by close observation because there may be enough swelling to occlude the urethra.

In the event of amputation, the transected piece should be kept clean and packed in ice until it can be sutured in place. Control of bleeding may require clamping and ligating vessels. If the lengthy procedure necessary to rejoin the penis seems inappropriate in an elderly man, the stump is simply trimmed and repaired.

Scrotum and Testes

Blunt trauma to the testicle causes either a contusion or a laceration of the testicle with associated hemorrhage. A contusion causes swelling, but not enough to obscure the testicular architecture, and can be managed with ice packs, analgesics, and rest with elevation of the testicles.

A major laceration of the testicle, in contrast, is best managed by immediate ice packs and analgesics and then usually orchiectomy. Attempted repair with drainage may be carried out, but usually unnecessarily prolongs the recovery.

NEUROGENIC DYSFUNCTION OF THE BLADDER

Retention of urine occurs with spinal cord and cauda equina injuries, infarction of parts of the spinal cord, transverse myelitis, and ruptured intervertebral disc. However, urinary retention is rarely the initial complaint. This problem is managed with temporary urethral catheter drainage.

GENITAL PROBLEMS

Phimosis with Balanoposthitis

Diabetes mellitus in particular causes mild recurrent infection leading to stenosis of the foreskin in the elderly individual who may have little interest in its retraction or in cleaning it within. As the foreskin tightens, severe infections can occur, with acute inflammation and edema of the foreskin and glans penis.

This infection is due to a coliform organism and is treated with antibiotics and warm soaks. Circumcision should follow resolution of the acute infection.

Paraphimosis

Tightening of the foreskin may be such that it can be retracted but not easily returned to its normal position. Caught snugly behind the glans penis, the skin and glans slowly swell until the foreskin can no longer be pulled back over the glans. This causes severe pain and can lead to local cellulitis.

It is usually possible to reduce the glans back under the foreskin by pressing it inward while pulling on the foreskin. Although this maneuver is painful, it gives the patient instant relief. Warm soaks and antibiotic therapy may be helpful after this reduction. In extreme cases it is necessary to incise the foreskin surgically to allow its release. After resolution of edema and infection, a proper circumcision is carried out.

Acute Epididymoorchitis

Infection of the epididymis and testicle may follow any urinary infection. Severe pain and swelling on the side affected, high fever, and chills follow. Walking becomes extremely difficult.

There is usually a history of voiding symptoms, such as dysuria and frequency. The onset of pain is rapid but not acute. Initial physical examination reveals the distended and tender epididymis, but later there is just a large tender reddened mass. Urinalysis usually reveals pyuria, and the white cell count is elevated.

Infection is due to coliform organisms, and appropriate antibiotics are given. Anti-inflammatory medications, such as ibuprofen, give quick symptomatic relief, as does injecting the spermatic cord with bupivacaine. In the very elderly, consideration is given to immediate orchiectomy. Investigation of the urinary tract is later carried out to seek a cause for the infection.

REFERENCES

1. Proceedings of the Regional Institutes on Geriatrics, Medical Education. *Geriatrics and Medical Education Proceedings*. Association of American Medical Colleges. Washington, DC, 1983, p 16.

2. Tilney NL, Lazarus JM: *Surgical Care of the Patient with Renal Failure*. Philadelphia, WB Saunders Co, 1982, pp 2–3.

3. Brendler H: Benign prostatic hyperplasia: Natural history, in Grayhach JT, Wilson JD, Scherbenske MJ (eds): *Benign Prostatic Hyperplasia*. Bethesda, MD, National Institutes of Health, 1975, pp 101–103.

4. Vaughn ED, Gillenwater JY: Diagnosis, characterization and management of postobstructive diuresis. *J Urol* 109:286–292, 1973.

5. Peterson LJ, Yarger WE, Schochen DD: Post obstructive diuresis: a varied syndrome. *J Urol* 113:190–194, 1975.

6. Morrison AS, Cole P: Epidemiology of urologic cancers, in Javadpour N (ed): *Principles and Management of Urologic Cancer*. Baltimore, Williams & Wilkins, 1979, p 8.

7. Klein LA, Koyle M, Berg S: The emergency management of patients with ureteral calculi. *J Urol* 129:938–940, 1983.

8. Bell DP, Frantz G: Urinary tract infections in the elderly. *Geriatrics* 38:42–48, 1983.

9. Curtis JR: Chronic renal failure. *The Practitioner* 220:904–910, 1978.

10. Hull AR: Complications of uremia. *Urol Clin North Am* 9:275–278, 1982.

11. Fry RE, Fry WJ: Renovascular emergencies. *Urol Clin North Am* 9:209–214, 1982.

12. Morehouse DD: Emergency management of urethral trauma. *Urol Clin North Am* 9:251–254, 1982.

13

Gynecologic Emergencies

Peggy L. McCall, MSN, RN, CNA

When an elderly woman comes to an emergency department (ED) for a gynecologic problem, she is often physically and psychologically uncomfortable. She may be experiencing pain, vaginal bleeding, or shock-like symptoms, or she may be a victim of sexual assault and trauma. The emergency practitioner should approach each woman in a careful and sensitive manner so that the experience will be less frightening, less embarrassing, and less traumatic.

The purposes of this chapter are to identify the geriatric gynecologic conditions frequently seen in the ED, outline their signs and symptoms, recommend treatment protocols and assessment techniques, and convey a holistic approach to patient care and discharge planning.

ASSESSMENT

Special assessment techniques that have been previously discussed in this text should always be considered in the triage of the geriatric gynecologic patient. In addition, a few basic principles should be followed. Information regarding the onset of signs and symptoms should be solicited in confidence, and privacy should be afforded for all aspects of the assessment and examination.[1] The emergency practitioner can further ensure the comfort needs of the woman by carefully explaining all procedures, by assisting in appropriate positioning and draping, by instructing her in the techniques of relaxation, and by providing emotional support at the time of examination.[1]

Before any procedures are begun, the elderly patient should be assisted in removing all her underclothing and any constricting garments. It is important for any woman, and especially an elderly woman, that her belongings be placed carefully in a bag or on hangers as they represent important parts of her identity.[1] Time and assistance should be provided to allow the patient to void so that the bladder is empty and does not interfere with the digital examination of any of the pelvic or abdominal structures. When the pelvic examination is completed, it is important to help the woman return to a comfortable position and to provide tissue paper or other cleansing agents to remove lubricants and secretions from the peri-anal area.

The mental status and emotional outlook of the elderly patient frequently impede one's ability to acquire a meaningful history. The obstetric/gynecologic history of an elderly woman is usually even more difficult to acquire. Unfortunately, many older women do not have a regular gynecologic examination because they mistakenly believe that the procedure is not necessary for women beyond the childbearing age.[2] Some find it an embarrassing and uncomfortable procedure, and they have more complex or disturbing medical problems that need attention. Therefore, neglect of gynecologic problems is very common among elderly women.[3]

The obstetric/gynecologic history should include the following information:

- number of pregnancies
- number of miscarriages
- frequency and type of surgeries
- any episode of bleeding
- amount and character of the bleeding
- menstrual history (approximate date of her last period)
- any evidence of infection, such as vaginal discharge or odors
- a history of sex habits in the later years

The urinary history is very important because pyelonephritis and urinary obstruction are common diseases in elderly women.[2] Frequency, dysuria, burning, dull backache, and fever are classic signs and symptoms that vary from mild to severe in these patients.

Because the elderly frequently have elimination problems, the assessment should always include a history of bowel habits.[4] To assess elimination, one should ask the patient whether any particular food creates a problem for her, how frequently and easily she defecates, the consistency of her stools, and whether she takes laxatives or enemas regularly. One should also establish if she needs assistance in going to the bathroom while she is hospitalized.

A drug history should always be included. One should record the name and dosage of any drug taken by the patient and the length of time she has been taking it and determine which prescribed drugs are not being taken by the patient.

SPECIFIC GYNECOLOGIC CONDITIONS

Vulva

The female genital area, as perhaps no other part of the body, reflects the changes of aging.[3] Vulvar skin changes are most prominent because this area had been under hormonal control in the past. There is a loss of hair and subcutaneous fat, and the labial folds flatten and tend to disappear into the surrounding skin. The skin appears thin, shiny, and avascular.[3]

As the endogenous estrogen level diminishes, the vulvar areas become more susceptible to inflammation and infections. Complaints of pruritus in the vulvar area become common, and itching frequently is accompanied by inflammation.[5] The patient responds to the pruritus and burning by scratching, which produces more trauma and introduces more infection. The results of this scratching are seen frequently in the ED as atrophic and hypertrophic vulvitis or "senile vulvitis."[3] Leukoplakia may also be noted on the vulva as a whitened thickening of the epithelium, which can later degenerate with the formation of cracks and fissures. This condition predisposes a woman to vulvar malignancies and should be followed closely by doing frequent biopsies.

The management of vulvar dermatitis can be quite complex because the etiology is often obscure and secondary infection and overtreatment are common. Before treatment is started, specific underlying causes should be ruled out. These include a number of dermatologic lesions and drug eruptions. Changes in the vulva may reflect such systemic diseases as diabetes, pernicious anemia, and hepatitis. The diagnostic workup should always include a urinalysis, a CBC, and determination of blood sugar and bilirubin levels. Culturing specimens from all vulvar lesions for monilia and bacteria is also considered essential.[3]

Emergency treatment in general should focus on patient/family education and topical application of soothing creams. Anti-inflammatory corticosteroid creams may also be prescribed for management of pruritus.[3] The importance of keeping the area clean and dry must be stressed to the patient and her family. Nutritional supplements should also be recommended. Any evidence of malnutrition, vitamin deficiency, or anemia should be corrected. During the acute phase, starch-water sitz baths (1 cup starch to a tub of warm water) and saline compresses are useful in controlling the itching and burning. Alkaline soaps and topical creams containing antihistamines should not be used.

Pruritus, irritation, and pain should be evaluated carefully to rule out carcinoma. The clitoris should be carefully inspected because it is a frequent site of malignancy in elderly females.[5] In general, any ulceration, no matter how superficial, or mass in the vulvar area must be referred to the obstetrics/gynecology service for biopsy. These lesions should not be treated with topical medications until a complete pathological evaluation has been done.

Vagina

The degenerative changes that occur in the vulva also occur in the vaginal canal. The epithelium thins, becomes avascular, and demonstrates a loss of elasticity. The canal appears smooth, shiny, dry, and pink tinged.[3] In parous females the vagina tends to roll outward. Vaginal secretions are scanty, and there is an alteration in the vaginal flora. The pH rises toward the alkaline range. These changes predispose the older female to the common infection of senile vaginitis,[2] the symptoms of which are soreness, pruritus, and burning of the vulva and the vagina. The area appears red with numerous petechiae. In progressive stages superficial ulcerations and bleeding may be noted. The condition is accompanied by a watery, purulent, or brown leukorrhea.[2,3] The management includes the application of estrogens locally as suppositories or creams. Acid douches may also be prescribed.[3]

The emergency practitioner should exercise extreme caution in prescribing suppositories and topical agents to elderly patients. One must ensure that they and/ or a reliable family member understand that the topical agents are not to be taken orally. The importance of the temperature of the douche water should also be emphasized, and it should be checked by a reliable family member. Good hygienic practices should be explained as being beneficial not only in the treatment of vaginitis but also in the prevention of this common condition.

Monilial vaginitis is unusual in elderly females except in the presence of diabetes mellitus or following antibiotic therapy. *Trichomonas vaginalis* vaginitis is also not as common in older as in younger patients in the reproductive years. However, the symptomatology, diagnosis, and treatment of these specific conditions are the same as in the younger age group.[3] Occasionally a forgotten or neglected pessary or other foreign body may cause vaginal ulceration and infections. These conditions usually respond promptly to the removal of the object and local hygienic measures.

Postmenopausal leukorrhea usually presents as a thin, watery, foul-smelling discharge that may be associated with pruritus and blood. This condition is generally caused by atrophy of the vagina, vulva, and uterus and is due to decreased estrogen levels.[5] Secondary infection is a frequent complication. This condition can also indicate a malignancy or foreign body. Any evidence of prolonged leukorrhea in elderly females makes further study and evaluation mandatory. Management should emphasize hygiene. The use of estrogen and antibiotics should be carefully individualized because of the complications of the drugs and the other disease processes that may be present.

Postmenopausal bleeding is a common complaint and must be considered a quasiemergency in this age group.[3] Evaluation should include a complete examination with pap smears, dilation and curettage (D&C), and biopsy. Sonograms and hysterograms are also considered important.[5] Vaginitis is the most common cause of postmenopausal bleeding; however, it can be associated with systemic diseases and carcinoma. A detailed history of estrogen injections is important in the evaluation of this condition. Treatment depends on the pathologic changes found.[3,5]

Cervix

The degenerative changes described for the vulva and vagina also occur in the aging cervix. The stroma atrophies and is largely replaced by connective tissue.

The cervix becomes smaller, and the endocervical epithelium also atrophies.[2,3] Occasionally the endocervical glands can seal over, forming Nabothian cysts. Secretions associated with these cysts may accumulate and cause fever, and a palpable, tender mass may form.[2] Cervical stenosis is significant because it may mask a carcinoma of the endometrium.[3] On examination the cervical canal must be probed for patency, and vaginal smears must be obtained to rule out malignancies. Endocervical polyps are frequently seen in this age group.[2,3] They are a common cause of postmenopausal vaginal bleeding, and although they are usually benign, excision and biopsy should be performed in all cases.[3]

Cancer of the cervix must be considered in any elderly woman who has vaginal bleeding or malodorous, blood-stained leukorrhea. The incidence, however, does decline significantly in women over the age of 60.[2,3] Pain is not a early symptom, and the growth of the tumor may be quite slow in the geriatric age group.[3] The patient may complain of fecal or urinary incontinence or urinary retention. Management should include a complete gynecologic examination with Pap smear and biopsies as indicated. Referral to the obstetric/gynecologic service should be initiated in the ED.

Uterus

The uterus decreases in size with age, becoming a fibrotic structure that is generally no larger than a normal cervix.[5] The atrophy may be so extreme that the emergency practitioner may think a supracervical hysterectomy has been performed in the past.[3] The endometrium becomes markedly atrophic so that frequently insufficient tissue is available for an adequate biopsy specimen.[3] However, the eodometrial tissue of the uterus never loses its ability to respond to hormonal stimulation. This is important because the administration of systemic hormones for various conditions, such as osteoporosis and menopause syndrome, may cause postmenopausal bleeding. Some patients may continue to secrete low levels of endogenous estrogens, a condition that contributes to endometrial hyperplasia and postmenopausal bleeding.[5]

Endometrial carcinoma is found more frequently in the geriatric population than is cervical carcinoma.[5] The tumor usually causes postmenopausal bleeding, and in early cases there may be no other physical finding. Ten percent of cases of postmenopausal bleeding can be linked to endometrial carcinoma. There is also a statistical relationship to obesity, hypertension, and diabetes in this age group.[3] Diagnosis is made by tissue examination. Because carcinoma of the endometrium accounts for 15% to 50% of all cases of postmenopausal bleeding, this condition must be investigated thoroughly and immediately.[3] A referral to the obstetric/gynecology department should be initiated in the ED for the patient with postmenopausal bleeding.

Myoma and endometrial polyps can also cause postmenopausal bleeding in geriatric patients.[3] It is important to investigate any increase in the size of a uterine myoma. A myoma may be forced through the cervix into the vagina by the shrinkage of the uterus. It then becomes a fibroid polyp and may cause postmenopausal bleeding. The diagnosis of these conditions, as for previous conditions causing postmenopausal bleeding, is by immediate and thorough tissue study.[3]

Fallopian Tubes

Conditions involving the fallopian tubes are rarely a geriatric problem. The incidence of carcinoma of the tube is extremely low. The tubes atrophy and appear pale, straight, and shortened.[3] If carcinoma does occur, unfortunately there are no early symptoms. There may be vaginal bleeding, discharge, and low abdominal pain. Occasionally Pap smears may be positive, and the biopsy may be negative.[3] The diagnosis is most often made by laparotomy. Surgery followed by external radiotherapy is the recommended treatment.[3]

Ovary

The geriatric ovaries are sclerotic, atrophic organs. They appear pale, thickened, and small, often measuring only 1 or 2 cm in length.[5] On pelvic examination they are rarely palpable. Ovarian cysts are not considered functional in this age group; they are considered new growths and must be investigated thoroughly.[3]

Ovarian carcinoma has a poor prognosis, because of the difficulty of early detection. Its incidence accounts for approximately 20% of all geriatric gynecologic malignancies.[5] The geriatric patient frequently has lower abdominal pain, multiple pelvic abdominal masses, and ascites. Recommended treatment includes immediate surgical exploration, radiation, and chemotherapy.[5]

Benign ovarian tumors are not uncommon in the elderly female. Because they can not be distinguished clinically from malignant tumors, immediate surgical exploration is mandatory.[3] These benign tumors may twist, hemorrhage, and rupture, just as in the younger age group, and may cause hemorrhage and shock.[6]

MOST COMMON GERIATRIC GYNECOLOGIC EMERGENCIES

Genital Prolapse

A frequent problem found in the geriatric gynecologic patient is perineal herniation. This condition results from the stretching and tearing of muscles during childbirth and the associated muscle weakness of advancing age. Cystocele, rectocele, and prolapse of the uterus are most likely to occur.[2]

Elderly females coming to the ED with uterine decensus have complaints that vary from a pressure sensation and "ball" in the vagina to complete procidentia with inversion of the vagina and a mass between the legs.[3] Associated with this problem are frequent complaints of back pain, pelvic "heaviness," and difficulty with bladder and bowel function, including attacks of cystitis, constipation, stress incontinence, or urinary retention.[3]

Because geriatric patients tolerate their disorders for long periods of time, it is not unusual to find on examination an edematous, inverted vaginal mass with an infected, ulcerated cervix.[5] Such a condition may be impossible to replace (into uterine cavity) in the ED due to the massive edema. Bedrest in the Trendelenburg position with soothing local applications is necessary before restoration of the vagina is possible.[3]

The management of a patient with complete genital prolapse is primarily surgical.[3] Vaginal pessaries are avoided as a permanent form of treatment because they fail to provide adequate support and tend to cause further ulceration and infection of the vaginal wall. They are to be used only as a temporary measure in the patient with severe medical contraindications to surgery.[3] Patient education, reassurance, and a referral to the obstetrics/gynecologic service for complete evaluation are recommended for this type of patient.

Urinary Retention

Bladder muscles weaken with age and may cause retention of large volumes of urine. In elderly females the most common cause of urinary retention is fecal impaction.[2] Symptoms of retention include urinary frequency, straining, dribbling, a palpable bladder, and a feeling by the individual that the bladder has not been emptied.[5]

Emergency management includes the determination of the cause of the retention, such as an impaction, meatal stenosis, or a neurogenic bladder.[2] Retention predisposes the elderly patient to the risk of developing an infection; therefore the use of a catheter to relieve the retention should be carefully evaluated.[6] The chances of infection can be minimal in single or intermittent catherization if the appropriate aseptic technique is used. Indwelling catheters should be avoided in management of urinary retention.[6]

Urinary Incontinence

A common and very bothersome problem of the elderly is urinary incontinence. It may be a serious problem as well as it frequently prevents the elderly from being cared for at home. Emergency health care providers must determine its underlying etiology to initiate appropriate management of the problem. A complete history, including onset, duration, symptoms of dysuria, hematuria, nocturia, and any associated pain, must be completely evaluated to treat this type of patient appropriately.[7] A complete physical examination, including pelvic examination to rule out pelvic tumors, is also recommended. Initial laboratory studies should include CBC (complete blood count), urinalysis, blood glucose, BUN, and creatinine. A referral to the urology and/or obstetric/gynecologic service should be initiated in the ED based on the history, physical examination, and preliminary laboratory studies.

Gynecologic causes of incontinence include uretheral caruncle, prolapsed uterus, and vaginitis.[5] In the geriatric patient with significant prolapse urinary symptoms are often prominent. They vary from residual urine, to chronic cystitis, to urgency frequency syndrome. If there is a urethrocele or loss of bladder neck support, the patient may also develop stress incontinence. As the prolapse progresses true stress incontinence disappears and may be replaced by urinary retention and overflow incontinence.[3]

In stress incontinence caused by pelvic support relaxation that results in the urethra-vesicle angle being disrupted, symptoms are brought on by walking, laughing, and coughing.[5] Management of this type of incontinence is by surgical repair. A ring pessary may be used as a temporary measure in nonsurgical patients.[5]

Vaginal Infection and Odors

Vaginal infections and odors are generally associated with poor hygiene in the geriatric female. Other causes may include monilial infections associated with diabetes, trichomonal vaginitis transmitted by intercourse, and leukorrhea due to malignancy or foreign bodies.[5] These conditions cause pruritus, which in turn may produce a secondary infection.[3]

The emergency management includes determination of the etiology of the infection by a complete examination with smears and cultures. Cleansing acid douches and such topical agents as estrogen creams should be prescribed to control the pruritus. Other types of vaginal creams may be indicated to treat the infection following the identification of the organism.[5]

Bowel Changes

Tenesmus and bowel changes are associated with rectocele, enterocele, and prolapsed uterus. The patient complaints and general condition must be thoroughly assessed prior to the consideration of definitive treatment.[5]

Constipation, flatulence, and fecal impactions are frequent problems in the elderly.[7] Presenting complaints include abdominal pain, rectal discomfort, and oozing fecal material around the impaction that is easily mistaken for diarrhea.[5] Treatment for constipation and flatus should focus on preventive measures. Emergency personnel must be aware of the concern the elderly have regarding their bowel habits and must attempt to understand their feelings. A complete history, including diet and bowel habits, should be obtained. Enemas and laxatives should only be prescribed carefully due to the risk of dehydration and electrolyte disturbances.[7] Fecal impaction should be gently removed digitally followed by insertion of a suppository. Patient discharge teaching should focus on nutritional counseling and encouragement of appropriate physical activity. A regular and adequate time for bowel movement should be encouraged.

Sexual Assault

The incidence of violent crimes, such as homicide and sexual assault, has risen rapidly during the past 15 years, especially in urban settings.[8] Rape is generally accepted by criminologists, psychologists, and other professionals working with victims and assailants as a crime of violence, rather than a sexual crime.[8] Elderly women are viewed by perpetrators of violent crime as easy victims because they are frail, physically weak, and often live alone. Many elderly women believe that rape is only a sexual crime against young women and do not consider themselves potential victims; therefore they do not exercise common precautions.[8]

In a study of 78 case histories of rape victims over the age of 50, physical force, including choking, pushing, and gagging, was used in 97% of the cases. Actual beatings occurred in 50% of the cases.[8] In 65% of the cases the rape was associated with robbery. A surprising finding was that in 43% of the cases the elderly victim freely admitted the rapist into her home, believing he was a repairman, official, or acquaintance.[8]

The elderly victim of sexual assault is frightened, humiliated, and frequently severely injured on admission to the ED. A complete physical assessment to determine priorities of care should be performed immediately on arrival. Special attention should be paid to the probability of injury of soft tissues, fractures, and internal organs. The attack could also exacerbate an existing chronic illness, such as a cardiovascular condition or arthritis.[8]

The gynecologic examination should include careful inspection of the external genitalia. The entire vagina must also be visualized in order not to overlook an associated but separate vagina injury.[1] The use of a narrow-blade speculum is recommended in the elderly woman to limit further vagina trauma. A digital rectal examination should also be performed.[9] Venereal disease prophylaxis is provided by procaine penicillin (4.8 m units) and probenecid (1 gm). Patients allergic to penicillin can be treated with alternative drugs, such as tetracycline.[9]

The completion of the rape evidence kit, including vaginal cultures, smears, nail scrapings, and collection of pubic hair, should be initiated as soon as possible. Careful factual documentation is necessary on the medical form provided with the sexual assault kit. Because this kit can be used in a court of law as legal evidence, the sexual assault kit must be opened in front of the patient and sealed immediately after use.[1] Adherence to local laws and procedures should be carefully followed by emergency providers in the collection of evidence.

It has not been determined if the psychological impact of rape is different in older women than in young women.[8] However, crisis intervention counseling by qualified individuals is considered vital in the emergency management of the rape victim.[1] Counselors working with elderly victims of rape must help them deal with the increased awareness of physical vulnerability, reduced resilience, old age, and the possibility of the imminence of death. The older victim frequently has to face the trauma of being violated sexually after perhaps years of sexual inactivity. Sodomy or oral sex may be especially traumatic to older women.[8] Continued counseling and follow-up by support individuals or groups is an important factor in the management of the sexual assault victims. Being aware of available resources in the community is the responsibility of emergency providers.

Frequent Related Disorders

Osteoporosis

Osteoporosis is a condition seen frequently in elderly females that is characterized by a decrease in bone mass. Women begin to lose cortical bone calcification approximately 10 years before menopause.[5] This increase in bone reabsorption in postmenopausal women is attributed to a lack of estrogen.[10]

Osteoporosis produces both cosmetic and functional disability. There is a high incidence of fractures among elderly females.[5] Secondary osteoarthritis and degenerative bone changes associated with vertebra compression fractures can cause not only "dowager hump" but also severe pain.[10]

Patients come to the ED with pathologic fractures that usually occur from minor or no apparent trauma. They may be completely asymptomatic or have pain secondary to the fracture. There may be spinal tenderness and postural changes. The most frequent sites of the fractures are the vertebra and femur.[10] Emergency management includes complete evaluation and treatment of the fractures, referral, and evaluation for possible estrogen therapy.[5] Estrogen replacement therapy for the treatment of osteoporosis must be carefully evaluated by the physician due to the increased incidence of endometrial and breast cancer.[5] Hypertension, blood clots, and myocardial infarctions may also be related to estrogen therapy.[5]

Breast Carcinoma

Breast cancer is the most common malignant condition in women.[5] It is found mostly in females 46–60 years of age, and it develops most frequently in individuals with a family history of breast cancer. Geriatric patients who in their younger years had premenstrual breast discomfort or breast swelling, especially cysts before menstruation, are more likely to develop cancer of the breast.[5]

The presenting sign is an unusual lump or thickening in the breast that is generally not painful. The incidence usually increases following menopause.[5] In geriatric patients, self-examination of the breast is generally infrequent, due to poor education and understanding of the disease. It is mandatory for emergency physicians to do a complete breast examination on all female patients regardless of age. Mammography should be part of the complete breast examination for all women over age 50.[5]

EMERGENCY GERIATRIC DIAGNOSTIC WORKUP

Diagnostic tests, bimanual examinations, and Pap smears should never be neglected in elderly women. The importance of yearly gynecologic examinations should be stressed in the ED to the geriatric patient and her family. The use of these procedures in the early diagnosis of reproductive tract complaints can be instrumental in the early detection of carcinoma.[5]

The following six points must be emphasized in the gynecologic evaluation of the geriatric patient:[3]

1. A biopsy must be done on any mass ulceration or persistently tender area of the vulva and vagina.[3]
2. The progressive changes of aging may alter the pH and bacterial flora of the genital tract and predispose the patient to infections. The pH and flora should be returned to normal by the use of buffered, acidifying medications; estrogenic applications; and/or specific antibacterial therapy to avoid chronic or recurrent infections.[3,5]
3. Vaginal bleeding must be considered as a quasiemergency in this age group requiring admission to the obstetric/gynecologic service for complete evaluation, including Pap smears, D&C, and cervical biopsy as minimal procedures to rule out uterine malignancy. Persistent vaginal bleeding with negative curettage could indicate a possible adnexal malignancy.[3]
4. Any lateral pelvic mass, regardless of size, is an indication for further evaluation. Any pelvic or abdominal mass in the pelvis with an increase in size, pain, or tenderness should be explored.[3]
6. Elderly women on prolonged steroid therapy should be limited regarding the use of estrogenic substances and be controlled at the lowest possible orally administered dosage range.[3,5] They should receive regular physical examinations.

Special Considerations for the Elderly Patient

Emergency providers have a unique opportunity to combine their interest in all subspecialties into one, emergency medicine. This requires the skill level well beyond those of a generalist. They must interact with individuals of all ages, socioeconomic circumstances, cultures, and religions. They must be sensitive to the special needs of individuals and their lifestyles as these factors are often significant to their health care.[11]

Age of the patient is an important factor to be kept in mind. The elderly woman in an ED is usually frightened and recognizes the loss of control in her life and fears further loss. All efforts should be made by emergency providers to allow her to maintain as much control as possible.[1]

The following seven methods should be helpful in achieving this goal:

1. Explain all procedures in a simple and untaxing manner.
2. Consider the frequent physical constraints of the elderly, such as impaired hearing, sight, and limited movement.
3. Remove as much extraneous noise and movement of others as possible.
4. Keep the elderly female covered and at a comfortable body temperature during the diagnostic examinations.
5. Give the elderly female time to recall or rehearse material to be learned. Written instruction sheets in simple meaningful terms are helpful.
6. Involve the family and other sources of support.
7. Provide community referrals.[12]

REFERENCES

1. McCall P, Varvel P: Obstetrical and gynecological emergencies, in Budassi SA, Barber JM (eds): *Emergency Nursing: Principles and Practice*. St. Louis, CV Mosby Co, 1981, pp 473–493.

2. Eliopoulos C: *Gerontological Nursing*. New York, Harper and Row, 1979, pp 110–117.

3. Birnbaum S: Geriatric gynecology, in *Working with Older People, Clinical Aspects of Aging*, Vol 4. Washington, DC, US Department of Health Education and Welfare, 1973, pp 149–155.

4. Hudson MF: Safeguard your elderly patient's health through accurate physical assessment. *Nursing 83*, November 1983, pp 58–64.

5. Elkowitz E: *Geriatric Medicine for the Primary Care Practitioner*. New York, Springer Publishing Company, 1981.

6. de Voogt HJ: Problems and dangers of catheterization in the elderly, in Folner AR, Schouten J (eds): *Geriatrics for the Practitioner*. Amsterdam, Excerpta Medica, 1981.

7 Pearson LF, Kotthoff ME: *Geriatric Clinical Protocols*. New York, JB Lippincott Company, 1979.

8. Davis LJ: Rape and older women, in Warner CG (ed): *Rape and Sexual Assault Management and Intervention*. Rockville, MD, Aspen Publishers, 1980, pp 94–118.

9. Hubbard LT, Gibbons WE (eds): *Handbook of Gynecologic Emergencies*. New York, Medical Examination Publishing Co, 1983.

10. Yen PK: Fractures and diet—what's the relationship. *Geriatric Nursing*. September/October 1981, pp 327–328.

11. Budassi SA, Barber JM: *Emergency Nursing: Principles and Practice*. St. Louis, CV Mosby Co, 1981.

12. Miller M: Patient teaching in the emergency department, in Budassi SA, Barber JM (eds): *Emergency Nursing: Principles and Practice*, St. Louis, CV Mosby Co, 1981, pp 214–227.

SUGGESTED READINGS

Gelin J: The aged American female. *J Gerontol Nurs* 6:69–73, 1980.

Statistical Abstract of the United States, ed 102. U.S. Department of Commerce, Bureau of the Census (102nd ed) National Data Book and Guide to Sources, 1981.

Wilson L, Simson, S.: *Establishing a Data Base on Emergency Services and the Elderly: Planning for Linkages Between Emergency Services, Long Term Care, and Health Related Services.* Dallas, Gerontology Services Administration, The University of Texas Health Service Center, 1981.

14

Ear, Nose, and Throat Emergencies

Lewis DeMent, MD, FACEP

Elderly patients with ear, nose, and throat (ENT) complaints pose a complicated challenge to the emergency physician. The discomfort of itching and ear pain in a healthy 20-year-old swimmer may in a 70-year-old diabetic patient be the initial stages of fulminant malignant external otitis, which, if not recognized, can lead to profound morbidity and death. For emergency physicians, suspicions about the cause of a complaint must be sharpened and focused in order to offer patients the best possible care. With the elderly who have complex past medical histories one cannot be too thorough.

This chapter describes ENT disease processes that cause the elderly person to see an emergency physician because of pain, fear, or sense of personal danger.

EAR

Infections

Although usually not an immediately life-threatening disease, ear infections can cause a great deal of pain in any aged patient.

Otitis Media

In general the older adult with acute otitis media has the same signs and symptoms as the young child; that is, ear pain, decreased hearing, and often fever. This condition usually follows an upper respiratory infection and is due to the lack of ventilation of the eustachian tube secondary to inflammation of the tube opening in the nasopharynx. It is thought that a vacuum develops in this closed system, and then fluid is secreted into the middle ear, providing a rich media for bacterial growth.

Physical findings include a red bulging tympanic membrane, lack of pain when the external ear is palpated, and possibly fluid visible behind the tympanic membrane. Pneumatic otoscopy usually reveals a tympanic membrane that does not move readily with air pressure. If the patient is in severe pain and if the tympanic membrane is bulging, myringotomy may be needed to provide comfort and to accelerate resolution of the healing process. Usually the patient can be treated with oral antibiotics, analgesics, and decongestants for comfort. In adults most of the infections are caused by *Pneumococcus, Hemophilus influenzae,* or *Streptococcus,*[1] and penicillin or amoxicillin is the initial drug of choice.

Most cases of otitis media are bilateral in the setting of an upper respiratory tract infection, although one ear may be affected more than the other. However, in the older adult the finding of a unilateral otitis media, especially in the absence of evidence of an upper respiratory infection, should alert the emergency physician to the possibility of a nasopharyngeal polyp or tumor as the cause of the eustachian tube dysfunction. Indirect nasopharyngeal laryngoscopy should be performed in an attempt to visualize the openings of the eustachian tube in the nasopharynx. Whether this procedure is successful in visualizing the abnormality, these patients need a thorough ENT examination. A benign cause should not be assumed.

External Otitis

In a like manner, external otitis has similar signs and symptoms in all age groups. As the size of the aged population increases and people are more active in their later years, even the typical swimmer's ear may be seen in the older adult. The signs and symptoms of external otitis are severe pain when the pinna or tragus is pulled, a swollen external auditory canal, and possibly superficial hemorrhage and large amounts of necrotic debris lying in a mucoid discharge. The infection is often caused by relatively minor trauma, such as caused by hairpins, cleaning the ear, or exposure to excessive moisture.[1]

Treatment consists of gentle cleaning of the canal with suction and placing a cotton wick through the stenotic canal so that medication can reach the inner parts of the auditory canal. Often a discharge from the canal emits a foul odor typical of the common *Pseudomonas* infection.[1] Ear drops containing polymixin-B, neomycin, and hydrocortisone used four times daily for a week usually clear these infections, providing the patient has kept water out of the ear and avoided excessive attempts to clean the ear, thereby causing further injury. Simple mucoid or keratin-containing drainage often responds to 2% acetic acid drops in the affected ear.

If small vesicles or furuncles are seen in the external canal,[2] they can be gently opened, and then an ointment or cream, such as polymyxin B, bacitracin, neomycin, or gentamicin, can be used to help heal these areas. When the skin of the external ear becomes inflamed as in impetigo or cellulitis, then appropriate broad-spectrum antistaphylococcal and antistreptococcal systemic antibiotics are appropriate.

Malignant External Otitis

The clinical picture of external otitis just described or a chronic external otitis not responding to the usual appropriate therapy in an elderly diabetic patient should alert the emergency physician to a potentially fatal disease.

Malignant external otitis was first described by Chandler in the late 1960s.[3] This disease is almost exclusively seen in the elderly diabetic patient. On examination, the patient is found to have a chronic external otitis with granulation tissue present on the floor of the external auditory canal at the cartilage-osseous junction portion of the canal. With gentle probing this tissue is found to be coming from a defect in the canal floor[4] and actually leads into the soft tissue at the base of the skull. There is tenderness behind the angle of the mandible, although with little external ear pain. It is a poor prognostic sign when cranial nerve VII is involved.

When the debris is cultured, the results indicate a *Pseudomonas* infection. These patients rarely respond to the usual treatment for external otitis, and the infection tends to involve bone, cartilage, nerves, and blood vessels.

Aggressive therapy is directed to surgical debridement and administration of systemic antibiotics, such as gentamicin IM 2 ml/kg/day and carbenicillin 24 gm/day, 1 gm IV given each hour, in an attempt to prevent the tragic sequelae of mastoiditis, osteomyelitis, meningitis, brain abscess, and death.[3] In Chandler's series of 38 patients in 1972, there was a 38% mortality, but after the aforementioned antibiotic regimen was started, the death rate dramatically decreased.[3] Most patients require hospitalization for several weeks. The emergency physician must be aware of this syndrome to avoid continuing the typical conservative local therapy that usually cures external otitis but only delays definitive therapy for this disease.

Ear Trauma

Trauma to the ear involves three anatomic areas: the external ear, the auditory canal, and the tympanic membrane or middle ear area. Most ear trauma in the elderly occurs as a result of falls, assaults, or auto accidents. However, canal trauma is also caused by the patient's attempt to clean the ear, and occasionally a tympanic membrane perforation is caused by the same method or more rarely by hot metal or lightning striking the patient.

Perforated Tympanic Membrane

Perforation of the tympanic membrane usually heals spontaneously and requires no surgical intervention. In the emergency department (ED) a rough measure of the patient's ability to hear should be recorded, and the patient should be advised not to put any foreign material, including water, into the ear. The patient is referred to the ENT specialist for a thorough audiological evaluation. However, in the elderly less air pressure is required to cause a perforation by blast injury than in a younger person so that the elderly are more vulnerable to the blast effect.[5] Also, the injuries caused by lightning and molten metal often heal very slowly if at all, and careful ENT follow-up is needed. Those patients whose perforation remains open for 3 months are considered for surgery. Only those patients with vertigo or perilymph leakage[5] soon after the accident may require early surgical intervention.

Canal Trauma

Trauma to the external canal is usually a small abrasion or laceration, which can simply be cleaned and treated with a local antibiotic ointment. In the healing period, the patient should try to avoid getting water and other foreign material in the ear.

External Ear Trauma

Trauma to the external ear must be carefully evaluated to avoid complications. Lacerations to the skin of the outer ear can be cleaned and closed with small interrupted 6-0 nylon sutures. If, however, the cartilage is also injured, it should be closed with absorbable sutures, and finally skin should be closed over it. Cartilage should not be left exposed; the risk of chondritis is high with resultant increased cosmetic deformity and the possibility of chronic infection.

After the outer ear is sutured, fluffed gauze should be placed in the postauricular area and a turban-style bandage applied to prevent the ear from collapsing and becoming deformed. If a deforming hematoma is found, it should be evacuated with a needle or incision and the ear bandaged as described previously to prevent deformity (cauliflower ear).

Sudden Hearing Loss

Sudden hearing loss occurs in all age groups and both sexes and is usually unilateral. There is no consensus in the literature on the etiology of this entity.[6] The main causes that have been considered are viral infections, vascular disorders, and lesions of the oval or round window. In a clinical sense the vascular theory is very attractive because it explains the sudden onset, tendency to recur, and the connections with hypercoagulable states of sudden hearing loss. However, the pathologic data are scanty, and most support the viral theory.[6] According to some data the three viral infections most likely to cause auditory failure are varicella zoster, measles, and mumps.[7] There is an increased hearing loss in the diabetic patient who is over 40 years old, but there is no difference found in the audiological patterns of diabetics as compared to controls.[8]

Approximately 63% of patients spontaneously recover their hearing. There does not seem to be a definite treatment protocol that has increased the percentage of patients who recover their hearing.[9] If a definite associated disease is found, such as a hypercoagulable state, then it makes sense to try the anticoagulant mode of therapy. Otherwise, the "shotgun" approach of vasodilators, histamines, and corticosteroids should be tried, with varying success and often disappointing results.

Vertigo

The elderly patient who arrives in the ED complaining of dizziness or vertigo needs a thorough examination. There are hundreds of causes of these symptoms, including simple viral infections, vascular diseases, and malignancy. The diagnostic approach must be organized to avoid overlooking the dangerous causes. If a life-threatening situation is not apparent on initial inspection, then a rapid assessment to rule out cardiac and major neurologic events is carried out. If one is left with the symptoms of vertigo or dizziness and finds spontaneous or positional nystagmus on examination, then the task becomes one of separating the central from the peripheral causes of nystagmus.

One of the more lucid descriptions of these patients has been provided by Lindeman.[10] In general, spontaneous nystagmus of a peripheral origin is characterized by horizontal or horizontorotatary direction, is usually bilateral, is accompanied by the subjective feeling of vertigo, and is usually suppressed by visual fixation. In contrast, the nystagmus of central origin is often vertical, unilateral, enhanced by visual fixation, and not necessarily accompanied by vertigo.

When the patient is subjected to position testing by being tilted quickly to the side from a sitting position, any eye changes that appear should be noted. In the nystagmus of peripheral origin there is usually a latent period of several seconds after the patient is tilted before the nystagmus starts. It then lasts only 1–2 min, demonstrates a crescendo-decrescendo pattern, is direction-fixed, fatigable, and reproduces the vertigo complaint.[10,11] Exactly the opposite signs are characteristic of central nystagmus; infatigability, sustained steady pattern, and changing direction are common.

In patients without hearing loss or tinnitus, the more likely peripheral disorders seen are benign positional vertigo and vestibular neuronitis.[11] In vestibular neuronitis, attacks occur intermittently much as in Meniere's disease, but hearing loss is not affected and the attack is not necessarily related to head position. Most of these elderly patients require hospitalization to manage their nausea and vomiting and to observe their course. They often benefit in the ED from sedatives or antihistamines, such as diphenhydramine or meclizine. Patients who have vertigo of central etiology and those who have nystagmus of peripheral origin and do not respond to appropriate treatment need a full evaluation by a neurospecialist.

A Neurosurgical Emergency

Vertigo that appears in the context of a transient ischemic attack (TIA) has usually been ascribed to the vertebrobasilar system.[12] If the patient has a TIA syndrome and a carotid bruit and develops vertigo when turning the head to the opposite side, a neurological emergency should be considered. This combination of findings has been shown to be a warning of immediate stroke related to occlusion of the carotid artery on the side of the bruit.[13] The patients who have had angiography show normal vertebrobasilar systems and total internal carotid occlusion.[13] It is thought that the stenotic internal carotid is kinked when the patient turns the head, and after endarterectomy these patients have complete resolution of their symptoms.[13]

NOSE

Infections

Nasal Vestibulitis

Although not a medical emergency, the pain associated with anterior nasal infection can cause a person to seek immediate aid. The history is usually one of progressive tenderness to palpation of the tip of the nose, often following an upper respiratory infection or a spell of dry weather that causes formation of a great deal of crust in the nose. This condition subsequently becomes more bothersome, and after the patient picks the nose, the nose becomes very tender. These infections are often staphylococcal and can be treated by the patient placing antibiotic ointment in small amounts in the nasal vestibule and applying intermittent moist heat to the nose. Resolution is usually achieved in a few days. One should advise the patient to use a lanolin-based ointment to prevent drying of the mucosa and help prevent future episodes.

Sinusitis

Paranasal sinusitis is usually a disease of young and middle-aged adults. Acute ethmoiditis in particular is more common in children;[14] however, the complications of sinusitis in the elderly adult can be severe. The elderly seek treatment later in the course of their disease than do younger people. In one study the patients over 60 years of age had experienced severe symptoms for several months before seeing a physician.[15]

The more dangerous complication of acute or chronic sinusitis is cavernous sinus thrombosis.[14] The patient may have been treated for weeks or months for a chronic sinusitis and then abruptly experience increased symptoms as the infection actually worsens.

To understand the clinical picture, one must recall the anatomy of the involved area. Several veins, including the ophthalmic, angular, ethmoid, superior ophthalmic, and inferior ophthalmic, have direct valveless connections to the cavernous sinuses (Figure 14–1). Cranial nerves III, IV, VI and the first two divisions of cranial nerve V, along with the internal carotid artery, pass through the cavernous sinus (Figure 14–2). Infections can travel intracranially through the

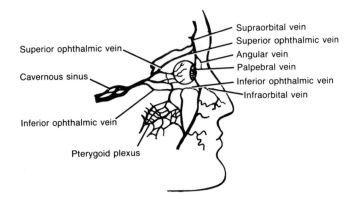

Figure 14–1 The venous drainage of the middle third of the face to the cavernous sinus.

Source: Reprinted with permission from *Journal of International College of Surgeons* (1963;40:66), Copyright © 1963, International College of Surgeons.

veins, and once inflammation has begun the sinus may become thrombosed, leading to the clinical syndrome that affects the nerves.[14,15]

The signs and symptoms progress from the previous state of sinus fullness to facial edema as the venous drainage of the face becomes obstructed. Then there may be retinal swelling, decreased vision, and extraocular muscle paralysis as the cranial nerves are involved. Paresthesias or anesthesia of the first and second divisions of cranial nerve V then follow, with frank meningitis and death close behind if not treated. The mortality rate continues to be in the 20% range even with modern antibiotic therapy.[14] In elderly debilitated or immunosuppressed patients mucormycosis of the sinuses may cause a less toxic but otherwise typical picture of cavernous sinus thrombosis.[15]

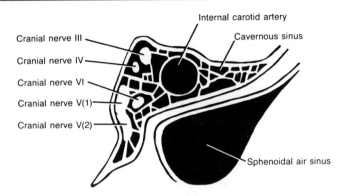

Figure 14–2 The anatomy of the cavernous sinus.

Source: Reprinted with permission from *Journal of International College of Surgeons* (1963;40:66), Copyright © 1963, International College of Surgeons.

Often there is no material available for culture, and the patient must be treated empirically yet aggressively. The treatment involves hospitalization and massive intravenous (IV) doses of broad-spectrum antibiotics, including those capable of treating penicillin-resistant, staphylococcal infections. In addition, consideration should be given to anticoagulation if the patient's general condition allows.[14]

Nasal Fracture

Nasal fractures, the most common of all facial fractures,[16] occur frequently in older persons. Because falling spells and blackouts are common among the elderly, as are assaults and automobile accidents, nasal trauma is common.

One of the duties of the emergency physician when examining a patient with a nasal injury is to evaluate the interior and exterior of the nose completely. The presence or absence of mucosal tears, septal deformities, or septal hematoma in particular should be evaluated because of the sequelae of septal necrosis, airway obstruction, and cosmetic deformity that may occur if the hematoma is not treated.[17]

The importance of clinical expertise in recognizing nasal fractures is often undervalued. Unlike most bony trauma in the body, a fractured nose may be associated with a perfectly normal x-ray film. It has been said that the most important single factor responsible for missing the diagnosis of facial fracture is a dependence on x-rays and films to make the diagnosis.[16] The keys to making the correct assessment are observation, palpation, and discussion with the patient. The presence of nasal deformity, crepitus on palpation, ecchymosis, and epistaxis suggest the diagnosis. It is imperative to question these patients about past trauma because the patient could have a simple contusion of a previously deformed nose. One of the most important pieces of information to obtain is the patient's perception of the presence or absence of a new nasal deformity.

If there is a great deal of edema, then the reduction can wait 5–7 days and be accomplished by the ENT physician. If there is little edema and the patient is otherwise stable, then the emergency physician may wish to effect reduction before increased swelling occurs a few hours later.

The treatment of nasal fracture in the elderly is not very different from the treatment in the younger person. The nose must be anesthetized sufficiently before reducing the fracture. This is accomplished by using either cocaine 5%[16] or topical lidocaine 4% with 1:1,000 epinephrine on cotton pledgets placed in the nostrils. In addition, an external nasal block using lidocaine 1% or Marcaine ½% is performed.

Walsham forceps are used to realign the bony pyramid by disimpacting the bone (Figure 14–3). Then the Asch septal forceps are used to straighten the septum and replace it in the vomerine groove if displaced. Finally the Salinger reduction instrument is used to contour the tip of the nose further.[16] Usually most bleeding is stopped as the nasal structures are reduced to their correct anatomic positions. Packs are then used only if bleeding persists. A plaster splint can be taped to the nose to afford protection while vasoconstricting nose drops, such as ¼% phenyl-

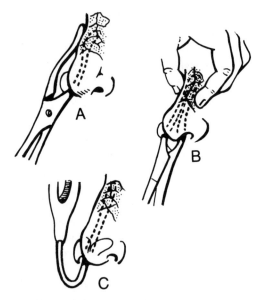

Figure 14–3 Closed reduction of nasal fractures. **A:** Walsham forceps; **B:** Asch septal forceps; **C:** Salinger reduction instrument.

Source: Reprinted with permission from *Journal of Trauma* (1975;15:322), Copyright © 1975, Williams & Wilkins Company, Baltimore.

---

ephrine hydrochloride, can be used during the first 3 days to aid in shrinking intranasal edema to ease breathing.

Epistaxis

Treating the elderly patient who has epistaxis can be a very challenging and often frightening experience. A 75-year-old patient who is anticoagulated and is in shock with a posterior epistaxis can provide the most experienced emergency physician plenty of opportunity to use his or her skills.

Etiology

The etiology of epistaxis in the elderly is multifactorial. Anterior bleeding is often the result of local causes, such as direct trauma, low relative humidity, recent upper respiratory infection with crust formations and mucosal drying, and such minor trauma as nose picking. The etiology of posterior bleeding, however, is more difficult to understand. Hypertension and atherosclerosis are routinely seen in the elderly patient with epistaxis, which is often posterior in a branch of the sphenopalatine artery where it bends or where the vessel is contained in a bony canal in the inferior turbinate.[18] As the nasal arteries age, there is degeneration of the vessels characterized by a loss of muscle in the tunica media vasorum and its replacement with collagen.[18] This has led to the idea that once these arteries bleed, they have less ability to contract and stop bleeding. There are of course more unusual causes of epistaxis, such as a ruptured internal carotid aneurysm that erodes through the paranasal sinuses and causes a near-fatal hemorrhage.[19]

Anatomy

To appreciate fully the clinical features of epistaxis, one must understand the vascular supply of the nose. Most patients with epistaxis have a bleeding site in the anterior part of the nasal septum known as Kiesselbach's plexus or Little's area, an area of convergence of several small blood vessels. In contrast, bleeding in the superior aspect of the posterior nasal cavity is usually from the anterior or posterior ethmoid arteries, and bleeding below the middle turbinate originates from branches of the sphenopalatine artery.[20] Another way of looking at the arterial distribution is to recognize that the area above the middle turbinate is supplied by the internal carotid artery, whereas the area below the middle turbinate is supplied by the external carotid branches (Figure 14–4).

Approach to the Patient

The initial task in treating epistaxis is to evaluate quickly the patient's general hemodynamic stability. Is the patient vigorous and has had only an hour of intermittent anterior bleeding? Or is the patient weak, pale, hypotensive, and gives a brief history of bleeding all night? If there is any question about the extent of bleeding, then the usual lifesaving measures of intravascular access, fluids, bloods, etc., are ordered. If the patient is stable, an orderly approach can be undertaken.

Almost all patients with epistaxis are apprehensive, and the physician who proceeds calmly to reassure the patient that everything is under control will have an extra assistant at hand if the bleeding is indeed great. Time taken to explain each step in the treatment will enhance a patient's cooperation so the procedures can be performed with skill and efficiency. If this rapport is established, sedatives are rarely needed. The patient and physician should be protected with aprons or gowns and the patient provided with facial tissue and an emesis basin.

Treating the Epistaxis

To control nasal bleeding effectively, the bleeding site must be found. Doing so requires a cooperative patient, a strong head light, suction equipment, and an organized approach to the nasal anatomy. The patient is instructed to blow out clots, pinch the nose closed, and breathe through the mouth while the ENT instrument tray is readied. Suction is then used to clear the nose. To see the bleeding artery, a nasal speculum is inserted to open vertically in one naris, then in the other. In the simplest case, a small vessel is seen to bleed in the Kiesselbach's plexus.[18,20] The nasal mucosa is then anesthetized with a cotton pledget soaked in

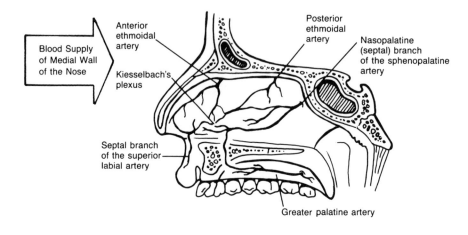

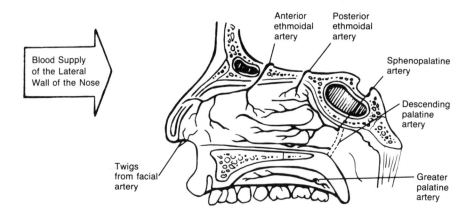

Figure 14–4 Blood supply of the nose.

Source: Reprinted with permission from *American Family Physician* (1976;14:78), Copyright © 1976, American Academy of Family Physicians.

a half-and-half mixture of 4% topical lidocine or 5% cocaine and 1:1,000 adrenalin. After the excess anesthetic is squeezed from the cotton, the pledget is placed in the nostril, and the patient is asked to pinch the nostrils closed for 3–4 min and breathe through the mouth. Obtaining full anesthesia if cocaine is used may require waiting 10 min.

When the cotton is removed, one can usually see small (feeder) vessels leading to the vessel that is bleeding. They are touched lightly with a silver nitrate stick, and then a new pledget is inserted. This sequence can be repeated until the main bleeder is bleeding slowly and it too can be cauterized with the silver nitrate stick. Often having an assistant hold the speculum while the physician applies suction and cautery simultaneously works well. In some cases electrocautery is required and seems to cauterize more quickly. In the unusual case of a persistent septal bleeder, a small piece of oxidized cellulose or absorbable gelatin sponge soaked in thrombin can be applied to the bleeding site to aid in the hemostasis. Large packs of these agents are to be avoided because they tend to become large and boggy masses that are difficult to remove later.

Anterior Packing. If, when the septum is examined, no bleeding site is found, the next most likely site is the anterior or posterior ends of the inferior turbinate laterally.[20] These areas can be best located by watching the suction tubing as a Frazier suction tip is gently inserted along the floor of the nose. A return of bright red blood gives a clue to the location of the bleeder. If the bleeder appears to be along the anterior aspect of the turbinate, it too may be cauterized if seen, but otherwise an anterior pack is needed.

To prepare for anterior packing, a cotton pledget soaked with the anesthetic agents previously described should be inserted deep into the nose. While waiting for the anesthetic to take effect, the pack itself should be prepared. A most effective pack is ¼ or ½ in by 6 ft petroleum jelly gauze. An antibiotic ointment, such as polymyxin-B, bacitracin, neomycin, or gentamicin, should be applied to the gauze because the incidence of sinusitis is increased with packs in place.

The anesthetic pledget should then be removed. The petroleum jelly gauze is inserted into the nose, starting with a loop about 4 in from the end of the gauze (Figure 14 5). This prevents the end of the gauze from being aspirated into the throat. Each loop is successively applied until the entire pack is in place. Most nostrils readily accommodate 6 ft of packing.

When the anterior packing is not sufficient or when it is apparent that the bleeding is coming from a truly posterior part of the nasal cavity, then a posterior pack is needed. The term ''posterior pack'' actually implies the combination of a posterior choanal pack and an anterior pack as previously described.

Posterior Packing. Although balloon catheters[20] have been used to control posterior bleeding, unless there is an extreme sense of emergency, a well-placed lamb's wool pack is probably more effective. It is during the placement of the posterior choanal pack that the rapport with the patient will be most appreciated. These packs are uncomfortable and at best give the patient a feeling of suffocation. It is very important to encourage the patient to breathe slowly through the mouth while the pack is being placed, and asking the patient to avoid biting the physician's fingers is also worthwhile.

The first step again is anesthesia. The anterior nose is anesthetized as previously described. The oral pharynx and uvula can be sprayed with Benzocaine to help retard the inevitable gag reflex.

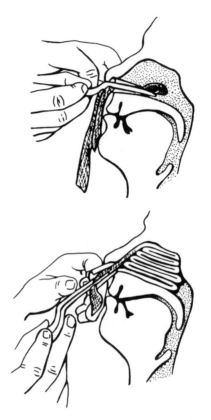

Figure 14–5 Anterior packing.

Source: Reprinted from *Procedures and Techniques in Emergency Medicine* (p 241) by RR Simon and BE Brenner with permission of Williams & Wilkins Company, Baltimore, © 1982.

A small rubber catheter is then placed through the nostril on the affected side and grabbed with forceps as it passes the uvula, bringing the end of the catheter through the mouth[20] (Figure 14–6). This is a natural pause in the procedure, and the patient can briefly rest while the two-string end of the lamb's wool pack is tied to the catheter. Then, while asking the patient to open the mouth wide, not to bite the physician's fingers, and to breathe through the mouth, the lamb's wool is placed behind the uvula with the fingers on one hand while the other hand pulls the catheter with the two strings through the nose. Again, there is a natural pause in the procedure so the patient can rest. The bleeding is now controlled because the physician can simply hold the pack by the two strings and pinch the nostrils, causing effective anterior-posterior tamponade. The anterior pack is then placed and the two strings tied over a roll of gauze, causing no pressure on the alae or columella. The remaining string dangling beyond the uvula is cut off at that level, which facilitates removal of the pack later.

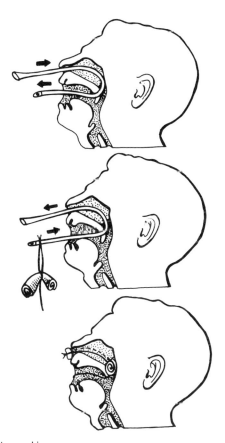

Figure 14–6 Posterior packing.

Source: Reprinted from *Procedures and Techniques in Emergency Medicine* (p 243) by RR Simon and BE Brenner with permission of Williams & Wilkins Company, Baltimore, © 1982.

Patients who have a posterior pack placed are at an increased risk for sinusitis,[20] and their general misery and potential for having life-threatening hemorrhage necessitate their hospitalization. Additional attention should be given to those patients who have chronic lung disease and a low PO_2 because the patient's PO_2 often decreases with a posterior pack in place.[21] A thorough inhospital workup is then done to rule out a coagulation disorder or occult nasopharyngeal pathology.

In some patients epistaxis may still be present after the unilateral anterior-posterior pack. The other nostril should then be packed in an anterior-posterior fashion, and most bleeding then stops. An occasional patient may have to go to surgery rather urgently to have a vessel ligated if a bilateral anterior-posterior pack does not control the bleeding.

A patient who arrives in the ED after nasal bleeding has stopped presents an interesting therapeutic question. Should the nose be cauterized or packed even though there is no bleeding? In many patients who bleed from the septum a small pimple-like area on the septum is seen. This is usually the artery that bled, and it should be cauterized.

If no septal site is found, the question of packing remains. After the physician explains the packing procedure, most patients, providing they are medically stable and have an adequate home situation, elect to go home and return if the bleeding recurs. This approach seems to make sense because it is very difficult to prevent recurrences by packing a nose when it is not bleeding.

An older patient who has experienced epistaxis should have a thorough ENT examination. Although simple anterior bleeding may be present, the patient should be evaluated to be certain that the bleeding does not represent the early signs of systemic disease, such as leukemia, or of local disease, such as nasopharyngeal cancer.

THROAT

It is not that the treatment of acute throat problems in the elderly differs so much from treatment in younger people; it is the heightened awareness of the potentially dangerous causes of throat problems in the elderly that, if overlooked, can have tragic consequences. Most throat complaints in the elderly person are related to difficulty in swallowing and pain. Although many of these symptoms may be chronic and annoying, some may be acute or prompt a visit to the ED because of their progressively worsening nature.

Infection

In general, throat infections are less common in the older adult than in the child or middle-aged person. Although pharyngitis may still be present in the elderly and an occasional patient with epiglottitis[22] may be encountered, an expanded differential diagnosis should be considered that includes diphtheria, Ludwig's angina, moniliasis, and pharyngitis associated with leukopenia. These more unusual causes of pharyngitis must be considered because the elderly are more likely to be debilitated or immunosuppressed and to have serious chronic underlying disease, such as diabetes or leukemia. These diseases usually require more treatment and follow-up care than most common causes of pharyngitis in the younger person.

Diphtheria

Although usually thought of as a disease of children, diphtheria strikes the adult population as well.[23] Once an epidemic begins in an area, a significant number of older persons are usually affected. During an epidemic from 1972 to 1975 in Seattle's "Skid Road" area, 11% of the cases and carriers were over 60 years old.[24] Recognizing the early cases in an epidemic can be a significant problem because the most common initial symptom is a sore throat,[25] even before the tell-tale "dirty" pharyngeal membrane develops.

Diphtheria immunizations are effective for approximately 10 years, but many older persons are not immunized. Because the mortality rate continues to be in the 10% range, a high index of suspicion is warranted.[25] Cardiac failure, otitis media, vocal cord paralysis, adrenal insufficiency, and pneumonia are a few of the complications that are known to occur, so early recognition is paramount. Antibiotics (penicillin and erythromycin) clear the body of the organism, but the mainstay of treatment is 40,000 to 100,000 units of antitoxin given intravenously after a scratch test is performed to check for antitoxin sensitivity.[23,25]

Ludwig's Angina

Ludwig's angina often occurs in the presence of poor oral hygiene in elderly debilitated men.[26] Infection spreads through minor traumatic lesions or infected teeth through the floor of the mouth and by definition involves sublingual and submaxillary spaces bilaterally.

These patients have a brawny cellulitis of the floor of the mouth, which tends to push the tongue upward. Because there is a danger of upper airway obstruction, these patients should be admitted to the intensive care unit. Pharyngeal cultures should be obtained before starting the patient on IV broad-spectrum antibiotics, including an aminoglycoside and a penicillinase-resistant penicillin. If a respiratory arrest occurs, a cricothyrotomy may have to be performed because routine tracheal intubation is often impossible because of the massive hypopharyngeal edema.[27]

Moniliasis

Moniliasis, which is usually seen in infants, may be seen in the elderly patient who has been on antibiotics or is immunosuppressed or debilitated from other chronic disease.[23] Even though the pain may not be severe as in other causes of pharyngitis, it nevertheless interferes with eating and swallowing. This condition is recognized by the white cheesy patches on the oral and pharyngeal mucosa that, when scraped off, reveal an erythematous base. The initial treatment consists of stopping antibiotics and starting nystatin suspension four times a day and, of course, searching for any underlying disorder.

Neutropenia

Almost any hematologic disorder that results in neutropenia can cause a severe sore throat secondary to local bacterial invasion. These patients often appear ill and febrile and have cervical adenitis. Agranulocytosis caused by medications may also be etiologic, in addition to primary hematologic disorders. The patient tends to deteriorate rapidly unless antibiotics are started quickly.[23]

Peritonsillar Abscess (Quinsy)

The presence of a peritonsillar abscess must be recognized because the usual treatment for pharyngitis with antibiotics is not sufficient. The typical history is one of persistent sore throat, odynophagia, and ear pain after antibiotic treatment.[28] On examination, the peritonsillar area is swollen and tends to push the uvula to the opposite side. Although this entity tends to occur in young and middle-aged adults, in the elderly patient this abscess may be superimposed on a tumor or in rare cases on an internal carotid aneurysm.[29] It takes little imagination to appreciate the horror and chaos associated with an inadvertent incision and drainage of the internal carotid artery in the ED.

Incision and drainage should be performed in the ED only if a definite non-pulsatile, fluctuant abscess is present and assistance is available to aid in suctioning the patient. With most elderly patients an ENT physician should be consulted and the patients admitted to the hospital. Abscesses that are not completely drained or that are treated late in their course may progress to peripharyngeal or retropharyngeal abscesses, which may be fatal if not treated.[23,28]

Cancer

A normal mouth and throat examination in the presence of sore throat symptoms should alert the physician to evaluate the hypopharynx thoroughly for malignancy. The common squamous cell cancers of the larynx are noted for causing pain on swallowing, hoarseness, and referred pain in the ear. This diagnosis should especially be considered in a chronic smoker or an alcoholic.[23] Any progressive sore throat, especially one that has persisted for 2–3 weeks or has recurred following antibiotic therapy, should be considered to represent a malignancy until proven otherwise. It is also rather characteristic of cancer that the throat pain may be transiently improved with antibiotic therapy and intensified by ingestion of citrus juices.[23] In a smoker who has a progressive history of a lump in the throat, the examiner must prove that a supraglottic tumor (typically squamous cell type) does not exist.[23,25]

Foreign Bodies

Foreign bodies in the pharynx and esophagus are commonly found in the elderly population. Often poor eyesight contributes to the problem; the person has difficulty seeing small objects, such as fish bones. There may be trouble in mastication in general and less sensation in the mouth because of the presence of dentures,[23] causing some objects to pass into the throat initially unnoticed.

Problems seen in the ED usually are caused by pharyngeal or esophageal foreign bodies. With the exception of chronic aspiration syndromes or acute "cafe coronary" presentations, foreign bodies that lodge in the glottis or trachea or are otherwise aspirated usually are expelled by the patient or found later when the patient develops pneumonia or other respiratory symptoms.

Pharyngeal

Small sharp objects usually stick in the tonsils, tongue, or periepiglottic area in the vallecula or pyriform sinuses.[23] Patients usually can localize foreign bodies that lie above the cricopharyngeus,[30] and it is mandatory to view these periepiglottic areas adequately when a patient complains of a localized pain. On occasion a foreign body can be seen in a tonsil simply by looking into the patient's mouth. Usually, however, either indirect laryngoscopy or direct laryngoscopy with a strong headlight and a large mirror to visualize the hypopharynx adequately is required. When a foreign body is seen, it can be grasped with a long clamp and removed.

If a thorough examination reveals no foreign body, then the examiner may wish to use plain x-ray films to find a foreign body if it is known to be opaque.[23] If the patient is otherwise asymptomatic, then the pharynx may have been only scratched and the patient will improve in 24 to 48 hours. If no improvement is noted, then more investigation is needed.

Esophageal

Although serious hemorrhage does not usually occur with esophageal foreign bodies,[31] esophageal obstruction and esophageal perforation with mediastinitis are known complications. There are also more severe but unusual complications, such as fatal hemorrhage from an esophageal foreign body that erodes into the aorta.[32] Esophageal foreign bodies usually become impacted at the cricopharyngeus, in the upper one-third of the esophagus, or at the gastroesophageal sphincter. Although local pain that increases with swallowing and is accompanied by hypersalivation is the classic triad for the diagnosis of an esophageal foreign body, the presence of hypersalivation alone after an episode of difficulty correlates highly with the presence of an esophageal foreign body.[33] An elderly patient who is drooling or hypersalivating after eating should be suspected of having at least a partially obstructing esophageal foreign body.

If the history suggests an object that is radio-opaque, such as a metal pin, plain x-ray films may reveal its location. It can then be removed by direct visualization during the esophagoscopy. If the history is one of choking on a bolus of food, then glucagon may be tried.[34] A dose of 1 mg is given intravenously, and the patient observed for a few minutes. As a smooth muscle relaxant, glucagon lowers the tone of the lower esophageal sphincter and allows the impacted bolus to pass into the stomach. If this treatment is not successful, then esophagoscopy may be required.

In general, when clinical signs of obstruction are present and a skilled endoscopist is available, there is little need to do a barium swallow because the barium tends to make the foreign body harder to see during esophagoscopy.[23] A barium swallow is better used to elucidate suspected motility problems and dysphagia. In that case, the irritating foreign body, such as a small piece of bay leaf, may not cause an esophageal obstruction, but might catch a swallowed barium-coated cotton ball, showing up well on the x-ray film during fluoroscopy.

Laryngeal Trauma

Fracture of the larynx usually is caused by an assault from a direct blow to the throat or an automobile accident when the neck strikes the dashboard or steering wheel. The diagnosis is made from the history and clinical findings of hoarseness, subcutaneous emphysema, stridor, hemoptysis, and often a flattened thyroid cartilage. A problem for the emergency physician then becomes how to protect an airway that may be already partially obstructed or may at any time become fully obstructed.

When laryngeal trauma is suspected, it is one of the few times in airway management when tracheal intubation is probably not the best initial choice. Some physicians feel that the airway may be compromised further by attempting to intubate the patient.[23,35] The sense of urgency the emergency physician feels may be the best determinant of which approach to use. If the patient is not in severe distress, then a more controlled but urgent tracheotomy may be a safer approach. This procedure is usually performed under local anesthesia by an ENT physician. Of course, if a patient is in immediate danger, intubation may have to be the first choice. The anatomy is usually distorted enough that a cricothyrotomy is not a good option. In more minor cases when a fractured larynx is suspected, an ENT specialist should evaluate the patient promptly because if surgery is required, the patients who have their surgery in the first 24 hours have fewer subsequent problems with breathing and speaking.[25,36]

REFERENCES

1. Walike JW: Management of acute ear infections. *Otolaryngol Clin North Am* 12:439–445, 1979.

2. Farmer HS: A guide for the treatment of external otitis. *Am Family Physician* 21:96–101, 1980.

3. Chandler JR: Pathogenesis and treatment of facial paralysis due to malignant external otitis. *Ann Oto Rhino Laryngol* 81:648–658, 1972.

4. Chandler JR: Malignant external otitis. *Laryngoscope* 78:1257–1293, 1968.

5. Griffin WL: A retrospective study of traumatic tympanic membrane perforation in a clinical practice. *Laryngoscope* 89:261–281, 1979.

6. Feldman H: Sudden hearing loss: A clinic survey. *Adv Otorhinolaryngol* 27:40–69, 1981.

7. Morrison AW: Acute deafness. *Br J Hosp* 19(3):237–42, 247–249, 1978.

8. Wilson WR, Laird N, Moo-Young G, et al: The relationship of idiopathic sudden hearing loss to diabetes mellitus. *Laryngoscope* 92:155–160, 1982.

9. Mattox DE: Medical management of sudden hearing loss. *Otolaryngol Head Neck Surg* 88:111–113, 1980.

10. Lindeman RC: Acute labyrinthine disorders. *Otolaryngol Clin North Am* 12:375–387, 1979.

11. Clemis JD, Becker GW: Vestibular neuronitis. *Otolaryngol Clin North Am* 6:139–155, 1973.

12. Heyman A, Leviton A, Millikan CH, et al: Report of the joint committee for stroke facilities. XI. Transient focal cerebral ischemia: Epidemiological and clinical aspects. *Stroke* 5:275–287, 1974.

13. Garner JT, Jacques S: Positional vertigo and bruit—a surgical emergency. *West J Med* 127:414–416, 1977.

14. Yarington Jr TC: Sinusitis as an emergency. *Otolaryngol Clin North Am* 12:447–454, 1979.

15. Sheffield RW, Cassisi NJ, Karlan MS: Complications of sinusitis. *Postgrad Med* 63:93–101, 1978.

16. Schultz RC, deVillers YT: Nasal fractures. *J Trauma* 15:319–327, 1975.

17. Jordan LW: Acute nasal and septal injuries. *Eye, Ear, Nose, Throat Monthly* 53:508–512, 1974.

18. Lingeman RE: Epistaxis. *Am Fam Physician* 14:79–83, 1976.

19. Polcyn JL: Epistaxis from rupture of aneurysm of internal carotid artery. *JAMA* 213:876, 1970.

20. DeWeese DD, Liebman EP, Norman FW, et al: From a to z in nosebleed control. *Patient Care* 66–83, 1978.

21. Lin YT, Orkin LR: Arterial hypoxemia in patient with anterior and posterior nasal packings. *Laryngoscope* 89:140–149, 1979.

22. Lindquist JR: Acute infections supraglottis in adults. *Ann Emerg Med* 9:256–259, 1980.

23. Cody DTR: *Diseases of the Ears, Nose and Throat*. Chicago, Year Book Medical Publishers Inc. 1981.

24. Pedersen AHB: Diphtheria on skid road, Seattle, Washington, 1972–75. *Pub Health Rep* 92:336–342, 1977.

25. Boies LR Jr et al: *Boies' Fundamentals of Otolaryngology*. Philadelphia, WB Saunders Co, 1978.

26. Meyers BR, Lawson W, Hirschman SZ: Ludwig's angina: Case report with review of bacteriology and current therapy. *Am J Med* 53:257–262, 1972.

27. Rosen P: *Emergency Medicine—Concepts and Clinical Practice*. St. Louis, CV Mosby Co, 1983.

28. Muller SP: Peritonsillar abscess: A prospective study of pathogens, treatment and morbidity. *Ear Nose Throat* 57:439–444, 1978.

29. Henry RC: Aneurysm of internal carotid artery presenting as a peritonsillar abscess. *J Laryngol Otol* 88:379–384, 1974.

30. Haglund S, Haverling M, Kuylenstierna R, et al: Radiographic diagnosis of foreign bodies in the esophagus. *J Laryngol Otol* 92:1117, 1978.

31. Norberg HP, Reyes HM: Complications of ornamental Christmas bulb ingestion—case report and review of literature. *Arch Surg* 110:1494–1495, 1975.

32. Singh B, Puri ND, Kakar PK, et al: A fatal denture in the esophagus. *J Laryngol Otol* 92:829, 1978.

33. Allen T: Suspected esophageal foreign body—choosing appropriate management. *JACEP* 8(3):101–105, 1979.

34. Glauser J, Lilja GP, Greenfeld B: Intravenous glucagon in the management of esophageal food obstruction. *JACEP* 8:228, 1979.

35. Olson NR: Surgical treatment of acute blunt laryngeal injuries. *Ann Otol Rhinol Laryngol* 87:716–721, 1978.

36. Leopold DA: Laryngeal trauma. *Arch Otolaryngol* 109:106–111, 1983.

15

Neurologic Emergencies

Mark M. Moy, MD, FACEP, FAAFP and Mark A. Shaffer, MD, FACEP

Neurologic emergencies present one of the most challenging tasks for the emergency physician. The challenge is especially magnified in elderly patients who often have complicating multisystem diseases and who ingest many drugs that influence the nervous system. In addition, the clinical features of many neurologic emergencies tend to overlap: A cerebrovascular accident may cause seizures, whereas a comatose patient may be postictal from a seizure. The physician's main goals in neurologic emergencies are (1) to preserve life by maintaining adequate respiration and circulation; (2) to preserve any viable, functional nervous tissue; (3) to determine the need for immediate neurosurgery; and (4) to correct complicating metabolic abnormalities.

COMA

True coma is a state of profound unconsciousness from which one cannot be aroused. However, the term "coma" in the emergency department (ED) is generally used to describe a spectrum of levels of consciousness between lethargy and absolute coma. In order for emergency medical personnel to communicate succinct, reproducible neurologic information to other health care providers, they should become familiar with the most popular coma scale at present, the Glasgow Coma Scale.[1] The scale is easy to remember and has been well tested for reproducibility between different observers (Table 15–1).

Coma is a pathologic disruption in the normal functioning of two neuronal systems: the reticular activating system (RAS) and the cerebral hemispheres. The RAS, a network of neurons in the midbrain connecting the cortex with the brainstem, is primarily responsible for consciousness, but large lesions of the hemispheres may also cause coma. The clinical challenge to the emergency physician is to determine which one of the two systems is at fault and then to

378

Table 15–1 Glasgow Coma Scale

Observations		Points
Eye Opening (E)	Spontaneous	4
	To speech	3
	To pain	2
	No response	1
Motor Response (M)	Obeys	6
	Localizes pain	5
	Withdraws (flex)	4
	Flexion posturing	3
	Extension posturing	2
	No responce	1
Verbalization (V)	Oriented	5
	Confused conversation	4
	Inappropriate words	3
	Incomprehensible	2
	No response	1

Total score = E + M + V (score of 3 to 15 possible)

Source: Lancet (1976;1:1081), Lancet Ltd, © 1976.

determine whether the cause is structural or metabolic. Structural lesions are local lesions that can be seen or held in one's hands, eg, a tumor, blood clot, or infarcted tissue. Metabolic comas imply a deficit of a vital metabolic substrate, such as oxygen or glucose, or the presence of circulating toxic materials.

This diagnostic challenge is especially heightened in an elderly patient. Whereas coma in the young usually reflects a single insult to the central nervous system (CNS), a decrease in consciousness in the elderly may reflect a combination of secondary effects of generalized or systemic organic disorders on the overall function of the CNS. The aged neurons and atherosclerotic vessels can compound the effects of any primary injury. In addition, many elderly patients take a number of medications that can alter consciousness.

Cardiorespiratory Problems

When a patient comes to the ED in a coma, the approach must be swift and systematic. The sequence of action begins with resuscitation of cardiorespiratory problems, followed by the neurologic examination, history, and laboratory and radiologic tests, and finally by definitive care. Whatever the cause, the immediate goal is always the same: to prevent further brain damage. This goal is achieved by paying initial attention to the ABCs: airway, breathing, and circulation. It is absolutely vital to maintain cerebral oxygenation and perfusion to prevent extension of damage to brain tissue. A flexible oropharyngeal airway should be placed to prevent partial pharyngeal obstruction, especially in the elderly because their pharyngeal and glossal tissues tend to be more hypotonic. The emergency physician should not hesitate to place an endotracheal tube if the patient has obvious labored breathing or apnea or if aspiration is likely. Once intubated, the physician has the option to use mechanical ventilation to hyperventilate the patient to reduce increased intracranial pressure.

An IV should always be started. After drawing some blood for laboratory tests, 50 ml of 50% dextrose should be injected to rule out hypoglycemia as the cause of the coma. An IV dose of 100 mg thiamine should be given after the administration of 50% dextrose to avoid the development of Wernicke's syndrome because malnutrition and alcoholism may be present in the elderly. The elderly are particularly susceptible to fluctuations in serum glucose. In addition, a dose of naloxone IV may prove to be therapeutic, as well as diagnostic. Normal saline should be used for the IV solution because it is preferred for use with phenytoin in case of seizures. The quantity of IV fluids to administer is difficult to determine in the elderly. Too much fluid may induce pulmonary edema or aggravate cerebral edema, whereas too little fluid may cause hypoperfusion in the elderly patient who is dehydrated. Because cerebral perfusion takes precedence over fluid restriction, enough fluid should be given to correct hypovolemic hypotension. After that, fluid should be kept to a minimum. Blood pressure, pulse, and urinary output should be used as guidelines for further fluid replacement. One of the most common causes of mental obtundation in the elderly is simple dehydration. If persistent hypotension is present, it will be necessary to monitor the patient's volume status with Swan-Ganz catheterization.

Neurologic Evaluation

Once the cardiorespiratory problems have been addressed, the next step is to perform a neurologic evaluation. The neurologic examination is geared to answer these two main questions, which dictate further definitive care: (1) is the coma due to a structural or metabolic cause, and (2) is the damage at the level of the midbrain (RAS) or above at the level of the hemispheres. The parts of the neurologic examination that help answer these questions are (1) level of consciousness, (2) motor response, (3) pupillary response, and (4) reflex ocular movements.

First, the level of consciousness must be assessed accurately. However, the level of consciousness in and of itself cannot differentiate between structural versus metabolic etiologies or locate the level of injury. The importance in assessing the level of consciousness lies not in any single reading but in any change in the level over a period of time. A deteriorating level of consciousness is an absolute emergency, because this implies that the injury is still in progress and must be stopped.

Second, the symmetry and nature of movement are recorded. As opposed to the level of consciousness, motor function does give important clues indicating the location and etiology of the coma. Any motor deficit, regardless of symmetry, implies a structural lesion until proven otherwise because metabolic comas rarely create focal motor deficits. Any asymmetry of movement—hemiparesis, asymmetric facies, or the like—implies that the injury is structural and probably above the midbrain at the level of the hemispheres. A primary injury at the level of the midbrain classically produces quadriparesis.

In addition, motor response gives the physician a rough measure of the depth of coma. When a patient is in light coma, stimulation elicits purposeful movement. In deeper coma, the patient responds with decorticate posturing: forced flexion of the arms with extension of the legs. The decerebrate response, when a patient responds to stimulus with forced extension of all limbs, occurs when the patient is deeper in coma. At the deepest stage, approaching death, the patient does not respond at all with any posturing.

Third, the pupils are examined for reactivity and size. Reactive, symmetrical small pupils usually indicate a metabolic etiology; the exceptions are atropinergic drugs and severe anoxia, both of which can lead to fixed, dilated pupils. One should worry about a structural lesion with any other pupil defect. Structural lesions located in the hemispheres can cause unilaterally enlarged, barely reactive pupils when herniation of midbrain structures compresses the third cranial nerve. Lesions lower in the midbrain usually produce midpositioned fixed pupils. A lesion lower yet in the pons results in the classic pinpoint pupils. However, one should never forget that the elderly often exhibit pupil changes as a result of chronic ocular diseases, such as glaucoma and cataracts, previous surgery, and ocular medications.

Finally, ocular motor reflexes are evaluated. As with other motor responses, any asymmetry of ocular movement implies a structural etiology. Patients in comas of metabolic etiology generally retain intact ocular reflex movements until near death when all reflexes disappear. Intact ocular reflex maneuvers, such as the oculocephalic or oculovestibular responses, indicate an intact midbrain. One should ensure that the cervical spine has been properly evaluated for trauma before testing for oculocephalic reflexes.

The goal of the remainder of the physical examination is to detect additional diagnostic clues. Fever suggests an infection-like meningoencephalitis, whereas hypothermia may indicate hypothermic coma or myxedema coma, both of which are particularly common in the elderly. Hypertension may be a cause of intracranial hemorrhage. Hypotension, in contrast, suggests myocardial failure, septic shock, myxedema coma, or an Addisonian crisis. The skull and fundi should be examined for evidence of cranial or intracranial injury. Finally, alcoholism is not uncommon in the elderly; consequently, one should not overlook hepatic encephalopathy or alcoholic intoxication and drug overdose.

Laboratory and Roentgenographic Studies

Laboratory studies and roentgenography are used to assist and confirm clinical diagnoses. When one suspects structural injury, especially if neurologic signs are deteriorating, an emergency neurosurgical consultation should be obtained. A CT scan is invaluable in the workup of acute coma. A positive CT scan is definitive for structural lesions, although a negative CT scan does not rule out small intracranial hemorrhages. With a negative CT scan, the emergency physician can feel relatively safe in performing a lumbar puncture to confirm infections or small subarachnoid hemorrhages. Metabolic comas warrant a vigorous search to identify the offending agent by use of chemical and toxicologic analysis of blood.

SEIZURES

A convulsive seizure is a paroxysmal discharge of a group of neurons that results in a transient impairment of sensation, movement, and consciousness. Epilepsy, which is a chronic disorder of recurrent seizures, has its onset early in life. As a rule, the later in life the onset of seizures, the greater the probability that the seizures are associated with some gross organic lesions or acute metabolic insult to the CNS. Therefore, the presentation of seizures in the elderly should alert the emergency physician to search aggressively for a correctable condition.

Types of Seizures

In general, seizures are classified into two broad categories: partial and generalized. Partial seizures arise from a single focus or multiple foci in the cortex. Typically, there is an aura followed by focal motor activity spreading from one involved area to another, followed by a postictal phase during which lethargy, confusion, headache, or focal weakness may last for many hours. The exact pattern of activity depends on the area of cortex involved. Psychomotor seizures, a subcategory of focal seizures, have a vast array of psychomotor, emotional, and visceral autonomic signs and symptoms.

Generalized seizures begin with a 30- to 60-sec tonic phase in which the patient suddenly loses consciousness, falls, stiffens, may stop breathing, become cyanotic, bite the tongue, and become incontinent. The following clonic phase consists of a rhythmic jerking of all body parts, labored respiration, frothing at the mouth, and then complete flaccidity. Postictally, the patient is usually somnolent, confused, and lethargic for a variable period of time. Status epilepticus is a state of recurrent seizures without recovery of baseline neurologic status in between seizures. This is an acute medical emergency for which aggressive treatment is mandatory before irreversible brain damage occurs. Lastly, patients may have focal manifestations, such as occur in epilepsia partialis continua, in which focal seizures may persist for weeks.

Causes

The major challenge in the elderly is to determine if a seizure has indeed occurred. With so many other possible neurologic entities in the elderly, such as confusional states, cerebrovascular accidents (CVAs), vertigo, transient ischemic attacks (TIAs), and Alzheimer's disease, that mimic seizures and postictal states, the differential diagnosis is considerable. Because of the physiologic effects of aging on neurons, vessels, and other organ systems, the elderly are particularly vulnerable to abnormal neuronal discharges resulting in seizure activity. In fact, the aging process itself, such as in Alzheimer's disease or parkinsonianism, can produce seizures. A drug-related etiology for acute seizure should be sought. The use of tranquilizers in the elderly invites complications because some reduce the seizure threshold either by use or by withdrawal. Heading this list are the major tranquilizers: phenothiazines, butyrophenones, and benzodiazepines. Tricyclic antidepressants have a propensity for precipitating a variety of CNS phenomena, among which is seizure activity. Other drugs known to produce seizure activity are IV penicillin, isoniazid (INH), amphetamines, β-adrenergic agonists, and theophylline.[2] Finally, alcohol, either by ingestion or by withdrawal, can induce seizure activity.

Metabolic disturbances are another major cause of seizures, especially in the elderly. The most common metabolic causes are associated with renal and hepatic failure and with disturbances related to diabetes mellitus. Focal seizures that result from renal failure may be the first symptom of this major metabolic derangement. However, systemic signs and symptoms of hepatic failure are usually evident before the onset of seizures. Diabetes mellitus produces seizures in nonketotic hyperosmolar states in which focal seizures may be the initial sign; these seizures are essentially unresponsive to the usual anticonvulsant therapy until the hyperosmolar metabolic state is corrected. The elderly neurons are very sensitive to fluctuations of serum glucose. Hypoglycemic seizures should always be suspected in an elderly diabetic, especially if the patient is on insulin therapy.

Vascular disorders are the most common cause of seizures in the elderly.[3] CVAs, whether hemorrhagic or thrombotic, can cause seizures. Seizures may also develop several months or years after an infarction, developing from the peri-infarction zone of damaged but still functional neurons. With their fragile vessels and increased dura space elderly patients are very prone to subdural hematomas after even trivial head trauma. The initial presentation may be a seizure even before the mass of the hematoma can produce functional deficits or depression of consciousness. Finally, such vascular disturbances as cardiac dysrhythmias and Stokes-Adams syndrome can produce seizures as a result of an acute anoxic episode.

Infection in older age groups can cause focal or generalized seizures. Fever or recent infection, especially of the head and neck region, should alert the physician to this cause of seizures. The elderly population has an increased frequency of diabetes, autoimmune disorders, and primary malignant lesions and, as a result, often take corticosteroids, immunosuppressant drugs, and radiation therapy. These disorders and therapeutic modes decrease the elderly's defenses against infection, such as meningitis and meningoencephalitis of viral and mycotic etiology.

Tumor as the cause of seizures should be suspected in an otherwise asymptomatic elderly individual. Primary tumors, meningiomas, and metastatic lesions dictate the use of the CT scan for definitive evaluation.

Treatment

As with comas, the initial approach to a seizing or postictal patient is to address the ABCs. As the airway, oxygenation, and perfusion are secured, seizure activity must be arrested. An IV of normal saline is started and blood sent for determination of antiepileptic drug plasma levels, biochemistry, blood counts, and arterial blood gases. One should first infuse 50 ml of 50% dextrose with thiamine 100 mg IV to avoid Wernicke's syndrome to rule out a hypoglycemic cause. There is no universal agreement on which anticonvulsant drugs to use first, but the literature shows that the five most commonly used are diazepam, phenytoin, phenobarbital, clonazepam, and lorazepam. It is agreed that all drugs should be administered intravenously to avoid the variable absorption of intramuscular injections. The most widely favored first-line drug is diazepam for the management of the acute seizures. A dose of 2 to 10 mg intravenously stops seizures in most elderly patients for about 30 min. The dose can be repeated to a maximum of 20 mg in 10 min if seizures recur. The elderly are particularly sensitive to respiratory depression secondary to the administration of diazepam and should be monitored closely. If no resolution of seizures occurs, phenytoin is usually injected IV at a rate of no more than 50 mg/min to a loading dose of 18 mg/kg in adult patients not previously receiving phenytoin. The elderly should receive the phenytoin at an even slower rate than 50 mg/min—probably around 20 to 30 mg/min—because they have a greater potential to develop side effects of cardiac arrhythmias and hypotension. The patient should be placed on a cardiac monitor and have the blood pressure monitored closely. A phenytoin serum level must be obtained at the conclusion of administration. Phenobarbital may be used next if no resolution of seizures occurs. Phenobarbital is administered intravenously at a rate of 25 to 50 mg/min to a maximum of 20 mg/kg. If seizures still have not stopped, intubation should be performed if not already done. If the seizures continue 30 min after the administration of phenobarbital, general anesthesia becomes necessary.[4] Because of the frailty of the elderly brain, a vigorous attempt should always be made to keep seizure activity to less than 30 min to avoid irreversible brain damage. The side effects of major motor seizures that must be addressed especially in the elderly are hyperthermia, hyperuricemia, and cerebral edema.

CEREBROVASCULAR ACCIDENTS

Cerebrovascular accidents (CVAs) or strokes refer to the clinical syndrome caused by two major pathologic processes: ischemia and hemorrhage. Ischemia, leading to infarction, is a result of vascular obstruction that may be caused by either the development of a thrombus in situ or embolization from a more central site. Hemorrhage can occur either intracerebrally through small vessel rupture within brain tissue or extracerebrally in the subarachnoid space usually through ruptured aneurysms. Neurons require a constant supply of glucose and oxygen, neither of which are stored within them. Therefore, when the blood supply is interrupted, it only takes minutes for neuronal function to cease. The important point for emergency care is that if blood supply is restored within 4–5 min during the ischemic stage, no permanent brain damage results.

Causes

The most common causes of cerebral ischemia are atherosclerosis and embolisms. Atherothrombosis is caused by clot formation at an ulcerated plaque. This clot may propagate until it either occludes the vessel or sheds emboli to plug more distant arteries. However, the picture is not always so simple, especially in the elderly. Thrombosis may occur secondary to meningitis, syphilitic arteritis, polyarteritis nodosa, thromboangiitis obliterans, and even vascular spasms. Aortocranial arteries may be occluded by tumors, and vertebral arteries may be occluded by arthritic changes of the cervical spine. Cerebral embolism, the other cause of ischemic infarcts, refers to the occlusion of a vessel usually by a thrombus; however, tumors, fat, air, or other foreign substances may also embolize. The most common cause of TIAs is microembolism from atherosclerotic plaques located in the cervical-cranial arteries.

Hemorrhages may result from rupture of a vessel anywhere within the cranial cavity. The most common cause of intraparenchymal hemorrhage is the rupture of microaneurysms caused by long-standing hypertension. About 80% of hypertensive intracerebral hemorrhages are fatal.[5] Subarachnoid hemorrhages occur when an aneurysm in the subarachnoid space ruptures, as in the case of arterial aneurysms of the Circle of Willis. The elderly are more prone to develop intracerebral hemorrhages caused by altered blood coagulation because of vessel fragility. Frequent causes of altered blood coagulation are anticoagulant therapy, neoplasms such as leukemias, blood dyscrasias, and even scurvy from malnutrition.

Management

An important first step in the management of strokes, as with other geriatric neurologic emergencies, is to determine if one has actually occurred. Other clinical entities may simulate acute strokes: postictal states, cardiac syncopes, such as Stokes-Adams syndrome, various comas, and encephalopathies. The emergency physician should not be too quick to assume that just a simple stroke has occurred and to admit the patient. A thorough history and physical examination with appropriate laboratory tests and roentgenograms must always be performed. Only after ruling out acute correctable conditions can the emergency physician allow admission.

A thorough history, including information about each systemic illness, such as diabetes, hypertension, and congestive heart failure, and about all current medications, should be obtained either from the patient and family or from the nursing home. Delayed information about any seizure activity, cardiac irregularities, headaches, audiovisual disturbances, mental changes, precipitating factors, and sensory, motor, or coordination deficits must be documented. In about one-third of the cases, one can elicit a history of recent TIAs causing focal neurologic symptoms, such as aphasia, paresis, visual defects, or paresthesias. The majority of CVAs result in a sudden onset of symptoms that reach maximum intensity within minutes to hours. A stroke is unlikely if the duration of time from the onset of symptoms to maximum deficits is greater than 24 hours. Generalized symptoms of headache, emesis, seizures, and coma are more common with acute hemorrhage.

The examination of the patient must rule out other acutely correctable causes of the patient's symptoms. The blood pressure is elevated in the majority of patients with hemorrhage and intracerebral infarction, but stays within normal limits with cerebral embolism. Hypertension with headache and focal neurologic signs in the elderly indicates a stroke (probably hemorrhagic) and not hypertensive encephalopathy until proven otherwise. Cardiac dysrhythmias, especially atrial fibrillation, are present in the majority of patients with a cerebral embolus. Alterations in rate and depth of respirations occur in 40% of patients with cerebral hemorrhages, 25% of cerebral embolism, and 10% of infarctions.[6] With a large hemorrhage or occlusion, the temperature may be elevated and the heart rate increased. A continued rise in temperature, pulse rate, and respiratory rate indicates that the vasomotor and thermoregulating centers have ceased to function.

The neurologic examination must determine if any focal neurologic deficit is present. Even in the comatose patient, movements of facies and extremities with and without stimuli can be observed. Subarachnoid hemorrhages usually do not cause focal neurologic deficits. Patients with brain infarction are usually alert, whereas brain hemorrhages cause mental obtundation. One should check for the presence of Babinski's sign. Examination of pupillary responses is complicated by the variation with different stages of cerebral damage and the presence of such complicating factors as previous ocular surgeries and medications. A homolateral, dilated, and fixed pupil implies uncal herniation and may be caused by a massive hemorrhage. Conjugate deviation of the eyes together usually occurs toward the lesion in hemispheric injury and away from the side of brainstem injury. Nuchal rigidity may occur with intracerebral but more often with subarachnoid hemorrhages. Because nuchal rigidity may also imply impending cerebellar herniation through the foramen magnum, lumbar punctures should be avoided until a CT scan is performed. Tendon reflexes are usually hyperactive on the side opposite the cerebral lesion. One clinical entity that should never be missed in the ED is cerebellar hemorrhage, which causes the triad of acute occipital headache, vertigo, and ataxia. This is a potentially correctable condition if immediate neurosurgery is performed. A delay in surgery often results in respiratory arrest due to compression of the medullary respiratory center.

Three radiologic tests are available to help in the early management of stroke: CT scan, radioisotope brain scanning, and arteriography. A CT scan of the brain is the examination of choice with any clinical picture suggesting stroke. The CT scan is normal if only ischemia has occurred. It does not show changes for about 12 hr after thrombotic infarctions. Hemorrhage, however, produces a positive CT scan at once unless the bleeding is minimal. The CT scan can also reveal the presence of edema, hydrocephalus, neoplasms, and subdural hematomas, all of which can mimic strokes. The isotope brain scan is a poor second choice if CT scan is unavailable because it is helpful only if it is positive. The isotope scan is usually negative with acute infarction and hemorrhage. It can, however, help in revealing such nonvascular lesions as tumors. Angiography should be considered with intracranial hemorrhage, progressing deterioration of neurologic signs, and suspicion of carotid occlusion.

The acute management of stroke involves preservation of life by addressing the ABCs. Adequate blood flow, oxygenation, and nutrients (glucose) to the brain are imperative if any recoverable brain tissue is to be saved. Every patient should be placed on oxygen; arterial blood gases should be used as a guide. One should always ensure patent airways by using nasal or oral pharyngeal airways and endotracheal intubation if necessary. Every patient should be infused with normal saline IV while blood samples are sent to the laboratory for state determinations of serum glucose, blood counts, and chemistries. Suspicion of hypoglycemia warrants immediate administration of 50% dextrose and thiamine. Any dysrhythmia that can compromise cardiac output should be treated aggressively. A systolic blood pressure less than 200 mm Hg and a diastolic less than 110 mm Hg probably should be left untreated because rapid lowering of blood pressure may lead to increased ischemia. Marked hypertension, however, may aggravate cerebral edema, hemorrhage, and cerebral vasospasms. A reasonable goal is to reduce diastolic pressure to about 100 mm Hg; systolic control is probably less critical. Nitroprusside is still the drug of choice for emergency treatment of severe hypertension. The use of anticoagulants and antiplatelet drugs should be reserved for inpatient management. Dexamethasone 10 mg intravenously can be given to patients with cerebral hemorrhages, although this treatment, which is still widely used, has not been proved to be definitely effective with cerebral infarction. Osmotic diuretics, such as mannitol, are helpful in reducing cerebral edema from hemorrhages. A lumbar puncture helps rule out infections and blood in the cerebral spinal fluid, but it should be done only after mass-producing lesions have been ruled out. If a patient's symptoms worsen, implying a stroke in progression, all vital signs should be reassessed, a repeat CT scan should be considered, and a vigorous search for complications from other organ systems, such as cardiovascular, hematologic, or renal, should be made.

TRANSIENT NEUROLOGIC SYMPTOMS

The elderly commonly come to the ED with transient neurologic symptoms. The burden for the emergency physician is to differentiate a TIA from all the other benign causes of temporary neurologic episodes. One may send patients home with a TIA only to have them return later with a full CVA. Other major concerns in the elderly include cardiac dysrhythmias, hypoglycemia, orthostatic hypotension, and acute labyrinthine disease.

TIAs are temporary neurologic deficits that last less than 24 hours. Depending on the vascular location affected, two general syndromes are described: the anterior circulation TIA and posterior circulation TIA. The anterior system involves the carotid system, and the patient has a history of hemiparesis, hemisensory loss, aphasias, and a monocular blindness. The posterior system involves the vertebrobasilar vessels and produces symptoms of diplopia, loss of binocular vision, vertigo, tinnitus, ataxia, dysarthria, and bilateral motor/sensory losses. The anterior TIA may be surgically correctible, whereas the posterior vessels usually do not lend themselves to surgery. A patient diagnosed as having had a TIA should be admitted for workup and observation.

The clinical history is the physician's most valuable aid in evaluating temporary neurologic symptoms. A comprehensive history, including past medical history, medications, and all events surrounding the present event, must be obtained before an accurate assessment can be made. The physical examination is focused on the CNS of course, but in the elderly attention should also be paid to the cardiovascular and any other system indicated by the past medical history. Orthostatic blood pressures should be determined. The patient should be placed on a monitor to detect dysrhythmias. Diagnostic testing should include an ECG, complete blood count, serum glucose, BUN, creatinine, and electrolytes. Arterial blood gases, ethanol levels, and roentgenograms should be obtained as indicated by history and physical examination. Often, even after a thorough history, physical examination, and diagnostic tests, the emergency physician still cannot pinpoint an exact diagnosis. Consultation with the patient's family physician and/or a neurologist may help determine the correct disposition for the patient.

HEADACHES

Headache is simply a symptom of some disease process, but it may represent clinical entities ranging from very benign to life-threatening disorders. When a patient feels that a headache is severe enough to warrant a visit to the ED, the emergency physician has the responsibility of taking the patient seriously and capably differentiating the benign from the serious causes. Three categories of headaches are commonly recognized: vascular headaches, such as migraine and cluster; muscular contraction headaches, such as tension headaches; and traction/inflammation headaches caused by tremors, neuralgia, arteritis, and the like. The emergency physician should be especially cautious in seeking out the traction/ inflammatory etiologies in the geriatric population because vascular headaches are much less common and the incidence of tumor and organic diseases of the nervous system is more frequent.[7]

It is important to understand which cerebral structures can sense pain. Brain tissue itself, bone, and most of the dura, pia, and arachnoid membranes are insensitive to pain. Brain parenchymal tumors, for example, do not produce pain until they cause pressure or tension on pain-sensitive structures. Any chemical, metabolic, or mechanical stimuli to the intracerebral vessels or extracerebral tissues can produce the symptom of headache. The important intracranial structures sensitive to pain are the arteries, veins, and cranial nerves V, IX, and X. Of course, extracranial structures such as skin, muscles, and teeth, are all sensitive to pain.

The Headache History

The key to proper diagnosis in patients with headache is a thorough, accurate history. In the emergency setting, the physician must pick up clues that can help rule out conditions that threaten the patient's life or mentation, such as subarachnoid hemorrhage, CVAs, infectious origins, hypertensive crisis, and space-occupying lesions. Key questions to ask are outlined in Table 15–2. It is also essential to take a full past history, family history of headaches, present illnesses, and medications.

If the patient has chronic headaches, the task is to find out why this headache warranted a visit to the ED. A present headache that differs in any way from the characteristics of previous headaches should be treated cautiously. A history of sudden severe pain ("worst headache in my life"), especially if associated with altered consciousness and nuchal signs, indicates a subarachnoid hemorrhage until proven otherwise. A headache that worsens with straining or changes in body

---

Table 15–2 Key Questions for Patients with Headaches

1. How does this headache compare with previous headaches? (severity)
2. Do you have frequent (chronic) headaches?
3. If yes, does this headache differ from your previous headaches?
4. Does the headache worsen with change in body position or straining?
5. When was the onset, and what is the duration of this headache?
6. Where does it hurt? (location)
7. Were there any prodromes? (aura)
8. Are there any associated symptoms? (eg, nausea)
9. Are there any neurologic deficits?
10. Are there any precipitating factors?
11. Are there any environmental factors?

position suggests intracerebral masses. A history of neurologic deficits may consist of a complicated migraine attack in the younger patient, but it implies a CVA in the elderly. Any history of fever, chills, and recent infection especially of the head or neck region in an elderly patient with headaches warrants a search for meningitis or encephalitis. Unilateral headaches, especially those alternating from side to side, are characteristic of vascular headaches. An aura is classic for migraines, but may indicate TIAs in the elderly. Associated neurologic deficits are especially important. Any visual defect mandates consideration of temporal arteritis, glaucoma, and strokes. Headaches with seizure activity or any neurologic deficit (motor, sensory, or coordination) require a CT scan to help rule out acute organic disorders. A full past history alerts the physician to headaches associated with metabolic or systemic disorders, such as infection, endocrine disorders, or hypertensive crises. A family history of migraines suggests a vascular etiology. Common medications that may cause headaches are outlined in Table 15–3. In addition, ethanol consumption should be investigated. Intracerebral hemorrhage should be considered if the elderly patient is on anticoagulants. Recent head trauma, no matter how trivial, may result in a subdural hematoma in the elderly. Miscellaneous information, such as the use of gas heaters at home, can point to carbon monoxide as a possible cause for headaches.

Physical Examination

The physical examination provides clues to life-threatening disorders and associated organic disorders that may cause headaches. Fever suggests an infectious cause, such as meningitis or brain abscess. High blood pressure may cause headaches, and if associated with changes in mentation, hypertensive encephalopathy should be assessed. Nuchal rigidity, although classically associated with meningitis, is also present commonly with subarachnoid hemorrhages. Fundoscopy should always be performed, but many tumors may be in neurologic silent zones and thus do not cause papilledema. Third and sixth nerve palsies are often related to aneurysms or increased intracranial pressure. Increased tenderness

---

Table 15–3 Headache-Causing Drugs

On Administration	On Withdrawal
Nitrates	Ergots
Indomethacin	Caffeine
Oral progestationals	Amphetamines
Vitamin B_2	Phenothiazines
Nicotinic acid	Clonidine
	Propranolol

Source: Adapted with permission from *Emergency Medicine* (1984;16:36), Copyright © July 1984, Cahners Publishing Company, Medical/Health Care Group.

of temporal areas suggests temporal arteritis. Some facial conditions that may cause pain are sinusitis, temporal mandibular joint syndrome, trigeminal neuralgia, otitis, and dental pain. Pseudotumor cerebri, although more common in the young, should be considered with the triad of headache, papilledema, and decreased visual acuity. Glaucoma should be considered when headaches are associated with painful red eyes. Headaches may result from referred pain from cervical arthritis. Respiratory disorders, such as COPD, can produce hypoxia or hypercapnia, which may result in vasodilation headaches. The presence of confusion or depressed mental status indicates a high probability of serious organic disorders.

Diagnostic Studies

Diagnostic tests are essential when an elderly patient presents with headaches. A complete blood count reveals such hematologic disorders as anemia. An erythrocyte sedimentation rate should be obtained if temporal arteritis is suspected. A serum glucose rules out hypoglycemia, which can cause headaches. Arterial blood gases and carboxyhemoglobin levels help rule out hypoxemia or carbon monoxide as the cause. Lumbar punctures can be performed to help diagnose intracranial infections and subarachnoid hemorrhage, but only after one is sure that increased intracranial pressure is not present. The spinal fluid pressure must always be checked before removing fluid. Skull films should be obtained only if clinically indicated. Plain skull films may reveal sinusitis, a shift of intracranial structures, pituitary enlargement, intracranial calcifications, and fractures. Suspicion of CVAs, intracranial hematoma, subarachnoid hemorrhage, increased intracranial pressure, and intracranial masses warrants an emergency CT scan. The CT scan is the single most valuable diagnostic tool available in evaluating suspicious headaches and is usually definitive for structural lesions.

Emergency Treatment

The emergency treatment of headache depends on the diagnosis. Admission to the hospital for further workup and definitive treatment is mandated for subarachnoid hemorrhage, intracranial hematoma or mass, CVAs, meningitis, temporal arteritis, glaucoma, and acute trigeminal neuralgia. Immediate neurosurgical consultation is needed for intracranial hemorrhages and signs of increased intracranial pressure. Hypertensive encephalopathy requires initiation of antihypertensive measures in the ED. Finally, if the emergency physician feels that the patient has a simple muscle contraction or vascular headache, pain relievers can be offered. Muscle relaxants and nonsteroidal anti-inflammatory drugs can be offered to patients with muscle contraction headaches. An injection of meperidine is an easy solution for vascular headaches, but has the adverse potential of addiction. Other medications presently advised for emergency treatment of migraines are corticosteroids, ergotamine, antiprostaglandins, and phenothiazines.

WEAKNESS

Weakness is a common complaint of the aged, and a certain amount can be expected because of the normal process of muscle atrophy from aging and disuse. When a patient complains of acute weakness, however, more serious disease entities should be considered (Table 15–4). An exact diagnosis in the ED is difficult because the patient's complaints are often nonspecific and weakness in the elderly can be the result of many neurologic and nonneurologic disorders. The emergency physician's task is to decide if the present weakness represents an acute life-threatening neuromuscular disorder that requires immediate admission and treatment or is a more benign condition that can be followed up on an outpatient basis.

History

A careful history is needed first. A past history of other organ system diseases, such as diabetes mellitus, cardiovascular disorders, renal failure, or COPD, requires individual evaluation to rule out those specific entities as the cause of the present weakness. A careful history should be taken of present medications and both prescription and over-the-counter drugs. The present history should determine the distribution of weakness, onset, and time of development. The weakness of periodic paralysis, botulism, and myasthenia gravis may evolve rather quickly over hours. It may take days for polio, polyneuropathies, and myopathies to develop. An ascending paralysis is classical for Guillain-Barré syndrome, whereas descending paralysis can occur with porphyria. A history of recent

---

Table 15–4 Differential Diagnosis of Acute Weakness

Peripheral neuropathies
  Guillain-Barré syndrome
  Tic paralysis
  Diphtheria
  Porphyria

Neuromuscular junction disorders
  Myasthenia gravis
  Botulism
  Organophosphate poisoning

Myopathies
  Inflammatory myopathy
  Periodic paralysis
  Rhabdomyolysis

Source: Adapted from *Neurologic Emergencies* (p 245) by MP Earnest with permission of Churchill Livingstone Inc, © 1983.

infection should suggest polio, diphtheria, viral myositis, and Guillain-Barré syndrome. Ocular complaints occur with myasthenia gravis, Guillain-Barré syndrome, tic paralysis, and diphtheria. Gastrointestinal signs of vomiting and diarrhea suggest exposure to toxic agents, such as arsenic, organophosphates, and *botulinum* toxin. A history of alcohol abuse suggests alcoholic myopathy and neuropathy. Associated pain is found in inflammatory myopathies, polymyalgia rheumatica, and certain neuritises.

Physical Examination

The physical examination should be used to confirm diagnostic suspicions elicited by the history. The vital signs can indicate cardiovascular, pulmonary, and infectious etiologies. Proximal muscle weakness is usually found in myasthenia gravis, parkinsonism, polymyalgia rheumatica, and Guillain-Barré syndrome. Distal weakness of hands and feet is more characteristic of polyneuropathies and radiculopathies. Ptosis and ophthalmoparesis are found with myasthenia gravis, botulism, and organophosphate poisoning. Large pupils are found with botulism, whereas small pupils are characteristic of organophosphate poisoning. Neurologic examination revealing sensory deficits—position, vibration, pain, temperature—suggests spinal cord compression. Any patient with progressing weakness in both legs has a spinal cord compression until proven otherwise. Delay in diagnosing an acute spinal cord compression, even by hours, may leave the patient paraplegic and incontinent.

A full diagnostic workup for weakness is impractical in the ED, but simple screening tests should be obtained. Minimum testing includes a complete blood count, electrolytes, glucose, BUN, and creatinine to rule out infectious etiologies, hypokalemia of periodic paralysis, diabetic neuropathy, and uremic neuropathy. Urinalysis detects myoglobinuria of rhabdomyolysis. Roentgenograms, ethanol level, drug screens, sedimentation rate, and arterial blood gases are obtained as indicated. Electrodiagnostic studies, lumbar puncture, and toxin assays may be obtained after admission.

Emergency Management

Emergency management of weakness includes treatment of any life-threatening disorder. Initial attention is paid to any respiratory complications of neuromuscular disease, such as inadequate respiratory drive, aspiration, pneumonia, and respiratory muscle exhaustion. One should initiate the administration of oxygen and obtain arterial blood gases. The patient may require endotracheal intubation if the respiratory drive is inadequate. The patient should be placed on a cardiac monitor to reveal any dysrhythmias caused by myopathies that affect cardiac muscle and autonomic dysfunction influences, ie, with Guillain-Barré syndrome. After oxygenation and circulation are ensured, attention is paid to correcting metabolic abnormalities, eg, potassium or glucose. A decision is then made to continue care on an inpatient or outpatient basis.

REFERENCES

1. Jennet B, Teasdale G, Braakman R, et al: Predicting outcome in individual patients after head injury. *Lancet* 1:1081, 1976.

2. Goldberg MA: Neurologic complications of drug therapy. *Primary Care* 11(4):591, 1984.

3. Dickinson ES: Seizure disorders in the elderly. *Primary Care* 9:135–143, 1982.

4. Delgado-Escueta AV, et al: Management of status epilepticus. *New Engl J Med* 306:1337–1340, 1982.

5. Merritt H: *A Textbook of Neurology*, ed 6. Philadelphia, Lea and Febiger Co, 1979, p 160.

6. Merritt H: *A Textbook of Neurology*, ed 6, Philadelphia, Lea and Febiger Co, 1979, p 167.

7. Rapoport AM, et al: Geriatric headaches. *Geriatrics* 38:83–87, 1983.

SUGGESTED READINGS

Carner LR, Hudgins RL, Espinosa RE, et al: Seizure beginning after the age of 60. *Arch Intern Med* 124:707–711, 1969.

DeReuch TS: Epilepsy in patients with cerebral infarcts. *J Neurol* 224:101–109, 1980.

Dhopesh KV, et al: A retrospective assessment of emergency department patients with complaint of headache. *Headache* 19:37–42, 1979.

Diamond S: Headache common but not ordinary. *Emerg Med* 16:36, 1984.

Earnest MP: *Neurologic Emergencies*, ed 1. New York, Churchill Livingstone Inc, 1983.

Friedman AP: Symposium on headache and related pain syndromes. *Med Clin North Am* 62:443–507, 1978.

Keichel W: *Clinical Aspects of Aging*. Baltimore, Williams & Wilkins Co, 1978.

Levy EE, et al: Prognosis in nontraumatic coma. *Ann Int Med* 94:293–301, 1981.

Miller B, McIntyre H: Evaluation of the comatose patient. *Primary Care* 11:693–706, 1984.

Paulson GW: Disorders of the central nervous system in the aged. *Med Clin North Am* 67:345–360, 1983.

Plum F, Posner J: *The Diagnosis of Stupor and Coma*, ed 3. Philadelphia, FA Davis, 1980.

Sabin TD: The differential diagnosis of stupor and coma. *New Engl J Med* 290:1062–1064, 1974.

Sherokman B, Massey EW: Evaluating loss of consciousness in the elderly. *J Am Geriatr Soc* 28:504–509, 1980.

16

Dermatologic Urgencies and Emergencies in the Elderly

Scott C. Edminster, MD, FACEP and Peter J. Lynch, MD

Dermatologic emergencies, particularly in the elderly, are in truth rare. However, there are a number of dermatologic conditions with acute onset that cause significant discomfort for the patient. These urgencies should be readily recognized and appropriately treated by emergency health care providers. Moreover, there are a number of systemic diseases in which the cutaneous manifestations, although not important themselves, provide a clue to the diagnosis and treatment. Less important dermatologic conditions likely to be encountered by the emergency health care provider are not covered here, but information about them is available in a problem-oriented algorithm devised by Lynch.[1,2]

URICARIA AND ANGIOEDEMA

Urticaria is perhaps the most common skin ailment seen in the emergency department (ED). Approximately 1/5 of the population experiences urticaria during their lifetimes, and many of these individuals have multiple episodes. Conceptually it is useful to think of urticaria as a reaction pattern, rather than as a single specific disease. In this way one can appreciate that many different etiologies are possible and that even the pathogenic pathways leading to urticaria may vary. Thus, acute urticarias are often immunologically mediated, whereas the mechanisms of chronic urticaria are generally unknown. Histamine is the predominant mediator of urticaria and angioedema. Other inflammatory mediators, such as slow reacting substances (SRS), serotonin, and bradykinin, play a more speculative role in their pathogenesis. Degranulation of mast cells (probably IgE mediated in anaphylactoid reactions) results in the release of these vasoactive mediators and consequent increased capillary permeability and extravasation of proteins and fluids into the skin. When this process occurs in the upper portion of the dermis, it is reflected clinically in the development of urticarial wheals. The confluence of such wheals leads to the development of polycyclic plaques. When the process occurs deep in the dermis or in the loose subcutaneous tissue, poorly marginated, skin-colored edema develops. This latter process is known as angioedema. For the purposes of this chapter, urticaria and angioedema are considered as a single process.

Etiology

A single specific cause for urticaria can be identified in only a relatively small proportion of cases. Nevertheless, because the removal of an identifiable cause is the single best approach to therapy, a search for the cause should be routinely carried out. In acute urticaria of abrupt onset the most commonly identified causes include medication reactions, reaction to the ingestion of certain foods, and reaction to infections. In chronic urticaria of 10 days or greater duration, psychologic stress, chronic viral infection, autoimmune disease, underlying malignancy, and reactions to food dyes and food preservatives are more likely causes.

Penicillin compounds and sulfa-derived products, including thiazides and sulfonylureas, are the most common offenders.[3] These medications should be suspected as the cause whenever they are being taken by a patient who has urticaria. Other medications associated with urticaria, although somewhat less frequently, are also listed in Table 16–1. Assessment of medications from this list depends to some degree on the time frame over which they have been administered. Specifically, urticaria and angioedema occurring as a result of a reaction to a medication are most likely to be encountered during the first month of therapy. The mechanism by which medications cause reactions is variable. When the onset of urticaria

---

Table 16–1 Drugs Capable of Causing Angioedema and/or Urticaria

ACTH	Griseofulvin (cold urticaria)	Pilocarpine
Aspirin	Insulin	Polio vaccine
Allopurinol	Iodides	Potassium sulfocyanate
Antimony	Liver extract	Procaine
Antipyrines	Methanol	Promethazine
Barbiturates	Meprobamate	Quinine
Bismuth	Mercury	Reserpine
Chloral hydrate	Morphine	Saccharin
Chlorpromazine	Opium	Stilbestrol
Cinchophen	Para-aminosalicylic acid	Sulfonamides
Eucalyptus	Penicillin	Thiamine chloride
Florides	Phenacetin	Thiouracil
Gold	Phenobarbital	

Source: Adapted from *Andrews' Diseases of the Skin,* 6th ed (pp 129–131) by AN Domonkos with permission of WB Saunders Company, © 1971.

or angioedema is acute, an IgE-mediated mechanism is most likely responsible. The mechanism responsible in other settings is less often identifiable, and in some instances, specifically with the opiates, a pharmacologic rather than immunologic mechanism may be important.[4]

The infections most commonly implicated in urticaria and angioedema include acute viral infections associated with upper respiratory disease, gastrointestinal (GI) disease, and flu-like syndromes. Chronic viral infections, such as mono-nucleosis and hepatitis B, are more often encountered in chronic urticaria. Among bacterial infections only those due to streptococci are commonly encountered. In some parts of the country coccidioidomycosis and histoplasmosis are important fungal infections. Foods most commonly incriminated include chocolate, fish, and nuts. In adults chronic urticaria may be related to food dyes, such as tartrazine, or food preservatives.

Noninfectious systemic diseases are sometimes associated with urticaria. A list of these diseases and other less common causes can be found in Table 16–2. In the elderly age group particular search should be made for malignancies, dyspro-teinemias, and autoimmune diseases.

Clinical Features and Diagnosis

Urticaria should be considered in the differential diagnosis of any nonscaling, nonpurpuric (blanchable) red eruption. The earliest lesions of urticaria may be macular, but by the time the patient has arrived in the ED, nearly all lesions are elevated and slightly palpable. The edematous wheal is the hallmark of the condition and is identified as a soft, sharply marginated, flat-topped papule. The color of the urticarial wheal depends on the amount of fluid present; the range is from light pink to dark red. These wheals frequently coalesce to form large polycyclic plaques. In some cases fading in the center results in an annular configuration as demonstrated in Figure 16–1. Urticaria and angioedema may occur on any part of the body and are almost always intensely pruritic. However, the lesions are rarely excoriated, but rather are transient. They change shape, resolve, and reappear in minutes to hours. This evanescence rarely occurs in other diseases and as such represents another diagnostic hallmark. The various patterns that urticarial lesions assume have no importance from a standpoint of etiology or therapy.

Angioedema may occur alone or concomitantly with urticaria. In general, the presence of angioedema makes the situation more urgent. Thus, health care providers involved in triage should recognize that skin-colored swelling of easily distensible tissues, such as the eyelids, earlobes, lips, external genitalia, and all mucous membranes, requires immediate attention to prevent the development of life-threatening swelling of the upper airway. The risk of such change is highest in anaphylaxis caused by reactions to medication or foods, but can also be seen in the rare disease, hereditary angioedema. The latter can be recognized by the relative absence of associated urticaria, a positive family history, the association of GI

Table 16–2 Common Causes of Urticaria

Cause	Common Responsible Factors
Altered endocrine state	Hyperthyroidism, pregnancy
Bacterial infection	Sinus, dental, tonsils, gallbladder, GI tract, respiratory, genitourinary
Contactants	Chemicals, cosmetics, topical medications, foods, textiles, marine animals, plants
Drugs	See Table 16–1
Foods	Fish, shellfish, eggs, cheese, milk, chocolate, berries, nuts, tomatoes
Fungal infection	Candidiasis, dermatophytosis
Heredity	Hereditary angioedema, familial cold urticaria, familial heat urticaria, vibratory angioedema
Inhalants	Animal danders, dust, mold spores, pollen, aerosols
Insect stings	Hymenoptera, fleas, mites, bedbugs
Internal disease	Systemic lupus erythematosus, rheumatic fever, juvenile rheumatoid arthritis, polymyositis, amyloidosis, polycythemia vera
Malignancy	Carcinoma, lymphoma, leukemia
Parasitic infections	Amebiasis, malaria, giardiasis, scabies, trichomoniasis
Physical agents	Cold, cholinergic urticaria, dermographism, heat, pressure, sunlight
Viral infection	Hepatitis, mononucleosis, coxsackie-virus

Source: Adapted with permission from *Medical Clinics of North America* (1980;64:867), Copyright © 1980, WB Saunders Company.

symptoms, and the precipitation by specific traumatic or stressful events. Angioedema of the airways rarely if ever presents after 24 hr in patients with urticaria, regardless of etiology.

Treatment

The first step in treatment is assessment of the mouth and upper airway. If edema is present in this location, epinephrine should be administered. Generally, 0.3–0.5 ml of a 1:1,000 aqueous solution is injected subcutaneously. In emergent settings epinephrine may be administered intravenously, but in dilutions of 1:10,000. Care should be taken when administering epinephrine to older indi-

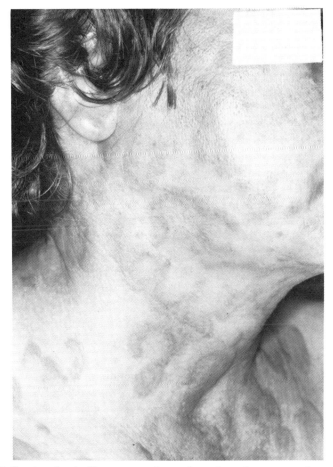

Figure 16–1 Gyrate urticaria. These nonscaling erythematous plaques may change rapidly and may form polycyclic and gyrate forms.

viduals because of its profound effects on the cardiovascular system. In particular, inadvertent IV administration of 1:1,000 dilutions may result in ventricular fibrillation.

Antihistamines are the mainstay of therapy. If urticaria or angioedema have been present for several hours or longer, antihistamines are best administered orally. Diphenhydramine (Benadryl) is time honored and cost effective. In adults it is generally administered initially in a 50-mg dose, which can be repeated in 4–6 hr if the hives have not disappeared. In chronic urticaria total daily doses greater than the usually recommended 200 mg/day are often needed. However, in the elderly, side effects both of sedation and atropine-like changes may limit the dose that can be administered. Hydroxyzine (Atarax, Vistaril) has been shown to be more potent than diphenhydramine in the prevention of histamine-induced wheals. It is, however, more sedating and significantly more costly. In the treatment of chronic urticaria it is often necessary to try different antihistamines until one is found that is effective. Cyproheptadine (Periactin) is a reasonable alternative because of its effect on mediators other than histamine. H_2 blockers, such as cimetidine (Tagamet), or ranitidine (Zantac) used alone, are not helpful in urticaria. It is possible, however, that the addition of an H_2 blocker to a full dose of H_1 antagonist may enhance its therapeutic effect.

Corticosteroids administered systemically can be useful agents in the treatment of urticaria.[4,5] These are rarely indicated for use by emergency health care providers. Corticosteroids applied topically are useless. However, topical treatment with local antipruritic lotions and tepid bathtub soaks for 30 or more minutes at a time are helpful adjuncts to standard pharmacologic therapy. Danazol, an androgenic hormone, is the preferred mode of long-term therapy in hereditary angioedema.[6] It has no role, however, in the treatment of other forms of urticaria.

The final step in therapy is the identification of any discernible cause. Obviously, the removal of that cause or the appropriate treatment of an associated disease, when identifiable, does much to prevent progression or recurrence of urticaria.

ERYTHEMA MULTIFORME BULLOSUM (STEVENS-JOHNSON SYNDROME)

Erythema multiforme bullosum (erythema multiforme major) is the most severe of the various forms of erythema multiforme. This syndrome, characterized by blister formation and the involvement of mucous membranes, has substantial morbidity and a mortality rate of approximately 5%.

Etiology

There are many possible causes of Stevens-Johnson syndrome. Those best documented include reactions to medication, especially sulfa-derived drugs,[7] and infections, particularly herpes simplex, mycoplasma, and histoplasma. Erythema multiforme bullosum may also be found in association with collagen vascular disease, malignancy, and immunizations.[8] Table 16–3 lists reported etiologic associations.

The pathogenesis of Stevens-Johnson syndrome is incompletely understood. Circulating immune complexes are often present and may even contain the putative antigen;[9] however, deposition of these complexes and activation of complement do not result in the typical histologic picture of a polymorphonuclear vasculitis. It is possible that delayed-type hypersensitivity also plays an important role in pathogenesis.[10] In any event the end result is a perivascular and upper dermal inflammatory infiltrate and formation of subepidermal blisters.

Table 16–3 Etiologic Associations of Erythema Multiforme Mentioned in the Medical Literature

I. Infections
  A. Viral
    1. Herpes simplex
    2. Infectious mononucleosis
    3. Vaccinia
    4. Orf
    5. Milker's nodules
    6. Mumps
    7. Measles
    8. Influenza
    9. Psittacosis
    10. Varicella/herpes zoster
    11. Lymphogranuloma
    12. Enterovirus infections
    13. Adenovirus infections
    14. Hepatitis B
  B. Bacterial
    1. Streptococcus
    2. Typhoid fever
    3. Pseudomonas
    4. Proteus
    5. Tularemia
    6. Vibrio parahemolyticus
    7. Dental infections
    8. Vincent's angina
    9. Pneumococcus
    10. Yersinia infections
    11. Legionnaire's disease
  C. Mycobacterial
    1. Tuberculosis
    2. Bacille Calmette Guérin
  D. Spirochetal-syphilis
  E. Mycoplasmal-mycoplasma pneumoniae
  F. Protozoan-trichomonas
  G. Fungal
    1. Histoplasmosis
    2. Coccidioidomycosis
    3. Dermatophyte infections

II. Immunizations or hyposensitization
  A. Horse serum
  B. Diphtheria-pertussis
  C. Polio vaccine
  D. Typhoid vaccine
  E. Pollen hyposensitization
  F. Poison ivy hyposensitization
  G. Measles vaccine

III. Systemic drugs
  A. Sulfonamides
  B. Penicillins
  C. Diphenylhydantoin
  D. Phenylbutazone
  E. Chlorpropamide
  F. Barbiturates
  G. Phenolphthalein
  H. Tetracycline
  I. Acetylsalicylic acid
  J. Alkylating agents
  K. Estrogens
  L. Arsenic
  M. Ethanol
  N. Carbamazepine
  O. Thiouracil
  P. Codeine
  Q. Trimethadione
  R. Chloramphenicol
  S. Thiacetazone
  T. Meprobamate
  U. Glutethimide
  V. Quinine
  W. Isoniazid
  X. Furosemide
  Y. Rifampin
  Z. Glucocorticoids
  AA. Zomepirac
  BB. Cimetidine
  CC. Clindamycin
  DD. Methotrexate
  EE. Thiabendazole
  FF. Ibuprofen
  GG. Ethosuximide
  HH. Benoxaprofen
  II. Fenoprofen

JJ. Minoxidil
KK. Sulindac
LL. Methaqualone
MM. Dapsone
NN. Glucagon
IV. Topical agents (chemical and drugs)
  A. 9-Bromofluorene
  B. Bulfonamides
  C. Anticholinergic eye drops
  D. Primula antigen
  E. Tropical Woods
  F. Fire Sponge
V. Neoplasms
  A. Leukemia
  B. Lymphoma
  C. Pelvic tumors
  D. Leiomyoma
VI. Connective tissue disease-lupus erythematosus
VII. Physical agents
  A. Sunlight
  B. X-irradiation of tumors
VIII. Food-margarine (emulsifying agent)
IX. Inhalants-methylparathion
X. Other diseases or conditions
  A. Inflammatory bowel disease
  B. Sarcoidosis
  C. Pregnancy
  D. Menstruation

Source: Adapted with permission from *Journal of the American Academy of Dermatology* (1983;8:770), Copyright © 1983, CV Mosby Company.

Clinical Features and Diagnosis

Stevens-Johnson syndrome should be considered in the differential diagnosis of the vesicular bullous diseases. The explosive onset; the occurrence of the cutaneous blisters on an erythematous base; the presence of some nonblistering, target-type lesions (Figure 16–2); the involvement of mucous membranes with blistering or erosive disease; and a distribution that frequently includes the palms and soles are features that help differentiate the condition from pemphigus, pemphigoid, and bullous impetigo.

These mucocutaneous lesions generally develop over 24–48 hr and are usually accompanied by a variable prodrome of constitutional signs and symptoms,

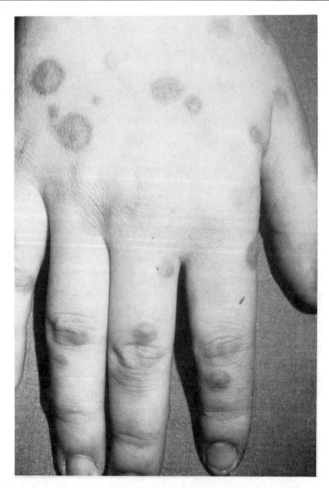

Figure 16–2 Erythema multiforme. Nonscaling, red target lesions on the dorsal surface of the hand.

including headache, malaise, fever, sore throat, myalgia, and arthralgia. Severe constitutional symptoms, such as tachycardia, tachypnea, and prostration, may also be present. In the most severe cases there is involvement of the internal mucous membranes leading to a picture of pneumonia and/or GI disturbances. Patients are often unable to eat because of the stomatitis, and dehydration may be caused by inadequate fluid intake.

Other potentially serious complications include severe eye involvement with resultant loss of vision, epistaxis, arthritis, pericarditis, cardiac dysrhythmias, hepatitis, glomerulonephritis, sepsis, seizures, and coma. The severity of these changes may prove fatal in a small percentage of the geriatric population.

Treatment

Hospitalization for IV fluid replacement is usually required. Systemic corticosteroids are usually administered even though at least one controlled study indicates no beneficial effect,[11] and none conclusively document a beneficial effect. When corticosteroids are used, they can be given as prednisone orally in a dosage of 2 mg/kg per day. Intramuscular or IV routes of administration may be required for patients with severe stomatitis. Topical application of corticosteroids is not indicated, but soaks may be soothing and useful, particularly if there is significant weeping or crust formation. Symptomatic relief from the painful stomatitis may be achieved with elixir of diphenhydramine, viscous lidocaine, or dyclonine solution. Secondary infections should be treated with appropriate antibiotics. Ophthalmologic consultation should be obtained when there is significant involvement of the eye.

TOXIC EPIDERMAL NECROLYSIS

Two different entities have been reported under the diagnosis of toxic epidermal necrolysis. The earliest recognized was that seen in infants and children as a result of staphylococcal infection (Ritter type). In this syndrome a toxic released by bacteria causes widespread cutaneous redness and sloughing of the upper layers of the epidermis. This disease is now more generally termed ''staphylococcal scaled skin syndrome.'' Because this disease is rarely seen in adults, it is not discussed further although its differentiating features can be found in Table 16–4.

The second and more important type of toxic epidermal necrolysis, Lyell type, is seen in adults generally as the result of a reaction to medication. It is characterized by redness of large areas of skin with subsequent sloughing of the entire thickness of the epidermis. Because the level of splitting in this disease is considerably deeper than that seen in staphylococcal scaled skin syndrome, toxic epidermal necrolysis of adults is associated with a longer duration, greater morbidity, and significant mortality.[12,13]

Table 16–4 Major Differential Diagnoses of Toxic Epidermal Necrolysis

	Toxic Epidermal Necrolysis	Staphylococcal Scaled Skin Syndrome
Patient age	Any (predominantly adults)	Rare in adults
Extent of bullae	Often widespread	Usually localized
Degree of exudation	4+	1+
Involvement of mucous membranes		
red	Yes	Yes
eroded	Yes	No
Level of epidermal split	Basement membrane zone	Granular layer
Mortality	10–40%	1–2%

Source: Adapted with permission from *Medical Clinics of North America* (1980;64:902), Copyright © 1980, WB Saunders Company.

Etiology

Toxic epidermal necrolysis in adults is generally directly related to the uses of medication. As in the Stevens-Johnson syndrome the sulfa-type drugs are most often incriminated. Phenytoin (Dilantin) is the next most common offender. Table 16–5 is a more complete list of drugs reported to cause toxic epidermal necrolysis. There have been a few scattered reports of causes other than medications, but most of these are single cases and without a convincing etiologic relationship.

The pathogenesis of toxic epidermal necrolysis is unknown, but because the histology is similar to that seen in the Stevens-Johnson syndrome, presumably the mechanisms of development are also similar.

Table 16–5 Drugs Capable of Causing Toxic Epidermal Necrolysis

Acetazolamide	Brompheniramine	Phenylbutazone
Allopurinol	Dapsone	Phenytoin
Aminopyrine	Gold salts	Salicylates
Antihistamines	Methyl salicylate	Polio vaccine
Antipyrines	Nitrofurantoin	Sulfonamides
Barbiturates	Penicillin	Tetracyclines
Boric acid powder	Phenolphthalein	Tolbutamide

Source: Adapted from *Andrews' Diseases of the Skin,* 6th ed (pp 129–131) by AN Domonkos with permission of WB Saunders Company, © 1971.

Clinical Features and Diagnosis

The earliest lesion seen in adults is nonscaling erythema. At this stage the differential diagnosis falls into the category of the vascular reactions. However, within a day or two blisters develop, and the differential diagnosis shifts to that of the vesicular bullous diseases. Unfortunately, the appearance of intact blisters is often time limited. Extension of the blistering process results in widespread confluence within 12–24 hr. At this point there is lifting, with subsequent shedding of large sheets of skin. The first clinical impression is almost always that of an extensive thermal burn.

Mucous membranes may be extensively involved. Mouth involvement with fissures and crusting (often hemorrhagic) leads to drooling and dehydration. Genital and rectal involvement causes painful urination and defecation. Eye involvement may also be seen.

Before the development of skin symptoms and signs there may be a brief prodrome of fatigue, fever, sore throat, and GI disease. Angina has been reported in some older patients. These symptoms and signs worsen quickly, and at the height of the illness, patients are seriously ill with fever, tachycardia, tachypnea, and sometimes coma. Complications may include acute renal failure, GI bleeding, and superimposed infection. If the patient does not succumb to these complications, gradual re-epithelialization of the skin occurs in the ensuing 14–28 days. Scarring is usually not troublesome, but there may be a decrease in visual acuity and loss of fingernails and hair.

Treatment

The treatment of toxic epidermal necrolysis is, for all intents and purposes, the same treatment given for an extreme second-degree burn. The problem of most immediate importance is fluid replacement. This should be started early because losses of 2–4 liters per day through the skin are not uncommon. Secondary infection is a common and significant problem. Topically applied silver sulfadiazine[14] (Silvadine) is usually used, despite its sulfa derivation. Although other topically applied medications with antibiotic efficacy can be used, care should be taken because absorption of materials not ordinarily considered toxic can be an important factor in these patients. Systemically administered antibiotics are also often used. Some investigators advocate the use of the newer porous surgical dressings or the use of artificial skin.[14] Pain control is important and generally requires the use of parenterally administered narcotics.

For those with less severe involvement, oral intake can sometimes be maintained through the use of viscous lidocaine, elixir of diphenhydramine, or Dyclone solution. For those with more severe involvement, consideration should be given to the use of parenteral alimentation. The use of systemic corticosteroids is controversial.[14] There is no proof that these are helpful, even though they are generally used. When the eyes are involved, an ophthalmologist should be consulted.

DISSEMINATED HERPES VIRUS INFECTIONS

The incidence of immunosuppression, as a result of disease or its treatment, has increased greatly in the geriatric population. Therefore, infections that are of little importance in the young adult may be life threatening in the elderly population.

Disseminated Herpes Simplex (Eczema Herpeticum, Kaposi's Varicelliform Eruption)

Dissemination of herpes simplex infection may occur cutaneously or systemically. Cutaneous dissemination generally requires the presence of a disturbed skin environment, such as underlying Darier's disease, pemphigus, thermal burn, atopic dermatitis, or other eczematous disease.

Clinical Features and Diagnosis

The initial lesions of disseminated herpes simplex are vesicular and are quite similar in appearance to those of conventional herpes labialis or genitalis. However, their appearance within the lesions of another skin disease disguises their morphology, and often the disease is not recognized until it has spread onto adjacent, otherwise normal skin. Often, but not always, there is a history or physical presence of preceding herpes labialis or genitalis. When the vesicles of herpes simplex disseminate, they lose their tendency to cluster and when occurring on otherwise normal skin generally are unassociated with underlying erythema. When fresh, these scattered vesicles are 3–4 mm in diameter and are filled with clear fluid. Mild itching may be present. Rather quickly, the fluid within the vesicles becomes cloudy, and within 48–72 hr the blister roofs break, leaving crusted lesions that are easily misdiagnosed as bacterial impetigo (Figure 16–3). Confirmation of a suspected diagnosis can be obtained through cytology (the Tzanck smear) or viral culture. Serologic evaluation is usually not helpful.

Fever and adenopathy may be seen in association with disseminated cutaneous herpes simplex. Pneumonitis, encephalitis, and hepatitis may also occur. Unfortunately, in the presence of an underlying systemic disease, it may be hard to tell whether any or all of these symptoms and signs are due to herpes or to the preceding problem.

Treatment

Localized herpes simplex requires no treatment even when it occurs in an immunocompromised host. Disseminated infection is generally treated with intravenously administered vidarabine (Vira-A) or acyclovir (Acyclovir).[15]

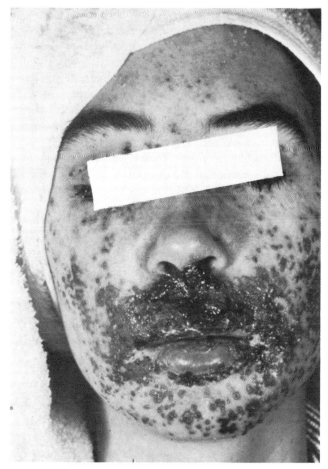

Figure 16–3 Kaposi's varicelliform eruption (Eczema herpeticum). Disseminated herpes simplex infection in an immunocompromised patient.

Disseminated Herpes Zoster

Clinical Features and Diagnosis

Localized herpes zoster (''shingles'') is usually readily recognized because of its unilateral dermatomal distribution and history of preceding segmental pain. The vesicles occur in clusters and are situated on a base of erythema. Individual vesicles are small, averaging 3 or 4 mm in diameter, but in the more severe case confluence may result in the appearance of larger lesions. The vesicular fluid is clear to cloudy gray; almost always a few vesicles contain some erythrocytes, a feature rarely if ever found in herpes simplex. Localized herpes zoster becomes an urgent problem only when the first branch of the trigeminal nerve is involved and there is accompanying eye involvement (Figure 16–4).

Dissemination of herpes zoster outside a single dermatome is cause for worry. The vesicles themselves, which are indistinguishable from those found in varicella, are not troublesome, but there is a high frequency of internal dissemination. Generalized toxicity is usually present, and often there are signs of meningoencephalitic involvement. Pneumonitis may also be present. Dissemination of this type is found only in debilitated individuals, the elderly,[16] or in those patients who are immunosuppressed because of cytotoxic therapy or underlying malignancy.[17] Patients with Hodgkin disease are at particularly high risk.

A clinical diagnosis of herpes zoster is best confirmed by viral cultures. As with herpes simplex, cytologic examination of a smear made with material taken from the base of a vesicle (the Tzanck test) is a very helpful screening test if positive.

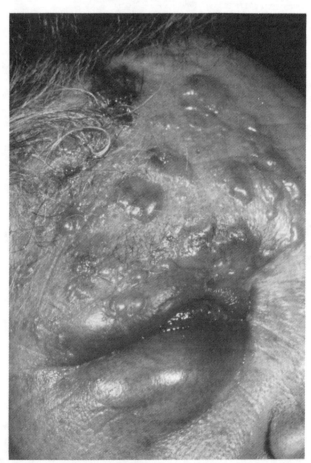

Figure 16–4 Herpes zoster of the face. Note vesiculation and massive swelling of the eyelid.

Treatment

The skin lesions should be treated symptomatically. Soaks (either wrapped or immersion) are particularly soothing. The nature of the soaking solution is not terribly important, and in most cases tap water suffices. Topically applied anesthetics (Quotane, Caladryl, etc.) are widely used, but are only marginally helpful and may, because of allergic sensitization, actually be detrimental. Pain is perhaps better controlled with systemically administered analgesics.

The use of systemically administered corticosteroids is controversial. There is evidence that large doses (60 mg of prednisone or its equivalent) decrease the incidence and severity of postherpetic neuralgia.[18] However, there is at least the theoretic possibility of the medication enhancing the likelihood of dissemination.

Specific antiviral therapy (intravenously administered vidarabine or acyclovir) is reserved for the seriously ill patient with evidence of cutaneous and visceral dissemination.

CONTACT DERMATITIS CAUSED BY POISON IVY

A sensitized individual subsequently exposed to plants of the poison ivy family is at risk for the development of severe bullous contact dermatitis. Recognition of the disease is not difficult if there has been a history of exposure 24–72 hr before its appearance. However, in the absence of a typical history the lesions resemble those seen in other blistering diseases. Clues to the morphologic recognition of plant-type contact dermatitis include (1) great variability in the size of the blisters, (2) a tendency for asymmetrical distribution, (3) angular-and-linear lesions, and (4) considerable accompanying inflammation and edema.

Many folk tales exist regarding poison ivy; education of the patient is part of the treatment. First, washing the skin vigorously, unless it can be accomplished within 30 min of contact, does not decrease the spread of disease. Second, the fluid in the blisters is not contagious. New lesions may continue to appear for several days, but this is not due to spread from old lesions. Third, if new lesions continue to appear for more than 4 days, there is likely to be continued exposure to plant antigen from clothing or other objects. Fourth, to prevent this kind of spread, soap-and-water washing of inanimate objects is sufficient; other forms of cleansing are not necessary.

Mild contact dermatitis caused by poison ivy can be treated with topically applied corticosteroids. When lesions are widespread or when there is involvement of the face, genitalia, hands, or feet, systemically administered corticosteroids are preferable.[1] Prednisone in a dose of 40 to 60 mg per day is given over a 10-day period.

BACTERIAL INTEGUMENTARY INFECTIONS

The most commonly encountered and potentially serious localized skin infections in order of skin depth involvement are cellulitis, furuncles, and necrotizing fasciitis. Generally, cellulitis and furuncles are not so urgent. However, necrotizing fasciitis is a serious, potentially life-threatening or limb-threatening disease. *Staphylococcus* is an etiologic bacteria common to all of these entities. *Streptococcus* is commonly implicated in cellulitis and in necrotizing fasciitis. The latter can also be caused by many different varieties of virulent gram-negative and anaerobic bacteria, including coliforms, *Bacteroides, Enterococcus,* and *Pseudomonas.*

Cellulitis

Cellulitis falls into the differential diagnosis of solid, nonscaling, red lesions. It may appear as a dome-shaped lesion (inflammatory nodule) or a flat-topped lesion (vascular reaction group).

A diagnosis of cellulitis is made clinically. Culture of material obtained by injection and aspiration of sterile saline into the involved skin has been widely advocated by purists, but in fact is rarely useful. The diagnostic hallmarks of bacterial cellulitis are sudden onset of a painful, tender, edematous, bright red, warm plaque generally in a single place but with no characteristic distribution. Constitutional symptoms, such as fever and malaise, may be present. Regional lymphadenitis and proximal lymphangitis may also be seen in more severe cases.

Cellulitis generally remains localized, but in the elderly, the diabetic, and the immunocompromised patient progressive spread and systemic infection may occur. Treatment consists of appropriate systemic antibiotics—penicillinase-resistant penicillin, erythromycin, or cephalosporin—local application of warm compresses, elevation, and rest of the involved part.[19]

Furuncles

Furuncles, as does cellulitis, fall into the differential diagnosis of solid, nonscaling, red lesions. They are slope-shouldered or dome-shaped (inflammatory nodule group). The diagnostic hallmarks are similar to those of cellulitis, but the rapidly arising, painful, tender, bright red lesions of furunculosis are nodular, rather than flat-topped. Occasionally a pustule is present at the summit. They may go on to become fluctuant and, in time, spontaneously drain. Large abscesses may form in certain untreated patients. An inflamed epidermoid cyst looks very much like a furuncle. Correct identification of an inflamed cyst requires elicitation of the history of a preceding noninflamed nodule. As with cellulitis, there is no characteristic location on the body. Constitutional symptoms are usually not present.

Treatment consists of systemic antibiotics—penicillinase–resistant penicillin, erythromycin, or cephalosporin—and the application of warm compresses to encourage fluctuance and spontaneous drainage. Fluctuant furuncles resolve most rapidly after they are incised and drained.

In general, furuncles are benign; however, in the elderly, the diabetic, and the potentially immunocompromised patient, treatment should be early and definitive to avoid local or systemic spread of infection.

Necrotizing Fasciitis

Necrotizing fasciitis is an acute necrotizing infection involving the dermal fascia. It should be considered in the differential diagnosis of both clear, fluid-filled, blistering lesions and solid, nonscaling, red lesions. Necrotizing fasciitis often appears, as does cellulitis, with rapid onset of edema, pain, and redness. It distinguishes itself, however, when yellow or serosanguinous fluid-filled blisters appear over the area of "cellulitis." Other points in differentiation include the occurrence of marked edema peripheral to the area of redness and, later, anesthesia of the central area (Figure 16–5). Within 1–2 days central patches of cyanosis appear and over the next day or two become gangrenous (Figure 16–6). Crepitus may be present on palpation. Soft tissues sometimes reveal gas formation.

Treatment consists of local surgical excision or debridement and concomitant administration of IV antibiotics that are active against *Streptococcus, Staphylococcus,* gram-negative coliforms, and anaerobic bacteria until cultures provide a rationale for more narrow-spectrum antibiotics.[19,20] As with other skin infections, the elderly, the diabetic, and the immunocompromised patients are particularly susceptible to local and systemic spread of infection when treatment is suboptimal.

DERMATOLOGIC MANIFESTATIONS OF SYSTEMIC DISEASE

Dermatologic manifestations of systemic disease may herald other signs and symptoms or may "clinch the diagnosis" when other manifestations appear in

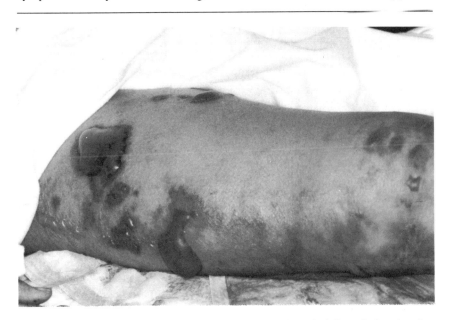

Figure 16–5 Necrotizing fasciitis. Note blistering areas overlying the inflamed edematous leg.

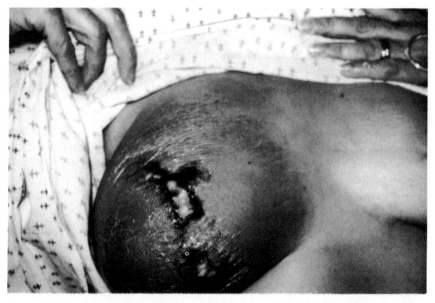

Figure 16–6 Necrotizing faciitis of the breast. Cultures grew coagulase positive *Staphylococcus aureus* organisms.

concert. Certain illnesses are less common or emergent than those already discussed, but are so closely associated with skin lesions that they are deserving of mention here. Other illnesses, although not consistently associated with skin changes, are serious enough to warrant mention as well.

Pruritus, with or without excoriation or lichenification (also occasional secondary eczematization), may occur with such systemic diseases as polycythemia vera, Hodgkin disease, lymphomas, liver disease (particularly cholestatic), and uremia.

Generalized hyperpigmentation, occurring most commonly in skin folds and intertriginous areas, may be a clue to the presence of malignancy (notably ectopic ACTH-producing lung tumors), advanced melanoma, adrenal failure (Addison disease), or hemochromatosis (bronze skin). Acanthosis nigricans occurs on the side of the neck, groin, and axilla, characteristically displaying soft, velvety ridges in the pigmented areas. In the nonobese adult patient, GI tumors are frequently associated.[1]

Hirsutism may be associated with Cushing syndrome, acromegaly, and some gonadal tumors.

Cutaneous ulcerations may be associated with rheumatoid arthritis, mycosis fungoides, certain deep fungal infections (sporotrichosis, coccidioidomycosis, histoplasmosis, and blastomycosis), and atypical mycobacterium infections to which the elderly and the immunocompromised patients are more vulnerable.

Exfoliative erythrodermatitis—eczematous disease covering 70% or more of the total body surface—may be seen as a drug reaction, but is also commonly associated with lymphomas, specifically Hodgkin disease, and mycosis fungoides. Dermatomyositis, characterized by violaceous edema of the upper eyelids and violaceous plaques on the elbows, knees, and knuckles, is found in approximately 50% of those patients with the autoimmune muscle disease of polymyocitis.

Patients with diabetes are likely to develop necrobiosis lipoidica diabeticorum, characterized by yellow plaques on the pretibial regions, in addition to being vulnerable to bacterial and fungal skin infections.

Skin findings have been noted in two-thirds of patients with the often fatal consumptive coagulopathy, disseminated intravascular coagulation, regardless of etiology.[21] Widespread, minute petechiae are most often seen due to platelet consumption.[22] Hemorrhagic bullae may be seen and purpura fulminans, a severe, rapidly fatal necrotizing vasculitis, may occur in late stages, but not so commonly in the elderly as in children.

There are a host of clinical syndromes falling under the general heading of vasculitis. Most forms of vasculitis are thought to be immunologic in origin, and classification is made primarily on the basis of vessel size and anatomic location. The best described and most commonly occurring forms of primary vasculitis are polyarteritis nodosa, lymphoid granulomatosis, Wegener's granulomatosis, thromboangiitis obliterans (Buerger disease), mucocutaneous lymph node syndrome, hypersensitivity vasculitis, and giant cell arteritis.[23] Vasculitis may be present as a component of other systemic diseases, such as systemic lupus erythematosus, rheumatoid arthritis, mixed cryoglobulinemias, polymyalgia rheumatica (with or without temporal arteritis), and subacute bacterial endocarditis. The skin manifestations common to most forms of vasculitis are petechiae, purpura, and ecchymoses. The purpura seen with vasculitis is usually palpable because it is caused by an infiltration of inflammatory leukocytes.[1] Vascular occlusion may occur, resulting in cutaneous ulceration or gangrene of the fingers or toes. Each variety of vasculitis has its own anatomic predilections, with most being widespread. Vasculitis should be considered in the differential diagnosis of nonblanchable, flat-topped, nonscaling, solid red lesions.

SUMMARY

Dermatologic emergencies in any age group are unusual. Toxic epidermal necrolysis and angioedema (with laryngeal edema) are true dermatologic emergencies that occur in the elderly. Dermatologic urgencies do occur more frequently in the elderly and should be recognized by the emergency health care provider. Certain systemic illnesses commonly have cutaneous manifestations that may assist in making a timely diagnosis and disposition.

REFERENCES

1. Lynch PJ: *Dermatology for the House Officer.* Baltimore, Williams & Wilkins Co. 1982.
2. Lynch PJ, Edminster SC: Dermatology for the non-dermatologist: A problem oriented system. *Ann Emerg Med* 13:603–606, 1984.

3. Dunagin WG, Milliken LE: Drug eruptions. *Med Clin North Am* 64:983–1001, 1980.
4. Monroe EW: Urticaria and urticarial vasculitis. *Med Clin North Am* 64:867–880, 1980.
5. Thompson JS: Urticaria and angioedema. *Ann Intern Med* 69:361–380, 1968.
6. Frank MM, Gelford JA, Atkinson JP: Hereditary angioedema: The clinical syndrome and its management (NIH Conference). *Ann Intern Med* 84:580–593, 1976.
7. Bianchine JR, Macarag PVJ, Lasagna L, et al: Drugs as etiologic factors in Stevens-Johnson syndrome. *Am J Med* 44:390–405, 1968.
8. Huff JC, Weston WL, Tonnesen MG: Erythema multiforme: A critical review of characteristics, diagnostic criteria, and causes. *J Am Acad Dermatol* 8:763–775, 1983.
9. Kazmierowski JA, Peizner DS, Wuepper KD: Herpes simplex antigen in immune complexes of patients with erythema multiforme. *JAMA* 247:2547–2550, 1982.
10. Tonnesen MG, Harrist TJ, Wintroub BU, et al: Erythema multiforme: Microvascular damage and infiltration of lymphocytes and basophils. *J Invest Dermatol* 80:282–286, 1983.
11. Rasmussen JE: Erythema multiforme in children: Response to treatment with systemic corticosteroids. *Br J Dermatol* 95:181–186, 1976.
12. Rist TC, Abele DC: Current concepts of toxic epidermal necrolysis. *South Med J* 68:22–26, 1975.
13. Amon RB, Dimon RL: Toxic epidermal necrolysis. *Arch Dermatol* 111:1433–1437, 1975.
14. Rasmussen JE: Toxic epidermal necrolysis. *Med Clin North Am* 64:901–918, 1980.
15. Corey L, Holmes KK: Genital herpes simplex virus infections: Current concepts in diagnosis, therapy, and prevention. *Ann Intern Med* 98:973–983, 1983.
16. Miller LH: Herpes zoster in the elderly. *Cutis* 18:427–432, 1976.
17. Dolin R, Reichman RC, Mazue MH, et al: Herpes zoster-varicella infections in immunosuppressed patients (NIH Conference). *Ann Intern Med* 89:375–378, 1978.
18. Eaglstein WH, Katz R, Brown JA: The effects of early corticosteroid therapy on the skin eruption and pain of herpes zoster. *JAMA* 211:1681–1683, 1970.
19. Hammar H, Wanger L: Erysipelas and necrotizing fasciitis. *Br J Dermatol* 96:409–419, 1977.
20. Koehn GG: Necrotizing fasciitis. *Arch Dermatol* 14:581–583, 1978.
21. Robboy SJ, Mihm MC, Colman RW, et al: The skin in disseminated intravascular coagulation: A prospective analysis of 36 cases. *Br J Dermatol* 88:221–229, 1973.
22. Coleman RW, Minna JD, Robboy SJ: Disseminated intravascular coagulation: A dermatologic disease. *Int J Dermatol* 16:47–51, 1977.
23. Fauci AS: The spectrum of vasculitis: Clinical, pathologic, immunologic, and therapeutic considerations. *Ann Intern Med* 84:660–676, 1978.

17

Burns in the Aged

Charles E. Copeland, MD, FACS

The population of the United States is aging, and it is estimated that by the year 2030 nearly 20% of the population will be 65 years of age or older.[1] The data base of the National Burn Exchange has identified an increased burn injury risk in the elderly; thus, the increasing numbers of aged persons represent a unique subset of potential burn patients.[2] This greater risk of burn injury among the elderly may be explained by visual and hearing losses, decreased sensory perception and motor strength, and mental and psychological features of aging,[3] which are responsible for an increasingly slower response to environmental events.

Furthermore, older burn patients are at greater risk of death than younger adults with the same extent of burn injury.[4] Persons 65 years of age and older account for a disproportionate share of the nearly 10,000 annual burn deaths.[5,6] This age-related increased mortality rate is attributed to decreased cardiac, pulmonary, and renal functional reserve as the consequence of biologic aging and acquired degenerative diseases. The severe metabolic stress of burn injury and the stress of burn wound sepsis may result in fatal cardiac, pulmonary, or renal complications. Careful cardiopulmonary and renal function monitoring and the prompt recognition and treatment of septic complications are even more important in older than younger burn patients if a satisfactory outcome is to be achieved.

EPIDEMIOLOGY

For burn victims of any age the common types of thermal injury include the following:

- flame burns as a result of residential fire and clothing ignition
- scalds from tap water in a bath or shower or by contact with hot liquids
- burns from contact with hot surfaces

415

- electrical burns
- chemical burns.

The most frequent types of thermal injury resulting in hospitalization are scalds and flame burns. In a 57-county, upstate New York study of 5,971 burn patients, scalds were responsible for 40% and flame injury for 37% of burn injuries resulting in hospitalization.[7] Twenty-seven percent of hospitalized scald injuries occurred in the 60-year-and-older age group that represented 15% of the general population.[8] A Florida study consisting of 1,297 patients demonstrated that the elderly, age 65 and older, had a proportionately larger number of burns greater than 30% of the body surface area (BSA).[9] Additionally, these patients had a much higher number of complications, such as burn shock, inhalation injury, renal failure, and septicemia. Sixty percent of the deaths occurred in this older age group.

The length of hospital stay for surviving thermally injured patients is dependent on a number of factors, including age. Older surviving burn patients with the same extent of injury as a younger counterpart remain in the hospital longer because of associated medical problems, reduced rehabilitation potential, and difficulties with posthospital placement.[4]

AGE-RELATED MORTALITY

The traditional factors of burn size—percentage of BSA burned, percentage of full thickness injury, patient age, and the presence or absence of inhalation injury—are important determinants of predicted mortality rates. An estimation of burn mortality on the basis of percentage of BSA burned and the patient's age are commonly determined by reference to grids,[10] data charts,[11] LA_{50} comparison tables,[12] or mortality contours[4] (Figure 17–1).

The results of 1,100 consecutive burns treated at the Institute of Surgical Research (ISR), Brooke Army Medical Center, which were tabulated according to age and extent of burn injury, clearly demonstrated a marked decrease in the LA_{50}—percentage of BSA burn that results in the death of 50% of the patients—in patients over 50 years of age.[13]

A simple scoring system that is especially useful in the emergency department (ED) in predicting whether an individual will survive a burn injury is the BAUX rule.[14] This method adds the patient's age to the percentage of BSA that is burned. A value of 75 of more indicates a poor prognosis and a high probability of death. For example, a 65-year-old patient with 25% BSA burn has a BAUX value of 90 and is at great risk. A modified BAUX rule that excludes patients less than 20 years of age predicts that a patient has a greater than 50% chance of death if the sum of the patient's age and the percentage of BSA burned exceeds 95.[15]

Age and burn size, although important factors, are only two variables that determine mortality. The presence of full thickness burns and associated inhala-

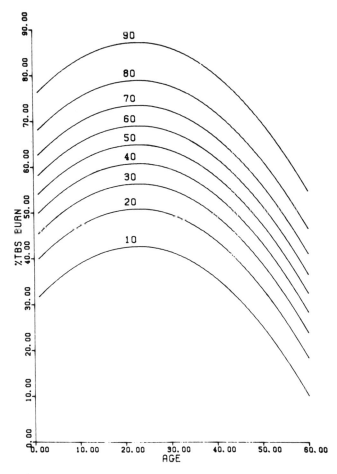

Figure 17-1 Mortality contours obtained from probit analysis of 937 consecutive patients treated at the New York Hospital-Cornell Medical Burn Center.

Source: Reprinted with permission from *Annals of Surgery* (1980;192:473), Copyright © 1980, JB Lippincott Company.

---

tion injury are also important determinants. The abbreviated burn severity index is a statistical model of five variables:

1. age
2. sex
3. percentage of BSA burn
4. the presence of full thickness burn
5. the presence of inhalation injury

Each variable has a scoring value, and the sum of the variables are applied to a reference table that provides a predicted mortality rate.[16] For example, a 61-year-old woman with a 25% BSA burn (part of which is full thickness) and an associated inhalation injury has a value of 10, indicating a severe threat to life and a probability of survival of only about 30%.

Studies of other potential predictors of mortality, such as pre-existing cardiovascular disease, renal disease, and liver disease, have shown these to have an adverse effect on survival.[17] Zawicki evaluated 1,295 burn patients using 12 possible predictor factors.[18] Six of these factors were the best discriminates between survival and nonsurvival:

1. age
2. BSA burn
3. full thickness area burned
4. prior bronchopulmonary disease
5. airway edema
6. abnormal PO_2

The best two-factor model included age and percentage of the BSA burned. The best three-factor model included an abnormal PO_2 as an indication of inhalation injury as well (Appendix 17–A).

The increased burn mortality rate with advancing age is often the result of single or multiple organ system failure as a consequence of the intense metabolic stress in a milieu of previously impaired cardiac, pulmonary, and renal functional reserve.

Cardiac Factors

The aging heart undergoes hypertrophy, and myocardial oxygen consumption is decreased.[19] An age-related decrease in cardiac output after the third decade of life approximates 1% a year.[20] Gerstenblith et al. state that "nearly every parameter of cardiovascular performance that has been measured suggests that the aging process impairs the response to exercise (stress)."[21] Hemodynamic stress and aging factors produce collagen changes with resulting fibrosis and degenerative calcification of the aortic valve and the mitral valve annulus of the heart.[22] Calcific aortic stenosis and mitral valve dysfunction are both etiologic factors in congestive heart failure and death.[23]

The incidence of cardiac arrhythmia increases with age and usually indicates the presence of concomitant cardiovascular disease, rather than being caused by the aging process alone.[24] Cardiac arrhythmias compromise the blood supply to vital organs, including the heart, and may also result in congestive heart failure and death.

Atypical symptoms of acute myocardial infarction as a result of coronary arteriosclerosis are common in the elderly. The absence of chest pain and such symptoms as confusion, dizziness, shortness of breath, and indigestion frequently occur in elderly myocardial infarction patients.[25]

A study of 107 burn patients 50 years of age or older treated at the ISR found 10 patients with acute myocardial infarctions. Curiously, chest pain was not a clinical feature, and in eight patients a clue to the diagnosis was a cardiac arrhythmia. None of the patients who had an acute myocardial infarction following a major body burn survived. Pruitt et al. cautioned that, in burn patients with pre-existing heart disease, "careful and frequent monitoring of cardiac status is required because of the grave consequences of myocardial infarction."[26]

Pulmonary Factors

With aging, changes in collagen and elastin copolymerization result in a decreased elastic property and increased rigidity of the lung.[27,28] This results in a decreased vital capacity (VC) and the 1 sec forced expiratory volume (FEV_1). Residual volume (RV) and functional residual capacity (FRC), on the other hand, increase with age.[29] The pulmonary diffusing capacity, a measure of alveolar capillary gas exchange, is decreased with the aging process, leading to a decreased arterial oxygen tension (PaO_2).[30,31] A combination of pulmonary changes associated with aging and acquired disease, such as asthma, chronic bronchitis, emphysema, and chronic obstructive pulmonary disease, that further derange lung function subjects the elderly patient to an increased risk of respiratory failure in situations of stress.

Pneumonia may result from bacterial colonization of the respiratory tract. In unburned patients over 40 years of age, the mortality rate for gram-negative pneumonia exceeded 80% and was nearly 50% with Staphylococcal pneumonia.[32] A review of 107 burn patients over 50 years of age showed that 35% developed pneumonia, with a mortality rate of 83.7%.[26]

Of 100 burn patients admitted to the Orange County Medical Center Burn Center, 22 had significant pulmonary complications. Nineteen (86%) of these patients died. It was concluded that pulmonary complications caused or contributed to the death of most patients who died from thermal injury.[33]

Renal Factors

The kidneys are vulnerable to age-induced functional deterioration. Such systemic illnesses as arteriosclerosis, hypertension, and diabetes mellitus further add to the risk of diminished renal function. With aging there is a loss of renal mass, and the number of functional nephrons is decreased.[34–36] Glomerular and tubular basement membranes are thickened, and there are progressive sclerotic changes in the larger renal vessels; in small vessels, hypertensive-like changes are seen in normotensive elderly patients.[37–39] These age-induced structural changes are accompanied by alterations in renal function.[40] After the third decade there is a decline in glomerular filtration rate, renal plasma flow, and tubular reabsorptive capacity.[34] As the glomerular filtration rate declines, the normal mean clearance of 120 ml diminishes to 80 ml/min in the elderly.[41]

With advancing age, muscle mass is reduced in proportion to the glomerular filtration rate and is not associated with an increase in serum creatinine. Estimation of creatinine clearance, therefore, is a more useful clinical indicator of renal function than is serum creatinine. A commonly used formula for predicting creatinine clearance at the bedside is as follows:[42]

$$\text{Creatinine Clearance} = \frac{140 - \text{Age} \times \text{Weight (kg)}}{72 \times \text{Serum Creatinine}}$$

Multiply Above by 0.85 for Women

A 65-year-old 70 kg man, for example, with a serum creatinine of 1.2 mg/dl (normal = 0.5-1.2 mg/dl) would have a creatinine clearance of 62.5 ml/min, a reduction of nearly 50% of renal function.

This formula is a valuable tool in calculating the degree of physiologic renal impairment in preparation for the administration of drugs that are excreted in the urine or when using potentially nephrotoxic drugs. Dosage adjustments are made by extending the administration interval or by reducing dosage prior to drug blood level determinations.[43]

The aging kidney has a diminished capacity to conserve salt and water.[44] In circumstances of limited water intake or increased insensible loss such as a burn, hypernatremia is common in the elderly. Likewise, water overloading with hyponatremia frequently occurs. The aged kidneys also have less adaptive capacity, and acute renal failure occurs with greater frequency in the geriatric age group.[45]

In the 107 burn patients in the older age group studied by Pruitt et al., 17 developed acute renal failure (16%), which was approximately five times the frequency in the younger burn population. Eight patients developed acute tubular necrosis within 6 days of admission. Later renal failure was attributed to an episode of hypotension in eight of nine patients.[26]

If renal failure is to be minimized in older burn patients, the physiologic response to fluid resuscitation must be closely monitored.

THE IMMUNE RESPONSE

Cell-mediated and humoral responses to foreign antigens are decreased with aging. This immune senescence is related to the involution of the thymus and an altered balance among T-lymphocytes. Although the total number of lymphocytes does not change, the number of helper or inducer T-lymphocytes is increased, and the number of suppressor or cytotoxic T-lymphocytes is decreased.[46] It has been demonstrated that more elderly individuals with impaired delayed hypersensitivity reactions died in a 2-year period than matched controls with maintained hypersensitivity response.[47] The total concentration of immunoglobulins remains the same with aging; however, there is a slight change in the distribution: IgG is increased, IgA is increased, and IgM is decreased.[16] The apparent increased susceptibility of the elderly to infections may be in part a consequence of immune senescence.

Because of a loss of protection provided by normal skin, infection is an inevitable consequence of an open-burn wound. Impairment of host defense mechanisms is a universal finding in severe burns and may allow burn-wound sepsis to occur or to advance to lethal septicemia. Humoral and cellular immunity have both been shown to be depressed after burn injury.[48,49] Adequate granulocyte response to infection is an important part of the host defense mechanism. Neutrophil dysfunction and the depression of opsonin levels after major burns have been identified.[50,51] This aberration in granulocyte function after thermal injury may play a primary role in development of fatal septicemia.[52] Cellular immunity, which also has a recognized role in host defense against sepsis, is suppressed after thermal injury and may be caused by an increase in suppressor cell lymphocytes.[53] High levels of suppressor cell activity accurately predicted mortality from sepsis.[54] These immunologic alterations in major burns are associated with increased septic complications and death.[49,55–57]

Improved antisepsis, bacteriologic monitoring of burn wounds, appropriate systemic antibiotic therapy, and early excision and grafting have reduced the incidence and severity of burn wound infection. Further improvement is anticipated with the development of additional topical antimicrobial agents and newer systemic antibiotics.

THE METABOLIC RESPONSE

Hypermetabolism characterizes the metabolic response of thermal injury and is related to the extent of the burn. Increased evaporative water loss through burned skin results in cooling and is an added stimulus to increasing the metabolic rate.[58] Catecholamines, which are elevated following thermal injury, are the primary mediator of the hypermetabolic response.[59] They increase the rate of cellular metabolism and are associated with a decrease in insulin and an increase in glucagon production.[60–62] The fasting blood sugar level is elevated following burn injury (postburn hyperglycemia) and correlates with the increased catecholamine excretion.[59] Although the increased metabolic rate and catecholamine excretion are not reduced by calorie and nitrogen administration, protein wasting is markedly diminished.[59] Following burn wound closure, sympathetic activity is returned to baseline, and the normal relationship between catecholamines and insulin and glucagon is re-established and is associated with weight gain.[59]

The catabolic consequences of major burn stress require close attention to nutritional status. Nutritional considerations are more important in elderly patients who may already be malnourished.[63] The caloric requirement of burn patients may be calculated by the following formula:[64]

Daily Calorie Requirement = 25 Kcal × Weight (kg) + 40 Kcal × %BSA Burn

For example, a 70-kg man with 50% BSA burn requires 3750 kilocalories (Kcalories) to minimize protein catabolism and weight loss. Following the initial postburn resuscitation, stabilization of fluid, and placement of a central venous catheter, the administration of a mixture of 25% dextrose and 4.25% amino acids can supply approximately 3,000 Kcalories per day. Nutritional support monitoring requires frequent determinations of the patient's weight, calorie intake, and blood and urine electrolytes and glucose.

FLUID RESUSCITATION AND MONITORING

Initial fluid resuscitation of adult patients with major BSA burns (25% BSA or greater) is accomplished by high-volume IV infusion of crystalloid solutions. Fluid resuscitation requires an accurate determination of the patient's weight and the percentage of BSA burned. In order to determine the area of BSA burned, one can refer to the Lund and Browder burn chart[65] or can apply the clinically useful Rule of Nines (Figure 17–2). The Rule of Nines ascribes 9% to each of the following BSAs:

- head and neck
- each arm
- each portion of the anterior torso above and below the xiphoid
- upper back

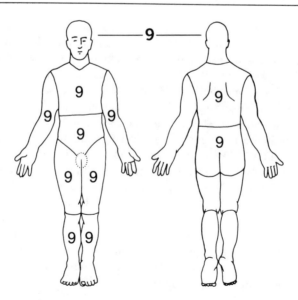

Figure 17–2 Rule of nines.

- lower back and buttocks
- each thigh
- each lower leg and foot.

As a check, a calculation of the unburned area should be made and the total should approximate as near as possible 100% BSA.

A variety of comparable formulas are available as guides in initial resuscitation. A commonly used regimen is that of Baxter and Shires, calculated by the following formula:[66]

$$4 \text{ ml} \times \text{kg} \times \% \text{ BSA Burn} = \text{Volume (Lactated Ringer's Solution)}$$

The volume of fluid calculated is administered as Lactated Ringer's Solution, with one-half given during the first 8 hr and one-quarter in each of the next 8 hr for a total of 16 hr. Written instructions must include the hourly rate of fluid administration. Colloid is generally not administered during the first 24 hr because of the initial increased capillary permeability, which returns to normal at approximately 18- to 24-hr postburn. Fluid administration during the second day is given as 5% glucose and water with the addition of colloid that can be calculated by the following formula:[67]

$$\text{Colloid Volume} = 0.5 \text{ ml} \times \text{kg} \times \% \text{ BSA Burn}$$

These formulas establish a guide for resuscitation that demands that the patient be continuously monitored for the response to therapy. An indwelling urinary catheter and a central venous pressure (CVP) line are critical in this regard. Urine output is observed for quantity and electrolyte content. The adult patient's urine output should be maintained at 40 to 50 ml per hour. Urinary sodium content should be maintained above 40 mEq/L. In addition to peripheral IV lines, a central venous catheter is used to monitor the effects of volume replacement. A CVP value of 10 cm of water is desirable. In instances where the CVP is low, additional fluid may be necessary; elevated CVP, providing that urinary output is adequate, may be an indication of volume overloading. An intra-arterial line may be necessary for blood pressure determinations and to provide ready access for the monitoring of arterial blood gases and pH to determine the effectiveness of volume resuscitation and ventilatory support in patients with associated inhalation injury. In the elderly patient, cardiac monitoring and daily chest roentgenographic examinations should be routine.

Most patients with severe burns can be successfully monitored by a CVP catheter, urinary output, and serum electrolyte studies. However, in instances of patients with a history of cardiovascular disease, it may be necessary to insert a pulmonary artery wedge catheter (Swan-Ganz catheter) in order to determine more precisely volume status and to measure cardiac output using the thermodilution technique. Insufficient resuscitation or hypovolemia may be indicated by oliguria with increasing urine specific gravity and normal or low CVP and low pulmonary artery wedge pressure (PAWP). Excessive resuscitation (overloading) is suspected with increased urine volumes, decreased urine specific gravity, high or rising CVP, and elevated PAWP.

During the second 24 hr, the most commonly encountered electrolyte abnormality is that of hypernatremia with an elevation in the serum sodium above 145 mEq/L. Hypernatremia, due to insufficient free water administration, is frequently caused by inadequate replacement of unrecognized evaporative water loss.[68] Treatment consists of the prompt administration of hypotonic or electrolyte free fluids.

Evaporative water loss may be estimated in the burn patient using the following formula:[69]

$$\text{ml per hour} = 25 + \%\text{BSA Burn} \times \text{Surface Area}$$

For example, a patient with 50% BSA burn and 1.7 square meters will have an evaporative water loss of 127 ml/hr or more than 3,000 ml/day.

Of the 107 older aged burn patients reviewed by Pruitt et al. 51% (55) patients received either slight to moderate underhydration or overhydration. The 32 patients receiving less fluids than required had an increased incidence of renal failure and a 71% mortality rate. Twenty-three patients received excessive fluid hydration; 28 developed pulmonary complications with a 56% mortality rate.[26] This clearly indicates the narrow margin permitted in the resuscitation of the elderly patient with major body burns and emphasizes the necessity of continuous monitoring of the response to therapy.

AGED SKIN AND THE BURN WOUND

Aging skin undergoes a number of biologic changes that alter its appearance and mechanical properties. There is flattening of the epidermal rete pegs and the dermal papillae.[70] Consequently, the thickness of both the epidermis and the dermis is decreased on various body sites in the older adult as compared to the young adult.[71] In addition to this thinning of skin, there are changes in collagen fiber length and cross-linkage that result in increased stiffness and decreased elasticity of skin after 40 years of age.[72]

These qualities of older skin render it more prone to such injury as burns and have been related to decreased separation of eschar during the postburn period. The observed slow separation of eschar in older patients was confirmed in a study of 49 patients who were 50 years of age or older.[26] The mean eschar separation time of 41 days was 10 to 20 days longer than in younger patients.

The characteristics of aged skin, its thinness, and loss of elasticity must be considered during surgical debridement and during the harvesting of donor isografts. Donor sites that are inadvertently deep will result in unnecessary delayed healing and excessive scarring.

Debridement and Skin Grafting

In the treatment of patients with major body burns, areas of full thickness burn injury require early excision and split thickness skin grafting. Surgical excision should be begun within the first week of admission, providing that the patient is hemodynamically stable.[73] The area of full thickness injury is excised, and split thickness grafts are applied either at the same operative procedure or at a subsequent planned procedure.

Burn patients undergoing debridement and grafting are at risk for hypothermia when exposed to the cooler environment of the operating room. Elderly patients are especially prone to impaired temperature homeostasis.[74] A decline in body temperature to 33.3°C (92°F) may result in serious cardiac arrhythmias.[75] It is essential that an esophageal or a rectal probe thermometer be used to monitor the patient's intraoperative body temperature and that there be routine cardiac monitoring. Prophylaxis should include prewarming of the operating room from 21.1°C (70°F) to 26.6°C (80°F), utilizing warming pads, and warming IV fluids and blood that are given.

The bacteriologic status of the preoperative burn wound should be known and appropriate antibiotic coverage instituted prior to, during, and following the surgical procedure. In a study of 46 patients with a mean full thickness burn of 19.4%, Peterson et al. found that excisional manipulation of the burn wound resulted in only a 1.6% incidence of perioperative septicemia. Of those patients, 47.8% had positive burn wound cultures before surgical excision; however, only four patients had 10^5 organisms/gram tissue on burn wound biopsy. It was concluded that excisional therapy in major burns did not result in high incidence of bacteremia and did not lead to fatal sepsis.[76]

Older burn patients whose hospital course is complicated by congestive failure, cardiac arrhythmias, or pulmonary problems may have surgical excision of the wound delayed in an attempt to further stabilization. Unnecessary delay, however, exposes the patient to the continued risk of bacterial wound colonization, burn wound sepsis, and death. In an early excision protocol study of 49 consecutive burn patients over the age of 50, 23 had BSA burns of greater than 20%. Thirty-five percent of the major burn patients died in the perioperative period; five of the eight deaths were a result of cardiovascular complications. Twelve of 14 patients requiring debridement and grafting survived, and 6 of these survivors had predicted mortality rates of 75% or greater.[77] Curreri et al. also demonstrated that aggressive early surgical excision in older burn patients can be accomplished without adversely affecting mortality.[4]

ASSOCIATED INJURIES AND ILLNESSES

During the emergency evaluation of burn patients, a detailed history of the injury event is vital. Falling during a fire, jumping from windows, industrial explosions, and burns sustained in vehicular accidents require examination of the patient as a multiply injured trauma victim. Fractures are not an uncommon injury associated with burns.[78-80] Elderly patients are particularly prone to severe head injury, fractures of the femur, and fractures of the forearm and wrist as a result of accidents.[81-83] Attention to the burn injury should not deter an evaluation of the burn patient in accordance with the principles of multiple trauma care. This includes a careful total body survey for cranial, spinal, thoracoabdominal, and musculoskeletal injuries.

Relevant information regarding pre-existing diseases is essential to the care of older burn patients. A medical history of cardiovascular disease, pulmonary disease, diabetes mellitus, seizure disorders, drug abuse, or alcoholism should be sought. When the patient is unable or reluctant to provide an adequate history, this information may be obtained by interviewing responsible family members.

A history of previous pulmonary disease is particularly important. Fires in enclosed areas, such as house fires, are frequently associated with smoke inhalation, a highly lethal related injury in burn patients. Inhalation injury and its complications are a major cause of death after serious burns.[84-88]

In a Cook County Hospital Burn Unit series of 914 patients, 9.2% sustained inhalation injury. Fifty-four percent of these patients died. In this study the presence of a 50% BSA burn with associated inhalation injury was universally fatal. Patients older than 60 years of age without inhalation injury had a 32.6% mortality; those with an inhalation injury had an 83.3% mortality.[89]

REHABILITATION

Rehabilitation of burn patients requires the participation of physicians, nurses, occupational therapists, physical therapists, clergy, clinical psychologists, and responsible family members. Physical therapy is begun on admission to the burn center. Daily active and passive exercises and range of motion are instituted to the upper and lower extremities, and isoprene splinting of burns across joint areas is accomplished. Following wound grafting, early ambulation, supervised stretching exercises, and participation of the patient in activities of daily living are encouraged and intensified. At the follow-up outpatient burn clinic, emphasis is placed on skin care, healing of recipient and donor sites, stretching exercises, continued splinting, and the application of pressure-gradient garments. When there is lessened improvement or increased loss of function, additional physical therapy may be required on an outpatient basis. Special attention is directed toward mobility of the shoulders, elbows, hands, and knees. Pressure-gradient garments are used to minimize hypertrophic scarring and to aid in preventing contractures. Family members caring for the patient are given instructions about the regimen and the goals of therapy. Home care nursing for supervised skin care and physical activity is required in elderly patients who have no family members available to help them.

Four problems encountered in the rehabilitation of elderly burn patients are:

1. lack of motivation
2. impaired mental status
3. decreased strength and flexibility
4. lowered state of health.

Motivation can be heightened if the patient understands that the goals of rehabilitation are reasonable and meaningful to the return of function and independence.[90]

Anxiety, depression, and delirium, common in elderly burn patients, should be recognized as a cause of inattentiveness and poor rehabilitation performance.[91,92] Muscle strength, joint flexibility, and mobility are rapidly reduced as a result of bedrest and inactivity, and ambulation and supervised exercise are essential.[93] A knowledge of the patient's preinjury occupation and leisure-time activity is useful in establishing rehabilitation goals.[3,94]

Older burn patients frequently have visual impairment, hearing loss, and postural balance problems that require the therapist to modify the pace of the rehabilitation program.[95-97]

In a carefully planned rehabilitation program as demonstrated by Dobbs and Curreri in 681 patients with 3,312 joints underlying surface burns, 85% of joints had a normal range of motion at the completion of treatment.[98]

PREVENTION

Older patients are at increased risk of sustaining burn injury and dying as a result of those injuries. Particular hazards are hot baths and showers, ignition of clothing, mishandling of flammable liquids, and house fires. A 4-year study of 1,049 adult burns at the University of California demonstrated that of 277 patients with scald injuries, 49 were admitted and 5 died; of 164 patients with flammable liquid injuries, 87 were admitted and 3 died; and in house fires, 52 patients were seen, of which 49 were admitted and 21 died. Forty-four percent of all deaths were the result of house fires. It was recommended that prevention programs include (1) a knowledge of scald danger in the home, (2) the safe home storage of flammable liquids, and (3) smoke-alarm systems for the early detection of house fires.[99]

In the United States there are 2,300 house fire deaths each year related to cigarette ignition sources alone. Mierley and Baker reviewed 55 house fire deaths in Baltimore; 56% of the related deaths were in fires caused by cigarette ignition.[100] The blood alcohol levels of 33 patients were examined, and it was found that the blood alcohol level was 0.10% or greater in 11 of 22 adults who died from cigarette-ignited house fires. To prevent injury and death in house fires, it was advised that escape routes be planned in advance and that alerting systems be installed.[100]

Physicians, nurses, and health care providers who work with the elderly should provide adult educational programs and disseminate information regarding home hazards for burn injury. A receptive and growing audience for this information is the membership of the American Association of Retired Persons. The Burn Prevention Committee of the American Burn Association has a resource list of books, cassette tapes, videotapes, pamphlets, posters, and brochures on burn prevention.[101]

It is recommended that the American Medical Association, the American College of Surgeons, and the American Trauma Society should further develop and distribute brochures and provide public service announcements on the prevention of burn injury. The Consumer Product Safety Commission, the National Safety Council, and the National Fire Commission on Fire Prevention and Control provide guidelines for burn prevention, developing protection standards, and recommending legislation.[100,102]

SUMMARY

Burn injury, a severe type of trauma, is particularly lethal to older patients. The great magnitude of the metabolic stress on cardiovascular, pulmonary, and renal reserves frequently results in fatal complications. Accurate monitoring of multiple organ systems and strict bacteriologic surveillance of the burn wound are crucial in order to identify and treat impending complications promptly. The rehabilitation of surviving older burn patients is lengthy, and satisfactory results are more difficult to achieve. If death and disability from burn injury in the older age group are to be prevented, then additional public education regarding environmental hazards will be required.

REFERENCES

1. Brody SJ: The graying of America. *Hospitals* 5:63–72, 1980.
2. Feller I, James MH, Jones CA: Burn epidemiology: Focus on youngsters and the aged. *J Burn Care Rehab* 3: (5):285–288, 1982.
3. Botwinick J: *Aging and Behavior*. New York, Springer Publishing Co Inc, 1973.
4. Curreri PW, et al: Analysis of survival and hospitalization time for 937 patients. *Ann Surg* 10:472–478, 1980.
5. *Fire In The United States*,   ed 2. Federal Emergency Management Agency, 1978.
6. Accident mortality at the older ages. *Stat Bull Metropolitan Life Insurance Co*, 63:10–12, 1982.
7. Feck G, Baptiste M: The epidemiology of burn injury in New York. *Public Health Rep* 7:312–318, 1979.
8. Feck G, Baptiste M: Preventing tap water burns. *Am J Public Health* 70:727, 1980.
9. Linn BS: Age differences in the severity and outcome of burns. *J Am Geriatr Soc* 28:118–123, 1980.
10. Bull JP, Fisher AJ: A study of mortality in a burns unit: A revised estimate. *Ann Surg* 139:269–274, 1984.

11. Feller I, Crane RH: National Burn Information Exchange. *Surg Clin N Am* 50:1425–1436, 1970.

12. Artz CP: Epidemiology—Causes and prognosis, in Artz CP, Moncrief JA, Pruitt BA Jr (eds): *Burns: A Team Approach.* Philadelphia, WB Saunders Co, 1979, p 21.

13. Pruitt BH, et al: Mortality in 1,100 consecutive burns treated at a burns unit. *Ann Surg* 3:396–401, 1964.

14. Tobiasen J, Hiebert J, Edlich R: Prediction of burn mortality. *Surg Gynec Obstet* 5:711–714, 1982.

15. Stern M, Waisbren B: Comparison of methods of predicting burn mortality. *Burns* 6:119–123, 1980.

16. Tobiasen J, Hiebert JH, Edlich RF: An abbreviated burn severity index. *Ann Emerg Med* 5:260–262, 1982.

17. Rittenbury MS, et al: Factors significantly affecting mortality in the burned patient. *J Trauma* 5:587–600, 1965.

18. Zawacki BE, et al: Multifactorial probit analysis of mortality in burned patients. *Ann Surg* 1:1–5, 1979.

19. Lakatta E, Yin FCP: Myocardial aging: Functional alterations and related cellular mechanisms. *Am J Phys* 242:H927–H941, 1982.

20. Brandfonbrener M, Landowne M, Shock NW: Changes in cardiac output with aging. *Circulation* 12:557–566, 1955.

21. Gerstenblith G, Lakatta EG, Weisfeldt MD: Age changes in myocardial function and exercise response. *Progress Cardiovasc Dis* 19:1–21, 1976.

22. Sell S, Scully RE: Aging changes in the aortic and mitral valves. *Am J Path* 46:345–355, 1965.

23. Rackley CE, et al: Mitral valve disease, in Hurst JW (ed): *The Heart*, ed 5. New York, McGraw-Hill Book Co, 1982.

24. Raftery EB, Cashman PM: Long-term recording of the electrocardiogram in a normal population. *Postgrad Med J* 52 (suppl 7):32–38, 1976.

25. Harris R: Cardiovascular diseases in the elderly. *Med Clin North Am* 67:379–394, 1983.

26. Pruitt BA Jr, Mason AD Jr, Hunt JL: Burn injury in the aged or high-risk patient, in Siege JH, Chadoff PD (eds): *The Aged and the High-Risk Surgical Patient.* New York, Grune & Stratton, 1976, pp 523–546.

27. Brandstetter R, Kazemi H: Aging and the respiratory system. *Med Clin North Am* 67:419–429, 1983.

28. Boucek RJ, Noble NL, Marks A: Age and the fibrous proteins of the human lungs. *Gerontologia* 5:150–157, 1961.

29. Greifenstein FE, et al: Pulmonary function studies in healthy men and women 50 years and older. *J Applied Phys* 4:641, 1952.

30. Hamer NAJ: The effect of age on the components of the pulmonary diffusing capacity. *Clin Sci* 23:85–93, 1962.

31. Cohn JE, et al: Maximal diffusing capacity of the lung of normal subjects of different ages. *J Applied Phys* 6:588–597, 1954.

32. Sullivan RJ, Dowdle WR, Marine WM: Adult pneumonia in a general hospital. *Arch Int Med* 129:935–942, 1972.

33. Achauer BM, et al: Pulmonary complications of burns: The major threat to the burn patient. *Ann Surg* 177:311–319, 1973.

34. Rowe JW: Aging and renal function. *Ann Rev Gerontol Geriatr* 1:161, 1980.

35. McLachlan MSF, et al: Vascular and glomerular changes in the aging kidney. *J Path* 121:65–78, 1977.

36. Sorensen FH: Quantitative studies of the renal corpuscles. *Acta Path Microbiol Scand* 85:356–366, 1977.

37. Ashworth CT, Erdmann RR, Arnold BS: Age changes in the renal basement membrane in rats. *Am J Path* 36:165–179, 1960.

38. Darmady EM, Offer J, Woodhouse MA: The parameters of the aging kidney. *J Path* 109:195–207, 1973.

39. Davidson AT, Talner LB, Down WM: A study of the radiographic appearance of the kidneys in an aging normotensive population. *Radiology* 92:975–983, 1969.

40. Friedman SA, Raizner AE, Soloman N: Functional defects in the aging kidney. *Ann Int Med* 76:41–45, 1972.

41. Davies DF, Shock NW: Age changes in glomerular filtration rate, effective renal plasma flow, and tubular excretory capacity in adult males. *J Clin Invest* 29:496–507, 1950.

42. Cockcroft DW, Gault MH: Prediction of creatinine clearance from serum creatinine. *Nephron* 16:31–41, 1976.

43. Bennett WM, et al: Guidelines for drug therapy in renal failure. *Ann Int Med* 86:754–783, 1977.

44. Rowe JW, Shock NW, DeFronzo RA: The influence of age on the renal response to water deprivation in man. *Nephron* 17:270–278, 1976.

45. Samly AH: Renal disease in the elderly. *Med Clin North Am* 67:463–480, 1983.

46. Weksler M: Senescence of the immune system. *Med Clin North Am* 67: 1983.

47. Roberts-Thomson IC, et al: Aging, immune response, and mortality. *Lancet* 2:368–370, 1974.

48. Munster AM, Hoagland HC, Pruitt BA: The effect of thermal injury on serum immunoglobulins. *Ann Surg* 172:965–969, 1970.

49. Munster AM, et al: Cell-mediated immunity after thermal injury. *Ann Surg* 177:139–143, 1973.

50. Alexander JW, et al: A sequential prospective analysis of immunologic abnormalities and infection following severe thermal injury. *Ann Surg* 188:809–816, 1978.

51. Lanser ME, Saba TM, Scovill WA: Opsonic glycoprotein (plasma fibronectin) levels after burn injury. *Ann Surg* 192:776–782, 1980.

52. Peterson V, et al: Regulation of granulopoiesis following severe thermal injury. *J Trauma* 23:19–24, 1983.

53. McIrvine AJ, et al: Depressed immune response in burn patients. *Ann Surg* 196:297–303, 1982.

54. Antonacci A, Good R, Gupta S: "T-cell subpopulations following thermal injury. *Surg Gynec Obstet* 155:1–8, 1982.

55. Alexander JW, et al: A comparison of immunologic profiles and their influence on bacteremia in surgical patients with a high risk of infection. *Surgery* 86:94–104, 1979.

56. Meakins J, et al: Delayed hypersensitivity: Indicator of acquired failure of host defenses in sepsis and trauma. *Ann Surg* 186:241–250, 1977.

57. Munster A, et al: Longitudinal assay of lymphocyte responsiveness in patients with major burns. *Ann Surg* 192:772–775, 1980.

58. Barr PO, et al: Oxygen consumption and water loss during treatment of burns with warm dry air. *Lancet* 1:164–168, 1968.

59. Wilmore DW, et al: Catecholamines: Mediator of the hypermetabolic response to thermal injury. *Ann Surg* 180:653–669, 1974.

60. Unger RH: Glucagon and the insulin: Glucagon ratio in diabetes and other catabolic illnesses. *Diabetes* 20:834–838, 1972.

61. Porte D Jr, et al: The effect of epinephrine on immunoreactive insulin levels in man. *J Clin Invest* 45:228–236, 1966.

62. Landsberg L, Young J: Fasting, feeding and regulation of the sympathetic nervous system. *New Engl J Med* 298:1295–1301, 1978.

63. Young EA: Nutrition, aging, and the aged. *Med Clin North Am* 67:295–313, 1983.

64. Curreri PW, et al: Dietary requirements of patients with major burns. *J Am Dietetic Assoc* 65:415–417, 1974.

65. Lund C, Browder N: The estimation of areas of burns. *Surg Gynec Obstet* 79:352–358, 1944.

66. Baxter CR, Shires T: Physiological response to crystalloid resuscitation of severe burns. *Ann NY Acad Sci* 150:874–894, 1968.

67. MacMillan B: Initial fluid replacement, in *Clinical Burn Therapy*, John Wright and Sons, 1982, p 64.

68. Warden G, et al: Hypernatremic state in hypermetabolic burn patients. *Arch Surg* 106:420–427, 1973.

69. Moncrief JA: Replacement therapy, Artz CP, Moncrief JA, Pruitt BA Jr (eds): *Burns: A Team Approach*. Philadelphia, WB Saunders Co, 1979, p 189.

70. Carter B: Dermatologic aspects of aging. *Med Clin North Am* 67.531–543, 1983.

71. Moncrief JA. The body's response to heat, in Artz CP, Moncrief JA, Pruitt BA Jr (eds): *Burns: A Team Approach*. Philadelphia, WB Saunders Co, 1979, p 27.

72. Ridge WV: Mechanical Properties of skin: A bioengineering study of skin structure. *J Applied Phys* 21:1602–1606, 1966.

73. Jurkiewicz MJ: Consensus summary on excisional therapy. *J Trauma* 19:933–934, 1979.

74. Collins D, et al: Accidental hypothermia and impaired temperature homeostasis in the elderly. *Br Med J* 1:353–356, 1977.

75. Rueler JB: Hypothermic, pathophysiology, clinical settings, and management. *Ann Int Med* 89:519–527, 1978.

76. Peterson S, Umphred E, Warden G: The incidence of bacteremia following burn wound excision. *J Trauma* 22:274–279, 1982.

77. Deitch E, Clothier J: Burns in the elderly: An early surgical approach. *J Trauma* 23:891–894, 1983.

78. Dowling J, Omer G, Moncrief JA: Treatment of fractures in burn patients. *J Trauma* 8:465–474, 1968.

79. Saffle J, et al: The management of fractures in thermally injured patients. *J Trauma* 23:902–910, 1983.

80. Purdue GF, et al: Burns in motor vehicle accidents. *J Trauma* 25:216–219, 1985.

81. Kirkpatrick J, Pearson J: Fatal cerebral injury in the elderly. *J Am Geriatr Soc* 26:489–496, 1978.

82. Brocklehurst JC, et al: Fracture of the femur in old age: A two-centre study of associated clinical factors and the cause of the fall. *Age Aging* 7:2–15, 1978.

83. Alffram P-A, Bauer GCH: Epidemiology of fractures of the forearm: A biomechanical investigation of bone strength. *J Bone Joint Surg* 1:105–114, 1962.

84. Achauer B, et al: Pulmonary complications of burns: The major threat to burn patients. *Ann Surg* 177:311–319, 1973.

85. DiVincenti F, Pruitt BA, Reckler J: Inhalation injuries. *J Trauma* 11:109–117, 1971.

86. Head JM: Inhalation injury in burns. *Am J Surg* 139:508–542, 1980.

87. Moylan J, Chan C-K: Inhalation injury—An increasing problem. *Ann Surg* 188:34–47, 1978.

88. Bartlett R, et al: Acute management of the upper airway in facial burns and smoke inhalation. *Arch Surg* 111:744–749, 1976.

89. Venus B, et al: Prophylactic intubation and continuous positive airway pressure in the management of inhalation injury in burn victims. *Crit Care Med* 9:519–523, 1981.

90. Hesse K, Campion E: Motivating the geriatric patient for rehabilitation. *Am Geriatr Soc* 10:586–589, 1983.
91. Andreasen NJC, et al: Management of emotional reactions in seriously burned adults. *New Engl J Med* 286:65–69, 1972.
92. Steiner H, Clark WR Jr: Psychiatric complications of burned adults: A classification. *J Trauma* 17:134–143, 1977.
93. Kottke F: The effects of limitation of activity upon the human body. *JAMA* 196:117–122, 1966.
94. Steinberg: *Care of the Geriatric Patient in the Tradition of E.V. Cowdry.* St. Louis, CV Mosby Co, 1983, pp 417 & 488.
95. MacLennan WJ, Hall MRP, Timothy JI: Postural hypotension in old age: Is it a disorder of the nervous system or of blood vessels? *Age Aging* 9:25–32, 1980.
96. Lipsitz L: The drop attack: A common geriatric symptom. *J Am Geriatr Soc* 31:617, 1983.
97. Williams W: Basilar arterial insufficiency. *Br Med J* 1:261, 1977.
98. Dobbs ER, Curreri PW: Burns: Analysis of results of physical therapy in 681 patients. *J Trauma* 12:242–248, 1972.
99. Jay K, et al: Burn epidemiology: A basis for burn prevention. *J Trauma* 17:943–947, 1977.
100. Mierley M, Baker S: Fatal house fires in an urban population. *JAMA* 249:1466–1468, 1983.
101. Dietzel SO: Burn prevention materials and resources. *J Burn Care Rehab* 3:317–324, 1982.
102. Beverley V: Reducing fire and burn. *Geriatrics* 5:106–110, 1976.

Appendix 17–A

Treatment Categories of Burn Patients

Major Burns
   2° > 25% BSA (>20%—children)
   3° > 10% BSA
   3° Face, eyes, ears, hands, feet, or perineum
   All inhalation injuries
   Electrical burns
   Burns complicated by fractures or other major trauma
   All poor-risk patients*

Moderate Burns
   2° 15% to 25% BSA (10%–20%—children)
   3° < 10% BSA
      And not involving: Face, eyes, ears, hands, feet, or perineum
      And excluding
   Inhalation injuries
   Electrical burns
   Burns complicated by fractures or other major trauma
   Poor-risk patients*

Minor Burns
   2° < 15% BSA (<10%—children)
   3° < 2% BSA
      And not involving: Face, eyes, ears, hands, feet, or perineum
      And excluding
   Inhalation injury
   Electrical burns
   Burns complicated by fractures or other major trauma
   Poor-risk patients*

*Poor-risk patients are defined as the elderly and patients with intercurrent disease.

18

Grief and Loss

Dominick Addario, MD and Janet Leigh Haley, BA

Emergency department (ED) personnel are aware that death is a subject few people want to discuss. Mental health professionals agree that an individual reacts to his or her own death with feelings of fantasy or a belief in immortality.[1] Some individuals fantasize that death will happen "to someone else" and dismiss the subject. Others fantasize that immortality is gained by living on through children or through creations or possessions that are left behind.[1] Freud pointed out, "It is indeed impossible to imagine our own death; whenever we attempt to do so, we can perceive that we are, in fact, still present as spectators."[2]

Most elderly individuals view death in a more accepting manner than do younger individuals. Older people have experienced the loss of family and friends, and according to psychological studies, thoughts of death are more frequent and more easily tolerated by them.[1,3] Nevertheless, it is unfair to assume that anyone, even an aged individual, is ever fully prepared to accept death.

Death is still an unknown that arouses feelings of denial, anger, bargaining, and grief. There is the physical termination of life for the deceased and the process of grief, with all its complexities, for the survivors.

GRIEF

ED staff who work with geriatric patients and their critical medical problems deal with death and acute grief on a daily basis.

Grief is the intense emotion that floods life when a person's inner security system is shattered by an acute loss. It is usually associated with the death of someone important in the person's life.[4] Grief caused by the loss of a loved companion can mean a succession of empty days and lonely nights. In the extreme, the grieving person might think that life is no longer worth living without the support and camaraderie of the one who is gone.

Mrs. T is a 79-year-old woman who, after 56 years of marriage and a 2-year illness of her husband, began experiencing multiple exacerbations of her cardiac illness after his death. The patient had a long-term hostile-dependent relationship with her husband that was characterized by ongoing conflict centering around his frequent absences from the home. Initially, these absences occurred because of his military career and later in life because of business. After his death, their long marriage, which had included a great deal of marital conflict, led to much ambivalence, remorse, and guilt on her part at his passing.

Although her husband had been a center of conflict in her life, he had also been her primary focus. She had few other friends or activities and found herself lonely and preoccupied by his death long after the initial grief period. She described herself to her physician: "How can you go on alone after 56 years with the same person?"

Grief can also be caused by the loss of senses, such as hearing, speech, eyesight, taste, and motor ability, or by the loss of physical and mental capabilities. In the geriatric individual, the fading of these senses can cause personal grief and grief in family members.

Grief is a cluster of adjustments, apprehensions, and uncertainties that strikes life in its forward progress and makes it difficult to reorganize and redirect the energies of life.[5]

Mrs. R's husband had died when she was 41 years old and he was 43 years old. She compensated for the loss by assuming a high-energy lifestyle; she was quite successful in business and a great source of energy and strength to her friends. From the age of 70 her eyesight began to deteriorate because of retinal disease. Her blindness led to increasing dependence on others where before she had been the primary provider of care. Her previous energy level, which had allowed her to cope with her internal feelings of remorse and at times to escape them, was no longer a vehicle of assistance to her. Her own vulnerability, which she had avoided over the years, was now met in the form of blindness and serious medical disabilities. Major alterations were taking place in her entire coping style as a result of the illness and the realization that she was as finite as her husband had been 30 years before.

Stages of Grief

To work through the stages of grief, a person must go through the process of mourning. Many individuals have specific ways of coping with grief; others are unprepared for the emotional confusion that results from loss and grief.

The first stage of grief is the immediate reaction of shock, disbelief, and denial of the reality that follows a major loss or the death of a loved one. This reaction usually occurs when the loss is sudden or when excessive denial existed before the loss.

The second stage begins as the shock recedes and the individual undergoes what Bowlby calls a "disorganization of personality" at this time of ultimate separation.[6] Symptoms of this stage include weeping, restlessness, inability to eat or sleep, and an indifference to personal appearance or the impression that is made on others. The bereaved individual experiences feelings of sadness, loneliness, helplessness, and anger.

As the bereaved individual accepts and learns to live with the loss, the third stage occurs: reorganization of personality. In this final stage of grieving the individual sees the loss in a new perspective, works through the bitter emotions, and is ready to approach new situations calmly.[6]

> Mr. S assisted his wife through a 3-year period of progressive deterioration as a result of diabetes, complicating atherosclerotic vascular disease, and congestive heart failure. He was extremely hopeful that she would survive. After two myocardial infarctions in 2 months she died one night suddenly. He awoke to find her motionless and discovered that she was dead.
>
> They had talked for many hours over the previous year about how she would survive and her illness would be defeated. He had never shared with her how he would feel if she died. For 2 hours he hesitated before calling an ambulance. He later explained that he was "numb." He said, "I sat in the other room and felt she would call me." As family began to arrive he started to talk about the experience and was extremely upset and preoccupied. He was more open than he had been for many years, according to his adult children. The primary focus of his grief dealt with his utter sense of aloneness and abandonment. He was angry at the physician because he had thought he had more time to spend with his wife. In the subsequent months he was supported by friends and family. His anger toward the medical community began to lessen. His previous hostility and indifference to his own life moved to a level of increasing interest in others, and he developed new friendships.

THE GERIATRIC PATIENT IN THE EMERGENCY DEPARTMENT

Three types of geriatric patients are brought into the ED:

1. The acute patient: The individual is mentally and physically active, self-sufficient, and has few complaints until a physical crisis precipitates the visit.

2. The chronic patient: The individual is brought to the ED because of a crisis during a long-term illness, is under the care of a physician, and might be in the terminal stage of a disease.
3. The psychosomatic patient:

- The dependent complainer is no stranger to the ED. Because of loneliness or a poor home situation or other problems, this individual uses somatic, autonomous complaints to communicate psychological needs and conflicts.
- The hostile complainer unconsciously attempts to create in others the same sense of helplessness, inadequacy, and ineptness or failure that is experienced in the complainer's own life.

THE FAMILY IN THE EMERGENCY DEPARTMENT

With geriatric patients the presence of the family in the ED is of enormous assistance to the staff. As a matter of policy, the family should be encouraged to be with the patient as an active member of the treatment team. A knowledgeable family member who has been responsible for the care of the patient can be helpful. By providing a history and emotional support, the family feels involved in the care of the loved one. This model of patient care is effectively used in pediatric care and would be of benefit in geriatric care.

If the patient is in a crisis situation—myocardial infarction, stroke, or major accident—and is possibly terminal, it is imperative that staff be able to administer to the needs of the patient without interference. It is difficult to perform duties while distraught family members and friends are in the area. Therefore, the family must be separated from the patient for a time. Most physicians agree that a potentially hostile situation can be defused by providing a staff member to explain procedures to the family and work as liaison with staff personnel.

Other contraindications to the presence of family in the ED include family members unable to cope with the pressures of the situation; the need for privacy to maintain the dignity of the patient; and technical limitations.

Mr. W had devotedly nursed his wife for 2 years as her health deteriorated from amyotrophic lateral sclerosis. One morning when he discovered she was breathing very shallowly, he contacted paramedics and she was taken to the ED. Once the ambulance arrived, Mr. W was sent to the business office of the ED to provide information, and his wife was taken to the treatment area where appropriate respiratory support and care was provided. After information was taken, Mr. W sat for over an hour waiting for someone to come out and discuss the case with him. This experience was very different from one he had had when an emergency had occurred with his wife 1 month before. At that time she was taken to another hospital, and he was allowed to be at his wife's bedside, where he had spent many hours assisting her and helping lessen her anxiety about the variety of acute technical measures that had been introduced into her care. She was much more easily managed at that time. This time, despite repeated visits to the clerk's window, he was reassured but told to "have a cup of coffee."

If death occurs, the emergency staff must be prepared for a variety of emotional responses from the family.

If the patient had a terminal illness, the family might already be mourning. Although still in shock, the family might feel relief that a painful and debilitating process has ended.

However, if the patient was vigorous and healthy before the crisis that resulted in a trip to the ED, the sudden shock of death might cause several emotional responses in the family:

- guilt over not having done enough for the patient. Guilt can be turned inward, causing depression; however, guilt often appears as anger against others as a substitute for anger against the self.
- anger that can be displaced toward the ED for not "having done enough" or against family or friends
- denial, an ongoing pattern used to soften the pain of acceptance. As shock recedes and reality returns, the loss will be acknowledged in one form or another and the work of mourning will finally begin.

DIGNITY AND DEATH

"A person's decision about death will be guided by what he, and others around him, believe is the significance of life, and therefore, of death. This is not something easily set down, nor readily universable (sic)."[7]

The ED physician and staff often must decide what measures should be taken to keep a terminally ill patient alive. There are no clear-cut norms for such a decision; experience and wisdom are needed to assess the various factors and to try to balance them against each other.[7] Many physicians agree that, despite a poor prognosis and despite age, each patient should receive no less care than any other patient. It is important for the physician to determine the feelings of the patient and, second, the feelings of the family regarding the patient's wish to survive the present acute event.

A patient might be brought to the ED because of a personal wish to avoid severe pain stemming from a terminal illness. The patient may not want extreme methods taken, such as being placed on a respirator, to prolong suffering from an illness with a poor prognosis.

If a terminal prognosis is made and the chances of recovery are nil, reducing pain and maintaining dignity are the primary objectives.

The enormous advances of modern medicine have created two misconceptions that are to the disadvantage of the dying individual and the family.

The first misconception is that there will always be a treatment or a medicine that can prevent death. A game can be played around dying as if the physician and the hospital have the power to postpone death indefinitely.[8]

According to Melvin Krant,[8] this misconception is based on the belief that a large number of therapeutic activities are available for patients with fatal illnesses and that these activities can postpone the moment of dying. Indeed, with modern surgery, rehabilitation, care, and intensive diagnostic facilities, some previously fatal illnesses now are curable. Additionally, the course of some fatal illnesses can be prolonged so that an individual goes into remission as if he or she were going to get better permanently. However, these victories tend to be short-lived, and people continue to die.

The second misconception is the fantasy of invulnerability and immortality achieved through one's lifestyle: the good survive and the indiscreet die young. Appropriate medical education about risk factors and health, such as the importance of a low cholesterol diet, proper exercise, and avoidance of smoking, have encouraged good health patterns. It has also created the fantasy that those who die do so as a consequence of poor self-care. This second misconception only encourages guilt, for there are some areas of life over which we have no control.

The reluctance of physicians to terminate treatment is understandable. The decision might pose a moral or religious problem for the physician who has been taught from the first days of medical school that death is an enemy to be defeated at all costs. Some physicians are now suggesting, however, that in certain circumstances, death can be a friend.[9]

Kastenbaum and Aisenberg[9] report that physicians often have to fulfill contradictory roles. They should be objective and scientific while being warm and personal. They must exert themselves with equal vigor to save all lives and yet are free to be selective on the type of care each patient should receive. They are responsible not only to themselves and their personal ethics but also to the community and the patient. They are sages and all-around authorities on life, but they are also technicians and repairpersons. Physicians have much influence over the general climate of thought and feeling and also over the functioning of others in the system, including the patient and the family.

The effect of the advances in medical technology in curing or alleviating once fatal diseases has also succeeded in extended the period of dying.[10] An article in the *New York Times*[11] pointed out that years ago death was a statement of fact; today it was become a dilemma of agonizing choices. The article discussed 123 patients who had died in 1 month at St. Luke's-Roosevelt Hospital Center in New York. Nearly half spent weeks knowing that death was imminent. Some died only after physicians, nurses, hospital attorneys, and families, ill equipped to deal with the agonizing ethical issues, found themselves having to choreograph the precise time and manner for life to end for these patients.[11]

Each patient must be considered on an individual basis, and each poses a moral and ethical question that physicians, staff, and family must answer. No matter what the outcome, arriving at the decision or not even making a decision but waiting for an illness to run its course can place enormous stress on the ED staff.

STRESS IN THE EMERGENCY DEPARTMENT

A study done by Feifel and colleagues[12] explored a very controversial possibility: On occasion many physicians choose their occupation because death is a personal problem for them. The study found that physicians and medical students have an above-average fear of death. Feifel found that, although other subjects would "feel bad" when learning of a death, a physician would be inclined to "reflect on my own mortality."[12]

Psychiatrist Avery Weisman states that unless a person's way of looking at life is broad enough to confront his or her own death or the death of those close, then that person has an incomplete perspective.[13]

Although medical professionals are trained to give specialized care to terminal patients, much of their behavior toward the dying resembles that of the layperson. Medical professionals suffer the same feelings such as guilt, denial, etc., despite their training. Realizing that working with the dying patient is traumatic, they understandably develop both standardized and idiosyncratic modes of coping.[14] These efforts to cope with death often adversely affect both the social and psychological aspects of patient care. Personnel in contact with a terminal patient are always somewhat disturbed by their own ineptness in handling the dying patient.[14] No profession seems more vulnerable to increased stresses than those in helping roles—physicians, nurses, psychiatrists, psychologists, and social workers—anyone whose role involves acting as a central figure to others who are dependent, ill, desperate, isolated, and suffering.[15]

Nurses and other health professionals face a great deal of stress because they give the majority of care to the patient. They work side by side with the physician in emergency situations. Additionally, they may be charged with being the liaison with the anxious family. If the patient dies, they need to feel they did a good job while the patient was alive.[10]

Health professionals need to recognize the stress inherent in both their professional and personal lives, to understand the specific ways that helping professionals are vulnerable to stress, and to devise ways to cope with the stress and grow within their professions.

A number of studies show that physicians are poor patients and tend to ignore symptoms of disease or problems in themselves, such as from cancer or myocardial infarction, and push aside any emotional strains they might be experiencing.[16] Drug abuse is more common among physicians, according to some studies, than among the general public, and it is estimated that 1% of all physicians in the United States will become addicted at some point, primarily to meperidine (Demerol). One study showed that one-third of all hospital time for hospitalized physicians occurred because of alcohol and drug abuse.[16] These findings can also be extended to other health professionals. Drug abuse and drug addiction among nurses are also high.

Because of the unique role that physicians have as healers and the prestige attached to the role of the physician, there is a tendency for physicians and other health professionals to become authority figures to the patient. From this comes the erroneous belief that all patients who improve do so as a result of specific care. The health professional then becomes vulnerable to feelings of omnipotence, idealism, and perfectionism, as well as a sense of guilt when patients do not survive.

Additionally, most health professionals find it impossible to leave their work at the office, clinic, or hospital.[15] Because individuals do not restrict their times of pain, suffering, and life crises to a predictable 8-hour day, the health professional is placed in the vulnerable position of being "on call" 24 hours each day. Schneider[15] points out that many professionals fall into the "meaningfulness trap." Because the work is meaningful and rewarding, it is increasingly difficult to leave it and make personal growth a priority.

Another major source of stress is that society, for a variety of reasons, has increasingly turned the task of caring for the chronically ill over to the health professional. Before 1930, over 80% of the deaths in the United States occurred in some place other than a hospital. This figure has since reversed, and in 1974, 80% of deaths occurred in the hospital.[16]

The hospital-based death is an increased source of stress for the health care professional for two reasons:

1. The health care professional is more likely than anyone else to encounter death and dying in society and in greater numbers than before.
2. Because hospitals are now the sites of most deaths, the health care professional encounters family, friends, and others unfamiliar with death who turn to the professional for assistance with their grief.[17]

Not only are physicians and staff personnel expected to possess technical and therapeutic skills to ease the dying process, they are expected to provide support, reassurance, and comfort to those in grief.[17]

Many patients come to the ED to die. Perhaps they choose to do so because they want to be in a supportive setting and to experience the fantasy that everything possible was done up until the last minute in this technical "promised land."

Unless health professionals are comfortable with their own grief process, however, they are unable to assist others with their grief. The very nature of the profession makes the experience of personal grief more difficult. Effective grief requires solitude, putting one's needs first, and being able to feel sadness, helplessness, and anger. All of these are mandated against by the role of the professional. An overly simplistic view of the health professionals' function as solely to preserve life handicaps their effectiveness with patients who need them at the time of death.

Coping with Stress

To cope with stress, the health professional needs to examine several areas of his or her life to decide whether they are causing excess stress. According to Bowden and Burstein,[17] these areas are the work environment, identity, and personal sources of stress.

Areas that should be explored in the work environment include the following:

- schedule (constantly on-call; called on demand)
- physical environment (high level of noise and confusion, lack of privacy, inadequate personal work space)
- available support groups provided as part of job
- availability of others to attend to patients or is the job indispensable?
- provisions on the job to meet one's specific emotional needs
- demands on time and energy that must be extended on job.

Issues relating to personal identity prompt the following questions:

- Is the job the most important area of your life?
- What expectations do you have of yourself?
- Do you want to be all things to all people?
- What other roles do you have? (spouse, parent, child, etc.)
- What happens when other roles conflict with your job? What are your priorities?

It is also important to reflect on the following issues:

- Do you consider yourself a "special" person?
- Do you expect others to take care of your needs because you take care of others?
- Do you sometimes feel that your role somehow grants you immunity from disease, illness, and the dying process that you witness in those for whom you care?

Personal sources of stress that need to be examined include recent changes in any of the following 13 elements:

1. family relationships
2. place of residence
3. income
4. status
5. friendships
6. health
7. health of others important to you
8. perspectives on what is meaningful in life
9. assumptions and beliefs carried from childhood, eg, no one important to me will die; I can handle anything; life is fair; I won't suffer pain, loss
10. safety of the environment
11. opportunities for relaxation
12. opportunities for exercise
13. enjoyment of day-to-day life.

Stress is any stimulus that requires the organism to adopt a change. Stress is related to life events and is based on the magnitude of adjustment that these events require.[18] Any source of stress has the potential to affect the health professional physically and emotionally, to alter the way the individual acts and thinks, and to change his or her values and attitudes.

To combat stress, time and solitude are needed to reflect on the change. Support groups and the insight of others can aid the process of understanding one's reaction to stress.[17]

It is important to recognize stress and have realistic alternatives to deal with it. These include the following:

- setting priorities
- implementing changes, such as
  —providing time for oneself each day
  —permitting the time to acknowledge transition in one's life
  —using regular ways of relaxing, such as meditation, music, or anaerobic or aerobic exercises
  —having support systems and psychotherapeutic or supervisory counseling
  —doing as much work as possible in groups
  —exploring ways to facilitate one's own grief process, if needed
  —developing a local support system with someone who cares about you

A self-care role model that can assist in relieving stress includes a checklist for exercise, diet, meditation, vacations and time off, space for self, enjoyment of work, and maintaining a sense of humor, especially about oneself. Individuals also need to give themselves permission to stop and to discover and acknowledge their limits.[17] Most importantly, the health professional needs to understand that taking care of oneself first enables one to provide better care for patients later.

REFERENCES

1. Spikes J: Grief, death and dying, in Busse EW, Blazer DG (eds): *Handbook of Geriatric Psychiatry*. New York, Van Nostrand, Reinhold, 1980, pp 415–417.

2. Freud S: Thoughts for times on war and death, in *Collected Papers IV*. London, The Hogarth Press, 1953.

3. Kalish RA, Reynolds DK: *Death and Ethnicity: A Psychocultural Study*. Los Angeles, University of Southern California Press, 1976, pp 131–135.

4. Marshall GN: *Facing Death and Grief*. New York, Prometheus Books, 1981, p 12.

5. Jackson EN: Grief, in Grollman EA (ed): *Concerning Death: A Practical Guide for the Living*. Boston, Beacon Press, 1974, pp 2–3.

6. Bowlby J: Process of mourning. *Int J Psychoanal* 42:13, 1961.

7. McMullin E: *Death and Decision*. American Association for the Advancement of Science. AAAS Selected Symposia Series. Boulder, Westview Press, 1978, pp 11–13.

8. Krant MJ: The doctor, fatal illness, and the family, in Grollman EA (ed): *Concerning Death: A Practical Guide for the Living*. Boston, Beacon Press, 1974, p 49.

9. Kastenbaum R, Aisenberg R: *The Psychology of Death*. New York, Springer Publishing Company, 1976, pp 171–174.

10. Rosoff SD: Death with dignity: Trends in death and dying legislation in the United States, in Dinsmore JL (ed): *Death and Dying: An Examination of Legislative and Policy Issues*. Georgetown University Health Policy Center, Washington, DC, 1976, pp 21–27.

11. Reported in the *New York Times*, January 15, 1985, p A1.

12. Feifel H, Hanson S, Jones R, et al.: Physicians consider death, *Proceedings of the 75th Annual Convention of the American Psychological Association,* vol 2. Washington, American Psychological Association, 1967, pp 201, 202.

13. Weisman AD: *On Dying and Denying*. New York, Behavioral Publications, 1972, p 21.

14. Strauss AL, Glaser BG: Awareness of dying, in Schoenberg B, Carr AC, Peretz D, et al (eds): *Loss and Grief: Psychological Management in Medical Practice*. New York, Columbia University Press, 1970, p 299.

15. Schneider J: Self care and the helping professions, in Pegg PF, Metze E (eds): *Death and Dying, A Quality of Life*. London, The Pittman Press, 1981, pp 97–100.

16. Reynolds DK, Kalish RN: The social ecology of dying: Observations of wards for the terminally ill. *Hosp Comm Psychiatry J* 25:147, 1974.

17. Bowden CL, Burstein AG: *Psychosocial Basis of Medical Practice*. Baltimore, Williams & Wilkins, 1974, pp 173–181, 217, 218.

18. Holmes TH, Rahe RH: The social readjustment rating scale. *J Psychosom Res* 11:213–218, 1967.

Index